# THE LIFE OF CHA

MRS GASKELL was born Elizabeth Cleghorn Stevenson in 1810. The daughter of a Unitarian, who was a civil servant and journalist, she was brought up after her mother's death by her aunt in Knutsford, Cheshire, which became the model not only for Cranford but also for Hollingford (in *Wives and Daughters*). In 1832 she married William Gaskell, a Unitarian minister in Manchester, with whom she lived very happily. Her first novel, *Mary Barton*, published in 1848, was immensely popular and brought her to the attention of Charles Dickens, who was looking for contributors to his new periodical, *Household Words*, for which she wrote the famous series of papers subsequently reprinted as *Cranford*. Her later novels include *Ruth* (1853), *North and South* (1854–5), *Sylvia's Lovers* (1863), and *Wives and Daughters* (1864–6). She also wrote many stories and her remarkable *Life of Charlotte Brontë*. She died in 1865.

CHARLOTTE BRONTË was born at Thornton, Yorkshire in 1816, the third child of Patrick and Maria Brontë. Her father was perpetual curate of Haworth, Yorkshire from 1820 until his death in 1861. Her mother died in 1821, leaving five daughters and a son. All of the girls except Anne were sent to a clergymen's daughters' boarding school (recalled as Lowood in *Jane Eyre*). Charlotte was employed as a teacher from 1835 to 1838, was subsequently a governess, and in 1842 went with her sister Emily to study languages in Brussels, where during 1843 she again worked as a teacher. She returned to Haworth in the following year, and in 1846 there appeared *Poems by Currer, Ellis, and Acton Bell*, the pseudonyms of Charlotte, Emily, and Anne. Charlotte's first novel, *The Professor*, was rejected by several publishers, and was not published until 1857. *Jane Eyre* was published (under the pseudonym Currer Bell) in 1847 and achieved immediate success. *Shirley* was published in 1849, and *Villette* in 1853, both pseudonymously. Charlotte married in 1854 the Revd A. B. Nicholls, her father's curate, but died in March 1855.

ANGUS EASSON is Research Professor of English at the University of Salford. He has edited Dickens's *The Old Curiosity Shop*, and Gaskell's *North and South*, *Cousin Phillis and Other Tales*, and *Wives and Daughters* for Oxford World's Classics. He has published a study of Elizabeth Gaskell and edited the Gaskell volume in the Critical Heritage series.

# OXFORD WORLD'S CLASSICS

*For over 100 years Oxford World's Classics have brought
readers closer to the world's great literature. Now with over 700
titles—from the 4,000-year-old myths of Mesopotamia to the
twentieth century's greatest novels—the series makes available
lesser-known as well as celebrated writing.*

*The pocket-sized hardbacks of the early years contained
introductions by Virginia Woolf, T. S. Eliot, Graham Greene,
and other literary figures which enriched the experience of reading.
Today the series is recognized for its fine scholarship and
reliability in texts that span world literature, drama and poetry,
religion, philosophy and politics. Each edition includes perceptive
commentary and essential background information to meet the
changing needs of readers.*

# OXFORD WORLD'S CLASSICS

---

## ELIZABETH GASKELL

# *The Life of Charlotte Brontë*

---

*Edited with an Introduction and Notes by*
**ANGUS EASSON**

**OXFORD**
UNIVERSITY PRESS

# OXFORD

UNIVERSITY PRESS

Great Clarendon Street, Oxford OX2 6DP

Oxford University Press is a department of the University of Oxford.
It furthers the University's objective of excellence in research, scholarship,
and education by publishing worldwide in

Oxford New York

Athens Auckland Bangkok Bogotá Buenos Aires Cape Town
Chennai Dar es Salaam Delhi Florence Hong Kong Istanbul Karachi
Kolkata Kuala Lumpur Madrid Melbourne Mexico City Mumbai Nairobi
Paris São Paulo Shanghai Singapore Taipei Tokyo Toronto Warsaw

with associated companies in Berlin Ibadan

Oxford is a registered trade mark of Oxford University Press
in the UK and in certain other countries

Published in the United States
by Oxford University Press Inc., New York

British Library Cataloguing in Publication Data

Data available

Library of Congress Cataloging in Publication Data
Gaskell, Elizabeth Cleghorn, 1810–1865.
The life of Charlotte Brontë / Elizabeth Gaskell; edited with an
introduction by Angus Easson.
(Oxford world's classics)
Includes bibliographical references and index.
1. Brontë, Charlotte, 1816–1855—Biography.   2. Women novelists,
English—19th century—Biography.   I. Easson, Angus.   II. Title.
III. Series.
PR4168.G3   1996   823'.8—dc20   95–491

ISBN 978–0–19–955476–8

15

Printed in Great Britain by
Clays Ltd, Elcograf S.p.A

# CONTENTS

# ACKNOWLEDGEMENTS

I WOULD like to thank all those who have helped me in various ways. All quotations from the manuscript of *The Life of Charlotte Brontë* and from the manuscripts of Patrick Brontë's letters are reproduced by courtesy of the Director and University Librarian, the John Rylands University Library of Manchester; I would like to thank him for his generosity in giving permission. The staff of the John Rylands (Deansgate Building) have been as helpful as ever, even amidst the trials of major rewiring. The Librarian of the Portico Library, Manchester, willingly gave access to the borrowers' register; Barbara Brill generously sent me her transcription of those records. The Manchester Central Public Library brought up books with speed. Ann Dinsdale of the Brontë Parsonage Museum answered my enquiries swiftly and effectively. I owe a particular debt to Margaret Smith, who has given immense and generous help from her extensive knowledge of the Brontës and of Charlotte's letters in particular. Through Margaret Smith, Sarah Fermi gave me useful information. Peter Henderson, the Walpole Librarian, The King's School, Canterbury, supplied me with a photocopy. Salford University granted me a term's study leave: the English Department made that leave possible, and extra administrative burdens were willingly taken on by Paul Callick and Colin Harrison. Other friends and colleagues at Salford and elsewhere who have given particular assistance are John Chapple, Ortwin de Graef, Geoff Harris, Peter Howell, John Keiger, Tony Lodge, Sue Powell, Phil Tomlinson, and Deirdre Toomey. At the Press, Judith Luna has waited patiently and given timely advice. The production staff, not least my copy-editor Alice Park, have been speedy and efficient, saving me from error and inconsistency. I would like to acknowledge a general debt to the *Brontë Society Transactions*, and to Alan Shelston's Penguin edition of *The Life*, of which I have been aware throughout my work, not least as a standard by which mine will be judged. Finally, my thanks to Bernard Jubb, who kept me on the rails (with trains and timetables) and willingly went on various Brontë outings.

# INTRODUCTION

In June 1855 Elizabeth Gaskell was surprised to receive a letter from the Reverend Patrick Brontë, asking, on behalf of himself and of his son-in-law, the Reverend Arthur Bell Nicholls, if she would write the life of his daughter, Charlotte Brontë, who had died on 31 March 1855.[1] The invitation was prompted by Ellen Nussey, Charlotte's friend since schooldays. Concerned about her friend's reputation and the biographical speculation of the press, Ellen had written to Patrick Brontë and Nicholls, demanding such fabrications be challenged and proposing Gaskell, a friend of Charlotte's and an established author, as 'official' biographer. The details which made Ellen so indignant were nothing new. Various biographical claims and speculations had appeared in reviews of the Brontës' work, while information of varying accuracy appeared in obituary notices and tributes after Charlotte's death. The Brontë sisters' linked pseudonyms (Acton, Currer, and Ellis Bell) had led to speculation as to whether they were three or one, male or female, while *Jane Eyre* proved fertile ground indeed: had its author been governess to Thackeray (known to have a mad wife), had its author forfeited the right to keep the company of respectable women?[2] The particular provocation for Ellen Nussey was an article in the June issue of *Sharpe's London Magazine*,[3] a fact not without its ironies in light of the subsequent invitation to Gaskell, since the article incorporates part of Gaskell's own account in a letter of her first meeting with Charlotte Brontë.[4] Despite Ellen's

---

[1] Patrick Brontë to Gaskell, 16 June 1855; John Rylands MS.

[2] One of the earliest reviews of the Brontës, a notice of the *Poems* of 1846 in the *Dublin University Magazine*, 28 (Oct. 1846), had suggested the Bells were but one author. Elizabeth Rigby, in the *Quarterly Review*, 84 (Dec. 1848), referred both to the Thackeray connection (made more seemingly plausible by Charlotte's dedication of the 2nd edition of *Jane Eyre* to Thackeray) and to Currer Bell's forfeiture of respectability if 'he' were a woman: hence Gaskell's later asperity in handling Rigby and the *Quarterly Review*. Even tributes could be inaccurate: Matthew Arnold's elegy, 'Haworth Churchyard', buries Anne at Haworth instead of Scarborough, while Harriet Martineau's obituary (*Daily News*, 6 Apr. 1855) claimed Charlotte lacked the strength to go walking on the moors.

[3] NS 6 (1855), 339-42.

[4] See J. G. Sharps, *Mrs Gaskell's Observation and Invention* (1970), pp.575-8: the article seems to have been written by the minor novelist Frank Smedley.

indignation, Mr Nicholls replied that he and Patrick Brontë thought that to take notice of it would give the piece undeserved importance—indeed, far from being upset, Patrick had laughed at the account given of himself.[5] Yet only a month later it was Patrick Brontë who wrote to Gaskell, asking her to undertake the biography.

Though surprised, Gaskell was not averse to the task. She determined to 'perform this grave duty laid upon me well and fully',[6] and in return Patrick sent her 'a few facts' about himself and his family.[7] Gaskell went across from Manchester to Haworth on 23 July and discussed the proposal with the two men. Patrick was enthusiastic; Nicholls not at all in favour, but going along with Patrick's wish. They brought out some letters and Patrick provided Gaskell next day with further biographical details.[8] As she left, Patrick's last words to Gaskell were, 'No quailing Mrs Gaskell! no drawing back!'[9]

If Gaskell had known of the difficulties, anxieties, and strains that writing *The Life of Charlotte Brontë* was to involve, she might well have quailed. What she felt first, though, was a duty on behalf of others—of Patrick Brontë, Ellen Nussey, Arthur Nicholls, and even more of Charlotte herself. The details of Charlotte's life must be given accurately, while the charges, both particular and general, levelled against Charlotte by the reviewers were to be refuted. Charlotte had been charged with coarseness, with representing love as the sole preoccupation of her characters. *Jane Eyre* had particularly been a transgressor.[10] Such charges Gaskell sought variously

---

[5] *The Brontës: Their Lives, Friendships and Correspondence*, ed. T. J. Wise and J. A. Symington (1932), iv. 189–90.

[6] *The Letters of Mrs Gaskell*, ed. J. A. V. Chapple and Arthur Pollard (1966), p. 349 (to George Smith, 18 June [1855]); hereafter given as *Letters*.

[7] Patrick Brontë to Elizabeth Gaskell, 20 June 1855; John Rylands MS. Patrick was already sounding what were to be keynotes in *The Life*: 'I never knew one, less selfish than she was, or more disposed to suffer, herself—to save others from suffering.'

[8] Patrick Brontë to Gaskell, 24 July 1855; John Rylands MS.

[9] *Letters*, p. 361.

[10] The charge of coarseness, which extended to the improper use of biblical allusions and language, and to a spirit of rebelliousness against the established order, can be usefully traced in Miriam Allott (ed.), *The Brontës: The Critical Heritage* (1974) ('coarseness' in Index, section II: 'characteristics'). Harriet Martineau, at Charlotte's insistence, had been severe in reviewing *Villette*, naming a morbid preoccupation with love as a fault of its characters (Allott, pp. 172–3). Charles Kingsley bears witness both to a common belief in coarseness and to Gaskell's success in *The Life*; in a letter of 14 May 1857 he praised 'the picture of a valiant woman made perfect by suffering' (Angus Easson (ed.), *Elizabeth Gaskell: The Critical Heritage* (1991), p. 398).

to repudiate. She vividly evoked the world of Haworth and the West Riding, partly to show that it was not Charlotte's nature but her environment that was rude and wild. She also counter-attacked those who had brought the charges: Elizabeth Rigby, an offender in the *Quarterly Review* article, was to be a particular target. Now, though, Gaskell had to turn to her task, which must begin with the gleaning of materials.

From the first appearance of *Jane Eyre* in 1847, Gaskell, like so many of its readers, had been possessed by the energy of the novel and fascinated by the mystery of its author's identity. Early on, through a network of friends and acquaintances, she had established that the mysterious 'Currer Bell' was a woman: 'Currer Bell (aha! what will you give me for a secret?) She's a she—that I will tell you'.[11] Then in August 1850, at the invitation of Sir James and Lady Kay-Shuttleworth, Gaskell went to Briery Close, near Windermere. There she first met Charlotte Brontë, an encounter that led to a friendship remarkable, despite its brevity, for warmth and intimacy, and one that determined the nature of *The Life* when it came to be written. Gaskell was struck by the childlike figure, 'a little wee dark person', dressed in black, and with hands like birds' claws.[12] Gaskell's sense of Charlotte as deprived and suffering suffuses *The Life*.

The biography rapidly expanded from the idea of a fairly brief memoir, perhaps no more than a preface to *The Professor*, Charlotte's as yet unpublished first novel. It was clear from the materials Gaskell had gathered by the end of 1855 that the work would be of some length, and it was to expand further. Writing occupied what time she could make throughout 1856. As she wrote, Gaskell sent sections to George Smith, Charlotte's publisher and friend, who was to publish the biography.[13] Smith criticized the work as it progressed, while Gaskell's husband, William, read it over for grammar and style, making his own occasional contributions. Gaskell took what opportunities she could for writing, a

---

[11] *Letters*, p. 93.     [12] Ibid., pp. 123, 127.

[13] Smith paid £800 for *The Life*, raising the proposed amount from £600 when Gaskell pointed out the time and expense involved in gathering materials; he delighted Gaskell by paying a further £200 for the revised 3rd edition, a task Gaskell felt to be an obligation on herself for the trouble Smith had been put to. For the payments, see *Letters*, pp. 430, 431–2, 495; the receipt for the original payment is in the Brontë Parsonage Museum (see *Brontë Society Transactions*, 19 (1986), 41).

day's rain allowing her to get twenty pages done;[14] she wrote from breakfast to five o'clock, later only until lunch. She paid for this in headaches, and then at the end of September she 'had a long fainting-fit one day ("quite promiscuous" as servants say)' and was forbidden work altogether.[15] By October, she was half-way through and estimated February 1857 as the end of her task. Printing began early in January and on 7 February she could announce, 'I have today finished my Life of Miss Brontë; and next week we set out for Rome'.[16] *The Life of Charlotte Brontë*, the first work to have Gaskell's name on the title-page, was widely noticed and mostly favourably received. If the reviews focused on Charlotte and the life of the Brontës, rather than the art of the biographer, there was praise for the authenticating mass of detail and for the portrait of the woman. Only with a retraction in *The Times* (30 May 1857) of any implications of impropriety against a lady (Mrs Robinson, the 'seducer' of Branwell Brontë), is a different note sounded, as Gaskell's veracity and judgement came to be doubted: the July *Blackwood's Magazine* pilloried her as 'a gossip and a gad-about' and the *Edinburgh Review* included her in an attack on trial by literature, where honour or virtue can be blown to the winds 'merely because it suits the humour of a romancer to rake up some imaginary or forgotten transgression'.[17]

In June 1857, on her return from Italy, Gaskell found a heap of correspondence waiting for her, some in praise of *The Life*, but more of it attacks on grounds of misrepresentation. Accepting the need for a revised edition of the work, she took on the task, despaired under domestic pressures, asked George Smith to find someone to act as editor, then found the time and set doggedly to do what had become painfully disagreeable. In September a third edition, revised but also expanded, appeared. The enterprise had been a demanding one, with a bitter taste at the end. Yet out of adversity, as well as love and loyalty, grew a biography, command-

---

[14] *Letters*, p. 395.        [15] Ibid., p. 415.

[16] Ibid., p. 443. For a fuller account of the getting of materials and the writing, see Angus Easson, *Elizabeth Gaskell* (1979), pp. 134-47. Print runs were 2,021 for the 1st edition, 2,200 for the 2nd edition (Juliet Barker, *The Brontës* (1994), p. 796).

[17] For a selection of reviews and responses, see *Elizabeth Gaskell: The Critical Heritage*, pp. 372-431 and 35-8; the *Blackwood*'s reviewer was Eneas Sweetland Dallas, the *Edinburgh*'s James Fitzjames Stephen.

ing in its structure and sure in its evocation of an individual and her milieu.

As Patrick Brontë observed when inviting Gaskell to write the biography, Gaskell was an established author, with novels such as *Mary Barton*, *Cranford*, and *Ruth* to her credit. But she was a writer of fiction, not a biographer, and she had to grapple with what biography meant. As she wrote to an old friend, during the biography's preparation, 'And I never *did* write a biography, and I don't exactly know how to set about it; you see I have to be accurate and keep to facts; a most difficult thing for a writer of fiction.'[18] The wryly amused tone suggests Gaskell's ability to balance her dedication and labour in the task against the pleasures and human oddities thrown up in the pursuit. From the first, she knew that she would need materials—facts and details and the voices of those who had known Charlotte Brontë—so that she could present the truth. But only as she worked and wrote did she come to realize how far biography is a work of collaboration, between author and subject, between author and the living, and how far that collaboration both advances and constrains the work. If a labour of love, the creation of a biography can yet be painful and frustrating. Gaskell had to find ways to establish Charlotte's background and formative experiences, to distinguish the trivial from the significant (however slight, even trivial, the significant might sometimes appear), and interpret Charlotte for the reader. For the biography was not, could not be, an objective memoir. From the first it was meant to be a defence and a vindication, to show Charlotte as 'a noble, true, and tender woman', a tribute to a dear friend. Gaskell never again attempted biography. Yet whatever reservations she might have personally, she had not failed in her endeavour. Re-creating the life of Charlotte Brontë demanded of Gaskell a complex process of response, adaptation, and determination. Out of that struggle, held to with honesty and determination, came an extraordinarily vivid and sensitive account. Charlotte Brontë, through Gaskell's handling and command of detail, is given to the reader, in all her pungent and strange individuality. In what follows I want to suggest Gaskell's struggle,

[18] To Harriet Anderson, née Carr, 15 Mar. [1856], in Sally Stonehouse, 'A Letter from Mrs Gaskell', *Brontë Society Transactions*, 20 (1991), 219.

while showing how she did more than just cope, for Gaskell turned
the demands of biography brilliantly to advantage.

Biography in the nineteenth century, unlike the novel, was not
a clearly established form. Earlier biographies had often been
eulogies, in which nothing ill or indeed of any specificity was to be
said of the dead, or else memoirs prefacing collected works, or
anecdotes of varying authenticity like those bundled together by
John Aubrey, the fascination of his 'Brief Lives' lying in their often
wonderfully incongruous juxtapositionings. In the eighteenth century, James Boswell's life of Samuel Johnson (1791) and its
predecessor, Richard Mason's life of the poet Thomas Gray (1775),
had revealed a subject through his letters. Much depends on the
nature and quality of the letters and not a little on the skill of the
biographer in using them. Boswell was concerned to vindicate a
public figure often characterized as boorish, gross, unmannerly,
and to raise him to heroic status. To do this, Boswell did not deny
the dirty linen or the physical oddities or the rudeness. Instead, he
incorporated them into an account of Johnson's hardships and
deprivations, seeking to make the man wholly known. The early
life in London—the night wanderings, the lack of patrons, the need
to make his own way; the revelations of his real charity—carrying
a prostitute collapsed in the street to his own house and looking
after her; his love of animals (the cats Hodge and Lily): all build
up in a sense that his least action is significant because part of a
whole truth. While nineteenth-century biography is often dull,
showing public men for public consumption (the tradition against
which Lytton Strachey, however superficial and specious his work,
so successfully reacted), it could be enlivened by the desire to
attack or to vindicate, to elevate or to reveal. Thomas Carlyle,
himself subjected after death to a biography that called out
counter-attacks, believed in biography as the representation of
great men. Yet greatness for Carlyle was not only revealed on the
stage of the big histories, of politics and battles and empire: people
seemingly obscure could, within the inwardness of their soul, live
a life as heroic as that of Cromwell or Napoleon or Frederick the
Great. In writing the life of his friend John Sterling (1851), who
died young with no evidence of achievement in the world, Carlyle
showed himself a practitioner in the biography of the hidden life,
realized through significant detail and written under a sense of

imperative. In the 'Conclusion' to his biography of Sterling, Carlyle insisted that to the question 'Why write the Life of Sterling?' the answer was that 'I imagine I had a commission higher than the world's, the dictate of Nature herself'. Gaskell knew Carlyle's work and she was surely struck by his sense of that 'higher commission', as well as by his use in the life of Sterling of the apparently trivial detail, the gift of a box of matches, for example. Carlyle wished to call 'the Sympathy of mortal hearts into action' and Gaskell wished to vindicate 'my dear friend Charlotte Brontë'.[19]

Initially, by way of materials, Gaskell had her own notes and retrieved some of her letters describing her meetings with Charlotte, while Patrick Brontë provided a skeleton biographical outline (not always accurate in detail) of himself and his family. A chronology had to be established, but Gaskell needed access to the life and hence the significance of her subject. On a sheet of paper, Gaskell copied two comments that suggest awareness of both external and internal life. The first stressed the need to get anecdotes, encapsulated history, since 'Character manifests itself in little things, just as a sunbeam finds its way through a chink'; the second, a direct reference to Charlotte, spoke of the 'truth of that wonderful infinite life in which there seems to have been so little of external fact or circumstances, and such a boundless sphere of feeling and intellect crammed within a silent existence'.[20] Gaskell travelled widely, to Haworth, but also to Cowan Bridge; to Casterton (where the Clergy Daughters' School was now located); to Thornton, where Charlotte had been born; to London to see George Smith and to visit the Chapter Coffee House; to Brussels to meet Constantin Heger, Charlotte's French teacher and, as

---

[19] Besides his accounts of public heroes in *On Heroes and Hero Worship* (1841), *Oliver Cromwell's Letters and Speeches* (1845), and *The History of Frederick the Great* (1858–65), Carlyle wrote two important essays on biography (1832; they come out of an extended review of Boswell's life of Johnson). For some discussion of the relationship between Gaskell's biography and Carlyle's life of Sterling, see my article, 'Domestic Romanticism: Elizabeth Gaskell and *The Life of Charlotte Brontë*', *Durham University Journal*, NS 42 (June 1981), 169–76. For a general discussion of biography, see Alan Shelston, *Biography*, Critical Idiom series (1971), and more particularly with respect to nineteenth-century biography, A. O. J. Cockshut, *Truth to Life: The Art of Biography in the Nineteenth Century* (1974), chs. 1–4.

[20] Both extracts are on a sheet bound up with the manuscript of *The Life*, in the John Rylands University Library of Manchester; the first is from the *Quarterly Review*, 98 (Mar. 1856), 297; the second from a letter of Anna Jameson's to Gaskell.

Gaskell discovered, the object of Charlotte's passion. At Haworth she spoke to those who knew the Brontës, amongst them, Martha Brown, a servant at the Parsonage; John Greenwood, who had sold the sisters writing paper, walking to Halifax rather than disappoint them of supplies; and Elizabeth Hardaker the pharmacist, who remembered when the servant Tabby broke her leg. Other contacts were made by letter: Miss Evans, for example, who had taught at the Clergy Daughters' School, or Mary Taylor, friend of Charlotte Brontë since schooldays at Roe Head and now settled in New Zealand. Chance lent its opportunities too, as when Gaskell met at dinner William Scoresby, ex-whaler and clergyman, who gave her accounts of West Riding life. All kinds of records were sought out: buildings, books, school reports, registers, and letters, while oral history plays its part, whether the testimony of the Burnley woman who nursed Mrs Brontë or the waiter at the Chapter Coffee House or the unnamed yet individual voices of Haworth. Again and again, Gaskell uses in *The Life* phrases like 'told me', 'informs me', 'writes to me', as authentication of her account. In the accretion of materials and voices can be sensed the influence of Walter Scott and of Macaulay, who had established the importance of social and personal history. Scott in his novels retrieved the past as human drama, while Macaulay in his *History of England* made—from plays, ballads, political lampoons, the state of the weather, details of meals and dress and behaviour—a vital palimpsest of the past. Gaskell's concern when she began as a novelist had been to give 'utterance' to the 'dumb people' of Manchester. Though her subject in *The Life* was articulate enough as the novels and letters show, in death she is dumb, and Gaskell's efforts raised up a cloud of witnesses, to authenticate the work and make Charlotte live.

In gathering this material, Gaskell also found herself collaborating with her informants. Even as a writer of fiction, Gaskell had not worked in splendid isolation. Her husband William looked over what she wrote, while friends, including Charlotte herself, were consulted during the gestation of *Ruth*. But here was a new sense of interaction. The positive side of such collaboration is obvious: it helped retrieve Charlotte's words, opinions, behaviour. The obverse is the control such witnesses sought to exercise. Gaskell had to co-operate for the value of their evidence and yet remain her own woman. People could be unexpectedly touchy. Even Patrick Brontë, while congratulating Gaskell on her work, 'done rightly, as I wish'd it to be', remarked on 'a few trifling mistakes, which . . . may be corrected in the Second Edition'.[21] Yet her energy in pursuit and her sympathy in contact (Gaskell had a happy gift of putting people at ease) ensured Gaskell a rich harvest from her collaborators.

To penetrate the inner life, Gaskell, modelling herself on Boswell, had particular recourse to Charlotte's letters, which in *The Life* show Charlotte developing from a gauche and self-conscious correspondent to a lively and penetrating commentator, even while Gaskell in her use of those same letters shows herself apt at seizing on the characteristic and distinctive. Not content with the half-dozen that Nicholls offered her on her visit to Haworth, Gaskell set about getting hold of all Charlotte's letters that she could, to reveal in the writer's shifting responses to her correspondents the facets of Charlotte's inner nature. It was to Ellen Nussey that Gaskell turned first. 'Mr Nicholls said that he thought that you were the person of all others to apply to',[22] and Ellen had indeed kept Charlotte's letters in a correspondence dating over twenty-four years. These she went through, deleting names (though not completely or consistently), before forwarding them to Gaskell. Even when Gaskell did not quote a letter, she might draw on it in paraphrase for information. She also saw and annotated letters not used, but which may have coloured her presentation of events, as when Patrick Brontë, baffled by his daughter's terrible silence at his opposition to her marrying Nicholls, wrote to Charlotte in the person of the Parsonage spaniel, Flossy.[23] Much has been made of Ellen's conventional nature: while this has some truth, Ellen had experience in her own family of extended physical and mental illnesses, and she was loyal to Charlotte as friend and confidante. Without Ellen, *The Life* could not have existed in anything like its range of detail and colour.

---

[21] 2 Apr. 1857, John Rylands MS; *Elizabeth Gaskell: The Critical Heritage*, pp. 373–4.
[22] *Letters*, p. 361.
[23] This letter of course is not *by* Charlotte, but Charlotte sent it to Ellen (19 Jan. 1853). Ellen passed it to Gaskell, who noted on the letter: 'Written to C. in the dog's name. Mr. B. dare not encounter again face to face C.'s sense of justice and Godly integrity, so he took this method of undermining Mr. N.' (*Brontë Society Transactions*, 12 (1953), 196–7).

The success of *Jane Eyre* had drawn Charlotte into correspondence with George Smith, head of her publishers, Smith, Elder,
whom some thought Charlotte had hoped to marry. He had been
generous and supportive to Charlotte as her publisher, and was to
prove so to Gaskell. Gaskell obviously had great hope of George
Smith's letters. At first, he let her have only a few, claiming the
rest contained 'matter of too purely personal nature to be generally
interesting'.[24] More were forthcoming, but in providing the letters,
George Smith enforced a measure of censorship on personal
details. Smith was clearly important in advising and guiding
Gaskell when she asked for advice in the process of writing, and
she looked to his professional expertise as the manuscript was
transferred into print, yet Gaskell regretted such losses, recognizing in Thackeray in tears over *Jane Eyre*, or Charlotte touched by
a fire provided in her bedroom, the human details that, like
sunbeams through chinks, could realize the power of the writer or
the spartan conditions of Haworth Parsonage.[25]

A biography by its nature extends into the life of many of its
readers. The biographer not only has to take account during
composition of the living who want their version written into the
record; after publication, there are the living who, through pressure groups or by invoking the law, object to how they are
represented. Here, truth, certainly as the biographer perceives it,
may be a victim. Mary Taylor, commenting on the difficulty of
biography, feared that Gaskell would raise a wasps' nest if she
spoke the truth of living people.[26] Some wasps Gaskell had tried
to avoid or at least was prepared for; she had recognized the need
for delicacy in writing about Patrick Brontë, about Nicholls, about
the Hegers. But she had also set herself to defend and vindicate Charlotte by telling the truth in ways that might well
give offence. 'Do you mind the law of libel?' she asked George

---

[24] *Letters*, p. 874.

[25] For Thackeray and for the bedroom fire, see notes to pp. 259 and 325. For George
Smith's role in securing Nicholls's agreement over the copyright of Charlotte's letters, see
Juliet Barker, *The Brontës*, pp. 794–5.

[26] To Ellen Nussey, 19 Apr.–10 May 1856; Joan Stevens, *Mary Taylor: Friend of
Charlotte Brontë* (1972), p. 126. It was presumably this letter that Gaskell reported to
George Smith: 'Does Mrs Gaskell know "what a nest of hornets she is pulling about her
ears?" ' (*Letters*, p. 446).

Smith;[27] the tone is humorous, but the intention was serious. Two subjects of Gaskell's 'libel' caused her (and others) much trouble. One was Mrs Robinson (now Lady Scott), the 'wicked seducer'[28] of Branwell as the Brontës saw her. The other, whom Gaskell perhaps did not expect to be a difficulty and had not named to George Smith, was the Reverend W. Carus Wilson or more properly his family, friends, and admirers, who proved to be legion.

Carus Wilson was founder of the Clergy Daughters' School, the cause, Gaskell believed, as did Charlotte herself, of the death of two of Charlotte's sisters and of Charlotte's emotional sufferings and stunted growth. Wilson, still alive in 1857, though retired through ill health from any active part in the school, was a clergyman of a kind easy to dislike, dogmatic and convinced of his own righteousness. The school was founded with good intentions, but there is no doubt that the first Cowan Bridge period of the Clergy Daughters' School saw bad management and unhealthy conditions in buildings, regime, and food. Carus Wilson took no part himself in the controversy, but a vociferous body sprang up on his behalf. While those determined to fault Gaskell's presentation of Cowan Bridge could do so (if the Brontës were already sickly children, their strength lowered by lack of animal food, how could Cowan Bridge be blamed for their death or stunted growth?), the weight of the evidence is that when the Brontës were there, there was poor management and poor provision. Gaskell, who had the account direct from Charlotte, remained convinced of the truth of her version. She made changes, but strengthened her case also—references to lack of animal food had been removed at Patrick Brontë's own insistence, while the evidence of the doctor was reinforced. Essentially, Gaskell needed to withdraw nothing of substance in her account.

On the other hand, the case of Mrs Robinson was and is problematical. The Brontës themselves, whatever blame they cast on their brother, believed she had seduced Branwell. Some of the claims originally made by Gaskell can be disproved: Mr Robinson's will has no reference to Branwell, for example. Yet Mrs Robinson

27 *Letters*, p. 418.
28 The phrase is Patrick Brontë's from his letter of 2 Apr. 1857.

did send a servant to Haworth with news of her husband's death, while sums of money reached Branwell through the Robinsons' doctor. It seems that there was something between Mrs Robinson and Branwell, sufficient for Mr Robinson to dismiss Branwell, yet not so as to lead him to change his will or his affection for his wife. Effectively Gaskell here had no option, except to rewrite the material. The biographer yielded to the threat of the law. While she still believed the essential truth of the liaison and of Mrs Robinson's responsibility, the Brontë version, the changes Gaskell made included the excision of rhetorical excess and bombast that was better gone. Doubtful and untrue details also went—for example, that Branwell's pockets were full of her letters when he died. The less hysterical, more measured presentation gives the truth of Branwell's wreck and the consequences for his family, without the irrelevant distractions of calls for repentance.

In fleshing out the bare chronology offered by Patrick Brontë, Gaskell crucially established the parameters of Charlotte's biography. First, Gaskell re-creates the particularity of life at Haworth, with its steep village street, the children going up to the moors, while below is the Yorkshire wool industry. She builds up a picture of domestic and village life, through her witnesses and through the Brontë children's diary letters and through Charlotte's later imagining of a typical Sunday kitchen scene, the dog and cat demanding scraps of mutton and Tabby boiling the potatoes to a glue. Nor is the larger world of Haworth and the West Riding neglected: indeed, in Gaskell's design it was part of the vindication of Charlotte, an environment that would help explain Charlotte's writing and show that the coarseness with which she stood charged was part and parcel of her experience. Yet if Gaskell felt by such accounts she had cleared Charlotte of deliberate revelling in coarseness, to us the fascination lies in the cross-over between ancient and modern, violence and cultivation. The ancient is apparent in landscape, traditions, character, and still powerfully present, for example, in the riotous opposition to Mr Redhead's institution at Haworth. The modern is apparent in the woollen mills and their masters; the Luddite disturbances (little more than forty years before Gaskell is writing, a mere four years before Charlotte was born), after which Patrick Brontë kept a loaded pistol in his bedroom at night; the strike in which

Patrick took the side of the men; the struggle for a proper water supply.

If Gaskell recalls the older world of Robin Hood and the ghostly story of Captain Batt's bloody footprint, an imaginative world of the past and of romance which entwines with the romantic side of Charlotte's imagination, she also evokes industrialization and that world of railways to which people like the Brontës quickly adapted themselves for travel and for investment. She evokes too the struggles for religious liberty and political reform, the 1848 Revolutions and the Crimean War. The world displayed is often savage or indifferent, people die frequently and suddenly, but it is too a world of music, of singers and concerts, of books and pictures, of periodicals and newspapers. If Charlotte's childhood list of 'painters whose work I wish to see' is very conventional, even old-fashioned by the time it was set down, it demonstrates how a world of the mind and culture crowded in upon the children at the Parsonage: the Brontës were often narrow, bigoted in politics and religion, but they none the less had access to ideas and art. Gaskell, too, explores and unveils the imaginative enclosure of the inner worlds of their invention. The Brontë novels can then be seen not as inexplicable and unprepared productions, but as the fruition of a long apprenticeship. From a fortnight of having the 'little writings' in her possession in July 1856, Gaskell was able to write the startling account of them. The Brontës, as Gaskell makes vividly apparent, did not sit in enrapt isolation, away from all the world, though it need not then be thought that they lived the kind of normal life that Gaskell herself led. They show the isolation characteristic of parsonage families. As children they kept together and were in many respects strange throughout their lives. The particularity of Gaskell's re-creation shows Charlotte as individual, not exemplary: as someone constrained by circumstances and her own nature at a time when many women, Gaskell and Harriet Martineau among them, were redefining roles and freedoms.

That the Brontës lived in Haworth Parsonage is of course a significant, not a casual fact. Gaskell, herself a clergyman's wife, appreciated the centrality of religion in Charlotte's experience (she quotes with approval Heger's comment that Charlotte was nourished on the Bible), even while her own liberal Unitarianism gave her a doctrinal tolerance and an (occasionally ironic) outsider's view. She establishes, besides the increasing tensions of an established church challenged in the West Riding and in the nineteenth century, the sense of opportunity that the Church, as exemplified in Patrick Brontë's career, gave through education and patronage. She conveys the power of Methodism as a force within the Church of England as well as a challenge to it, and the pervasive force of evangelicalism, particularly that of Charles Simeon. Simeon's evangelicalism, with its stress on Calvinistic doctrine, personal conversion, the individual speaking to God without other human mediation, is part of the fabric of *The Life*, significantly in Carus Wilson and the Clergy Daughters' School, almost (but not quite) casually in the preachers Charlotte wanted to hear in London. While Charlotte, like her father, rejected the doctrinal extremes of evangelicalism, its seriousness can be felt in Jane Eyre's inward debate after the interrupted marriage cere-mony, and is at the core of Lucy Snowe's confrontation of a European world that she believes interposes the priest between the individual and God, not just in religion but in all relationships. Gaskell also, if more cautiously, touches on Charlotte's own attraction (often expressed as strong repulsion) to the Catholic Church: Charlotte's ambivalence reveals her emotional rather than intellectual response to religion.

It was while abroad, as Gaskell makes clear, for all the childhood excitements of Catholic Emancipation, that Charlotte was most aware of Catholicism. 'Abroad', indeed, is a theme crucial to Charlotte's life and to her writings: two of her novels are set largely in Brussels, while the East and West Indies have a part in *Jane Eyre*, the European struggle between French and English in *Shirley*. Gaskell herself delighted in Europe: she set out for Rome immediately on completion of *The Life*, and in France was as ready to converse with a gardener at Saint-Germain-en-Laye as with her friend Mme Mohl in Paris. For Charlotte, going abroad to acquire French was a prerequisite in setting up a school; if the language could have been acquired without going abroad, Charlotte would have embraced that option. The experience proved deeply disturb-ing and while it was only intensely disagreeable in her second year—when she was without Emily; when Heger, an increasing object of desire, was no longer teaching her or indeed had much time for her—it was one that stimulated Charlotte's prejudices rather than her curiosity.[29] Yet Gaskell, though discreetly eliding Charlotte's obsession with Heger, both depicts that experience and shows how without it, neither *The Professor* nor *Villette* would have been written—and not just because Brussels provided the material of the teacher abroad. The Belgian experience provided the clash of systems, in which the English character must struggle, endure, and eventually survive on his or her own terms.

Throughout her work on the biography, Gaskell was aiming for the truth. That desire for truth, and through it the defence and vindication of Charlotte, appears in the book's shaping ideas—that Charlotte had suffered doubly as a woman. In her personal life, she knew deprivation and loss, while in her artistic life, despite her fame, she had been taunted as coarse and had none of the advantages that a man might take for granted. These points are made first for the reader by the epigraph, from Elizabeth Barrett Browning's *Aurora Leigh*, a woman's poem about the woman artist. They are at the heart also of Mary Taylor's letter, giving her reminiscences of Charlotte and her interpretation of Charlotte's life, which helps structure the work. It is a high view of her life, enforcing Gaskell's own recognition on first meeting Charlotte, of someone who had suffered. Mary described how, before she emigrated, she took farewell of Charlotte and urged her also to leave home. Gaskell quotes this passage (p. 220) and in the manuscript continued to transcribe Mary's letter:

She thought much of her duty, and had loftier and clearer notions of it than most people, and held fast to them with more success. It was done, it seems to me, with much more difficulty than people have of stronger nerves, and better fortunes. All her life was but labour and pain, and she never threw down the burden for the sake of present pleasure.

Gaskell then transferred this passage to the very end of *The Life*, where it seems to stand as the summation of Charlotte's life. The hero has scope in physical action, in a struggle with the world out in the world: the domestic sphere of the heroine is more painful

---

[29] Her comment to Emily that the inhabitants of the Pensionnat Heger were at 'their idolatrous "messe" ', its roots in a deeply protestant contempt for eucharistic doctrine, is more than a passing sarcasm. The names used in *Villette* are also scornful of Belgium: see Margaret Smith's notes to *Villette*, and Georgia S. Dunbar, 'Proper Names in *Villette*', *Nineteenth-Century Fiction*, 15 (June 1960), 77–80.

because of its passivity. But whatever Gaskell takes of Mary Taylor's idea of Charlotte's suffering, she finds it in the end essentially negative. Mary, for all her own sense of liberation, could only view the world cynically, representing it as rejecting Charlotte. If that were so, to what end has Gaskell written? She might as well have compiled a personal record and left it to her children, as she once thought to do.[30] If there is only Mary Taylor's 'world' that rejects, then how is Charlotte Brontë ever to be known by it? The suffering darkness of Charlotte's life is set against the uncomprehending darkness of the world. But Gaskell has realized another Charlotte and sketched an alternative world, even while she accepts a truth in Mary Taylor's version. Charlotte, in all her shyness, her strangeness, is made known, the outer and the inner life conveyed: her moods of depression and of exaltation; her fears of loneliness—and of ghost stories; her intense appreciation of the Bible, poetry, music, the theatre; her love of her family—even, in due course, of Nicholls. And she is portrayed in a world which may find her strange, but thinks it worth while *not* to reject her: a world represented in *The Life* by Ellen Nussey, Margaret Wooler, Constantin Heger, George Smith, Thackeray, and by Gaskell herself. It is to this world, of which Gaskell makes her readers a part, that Gaskell offers in the end, triumphantly, 'her dear friend, Charlotte Brontë'.

Elizabeth Gaskell's work stands as parent of all subsequent biography of the Brontës. After Gaskell, indeed, there was a long interval before another Brontë biography appeared. Ellen Nussey published her reminiscences of Charlotte in 1871, but the next formal biography was that of T. Wemyss Reid (1877). He felt able to write freely where respect for the living constrained Gaskell, while he aimed also to correct the impression, so powerfully

---

[30] Gaskell had written to George Smith in June 1855 of her determination to note down what she could remember of Charlotte, meaning it to be a record for her children (*Letters*, p. 347). She was not alone in keeping such records: Richard Monckton Milnes, a friend of Gaskell and the biographer of Keats, made notes about Charlotte and his later investigation of Branwell Brontë. The jottings about Charlotte in his Commonplace Books (Houghton papers, Trinity College, Cambridge) are a jumble of opinion, misinformation, and anecdote: Patrick Brontë is her 'tyrannical scriptural father,—a scholarly man who married late & was disgusted with family life', and there are the anecdotes of the sisters walking round the table at night and of the shocked response of a parent: ' "What do you mean, my dear? Love your governess?" ' (see pp. 247 and 136). Juliet Barker has found and discusses the Branwell material (*The Brontës*, ch. 28).

rendered by Gaskell, of Charlotte's 'extreme depression of spirits'. Attention turned to other members of the family. Mary Duclaux wrote a speculative life of Emily (1883) and F. A. Leyland, whose brother had been a friend of Branwell's, published in 1886 *The Brontë Family, with Special Reference to Patrick Branwell Brontë*, more apologia than biography. Towards the end of the century, Clement Shorter sought out Arthur Bell Nicholls in Ireland, and secured possession of manuscripts and material objects, including the Brontë juvenilia, unseen since Gaskell's reproduction of a page in *The Life*. This coup gave immense importance to Shorter's four books, produced between 1896 and 1914, on Charlotte and her circle. Another revelation came with the generous gift to the British Museum by the Heger family of Charlotte's letters to her Belgian teacher, published in M. H. Spielmann's *The Inner History of the Brontë–Heger Letters* (1919) and stimulating interest in an area where Gaskell had been extremely and deliberately circumspect. More recent biography, described in the Further Reading section, has explored further the individual Brontës and sought to dispel the shadows of Gaskell's work, whether those cast by the sufferings of her subject or by the obscurities dictated by tact or lack of information. Yet even at their most corrective, they pay homage in their flair for detail and their biographical architectonics to Elizabeth Gaskell as the great original in Charlotte Brontë's biography.

# NOTE ON THE TEXT

ELIZABETH GASKELL began writing *The Life of Charlotte Brontë* in early 1856, while still pursuing information, so that, for example, the long account of the writing and publication of *Jane Eyre* (pp. 258–65) was based on information from the publisher George Smith, still 'to come', as Gaskell noted on the manuscript at that point in her narrative. The manuscript, a work of collaboration both in its many contributors and in the copying and correction done in it physically by Gaskell's husband William and by her daughters Marianne and Meta, is now in the John Rylands University Library of Manchester. Its approximately 680 pages (665 numbered pages plus additional sheets) are handsomely bound in two volumes that correspond almost but not exactly to the two-volume division of the printed work. It is complete (except for a few lines at the end of vol. I of the manuscript) and is the copy sent to the printers, being marked up with the names of the compositors, though it is not in all respects identical to the biography as published.

The pressure Gaskell wrote under allowed her little time for detailed revision, yet the demands of accuracy, of tact and discretion, besides the incorporation of material as it came to hand, mean that there are many changes, deletions, additions in what is in bulk the original and only manuscript. The evidence survives of some rewriting: there is an original and its fair copy of one page (both numbered 615: one is bound in its proper sequence, the other with the additions for the Third Edition at the end of vol. II of the manuscript), while another, extended manuscript passage, the account of the 'pop' visit to London by Charlotte and Anne in July 1848, for which we know there was once another and earlier manuscript version, which has not survived, is substantially different from the printed text (see p. 281 note). The differences between the manuscript and the First Edition arise because *The Life* is an example of work in process, not only within its writing but also within its production in printed form. The manuscript as it stands does not provide the text of the biography: it is distinctly different not only in features of punctuation and mechanical presentation (the chapter divisions, which Gaskell only sketchily indicated in the manuscript, for example), but also in grammatical and stylistic changes, and omissions and rewritings. The omissions, even when not deleted, are clearly deliberate: Gaskell's family copyists transcribed letters that Gaskell then edited in manuscript, while Gaskell (or her publisher) recognized on occasions that the biographer's self-imposed limits (in not speaking ill of the living, for example) had been overstepped. This process of change also occurs in a limited way in the Second Edition and quite fundamentally in the Third Edition. No material has been incorporated into the *text* of this edition from the manuscript, though the manuscript is important for emendations. The Explanatory Notes offer the more interesting examples of Gaskell's deleted and undeleted material and indicate the treatment of Charlotte Brontë's letters. Material from Charlotte's letters, in the manuscript but not printed, is not usually given, since it has mostly been printed elsewhere and all of it is in Margaret Smith's Clarendon edition of Charlotte's letters.

The First Edition appeared in two volumes on 25 March 1857. The setting up had proceeded rapidly, with initial difficulties, like the lack of Es with the diaeresis (Ë) for 'BRONTË' in the running headlines (note on MS p. 21 verso), soon being overcome. Gaskell and probably her publisher rewrote on the proofs (or, if separately, in manuscript that, like the proofs, has not survived), this rewriting being both stylistic (grammar, phrasing, avoidance of repetition of words) and substantive. Proof-reading seems to have been by light of nature, that is, without reference to the manuscript, and while the printers worked to a high standard and proof-reading was good (the First Edition has very few literal misprints), what are clearly misreadings of the manuscript (as against corrections at proof-stage) slipped through. Perhaps the most interesting example of this misreading, because in a passage that was progressively corrupted in the First and Second Editions and which besides has rightly attracted readers' attention, is the account of the sisters gathering in the evening to walk about the room and to discuss their writing. The First Edition says they began 'their study, pacing' the room, for the manuscript's 'their steady pacing': in the Second Edition, the oddity of phrasing was recognized and without any reference back to the manuscript the word 'beginning' was

changed to 'commencing', which while it fitted better with 'their
study', corrupted Gaskell's account yet further (see Textual Variants to p. 247 for details of these two examples and a third
misreading in the same vivid passage). This edition reverts here to
the reading of the manuscript and to Gaskell's intentions.

Gaskell, away in Italy, heard nothing of the work's publication
or reception, and only in Venice, on her way home, first saw a
copy, in the English-language edition produced for sale on the
Continent by the German publisher Tauchnitz. But so successful
was the work that a Second Edition had been called for and
appeared in two volumes in April 1857. It has been common (as I
myself have always done) to speak of this as a reprint or reissue
rather than a distinct edition. True, being entirely reset, it is not a
reprint from the original type-setting, but since the publishers had
no communication with Gaskell, it could not offer authorial
changes. Yet it does have changes, which subsequently acquired
authorial authority. There are a significant number of variants from
the First Edition (more than 90, excluding numerous changes,
mainly with regard to accents, in the French passages), all of them,
with one exception, being stylistic and grammatical. Given their
nature, it is reasonable to conjecture that they were all or mostly
made by William Gaskell: Gaskell looked to her husband to pick
up on stylistic details and phrasing and on grammar. All these
changes were accepted by Gaskell into the Third Edition, except,
oddly, the one substantive change, an anecdotal footnote about
Tabby (see p. 63 note). The only person who seems previously to
have noticed this anecdote is Clement Shorter in his edition of *The
Life* (1900, p. xxvii), though he mistakenly claims it is 'the only
variation between the two issues'. One result of these changes,
intelligently done though they are, was the treating of all the text
as though it were entirely by Gaskell and therefore legitimately
subject to the changes she expected her husband to make. Charlotte Brontë's letters, therefore, were subjected to the same treatment in their grammar. The present edition restores Charlotte's
own words where the change is made in the Second Edition.

When Gaskell returned to England in June 1857 she met the full
force of the wasps' nest she had stirred up and it momentarily
overwhelmed her. A revised edition of *The Life* was needed. The
statements about Mrs Robinson (Lady Scott) had, in Gaskell's

absence, been legally withdrawn, while the supporters of the Revd W. Carus Wilson were clamorous in his defence. In setting about the revisions, Gaskell took on board the changes made in the Second Edition (we may reasonably conjecture, though there is no evidence, that she was told of them, in general if not in detail). Gaskell apparently used a copy of the Second Edition for keying in and inserting her additions—all its changes appear in the Third Edition and these should in general principle therefore be incorporated where Gaskell's own words are concerned. Since, though, she did not systematically approve each variation, some discretion is both possible and necessary in this process.

Mary Taylor had declared that the new version would be mutilated, but the Third Edition has authority for a number of reasons. First and foremost, its revisions are authorial. In the course of her work, Gaskell not only removed and rewrote things that gave offence, but also incorporated new material, on the Yorkshire background, for example. She also deleted or softened some of her rhetorical excesses, an aesthetic gain, and by so doing opened out the possibility of debate, even while standing by her own beliefs and interpretations. The manuscript additions and revisions vary between small changes (for example, directing the printers that 'Miss Wooler' should become 'Miss W——' throughout) and passages of some length. Those that survive, with the exception of a page preserved in Manchester Central Public Library, are bound up with the manuscript in the John Rylands University Library of Manchester (see the Explanatory Notes for details). Manuscript material known not to survive includes a letter from Gaskell's friend and legal adviser, William Shaen, giving corrections that she asked to be incorporated (*Letters*, pp. 462–3). The Third Edition appeared in two volumes at the end of August 1857.

The present edition, based on the Third Edition (there is no evidence that Gaskell was concerned with any subsequent issue of the work), takes account of the manuscript, the first two editions, and also the text of Charlotte Brontë's letters. The changes of this edition from the text of the Third Edition (145 in all, listed in the Textual Variants at the end of the volume) involve in the main (i) emendations from the manuscript or (ii) a rejection of misreadings introduced by the Second Edition. In both cases caution is needed. The manuscript, as already indicated, was a stage in the composition (the main stage, of course); it cannot therefore simply be assumed that all changes from it are misreadings allowed to stand by 'light of nature' proof-reading. On a conservative basis, 100 changes have been made on the authority of the manuscript (including a few from the manuscript additions to the Third Edition). In the case of the Second Edition, while Gaskell accepted its changes and they so far have authorial authority, no change of itself has specific authorial sanction. I have therefore gone back to the First Edition when the change in the Second Edition does not make good sense or is merely arbitrary or seems to be a printing error or omission. The Second Edition's changes in the text of letters by Charlotte Brontë have also been rejected. On this basis, itself conservatively applied, 28 changes from the Second Edition are made, of which the majority are reversions to the original and proper readings of Charlotte's letters. There is one reversion to the First Edition (p. 116, 'Legh' for 'Leigh') where the manuscript had misspelt the name, and where the Second Edition independently reverted to the incorrect spelling. Purely editorial changes are very few.

Two special features need a little more notice. This edition's treatment of Charlotte Brontë's letters, an important component of *The Life*, has already been explained; changes made to the letters in the Second Edition are rejected in favour of the First Edition. This policy, by restoring what Charlotte herself wrote, also helps vindicate Gaskell from the suggestion that she was cavalier in handling these letters. While not claiming a scholarly exactness for her, I would stress that Gaskell is generally careful and accurate in reproduction and in indicating how the letters are handled. That she edits and omits was part of her authorial policy, made explicit in the work itself: nothing offensive about the living should appear and she omits in the Third Edition a passage which violated this principle (see p. 406 note). In 4 emendations I have gone back beyond Gaskell's manuscript to Charlotte's original. The question might arise, whether an edition could go back directly and restore Charlotte's own texts in full: but Gaskell was consciously and deliberately working with these letters and this, after all, is an edition of *The Life of Charlotte Brontë*. Where Gaskell's manuscript allows it I have gone back to Charlotte's words; where that manuscript is quite clear, as with 'sniggle' and '*mais*' (p. 152),

Gaskell's version has been retained. In the case of the four exceptions, where the manuscript and printed editions are in some measure at odds and the text of Charlotte's letter is given, I would, if challenged, revert to Gaskell's manuscript rather than abandon Gaskell's representation of Charlotte's words.

The other area that needs comment is the passages of French. There are two substantial exercises in French composition, and letters by Charlotte, by Heger, and by an anonymous French lady. This edition is the first to offer translations of them all and indeed gives the first translation ever of several of them, including 'Peter the Hermit': literalness rather than grace has been aimed at. The French passages offer a particular editorial problem, on which I have taken the opportunity of Gaskell's authority to cut the Gordian knot. The texts Gaskell had, including the two French exercises, were often accented very lightly (Heger was clearly relaxed about this formal aspect) and at various stages, in the First Edition, in the Second Edition (arbitrarily and inconsistently), and in the Third Edition at Gaskell's own behest (*Letters*, p. 464), accents were put in and the French occasionally corrected. Since Gaskell accepted and indeed endorsed these changes, they are reproduced as in the Third Edition. The exception to this is in 'Peter the Hermit', where a phrase from the manuscript is included, omitted in printing because it was crossed through to represent a crossing out by Charlotte: despite Heger's marginal comment, 'Why this deletion?', when the printed text has never shown a deletion, the phrase's absence has not previously been noted.

Oxford house style is followed throughout in the use of full stops after abbreviations, chapter headings, running headlines, and titles, and in the use of single and double inverted commas. Because page settings do not correspond to those of Ed. 3, not all the right-hand headlines are included. A few obvious printing errors have been silently corrected.

# NOTE ON THE NOTES

EDITORIAL notes are keyed in by asterisks (*); Gaskell's own notes are keyed in by numerals and given at the foot of the page.

Unless otherwise indicated in the text or notes, all letters are addressed to Ellen Nussey. In the text Gaskell's own abbreviations are E. = Ellen Nussey; W. = Margaret Wooler; Mary (or Mary T. or Polly) = Mary Taylor.

# FURTHER READING

THE Brontë biography is well covered, though new facts as well as new interpretations continue to emerge. For Patrick Brontë, the standard life is still John Lock and W. T. Dixon, *A Man of Sorrow: The Life, Letters and Times of the Rev. Patrick Brontë 1777–1861* (1965), which has much information, though of the 'veins stood out like whip-cords' school of writing. A major claim to the Brontë children has been made by Winifred Gérin in her tetralogy: *Anne Brontë* (1959; rev. 1976); *Branwell Brontë* (1961); *Charlotte Brontë: The Evolution of Genius* (1967); *Emily Brontë* (1971). Though challenged on detail, Gérin's biographies are excellent as narratives and very full on the milieu. Rebecca Fraser, *Charlotte Brontë* (1988), gives a good account and takes recent scholarship on board. Lyndall Gordon's *Charlotte Brontë: A Passionate Life* (1994) is primarily an interpretative study. The most recent work, of immense scholarship, takes account of the Brontës as a family: Juliet Barker's *The Brontës* (1994) goes back again and again to seek evidence for what has been assumed or left uninvestigated, while conducting at length a forceful narrative. The letters of the Brontës have until now been ill-served. The edition by T. J. Wise and J. A. Symington, *The Brontës: Their Lives, Friendships and Correspondence* (4 vols., 1932; repr. in 2 vols., 1980), has long been recognized as unreliable, yet it was the only collection and contains much that is undoubtedly useful. For Charlotte Brontë's letters, it is now replaced by Margaret Smith's edition (3 vols.; 1995– ), with full reliable texts and annotations. The novels have all been edited in the Clarendon Brontë and transferred in paperback to World's Classics: as well as good texts these provide good notes and various appendices. Christine Alexander has provided *A Bibliography of The Manuscripts of Charlotte Brontë* (1982), and a study of the juvenilia, the *Early Writings of Charlotte Brontë* (1983), and is currently editing the *Early Writings of Charlotte Brontë* (3 vols. to date, 1987– ). Two of Charlotte's friends are covered by Barbara Whitehead's study of Ellen Nussey, *Charlotte Brontë and Her 'Dearest Nell'* (1993), and in a rather more specialized way by Joan Stevens, *Mary Taylor: Friend of Charlotte Brontë* (1972).

George Smith is studied in a series of chapters by Jenifer Glynn's *Prince of Publishers: A Biography of George Smith* (1986).

On Gaskell, the best recent biography is Jenny Uglow, *Elizabeth Gaskell: A Habit of Stories* (1993), which has a lively account of *The Life*'s writing and nature. Winifred Gérin's *Elizabeth Gaskell: A Biography* (1976), though sympathetic, is lightweight on detail. For the writing and the reception of *The Life*, see Angus Easson, *Elizabeth Gaskell* (1979), still the fullest account of the composition and manuscript. Gaskell's letters, besides being wonderful to read, shed light on her friendship with Charlotte and the various stages of *The Life* (*The Letters of Mrs Gaskell*, ed. J. A. V. Chapple and Arthur Pollard, 1966; *Further Letters of Mrs Gaskell*, ed. John Chapple and Alan Shelston, 2000).

For the reception of the Brontë novels in their own time, see Miriam Allott (ed.), *The Brontës: The Critical Heritage* (1974), which includes a selection of responses to *The Life*: these latter are amplified by Angus Easson (ed.), *Elizabeth Gaskell: The Critical Heritage* (1991). Of more specialized studies, Elisabeth Jay, *The Religion of the Heart: Anglican Evangelicanism and the Nineteenth-Century Novel* (1979), is good on the nature of evangelicanism, while Enid Duthie, *The Foreign Vision of Charlotte Brontë* (1975), is excellent on Charlotte in Belgium and her learning French. In following the Brontë trail, Eddie Flintoff's *In the Steps of the Brontës* (1993) is a good guide.

Amongst articles should be mentioned Angus Easson, 'Domestic Romanticism: Elizabeth Gaskell and *The Life of Charlotte Brontë*', *Durham University Journal*, NS 42 (June 1981), 169–76; Suzann Bick, 'Clouding the "Severe Truth": Elizabeth Gaskell's Strategy in *The Life of Charlotte Brontë*', *Essays in Arts and Sciences*, 11 (1982), 33–47; Marnie Jones, 'George Smith's Influence on *The Life of Charlotte Brontë*', *Brontë Society Transactions*, 18 (1984), 279–85; Harold Fromm, 'The Lives and Deaths of Charlotte Brontë: A Case of Literary Politics', *Hudson Review*, 40/2 (1987), 233–50; and Alison Kershaw, 'The Business of a Woman's Life: Elizabeth Gaskell's *Life of Charlotte Brontë*', *Brontë Society Transactions*, 20 (1990), 11–24. The *Brontë Society Transactions* are generally useful. Finally, A. O. J. Cockshut's *Truth to Life: The Art of Biography in the Nineteenth Century* (1974) discusses biography generally, though without mentioning either Gaskell or Charlotte Brontë.

# A CHRONOLOGY OF
# ELIZABETH GASKELL

1810 (29 Sept.) Elizabeth Cleghorn Stevenson, second surviving child
of William Stevenson and Elizabeth Holland, born in Chelsea.

1811 (Nov.) After her mother's death, Elizabeth is taken to Knutsford
to live with her Aunt Hannah Lumb.

1822–7 Attends school at Misses Byerley's in Warwick and Stratford-
upon-Avon.

1828–9 Her elder brother, John Stevenson (b. 1799), disappears while on
a voyage to India. Elizabeth goes to Chelsea to live with her father
and stepmother.

1829 (22 Mar.) Elizabeth's father dies; she goes to Newcastle upon
Tyne, to the home of the Revd William Turner.

1831 Spends much of this year in Edinburgh with Mr Turner's
daughter. Visits Manchester.

1832 (30 Aug.) Marries the Revd William Gaskell, assistant Minister at
Cross Street Chapel, Manchester, at St John's Parish Church,
Knutsford. They live at 14 Dover Street, Manchester.

1833 Her first child, a daughter, born dead.

1834 Her second daughter, Marianne, born.

1837 A poem, 'Sketches among the Poor', by Mr and Mrs Gaskell,
appears in *Blackwood's Magazine* (Jan.). Her third daughter,
Margaret Emily (Meta), born. Mrs Hannah Lumb dies.

1840 Her description of Clopton Hall included by William Howitt in
*Visits to Remarkable Places*.

1841 Mr and Mrs Gaskell visit the Continent, touring the Rhine
country.

1842 Her fourth daughter, Florence Elizabeth, born. The family move
to 121 Upper Rumford Street, Manchester.

1844 Her only son, William, born; dies of scarlet fever at Festiniog,
1845.

1846 Her fifth daughter, Julia Bradford, born.

1848 'Christmas Storms and Sunshine' in *Howitt's Journal*. Her first
novel, *Mary Barton*, published.

1849 Visits London, where she meets Dickens and other literary figures.
Meets Wordsworth while on holiday in Ambleside.

1850 The family move to 84 Plymouth Grove, Manchester. Dickens
invites Gaskell to contribute to *Household Words*: 'Lizzie Leigh'
begins in first number, followed by 'The Well of Pen Morfa' and

'The Heart of John Middleton'. *The Moorland Cottage* published. (Aug.) First meets Charlotte Brontë.

1851    Continues to write for *Household Words*, the first episode of *Cranford* appearing in Dec. Visited by Charlotte Brontë in June. Her portrait, now in the National Portrait Gallery, drawn by Richmond.

1852    Gives Charlotte Brontë the outline of *Ruth* (Apr.). Visited by Dickens (Sept.).

1853    *Ruth* (Jan.) and *Cranford* (June) published. Begins *North and South*. (Apr. and Aug.) Visits exchanged with Charlotte Brontë.

1854    (Sept.) *North and South* begins to appear in *Household Words*. Her husband succeeds as Minister of Cross Street Chapel, Manchester. Visits France with Marianne: meets Mme Mohl and William W. Story. Meets Florence Nightingale in London. Last meeting with Charlotte Brontë (May).

1855    *North and South* and *Lizzie Leigh and Other Stories* published. In June, Charlotte Brontë's father asks her to write his daughter's *Life*. She and Meta spend a month in Paris with Mme Mohl.

1857    *Life of Charlotte Brontë* published. Visits Paris and Rome with her two eldest daughters and Catherine Winkworth.

1859    *Round the Sofa and Other Tales* published. Visits Whitby where she collects material for *Sylvia's Lovers*. Takes her daughters Meta and Florence to Germany, returning via Paris.

1860    *Right at Last and Other Tales* published. 'Curious, if True' in *The Cornhill*. Visits to France.

1862    Visits Paris, Normandy, and Brittany with Meta and a friend, returning to London for the Exhibition. Back in Manchester she over-exerts herself in relief work among the workmen, and has to recuperate. Writes a Preface to Vecchi's *Garibaldi*.

1863    'Cousin Phillis' in *The Cornhill*. *Sylvia's Lovers* published by Smith, Elder. Visits Mme Mohl in Paris, going on to Rome with three of her daughters. Her daughter Florence marries.

1864    *Wives and Daughters* begins to appear in *The Cornhill*.

1865    *Cousin Phillis and Other Tales* and *The Grey Woman and Other Tales* published. Visits Dieppe, and Mme Mohl in Paris. Buys a house, The Lawns, nr. Holybourne in Hampshire, and dies there suddenly on 12 Nov.

1866    *Wives and Daughters* published posthumously.

# A CHRONOLOGY OF
# CHARLOTTE BRONTË

| | |
|---|---|
| 1816 | (21 Apr.) Born at Thornton, Bradford, Yorkshire, third child of Patrick and Maria Brontë. |
| 1817 | (26 June) Patrick Branwell Brontë born. |
| 1818 | (30 July) Emily Jane Brontë born. |
| 1820 | (17 Jan.) Anne Brontë born. |
| | (20 Apr.) The Brontës move to Haworth, near Keighley, Yorkshire. |
| 1821 | (15 Sept.) Mrs Brontë dies. |
| 1824 | (10 Aug.) Charlotte arrives at Cowan Bridge school, Lancashire; (25 Nov.) joined by Emily. |
| 1825 | (6 May) Charlotte's elder sister Maria dies, |
| | (1 June) Elizabeth, Charlotte, and Emily return to Haworth. |
| | (15 June) Elizabeth Brontë dies. |
| 1825–30 | Brontë children at home under supervision of their aunt, Elizabeth Branwell. |
| 1831 | (Jan.) Charlotte arrives at Miss Wooler's school, Roe Head, near Mirfield, Yorkshire. |
| 1832 | (May) Charlotte leaves Roe Head. |
| 1835 | (July) Charlotte returns to Roe Head as teacher. |
| 1837 | (May) Miss Wooler's school moves to Dewsbury Moor. |
| 1838 | (Dec.) Charlotte leaves Dewsbury Moor. |
| 1839 | (Mar.) Refuses Henry Nussey's proposal of marriage. |
| | (May) Governess at Mrs Sidgwick's at Stonegappe, Lothersdale. |
| | (July) Leaves Stonegappe. |
| | (July) Refuses Mr Bryce's proposal. |
| | (Aug.–Sept.) Holiday with Ellen Nussey at Easton and Bridlington. |
| 1840 | With Emily at Haworth. |
| 1841 | (Mar.) Governess at Mrs White's, Upperwood House, Rawdon, near Bradford. |
| | (Dec.) Leaves Upperwood House. |
| 1842 | (Feb.) Goes with Emily to Mme Heger's school in Brussels. |
| | (29 Oct.) Miss Branwell dies at Haworth. |
| | (Nov.) Charlotte and Emily return to Haworth. |
| 1843 | (Jan.) Charlotte returns alone to Brussels. |
| 1844 | (Jan.) Charlotte leaves Brussels for Haworth; |
| | (July) Occupied with project of school at Haworth Parsonage. |

1844–5    Letters from Charlotte to M. Heger written.

1845      (July) Branwell receives dismissal from his post as tutor.

1846      (May) Publication of *Poems* by Currer, Ellis, and Acton Bell (Charlotte, Emily, and Anne).

          (Apr. 1846–July 1847) *The Professor* offered, without success, to various publishers.

          (Aug.) *Jane Eyre* begun.

1847      (Oct.) *Jane Eyre* published.

          (Dec.) *Wuthering Heights* (by Emily Brontë) and *Agnes Grey* (by Anne Brontë) published.

1848      (June) Anne's *The Tenant of Wildfell Hall* published. (July) Charlotte and Anne visit their publishers in London to prove the separate identity of the 'Bells'.

          (24 Sept.) Branwell dies.

          (19 Dec.) Emily dies.

1849      (28 May) Anne dies.

          (Oct.) *Shirley* published.

          (Nov.–Dec.) Charlotte visits London; meets Thackeray.

1850      (May–June) Visits London, sits for portrait to Richmond.

          (July) Visits Edinburgh.

          (Aug.) Meets Elizabeth Gaskell during visit to Kay-Shuttleworths.

1851      (May–June) Visits London for the Exhibition; visits Elizabeth Gaskell in Manchester. Begins writing *Villette*.

1852      *Villette* completed.

1853      (Jan.) Last visit to London.

          (Jan.) *Villette* published.

          (Apr.) Visits Elizabeth Gaskell in Manchester; Gaskell visits her at Haworth (Sept.).

1854      Visits Elizabeth Gaskell in Manchester.

          (June) Marries Revd A. B. Nicholls.

1855      (31 Mar.) Dies at Haworth.

# THE LIFE OF
# CHARLOTTE BRONTË

'O my God,
————————Thou hast knowledge, only Thou,
How dreary 'tis for women to sit still
On winter nights by solitary fires
And hear the nations praising them far off.'

AURORA LEIGH.*

# CONTENTS OF VOL. I

Extract from the introduction to 'Tales of the Islanders'—'History of the year 1829'—Charlotte's taste for Art—Extracts from other early writings in MS—Charlotte's mental tendencies and home duties—A strange occurrence at the Parsonage—A youthful effusion in verse     63

## CHAPTER VI

Personal description of Charlotte Brontë—Miss W——'s school at Roe Head—Oakwell Hall and its legends—Charlotte's first appearance at school—Her youthful character and political feelings—School days at Roe Head—Mr Cartwright and the Luddites—Mr Roberson of Heald's Hall—Chapel scenes and other characteristics of Heckmondwike and Gomersall     76

## CHAPTER VII

Charlotte Brontë leaves school, and returns home to instruct her sisters—Studies and books at the Parsonage—Visit from a school friend—Letters to a friend visiting London for the first time—On the choice of books—On dancing—Character and talents of Branwell Brontë—Plans for his advancement—Prospect of separation     94

## CHAPTER VIII

Charlotte as teacher at Miss W——'s school—Emily's home-sickness—Letters indicative of Charlotte's despondency and melancholy—The sisters at home—Winter evenings at Haworth—Charlotte writes to Southey, and Branwell to Wordsworth—Branwell's letter and verses—Prospect of losing the society of a friend—Charlotte's correspondence with Southey—Letter written in a state of despondency—Accident to the old servant, and characteristic kindness of the Brontës—Symptoms of illness in Anne Brontë—Charlotte's first proposal of marriage—Charlotte and Anne go out as governesses—Charlotte's experience of governess life—Advent of the first Curate at Haworth—A second proposal of marriage—A visit to the sea-side     109

## CHAPTER IX

Branwell Brontë still at home—Miss Branwell and her nieces—Plan of keeping a school—Charlotte commences her first story—The Curates at Haworth—Charlotte's sentiments on marriage—She seeks and obtains a situation as governess     145

## CHAPTER X

## CHAPTER XI

## CHAPTER XII

## CHAPTER XIII

## CHAPTER XIV

# CONTENTS OF VOL. II

## CHAPTER I

## CHAPTER II

## CHAPTER III

## CHAPTER IV

## CHAPTER V

## CHAPTER VI

## CHAPTER VII

## CHAPTER VIII

## CHAPTER IX

## CHAPTER X

## CHAPTER XI

## CHAPTER XII

## CHAPTER XIII

## CHAPTER XIV

# LIFE OF CHARLOTTE BRONTË
# VOLUME I

## CHAPTER I

THE Leeds and Skipton railway runs along a deep valley of the Aire; a slow and sluggish stream, compared to the neighbouring river of Wharfe. Keighley station* is on this line of railway, about a quarter of a mile from the town of the same name. The number of inhabitants and the importance of Keighley have been very greatly increased during the last twenty years, owing to the rapidly extended market for worsted manufactures, a branch of industry that mainly employs the factory population of this part of Yorkshire, which has Bradford for its centre and metropolis.

Keighley is in process of transformation from a populous, old-fashioned village, into a still more populous and flourishing town. It is evident to the stranger, that as the gable-ended houses, which obtrude themselves corner-wise on the widening street, fall vacant, they are pulled down to allow of greater space for traffic, and a more modern style of architecture. The quaint and narrow shop-windows of fifty years ago, are giving way to large panes and plate-glass. Nearly every dwelling seems devoted to some branch of commerce. In passing hastily through the town, one hardly perceives where the necessary lawyer and doctor can live, so little appearance is there of any dwellings of the professional middle-class, such as abound in our old cathedral towns. In fact, nothing can be more opposed than the state of society, the modes of thinking, the standards of reference on all points of morality, manners, and even politics and religion, in such a new manufacturing place as Keighley in the north, and any stately, sleepy, picturesque cathedral town in the south. Yet the aspect of Keighley promises well for future stateliness, if not picturesqueness. Grey stone abounds; and the rows of houses built of it have a kind of solid grandeur connected with their uniform and enduring lines.

The frame-work of the doors, and the lintels of the windows, even in the smallest dwellings, are made of blocks of stone. There is no painted wood to require continual beautifying, or else present a shabby aspect; and the stone is kept scrupulously clean by the notable Yorkshire housewifes. Such glimpses into the interior as a passer-by obtains, reveal a rough abundance of the means of living, and diligent and active habits in the women. But the voices of the people are hard, and their tones discordant, promising little of the musical taste that distinguishes the district, and which has already furnished a Carrodus to the musical world.* The names over the shops (of which the one just given is a sample) seem strange even to an inhabitant of the neighbouring county, and have a peculiar smack and flavour of the place.

The town of Keighley never quite melts into country on the road to Haworth, although the houses become more sparse as the traveller journeys upwards to the grey round hills that seem to bound his journey in a westerly direction. First come some villas; just sufficiently retired from the road to show that they can scarcely belong to any one liable to be summoned in a hurry, at the call of suffering or danger, from his comfortable fire-side; the lawyer, the doctor, and the clergyman, live at hand, and hardly in the suburbs, with a screen of shrubs for concealment.

In a town one does not look for vivid colouring; what there may be of this is furnished by the wares in the shops, not by foliage or atmospheric effects; but in the country some brilliancy and vividness seems to be instinctively expected, and there is consequently a slight feeling of disappointment at the grey neutral tint of every object, near or far off, on the way from Keighley to Haworth. The distance is about four miles; and, as I have said, what with villas, great worsted factories, rows of workmen's houses, with here and there an old-fashioned farm-house and outbuildings, it can hardly be called 'country' any part of the way. For two miles the road passes over tolerably level ground, distant hills on the left, a 'beck' flowing through meadows on the right, and furnishing water power, at certain points, to the factories built on its banks. The air is dim and lightless with the smoke from all these habitations and places of business. The soil in the valley (or 'bottom,' to use the local term) is rich; but, as the road begins to ascend, the vegetation becomes poorer; it does not flourish, it merely exists; and, instead of trees, there are only bushes and shrubs about the dwellings. Stone dykes are everywhere used in place of hedges; and what crops there are, on the patches of arable land, consist of pale, hungry-looking, grey-green oats. Right before the traveller on this road rises Haworth village; he can see it for two miles before he arrives, for it is situated on the side of a pretty steep hill, with a background of dun and purple moors, rising and sweeping away yet higher than the church, which is built at the very summit of the long narrow street. All round the horizon there is this same line of sinuous wave-like hills; the scoops into which they fall only revealing other hills beyond, of similar colour and shape, crowned with wild, bleak moors—grand, from the ideas of solitude and loneliness which they suggest, or oppressive from the feeling which they give of being pent-up by some monotonous and illimitable barrier, according to the mood of mind in which the spectator may be.

For a short distance the road appears to turn away from Haworth, as it winds round the base of the shoulder of a hill; but then it crosses a bridge over the 'beck,' and the ascent through the village begins. The flag-stones with which it is paved are placed end-ways, in order to give a better hold to the horses' feet; and, even with this help, they seem to be in constant danger of slipping backwards. The old stone houses are high compared to the width of the street, which makes an abrupt turn before reaching the more level ground at the head of the village, so that the steep aspect of the place, in one part, is almost like that of a wall. But this surmounted, the church lies a little off the main road on the left; a hundred yards, or so, and the driver relaxes his care, and the horse breathes more easily, as they pass into the quiet little by-street that leads to Haworth Parsonage.* The churchyard is on one side of this lane, the school-house and the sexton's dwelling (where the curates formerly lodged) on the other.

The parsonage stands at right angles to the road, facing down upon the church; so that, in fact, parsonage, church, and belfried school-house, form three sides of an irregular oblong, of which the fourth is open to the fields and moors that lie beyond. The area of this oblong is filled up by a crowded churchyard, and a small garden or court in front of the clergyman's house. As the entrance to this from the road is at the side, the path goes round the corner into the little plot of ground. Underneath the windows is a narrow flower-border, carefully tended in days of yore, although only the most hardy plants could be made to grow there. Within the stone wall, which keeps out the surrounding churchyard, are bushes of elder and lilac; the rest of the ground is occupied by a square grass-plot and a gravel walk. The house is of grey stone, two stories high, heavily roofed with flags, in order to resist the winds that might strip off a lighter covering. It appears to have been built about a hundred years ago, and to consist of four rooms on each story; the two windows on the right (as the visitor stands with his back to the church, ready to enter in at the front door) belonging to Mr Brontë's study, the two on the left to the family sitting-room. Everything about the place tells of the most dainty order, the most exquisite cleanliness. The door-steps are spotless; the small old-fashioned window-panes glitter like looking-glass. Inside and outside of that house cleanliness goes up into its essence, purity.

The little church lies, as I mentioned, above most of the houses in the village; and the graveyard rises above the church, and is terribly full of upright tombstones.* The chapel or church claims greater antiquity than any other in that part of the kingdom; but there is no appearance of this in the external aspect of the present edifice, unless it be in the two eastern windows, which remain unmodernized, and in the lower part of the steeple. Inside, the character of the pillars shows that they were constructed before the reign of Henry VII. It is probable that there existed on this ground, a 'field-kirk,' or oratory, in the earliest times; and, from the archbishop's registry at York, it is ascertained that there was a chapel at Haworth in 1317. The inhabitants refer inquirers concerning the date to the following inscription on a stone in the church tower:—

'Hic fecit Cænobium Monachorum Auteste fundator. A. D. sexcentissimo.'*

That is to say, before the preaching of Christianity in Northumbria. Whitaker says that this mistake originated in the illiterate copying out, by some modern stone-cutter, of an inscription in the character of Henry the Eighth's time on an adjoining stone:—

'Orate pro bono statu Eutest Tod.'

'Now every antiquary knows that the formula of prayer "bono statu" always refers to the living. I suspect this singular Christian name has been mistaken by the stone-cutter for Austet, a contraction of Eustatius, but the word Tod, which has been mis-read for the Arabic figures 600 is perfectly fair and legible. On the presumption of this foolish claim to antiquity, the people would needs set up for independence, and contest the right of the Vicar of Bradford to nominate a curate at Haworth.'

I have given this extract, in order to explain the imaginary groundwork of a commotion which took place in Haworth about five and thirty years ago, to which I shall have occasion to allude again more particularly.

The interior of the church is common-place; it is neither old enough nor modern enough to compel notice. The pews are of black oak, with high divisions; and the names of those to whom they belong are painted in white letters on the doors. There are neither brasses, nor altar-tombs, nor monuments, but there is a mural tablet on the right-hand side of the communion-table, bearing the following inscription:—

HERE
LIE THE REMAINS OF
## MARIA BRONTË, WIFE
OF THE
REV. P. BRONTË, A.B., MINISTER OF HAWORTH.
HER SOUL
DEPARTED TO THE SAVIOUR, SEPT. 15TH, 1821,
IN THE 39TH YEAR OF HER AGE.

'Be ye also ready: for in such an hour as ye think not the Son of Man cometh.'—Matthew xxiv. 44.

ALSO HERE LIE THE REMAINS OF
## MARIA BRONTË, DAUGHTER OF THE AFORESAID;
SHE DIED ON THE
6TH OF MAY, 1825, IN THE 12TH YEAR OF HER AGE;
AND OF
## ELIZABETH BRONTË, HER SISTER,
WHO DIED JUNE 15TH, 1825, IN THE 11TH YEAR OF HER AGE.

'Verily I say unto you, Except ye be converted, and become as little children, ye shall not enter into the kingdom of heaven.'—Matthew xviii. 3.

HERE ALSO LIE THE REMAINS OF

## PATRICK BRANWELL BRONTË,

WHO DIED SEPT. 24TH, 1848, AGED 30 YEARS;

AND OF

## EMILY JANE BRONTË,

WHO DIED DEC. 19TH, 1848, AGED 29 YEARS,

SON AND DAUGHTER OF THE

REV. P. BRONTË , INCUMBENT.

THIS STONE IS ALSO DEDICATED TO THE

## MEMORY OF ANNE BRONTË,[1]

YOUNGEST DAUGHTER OF THE REV. P. BRONTË, A.B.

SHE DIED, AGED 27 YEARS, MAY 28TH, 1849,

AND WAS BURIED AT THE OLD CHURCH, SCARBORO'.

At the upper part of this tablet ample space is allowed between the lines of the inscription; when the first memorials were written down, the survivors, in their fond affection, thought little of the margin and verge they were leaving for those who were still living. But as one dead member of the household follows another fast to the grave, the lines are pressed together, and the letters become small and cramped. After the record of Anne's death, there is room for no other.

But one more of that generation—the last of that nursery of six little motherless children—was yet to follow, before the survivor, the childless and widowed father, found his rest. On another tablet, below the first, the following record has been added to that mournful list:—

ADJOINING LIE THE REMAINS OF

## CHARLOTTE, WIFE

OF THE

REV. ARTHUR BELL NICHOLLS, A.B.,

AND DAUGHTER OF THE REV. P. BRONTË, A.B., INCUMBENT.

SHE DIED MARCH 31ST, 1855, IN THE 39TH

YEAR OF HER AGE.

---

[1] A reviewer pointed out the discrepancy between the age (twenty-seven years) assigned, on the mural tablet, to Anne Brontë at the time of her death in 1849, and the alleged fact that she was born at Thornton, from which place Mr Brontë removed on February 25th, 1820. I was aware of the discrepancy, but I did not think it of sufficient consequence to be rectified by an examination of the register of births. Mr Brontë's own words, on which I grounded my statement as to the time of Anne Brontë's birth, are as follows:—

'In Thornton, Charlotte, Patrick Branwell, Emily Jane, and Anne were born.' And such of the inhabitants of Haworth as have spoken on the subject say that all the children of Mr and Mrs Brontë were born before they removed to Haworth. There is probably some mistake in the inscription on the tablet.*

FOR a right understanding of the life of my dear friend, Charlotte Brontë, it appears to me more necessary in her case than in most others, that the reader should be made acquainted with the peculiar forms of population and society amidst which her earliest years were passed, and from which both her own and her sisters' first impressions of human life must have been received. I shall endeavour, therefore, before proceeding further with my work, to present some idea of the character of the people of Haworth, and the surrounding districts.

Even an inhabitant of the neighbouring county of Lancaster is struck by the peculiar force of character which the Yorkshiremen display. This makes them interesting as a race; while, at the same time, as individuals, the remarkable degree of self-sufficiency they possess gives them an air of independence rather apt to repel a stranger. I use this expression 'self-sufficiency' in the largest sense. Conscious of the strong sagacity and the dogged power of will which seem almost the birthright of the natives of the West Riding, each man relies upon himself, and seeks no help at the hands of his neighbour. From rarely requiring the assistance of others, he comes to doubt their power of bestowing it: from the general success of his efforts, he grows to depend upon them, and to over-esteem his own energy and power. He belongs to that keen, yet short-sighted class, who consider suspicion of all whose honesty is not proved as a sign of wisdom. The practical qualities of a man are held in great respect; but the want of faith in strangers and untried modes of action, extends itself even to the manner in which the virtues are regarded; and if they produce no immediate and tangible result, they are rather put aside as unfit for this busy, striving world; especially if they are more of a passive than an active character. The affections are strong, and their foundations lie deep: but they are not—such affections seldom are—wide-spreading; nor do they show themselves on the surface. Indeed, there is little display of any of the amenities of life among this wild, rough population. Their accost is curt; their accent and tone of speech blunt and harsh. Something of this may, probably, be attributed to the freedom of mountain air and of isolated hill-side life; something be derived from their rough Norse ancestry. They have a quick perception of character, and a keen sense of humour; the dwellers among them must be prepared for certain uncomplimentary, though most likely true, observations, pithily expressed. Their feelings are not easily roused, but their duration is lasting. Hence there is much close friendship and faithful service; and for a correct exemplification of the form in which the latter frequently appears, I need only refer the reader of 'Wuthering Heights' to the character of 'Joseph.'

From the same cause come also enduring grudges, in some cases amounting to hatred, which occasionally has been bequeathed from generation to generation. I remember Miss Brontë once telling me that it was a saying round about Haworth, 'Keep a stone in thy pocket seven year; turn it, and keep it seven year longer, that it may be ever ready to thine hand when thine enemy draws near.'*

The West Riding men are sleuth-hounds in pursuit of money. Miss Brontë related to my husband a curious instance illustrative of this eager desire for riches.* A man that she knew, who was a small manufacturer, had engaged in many local speculations, which had always turned out well, and thereby rendered him a person of some wealth. He was rather past middle age, when he bethought him of insuring his life; and he had only just taken out his policy, when he fell ill of an acute disease which was certain to end fatally in a very few days. The doctor, half-hesitatingly, revealed to him his hopeless state. 'By jingo!' cried he, rousing up at once into the old energy, 'I shall *do* the insurance company! I always was a lucky fellow!'

These men are keen and shrewd; faithful and persevering in following out a good purpose, fell in tracking an evil one. They are not emotional; they are not easily made into either friends or enemies; but once lovers or haters, it is difficult to change their feeling. They are a powerful race both in mind and body, both for good and for evil.

The woollen manufacture was introduced into this district in the days of Edward III.* It is traditionally said that a colony of Flemings came over and settled in the West Riding to teach the inhabitants what to do with their wool. The mixture of agricultural with manufacturing labour that ensued and prevailed in the West

Riding up to a very recent period, sounds pleasant enough at this distance of time, when the classical impression is left, and the details forgotten, or only brought to light by those who explore the few remote parts of England where the custom still lingers. The idea of the mistress and her maidens spinning at the great wheels while the master was abroad, ploughing his fields, or seeing after his flocks on the purple moors, is very poetical to look back upon; but when such life actually touches on our own days, and we can hear particulars from the lips of those now living, there come out details of coarseness—of the uncouthness of the rustic mingled with the sharpness of the tradesman—of irregularity and fierce lawlessness—that rather mar the vision of pastoral innocence and simplicity. Still, as it is the exceptional and exaggerated characteristics of any period that leave the most vivid memory behind them, it would be wrong, and in my opinion faithless, to conclude that such and such forms of society and modes of living were not best for the period when they prevailed, although the abuses they may have led into, and the gradual progress of the world, have made it well that such ways and manners should pass away for ever, and as preposterous to attempt to return to them, as it would be for a man to return to the clothes of his childhood.

The patent granted to Alderman Cockayne, and the further restrictions imposed by James I on the export of undyed woollen cloths (met by a prohibition on the part of the States of Holland of the import of English-dyed cloths), injured the trade of the West Riding manufacturers considerably. Their independence of character, their dislike of authority, and their strong powers of thought, predisposed them to rebellion against the religious dictations of such men as Laud, and the arbitrary rule of the Stuarts; and the injury done by James and Charles to the trade by which they gained their bread, made the great majority of them Commonwealth men. I shall have occasion afterwards to give one or two instances of the warm feelings and extensive knowledge on subjects of both home and foreign politics existing at the present day in the villages lying west and east of the mountainous ridge that separates Yorkshire and Lancashire; the inhabitants of which are of the same race and possess the same quality of character.

The descendants of many who served under Cromwell at Dunbar, live on the same lands as their ancestors occupied then;

and perhaps there is no part of England where the traditional and fond recollections of the Commonwealth have lingered so long as in that inhabited by the woollen manufacturing population of the West Riding, who had the restrictions taken off their trade by the Protector's admirable commercial policy. I have it on good authority that, not thirty years ago, the phrase, 'in Oliver's days,' was in common use to denote a time of unusual prosperity. The class of Christian names prevalent in a district is one indication of the direction in which its tide of hero-worship sets. Grave enthusiasts in politics or religion perceive not the ludicrous side of those which they give to their children; and some are to be found, still in their infancy, not a dozen miles from Haworth, that will have to go through life as Lamartine, Kossuth, and Dembinsky.* And so there is a testimony to what I have said, of the traditional feeling of the district, in the fact that the Old Testament names in general use among the Puritans are yet the prevalent appellations in most Yorkshire families of middle or humble rank, whatever their religious persuasion may be. There are numerous records, too, that show the kindly way in which the ejected ministers were received by the gentry, as well as by the poorer part of the inhabitants, during the persecuting days of Charles II.* These little facts all testify to the old hereditary spirit of independence, ready ever to resist authority which was conceived to be unjustly exercised, that distinguishes the people of the West Riding to the present day.

The parish of Halifax touches that of Bradford, in which the chapelry of Haworth is included; and the nature of the ground in the two parishes is much of the same wild and hilly description. The abundance of coal, and the number of mountain streams in the district, make it highly favourable to manufactures; and accordingly, as I stated, the inhabitants have for centuries been engaged in making cloth, as well as in agricultural pursuits. But the intercourse of trade failed, for a long time, to bring amenity and civilization into these outlying hamlets, or widely scattered dwellings. Mr Hunter, in his 'Life of Oliver Heywood,'* quotes a sentence out of a memorial of one James Rither, living in the reign of Elizabeth, which is partially true to this day:—

'They have no superior to court, no civilities to practise: a sour and sturdy humour is the consequence, so that a stranger is shocked by a tone of defiance in every voice, and an air of fierceness in every countenance.'

Even now, a stranger can hardly ask a question without receiving some crusty reply, if, indeed, he receive any at all. Sometimes the sour rudeness amounts to positive insult. Yet, if the 'foreigner' takes all this churlishness good-humouredly, or as a matter of course, and makes good any claim upon their latent kindliness and hospitality, they are faithful and generous, and thoroughly to be relied upon. As a slight illustration of the roughness that pervades all classes in these out-of-the-way villages, I may relate a little adventure which happened to my husband and myself, three years ago, at Addingham—*

> From Penigent to Pendle Hill,
> From Linton to Long-*Addingham*
> And all that Craven coasts did tell, &c.—

one of the places that sent forth its fighting men to the famous old battle of Flodden Field, and a village not many miles from Haworth.

We were driving along the street, when one of those ne'er-do-weel lads who seem to have a kind of magnetic power for misfortunes, having jumped into the stream that runs through the place, just where all the broken glass and bottles are thrown, staggered naked and nearly covered with blood into a cottage before us. Besides receiving another bad cut in the arm, he had completely laid open the artery, and was in a fair way of bleeding to death—which, one of his relations comforted him by saying, would be likely to 'save a deal o' trouble.'

When my husband had checked the effusion of blood with a strap that one of the bystanders unbuckled from his leg, he asked if a surgeon had been sent for.

'Yoi,' was the answer; 'but we dunna think he'll come.'

'Why not?'

'He's owd, yo seen, and asthmatic, and it's up-hill.'

My husband, taking a boy for his guide, drove as fast as he could to the surgeon's house, which was about three-quarters of a mile off, and met the aunt of the wounded lad leaving it.

'Is he coming?' inquired my husband.

'Well, he didna' say he wouldna' come.'

'But tell him the lad may bleed to death.'

'I did.'

'And what did he say?'

'Why, only, "D——n him; what do I care?" '

It ended, however, in his sending one of his sons, who, though not brought up to 'the surgering trade,' was able to do what was necessary in the way of bandages and plasters. The excuse made for the surgeon was, that 'he was near eighty, and getting a bit doited, and had had a matter o' twenty childer.'

Among the most unmoved of the lookers-on was the brother of the boy so badly hurt; and while he was lying in a pool of blood on the flag floor, and crying out how much his arm was 'warching,' his stoical relation stood coolly smoking his bit of black pipe, and uttered not a single word of either sympathy or sorrow.

Forest customs, existing in the fringes of dark wood, which clothed the declivity of the hills on either side, tended to brutalize the population until the middle of the seventeenth century.* Execution by beheading was performed in a summary way upon either men or women who were guilty of but very slight crimes; and a dogged, yet in some cases fine, indifference to human life was thus generated. The roads were so notoriously bad, even up to the last thirty years, that there was little communication between one village and another; if the produce of industry could be conveyed at stated times to the cloth market of the district, it was all that could be done; and, in lonely houses on the distant hill-side, or by the small magnates of secluded hamlets, crimes might be committed almost unknown, certainly without any great uprising of popular indignation calculated to bring down the strong arm of the law. It must be remembered that in those days there was no rural constabulary; and the few magistrates left to themselves, and generally related to one another, were most of them inclined to tolerate eccentricity, and to wink at faults too much like their own.

Men hardly past middle life talk of the days of their youth, spent in this part of the country, when, during the winter months, they rode up to the saddle-girths in mud; when absolute business was the only reason for stirring beyond the precincts of home; and when that business was conducted under a pressure of difficulties which they themselves, borne along to Bradford market in a swift

first-class carriage, can hardly believe to have been possible. For
instance, one woollen manufacturer* says that, not five and twenty
years ago, he had to rise betimes to set off on a winter's morning
in order to be at Bradford with the great waggon-load of goods
manufactured by his father: this load was packed over-night, but
in the morning there was great gathering around it, and flashing of
lanterns, and examination of horses' feet, before the ponderous
waggon got under way; and then some one had to go groping here
and there, on hands and knees, and always sounding with a staff
down the long, steep, slippery brow, to find where the horses
might tread safely, until they reached the comparative easy-going
of the deep-rutted main road. People went on horseback over the
upland moors, following the tracks of the pack-horses that carried
the parcels, baggage, or goods from one town to another, between
which there did not happen to be a highway.

But in winter, all such communication was impossible, by reason
of the snow which lay long and late on the bleak high ground. I
have known people who, travelling by the mail-coach over Blackstone Edge,* had been snowed up for a week or ten days at the
little inn near the summit, and obliged to spend both Christmas
and New Year's Day there, till the store of provisions laid in for
the use of the landlord and his family falling short before the
inroads of the unexpected visitors, they had recourse to the
turkeys, geese, and Yorkshire pies with which the coach was laden;
and even these were beginning to fail, when a fortunate thaw
released them from their prison.

Isolated as the hill villages may be, they are in the world,
compared with the loneliness of the grey ancestral houses to be
seen here and there in the dense hollows of the moors. These
dwellings are not large, yet they are solid and roomy enough for
the accommodation of those who live in them, and to whom the
surrounding estates belong. The land has often been held by one
family since the days of the Tudors; the owners are, in fact, the
remains of the old yeomanry—small squires, who are rapidly
becoming extinct as a class, from one of two causes. Either the
possessor falls into idle, drinking habits, and so is obliged eventually to sell his property: or he finds, if more shrewd and
adventurous, that the 'beck' running down the mountain-side, or
the minerals beneath his feet, can be turned into a new source of

wealth; and leaving the old plodding life of a landowner with small capital, he turns manufacturer, or digs for coal, or quarries for stone.

Still there are those remaining of this class—dwellers in the lonely houses far away in the upland districts—even at the present day, who sufficiently indicate what strange eccentricity—what wild strength of will—nay, even what unnatural power of crime was fostered by a mode of living in which a man seldom met his fellows, and where public opinion was only a distant and inarticulate echo of some clearer voice sounding behind the sweeping horizon.

A solitary life cherishes mere fancies until they become manias. And the powerful Yorkshire character, which was scarcely tamed into subjection by all the contact it met with in 'busy town or crowded mart,'* has before now broken out into strange wilfulness in the remoter districts. A singular account was recently given me* of a landowner (living, it is true, on the Lancashire side of the hills, but of the same blood and nature as the dwellers on the other) who was supposed to be in the receipt of seven or eight hundred a year, and whose house bore marks of handsome antiquity, as if his forefathers had been for a long time people of consideration. My informant was struck with the appearance of the place, and proposed to the countryman who was accompanying him, to go up to it and take a nearer inspection. The reply was, 'Yo'd better not; he'd threap yo' down th' loan.* He's let fly at some folk's legs, and let shot lodge in 'em afore now, for going too near to his house.' And finding, on closer inquiry, that such was really the inhospitable custom of this moorland squire, the gentleman gave up his purpose. I believe that the savage yeoman is still living.

Another squire, of more distinguished family and larger property—one is thence led to imagine of better education, but that does not always follow—died at his house, not many miles from Haworth, only a few years ago. His great amusement and occupation had been cock-fighting. When he was confined to his chamber with what he knew would be his last illness, he had his cocks brought up there, and watched the bloody battle from his bed. As his mortal disease increased, and it became impossible for him to turn so as to follow the combat, he had looking-glasses arranged in such a manner, around and above him, as he lay, that he could still see the cocks fighting. And in this manner he died.

These are merely instances of eccentricity compared to the tales of positive violence and crime that have occurred in these isolated dwellings, which still linger in the memories of the old people of the district, and some of which were doubtless familiar to the authors of 'Wuthering Heights' and 'The Tenant of Wildfell Hall.'

The amusements of the lower classes could hardly be expected to be more humane than those of the wealthy and better educated. The gentleman, who has kindly furnished me with some of the particulars I have given, remembers the bull-baitings at Rochdale, not thirty years ago. The bull was fastened by a chain or rope to a post in the river. To increase the amount of water, as well as to give their workpeople the opportunity of savage delight, the masters were accustomed to stop their mills on the day when the sport took place. The bull would sometimes wheel suddenly round, so that the rope by which he was fastened swept those who had been careless enough to come within its range down into the water, and the good people of Rochdale had the excitement of seeing one or two of their neighbours drowned, as well as of witnessing the bull baited, and the dogs torn and tossed.

The people of Haworth were not less strong and full of character than their neighbours on either side of the hill. The village lies embedded in the moors, between the two counties, on the old road between Keighley and Colne. About the middle of the last century, it became famous in the religious world as the scene of the ministrations of the Rev. William Grimshaw,* curate of Haworth for twenty years. Before this time, it is probable that the curates were of the same order as one Mr Nicholls,* a Yorkshire clergyman in the days immediately succeeding the Reformation, who was 'much addicted to drinking and company-keeping,' and used to say to his companions, 'You must not heed me but when I am got three feet above the earth,' that was, into the pulpit.

Mr Grimshaw's life was written by Newton, Cowper's friend;* and from it may be gathered some curious particulars of the manner in which a rough population were swayed and governed by a man of deep convictions, and strong earnestness of purpose. It seems that he had not been in any way remarkable for religious zeal, though he had led a moral life, and been conscientious in fulfilling his parochial duties, until a certain Sunday in September, 1744, when the servant, rising at five, found her master already engaged in prayer; she stated that, after remaining in his chamber for some time, he went to engage in religious exercises in the house of a parishioner, then home again to pray; thence, still fasting, to the church, where, as he was reading the second lesson, he fell down, and, on his partial recovery, had to be led from the church. As he went out, he spoke to the congregation, and told them not to disperse, as he had something to say to them, and would return presently. He was taken to the clerk's house, and again became insensible. His servant rubbed him, to restore the circulation; and when he was brought to himself 'he seemed in a great rapture,' and the first words he uttered were 'I have had a glorious vision from the third heaven.' He did not say what he had seen, but returned into the church, and began the service again, at two in the afternoon, and went on until seven.

From this time he devoted himself, with the fervour of a Wesley, and something of the fanaticism of a Whitfield,* to calling out a religious life among his parishioners. They had been in the habit of playing at foot-ball on Sunday, using stones for this purpose; and giving and receiving challenges from other parishes. There were horse-races held on the moors just above the village, which were periodical sources of drunkenness and profligacy. Scarcely a wedding took place without the rough amusement of foot-races, where the half-naked runners were a scandal to all decent strangers. The old custom of 'arvills,' or funeral feasts, led to frequent pitched battles between the drunken mourners. Such customs were the outward signs of the kind of people with whom Mr Grimshaw had to deal. But, by various means, some of the most practical kind, he wrought a great change in his parish. In his preaching he was occasionally assisted by Wesley and Whitfield, and at such times the little church proved much too small to hold the throng that poured in from distant villages, or lonely moorland hamlets; and frequently they were obliged to meet in the open air; indeed, there was not room enough in the church even for the communicants. Mr Whitfield was once preaching in Haworth, and made use of some such expression, as that he hoped there was no need to say much to this congregation, as they had sat under so pious and godly a minister for so many years; 'whereupon Mr Grimshaw stood up in his place, and said with a loud voice, "Oh, sir! for God's sake do not speak so. I pray you do not flatter them. I fear

the greater part of them are going to hell with their eyes open." '
But if they were so bound, it was not for want of exertion on Mr
Grimshaw's part to prevent them. He used to preach twenty or
thirty times a week in private houses. If he perceived any one
inattentive to his prayers, he would stop and rebuke the offender,
and not go on till he saw every one on their knees. He was very
earnest in enforcing the strict observance of Sunday; and would
not even allow his parishioners to walk in the fields between
services. He sometimes gave out a very long Psalm (tradition says
the 119th), and while it was being sung, he left the reading-desk,
and taking a horsewhip went into the public-houses, and flogged
the loiterers into church. They were swift who could escape the
lash of the parson by sneaking out the back way. He had strong
health and an active body, and rode far and wide over the hills,
'awakening' those who had previously had no sense of religion. To
save time, and be no charge to the families at whose houses he held
his prayer-meetings, he carried his provisions with him; all the
food he took in the day on such occasions consisting simply of a
piece of bread and butter, or dry bread and a raw onion.

The horse-races were justly objectionable to Mr Grimshaw; they
attracted numbers of profligate people to Haworth, and brought a
match to the combustible materials of the place, only too ready to
blaze out into wickedness. The story is, that he tried all means of
persuasion, and even intimidation, to have the races discontinued,
but in vain. At length, in despair, he prayed with such fervour of
earnestness that the rain came down in torrents, and deluged the
ground, so that there was no footing for man or beast, even if the
multitude had been willing to stand such a flood let down from
above. And so Haworth races were stopped, and have never been
resumed to this day. Even now the memory of this good man is
held in reverence, and his faithful ministrations and real virtues are
one of the boasts of the parish.

But after his time, I fear there was a falling back into the wild
rough heathen ways, from which he had pulled them up, as it were,
by the passionate force of his individual character. He had built a
chapel for the Wesleyan Methodists, and not very long after the
Baptists established themselves in a place of worship.* Indeed, as
Dr Whitaker says, the people of this district are 'strong religionists;' only, fifty years ago, their religion did not work down into

their lives. Half that length of time back, the code of morals seemed to be formed upon that of their Norse ancestors. Revenge was handed down from father to son as an hereditary duty; and a great capability for drinking, without the head being affected, was considered as one of the manly virtues. The games of foot-ball on Sundays, with the challenges to the neighbouring parishes, were resumed, bringing in an influx of riotous strangers to fill the public-houses, and make the more sober-minded inhabitants long for good Mr Grimshaw's stout arm, and ready horse-whip. The old custom of 'arvills' was as prevalent as ever. The sexton, standing at the foot of the open grave, announced that the 'arvill' would be held at the Black Bull,* or whatever public-house might be fixed upon by the friends of the dead; and thither the mourners and their acquaintances repaired. The origin of the custom had been the necessity of furnishing some refreshment for those who came from a distance, to pay the last mark of respect to a friend. In the life of Oliver Heywood there are two quotations,* which show what sort of food was provided for 'arvills' in quiet Nonconformist connections in the seventeenth century; the first (from Thoresby) tells of 'cold possets, stewed prunes, cake, and cheese,' as being the arvill after Oliver Heywood's funeral. The second gives, as rather shabby, according to the notion of the times (1673), 'nothing but a bit of cake, draught of wine, piece of rosemary, and pair of gloves.'

But the arvills at Haworth were often far more jovial doings. Among the poor, the mourners were only expected to provide a kind of spiced roll for each person; and the expense of the liquors—rum, or ale, or a mixture of both called 'dog's nose'—was generally defrayed by each guest placing some money on a plate, set in the middle of the table. Richer people would order a dinner for their friends. At the funeral of Mr Charnock* (the next successor but one to Mr Grimshaw in the incumbency), above eighty people were bid to the arvill, and the price of the feast was 4s. 6d. per head, all of which was defrayed by the friends of the deceased. As few 'shirked their liquor,' there were very frequently 'up-and-down-fights' before the close of the day; sometimes with the horrid additions of 'pawsing' and 'gouging,' and biting.

Although I have dwelt on the exceptional traits in the characteristics of these stalwart West-Ridingers, such as they were in the

first quarter of this century, if not a few years later, I have little
doubt that in the every-day life of the people so independent,
wilful, and full of grim humour, there would be much found even
at present that would shock those accustomed only to the local
manners of the south; and, in return, I suspect the shrewd,
sagacious, energetic Yorkshireman would hold such 'foreigners' in
no small contempt.

I have said, it is most probable that where Haworth Church now
stands, there was once an ancient 'field-kirk,' or oratory. It
occupied the third or lowest class of ecclesiastical structures,
according to the Saxon law,* and had no right of sepulture, or
administration of sacraments. It was so called because it was built
without enclosure, and open to the adjoining fields or moors. The
founder, according to the laws of Edgar, was bound, without
subtracting from his tithes, to maintain the ministering priest out
of the remaining nine parts of his income. After the Reformation,
the right of choosing their clergyman, at any of those chapels of
ease which had formerly been field-kirks, was vested in the
freeholders and trustees, subject to the approval of the vicar of the
parish. But owing to some negligence, this right has been lost to
the freeholders and trustees at Haworth, ever since the days of
Archbishop Sharp; and the power of choosing a minister has lapsed
into the hands of the Vicar of Bradford. So runs the account,
according to one authority.

Mr Brontë says,*—'This living has for its patrons the Vicar of
Bradford and certain trustees. My predecessor took the living with
the consent of the Vicar of Bradford, but in opposition to the
trustees; in consequence of which he was so opposed that, after
only three weeks' possession, he was compelled to resign.' A
Yorkshire gentleman,* who has kindly sent me some additional
information on this subject since the second edition of my work
was published, writes thus:—

'The sole right of presentation to the incumbency of Haworth is
vested in the Vicar of Bradford. He only can present. The funds,
however, from which the clergyman's stipend mainly proceeds, are
vested in the hands of trustees, who have the power to withhold
them, if a nominee is sent of whom they disapprove. On the
decease of Mr Charnock, the Vicar first tendered the preferment
to Mr Brontë, and he went over to his expected cure. He was told

that towards himself they had no personal objection; but that as a nominee of the Vicar he would not be received. He therefore retired, with the declaration that if he could not come with the approbation of the parish, his ministry could not be useful. Upon this the attempt was made to introduce Mr Redhead.

'When Mr Redhead was repelled, a fresh difficulty arose. Some one must first move towards a settlement, but a spirit being evoked which could not be allayed, action became perplexing. The matter had to be referred to some independent arbitrator, and my father was the gentleman to whom each party turned its eye. A meeting was convened, and the business settled by the Vicar's conceding the choice to the trustees, and their acceptance of the Vicar's presentation. That choice forthwith fell on Mr Brontë, whose promptness and prudence had won their hearts.'

In conversing on the character of the inhabitants of the West Riding with Dr Scoresby,* who had been for some time Vicar of Bradford, he alluded to certain riotous transactions which had taken place at Haworth on the presentation of the living to Mr Redhead, and said that there had been so much in the particulars indicative of the character of the people, that he advised me to inquire into them. I have accordingly done so, and, from the lips of some of the survivors among the actors and spectators, I have learnt the means taken to eject the nominee of the Vicar.

The previous incumbent had been the Mr Charnock whom I have mentioned as next but one in succession to Mr Grimshaw. He had a long illness which rendered him unable to discharge his duties without assistance, and Mr Redhead gave him occasional help, to the great satisfaction of the parishioners, and was highly respected by them during Mr Charnock's lifetime. But the case was entirely altered when, at Mr Charnock's death in 1819, they conceived that the trustees had been unjustly deprived of their rights by the Vicar of Bradford, who appointed Mr Redhead as perpetual curate.*

The first Sunday he officiated, Haworth Church was filled even to the aisles; most of the people wearing the wooden clogs of the district. But while Mr Redhead was reading the second lesson, the whole congregation, as by one impulse, began to leave the church, making all the noise they could with clattering and clumping of clogs, till, at length, Mr Redhead and the clerk were the only two left to continue the service. This was bad enough, but the next Sunday the proceedings were far worse. Then, as before, the church was well filled, but the aisles were left clear; not a creature, not an obstacle was in the way. The reason for this was made evident about the same time in the reading of the service as the disturbances had begun the previous week. A man rode into the church upon an ass, with his face turned towards the tail, and as many old hats piled on his head, as he could possibly carry. He began urging his beast round the aisles, and the screams, and cries, and laughter of the congregation entirely drowned all sound of Mr Redhead's voice; and, I believe, he was obliged to desist.

Hitherto they had not proceeded to anything like personal violence; but on the third Sunday they must have been greatly irritated at seeing Mr Redhead, determined to brave their will, ride up the village street, accompanied by several gentlemen from Bradford. They put up their horses at the Black Bull—the little inn close upon the churchyard, for the convenience of arvills as well as for other purposes—and went into church. On this the people followed, with a chimney-sweeper, whom they had employed to clean the chimneys of some out-buildings belonging to the church that very morning, and afterwards plied with drink till he was in a state of solemn intoxication. They placed him right before the reading-desk, where his blackened face nodded a drunken, stupid assent to all that Mr Redhead said. At last, either prompted by some mischief-maker, or from some tipsy impulse, he clambered up the pulpit stairs, and attempted to embrace Mr Redhead. Then the profane fun grew fast and furious. Some of the more riotous pushed the soot-covered chimney-sweeper against Mr Redhead, as he tried to escape. They threw both him and his tormentor down on the ground in the church-yard where the soot-bag had been emptied, and, though, at last, Mr Redhead escaped into the Black Bull, the doors of which were immediately barred, the people raged without, threatening to stone him and his friends. One of my informants is an old man, who was the landlord of the inn at the time,* and he stands to it that such was the temper of the irritated mob, that Mr Redhead was in real danger of his life. This man, however, planned an escape for his unpopular inmates. The Black Bull is near the top of the long, steep Haworth street, and at the bottom, close by the bridge, on the road to

Keighley, is a turnpike. Giving directions to his hunted guests to steal out at the back door (through which, probably, many a ne'er-do-weel has escaped from good Mr Grimshaw's horsewhip), the landlord and some of the stable-boys rode the horses belonging to the party from Bradford backwards and forwards before his front door, among the fiercely-expectant crowd. Through some opening between the houses, those on the horses saw Mr Redhead and his friends creeping along behind the street; and then, striking spurs, they dashed quickly down to the turnpike; the obnoxious clergyman and his friends mounted in haste, and had sped some distance before the people found out that their prey had escaped, and came running to the closed turnpike gate.

This was Mr Redhead's last appearance at Haworth for many years. Long afterwards, he came to preach,* and in his sermon to a large and attentive congregation he good-humouredly reminded them of the circumstances which I have described. They gave him a hearty welcome, for they owed him no grudge; although before they had been ready enough to stone him, in order to maintain what they considered to be their rights.

The foregoing account, which I heard from two of the survivors, in the presence of a friend who can vouch for the accuracy of my repetition, has to a certain degree been confirmed by a letter from the Yorkshire gentleman, whose words I have already quoted.*

'I am not surprised at your difficulty in authenticating matter of fact. I find this in recalling what I have heard, and the authority on which I have heard anything. As to the donkey tale, I believe you are right. Mr Redhead and Dr Ramsbotham, his son-in-law, are no strangers to me. Each of them has a niche in my affections.

'I have asked, this day, two persons who lived in Haworth at the time to which you allude, the son and daughter of an acting trustee, and each of them between sixty and seventy years of age, and they assure me that the donkey was introduced. One of them says it was mounted by a half-witted man, seated with his face towards the tail of the beast, and having several hats piled on his head. Neither of my informants was, however, present at these edifying services. I believe that no movement was made in the church on either Sunday, until the whole of the authorised reading-service was gone through, and I am sure that nothing was more remote from the more respectable party than any personal antagonism toward Mr Redhead. He was one of the most amiable and worthy of men, a man to myself endeared by many ties and obligations. I never heard before your book that the sweep ascended the pulpit steps. He was present, however, in the clerical habiliments of his order*..... I may also add that among the many who were present at those sad Sunday orgies the majority were non-residents, and came from those moorland fastnesses on the outskirts of the parish locally designated as "ovver th' steyres," one stage more remote than Haworth from modern civilisation.

'To an instance or two more of the rusticity of the inhabitants of the chapelry of Haworth, I may introduce you.

'A Haworth carrier called at the office of a friend of mine to deliver a parcel on a cold winter's day, and stood with the door open. "Robin! shut the door!" said the recipient. "Have you no doors in your country?" "Yoi," responded Robin, "we hev, but we nivver steik 'em." I have frequently remarked the number of doors open even in winter.

'When well directed, the indomitable and independent energies of the natives of this part of the country are invaluable; dangerous when perverted. I shall never forget the fierce actions and utterances of one suffering from delirium tremens. Whether in its wrath, disdain, or its dismay, the countenance was infernal. I called once upon a time on a most respectable yeoman, and I was, in language earnest and homely, pressed to accept the hospitality of the house. I consented. The word to me was, "Nah, Maister, yah mun stop an hev sum te-ah, yah mun, eah, yah mun." A bountiful table was soon spread; at all events, time soon went while I scaled the hills to see "t' maire at wor thretty year owd, an't' foile at wor fower." On sitting down to the table, a venerable woman officiated, and after filling the cups, she thus addressed me: "Nah, Maister, yah mun loawze th' taible" (loose the table). The master said, "Shah meeans yah mun sey t' greyce." I took the hint, and uttered the blessing.

'I spoke with an aged and tried woman at one time, who, after recording her mercies, stated, among others, her powers of speech, by asserting "Thank the Lord, ah nivver wor a meilly-meouthed wumman." I feel particularly at fault in attempting the ortho-graphy of the dialect, but must excuse myself by telling you that I once saw a letter in which the word I have just now used (excuse) was written "ecksqueaize!"

'There are some things, however, which rather tend to soften the idea of the rudeness of Haworth. No rural district has been more markedly the abode of musical taste and acquirement, and this at a period when it was difficult to find them to the same extent apart from towns in advance of their times. I have gone to Haworth and found an orchestra to meet me, filled with local performers, vocal and instrumental, to whom the best works of Handel, Haydn, Mozart, Marcello,* &c. &c., were familiar as household words. By knowledge, taste, and voice, they were markedly separate from ordinary village choirs, and have been put in extensive requisition for the solo and chorus of many an imposing festival. One man still survives, who, for fifty years has had one of the finest tenor voices I ever heard, and with it a refined and cultivated taste. To him and to others many inducements have been offered to migrate; but the loom, the association, the mountain air have had charms enow to secure their continuance at home. I love the recollection of their performance; that recollection extends over more than sixty years. The attachments, the antipathies, and the hospitalities of the district are ardent, hearty, and homely. Cordiality in each is the prominent characteristic. As a people, these mountaineers have ever been accessible to gentleness and truth, so far as I have known them; but excite suspicion or resentment, and they give emphatic and not impotent resistance. Compulsion they defy.

'I accompanied Mr Heap* on his first visit to Haworth after his accession to the vicarage of Bradford. It was on Easter day, either 1816 or 1817. His predecessor, the venerable John Crosse, known as the "blind vicar," had been inattentive to the vicarial claims. A searching investigation had to be made and enforced, and as it proceeded stout and sturdy utterances were not lacking on the part of the parishioners. To a spectator, though rude, they were amusing, and significant, foretelling what might be expected, and what was afterwards realised, on the advent of a new incumbent, if they deemed him an intruder.

'From their peculiar parochial position and circumstances, the inhabitants of the chapelry have been prompt, earnest, and persevering in their opposition to church-rates. Athough ten miles from the mother-church, they were called upon to defray a large proportion of this obnoxious tax,—I believe one fifth.

'Besides this, they had to maintain their own edifice, &c. &c. They resisted, therefore, with energy, that which they deemed to be oppression and injustice. By scores would they wend their way from the hills to attend a vestry meeting at Bradford, and in such service failed not to show less of the *suaviter in modo* than the *fortiter in re.** Happily such occasion for their action has not occurred for many years.

'The use of patronymics has been common in this locality. Inquire for a man by his Christian name and surname, and you may have some difficulty in finding him: ask, however, for "George o' Ned's," or "Dick o' Bob's," or "Tom o' Jack's," as the case may be, and your difficulty is at an end. In many instances the person is designated by his residence. In my early years I had occasion to inquire for Jonathan Whitaker, who owned a considerable farm in the township. I was sent hither and thither, until it occurred to me to ask for "Jonathan o' th' Yate."* My difficulties were then at an end. Such circumstances arise out of the settled character and isolation of the natives.

'Those who have witnessed a Haworth wedding when the parties were above the rank of labourers, will not easily forget the scene. A levy was made on the horses of the neighbourhood, and a merry cavalcade of mounted men and women, single or double, traversed the way to Bradford church. The inn and church appeared to be in natural connection, and as the labours of the Temperance Society had then to begin,* the interests of sobriety were not always consulted. On remounting their steeds they commenced with a race, and not unfrequently an inebriate or unskilful horseman or woman was put *hors de combat*. A race also was frequent at the end of these wedding expeditions, from the bridge to the toll-bar at Haworth. The race-course you will know to be anything but level.'

Into the midst of this lawless, yet not unkindly population, Mr Brontë brought his wife and six little children, in February, 1820. There are those yet alive who remember seven heavily-laden carts lumbering slowly up the long stone street, bearing the 'new parson's' household goods to his future abode.

One wonders how the bleak aspect of her new home—the low, oblong, stone parsonage, high up, yet with a still higher back-ground of sweeping moors—struck on the gentle, delicate wife, whose health even then was failing.

# CHAPTER III

THE Rev. Patrick Brontë is a native of the County Down in Ireland.* His father Hugh Brontë, was left an orphan at an early age. He came from the south to the north of the island, and settled in the parish of Ahaderg, near Loughbrickland. There was some family tradition that, humble as Hugh Brontë's circumstances were, he was the descendant of an ancient family. But about this neither he nor his descendants have cared to inquire. He made an early marriage, and reared and educated ten children on the proceeds of the few acres of land which he farmed. This large family were remarkable for great physical strength, and much personal beauty. Even in his old age, Mr Brontë is a striking-looking man, above the common height, with a nobly-shaped head, and erect carriage. In his youth he must have been unusually handsome.

He was born on Patrickmas day (March 17), 1777, and early gave tokens of extraordinary quickness and intelligence. He had also his full share of ambition; and of his strong sense and forethought there is a proof in the fact, that, knowing that his father could afford him no pecuniary aid, and that he must depend upon his own exertions, he opened a public school at the early age of sixteen; and this mode of living he continued to follow for five or six years. He then became a tutor in the family of the Rev. Mr Tighe, rector of Drumgooland parish. Thence he proceeded to St John's College, Cambridge,* where he was entered in July, 1802, being at the time five-and-twenty years of age. After nearly four years' residence, he obtained his B.A. degree, and was ordained to a curacy in Essex, whence he removed into Yorkshire. The course of life of which this is the outline, shows a powerful and remarkable character, originating and pursuing a purpose in a resolute and independent manner. Here is a youth—a boy of sixteen—separating himself from his family, and determining to maintain himself; and that, not in the hereditary manner by agricultural pursuits, but by the labour of his brain.

I suppose, from what I have heard, that Mr Tighe became strongly interested in his children's tutor, and may have aided him, not only in the direction of his studies, but in the suggestion of an English university education, and in advice as to the mode in which he should obtain entrance there. Mr Brontë has now no trace of his Irish origin remaining in his speech;* he never could have shown his Celtic descent in the straight Greek lines and long oval of his face; but at five-and-twenty, fresh from the only life he had ever known, to present himself at the gates of St John's proved no little determination of will, and scorn of ridicule.

While at Cambridge, he became one of a corps of volunteers, who were then being called out all over the country to resist the apprehended invasion by the French. I have heard him allude, in late years, to Lord Palmerston* as one who had often been associated with him then in the mimic military duties which they had to perform.

We take him up now settled as a curate at Hartshead,* in Yorkshire—far removed from his birth-place and all his Irish connections; with whom, indeed, he cared little to keep up any intercourse, and whom he never, I believe, re-visited after becoming a student at Cambridge.

Hartshead is a very small village, lying to the east of Huddersfield and Halifax; and, from its high situation—on a mound, as it were, surrounded by a circular basin—commanding a magnificent view. Mr Brontë resided here for five years; and, while the incumbent of Hartshead, he wooed and married Maria Branwell.*

She was the third daughter of Mr Thomas Branwell, merchant, of Penzance. Her mother's maiden name was Carne: and, both on father's and mother's side, the Branwell family were sufficiently well descended to enable them to mix in the best society that Penzance then afforded. Mr and Mrs Branwell would be living— their family of four daughters and one son, still children—during the existence of that primitive state of society which is well described by Dr Davy in the life of his brother.*

'In the same town, when the population was about 2,000 persons, there was only one carpet, the floors of rooms were sprinkled with sea-sand, and there was not a single silver fork.

'At that time, when our colonial possessions were very limited, our army and navy on a small scale, and there was comparatively little demand for intellect, the younger sons of gentlemen were often of necessity brought up to some trade or mechanical art, to which no discredit, or loss of caste, as it were, was attached. The eldest son, if not allowed to remain an idle country squire, was sent to Oxford or Cambridge, preparatory to his engaging in one of the three liberal professions of divinity, law, or physic; the second son was perhaps apprenticed to a surgeon or apothecary, or a solicitor; the third to a pewterer or watchmaker; the fourth to a packer or mercer, and so on, were there more to be provided for.

'After their apprenticeships were finished, the young men almost invariably went to London to perfect themselves in their respective trade or art: and on their return into the country, when settled in business, they were not excluded from what would now be considered genteel society. Visiting then was conducted differently from what it is at present. Dinner-parties were almost unknown, excepting at the annual feast-time. Christmas, too, was then a season of peculiar indulgence and conviviality, and a round of entertainments was given, consisting of tea and supper. Excepting at these two periods, visiting was almost entirely confined to tea-parties, which assembled at three o'clock, broke up at nine, and the amusement of the evening was commonly some round game at cards, as Pope Joan, or Commerce. The lower class was then extremely ignorant, and all classes were very superstitious; even the belief in witches maintained its ground, and there was an almost unbounded credulity respecting the supernatural and monstrous. There was scarcely a parish in the Mount's Bay that was without a haunted house, or a spot to which some story of supernatural horror was not attached. Even when I was a boy, I remember a house in the best street of Penzance which was uninhabited because it was believed to be haunted, and which young people walked by at night at a quickened pace, and with a beating heart. Amongst the middle and higher classes there was little taste for literature, and still less for science, and their pursuits were rarely of a dignified or intellectual kind. Hunting, shooting, wrestling, cock-fighting, generally ending in drunkenness, were what they most delighted in. Smuggling was carried on to a great extent; and drunkenness, and a low state of morals, were naturally associated with it. Whilst smuggling was the means of acquiring wealth to bold and reckless adventurers, drunkenness and dissipation occasioned the ruin of many respectable families.'

I have given this extract because I conceive it bears some reference to the life of Miss Brontë, whose strong mind and vivid imagination must have received their first impressions either from the servants (in that simple household, almost friendly companions during the greater part of the day) retailing the traditions or the news of Haworth village; or from Mr Brontë, whose intercourse with his children appears to have been considerably restrained, and whose life, both in Ireland and at Cambridge, had been spent under peculiar circumstances; or from her aunt, Miss Branwell,* who came to the parsonage, when Charlotte was only six or seven years old, to take charge of her dead sister's family. This aunt was older than Mrs Brontë, and had lived longer among the Penzance society, which Dr Davy describes. But in the Branwell family itself, the violence and irregularity of nature did not exist. They were Methodists,* and, as far as I can gather, a gentle and sincere piety gave refinement and purity of character. Mr Branwell, the father, according to his descendants' account, was a man of musical talent. He and his wife lived to see all their children grown up, and died within a year of each other—he in 1808, she in 1809, when their daughter Maria was twenty-five or twenty-six years of age. I have been permitted to look over a series of nine letters, which were addressed by her to Mr Brontë, during the brief term of their engagement in 1812.* They are full of tender grace of expression, and feminine modesty; pervaded by the deep piety to which I have alluded as a family characteristic. I shall make one or two extracts from them, to show what sort of a person was the mother of Charlotte Brontë: but first, I must state the circumstances under which this Cornish lady met the scholar from Ahaderg, near Loughbrickland. In the early summer of 1812, when she would be twenty-nine, she came to visit her uncle, the Reverend John Fennel,* who was at that time a clergyman of the Church of England, living near Leeds, but who had previously been a Methodist minister. Mr Brontë was the incumbent of Hartshead; and had the reputation in the neighbourhood of being a very handsome fellow, full of Irish enthusiasm, and with something of an Irishman's capability of falling easily in love. Miss Branwell was extremely small in person; not pretty, but very elegant, and always dressed with a quiet simplicity of taste, which accorded well with her general character, and of which some of the details call to mind the style of dress preferred by her daughter for her favourite heroines. Mr Brontë was soon captivated by the little, gentle creature, and this time declared that it was for life. In her first letter to him, dated August 26th, she seems almost surprised to find herself engaged, and alludes to the short time which she has known him. In the rest there are touches reminding one of Juliet's—

> 'But trust me, gentleman, I'll prove more true
> Than those that have more cunning to be strange.'*

There are plans for happy pic-nic parties to Kirkstall Abbey,* in the glowing September days, when 'Uncle, Aunt, and Cousin Jane,'—the last engaged to a Mr Morgan, another clergyman*— were of the party; all since dead, except Mr Brontë. There was no opposition on the part of any of her friends to her engagement. Mr and Mrs Fennel sanctioned it, and her brother and sisters in far-away Penzance appear fully to have approved of it. In a letter dated September 18th, she says:—

'For some years I have been perfectly my own mistress, subject to no control whatever; so far from it, that my sisters, who are many years older than myself, and even my dear mother, used to consult me on every occasion of importance, and scarcely ever doubted the propriety of my opinions and actions: perhaps you will be ready to accuse me of vanity in mentioning this, but you must consider that I do not boast of it. I have many times felt it a disadvantage, and although, I thank God, it has never led me into error, yet, in circumstances of uncertainty and doubt, I have deeply felt the want of a guide and instructor.' In the same letter she tells Mr Brontë, that she has informed her sisters of her engagement, and that she should not see them again so soon as she had intended. Mr Fennel, her uncle, also writes to them by the same post in praise of Mr Brontë.

The journey from Penzance to Leeds in those days was both very long and very expensive; the lovers had not much money to spend in unnecessary travelling, and, as Miss Branwell had neither father nor mother living, it appeared both a discreet and seemly arrangement that the marriage should take place from her uncle's house. There was no reason either why the engagement should be prolonged. They were past their first youth; they had means sufficient for their unambitious wants; the living of Hartshead is rated in the Clergy List at 202*l.* per annum,* and she was in the receipt of a small annuity (50*l.* I have been told) by the will of her father. So, at the end of September, the lovers began to talk about taking a house, for I suppose that Mr Brontë up to that time had been in lodgings; and all went smoothly and successfully with a view to their marriage in the ensuing winter, until November, when a misfortune happened, which she thus patiently and prettily describes:—*

'I suppose you never expected to be much the richer for me, but I am sorry to inform you that I am still poorer than I thought myself. I mentioned having sent for my books, clothes, &c. On Saturday evening, about the time when you were writing the description of your imaginary shipwreck, I was reading and feeling the effects of a real one, having then received a letter from my sister giving me an account of the vessel in which she had sent my box being stranded on the coast of Devonshire, in consequence of which the box was dashed to pieces with the violence of the sea, and all my little property, with the exception of a very few articles, being swallowed up in the mighty deep. If this should not prove the prelude to something worse I shall think little of it, as it is the first disastrous circumstance which has occurred since I left my home.'

The last of these letters is dated December the 5th. Miss Branwell and her cousin intended to set about making the wedding-cake in the following week, so the marriage could not be far off. She had been learning by heart a 'pretty little hymn' of Mr Brontë's composing;* and reading Lord Lyttelton's 'Advice to a Lady,'* on which she makes some pertinent and just remarks, showing that she thought as well as read. And so Maria Branwell fades out of sight; we have no more direct intercourse with her; we hear of her as Mrs Brontë, but it is as an invalid, not far from death; still patient, cheerful, and pious. The writing of these letters is elegant and neat;* while there are allusions to household occupations—such as making the wedding-cake—there are also allusions to the books she has read, or is reading, showing a well-cultivated mind. Without having anything of her daughter's rare talents, Mrs Brontë must have been, I imagine, that unusual character, a well-balanced and consistent woman. The style of the letters is easy and good; as is also that of a paper from the same hand, entitled 'The Advantages of Poverty in Religious Concerns,'* which was written rather later, with a view to publication in some periodical.

She was married, from her uncle's house, in Yorkshire, on the 29th of December, 1812;* the same day was also the wedding-day of her younger sister, Charlotte Branwell, in distant Penzance. I do not think that Mrs Brontë ever revisited Cornwall, but she has left a very pleasant impression on the minds of those relations who yet survive; they speak of her as 'their favourite aunt, and one to whom they, as well as all the family, looked up, as a person of talent and great amiability of disposition;' and, again, as 'meek and retiring, while possessing more than ordinary talents, which she inherited from her father, and her piety was genuine and unobtrusive.'

Mr Brontë remained for five years at Hartshead, in the parish of Dewsbury. There he was married, and his two children, Maria and Elizabeth,* were born. At the expiration of that period, he had the living of Thornton, in Bradford parish.* Some of those great West Riding parishes are almost like bishoprics for their amount of population and number of churches. Thornton church is a little episcopal chapel of ease, rich in Nonconformist monuments, as of Accepted Lister and his friend Dr Hall.* The neighbourhood is desolate and wild; great tracts of bleak land, enclosed by stone dykes, sweeping up Clayton heights. The church itself looks ancient and solitary, and as if left behind by the great stone mills of a flourishing Independent firm, and the solid square chapel built by the members of that denomination.* Altogether not so pleasant a place as Hartshead, with its ample outlook over cloud-shadowed, sun-flecked plain, and hill rising beyond hill to form the distant horizon.

Here, at Thornton, Charlotte Brontë was born, on the 21st of April, 1816. Fast on her heels followed Patrick Branwell, Emily Jane, and Anne.* After the birth of this last daughter, Mrs Brontë's health began to decline. It is hard work to provide for the little tender wants of many young children where the means are but limited. The necessaries of food and clothing are much more easily supplied than the almost equal necessaries of attendance, care, soothing, amusement, and sympathy. Maria Brontë, the eldest of six, could only have been a few months more than six years old, when Mr Brontë removed to Haworth, on February 25th, 1820.* Those who knew her there, describe her as grave, thoughtful, and quiet, to a degree far beyond her years. Her childhood was no childhood; the cases are rare in which the possessors of great gifts have known the blessings of that careless happy time; *their* unusual powers stir within them, and, instead of the natural life of perception—the objective, as the Germans call it—they begin the deeper life of reflection—the subjective.

Little Maria Brontë was delicate and small in appearance, which seemed to give greater effect to her wonderful precocity of intellect. She must have been her mother's companion and help-mate in many a household and nursery experience, for Mr Brontë was, of course, much engaged in his study; and besides, he was not naturally fond of children, and felt their frequent appearance on the scene as a drag both on his wife's strength, and as an interruption to the comfort of the household.

Haworth Parsonage is—as I mentioned in the first chapter—an oblong stone house, facing down the hill on which the village stands, and with the front door right opposite to the western door of the church, distant about a hundred yards. Of this space twenty yards or so in depth are occupied by the grassy garden, which is scarcely wider than the house. The graveyard lies on two sides of the house and garden.* The house consists of four rooms on each floor, and is two stories high. When the Brontës took possession, they made the larger parlour, to the left of the entrance, the family sitting-room, while that on the right was appropriated to Mr Brontë as a study. Behind this was the kitchen; behind the former, a sort of flagged store-room. Up-stairs were four bed-chambers of similar size, with the addition of a small apartment over the passage, or 'lobby' as we call it in the north. This was to the front, the staircase going up right opposite to the entrance. There is the pleasant old fashion of window seats all through the house; and one can see that the parsonage was built in the days when wood was plentiful, as the massive stair-banisters, and the wainscots, and the heavy window-frames testify.

This little extra up-stairs room was appropriated to the child-ren.* Small as it was, it was not called a nursery; indeed, it had not the comfort of a fireplace in it; the servants—two affectionate, warm-hearted sisters,* who cannot now speak of the family without tears—called the room the 'children's study.' The age of the eldest student was perhaps by this time seven.

The people in Haworth were none of them very poor. Many of them were employed in the neighbouring worsted mills; a few were mill-owners and manufacturers in a small way; there were also some shopkeepers for the humbler and every-day wants; but for medical advice, for stationery, books, law, dress, or dainties, the inhabitants had to go to Keighley. There were several Sunday-schools; the Baptists had taken the lead in instituting them, the Wesleyans had followed, the Church of England had brought up the rear. Good Mr Grimshaw, Wesley's friend, had built a humble Methodist chapel, but it stood close to the road leading on to the moor; the Baptists then raised a place of worship, with the distinction of being a few yards back from the highway; and the Methodists have since thought it well to erect another and a larger chapel, still more retired from the road. Mr Brontë was ever on kind and friendly terms with each denomination as a body; but from individuals in the village the family stood aloof, unless some direct service was required, from the first. 'They kept themselves very close,' is the account given by those who remember Mr and Mrs Brontë's coming amongst them. I believe many of the Yorkshiremen would object to the system of parochial visiting; their surly independence would revolt from the idea of any one having a right, from his office, to inquire into their condition, to counsel, or to admonish them. The old hill-spirit lingers in them, which coined the rhyme, inscribed on the under part of one of the seats in the Sedilia of Whalley Abbey, not many miles from Haworth,

'Who mells wi' what another does
Had best go home and shoe his goose.'*

I asked an inhabitant of a district close to Haworth, what sort of a clergyman they had at the church which he attended.

'A rare good one,' said he: 'he minds his own business, and ne'er troubles himself with ours.'

Mr Brontë was faithful in visiting the sick, and all those who sent for him, and diligent in attendance at the schools; and so was his daughter Charlotte too; but, cherishing and valuing privacy themselves, they were perhaps over-delicate in not intruding upon the privacy of others.

From their first going to Haworth, their walks were directed rather out towards the heathery moors, sloping upwards behind the parsonage, than towards the long descending village street. A good old woman,* who came to nurse Mrs Brontë in the illness—an internal cancer—which grew and gathered upon her, not many months after her arrival at Haworth, tells me that at that time the six little creatures used to walk out, hand in hand, towards the glorious wild moors, which in after days they loved so passionately; the elder ones taking thoughtful care for the toddling wee things.

They were grave and silent beyond their years; subdued, probably, by the presence of serious illness in the house; for, at the time which my informant speaks of, Mrs Brontë was confined to the bed-room from which she never came forth alive. 'You would not have known there was a child in the house, they were such still, noiseless, good little creatures. Maria would shut herself up' (Maria, but seven!) 'in the children's study with a newspaper, and be able to tell one everything when she came out; debates in parliament, and I don't know what all. She was as good as a mother to her sisters and brother. But there never were such good children. I used to think them spiritless, they were so different to any children I had ever seen.* They were good little creatures. Emily was the prettiest.'

Mrs Brontë was the same patient, cheerful person as we have seen her formerly; very ill, suffering great pain, but seldom if ever complaining; at her better times begging her nurse to raise her in bed to let her see her clean the grate, 'because she did it as it was done in Cornwall;' devotedly fond of her husband, who warmly repaid her affection, and suffered no one else to take the night-nursing; but, according to my informant, the mother was not very anxious to see much of her children, probably because the sight of them, knowing how soon they were to be left motherless, would have agitated her too much. So the little things clung quietly together, for their father was busy in his study and in his parish, or with their mother, and they took their meals alone; sat reading, or whispering low, in the 'children's study,' or wandered out on the hill-side, hand in hand.

The ideas of Rousseau and Mr Day on education* had filtered down through many classes, and spread themselves widely out. I imagine, Mr Brontë must have formed some of his opinions on the management of children from these two theorists. His practice was not half so wild or extraordinary as that to which an aunt of mine was subjected by a disciple of Mr Day's. She had been taken by this gentleman and his wife, to live with them as their adopted child, perhaps about five-and-twenty years before the time of which I am writing. They were wealthy people and kind hearted, but her food and clothing were of the very simplest and rudest description, on Spartan principles. A healthy, merry child, she did not much care for dress or eating; but the treatment which she felt as a real cruelty was this. They had a carriage, in which she and the favourite dog were taken an airing on alternate days; the creature whose turn it was to be left at home being tossed in a blanket—an operation which my aunt especially dreaded. Her affright at the tossing was probably the reason why it was persevered in. Dressed-up ghosts had become common, and she did not care for them, so the blanket exercise was to be the next mode of hardening her nerves. It is well known that Mr Day broke off his intention of marrying Sabrina, the girl whom he had educated for this purpose, because, within a few weeks of the time fixed for the wedding, she was guilty of the frivolity, while on a visit from home, of wearing thin sleeves. Yet Mr Day and my aunt's relations were benevolent people, only strongly imbued with the crotchet that by a system of training might be educed the hardihood and simplicity of the ideal savage, forgetting the terrible isolation of feelings and habits which their pupils would experience, in the future life which they must pass among the corruptions and refinements of civilization.

Mr Brontë wished to make his children hardy, and indifferent to the pleasures of eating and dress. In the latter he succeeded, as far as regarded his daughters.*

His strong, passionate, Irish nature was, in general, compressed down with resolute stoicism; but it was there notwithstanding all his philosophic calm and dignity of demeanour; though he did not speak when he was annoyed or displeased.* Mrs Brontë, whose sweet nature thought invariably of the bright side, would say, 'Ought I not to be thankful that he never gave me an angry word?'*

Mr Brontë was an active walker, stretching away over the moors for many miles, noting in his mind all natural signs of wind and weather, and keenly observing all the wild creatures that came and

went in the loneliest sweeps of the hills. He has seen eagles
stooping low in search of food for their young; no eagle is ever seen
on those mountain slopes now.

He fearlessly took whatever side in local or national politics
appeared to him right. In the days of the Luddites,* he had been
for the peremptory interference of the law, at a time when no
magistrate could be found to act, and all the property of the West
Riding was in terrible danger. He became unpopular then among
the millworkers, and he esteemed his life unsafe if he took his long
and lonely walks unarmed; so he began the habit, which has
continued to this day, of invariably carrying a loaded pistol about
with him. It lay on his dressing-table with his watch; with his
watch it was put on in the morning; with his watch it was taken
off at night.

Many years later, during his residence at Haworth, there was a
strike;* the hands in the neighbourhood felt themselves aggrieved
by the masters, and refused to work: Mr Brontë thought that they
had been unjustly and unfairly treated, and he assisted them by all
the means in his power to 'keep the wolf from their doors,' and
avoid the incubus of debt. Several of the more influential inhabitants of Haworth and the neighbourhood were mill-owners; they
remonstrated pretty sharply with him, but he believed that his
conduct was right, and persevered in it.

His opinions might be often both wild and erroneous, his
principles of action eccentric and strange, his views of life partial,
and almost misanthropical; but not one opinion that he held could
be stirred or modified by any worldly motive: he acted up to his
principles of action; and, if any touch of misanthropy mingled with
his view of mankind in general, his conduct to the individuals who
came in personal contact with him did not agree with such view.
It is true that he had strong and vehement prejudices, and was
obstinate in maintaining them, and that he was not dramatic
enough in his perceptions to see how miserable others might be in
a life that to him was all-sufficient. But I do not pretend to be able
to harmonize points of character, and account for them, and bring
them all into one consistent and intelligible whole. The family with
whom I have now to do shot their roots down deeper than I can
penetrate. I cannot measure them, much less is it for me to judge
them. I have named these instances of eccentricity in the father

because I hold the knowledge of them to be necessary for a right understanding of the life of his daughter.

Mrs Brontë died in September, 1821,* and the lives of those quiet children must have become quieter and lonelier still. Charlotte tried hard, in after years, to recall the remembrance of her mother, and could bring back two or three pictures of her. One was when, sometime in the evening light, she had been playing with her little boy, Patrick Branwell, in the parlour of Haworth Parsonage. But the recollections of four or five years old are of a very fragmentary character.

Owing to some illness of the digestive organs, Mr Brontë was obliged to be very careful about his diet; and, in order to avoid temptation, and possibly to have the quiet necessary for digestion, he had begun, before his wife's death, to take his dinner alone,—a habit which he always retained. He did not require companionship, therefore he did not seek it, either in his walks, or in his daily life. The quiet regularity of his domestic hours was only broken in upon by churchwardens, and visitors on parochial business; and sometimes by a neighbouring clergyman, who came down the hills, across the moors, to mount up again to Haworth Parsonage, and spend an evening there. But, owing to Mrs Brontë's death so soon after her husband had removed into the district, and also to the distances, and the bleak country to be traversed, the wives of these clerical friends did not accompany their husbands; and the daughters grew up out of childhood into girlhood bereft, in a singular manner, of all such society as would have been natural to their age, sex, and station.*

But the children did not want society. To small infantine gaieties they were unaccustomed. They were all in all to each other. I do not suppose that there ever was a family more tenderly bound to each other. Maria read the newspapers, and reported intelligence to her younger sisters which it is wonderful they could take an interest in. But I suspect that they had no 'children's books,' and that their eager minds 'browzed undisturbed among the wholesome pasturage of English literature,' as Charles Lamb expresses it.* The servants of the household appear to have been much impressed with the little Brontës' extraordinary cleverness. In a letter which I had from him on this subject, their father writes:—'The servants often said that they had never seen such a clever little

child' (as Charlotte), 'and that they were obliged to be on their
guard as to what they said and did before her. Yet she and the
servants always lived on good terms with each other.'*

These servants are yet alive; elderly women residing in Bradford.
They retain a faithful and fond recollection of Charlotte, and speak
of her unvarying kindness from the 'time when she was ever such
a little child!' when she would not rest till she had got the old
disused cradle sent from the parsonage to the house where the
parents of one of them lived, to serve for a little infant sister. They
tell of one long series of kind and thoughtful actions from this early
period to the last weeks of Charlotte Brontë's life; and, though she
had left her place many years ago, one of these former servants
went over from Bradford to Haworth on purpose to see Mr Brontë,
and offer him her true sympathy, when his last child died. I may
add a little anecdote* as a testimony to the admirable character of
the likeness of Miss Brontë prefixed to this volume. A gentleman
who had kindly interested himself in the preparation of this
memoir took the first volume, shortly after the publication, to the
house of this old servant, in order to show her the portrait. The
moment she caught a glimpse of the frontispiece, 'There she is,' in
a minute she exclaimed. 'Come, John, look!' (to her husband); and
her daughter was equally struck by the resemblance. There might
not be many to regard the Brontës with affection, but those who
once loved them, loved them long and well.

I return to the father's letter. He says:—

'When mere children, as soon as they could read and write,
Charlotte and her brother and sisters used to invent and act little
plays of their own, in which the Duke of Wellington, my daughter
Charlotte's hero, was sure to come off conqueror; when a dispute
would not unfrequently arise amongst them regarding the comparative merits of him, Buonaparte, Hannibal, and Cæsar. When
the argument got warm, and rose to its height, as their mother was
then dead, I had sometimes to come in as arbitrator, and settle the
dispute according to the best of my judgment. Generally, in the
management of these concerns, I frequently thought that I discovered signs of rising talent, which I had seldom or never before
seen in any of their age. . . . . A circumstance now occurs to my
mind which I may as well mention. When my children were very
young, when, as far as I can remember, the oldest was about ten

years of age, and the youngest about four, thinking that they knew
more than I had yet discovered, in order to make them speak with
less timidity, I deemed that if they were put under a sort of cover
I might gain my end; and happening to have a mask in the house,
I told them all to stand and speak boldly from under cover of the
mask.

'I began with the youngest (Anne, afterwards Acton Bell), and
asked what a child like her most wanted; she answered, "Age and
experience."* I asked the next (Emily, afterwards Ellis Bell), what
I had best do with her brother Branwell, who was sometimes a
naughty boy; she answered, "Reason with him, and when he won't
listen to reason, whip him." I asked Branwell what was the best
way of knowing the difference between the intellects of man and
woman; he answered, "By considering the difference between them
as to their bodies." I then asked Charlotte what was the best book
in the world; she answered, "The Bible." And what was the next
best; she answered, "The Book of Nature." I then asked the next
what was the best mode of education for a woman; she answered,
"That which would make her rule her house well." Lastly, I asked
the oldest what was the best mode of spending time; she answered,
"By laying it out in preparation for a happy eternity." I may not
have given precisely their words, but I have nearly done so, as they
made a deep and lasting impression on my memory. The substance, however, was exactly what I have stated.'

The strange and quaint simplicity of the mode taken by the father
to ascertain the hidden characters of his children, and the tone and
character of these questions and answers, show the curious education
which was made by the circumstances surrounding the Brontës. They
knew no other children. They knew no other modes of thought than
what were suggested to them by the fragments of clerical conversation
which they overheard in the parlour, or the subjects of village and
local interest which they heard discussed in the kitchen. Each had
their own strong characteristic flavour.

They took a vivid interest in the public characters, and the local
and the foreign as well as home politics discussed in the newspapers. Long before Maria Brontë died, at the age of eleven, her
father used to say he could converse with her on any of the leading
topics of the day with as much freedom and pleasure as with any
grown-up person.

# CHAPTER IV

ABOUT a year after Mrs Brontë's death, an elder sister, as I have before mentioned, came from Penzance to superintend her brother-in-law's household, and look after his children.* Miss Branwell was, I believe, a kindly and conscientious woman, with a good deal of character, but with the somewhat narrow ideas natural to one who had spent nearly all her life in the same place. She had strong prejudices, and soon took a distaste to Yorkshire. From Penzance, where plants which we in the north call greenhouse flowers grow in great profusion, and without any shelter even in the winter, and where the soft warm climate allows the inhabitants, if so disposed, to live pretty constantly in the open air, it was a great change for a lady considerably past forty to come and take up her abode in a place where neither flowers nor vegetables would flourish, and where a tree of even moderate dimensions might be hunted for far and wide; where the snow lay long and late on the moors, stretching bleakly and barely far up from the dwelling which was henceforward to be her home; and where often, on autumnal or winter nights, the four winds of heaven seemed to meet and rage together, tearing round the house as if they were wild beasts striving to find an entrance. She missed the small round of cheerful, social visiting perpetually going on in a country town; she missed the friends she had known from her childhood, some of whom had been her parents' friends before they were hers; she disliked many of the customs of the place, and particularly dreaded the cold damp arising from the flag floors in the passages and parlours of Haworth Parsonage. The stairs, too, I believe, are made of stone;* and no wonder, when stone quarries are near, and trees are far to seek. I have heard that Miss Branwell always went about the house in patterns, clicking up and down the stairs, from her dread of catching cold. For the same reason, in the later years of her life, she passed nearly all her time, and took most of her meals, in her bed-room. The children respected her, and had that sort of affection for her which is generated by esteem; but I do not think they ever freely loved her. It was a severe trial for any one at her time of life to change neighbourhood and habitation so entirely as she did; and the greater her merit.

I do not know whether Miss Branwell taught her nieces anything besides sewing, and the household arts in which Charlotte afterwards was such an adept. Their regular lessons were said to their father; and they were always in the habit of picking up an immense amount of miscellaneous information for themselves. But a year or so before this time, a school had been begun in the North of England for the daughters of clergymen. The place was Cowan Bridge,* a small hamlet on the coach-road between Leeds and Kendal, and thus easy of access from Haworth, as the coach ran daily, and one of its stages was at Keighley. The yearly expense for each pupil (according to the entrance-rules given in the Report for 1842,* and I believe they had not been increased since the establishment of the schools in 1823) was as follows:—

'Rule 11. The terms for clothing, lodging, boarding, and educating, are 14*l.* a year; half to be paid in advance, when the pupils are sent; and also 1*l.* entrance-money, for the use of books, &c. The system of education comprehends history, geography, the use of the globes, grammar, writing and arithmetic, all kinds of needlework, and the nicer kinds of household work—such as getting up fine linen, ironing, &c. If accomplishments are required, an additional charge of 3*l.* a year is made for music or drawing, each.'

Rule 3rd requests that the friends will state the line of education desired in the case of every pupil, having a regard to her future prospects.

Rule 4th states the clothing and toilette articles which a girl is expected to bring with her; and thus concludes: 'The pupils all appear in the same dress. They wear plain straw cottage bonnets; in summer white frocks on Sundays, and nankeen on other days; in winter, purple stuff frocks, and purple cloth cloaks. For the sake of uniformity, therefore, they are required to bring 3*l.* in lieu of frocks, pelisse, bonnet, tippet, and frills; making the whole sum which each pupil brings with her to the school—

7*l.* half-year in advance.
1*l.* entrance for books.
1*l.* entrance for clothes.

The 8th rule is,—'All letters and parcels are inspected by the superintendent;' but this is a very prevalent regulation in all young ladies' schools, where I think it is generally understood that the schoolmistress may exercise this privilege, although it is certainly unwise in her to insist too frequently upon it.

There is nothing at all remarkable in any of the other regulations, a copy of which was doubtless in Mr Brontë's hands when he formed the determination to send his daughters to Cowan Bridge School; and he accordingly took Maria and Elizabeth thither in July, 1824.

I now come to a part of my subject which I find great difficulty in treating, because the evidence relating to it on each side is so conflicting that it seems almost impossible to arrive at the truth. Miss Brontë more than once said to me, that she should not have written what she did of Lowood in 'Jane Eyre,' if she had thought the place would have been so immediately identified with Cowan Bridge,* although there was not a word in her account of the institution but what was true at the time when she knew it; she also said that she had not considered it necessary, in a work of fiction, to state every particular with the impartiality that might be required in a court of justice, nor to seek out motives, and make allowances for human failings, as she might have done, if dispassionately analyzing the conduct of those who had the superintendence of the institution. I believe she herself would have been glad of an opportunity to correct the over-strong impression which was made upon the public mind by her vivid picture, though even she, suffering her whole life long, both in heart and body, from the consequences of what happened there, might have been apt, to the last, to take her deep belief in facts for the facts themselves—her conception of truth for the absolute truth.

In some of the notices* of the previous editions of this work, it is assumed that I derived the greater part of my information with regard to her sojourn at Cowan Bridge from Charlotte Brontë herself. I never heard her speak of the place but once, and that was on the second day of my acquaintance with her. A little child on that occasion expressed some reluctance to finish eating his piece of bread at dinner; and she, stooping down, and addressing him in a low voice, told him how thankful she should have been at his age for a piece of bread; and when we—though I am not sure if I myself spoke—asked her some question as to the occasion she alluded to, she replied with reserve and hesitation, evidently shying away from what she imagined might lead to too much conversation on one of her books. She spoke of the oat-cake at Cowan Bridge (the clap-bread of Westmorland) as being different to the leaven-raised oat-cake of Yorkshire, and of her childish distaste for it. Some one present made an allusion to a similar childish dislike in the true tale of 'The terrible knitters o' Dent' given in Southey's 'Common-place Book:'* and she smiled faintly, but said that the mere difference in food was not all: that the food itself was spoilt by the dirty carelessness of the cook, so that she and her sisters disliked their meals exceedingly; and she named her relief and gladness when the doctor condemned the meat, and spoke of having seen him spit it out. These are all the details I ever heard from her. She so avoided particularizing, that I think Mr Carus Wilson's name never passed between us.

I do not doubt the general accuracy of my informants,—of those who have given, and solemnly repeated, the details that follow,—but it is only just to Miss Brontë to say that I have stated above pretty nearly all that I ever heard on the subject from her.

A clergyman, living near Kirby Lonsdale, the Reverend William Carus Wilson,* was the prime mover in the establishment of this school. He was an energetic man, sparing no labour for the accomplishment of his ends. He saw that it was an extremely difficult task for clergymen with limited incomes to provide for the education of their children; and he devised a scheme, by which a certain sum was raised annually by subscription, to complete the amount required to furnish a solid and sufficient English education, for which the parent's payment of 14*l.* a year would not have been sufficient. Indeed, that made by the parents was considered to be exclusively appropriated to the expenses of lodging and boarding, and the education provided for by the subscriptions. Twelve trustees were appointed; Mr Wilson being not only a trustee, but the treasurer and secretary; in fact, taking most of the business arrangements upon himself; a responsibility which appropriately fell to him, as he lived nearer the school than any one else who was interested in it. So his character for prudence and judgment was to a certain degree implicated in the success or failure of Cowan Bridge School; and the working of it was for many years the great object and interest of his life. But he was apparently unacquainted with the prime element in good administration—seeking out thoroughly competent persons to fill each department, and then making them responsible for, and judging them by, the result, without perpetual interference\* with the details.

So great was the amount of good which Mr Wilson did, by his constant, unwearied superintendence, that I cannot help feeling sorry that, in his old age and declining health, the errors which he was believed to have committed, should have been brought up against him in a form which received such wonderful force from the touch of Miss Brontë's great genius. No doubt whatever can be entertained of the deep interest which he felt in the success of the school. As I write, I have before me his last words on giving up the secretaryship in 1850: he speaks of the 'withdrawal, from declining health, of an eye, which, at all events, has loved to watch over the schools with an honest and anxious interest;'—and again he adds, 'that he resigns, therefore, with a desire to be thankful for all that God has been pleased to accomplish through his instrumentality (the infirmities and unworthinesses of which he deeply feels and deplores).'

Cowan Bridge is a cluster of some six or seven cottages, gathered together at both ends of a bridge, over which the high road from Leeds to Kendal crosses a little stream, called the Leck. This high road is nearly disused now; but formerly, when the buyers from the West Riding manufacturing districts had frequent occasion to go up into the North to purchase the wool of the Westmoreland and Cumberland farmers, it was doubtless much travelled; and perhaps the hamlet of Cowan Bridge had a more prosperous look than it bears at present. It is prettily situated; just where the Leck-fells swoop into the plain; and by the course of the beck alder-trees and willows and hazel bushes grow. The current of the stream is interrupted by broken pieces of grey rock; and the waters flow over a bed of large round white pebbles, which a flood heaves up and moves on either side out of its impetuous way till in some parts they almost form a wall. By the side of the little, shallow, sparkling, vigorous Leck, run long pasture fields, of the fine short grass common in high land; for though Cowan Bridge is situated on a plain, it is a plain from which there is many a fall and long

descent before you and the Leck reach the valley of the Lune. I
can hardly understand how the school there came to be so
unhealthy, the air all round about was so sweet and thyme-scented,
when I visited it last summer. But at this day, every one knows
that the site of a building intended for numbers should be chosen
with far greater care than that of a private dwelling, from the
tendency to illness, both infectious and otherwise, produced by the
congregation of people in close proximity.

The house is still remaining that formed part of that occupied
by the school. It is a long, low bow-windowed cottage, now divided
into two dwellings. It stands facing the Leck, between which and
it intervenes a space, about seventy yards deep, that was once the
school garden. This original house* was an old dwelling of the
Picard family, which they had inhabited for two generations. They
sold it for school purposes, and an additional building was erected,
running at right angles from the older part. This new part was
devoted expressly to school-rooms, dormitories, &c.; and after the
school was removed to Casterton, it was used for a bobbin-mill
connected with the stream, where wooden reels were made out of
the alders, which grow profusely in such ground as that surrounding Cowan Bridge. This mill is now destroyed. The present cottage
was, at the time of which I write, occupied by the teachers' rooms,
the dining-room and kitchens, and some smaller bed-rooms. On
going into this building, I found one part, that nearest to the high
road, converted into a poor kind of public-house, then to let, and
having all the squalid appearance of a deserted place, which
rendered it difficult to judge what it would look like when neatly
kept up, the broken panes replaced in the windows, and the
rough-cast (now cracked and discoloured) made white and whole.
The other end forms a cottage, with the low ceilings and stone
floors of a hundred years ago; the windows do not open freely and
widely; and the passage up-stairs, leading to the bed-rooms, is
narrow and tortuous: altogether, smells would linger about the
house, and damp cling to it. But sanitary matters were little
understood thirty years ago; and it was a great thing to get a roomy
building close to the high road, and not too far from the habitation
of Mr Wilson, the originator of the educational scheme. There was
much need of such an institution; numbers of ill-paid clergymen
hailed the prospect with joy, and eagerly put down the names of

their children as pupils when the establishment should be ready to receive them. Mr Wilson was, no doubt, pleased by the impatience with which the realisation of his idea was anticipated, and opened the school with less than a hundred pounds in hand, and with pupils, the number of whom varies according to different accounts; Mr W. W. Carus Wilson, the son of the founder, giving it as seventy; while Mr Shepheard, the son-in-law, states it to have been only sixteen.*

Mr Wilson felt, most probably, that the responsibility of the whole plan rested upon him. The payment made by the parents was barely enough for food and lodging; the subscriptions did not flow very freely into an untried scheme; and great economy was necessary in all the domestic arrangements. He determined to enforce this by frequent personal inspection; carried perhaps to an unnecessary extent,* and leading occasionally to a meddling with little matters, which had sometimes the effect of producing irritation of feeling. Yet, although there was economy in providing for the household, there does not appear to have been any parsimony. The meat, flour, milk, &c., were contracted for, but were of very fair quality; and the dietary, which has been shown to me in manuscript, was neither bad nor unwholesome; nor, on the whole, was it wanting in variety. Oatmeal porridge for breakfast; a piece of oat-cake for those who required luncheon; baked and boiled beef, and mutton, potato-pie, and plain homely puddings of different kinds for dinner. At five o'clock, bread and milk for the younger ones; and one piece of bread (this was the only time at which the food was limited) for the elder pupils, who sat up till a later meal of the same description.

Mr Wilson himself ordered in the food, and was anxious that it should be of good quality. But the cook, who had much of his confidence, and against whom for a long time no one durst utter a complaint, was careless, dirty, and wasteful. To some children oatmeal porridge is distasteful, and consequently unwholesome, even when properly made; at Cowan Bridge School it was too often sent up, not merely burnt, but with offensive fragments of other substances discoverable in it. The beef, that should have been carefully salted before it was dressed, had often become tainted from neglect; and girls, who were schoolfellows with the Brontës, during the reign of the cook of whom I am speaking, tell me that the house seemed to be pervaded, morning, noon, and night, by the odour of rancid fat that steamed out of the oven in which much of their food was prepared. There was the same carelessness in making the puddings; one of those ordered was rice boiled in water, and eaten with a sauce of treacle and sugar; but it was often uneatable, because the water had been taken out of the rain-tub, and was strongly impregnated with the dust lodging on the roof, whence it had trickled down into the old wooden cask, which also added its own flavour to that of the original rain water. The milk, too, was often 'bingy,' to use a country expression for a kind of taint that is far worse than sourness, and suggests the idea that it is caused by want of cleanliness about the milk pans, rather than by the heat of the weather. On Saturdays, a kind of pie, or mixture of potatoes and meat, was served up, which was made of all the fragments accumulated during the week. Scraps of meat from a dirty and disorderly larder, could never be very appetizing; and, I believe, that this dinner was more loathed than any in the early days of Cowan Bridge School. One may fancy how repulsive such fare would be to children whose appetites were small, and who had been accustomed to food, far simpler perhaps, but prepared with a delicate cleanliness that made it both tempting and whole-some. At many a meal the little Brontës went without food, although craving with hunger. They were not strong when they came, having only just recovered from a complication of measles and hooping-cough: indeed, I suspect they had scarcely recovered; for there was some consultation on the part of the school authorities whether Maria and Elizabeth should be received or not, in July 1824. Mr Brontë came again, in the September of that year, bring-ing with him Charlotte and Emily to be admitted as pupils.*

It appears strange that Mr Wilson should not have been informed by the teachers of the way in which the food was served up; but we must remember that the cook had been known for some time to the Wilson family, while the teachers were brought together for an entirely different work—that of education. They were expressly given to understand that such was their department; the buying in and management of the provisions rested with Mr Wilson and the cook. The teachers would, of course, be unwilling to lay any complaints on the subject before him.*

There was another trial of health common to all the girls. The path from Cowan Bridge to Tunstall Church,* where Mr Wilson preached, and where they all attended on the Sunday, is more than two miles in length, and goes sweeping along the rise and fall of the unsheltered country, in a way to make it a fresh and exhilarating walk in summer, but a bitter cold one in winter, especially to children like the delicate little Brontës, whose thin blood flowed languidly in consequence of their feeble appetites rejecting the food prepared for them, and thus inducing a half starved condition. The church was not warmed, there being no means for this purpose. It stands in the midst of fields, and the damp mist must have gathered round the walls, and crept in at the windows. The girls took their cold dinner with them, and ate it between the services, in a chamber over the entrance, opening out of the former galleries. The arrangements for this day were peculiarly trying to delicate children, particularly to those who were spiritless and longing for home, as poor Maria Brontë must have been; for her ill health was increasing, and the old cough, the remains of the hooping-cough, lingered about her.*

She was far superior in mind to any of her play-fellows and companions, and was lonely amongst them from that very cause; and yet she had faults so annoying that she was in constant disgrace with her teachers, and an object of merciless dislike to one of them, who is depicted as 'Miss Scatcherd' in 'Jane Eyre,'* and whose real name I will be merciful enough not to disclose. I need hardly say, that Helen Burns is as exact a transcript of Maria Brontë as Charlotte's wonderful power of reproducing character could give. Her heart, to the latest day on which we met, still beat with unavailing indignation at the worrying and the cruelty to which her gentle, patient, dying sister had been subjected by this woman. Not a word of that part of 'Jane Eyre' but is a literal repetition of scenes between the pupil and the teacher. Those who had been pupils at the same time knew who must have written the book from the force with which Helen Burns' sufferings are described. They had, before that, recognised the description of the sweet dignity and benevolence of Miss Temple* as only a just tribute to the merits of one whom all that knew her appear to hold in honour; but when Miss Scatcherd was held up to opprobrium they also recognised in the writer of 'Jane Eyre' an unconsciously avenging sister of the sufferer.

One of their fellow-pupils, among other statements even worse, gives me the following:—The dormitory in which Maria slept was a long room, holding a row of narrow little beds on each side, occupied by the pupils; and at the end of this dormitory there was a small bed-chamber opening out of it, appropriated to the use of Miss Scatcherd. Maria's bed stood nearest to the door of this room. One morning, after she had become so seriously unwell as to have had a blister applied to her side* (the sore from which was not perfectly healed), when the getting-up bell was heard, poor Maria moaned out that she was so ill, so very ill, she wished she might stop in bed; and some of the girls urged her to do so, and said they would explain it all to Miss Temple, the superintendent. But Miss Scatcherd was close at hand, and her anger would have to be faced before Miss Temple's kind thoughtfulness could interfere; so the sick child began to dress, shivering with cold, as, without leaving her bed, she slowly put on her black worsted stockings over her thin white legs (my informant spoke as if she saw it yet, and her whole face flashed out undying indignation). Just then Miss Scatcherd issued from her room, and, without asking for a word of explanation from the sick and frightened girl, she took her by the arm, on the side to which the blister had been applied, and by one vigorous movement whirled her out into the middle of the floor, abusing her all the time for dirty and untidy habits. There she left her. My informant says, Maria hardly spoke, except to beg some of the more indignant girls to be calm; but, in slow, trembling movements, with many a pause, she went down stairs at last,—and was punished for being late.

Any one may fancy how such an event as this would rankle in Charlotte's mind. I only wonder that she did not remonstrate against her father's decision to send her and Emily back to Cowan Bridge, after Maria's and Elizabeth's deaths. But frequently children are unconscious of the effect which some of their simple revelations would have in altering the opinions entertained by their friends of the persons placed around them. Besides, Charlotte's earnest vigorous mind saw, at an unusually early age, the immense importance of education, as furnishing her with tools which she had the strength and the will to wield, and she would be aware that the Cowan Bridge education was, in many points, the best that her father could provide for her.

Before Maria Brontë's death, that low fever broke out, in the spring of 1825, which is spoken of in 'Jane Eyre.'* Mr Wilson was

extremely alarmed at the first symptoms of this.* He went to a kind
motherly woman, who had had some connection with the school—
as laundress, I believe—and asked her to come and tell him what
was the matter with them. She made herself ready, and drove with
him in his gig. When she entered the school-room, she saw from
twelve to fifteen girls lying about; some resting their aching heads
on the table, others on the ground; all heavy-eyed, flushed,
indifferent, and weary, with pains in every limb. Some peculiar
odour, she says, made her recognise that they were sickening for
'the fever;' and she told Mr Wilson so, and that she could not stay
there for fear of conveying the infection to her own children; but
he half commanded, and half intreated her to remain and nurse
them; and finally mounted his gig and drove away, while she was
still urging that she must return to her own house, and to her
domestic duties, for which she had provided no substitute. However, when she was left in this unceremonious manner, she
determined to make the best of it; and a most efficient nurse she
proved: although, as she says, it was a dreary time.

Mr Wilson supplied everything ordered by the doctors, of the
best quality and in the most liberal manner;* the invalids were
attended by Dr Batty, a very clever surgeon in Kirby, who had had
the medical superintendence of the establishment from the beginning, and who afterwards became Mr Wilson's brother-in-law. I
have heard from two witnesses besides Charlotte Brontë, that Dr
Batty condemned the preparation of the food by the expressive
action of spitting out a portion of it. He himself, it is but fair to
say, does not remember this circumstance, nor does he speak of the
fever itself as either alarming or dangerous. About forty of the girls
suffered from this, but none of them died at Cowan Bridge; though
one died at her own home, sinking under the state of health which
followed it. None of the Brontës had the fever. But the same
causes, which affected the health of the other pupils through
typhus, told more slowly, but not less surely, upon their constitutions. The principal of these causes was the food.

The bad management of the cook was chiefly to be blamed for
this; she was dismissed, and the woman who had been forced
against her will to serve as head nurse, took the place of housekeeper; and henceforward the food was so well prepared that no
one could ever reasonably complain of it.* Of course it cannot be

expected that a new institution, comprising domestic and educational arrangements for nearly a hundred persons, should work quite smoothly at the beginning.

All this occurred during the first two years of the establishment, and in estimating* its effect upon the character of Charlotte Brontë, we must remember that she was a sensitive, thoughtful child, capable of reflecting deeply, if not of analyzing truly; and peculiarly susceptible, as are all delicate and sickly children, to painful impressions. What the healthy suffer from but momentarily and then forget, those who are ailing brood over involuntarily and remember long,—perhaps with no resentment, but simply as a piece of suffering that has been stamped into their very life. The pictures, ideas, and conceptions of character received into the mind of the child of eight years old, were destined to be reproduced in fiery words a quarter of a century afterwards. She saw but one side of Mr Wilson's character; and many of those who knew him at that time assure me of the fidelity with which this is represented, while at the same time they regret that the delineation should have obliterated, as it were, nearly all that was noble or conscientious. And that there were grand and fine qualities in Mr Wilson, I have received abundant evidence. Indeed for several weeks past I have received letters almost daily, bearing on the subject of this chapter; some vague, some definite; many full of love and admiration for Mr Wilson, some as full of dislike and indignation; few containing positive facts. After giving careful consideration to this mass of conflicting evidence, I have made such alterations and omissions in this chapter as seem to me to be required. It is but just to state that the major part of the testimony with which I have been favoured from old pupils is in high praise of Mr Wilson. Among the letters that I have read, there is one whose evidence ought to be highly respected. It is from the husband of 'Miss Temple.'* She died last year, but he, a clergyman, thus wrote in reply to a letter addressed to him on the subject by one of Mr Wilson's friends:— 'Often have I heard my late dear wife speak of her sojourn at Cowan Bridge; always in terms of admiration of Mr Carus Wilson, his parental love to his pupils, and their love for him; of the food and general treatment in terms of approval. I have heard her allude to an unfortunate cook, who used at times to spoil the porridge, but who, she said, was soon dismissed.'

The recollections left of the four Brontë sisters at this period of their lives, on the minds of those who associated with them, are not very distinct. Wild, strong hearts, and powerful minds, were hidden under an enforced propriety and regularity of demeanour and expression, just as their faces had been concealed by their father, under his stiff, unchanging mask. Maria was delicate, unusually clever and thoughtful for her age, gentle, and untidy. Of her frequent disgrace from this last fault—of her sufferings, so patiently borne—I have already spoken. The only glimpse we get of Elizabeth, through the few years of her short life, is contained in a letter which I have received from 'Miss Temple.' 'The second, Elizabeth, is the only one of the family of whom I have a vivid recollection, from her meeting with a somewhat alarming accident, in consequence of which I had her for some days and nights in my bed-room, not only for the sake of greater quiet, but that I might watch over her myself. Her head was severely cut, but she bore all the consequent suffering with exemplary patience, and by it won much upon my esteem. Of the two younger ones (if two there were) I have very slight recollections, save that one, a darling child, under five years of age, was quite the pet nursling of the school.' This last would be Emily. Charlotte was considered the most talkative of the sisters—a 'bright, clever little child.' Her great friend was a certain 'Mellany Hane'* (so Mr Brontë spells the name), whose brother paid for her schooling, and who had no remarkable talent except for music, which her brother's circumstances forbade her to cultivate. She was 'a hungry, good-natured, ordinary girl;' older than Charlotte, and ever ready to protect her from any petty tyranny or encroachments on the part of the elder girls. Charlotte always remembered her with affection and gratitude.

I have quoted the word 'bright' in the account of Charlotte. I suspect that this year of 1825 was the last time it could ever be applied to her. In the spring of it, Maria became so rapidly worse that Mr Brontë was sent for. He had not previously been aware of her illness, and the condition in which he found her was a terrible shock to him. He took her home by the Leeds coach, the girls crowding out into the road to follow her with their eyes over the bridge, past the cottages, and then out of sight for ever. She died a very few days after her arrival at home. Perhaps the news of her death, falling suddenly into the life of which her patient existence had formed a part, only a little week or so before, made those who remained at Cowan Bridge look with more anxiety on Elizabeth's symptoms, which also turned out to be consumptive. She was sent home in charge of a confidential servant of the establishment; and she, too, died in the early summer of that year. Charlotte was thus suddenly called into the responsibilities of eldest sister in a motherless family. She remembered how anxiously her dear sister Maria had striven, in her grave earnest way, to be a tender helper and a counsellor to them all; and the duties that now fell upon her seemed almost like a legacy from the gentle little sufferer so lately dead.

Both Charlotte and Emily returned to school after the Midsummer holidays in this fatal year.* But before the next winter it was thought desirable to advise their removal, as it was evident that the damp situation of the house at Cowan Bridge did not suit their health.[1]

[1] With regard to my own opinion of the present school, I can only give it as formed after what was merely a cursory and superficial inspection, as I do not believe that I was in the house above half an hour; but it was and is this,—that the house at Casterton seemed thoroughly healthy and well kept, and is situated in a lovely spot; that the pupils looked bright, happy and well, and that the lady superintendent was a most prepossessing looking person, who, on my making some inquiry as to the accomplishments taught to the pupils, said that the scheme of education was materially changed since the school had been opened. I would have inserted this testimony in the first edition, had I believed that any weight could be attached to an opinion formed on such slight and superficial grounds.*

# CHAPTER V

FOR the reason just stated, the little girls were sent home in the autumn of 1825, when Charlotte was little more than nine years old.

About this time, an elderly woman of the village came to live as servant at the parsonage.* She remained there, as a member of the household, for thirty years; and from the length of her faithful service, and the attachment and respect which she inspired, is deserving of mention. Tabby was a thorough specimen of a Yorkshire woman of her class, in dialect, in appearance, and in character. She abounded in strong practical sense and shrewdness. Her words were far from flattery; but she would spare no deeds in the cause of those whom she kindly regarded. She ruled the children pretty sharply; and yet never grudged a little extra trouble to provide them with such small treats as came within her power. In return, she claimed to be looked upon as a humble friend; and, many years later, Miss Brontë told me that she found it somewhat difficult to manage, as Tabby expected to be informed of all the family concerns, and yet had grown so deaf that what was repeated to her became known to whoever might be in or about the house. To obviate this publication of what it might be desirable to keep secret, Miss Brontë used to take her out for a walk on the solitary moors; where, when both were seated on a tuft of heather, in some high lonely place, she could acquaint the old woman, at leisure, with all that she wanted to hear.

Tabby had lived in Haworth in the days when the pack-horses went through once a week, with their tinkling bells and gay worsted adornment, carrying the produce of the country from Keighley over the hills to Colne and Burnley. What is more, she had known the 'bottom,' or valley, in those primitive days when the fairies frequented the margin of the 'beck' on moonlight nights, and had known folk who had seen them. But that was when there were no mills in the valleys; and when all the wool-spinning was done by hand in the farm-houses round. 'It wur the factories as had driven 'em away,' she said. No doubt she had many a tale to tell of by-gone days of the country-side; old ways of living, former inhabitants, decayed gentry, who had melted away, and whose places knew them no more; family tragedies, and dark superstitious dooms; and in telling these things, without the least consciousness that there might ever be anything requiring to be softened down, would give at full length the bare and simple details.

Miss Branwell instructed the children at regular hours in all she could teach, making her bed-chamber into their school-room. Their father was in the habit of relating to them any public news in which he felt an interest; and from the opinions of his strong and independent mind they would gather much food for thought; but I do not know whether he gave them any direct instruction. Charlotte's deep thoughtful spirit appears to have felt almost painfully the tender responsibility which rested upon her with reference to her remaining sisters. She was only eighteen months older than Emily; but Emily and Anne were simply companions and playmates, while Charlotte was motherly friend and guardian to both; and this loving assumption of duties beyond her years, made her feel considerably older than she really was.

Patrick Branwell, their only brother, was a boy of remarkable promise, and, in some ways, of extraordinary precocity of talent. Mr Brontë's friends advised him to send his son to school; but, remembering both the strength of will of his own youth and his mode of employing it, he believed that Patrick was better at home, and that he himself could teach him well, as he had taught others before. So Patrick, or as his family called him—Branwell, remained at Haworth, working hard for some hours a day with his father; but, when the time of the latter was taken up with his parochial duties, the boy was thrown into chance companionship with the lads of the village—for youth will to youth, and boys will to boys.

Still, he was associated in many of his sisters' plays and amusements. These were mostly of a sedentary and intellectual nature. I have had a curious packet confided to me,* containing an immense amount of manuscript, in an inconceivably small space; tales, dramas, poems, romances, written principally by Charlotte, in a hand which it is almost impossible to decipher without the aid of a magnifying glass. No description will give so good an idea of the extreme minuteness of the writing as the annexed fac-simile of a page.*

Among these poems there is a set of her works, which, I say, is a curious proof how early the taste for literary composition had seized upon her.

# THE · SECRET
## CHAPTER THE 1st

*[The main body of the page is a facsimile of a page of minute handwriting, largely illegible.]*

continued in 'The Spirit of a Solitude, &c., &c., &c., &c.' ...
Poems 2. The Glass Town a Song 3. The Silver Cup a Tale 4.
The Tales and Vist... in the Desert a Poem 5. Conversations 11.
Scene on the Great Bridge 12. Song of the Ancient Britons 13.
Scene in my Inn a Tale, &c. An Interesting Passage in the lives
of some of the Eminent Men of Leisure 17. Blood of the Glass Town 8.
14. The Search after Happiness a Tale in the 'Tragedy of the

Among these papers there is a list of her works,* which I copy, as a curious proof how early the rage for literary composition had seized upon her:—

CATALOGUE OF MY BOOKS, WITH THE PERIOD OF THEIR
COMPLETION UP TO AUGUST 3RD, 1830.

Two romantic tales in one volume; viz., The Twelve Adventurers and the Adventures in Ireland, April 2nd, 1829.

The Search after Happiness, a Tale, Aug. 1st, 1829.

Leisure Hours, a Tale, and two Fragments, July 6th, 1829.

The Adventures of Edward de Crack, a Tale, Feb. 2nd, 1830.

The Adventures of Ernest Alembert, a Tale, May 26th, 1830.

An interesting Incident in the Lives of some of the most eminent Persons of the Age, a Tale, June 10th, 1830.

Tales of the Islanders, in four volumes. Contents of the 1st Vol.:—1. An Account of their Origin; 2. A Description of Vision Island; 3. Ratten's Attempt; 4. Lord Charles Wellesley and the Marquis of Douro's Adventure; completed June 31st, 1829. 2nd Vol.:—1. The School-rebellion; 2. The strange Incident in the Duke of Wellington's Life; 3. Tale to his Sons; 4. The Marquis of Douro and Lord Charles Wellesley's Tale to his little King and Queens; completed Dec. 2nd, 1829. 3rd Vol.:—1. The Duke of Wellington's Adventure in the Cavern; 2. The Duke of Wellington and the little King's and Queen's visit to the Horse-Guards; completed May 8th, 1830. 4th Vol.:—1. The three old Washerwomen of Strathfieldsaye; 2. Lord C. Wellesley's Tale to his Brother; completed July 30th, 1830.

Characters of Great Men of the Present Age, Dec. 17th, 1829.

The Young Men's Magazines, in Six Numbers, from August to December, the latter months double number, completed December the 12th, 1829. General index to their contents:—1. A True Story; 2. Causes of the War; 3. A Song; 4. Conversations; 5. A True Story continued; 6. The Spirit of Cawdor; 7. Interior of a Pot-house, a Poem; 8. The Glass Town, a Song; 9. The Silver Cup, a Tale; 10. The Table and Vase in the Desert, a Song; 11. Conversations; 12. Scene on the Great Bridge; 13. Song of the Ancient Britons; 14. Scene in my Tun, a Tale; 15. An American Tale; 16. Lines written on seeing the Garden of a Genius; 17. The Lay of the Glass Town; 18. The Swiss Artist, a Tale; 19. Lines on the Transfer of this

Magazine; 20. On the Same, by a different hand; 21. Chief Genii in Council; 22. Harvest in Spain; 23. The Swiss Artist continued; 24. Conversations.

The Poetaster, a Drama, in 2 volumes, July 12th, 1830.

A Book of Rhymes, finished December 17th, 1829. Contents:— 1. The Beauty of Nature; 2. A short Poem; 3. Meditations while Journeying in a Canadian Forest; 4. A Song of an Exile; 5. On Seeing the Ruins of the Tower of Babel; 6. *A Thing of* 14 *lines;* 7. Lines written on the Bank of a River one fine Summer Evening; 8. Spring, a Song; 9. Autumn, a Song.

Miscellaneous Poems, finished May 30th, 1830. Contents:—1. The Churchyard; 2. Descriptions of the Duke of Wellington's Palace on the Pleasant Banks of the Lusiva; this article is a small prose tale or incident; 3. Pleasure; 4. Lines written on the Summit of a high Mountain of the North of England; 5. Winter; 6. Two Fragments, namely, 1st, The Vision; 2nd, A Short untitled Poem; the Evening Walk, a Poem, June 23rd, 1830.

Making in the whole twenty-two volumes.

C. BRONTË , *August* 3. 1830.

As each volume contains from sixty to a hundred pages, and the size of the page lithographed is rather less than the average, the amount of the whole seems very great, if we remember that it was all written in about fifteen months. So much for the quantity; the quality strikes me as of singular merit for a girl of thirteen or fourteen. Both as a specimen of her prose style at this time, and also as revealing something of the quiet domestic life led by these children, I take an extract from the introduction to 'Tales of the Islanders,' the title of one of their 'Little Magazines:'—*

'June the 31st, 1829.

'The play of the "Islanders" was formed in December, 1827, in the following manner. One night, about the time when the cold sleet and stormy fogs of November are succeeded by the snow-storms, and high piercing night-winds of confirmed winter, we were all sitting round the warm blazing kitchen fire, having just concluded a quarrel with Tabby concerning the propriety of lighting a candle, from which she came off victorious, no candle having been produced. A long pause succeeded, which was at last broken by Branwell saying, in a lazy manner, "I don't know what to do." This was echoed by Emily and Anne.

'*Tabby*. "Wha ya may go t'bed."

'*Branwell*. "I'd rather do anything than that."

'*Charlotte*. "Why are you so glum to-night, Tabby? Oh! suppose we had each an island of our own."

'*Branwell*. "If we had I would choose the Island of Man."

'*Charlotte*. "And I would choose the Isle of Wight."

'*Emily*. "The Isle of Arran for me."

'*Anne*. "And mine should be Guernsey."

'We then chose who should be chief men in our islands.* Branwell chose John Bull, Astley Cooper, and Leigh Hunt; Emily, Walter Scott, Mr Lockhart, Johnny Lockhart; Anne, Michael Sadler, Lord Bentinck, Sir Henry Halford. I chose the Duke of Wellington and two sons, Christopher North and Co., and Mr Abernethy. Here our conversation was interrupted by the, to us, dismal sound of the clock striking seven, and we were summoned off to bed. The next day we added many others to our list of men, till we got almost all the chief men of the kingdom. After this, for a long time, nothing worth noticing occurred. In June, 1828, we erected a school on a fictitious island, which was to contain 1,000 children. The manner of the building was as follows. The Island was fifty miles in circumference, and certainly appeared more like the work of enchantment than anything real,' &c.

Two or three things strike me much in this fragment; one is the graphic vividness with which the time of the year, the hour of the evening, the feeling of cold and darkness outside, the sound of the night-winds sweeping over the desolate snow-covered moors, coming nearer and nearer, and at last shaking the very door of the room where they were sitting—for it opened out directly on that bleak, wide expanse—is contrasted with the glow, and busy brightness of the cheerful kitchen where these remarkable children are grouped. Tabby moves about in her quaint country-dress, frugal, peremptory, prone to find fault pretty sharply, yet allowing no one else to blame her children, we may feel sure. Another noticeable fact is the intelligent partisanship with which they choose their great men, who are almost all stanch Tories of the time. Moreover, they do not confine themselves to local heroes; their range of choice has been widened by hearing much of what is not usually considered to interest children. Little Anne, aged scarcely eight, picks out the politicians of the day for her chief men.

There is another scrap of paper, in this all but illegible hand-writing, written about this time, and which gives some idea of the sources of their opinions.

#### THE HISTORY OF THE YEAR 1829.*

'Once Papa lent my sister Maria a book. It was an old geo-graphy-book; she wrote on its blank leaf, "Papa lent me this book." This book is a hundred and twenty years old; it is at this moment lying before me. While I write this I am in the kitchen of the Parsonage, Haworth; Tabby, the servant, is washing up the breakfast-things, and Anne, my youngest sister (Maria was my eldest), is kneeling on a chair, looking at some cakes which Tabby has been baking for us. Emily is in the parlour, brushing the carpet. Papa and Branwell are gone to Keighley. Aunt is up-stairs in her room, and I am sitting by the table writing this in the kitchen. Keighley is a small town four miles from here. Papa and Branwell are gone for the newspaper, the "Leeds Intelligencer," a most excellent Tory newspaper, edited by Mr Wood, and the proprietor, Mr Henneman. We take two and see three newspapers a week. We take the "Leeds Intelligencer," Tory, and the "Leeds Mercury," Whig, edited by Mr Baines, and his brother, son-in-law, and his two sons, Edward and Talbot. We see the "John Bull;" it is a high Tory, very violent. Mr Driver lends us it, as likewise "Blackwood's Magazine,"* the most able periodical there is. The Editor is Mr Christopher North, an old man seventy-four years of age; the 1st of April is his birth-day; his company are Timothy Tickler, Morgan O'Doherty, Macrabin Mordecai, Mullion, War-nell, and James Hogg, a man of most extraordinary genius, a Scottish shepherd. Our plays were established; "Young Men," June, 1826; "Our Fellows," July, 1827; "Islanders," December, 1827. These are our three great plays, that are not kept secret. Emily's and my best plays were established the 1st of December, 1827; the others March, 1828. Best plays mean secret plays; they are very nice ones. All our plays are very strange ones. Their nature I need not write on paper, for I think I shall always remember them. The "Young Men's" play took its rise from some wooden soldiers Branwell had: "Our Fellows" from "Æsop's Fables;" and the "Islanders" from several events which happened. I will sketch out the origin of our plays more explicitly if I can. First, "Young Men." Papa bought Branwell some wooden soldiers at Leeds; when Papa came home it was night, and we were in bed, so next morning Branwell came to our door with a box of soldiers. Emily and I jumped out of bed, and I snatched up one and exclaimed, "This is the Duke of Wellington! This shall be the Duke!" When I had said this Emily likewise took one up and said it should be hers; when Anne came down, she said one should be hers. Mine was the prettiest of the whole, and the tallest, and the most perfect in every part. Emily's was a grave-looking fellow, and we called him "Gravey." Anne's was a queer little thing, much like herself, and we called him "Waiting-Boy." Branwell chose his, and called him "Buonaparte." '

The foregoing extract shows something of the kind of reading in which the little Brontës were interested; but their desire for knowledge must have been excited in many directions, for I find a "list of painters whose works I wish to see,"* drawn up by Charlotte when she was scarcely thirteen:—

'Guido Reni, Julio Romano, Titian, Raphael, Michael Angelo, Correggio, Annibal Caracci, Leonardo da Vinci, Fra Bartolomeo, Carlo Cignani, Vandyke, Rubens, Bartolomeo Ramerghi.'

Here is this little girl, in a remote Yorkshire parsonage, who has probably never seen anything worthy the name of a painting in her life, studying the names and characteristics of the great old Italian and Flemish masters, whose works she longs to see sometime, in the dim future that lies before her! There is a paper remaining which contains minute studies of, and criticisms upon, the engravings in 'Friendship's Offering for 1829;'* showing how she had early formed those habits of close observation, and patient analysis of cause and effect, which served so well in after-life as handmaids to her genius.

The way in which Mr Brontë made his children sympathise with him in his great interest in politics, must have done much to lift them above the chances of their minds being limited or tainted by petty local gossip. I take the only other remaining personal fragment out of 'Tales of the Islanders;'* it is a sort of apology, contained in the introduction to the second volume, for their not having been continued before; the writers had been for a long time too busy, and latterly too much absorbed in politics.

'Parliament was opened, and the great Catholic question* was brought forward, and the Duke's measures were disclosed, and all was slander, violence, party-spirit, and confusion. Oh, those six months, from the time of the King's speech to the end! Nobody could write, think, or speak on any subject but the Catholic question, and the Duke of Wellington, and Mr Peel. I remember the day when the Intelligence Extraordinary came with Mr Peel's speech in it, containing the terms on which the Catholics were to be let in! With what eagerness Papa tore off the cover, and how we all gathered round him, and with what breathless anxiety we listened, as one by one they were disclosed, and explained, and argued upon so ably, and so well! and then when it was all out, how aunt said that she thought it was excellent, and that the Catholics could do no harm with such good security! I remember also the doubts as to whether it would pass the House of Lords, and the prophecies that it would not; and when the paper came which was to decide the question, the anxiety was almost dreadful with which we listened to the whole affair: the opening of the doors; the hush; the royal dukes in their robes, and the great duke in green sash and waistcoat; the rising of all the peeresses when he rose; the reading of his speech—Papa saying that his words were like precious gold; and lastly, the majority of one to four (sic) in favour of the Bill. But this is a digression.' &c. &c.

This must have been written when she was between thirteen and fourteen.

It will be interesting to some of my readers to know what was the character of her purely imaginative writing at this period. While her description of any real occurrence is, as we have seen, homely, graphic, and forcible, when she gives way to her powers of creation, her fancy and her language alike run riot, sometimes to the very borders of apparent delirium. Of this wild weird writing, a single example will suffice. It is a letter to the editor of one of the 'Little Magazines.'*

'SIR,—It is well known that the Genii have declared that unless they perform certain arduous duties every year, of a mysterious nature, all the worlds in the firmament will be burnt up, and gathered together in one mighty globe, which will roll in solitary grandeur through the vast wilderness of space, inhabited only by the four high princes of the Genii, till time shall be succeeded by Eternity; and the impudence of this is only to be paralleled by another of their assertions, namely, that by their magic might they can reduce the world to a desert, the purest waters to streams of livid poison, and the clearest lakes to stagnant waters, the pestilential vapours of which shall slay all living creatures, except the blood-thirsty beast of the forest, and the ravenous bird of the rock. But that in the midst of this desolation the palace of the Chief Geni shall rise sparkling in the wilderness, and the horrible howl of their war-cry shall spread over the land at morning, at noontide and night; but that they shall have their annual feast over the bones of the dead, and shall yearly rejoice with the joy of victors. I think, sir, that the horrible wickedness of this needs no remark, and therefore I haste to subscribe myself, &c.

'*July* 14. 1829.'

It is not unlikely that the foregoing letter may have had some allegorical or political reference, invisible to our eyes, but very clear to the bright little minds for whom it was intended. Politics were evidently their grand interest; the Duke of Wellington their demi-god. All that related to him belonged to the heroic age. Did Charlotte want a knight-errant, or a devoted lover, the Marquis of Douro, or Lord Charles Wellesley, came ready to her hand. There is hardly one of her prose-writings at this time in which they are not the principal personages, and in which their 'august father' does not appear as a sort of Jupiter Tonans, or Deus ex Machinâ.*

As one evidence how Wellesley haunted her imagination, I copy out a few of the titles to her papers in the various magazines.*

'Liffey Castle,' a Tale by Lord C. Wellesley.

'Lines to the River Aragua,' by the Marquis of Douro.

'An Extraordinary Dream,' by Lord C. Wellesley.

'The Green Dwarf, a Tale of the Perfect Tense,' by the Lord Charles Albert Florian Wellesley.

'Strange Events,' by Lord C. A. F. Wellesley.

Life in an isolated village, or a lonely country-house, presents many little occurrences which sink into the mind of childhood, there to be brooded over. No other event may have happened, or be likely to happen, for days, to push one of these aside, before it has assumed a vague and mysterious importance. Thus, children leading a secluded life are often thoughtful and dreamy: the impressions made upon them by the world without—the unusual sights of earth and sky—the accidental meetings with strange faces and figures (rare occurrences in those out-of-the-way places)—are sometimes magnified by them into things so deeply significant as to be almost supernatural. This peculiarity I perceive very strongly in Charlotte's writings at this time. Indeed, under the circumstances, it is no peculiarity. It has been common to all, from the Chaldean shepherds*—'the lonely herdsman stretched on the soft grass through half a summer's day'—the solitary monk—to all whose impressions from without have had time to grow and vivify in the imagination, till they have been received as actual personifications, or supernatural visions, to doubt which would be blasphemy.

To counterbalance this tendency in Charlotte, was the strong common sense natural to her, and daily called into exercise by the requirements of her practical life. Her duties were not merely to learn her lessons, to read a certain quantity, to gain certain ideas: she had, besides, to brush rooms, to run errands up and down stairs, to help in the simpler forms of cooking, to be by turns play-fellow and monitress to her younger sisters and brother, to make and to mend, and to study economy under her careful aunt. Thus we see that, while her imagination received vivid impressions, her excellent understanding had full power to rectify them before her fancies became realities. On a scrap of paper, she has written down the following relation:—*

'June 22. 1830, 6 o'clock P.M.
'Haworth, near Bradford.

'The following strange occurrence happened on the 22nd of June, 1830:—At that time Papa was very ill, confined to his bed, and so weak that he could not rise without assistance. Tabby and I were alone in the kitchen, about half past nine ante-meridian. Suddenly we heard a knock at the door; Tabby rose and opened it. An old man appeared, standing without, who accosted her thus:—

'*Old Man.*—"Does the parson live here?"
'*Tabby.*—"Yes."

'*Old Man.*—"I wish to see him."
'*Tabby.*—"He is poorly in bed."
'*Old Man.*—"I have a message for him."
'*Tabby.*—"Who from?"
'*Old Man.*—"From the Lord."
'*Tabby.*—"Who?"
'*Old Man.*—"The Lord. He desires me to say that the bridegroom is coming,* and that we must prepare to meet him; that the cords are about to be loosed, and the golden bowl broken; the pitcher broken at the fountain."

'Here he concluded his discourse, and abruptly went his way. As Tabby closed the door, I asked her if she knew him. Her reply was, that she had never seen him before, nor any one like him. Though I am fully persuaded that he was some fanatical enthusiast, well meaning perhaps, but utterly ignorant of true piety; yet I could not forbear weeping at his words, spoken so unexpectedly at that particular period.'

Though the date of the following poem* is a little uncertain, it may be most convenient to introduce it here. It must have been written before 1833, but how much earlier there are no means of determining. I give it as a specimen of the remarkable poetical talent shown in the various diminutive writings of this time; at least, in all of them which I have been able to read.

### THE WOUNDED STAG.

Passing amid the deepest shade
    Of the wood's sombre heart,
Last night I saw a wounded deer
    Laid lonely and apart.

Such light as pierced the crowded boughs
    (Light scattered, scant and dim,)
Passed through the fern that formed his couch
    And centred full on him.

Pain trembled in his weary limbs,
    Pain filled his patient eye,
Pain-crushed amid the shadowy fern
    His branchy crown did lie.

Where were his comrades? where his mate?
　All from his death-bed gone!
And he, thus struck and desolate,
　Suffered and bled alone.

Did he feel what a man might feel
　Friend-left, and sore distrest?
Did Pain's keen dart, and Grief's sharp sting
　Strive in his mangled breast?

Did longing for affection lost
　Barb every deadly dart;
Love unrepaid, and Faith betrayed,
　Did these torment his heart?

No! leave to man his proper doom!
　These are the pangs that rise
Around the bed of state and gloom,
　Where Adam's offspring dies!

# CHAPTER VI

THIS is perhaps a fitting time to give some personal description of Miss Brontë. In 1831, she was a quiet, thoughtful girl, of nearly fifteen years of age, very small in figure—'stunted' was the word she applied to herself,—but as her limbs and head were in just proportion to the slight, fragile body, no word in ever so slight a degree suggestive of deformity could properly be applied to her; with soft, thick, brown hair, and peculiar eyes, of which I find it difficult to give a description, as they appeared to me in her later life. They were large and well shaped; their colour a reddish brown; but if the iris was closely examined, it appeared to be composed of a great variety of tints. The usual expression was of quiet, listening intelligence; but now and then, on some just occasion for vivid interest or wholesome indignation, a light would shine out, as if some spiritual lamp had been kindled, which glowed behind those expressive orbs. I never saw the like in any other human creature. As for the rest of her features, they were plain, large, and ill set; but, unless you began to catalogue them, you were hardly aware of the fact, for the eyes and power of the countenance over-balanced every physical defect; the crooked mouth and the large nose were forgotten, and the whole face arrested the attention, and presently attracted all those whom she herself would have cared to attract. Her hands and feet were the smallest I ever saw; when one of the former was placed in mine, it was like the soft touch of a bird in the middle of my palm. The delicate long fingers had a peculiar fineness of sensation, which was one reason why all her handiwork, of whatever kind—writing, sewing, knitting—was so clear in its minuteness. She was remarkably neat in her whole personal attire; but she was dainty as to the fit of her shoes and gloves.

I can well imagine that the grave serious composure, which, when I knew her, gave her face the dignity of an old Venetian portrait, was no acquisition of later years, but dated from that early age when she found herself in the position of an elder sister to motherless children. But in a girl only just entered on her teens, such an expression would be called (to use a country phrase) 'old-fashioned;' and in 1831, the period of which I now write, we must think of her as a little, set, antiquated girl, very quiet in manners, and very quaint in dress; for besides the influence exerted by her father's ideas concerning the simplicity of attire befitting the wife and daughters of a country clergyman,* her aunt, on whom the duty of dressing her nieces principally devolved, had never been in society since she left Penzance, eight or nine years before, and the Penzance fashions of that day were still dear to her heart.

In January, 1831, Charlotte was sent to school again.* This time she went as a pupil to the Miss W——,* who lived at Roe Head, á cheerful roomy country house, standing a little apart in a field, on the right of the road from Leeds to Huddersfield. Three tiers of old-fashioned semicircular bow windows run from basement to roof; and look down upon a long green slope of pasture-land, ending in the pleasant woods of Kirklees, Sir George Armitage's park. Although Roe Head and Haworth are not twenty miles apart, the aspect of the country is as totally dissimilar as if they enjoyed a different climate. The soft curving and heaving landscape round the former gives a stranger the idea of cheerful airiness on the heights, and of sunny warmth in the broad green valleys below. It is just such a neighbourhood as the monks loved, and traces of the old Plantagenet times are to be met with everywhere, side by side with the manufacturing interests of the West Riding of to-day. There is the park of Kirklees, full of sunny glades, speckled with black shadows of immemorial yew-trees; the grey pile of building, formerly a 'House of professed Ladies;' the mouldering stone in the depth of the wood, under which Robin Hood is said to lie; close outside the park, an old stone-gabled house, now a roadside inn, but which bears the name of the 'Three Nuns,' and has a pictured sign to correspond. And this quaint old inn is frequented by fustian-dressed mill-hands from the neighbouring worsted factories, which strew the high road from Leeds to Huddersfield, and form the centres round which future villages gather. Such are the contrasts of modes of living, and of times and seasons, brought before the traveller on the great roads that traverse the West Riding. In no other part of England, I fancy, are the centuries brought into such close, strange contact as in the district in which Roe Head is situated. Within six miles of Miss W——'s house—on the left of the road, coming from Leeds—lie the remains of Howley Hall,* now the property of Lord Cardigan, but formerly belonging to a branch of the Saviles. Near to it is Lady Anne's well; 'Lady Anne,' according to tradition, having been worried and eaten by wolves as she sat at the well, to which the indigo-dyed factory people from Birstall and Batley woollen mills would formerly repair on Palm Sunday, when the waters possess remarkable medicinal efficacy; and it is still believed by some that they assume a strange variety of colours at six o'clock on the morning of that day.

All round the lands held by the farmer who lives in the remains of Howley Hall are stone houses of to-day, occupied by the people who are making their living and their fortunes by the woollen mills that encroach upon and shoulder out the proprietors of the ancient halls. These are to be seen in every direction, picturesque, many-gabled, with heavy stone carvings of coats of arms for heraldic ornament; belonging to decayed families, from whose ancestral lands field after field has been shorn away, by the urgency of rich manufacturers pressing hard upon necessity.

A smoky atmosphere surrounds these old dwellings of former Yorkshire squires, and blights and blackens the ancient trees that overshadow them; cinder-paths lead up to them; the ground round about is sold for building upon; but still the neighbours, though they subsist by a different state of things, remember that their forefathers lived in agricultural dependence upon the owners of these halls; and treasure up the traditions connected with the stately households that existed centuries ago. Take Oakwell Hall,* for instance. It stands in a pasture-field, about a quarter of a mile from the high road. It is but that distance from the busy whirr of the steam-engines employed in the woollen mills at Birstall; and if you walk to it from Birstall Station about meal-time, you encounter strings of mill-hands, blue with woollen dye, and cranching in hungry haste over the cinder-paths bordering the high road. Turning off from this to the right, you ascend through an old pasture-field, and enter a short by-road, called the 'Bloody Lane'— a walk haunted by the ghost of a certain Captain Batt, the reprobate proprietor of an old hall close by, in the days of the Stuarts. From the 'Bloody Lane,' overshadowed by trees, you come into the field in which Oakwell Hall is situated. It is known in the neighbourhood to be the place described as 'Field Head,' Shirley's residence. The enclosure in front, half court, half garden; the panelled hall, with the gallery opening into the bed-chambers running round; the barbarous peach-coloured drawing-room; the bright look-out through the garden-door upon the grassy lawns and terraces behind, where the soft-hued pigeons still love to coo and strut in the sun,—are described in 'Shirley.' The scenery of that fiction lies close around; the real events which suggested it took place in the immediate neighbourhood.

They show a bloody footprint in a bed-chamber of Oakwell Hall, and tell a story connected with it, and with the lane by which the house is approached. Captain Batt was believed to be far away; his family was at Oakwell; when in the dusk, one winter evening, he came stalking along the lane, and through the hall, and up the stairs, into his own room, where he vanished. He had been killed in a duel in London that very same afternoon of December 9th, 1684.

The stones of the Hall formed part of the more ancient vicarage, which an ancestor of Captain Batt's had seized in the troublous times for property which succeeded the Reformation. This Henry Batt possessed himself of houses and money without scruple; and, at last, stole the great bell of Birstall Church, for which sacrilegious theft a fine was imposed on the land, and has to be paid by the owner of the Hall to this day.

But the Oakwell property passed out of the hands of the Batts at the beginning of the last century; collateral descendants succeeded, and left this picturesque trace of their having been. In the great hall hangs a mighty pair of stag's horns, and dependent from them a printed card, recording the fact that, on the 1st of September, 1763, there was a great hunting-match, when this stag was slain; and that fourteen gentlemen shared in the chase, and dined on the spoil in that hall, along with Fairfax Fearneley, Esq., the owner. The fourteen names are given, doubtless 'mighty men of yore;' but, among them all, Sir Fletcher Norton, Attorney-General, and Major-General Birch were the only ones with which I had any association in 1855. Passing on from Oakwell there lie houses right and left, which were well known to Miss Brontë when she lived at Roe Head, as the hospitable homes of some of her school-fellows. Lanes branch off for three or four miles* to heaths and commons on the higher ground, which formed pleasant walks on holidays, and then comes the white gate into the field-path leading to Roe Head itself.

One of the bow-windowed rooms on the ground floor, with the pleasant look-out I have described, was the drawing-room; the other was the school-room. The dining-room was on one side of the door, and faced the road.

The number of pupils, during the year and a half* Miss Brontë was there, ranged from seven to ten; and as they did not require the whole of the house for their accommodation, the third story was unoccupied, except by the ghostly idea of a lady, whose rustling silk gown was sometimes heard by the listeners at the foot of the second flight of stairs.

The kind motherly nature of Miss W——, and the small number of the girls, made the establishment more like a private family than a school. Moreover, she was a native of the district immediately surrounding Roe Head, as were the majority of her pupils. Most likely Charlotte Brontë, in coming from Haworth, came the greatest distance of all. 'E.'s'* home was five miles away; two other dear friends* (the Rose and Jessie Yorke of 'Shirley') lived still nearer; two or three came from Huddersfield; one or two from Leeds.

I shall now quote from a valuable letter which I have received from 'Mary,'* one of these early friends; distinct and graphic in expression, as becomes a cherished associate of Charlotte Brontë's. The time referred to is her first appearance at Roe Head, on January 19th, 1831.

'I first saw her coming out of a covered cart, in very old-fashioned clothes, and looking very cold and miserable. She was coming to school at Miss W——'s. When she appeared in the school-room, her dress was changed, but just as old. She looked a little old woman, so short-sighted that she always appeared to be seeking something, and moving her head from side to side to catch a sight of it. She was very shy and nervous, and spoke with a strong Irish accent.* When a book was given her, she dropped her head over it till her nose nearly touched it, and when she was told to hold her head up, up went the book after it, still close to her nose, so that it was not possible to help laughing.'

This was the first impression she made upon one of those whose dear and valued friend she was to become in after-life. Another of the girls recalls her first sight of Charlotte, on the day she came, standing by the school-room window, looking out on the snowy landscape, and crying, while all the rest were at play. 'E.' was younger than she, and her tender heart was touched by the apparently desolate condition in which she found the oddly-dressed, odd-looking little girl that winter morning, as 'sick for home she stood in tears,'* in a new strange place, among new strange people. Any over-demonstrative kindness would have scared the wild little maiden from Haworth; but 'E.' (who is shadowed forth in the Caroline Helstone of 'Shirley') managed to win confidence, and was allowed to give sympathy.

To quote again from 'Mary's' letter:—

'We thought her very ignorant, for she had never learnt grammar at all, and very little geography.'

This account of her partial ignorance is confirmed by her other school-fellows. But Miss W—— was a lady of remarkable intelligence and of delicate tender sympathy. She gave a proof of this in her first treatment of Charlotte. The little girl was well-read, but not well-grounded. Miss W—— took her aside and told her she was afraid that she must place her in the second class for some time, till she could overtake the girls of her own age in the knowledge of grammar, &c.; but poor Charlotte received this announcement with so sad a fit of crying, that Miss W——'s kind heart was softened, and she wisely perceived that, with such a girl, it would be better to place her in the first class, and allow her to make up by private study in those branches where she was deficient.

'She would confound us by knowing things that were out of our range altogether. She was acquainted with most of the short pieces of poetry that we had to learn by heart; would tell us the authors, the poems they were taken from, and sometimes repeat a page or two, and tell us the plot. She had a habit of writing in italics (printing characters),* and said she had learnt it by writing in their magazine. They brought out a "magazine" once a month, and wished it to look as like print as possible. She told us a tale out of it. No one wrote in it, and no one read it, but herself, her brother, and two sisters. She promised to show me some of these magazines, but retracted it afterwards, and would never be persuaded to do so. In our play hours she sate, or stood still, with a book, if

possible. Some of us once urged her to be on our side in a game
at ball. She said she had never played, and could not play. We
made her try, but soon found that she could not see the ball, so we
put her out. She took all our proceedings with pliable indifference,
and always seemed to need a previous resolution to say "No" to
anything. She used to go and stand under the trees in the
play-ground, and say it was pleasanter. She endeavoured to explain
this, pointing out the shadows, the peeps of sky, &c. We understood but little of it. She said that at Cowan Bridge she used to
stand in the burn, on a stone, to watch the water flow by. I told
her she should have gone fishing; she said she never wanted. She
always showed physical feebleness in everything. She ate no animal
food at school. It was about this time I told her she was very ugly.
Some years afterwards, I told her I thought I had been very
impertinent. She replied, "You did me a great deal of good, Polly,
so don't repent of it." She used to draw much better, and more
quickly, than anything we had seen before, and knew much about
celebrated pictures and painters. Whenever an opportunity offered
of examining a picture or cut of any kind, she went over it
piecemeal, with her eyes close to the paper, looking so long that
we used to ask her "what she saw in it." She could always see
plenty, and explained it very well. She made poetry and drawing
at least exceedingly interesting to me; and then I got the habit,
which I have yet, of referring mentally to her opinion on all
matters of that kind, along with many more, resolving to describe
such and such things to her, until I start at the recollection that I
never shall.'

To feel the full force of this last sentence—to show how steady
and vivid was the impression which Miss Brontë made on those
fitted to appreciate her—I must mention that the writer of this
letter, dated January 18th, 1856, in which she thus speaks of
constantly referring to Charlotte's opinion, has never seen her for
eleven years, nearly all of which have been passed among strange
scenes, in a new continent, at the antipodes.

'We used to be furious politicians, as one could hardly help
being in 1832.* She knew the names of the two ministries; the one
that resigned, and the one that succeeded and passed the Reform
Bill. She worshipped the Duke of Wellington, but said that Sir
Robert Peel was not to be trusted; he did not act from principle

like the rest, but from expediency. I, being of the furious radical party, told her "how could any of them trust one another; they were all of them rascals!" Then she would launch out into praises of the Duke of Wellington, referring to his actions; which I could not contradict, as I knew nothing about him. She said she had taken interest in politics ever since she was five years old. She did not get her opinions from her father—that is, not directly—but from the papers, &c. he preferred.'

In illustration of the truth of this, I may give an extract from a letter to her brother, written from Roe Head, May 17th, 1832:—
'Lately I had begun to think that I had lost all the interest which I used formerly to take in politics; but the extreme pleasure I felt at the news of the Reform Bill's being thrown out by the House of Lords, and of the expulsion, or resignation, of Earl Grey, &c., convinced me that I have not as yet lost all my penchant for politics. I am extremely glad that aunt has consented to take in "Frazer's Magazine;"* for, though I know from your description of its general contents it will be rather uninteresting when compared with "Blackwood," still it will be better than remaining the whole year without being able to obtain a sight of any periodical whatever; and such would assuredly be our case, as, in the little wild moorland village where we reside, there would be no possibility of borrowing a work of that description from a circulating library. I hope with you that the present delightful weather may contribute to the perfect restoration of our dear papa's health; and that it may give aunt pleasant reminiscences of the salubrious climate of her native place,' &c.

To return to 'Mary's' letter.

'She used to speak of her two elder sisters, Maria and Elizabeth, who died at Cowan Bridge. I used to believe them to have been wonders of talent and kindness. She told me, early one morning, that she had just been dreaming; she had been told that she was wanted in the drawing-room, and it was Maria and Elizabeth. I was eager for her to go on, and when she said there was no more, I said, "Well! but go on! *Make it out!* I know you can." She said she would not; she wished she had not dreamed, for it did not go on nicely; they were changed; they had forgotten what they used to care for. They were very fashionably dressed, and began criticising the room, &c.

'This habit of "making out" interests for themselves, that most children get who have none in actual life, was very strong in her. The whole family used to "make out" histories, and invent characters and events. I told her sometimes they were like growing potatoes in a cellar. She said, sadly, "Yes! I know we are!"

'Some one at school* said she "was always talking about clever people; Johnson, Sheridan, &c." She said, "Now you don't know the meaning of *clever;* Sheridan might be clever; yes, Sheridan was clever,—scamps often are; but Johnson hadn't a spark of cleverality in him." No one appreciated the opinion; they made some trivial remark about "*cleverality*," and she said no more.

'This is the epitome of her life. At our house she had just as little chance of a patient hearing, for though not school-girlish, we were more intolerant. We had a rage for practicality, and laughed all poetry to scorn. Neither she nor we had any idea but that our opinions were the opinions of all the *sensible* people in the world, and we used to astonish each other at every sentence. . . . . Charlotte, at school, had no plan of life beyond what circumstances made for her. She knew that she must provide for herself, and chose her trade; at least chose to begin it at once. Her idea of self-improvement ruled her even at school. It was to cultivate her tastes. She always said there was enough of hard practicality, and *useful* knowledge forced on us by necessity, and that the thing most needed was to soften and refine our minds. She picked up every scrap of information concerning painting, sculpture, poetry, music, &c., as if it were gold.'

What I have heard of her school days from other sources, confirms the accuracy of the details in this remarkable letter. She was an indefatigable student: constantly reading and learning; with a strong conviction of the necessity and value of education, very unusual in a girl of fifteen. She never lost a moment of time, and seemed almost to grudge the necessary leisure for relaxation and play-hours, which might be partly accounted for by the awkward-ness in all games occasioned by her shortness of sight. Yet, in spite of these unsociable habits, she was a great favourite with her school-fellows. She was always ready to try and do what they wished, though not sorry when they called her awkward, and left her out of their sports. Then, at night, she was an invaluable story-teller, frightening them almost out of their wits as they lay

in bed. On one occasion the effect was such that she was led to
scream out loud, and Miss W——, coming up-stairs, found that
one of the listeners had been seized with violent palpitations, in
consequence of the excitement produced by Charlotte's story.

Her indefatigable craving for knowledge tempted Miss W——
on into setting her longer and longer tasks of reading for examination; and towards the end of the year and a half that she remained
as a pupil at Roe Head, she received her first bad mark for an
imperfect lesson. She had had a great quantity of Blair's 'Lectures
on Belles Lettres'* to read; and she could not answer some of the
questions upon it; Charlotte Brontë had a bad mark. Miss W——
was sorry, and regretted that she had set Charlotte so long a task.*
Charlotte cried bitterly. But her school-fellows were more than
sorry—they were indignant. They declared that the infliction of
ever so slight a punishment on Charlotte Brontë was unjust—for
who had tried to do her duty like her?—and testified their feeling
in a variety of ways, until Miss W——, who was in reality only too
willing to pass over her good pupil's first fault, withdrew the bad
mark; and the girls all returned to their allegiance except 'Mary,'
who took her own way during the week or two that remained of
the half-year, choosing to consider that Miss W——, in giving
Charlotte Brontë so long a task, had forfeited her claim to
obedience of the school regulations.

The number of pupils was so small that the attendance to certain
subjects at particular hours, common in larger schools, was not
rigidly enforced. When the girls were ready with their lessons, they
came to Miss W—— to say them. She had a remarkable knack of
making them feel interested in whatever they had to learn. They
set to their studies, not as to tasks or duties to be got through, but
with a healthy desire and thirst for knowledge, of which she had
managed to make them perceive the relishing savour. They did not
leave off reading and learning as soon as the compulsory pressure
of school was taken away. They had been taught to think, to
analyse, to reject, to appreciate. Charlotte Brontë was happy in the
choice made for her of the second school to which she was sent.
There was a robust freedom in the out-of-doors life of her
companions. They played at merry games in the fields round the
house: on Saturday half-holidays they went long scrambling walks
down mysterious shady lanes, then climbing the uplands, and thus

gaining extensive views over the country, about which so much had to be told, both of its past and present history.

Miss W—— must have had in great perfection the French art, 'conter,' to judge from her pupil's recollections of the tales* she related during these long walks, of this old house, or that new mill, and of the states of society consequent on the changes involved by the suggestive dates of either building. She remembered the times when watchers or wakeners in the night heard the distant word of command, and the measured tramp of thousands of sad desperate men receiving a surreptitious military training, in preparation for some great day which they saw in their visions, when right should struggle with might and come off victorious: when the people of England, represented by the workers of Yorkshire, Lancashire, and Nottinghamshire, should make their voice heard in a terrible slogan, since their true and pitiful complaints could find no hearing in parliament. We forget, now-a-days, so rapid have been the changes for the better, how cruel was the condition of numbers of labourers at the close of the great Peninsular war. The half-ludicrous nature of some of their grievances has lingered on in tradition; the real intensity of their sufferings has become forgotten. They were maddened and desperate; and the country, in the opinion of many, seemed to be on the verge of a precipice, from which it was only saved by the prompt and resolute decision of a few in authority. Miss W—— spoke of those times; of the mysterious nightly drillings; of thousands on lonely moors; of the muttered threats of individuals too closely pressed upon by necessity to be prudent; of the overt acts, in which the burning of Cartwright's mill took a prominent place; and these things sank deep into the mind of one, at least, among her hearers.

Mr Cartwright was the owner of a factory called Rawfolds, in Liversedge, not beyond the distance of a walk from Roe Head. He had dared to employ machinery for the dressing of woollen cloth, which was an unpopular measure in 1812, when many other circumstances conspired to make the condition of the mill-hands unbearable from the pressure of starvation and misery. Mr Cartwright was a very remarkable man, having, as I have been told, some foreign blood in him, the traces of which were very apparent in his tall figure, dark eyes and complexion, and singular, though gentlemanly bearing. At any rate, he had been much abroad, and spoke French well, of itself a suspicious circumstance to the bigoted nationality of those days. Altogether he was an unpopular man, even before he took the last step of employing shears, instead of hands, to dress his wool. He was quite aware of his unpopularity, and of the probable consequences. He had his mill prepared for an assault. He took up his lodgings in it; and the doors were strongly barricaded at night. On every step of the stairs there was placed a roller, spiked with barbed points all round, so as to impede the ascent of the rioters, if they succeeded in forcing the doors.

On the night of Saturday the 11th of April, 1812, the assault was made. Some hundreds of starving cloth-dressers assembled in the very field near Kirklees that sloped down from the house which Miss W—— afterwards inhabited, and were armed by their leaders with pistols, hatchets, and bludgeons, many of which had been extorted by the nightly bands that prowled about the country, from such inhabitants of lonely houses as had provided themselves with these means of self-defence. The silent sullen multitude marched in the dead of that spring-night to Rawfolds, and giving tongue with a great shout, roused Mr Cartwright up to the knowledge that the long-expected attack was come. He was within walls, it is true; but against the fury of hundreds he had only four of his own workmen and five soldiers to assist him. These ten men, however, managed to keep up such a vigorous and well-directed fire of musketry that they defeated all the desperate attempts of the multitude outside to break down the doors, and force a way into the mill; and, after a conflict of twenty minutes, during which two of the assailants were killed and several wounded, they withdrew in confusion, leaving Mr Cartwright master of the field, but so dizzy and exhausted, now the peril was past, that he forgot the nature of his defences, and injured his leg rather seriously by one of the spiked rollers, in attempting to go up his own staircase. His dwelling was near the factory. Some of the rioters vowed that, if he did not give in, they would leave this, and go to his house, and murder his wife and children. This was a terrible threat, for he had been obliged to leave his family with only one or two soldiers to defend them. Mrs Cartwright knew what they had threatened; and on that dreadful night, hearing, as she thought, steps approaching, she snatched up her two infant children, and put them in a basket up the great chimney, common in old-fashioned Yorkshire houses.* One of the two children who had been thus stowed away used to point out with pride, after she had grown up to woman's estate, the marks of musket shot, and the traces of gunpowder on the walls of her father's mill. He was the first that had offered any resistance to the progress of the 'Luddites,' who had become by this time so numerous as almost to assume the character of an insurrectionary army. Mr Cartwright's conduct was so much admired by the neighbouring mill-owners that they entered into a subscription for his benefit, which amounted in the end to 3,000*l*.

Not much more than a fortnight after this attack on Rawfolds, another manufacturer who employed the obnoxious machinery was shot down in broad daylight, as he was passing over Crossland Moor, which was skirted by a small plantation in which the murderers lay hidden. The readers of 'Shirley' will recognise these circumstances, which were related to Miss Brontë years after they occurred, but on the very spots where they took place, and by persons who remembered full well those terrible times of insecurity to life and property on the one hand, and of bitter starvation and blind ignorant despair on the other.

Mr Brontë himself had been living amongst these very people in 1812, as he was then clergyman at Hartshead, not three miles from Rawfolds; and, as I have mentioned, it was in these perilous times that he began his custom of carrying a loaded pistol continually about with him. For not only his Tory politics, but his love and regard for the authority of the law, made him despise the cowardice of the surrounding magistrates, who, in their dread of the Luddites, refused to interfere so as to prevent the destruction of property. The clergy of the district were the bravest men by far.

There was a Mr Roberson of Heald's Hall,* a friend of Mr Brontë's, who has left a deep impression of himself on the public mind. He lived near Heckmondwike, a large, straggling, dirty village, not two miles from Roe Head. It was principally inhabited by blanket weavers, who worked in their own cottages; and Heald's Hall is the largest house in the village, of which Mr Roberson was the vicar. At his own cost, he built a handsome church at Liversedge, on a hill opposite the one on which his house stood, which was the first attempt in the West Riding to meet the wants

of the overgrown population, and made many personal sacrifices
for his opinions, both religious and political, which were of the true
old-fashioned Tory stamp. He hated everything which he fancied
had a tendency towards anarchy. He was loyal in every fibre to
Church and king; and would have proudly laid down his life, any
day, for what he believed to be right and true. But he was a man
of an imperial will, and by it he bore down opposition, till tradition
represents him as having something grimly demoniac about him.
He was intimate with Cartwright, and aware of the attack likely to
be made on his mill; accordingly, it is said, he armed himself and
his household, and was prepared to come to the rescue, in the
event of a signal being given that aid was needed. Thus far is likely
enough. Mr Roberson had plenty of warlike spirit in him, man of
peace though he was.

But, in consequence of his having taken the unpopular side,
exaggerations of his character linger as truth in the minds of the
people; and a fabulous story is told of his forbidding any one to
give water to the wounded Luddites, left in the mill-yard, when
he rode in the next morning to congratulate his friend Cartwright on his successful defence. Moreover, this stern, fearless
clergyman had the soldiers that were sent to defend the neighbourhood billeted at his house; and this deeply displeased the workpeople, who were to be intimidated by the red-coats. Although not
a magistrate, he spared no pains to track out the Luddites
concerned in the assassination I have mentioned; and was so
successful in his acute unflinching energy, that it was believed he
had been supernaturally aided; and the country people, stealing
into the field surrounding Heald's Hall on dusky winter evenings,
years after this time, declared that through the windows they saw
Parson Roberson dancing, in a strange red light, with black demons
all whirling and eddying round him. He kept a large boys' school;
and made himself both respected and dreaded by his pupils. He
added a grim kind of humour to his strength of will; and the
former quality suggested to his fancy strange out-of-the-way kinds
of punishment for any refractory pupils: for instance, he made
them stand on one leg in a corner of the school-room, holding a
heavy book in each hand; and once, when a boy had run away
home, he followed him on horseback, reclaimed him from his
parents, and, tying him by a rope to the stirrup of his saddle, made

him run alongside of his horse for the many miles they had to traverse before reaching Heald's Hall.

One other illustration of his character may be given. He discovered that his servant Betty had 'a follower;' and, watching his time till Richard was found in the kitchen, he ordered him into the dining-room, where the pupils were all assembled. He then questioned Richard whether he had come after Betty; and on his confessing the truth, Mr Roberson gave the word, 'Off with him, lads, to the pump!' The poor lover was dragged to the court-yard, and the pump set to play upon him; and, between every drenching, the question was put to him, 'Will you promise not to come after Betty again?' For a long time Richard bravely refused to give in; when 'Pump again, lads!' was the order. But, at last, the poor soaked 'follower' was forced to yield, and renounce his Betty.

The Yorkshire character of Mr Roberson would be incomplete if I did not mention his fondness for horses. He lived to be a very old man, dying some time nearer to 1840 than 1830; and even after he was eighty years of age, he took great delight in breaking refractory steeds; if necessary, he would sit motionless on their backs for half-an-hour or more, to bring them to. There is a story current that once, in a passion, he shot his wife's favourite horse, and buried it near a quarry, where the ground, some years after, miraculously opened and displayed the skeleton; but the real fact is, that it was an act of humanity to put a poor old horse out of misery; and that, to spare it pain, he shot it with his own hands, and buried it where, the ground sinking afterwards by the working of a coal-pit, the bones came to light. The traditional colouring shows the animus with which his memory is regarded by one set of people. By another, the neighbouring clergy, who remember him riding, in his old age, down the hill on which his house stood, upon his strong white horse—his bearing proud and dignified, his shovel hat bent over and shadowing his keen eagle eyes—going to his Sunday duty, like a faithful soldier that dies in harness—who can appreciate his loyalty to conscience, his sacrifices for duty, and his stand by his religion—his memory is venerated. In his extreme old age, a rubric-meeting* was held, at which his clerical brethren gladly subscribed to present him with a testimonial of their deep respect and regard.

This is a specimen of the strong character not seldom manifested by the Yorkshire clergy of the Established Church. Mr Roberson was a friend of Charlotte Brontë's father; lived within a couple of miles of Roe Head while she was at school there; and was deeply engaged in transactions, the memory of which was yet recent when she heard of them, and of the part which he had had in them.

I may now say a little on the character of the Dissenting population immediately surrounding Roe Head; for the 'Tory and clergyman's daughter,' 'taking interest in politics ever since she was five years old,' and holding frequent discussions with such of the girls as were Dissenters and Radicals, was sure to have made herself as much acquainted as she could with the condition of those to whom she was opposed in opinion.

The bulk of the population were Dissenters, principally Independents.* In the village of Heckmondwike, at one end of which Roe Head is situated, there were two large chapels, belonging to that denomination, and one to the Methodists, all of which were well filled two or three times on a Sunday, besides having various prayer-meetings, fully attended, on week-days. The inhabitants were a chapel-going people, very critical about the doctrine of their sermons, tyrannical to their ministers, and violent Radicals in politics. A friend,* well acquainted with the place when Charlotte Brontë was at school, has described some events which occurred then among them:—

'A scene, which took place at the Lower Chapel at Heckmondwike, will give you some idea of the people at that time. When a newly-married couple made their appearance at chapel, it was the custom to sing the Wedding Anthem, just after the last prayer, and as the congregation was quitting the chapel. The band of singers who performed this ceremony expected to have money given them, and often passed the following night in drinking; at least, so said the minister of the place; and he determined to put an end to this custom. In this he was supported by many members of the chapel and congregation; but so strong was the democratic element, that he met with the most violent opposition, and was often insulted when he went into the street. A bride was expected to make her first appearance, and the minister told the singers not to perform the anthem. On their declaring they would, he had the large pew which they usually occupied locked; they broke it open: from the pulpit he told the congregation that, instead of their singing a hymn, he would read a chapter; hardly had he uttered the first

word, before up rose the singers, headed by a tall, fierce-looking
weaver, who gave out a hymn, and all sang it at the very top of
their voices, aided by those of their friends who were in the chapel.
Those who disapproved of the conduct of the singers, and sided
with the minister, remained seated till the hymn was finished.
Then he gave out the chapter again, read it, and preached. He was
just about to conclude with prayer, when up started the singers and
screamed forth another hymn. These disgraceful scenes were
continued for many weeks, and so violent was the feeling, that the
different parties could hardly keep from blows as they came
through the chapel-yard. The minister, at last, left the place, and
along with him went many of the most temperate and respectable
part of the congregation, and the singers remained triumphant.

'I believe that there was such a violent contest respecting the
choice of a pastor, about this time, in the Upper Chapel at
Heckmondwike, that the Riot Act had to be read at a church-
meeting.'

Certainly, the *soi-disant* Christians who forcibly ejected Mr
Redhead at Haworth, ten or twelve years before, held a very
heathen brotherhood with the *soi-disant* Christians of Heckmondwike; though the one set might be called members of the Church
of England, and the other Dissenters.

The letter from which I have taken the above extract relates
throughout to the immediate neighbourhood of the place where
Charlotte Brontë spent her school days, and describes things as
they existed at that very time. The writer says,—'Having been
accustomed to the respectful manners of the lower orders in the
agricultural districts, I was, at first, much disgusted and somewhat
alarmed at the great freedom displayed by the working classes of
Heckmondwike and Gomersall to those in a station above them.
The term "lass," was as freely applied to any young lady, as the
word "wench" is in Lancashire. The extremely untidy appearance
of the villages shocked me not a little, though I must do the
housewives the justice to say that the cottages themselves were not
dirty, and had an air of rough plenty about them (except when
trade was bad), that I had not been accustomed to see in the
farming districts. The heap of coals on one side of the house-door,
and the brewing tubs on the other, and the frequent perfume of
malt and hops as you walked along, proved that fire and "home-

brewed" were to be found at almost every man's hearth. Nor was hospitality, one of the main virtues of Yorkshire, wanting. Oat-cake, cheese, and beer, were freely pressed upon the visitor.

'There used to be a yearly festival, half religious, half social, held at Heckmondwike, called "The Lecture."* I fancy it had come down from the times of the Nonconformists. A sermon was preached by some stranger at the Lower Chapel, on a week-day evening, and the next day two sermons in succession were de-livered at the Upper Chapel. Of course, the service was a very long one, and as the time was June, and the weather often hot, it used to be regarded by myself and my companions as no pleasurable way of passing the morning. The rest of the day was spent in social enjoyment; great numbers of strangers flocked to the place; booths were erected for the sale of toys and gingerbread (a sort of "Holy Fair"); and the cottages, having had a little extra paint and white-washing, assumed quite a holiday look.

'The village of Gomersall' (where Charlotte Brontë's friend 'Mary' lived with her family), 'which was a much prettier place than Heckmondwike, contained a strange-looking cottage, built of rough unhewn stones, many of them projecting considerably, with uncouth heads and grinning faces carved upon them; and upon a stone above the door was cut, in large letters, "SPITE HALL."* It was erected by a man in the village, opposite to the house of his enemy, who had just finished for himself a good house, command-ing a beautiful view down the valley, which this hideous building quite shut out.'

Fearless—because this people were quite familiar to all of them—amidst such a population, lived and walked the gentle Miss W——'s eight or nine pupils. She herself was born and bred among this rough, strong, fierce set, and knew the depth of goodness and loyalty that lay beneath their wild manners and insubordinate ways. And the girls talked of the little world around them, as if it were the only world that was; and had their opinions and their parties, and their fierce discussions like their elders—possibly, their betters. And among them, beloved and respected by all, laughed at occasionally by a few, but always to her face—lived, for a year and a half, the plain, short-sighted, oddly-dressed, studious little girl they called Charlotte Brontë.

Miss Brontë left Roe Head in 1832, having won the affectionate regard both of her teacher and her school-fellows, and having formed there the two fast friendships which lasted her whole life long; the one with 'Mary,' who has not kept her letters; the other with 'E.,' who has kindly entrusted me with a large portion of Miss Brontë's correspondence with her.* This she has been induced to do by her knowledge of the urgent desire on the part of Mr Brontë that the life of his daughter should be written, and in compliance with a request from her husband that I should be permitted to have the use of these letters, without which such a task could be but very imperfectly executed. In order to shield this friend, however, from any blame or misconstruction, it is only right to state that, before granting me this privilege, she throughout most carefully and completely effaced the names of the persons and places which occurred in them; and also that such information as I have obtained from her bears reference solely to Miss Brontë and her sisters, and not to any other individuals whom I may find it necessary to allude to in connexion with them.

In looking over the earlier portion of this correspondence, I am struck afresh by the absence of hope, which formed such a strong characteristic in Charlotte. At an age when girls, in general, look forward to an eternal duration of such feelings as they or their friends entertain, and can therefore see no hindrance to the fulfilment of any engagements dependent on the future state of the affections, she is surprised that 'E.' keeps her promise to write. In after-life, I was painfully impressed with the fact, that Miss Brontë never dared to allow herself to look forward with hope; that she had no confidence in the future; and I thought, when I heard of the sorrowful years she had passed through, that it had been this pressure of grief which had crushed all buoyancy of expectation out of her. But it appears from the letters, that it must have been, so to speak, constitutional; or, perhaps, the deep pang of losing her two elder sisters combined with a permanent state of bodily weakness in producing her hopelessness. If her trust in God had been less strong, she would have given way to unbounded anxiety, at many a period of her life. As it was, we shall see, she made a great and successful effort to leave 'her times in His hands.'*

After her return home, she employed herself in teaching her sisters, over whom she had had superior advantages. She writes thus, July 21st, 1832, of her course of life at the parsonage:—

'An account of one day is an account of all. In the morning, from nine o'clock till half-past twelve, I instruct my sisters, and draw; then we walk till dinner-time. After dinner I sew till tea-time, and after tea I either write, read, or do a little fancy-work, or draw, as I please. Thus, in one delightful, though somewhat monotonous course, my life is passed. I have been only out twice to tea since I came home. We are expecting company this afternoon, and on Tuesday next we shall have all the female teachers of the Sunday-school to tea.'

I may here introduce a quotation from a letter which I have received from 'Mary' since the publication of the previous editions of this memoir.*

'Soon after leaving school she admitted reading something of Cobbett's.* "She did not like him," she said; "but all was fish that came to her net." At this time she wrote to me that reading and drawing were the only amusements she had, and that her supply of books was very small in proportion to her wants. She never spoke of her aunt. When I saw Miss Branwell she was a very precise person, and looked very odd, because her dress, &c., was so utterly out of fashion. She corrected one of us once for using the word "spit" or "spitting." She made a great favourite of Branwell. She made her nieces sew, with purpose or without, and as far as possible discouraged any other culture. She used to keep the girls sewing charity clothing, and maintained to me that it was not for the good of the recipients, but of the sewers. "It was proper for them to do it," she said. Charlotte never was "in wild excitement" that I know of. When in health she used to talk better, and indeed when in low spirits never spoke at all. She needed her best spirits to say what was in her heart, for at other times she had not courage. She never gave decided opinions at such times. . . . .

'Charlotte said she could get on with any one who had a bump at the top of their heads (meaning conscientiousness).* I found that I seldom differed from her, except that she was far too tolerant of stupid people, if they had a grain of kindness in them.'

It was about this time that Mr Brontë provided his children with a teacher in drawing,* who turned out to be a man of considerable talent, but very little principle. Although they never attained to anything like proficiency, they took great interest in acquiring this art; evidently, from an instinctive desire to express their powerful imaginations in visible forms. Charlotte told me, that at this period of her life, drawing, and walking out with her sisters, formed the two great pleasures and relaxations of her day.

The three girls used to walk upwards toward the 'purple-black' moors, the sweeping surface of which was broken by here and there a stone-quarry; and if they had strength and time to go far enough, they reached a waterfall,* where the beck fell over some rocks into the 'bottom.' They seldom went downwards through the village. They were shy of meeting even familiar faces, and were scrupulous about entering the house of the very poorest uninvited. They were steady teachers at the Sunday-school, a habit which Charlotte kept up very faithfully, even after she was left alone; but they never faced their kind voluntarily, and always preferred the solitude and freedom of the moors.

In the September of this year, Charlotte went to pay her first visit to her friend 'E.' It took her into the neighbourhood of Roe Head, and brought her into pleasant contact with many of her old school-fellows. After this visit, she and her friend seem to have agreed to correspond in French, for the sake of improvement in the language. But this improvement could not be great, when it could only amount to a greater familiarity with dictionary words, and when there was no one to explain to them that a verbal translation of English idioms hardly constituted French composition; but the effort was laudable, and of itself shows how willing they both were to carry on the education which they had begun under Miss W——. I will give an extract which, whatever may be thought of the language, is graphic enough, and presents us with a happy little family picture; the eldest sister returning home to the two younger, after a fortnight's absence.*

'J'arrivait à Haworth en parfaite sauveté sans le moindre accident ou malheur. Mes petites sœurs couraient hors de la maison pour me rencontrer aussitôt que la voiture se fit voir, et elles m'embras-saient avec autant d'empressement, et de plaisir, comme si j'avais

été absente pour plus d'an. Mon Papa, ma Tante, et le monsieur dont
mon frère avoit parlé, furent tous assemblés dans le Salon, et en peu
de temps je m'y rendis aussi. C'est souvent l'ordre du Ciel que quand
on a perdu un plaisir il y en a un autre prêt à prendre sa place. Ainsi
je venoit de partir de très-chers amis, mais tout à l'heure je revins à
des parens aussi chers et bons dans le moment. Même que vous me
perdiez (ose-je croire que mon départ vous était un chagrin?) vous
attendites l'arrivée de votre frère, et de votre sœur. J'ai donné à mes
sœurs les pommes que vous leur envoyiez avec tant de bonté; elles
disent qu'elles sont sûr que Mademoiselle E. est très-aimable et bonne;
l'une et l'autre sont extrêmement impatientes de vous voir; j'espère
qu'en peu de mois elles auront ce plaisir.'

But it was some time yet before the friends could meet, and
meanwhile they agreed to correspond once a month. There were
no events to chronicle in the Haworth letters. Quiet days, occupied
in teaching, and feminine occupations in the house, did not present
much to write about; and Charlotte was naturally driven to criticise
books.*

Of these there were many in different plights, and according to
their plight, kept in different places. The well-bound were ranged
in the sanctuary of Mr Brontë's study; but the purchase of books
was a necessary luxury to him, and as it was often a choice between
binding an old one, or buying a new one, the familiar volume,
which had been hungrily read by all the members of the family,
was sometimes in such a condition that the bed-room shelf was
considered its fitting place. Up and down the house, were to be
found many standard works of a solid kind.* Sir Walter Scott's
writings, Wordsworth's and Southey's poems were among the
lighter literature; while, as having a character of their own—earnest, wild, and occasionally fanatical—may be named some of the
books which came from the Branwell side of the family—from the
Cornish followers of the saintly John Wesley—and which are
touched on in the account of the works to which Caroline Helstone
had access in 'Shirley:'*—'Some venerable Lady's Magazines, that
had once performed a voyage with their owner, and undergone a
storm'—(possibly part of the relics of Mrs Brontë's possessions,
contained in the ship wrecked on the coast of Cornwall)—'and
whose pages were stained with salt water! some mad Methodist
Magazines full of miracles and apparitions, and preternatural

warnings, ominous dreams, and frenzied fanaticism; and the equally mad letters of Mrs Elizabeth Rowe from the Dead to the Living.'

Mr Brontë encouraged a taste for reading in his girls; and though Miss Branwell kept it in due bounds, by the variety of household occupations, in which she expected them not merely to take a part, but to become proficients, thereby occupying regularly a good portion of every day, they were allowed to get books from the circulating library at Keighley; and many a happy walk, up those long four miles, must they have had, burdened with some new book, into which they peeped as they hurried home. Not that the books were what would generally be called new; in the beginning of 1833, the two friends seem almost simultaneously to have fallen upon 'Kenilworth,'* and Charlotte writes as follows about it:—*

'I am glad you like "Kenilworth;" it is certainly more resembling a romance than a novel: in my opinion, one of the most interesting works that ever emanated from the great Sir Walter's pen. Varney is certainly the personification of consummate villainy; and in the delineation of his dark and profoundly artful mind, Scott exhibits a wonderful knowledge of human nature, as well as a surprising skill in embodying his perceptions, so as to enable others to become participators in that knowledge.'

Commonplace as this extract may seem, it is noteworthy on two or three accounts: in the first place, instead of discussing the plot or story, she analyses the character of Varney; and next, she, knowing nothing of the world, both from her youth and her isolated position, has yet been so accustomed to hear 'human nature' distrusted, as to receive the notion of intense and artful villainy without surprise.

What was formal and set in her way of writing to 'E.' diminished as their personal acquaintance increased, and as each came to know the home of the other; so that small details concerning people and places had their interest and their significance. In the summer of 1833, she wrote* to invite her friend to come and pay her a visit. 'Aunt thought it would be better' (she says) 'to defer it until about the middle of summer, as the winter, and even the spring seasons, are remarkably cold and bleak among our mountains.'

The first impression made on the visitor by the sisters of her school-friend was, that Emily was a tall, long-armed girl, more fully grown than her elder sister; extremely reserved in manner. I distinguish reserve from shyness, because I imagine shyness would please, if it knew how; whereas, reserve is indifferent whether it pleases or not. Anne, like her eldest sister, was shy; Emily was reserved.

Branwell was rather a handsome boy, with 'tawny' hair, to use Miss Brontë's phrase for a more obnoxious colour.* All were very clever, original, and utterly different to any people or family 'E.' had ever seen before. But, on the whole, it was a happy visit to all parties. Charlotte says, in writing to 'E.,'* just after her return home—'Were I to tell you of the impression you have made on every one here, you would accuse me of flattery. Papa and aunt are continually adducing you as an example for me to shape my actions and behaviour by. Emily and Anne say "they never saw any one they liked so well as you." And Tabby, whom you have absolutely fascinated, talks a great deal more nonsense about your ladyship than I care to repeat. It is now so dark that, notwithstanding the singular property of seeing in the night-time, which the young ladies at Roe Head used to attribute to me, I can scribble no longer.'*

To a visitor at the parsonage, it was a great thing to have Tabby's good word. She had a Yorkshire keenness of perception into character, and it was not everybody she liked.

Haworth is built with an utter disregard of all sanitary conditions: the great old churchyard lies above all the houses, and it is terrible to think how the very water-springs of the pumps below must be poisoned. But this winter of 1833–4 was particularly wet and rainy, and there were an unusual number of deaths in the village.* A dreary season it was to the family in the parsonage: their usual walks obstructed by the spongy state of the moors—the passing and funeral bells so frequently tolling, and filling the heavy air with their mournful sound—and, when they were still, the 'chip, chip' of the mason, as he cut the grave-stones in a shed close by. In many, living, as it were, in a churchyard, and with all the sights and sounds connected with the last offices to the dead things of every-day occurrence, the very familiarity would have bred indifference. But it was otherwise with Charlotte Brontë. One of her friends says:*—'I have seen her turn pale and feel faint when, in Hartshead church, some one accidentally remarked that we were

walking over graves. Charlotte was certainly afraid of death. Not
only of dead bodies, or dying people. She dreaded it as something
horrible. She thought we did not know how long the "moment of
dissolution" might really be, or how terrible. This was just such a
terror as only hypochondriacs can provide for themselves. She told
me long ago that a misfortune was often preceded by the dream
frequently repeated which she gives to "Jane Eyre,"* of carrying a
little wailing child, and being unable to still it. She described
herself as having the most painful sense of pity for the little thing,
lying *inert*, as sick children do, while she walked about in some
gloomy place with it, such as the aisle of Haworth Church. The
misfortunes she mentioned were not always to herself. She thought
such sensitiveness to omens was like the cholera, present to
susceptible people,—some feeling more, some less.'

About the beginning of 1834, 'E.' went to London for the first
time. The idea of her friend's visit seems to have stirred Charlotte
strangely. She appears to have formed her notions of its probable
consequences from some of the papers in the 'British Essayists,'*
'The Rambler,' 'The Mirror,' or 'The Lounger,' which may have
been among the English classics on the parsonage book-shelves; for
she evidently imagines that an entire change of character for the
worse is the usual effect of a visit to 'the great metropolis,' and is
delighted to find that 'E.' is 'E.' still. And, as her faith in her
friend's stability is restored, her own imagination is deeply moved
by the idea of what great wonders are to be seen in that vast and
famous city.

'Haworth, February 20th, 1834.

'Your letter gave me real and heartfelt pleasure, mingled with no
small share of astonishment. Mary had previously informed me of
your departure for London, and I had not ventured to calculate on
any communication from you while surrounded by the splendours
and novelties of that great city, which has been called the
mercantile metropolis of Europe. Judging from human nature, I
thought that a little country girl, for the first time in a situation so
well calculated to excite curiosity, and to distract attention, would
lose all remembrance, for a time at least, of distant and familiar
objects, and give herself up entirely to the fascination of those
scenes which were then presented to her view. Your kind, interest-

ing, and most welcome epistle showed me, however, that I had been both mistaken and uncharitable in these suppositions. I was greatly amused at the tone of nonchalance which you assumed, while treating of London and its wonders. Did you not feel awed while gazing at St Paul's and Westminister Abbey? Had you no feeling of intense and ardent interest, when in St James's you saw the palace where so many of England's kings have held their courts, and beheld the representations of their persons on the walls? You should not be too much afraid of appearing *country-bred;* the magnificence of London has drawn exclamations of astonishment from travelled men, experienced in the world, its wonders and beauties. Have you yet seen anything of the great personages whom the sitting of Parliament now detains in London—the Duke of Wellington, Sir Robert Peel, Earl Grey, Mr Stanley, Mr O'Connell?* If I were you, I would not be too anxious to spend my time in reading whilst in town. Make use of your own eyes for the purposes of observation now, and, for a time at least, lay aside the spectacles with which authors would furnish us.'

In a postscript she adds:—

'Will you be kind enough to inform me of the number of performers in the King's military band?'

And in something of the same strain she writes on

'June 19th.*

'MY *own* DEAR E.,
'I may rightfully and truly call you so now. You *have* returned or *are* returning from London—from the great city which is to me as apocryphal as Babylon, or Nineveh, or ancient Rome. You are withdrawing from the world (as it is called), and bringing with you—if your letters enable me to form a correct judgment—a heart as unsophisticated, as natural, as true, as that you carried there. I am slow, *very* slow, to believe the protestations of another; I know my own sentiments, I can read my own mind, but the minds of the rest of man and woman kind are to me sealed volumes, hieroglyphical scrolls, which I cannot easily either unseal or decipher. Yet time, careful study, long acquaintance, overcome most difficulties; and, in your case, I think they have succeeded well in bringing to light and construing that hidden language,

whose turnings, windings, inconsistencies, and obscurities, so
frequently baffle the researches of the honest observer of human
nature. . . . I am truly grateful for your mindfulness of so obscure
a person as myself, and I hope the pleasure is not altogether selfish; I
trust it is partly derived from the consciousness that my friend's
character is of a higher, a more steadfast order than I was once
perfectly aware of. Few girls would have done as you have done—
would have beheld the glare, and glitter, and dazzling display of
London with dispositions so unchanged, heart so uncontaminated. I
see no affectation in your letters, no trifling, no frivolous contempt of
plain, and weak admiration of showy persons and things.'

In these days of cheap railway trips, we may smile at the idea of
a short visit to London having any great effect upon the character,
whatever it may have upon the intellect. But her London—her
great apocryphal city—was the 'town' of a century before, to which
giddy daughters dragged unwilling papas, or went with injudicious
friends, to the detriment of all their better qualities, and sometimes
to the ruin of their fortunes; it was the Vanity Fair of the 'Pilgrim's
Progress' to her.

But see the just and admirable sense with which she can treat a
subject of which she is able to overlook all the bearings.

'Haworth, July 4th, 1834.

'In your last, you request me to tell you of your faults. Now,
really, how can you be so foolish! I *won't* tell you of your faults,
because I don't know them. What a creature would that be, who,
after receiving an affectionate and kind letter from a beloved
friend, should sit down and write a catalogue of defects by way of
answer! Imagine me doing so, and then consider what epithets you
would bestow on me. Conceited, dogmatical, hypocritical, little
humbug, I should think, would be the mildest. Why, child! I've
neither time nor inclination to reflect on your *faults* when you are
so far from me, and when, besides, kind letters and presents, and
so forth, are continually bringing forth your goodness in the most
prominent light. Then, too, there are judicious relations always
round you, who can much better discharge that unpleasant office.
I have no doubt their advice is completely at your service; why
then should I intrude mine? If you will not hear *them*, it will be

vain though one should rise from the dead to instruct you.* Let us
have no more nonsense, if you love me. Mr —— is going to be
married, is he?* Well, his wife elect appeared to me to be a clever
and amiable lady, as far as I could judge from the little I saw of
her, and from your account. Now to that flattering sentence must
I tack on a list of her faults? You say it is in contemplation for you
to leave ——.* I am sorry for it. —— is a pleasant spot, one of the
old family halls of England, surrounded by lawn and woodland,
speaking of past times, and suggesting (to me at least) happy
feelings. M. thought you grown less, did she? I am not grown a
bit, but as short and dumpy as ever. You ask me to recommend
you some books for your perusal. I will do so in as few words as I
can. If you like poetry, let it be first-rate; Milton, Shakspeare,
Thomson, Goldsmith, Pope (if you will, though I don't admire
him), Scott, Byron, Campbell, Wordsworth, and Southey.* Now
don't be startled at the names of Shakspeare and Byron. Both these
were great men, and their works are like themselves. You will
know how to choose the good, and to avoid the evil; the finest
passages are always the purest, the bad are invariably revolting; you
will never wish to read them over twice. Omit the comedies of
Shakspeare, and the Don Juan, perhaps the Cain, of Byron, though
the latter is a magnificent poem, and read the rest fearlessly; that
must indeed be a depraved mind which can gather evil from Henry
VIII, from Richard III, from Macbeth, and Hamlet, and Julius
Cæsar. Scott's sweet, wild, romantic poetry can do you no harm.
Nor can Wordsworth's, nor Campbell's, nor Southey's—the greatest part at least of his; some is certainly objectionable. For history,
read Hume, Rollin, and the Universal History, if you *can;* I never
did. For fiction, read Scott alone; all novels after his are worthless.
For biography, read Johnson's Lives of the Poets, Boswell's Life
of Johnson, Southey's Life of Nelson, Lockhart's Life of Burns,
Moore's Life of Sheridan, Moore's Life of Byron, Wolfe's Remains. For natural history, read Bewick and Audubon, and Goldsmith and White's History of Selborne. For divinity, your brother
will advise you there. I can only say, adhere to standard authors,
and avoid novelty.'

From this list, we see that she must have had a good range of
books from which to choose her own reading.* It is evident, that
the womanly consciences of these two correspondents were

anxiously alive to many questions discussed among the stricter religionists. The morality of Shakspeare needed the confirmation of Charlotte's opinion to the sensitive 'E.;' and a little later, she inquired whether dancing was objectionable, when indulged in for an hour or two in parties of boys and girls. Charlotte replies,* 'I should hesitate to express a difference of opinion from Mr ——, or from your excellent sister, but really the matter seems to me to stand thus. It is allowed on all hands, that the sin of dancing consists not in the mere action of "shaking the shanks" (as the Scotch say), but in the consequences that usually attend it; namely, frivolity and waste of time; when it is used only, as in the case you state, for the exercise and amusement of an hour among young people (who surely may without any breach of God's commandments be allowed a little light-heartedness), these consequences cannot follow. Ergo (according to my manner of arguing), the amusement is at such times perfectly innocent.'

Although the distance between Haworth and B——* was but seventeen miles, it was difficult to go straight from the one to the other without hiring a gig or vehicle of some kind for the journey. Hence a visit from Charlotte required a good deal of pre-arrangement. *The* Haworth gig was not always to be had; and Mr Brontë was often unwilling to fall into any arrangement for meeting at Bradford or other places, which would occasion trouble to others. The whole family had an ample share of that sensitive pride which led them to dread incurring obligations, and to fear 'outstaying their welcome' when on any visit. I am not sure whether Mr Brontë did not consider distrust of others as a part of that knowledge of human nature on which he piqued himself. His precepts to this effect, combined with Charlotte's lack of hope, made her always fearful of loving too much; of wearying the objects of her affection; and thus she was often trying to restrain her warm feelings, and was ever chary of that presence so invariably welcome to her true friends. According to this mode of acting, when she was invited for a month, she stayed but a fortnight amidst 'E.'s' family, to whom every visit only endeared her the more, and by whom she was received with that kind of quiet gladness with which they would have greeted a sister.

She still kept up her childish interest in politics. In March, 1835,* she writes: 'What do you think of the course politics are taking? I make this inquiry, because I now think you take a wholesome interest in the matter; formerly you did not care greatly about it.\* B., you see, is triumphant. Wretch! I am a hearty hater, and if there is any one I thoroughly abhor, it is that man. But the Opposition is divided, Red-hots, and Luke-warms; and the Duke (par-excellence *the* Duke), and Sir Robert Peel show no signs of insecurity, though they have been twice beat; so "Courage, mon amie," as the old chevaliers used to say, before they joined battle.'

In the middle of the summer of 1835, a great family plan was mooted at the parsonage. The question was, to what trade or profession should Branwell be brought up? He was now nearly eighteen; it was time to decide. He was very clever, no doubt; perhaps, to begin with, the greatest genius in this rare family. The sisters hardly recognised their own, or each others' powers, but they knew *his*. The father, ignorant of many failings in moral conduct, did proud homage to the great gifts of his son; for Branwell's talents were readily and willingly brought out for the entertainment of others. Popular admiration was sweet to him. And this led to his presence being sought at 'arvills' and all the great village gatherings, for the Yorkshire men have a keen relish for intellect; and it likewise procured him the undesirable distinction of having his company recommended by the landlord of the Black Bull\* to any chance traveller who might happen to feel solitary or dull over his liquor. 'Do you want some one to help you with your bottle, sir? If you do, I'll send up for Patrick' (so the villagers called him till the day of his death, though in his own family he was always 'Branwell'). And while the messenger went, the landlord entertained his guest with accounts of the wonderful talents of the boy, whose precocious cleverness, and great conversational powers, were the pride of the village. The attacks of ill health to which Mr Brontë had been subject of late years, rendered it not only necessary that he should take his dinner alone (for the sake of avoiding temptations to unwholesome diet), but made it also desirable that he should pass the time directly succeeding his meals in perfect quiet. And this necessity, combined with due attention to his parochial duties, made him partially ignorant how his son employed himself out of lesson-time. His own youth had been spent among people of the same conventional rank as those into whose companionship Branwell was now thrown; but he had had a strong will, and an earnest and persevering ambition, and a resoluteness of purpose which his weaker son wanted.*

It is singular how strong a yearning the whole family had towards the art of drawing. Mr Brontë had been very solicitous to get them good instruction; the girls themselves loved everything connected with it—all descriptions or engravings of great pictures; and, in default of good ones, they would take and analyse any print or drawing which came in their way, and find out how much thought had gone to its composition, what ideas it was intended to suggest, and what it *did* suggest. In the same spirit, they laboured to design imaginations of their own; they lacked the power of execution, not of conception. At one time, Charlotte had the notion of making her living as an artist, and wearied her eyes in drawing with pre-Raphaelite minuteness, but not with pre-Raphaelite accuracy,* for she drew from fancy rather than from nature.

But they all thought there could be no doubt about Branwell's talent for drawing. I have seen an oil painting of his,* done I know not when, but probably about this time. It was a group of his sisters, life size, three-quarters' length; not much better than sign-painting, as to manipulation; but the likenesses were, I should think, admirable. I could only judge of the fidelity with which the other two were depicted, from the striking resemblance which Charlotte, upholding the great frame of canvas, and consequently standing right behind it, bore to her own representation, though it must have been ten years and more since the portraits were taken. The picture was divided, almost in the middle, by a great pillar. On the side of the column which was lighted by the sun, stood Charlotte, in the womanly dress of that day of gigot sleeves and large collars. On the deeply shadowed side, was Emily, with Anne's gentle face resting on her shoulder. Emily's countenance struck me as full of power; Charlotte's of solicitude; Anne's of tenderness. The two younger seemed hardly to have attained their full growth, though Emily was taller than Charlotte; they had cropped hair, and a more girlish dress. I remember looking on those two sad, earnest, shadowed faces, and wondering whether I could trace the mysterious expression which is said to foretell an early death. I had some fond superstitious hope that the column divided their fates from hers, who stood apart in the canvas, as in life she survived. I liked to see that the bright side of the pillar was towards *her*—that the light in the picture fell on *her:* I might more truly have sought in her presentment—nay, in her living face—for the sign of death in her prime. They were good likenesses, however badly executed. From thence I should guess his family augured truly that, if Branwell had but the opportunity, and, alas! had but the moral qualities, he might turn out a great painter.

The best way of preparing him to become so appeared to be to send him as a pupil to the Royal Academy.* I dare say, he longed and yearned to follow this path, principally because it would lead him to that mysterious London—that Babylon the great—which seems to have filled the imaginations and haunted the minds of all the younger members of this recluse family. To Branwell it was more than a vivid imagination, it was an impressed reality. By dint of studying maps, he was as well acquainted with it, even down to its by-ways, as if he had lived there.* Poor misguided fellow! this craving to see and know London, and that stronger craving after fame, were never to be satisfied. He was to die at the end of a short and blighted life. But in this year of 1835, all his home kindred were thinking how they could best forward his views, and how help him up to the pinnacle where he desired to be. What their plans were, let Charlotte explain. These are not the first sisters who have laid their lives as a sacrifice before their brother's idolized wish. Would to God they might be the last who met with such a miserable return!

'Haworth, July 6th, 1835.*

'I had hoped to have had the extreme pleasure of seeing you at Haworth this summer, but human affairs are mutable, and human resolutions must bend to the course of events. We are all about to divide, break up, separate. Emily is going to school, Branwell is going to London, and I am going to be a governess. This last determination I formed myself, knowing that I should have to take the step sometime, "and better sune as syne," to use the Scotch proverb; and knowing well that papa would have enough to do with his limited income, should Branwell be placed at the Royal Academy, and Emily at Roe Head. Where am I going to reside? you will ask. Within four miles of you, at a place neither of us are unacquainted with, being no other than the identical Roe Head mentioned above. Yes! I am going to teach in the very school where I was myself taught. Miss W—— made me the offer, and I preferred it to one or two proposals of private governess-ship, which I had before received. I am sad—very sad—at the thoughts of leaving home; but duty—necessity—these are stern mistresses, who will not be disobeyed. Did I not once say you ought to be thankful for your independence? I felt what I said at the time, and I repeat it now with double earnestness; if anything would cheer me, it is the idea of being so near you. Surely, you and Polly will come and see me; it would be wrong in me to doubt it; you were never unkind yet. Emily and I leave home on the 27th of this month; the idea of being together consoles us both somewhat, and, truth, since I must enter a situation, "My lines have fallen in pleasant places."* I both love and respect Miss W——.'

# CHAPTER VIII

On the 29th of July, 1835, Charlotte, now little more than nineteen years old, went as teacher to Miss W——'s. Emily accompanied her as a pupil; but she became literally ill from home-sickness, and could not settle to anything, and after passing only three months at Roe Head, returned to the parsonage and the beloved moors.

Miss Brontë gives the following reasons as those which prevented Emily's remaining at school, and caused the substitution of her younger sister in her place at Miss W——'s:—

'My sister Emily loved the moors. Flowers brighter than the rose bloomed in the blackest of the heath for her;—out of a sullen hollow in a livid hill-side, her mind could make an Eden. She found in the bleak solitude many and dear delights; and not the least and best-loved was—liberty. Liberty was the breath of Emily's nostrils; without it she perished. The change from her own home to a school, and from her own very noiseless, very secluded, but unrestricted and unartificial mode of life, to one of disciplined routine (though under the kindest auspices), was what she failed in enduring. Her nature proved here too strong for her fortitude. Every morning, when she woke, the vision of home and the moors rushed on her, and darkened and saddened the day that lay before her. Nobody knew what ailed her but me. I knew only too well. In this struggle her health was quickly broken: her white face, attenuated form, and failing strength, threatened rapid decline. I felt in my heart she would die, if she did not go home, and with this conviction obtained her recall. She had only been three months at school; and it was some years before the experiment of sending her from home was again ventured on.'*

This physical suffering on Emily's part when absent from Haworth, after recurring several times under similar circumstances, became at length so much an acknowledged fact, that whichever was obliged to leave home, the sisters decided that Emily must remain there, where alone she could enjoy anything like good health. She left it twice again in her life; once going as teacher to a school in Halifax for six months, and afterwards accompanying

Charlotte to Brussels for ten. When at home, she took the principal part of the cooking upon herself, and did all the household ironing; and after Tabby grew old and infirm, it was Emily who made all the bread for the family; and any one passing by the kitchen-door, might have seen her studying German out of an open book, propped up before her, as she kneaded the dough; but no study, however interesting, interfered with the goodness of the bread, which was always light and excellent. Books were, indeed, a very common sight in that kitchen; the girls were taught by their father theoretically, and by their aunt practically, that to take an active part in all household work was, in their position, woman's simple duty; but, in their careful employment of time, they found many an odd five minutes for reading while watching the cakes, and managed the union of two kinds of employment better than King Alfred.*

Charlotte's life at Miss W——'s was a very happy one, until her health failed. She sincerely loved and respected the former school-mistress, to whom she was now become both companion and friend. The girls were hardly strangers to her, some of them being younger sisters of those who had been her own playmates. Though the duties of the day might be tedious and monotonous, there were always two or three happy hours to look forward to in the evening, when she and Miss W—— sat together—sometimes late into the night—and had quiet pleasant conversations, or pauses of silence as agreeable, because each felt that as soon as a thought or remark occurred which they wished to express, there was an intelligent companion ready to sympathise, and yet they were not compelled to 'make talk.'*

Miss W—— was always anxious to afford Miss Brontë every opportunity of recreation in her power; but the difficulty often was to persuade her to avail herself of the invitations which came, urging her to spend Saturday and Sunday with 'E.' and 'Mary,' in their respective homes, that lay within the distance of a walk. She was too apt to consider, that allowing herself a holiday was a dereliction of duty, and to refuse herself the necessary change, from something of an over-ascetic spirit, betokening a loss of healthy balance in either body or mind. Indeed, it is clear that such was the case, from a passage, referring to this time, in the letter of 'Mary' from which I have before given extracts.

'Three years after'—(the period when they were at school together)—'I heard that she had gone as teacher to Miss W——'s. I went to see her, and asked how she could give so much for so little money, when she could live without it. She owned that, after clothing herself and Anne, there was nothing left, though she had hoped to be able to save something. She confessed it was not brilliant, but what could she do? I had nothing to answer. She seemed to have no interest or pleasure beyond the feeling of duty, and, when she could get, used to sit alone, and "make out." She told me afterwards, that one evening she had sat in the dressing-room until it was quite dark, and then observing it all at once, had taken sudden fright.' No doubt she remembered this well when she described a similar terror getting hold upon Jane Eyre. She says in the story, 'I sat looking at the white bed and overshadowed walls—occasionally turning a fascinated eye towards the gleaming mirror—I began to recall what I had heard of dead men troubled in their graves. . . . I endeavoured to be firm; shaking my hair from my eyes, I lifted my head and tried to look boldly through the dark room; at this moment, a ray from the moon penetrated some aperture in the blind. No! moonlight was still, and this stirred. . . . prepared as my mind was for horror, shaken as my nerves were by agitation, I thought the swift-darting beam was a herald of some coming vision from another world. My heart beat thick, my head grew hot; a sound filled my ears which I deemed the rustling of wings; something seemed near me.'[1]

'From that time,' Mary adds, 'her imaginations became gloomy or frightful; she could not help it, nor help thinking. She could not forget the gloom, could not sleep at night, nor attend in the day.

'She told me that one night,* sitting alone, about this time, she heard a voice repeat these lines:

> "Come thou high and holy feeling,
> Shine o'er mountain, flit o'er wave,
> Gleam like light o'er dome and shieling.—"

'There were eight or ten more lines which I forget. She insisted that she had not made them, that she had heard a voice repeat them. It is possible that she had read them, and unconsciously

---

[1] 'Jane Eyre,' Vol. I, page 20.*

recalled them. They are not in the volume of poems which the sisters published. She repeated a verse of Isaiah, which she said had inspired them, and which I have forgotten. Whether the lines were recollected or invented, the tale proves such habits of sedentary, monotonous solitude of thought, as would have shaken a feebler mind.'

Of course, the state of health thus described came on gradually, and is not to be taken as a picture of her condition in 1836. Yet even then there is a despondency in some of her expressions, that too sadly reminds one of some of Cowper's letters.* And it is remarkable how deeply his poems impressed her. His words, his verses, came more frequently to her memory, I imagine, than those of any other poet.

'Mary' says: 'Cowper's poem, "The Castaway," was known to them all, and they all at times appreciated, or almost appropriated it. Charlotte told me once that Branwell had done so; and though his depression was the result of his faults, it was in no other respect different from hers. Both were not mental but physical illnesses. She was well aware of this, and would ask how that mended matters, as the feeling was there all the same, and was not removed by knowing the cause. She had a larger religious toleration than a person would have who had never questioned, and the manner of recommending religion was always that of offering comfort, not fiercely enforcing a duty. One time I mentioned that some one had asked me what religion I was of (with the view of getting me for a partizan), and that I had said that that was between God and me;—Emily (who was lying on the hearth-rug) exclaimed, "That's right." This was all I ever heard Emily say on religious subjects. Charlotte was free from religious depression when in tolerable health; when that failed, her depression returned. You have probably seen such instances. They don't get over their difficulties; they forget them, when their stomach (or whatever organ it is that inflicts such misery on sedentary people) will let them. I have heard her condemn Socinianism, Calvinism,* and many other "isms" inconsistent with Church of Englandism. I used to wonder at her acquaintance with such subjects.'

'May 10th, 1836.

'I was struck with the note you sent me with the umbrella; it showed a degree of interest in my concerns which I have no right to expect from any earthly creature. I won't play the hypocrite; I won't answer your kind, gentle, friendly questions in the way you wish me to. Don't deceive yourself by imagining I have a bit of real goodness about me. My darling, if I were like you, I should have my face Zion-ward, though prejudice and error might occasionally fling a mist over the glorious vision before me—but I *am not like you*. If you knew my thoughts, the dreams that absorb me, and the fiery imagination that at times eats me up, and makes me feel society, as it is, wretchedly insipid, you would pity and I dare say despise me. But I know the treasures of the *Bible;* I love and adore them. I can *see* the Well of Life in all its clearness and brightness; but when I stoop down to drink of the pure waters they fly from my lips as if I were Tantalus.*

'You are far too kind and frequent in your invitations. You puzzle me. I hardly know how to refuse, and it is still more embarrassing to accept. At any rate, I cannot come this week, for we are in the very thickest *melée* of the Repetitions.* I was hearing the terrible fifth section when your note arrived. But Miss Wooler* says I must go to Mary next Friday, as she promised for me on Whit-Sunday; and on Sunday morning I will join you at church, if it be convenient, and stay till Monday. There's a free and easy proposal! Miss W—— has driven me to it. She says her character is implicated.'

Good, kind Miss W——! however monotonous and trying were the duties Charlotte had to perform under her roof, there was always a genial and thoughtful friend watching over her, and urging her to partake of any little piece of innocent recreation that might come in her way. And in those Midsummer holidays of 1836, her friend E. came to stay with her at Haworth, so there was one happy time secured.

Here follows a series of letters, not dated, but belonging to the latter portion of this year; and again we think of the gentle and melancholy Cowper.

'My *dear dear* E.,*
'I am at this moment trembling all over with excitement, after reading your note; it is what I never received before—it is the unrestrained pouring out of a warm, gentle, generous heart. . . . . I

thank you with energy for this kindness. I will no longer shrink from answering your questions. I *do* wish to be better than I am. I pray fervently sometimes to be made so. I have stings of conscience, visitings of remorse, glimpses of holy, of inexpressible things, which formerly I used to be a stranger to; it may all die away, and I may be in utter midnight, but I implore a merciful Redeemer, that, if this be the dawn of the gospel, it may still brighten to perfect day. Do not mistake me—do not think I am good; I only wish to be so. I only hate my former flippancy and forwardness. Oh! I am no better than ever I was. I am in that state of horrid, gloomy uncertainty that, at this moment, I would submit to be old, grey-haired, to have passed all my youthful days of enjoyment, and to be settling on the verge of the grave, if I could only thereby ensure the prospect of reconciliation to God, and redemption through his Son's merits. I never was exactly careless of these matters, but I have always taken a clouded and repulsive view of them; and now, if possible, the clouds are gathering darker, and a more oppressive despondency weighs on my spirits. You have cheered me, my darling; for one moment, for an atom of time, I thought I might call you my own sister in the spirit; but the excitement is past, and I am now as wretched and hopeless as ever. This very night I will pray as you wish me. May the Almighty hear me compassionately! and I humbly hope he will, for you will strengthen my polluted petitions with your own pure requests. All is bustle and confusion round me, the ladies pressing with their sums and their lessons. . . . . . If you love me, *do, do, do* come on Friday: I shall watch and wait for you, and if you disappoint me I shall weep. I wish you could know the thrill of delight which I experienced, when, as I stood at the dining-room window, I saw ——,* as he whirled past, toss your little packet over the wall.'

Huddersfield market-day* was still the great period for events at Roe Head. Then girls, running round the corner of the house and peeping between tree-stems, and up a shadowy lane, could catch a glimpse of a father or brother driving to market in his gig; might, perhaps, exchange a wave of the hand; or see, as Charlotte Brontë did from the window,* a white packet tossed over the wall, by some swift strong motion of an arm, the rest of the traveller's body unseen.

'Weary with a day's hard work. . . . I am sitting down to write a few lines to my dear E. Excuse me if I say nothing but nonsense, for my mind is exhausted and dispirited. It is a stormy evening, and the wind is uttering a continual moaning sound, that makes me feel very melancholy. At such times—in such moods as these—it is my nature to seek repose in some calm tranquil idea, and I have now summoned up your image to give me rest. There you sit, upright and still in your black dress, and white scarf, and pale marble-like face—just like reality. I wish you would speak to me. If we should be separated—if it should be our lot to live at a great distance, and never to see each other again—in old age, how I should conjure up the memory of my youthful days, and what a melancholy pleasure I should feel in dwelling on the recollection of my early friend! . . . . I have some qualities that make me very miserable, some feelings that you can have no participation in—that few, very few, people in the world can at all understand. I don't pride myself on these peculiarities. I strive to conceal and suppress them as much as I can; but they burst out sometimes, and then those who see the explosion despise me, and I hate myself for days afterwards. . . I have just received your epistle and what accompanied it. I can't tell what should induce you and your sisters to waste your kindness on such a one as me. I'm obliged to them, and I hope you'll tell them so. I'm obliged to you also, more for your note than for your present. The first gave me pleasure, the last something like pain.'

The nervous disturbance, which is stated to have troubled her while she was at Miss W——'s, seems to have begun to distress her about this time; at least, she herself speaks of her irritable condition, which was certainly only a temporary ailment.

'You have been very kind to me of late, and have spared me all those little sallies of ridicule, which, owing to my miserable and wretched touchiness of character, used formerly to make me wince, as if I had been touched with a hot iron; things that nobody else cares for, enter into my mind and rankle there like venom. I know these feelings are absurd, and therefore I try to hide them, but they only sting the deeper for concealment.'

Compare this state of mind with the gentle resignation with which she had submitted to be put aside as useless, or told of her ugliness by her schoolfellows, only three years before.

'My life since I saw you has passed as monotonously and unbroken as ever; nothing but teach, teach, teach, from morning till night. The greatest variety I ever have is afforded by a letter from you, or by meeting with a pleasant new book. The "Life of Oberlin," and "Legh Richmond's Domestic Portraiture,"* are the last of this description. The latter work strongly attracted and strangely fascinated my attention. Beg, borrow, or steal it without delay; and read the "Memoir of Wilberforce,"—that short record of a brief uneventful life; I shall never forget it; it is beautiful, not on account of the language in which it is written, not on account of the incidents it details, but because of the simple narrative it gives of a young talented sincere Christian.'

About this time Miss W—— removed her school from the fine, open, breezy situation of Roe Head, to Dewsbury Moor,* only two or three miles distant. Her new residence was on a lower site, and the air was less exhilarating to one bred in the wild hill-village of Haworth. Emily had gone as teacher to a school at Halifax,* where there were nearly forty pupils.

'I have had one letter from her since her departure,' writes Charlotte, on October 2nd, 1836:* 'it gives an appalling account of her duties; hard labour from six in the morning to eleven at night, with only one half-hour of exercise between. This is slavery. I fear she can never stand it.'

When the sisters met at home in the Christmas holidays, they talked over their lives, and the prospect which they afforded of employment and remuneration. They felt that it was a duty to relieve their father of the burden of their support, if not entirely, or that of all three, at least that of one or two; and, naturally, the lot devolved upon the elder ones to find some occupation which would enable them to do this. They knew that they were never likely to inherit much money. Mr Brontë had but a small stipend, and was both charitable and liberal. Their aunt had an annuity of 50*l.*, but it reverted to others at her death, and her nieces had no right, and were the last persons in the world to reckon upon her savings. What could they do? Charlotte and Emily were trying teaching, and, as it seemed, without much success. The former, it is true, had the happiness of having a friend for her employer, and of being surrounded by those who knew her and loved her; but her salary was too small for her to save out of it; and her education did not entitle her to a larger. The sedentary and monotonous nature of the life, too, was preying upon her health and spirits, although, with necessity 'as her mistress,' she might hardly like to acknow-ledge this even to herself. But Emily—that free, wild, untameable spirit, never happy nor well but on the sweeping moors that gathered round her home—that hater of strangers, doomed to live amongst them, and not merely to live but to slave in their service—what Charlotte could have borne patiently for herself, she could not bear for her sister. And yet what to do? She had once hoped that she herself might become an artist, and so earn her livelihood; but her eyes had failed her in the minute and useless labour which she had imposed upon herself with a view to this end.

It was the household custom among these girls to sew till nine o'clock at night. At that hour, Miss Branwell generally went to bed, and her nieces' duties for the day were accounted done. They put away their work, and began to pace the room backwards and forwards, up and down,—as often with the candles extinguished, for economy's sake, as not,—their figures glancing into the fire-light, and out into the shadow, perpetually. At this time, they talked over past cares, and troubles; they planned for the future, and consulted each other as to their plans. In after years this was the time for discussing together the plots of their novels. And again, still later, this was the time for the last surviving sister to walk alone, from old accustomed habit, round and round the desolate room, thinking sadly upon the 'days that were no more.'* But this Christmas of 1836 was not without its hopes and daring aspirations. They had tried their hands at story-writing, in their miniature magazine, long ago; they all of them 'made out' perpe-tually. They had likewise attempted to write poetry; and had a modest confidence that they had achieved a tolerable success. But they knew that they might deceive themselves, and that sisters' judgments of each other's productions were likely to be too partial to be depended upon. So Charlotte, as the eldest, resolved to write to Southey.* I believe (from an expression in a letter to be noticed hereafter), that she also consulted Coleridge; but I have not met with any part of that correspondence.

On December 29th, her letter to Southey was despatched; and from an excitement not unnatural in a girl who has worked herself up to the pitch of writing to a Poet Laureate and asking his opinion of her poems, she used some high-flown expressions, which, probably, gave him the idea that she was a romantic young lady, unacquainted with the realities of life.

This, most likely, was the first of those adventurous letters that passed through the little post-office of Haworth. Morning after morning of the holidays slipped away, and there was no answer; the sisters had to leave home, and Emily to return to her distasteful duties, without knowing even whether Charlotte's letter had ever reached its destination.

Not dispirited, however, by the delay, Branwell determined to try a similar venture, and addressed the following remarkable letter to Wordsworth.* It was given by the poet to Mr Quillinan in 1850, after the name of Brontë had become known and famous. I have no means of ascertaining what answer was returned by Mr Wordsworth; but that he considered the letter remarkable may, I think, be inferred both from its preservation, and its recurrence to his memory when the real name of Currer Bell was made known to the public.

'Haworth, near Bradford,
'Yorkshire, January 19. 1837.

'SIR,—I most earnestly entreat you to read and pass your judgment upon what I have sent you, because from the day of my birth to this the nineteenth year of my life, I have lived among secluded hills, where I could neither know what I was, or what I could do. I read for the same reason that I ate or drank; because it was a real craving of nature. I wrote on the same principle as I spoke—out of the impulse and feelings of the mind; nor could I help it, for what came, came out, and there was the end of it. For as to self-conceit, that could not receive food from flattery, since to this hour, not half a dozen people in the world know that I have ever penned a line.

'But a change has taken place now, sir: and I am arrived at an age wherein I must do something for myself: the powers I possess must be exercised to a definite end, and as I don't know them myself I must ask of others what they are worth. Yet there is not

one here to tell me; and still, if they are worthless, time will
henceforth be too precious to be wasted on them.

'Do pardon me, sir, that I have ventured to come before one
whose works I have most loved in our literature, and who most has
been with me a divinity of the mind,—laying before him one of
my writings, and asking of him a judgment of its contents. I must
come before some one from whose sentence there is no appeal; and
such a one is he who has developed the theory of poetry as well as
its practice, and both in such a way as to claim a place in the
memory of a thousand years to come.

'My aim, sir, is to push out into the open world, and for this I
trust not poetry alone—that might launch the vessel, but could not
bear her on; sensible and scientific prose, bold and vigorous efforts
in my walk in life, would give a farther title to the notice of the
world; and then again poetry ought to brighten and crown that
name with glory; but nothing of all this can be ever begun without
means, and as I don't possess these, I must in every shape strive
to gain them. Surely, in this day, when there is not a *writing* poet
worth a sixpence, the field must be open, if a better man can step
forward.

'What I send you is the Prefatory Scene of a much longer subject,
in which I have striven to develope strong passions and weak
principles struggling with a high imagination and acute feelings, till,
as youth hardens towards age, evil deeds and short enjoyments end in
mental misery and bodily ruin. Now, to send you the whole of this
would be a mock upon your patience; what you see, does not even
pretend to be more than the description of an imaginative child. But
read it, sir; and, as you would hold a light to one in utter darkness—as
you value your own kind-heartedness—*return* me an *answer*, if but one
word, telling me whether I should write on, or write no more. Forgive
undue warmth, because my feelings in this matter cannot be cool; and
believe me, sir, with deep respect,

'Your really humble servant,
'P. B. BRONTË.'

The poetry enclosed seems to me by no means equal to parts of
the letter; but, as every one likes to judge for himself, I copy the
six opening stanzas—about a third of the whole, and certainly not
the worst.*

So where he reigns in glory bright,
Above those starry skies of night,
Amid his paradise of light
    Oh, why may I not be?

Oft when awake on Christmas morn,
In sleepless twilight laid forlorn,
Strange thoughts have o'er my mind been borne,
    How He has died for me.

And oft within my chamber lying,
Have I awaked myself with crying
From dreams, where I beheld Him dying
    Upon the accursed Tree.

And often has my mother said,
While on her lap I laid my head,
She feared for time I was not made,
    But for Eternity.

So 'I can read my title clear,
    To mansions in the skies,
And let me bid farewell to fear,
    And wipe my weeping eyes.'

I'll lay me down on this marble stone,
    And set the world aside,
To see upon her ebon throne
    The Moon in glory ride.

Soon after Charlotte returned to Dewsbury Moor, she was distressed by hearing that her friend 'E.' was likely to leave the neighbourhood for a considerable length of time.

'Feb. 20th.*

'What shall I do without you? How long are we likely to be separated? Why are we to be denied each other's society? It is an inscrutable fatality. I long to be with you, because it seems as if two or three days, or weeks, spent in your company would beyond measure strengthen me in the enjoyment of those feelings which I have so lately begun to cherish. You first pointed out to me that way in which I am so feebly endeavouring to travel, and now I cannot keep you by my side, I must proceed sorrowfully alone. Why are we to be divided? Surely, it must be because we are in danger of loving each other too well—of losing sight of the *Creator* in idolatry of the *creature*. At first, I could not say "Thy will be done!"\* I felt rebellious, but I knew it was wrong to feel so. Being left a moment alone this morning, I prayed fervently to be enabled to resign myself to *every* decree of God's will, though it should be dealt forth by a far severer hand than the present disappointment; since then I have felt calmer and humbler, and consequently happier. Last Sunday I took up my Bible in a gloomy state of mind: I began to read—a feeling stole over me such as I have not known for many long years—a sweet, placid sensation, like those, I remember, which used to visit me when I was a little child, and, on Sunday evenings in summer, stood by the open window reading the life of a certain French nobleman,\* who attained a purer and higher degree of sanctity than has been known since the days of the early martyrs.'

'E.'s' residence was equally within a walk from Dewsbury Moor as it had been from Roe Head; and on Saturday afternoons both 'Mary' and she used to call upon Charlotte, and often endeavoured to persuade her to return with them, and be the guest of one of them till Monday morning; but this was comparatively seldom. Mary says:—'She visited us twice or thrice when she was at Miss W——'s. We used to dispute about politics and religion. She, a Tory and clergyman's daughter, was always in a minority of one in our house of violent Dissent and Radicalism. She used to hear over again, delivered *with authority*, all the lectures I had been used to give her at school on despotic aristocracy, mercenary priesthood, &c. She had not energy to defend herself; sometimes she owned to a *little* truth in it, but generally said nothing. Her feeble health gave her her yielding manner, for she could never oppose any one without gathering up all her strength for the struggle. Thus she would let me advise and patronise most imperiously, sometimes picking out any grain of sense there might be in what I said, but never allowing any one materially to interfere with her independence of thought and action. Though her silence sometimes left one under the impression that she agreed when she did not, she never gave a flattering opinion, and thus her words were golden, whether for praise or blame.'

'Mary's' father\* was a man of remarkable intelligence, but of strong, not to say violent prejudices, all running in favour of

Republicanism and Dissent. No other county but Yorkshire could have produced such a man. His brother had been a *détenu* in France, and had afterwards voluntarily taken up his residence there. Mr T. himself had been much abroad, both on business and to see the great continental galleries of paintings. He spoke French perfectly, I have been told, when need was; but delighted usually in talking the broadest Yorkshire. He bought splendid engravings of the pictures which he particularly admired, and his house was full of works of art and of books; but he rather liked to present his rough side to any stranger or newcomer; he would speak his broadest, bring out his opinions on Church and State in their most startling forms, and, by and by, if he found his hearer could stand the shock, he would involuntarily show his warm kind heart, and his true taste, and real refinement. His family of four sons and two daughters were brought up on Republican principles; independence of thought and action was encouraged; no 'shams' tolerated. They are scattered far and wide: Martha, the younger daughter, sleeps in the Protestant cemetery at Brussels; Mary is in New Zealand; Mr T. is dead. And so life and death have dispersed the circle of 'violent Radicals and Dissenters' into which, twenty years ago, the little, quiet, resolute clergyman's daughter was received and by whom she was truly loved and honoured.

January and February of 1837 had passed away, and still there was no reply from Southey. Probably she had lost expectation and almost hope when at length, in the beginning of March, she received the letter inserted in Mr C. C. Southey's life of his Father,* vol. VI. p. 327.

After accounting for his delay in replying to hers by the fact of a long absence from home, during which his letters had accumulated, whence 'it has lain unanswered till the last of a numerous file, not from disrespect or indifference to its contents, but because in truth it is not an easy task to answer it, nor a pleasant one to cast a damp over the high spirits and the generous desires of youth,' he goes on to say: 'What you are I can only infer from your letter, which appears to be written in sincerity, though I may suspect that you have used a fictitious signature. Be that as it may, the letter and the verses bear the same stamp, and I can well understand the state of mind they indicate.'

* * *

'It is not my advice that you have asked as to the direction of your talents, but my opinion of them, and yet the opinion may be worth little, and the advice much. You evidently possess, and in no inconsiderable degree, what Wordsworth calls the "faculty of verse."* I am not depreciating it when I say that in these times it is not rare. Many volumes of poems are now published every year without attracting public attention, any one of which if it had appeared half a century ago, would have obtained a high reputation for its author. Whoever, therefore, is ambitious of distinction in this way ought to be prepared for disappointment.

'But it is not with a view to distinction that you should cultivate this talent, if you consult your own happiness. I, who have made literature my profession, and devoted my life to it, and have never for a moment repented of the deliberate choice, think myself, nevertheless, bound in duty to caution every young man who applies as an aspirant to me for encouragement and advice, against taking so perilous a course. You will say that a woman has no need of such a caution; there can be no peril in it for her. In a certain sense this is true; but there is a danger of which I would, with all kindness and all earnestness, warn you. The day dreams in which you habitually indulge are likely to induce a distempered state of mind; and in proportion as all the ordinary uses of the world seem to you flat and unprofitable,* you will be unfitted for them without becoming fitted for anything else. Literature cannot be the business of a woman's life, and it ought not to be. The more she is engaged in her proper duties, the less leisure will she have for it, even as an accomplishment and a recreation. To those duties you have not yet been called, and when you are you will be less eager for celebrity. You will not seek in imagination for excitement, of which the vicissitudes of this life, and the anxieties from which you must not hope to be exempted, be your state what it may, will bring with them but too much.

'But do not suppose that I disparage the gift which you possess; nor that I would discourage you from exercising it. I only exhort you so to think of it, and so to use it, as to render it conducive to your own permanent good. Write poetry for its own sake; not in a spirit of emulation, and not with a view to celebrity; the less you aim at that the more likely you will be to deserve and finally to obtain it. So written, it is wholesome both for the heart and soul; it may be made the surest means, next to religion, of soothing the mind and elevating it. You may embody in it your best thoughts and your wisest feelings, and in so doing discipline and strengthen them.

'Farewell, madam. It is not because I have forgotten that I was once young myself, that I write to you in this strain; but because I remember it. You will neither doubt my sincerity nor my good will; and however ill what has here been said may accord with your present views and temper, the longer you live the more reasonable it will appear to you. Though I may be but an ungracious adviser, you will allow me, therefore, to subscribe myself, with the best wishes for your happiness here and hereafter, your true friend,

'ROBERT SOUTHEY.'

I was with Miss Brontë when she received Mr Cuthbert Southey's note,* requesting her permission to insert the foregoing letter in his father's life. She said to me, 'Mr Southey's letter was kind and admirable; a little stringent, but it did me good.'

It is partly because I think it so admirable, and partly because it tends to bring out her character, as shown in the following reply, that I have taken the liberty of inserting the foregoing extracts from it.

'March 16th.

'SIR,

'I cannot rest till I have answered your letter, even though by addressing you a second time I should appear a little intrusive; but I must thank you for the kind and wise advice you have condescended to give me. I had not ventured to hope for such a reply; so considerate in its tone, so noble in its spirit. I must suppress what I feel, or you will think me foolishly enthusiastic.

'At the first perusal of your letter, I felt only shame and regret that I had ever ventured to trouble you with my crude rhapsody; I felt a painful heat rise to my face when I thought of the quires of paper I had covered with what once gave me so much delight, but which now was only a source of confusion; but, after I had thought a little and read it again and again, the prospect seemed to clear. You do not forbid me to write; you do not say that what I

write is utterly destitute of merit. You only warn me against the
folly of neglecting real duties, for the sake of imaginative pleasures;
of writing for the love of fame; for the selfish excitement of
emulation. You kindly allow me to write poetry for its own sake,
provided I leave undone nothing which I ought to do, in order to
pursue that single, absorbing, exquisite gratification. I am afraid,
sir, you think me very foolish. I know the first letter I wrote to you
was all senseless trash from beginning to end; but I am not
altogether the idle dreaming being it would seem to denote. My
father is a clergyman of limited, though competent income, and I
am the eldest of his children. He expended quite as much in my
education as he could afford in justice to the rest. I thought it
therefore my duty, when I left school, to become a governess. In
that capacity I find enough to occupy my thoughts all day long,
and my head and hands too, without having a moment's time for
one dream of the imagination. In the evenings, I confess, I do
think, but I never trouble any one else with my thoughts. I
carefully avoid any appearance of pre-occupation and eccentricity,
which might lead those I live amongst to suspect the nature of my
pursuits. Following my father's advice—who from my childhood
has counselled me just in the wise and friendly tone of your
letter—I have endeavoured not only attentively to observe all the
duties a woman ought to fulfil, but to feel deeply interested in
them. I don't always succeed, for sometimes when I'm teaching or
sewing I would rather be reading or writing; but I try to deny
myself; and my father's approbation amply rewarded me for the
privation. Once more allow me to thank you with sincere gratitude.
I trust I shall never more feel ambitious to see my name in print:
if the wish should rise I'll look at Southey's letter, and suppress it.
It is honour enough for me that I have written to him, and received
an answer. That letter is consecrated; no one shall ever see it, but
papa and my brother and sisters. Again I thank you. This incident,
I suppose, will be renewed no more; if I live to be an old woman,
I shall remember it thirty years hence as a bright dream. The
signature which you suspected of being fictitious is my real name.
Again, therefore, I must sign myself,

'C. Brontë.'

'P. S.—Pray, sir, excuse me for writing to you a second time; I
could not help writing, partly to tell you how thankful I am for

your kindness, and partly to let you know that your advice shall not be wasted; however sorrowfully and reluctantly it may be at first followed.

'C. B.'

I cannot deny myself the gratification of inserting Southey's reply:—*

'Keswick, March 22. 1837.

'DEAR MADAM,

'Your letter has given me great pleasure, and I should not forgive myself if I did not tell you so. You have received admonition as considerately and as kindly as it was given. Let me now request that, if you ever should come to these lakes while I am living here, you will let me see you. You would then think of me afterwards with the more good will, because you would perceive that there is neither severity nor moroseness in the state of mind to which years and observation have brought me.

'It is, by God's mercy, in our power to attain a degree of self-government, which is essential to our own happiness, and contributes greatly to that of those around us. Take care of over-excitement, and endeavour to keep a quiet mind (even for your health it is the best advice that can be given you): your moral and spiritual improvement will then keep pace with the culture of your intellectual powers.

'And now, Madam, God bless you!

'Farewell, and believe me to be your sincere friend,

'ROBERT SOUTHEY.'

Of this second letter also she spoke, and told me that it contained an invitation for her to go and see the poet if ever she visited the Lakes. 'But there was no money to spare,' said she, 'nor any prospect of my ever earning money enough to have the chance of so great a pleasure, so I gave up thinking of it.' At the time we conversed together on the subject we were at the Lakes. But Southey was dead.*

This 'stringent' letter made her put aside, for a time, all idea of literary enterprise. She bent her whole energy towards the fulfilment of the duties in hand; but her occupation was not sufficient food for her great forces of intellect, and they cried out perpetually, 'Give, give,' while the comparatively less breezy* air of Dewsbury Moor told upon her health and spirits more and more. On August 27. 1837,* she writes:—

'I am again at Dewsbury, engaged in the old business,—teach, teach, teach. . . . *When will you come home?* Make haste! You have been at Bath long enough for all purposes; by this time you have acquired polish enough, I am sure; if the varnish is laid on much thicker, I am afraid the good wood underneath will be quite concealed, and your Yorkshire friends won't stand that. Come, come. I am getting really tired of your absence. Saturday after Saturday comes round, and I can have no hope of hearing your knock at the door, and then being told that "Miss E. is come." Oh dear! in this monotonous life of mine, that was a pleasant event. I wish it would recur again; but it will take two or three interviews before the stiffness—the estrangement of this long separation—will wear away.'

About this time she forgot to return a work-bag she had borrowed, by a messenger, and in repairing her error she says:—*
'These aberrations of memory warn me pretty intelligibly that I am getting past my prime.' Ætat 21! And the same tone of despondency runs through the following letter:—*

'I wish exceedingly that I could come to you before Christmas, but it is impossible; another three weeks must elapse before I shall again have my comforter beside me, under the roof of my own dear quiet home. If I could always live with you, and daily read the Bible with you—if your lips and mine could at the same time drink the same draught, from the same pure fountain of mercy—I hope, I trust, I might one day become better, far better than my evil, wandering thoughts, my corrupt heart, cold to the spirit and warm to the flesh, will now permit me to be. I often plan the pleasant life which we might lead together, strengthening each other in that power of self-denial, that hallowed and glowing devotion, which the first saints of God often attained to. My eyes fill with tears when I contrast the bliss of such a state, brightened by hopes of the future, with the melancholy state I now live in, uncertain that

I ever felt true contrition, wandering in thought and deed, longing for holiness, which I shall *never, never* obtain, smitten at times to the heart with the conviction that ghastly Calvinistic doctrines are true*—darkened, in short, by the very shadows of spiritual death. If Christian perfection be necessary to salvation, I shall never be saved; my heart is a very hot-bed for sinful thoughts, and when I decide on an action I scarcely remember to look to my Redeemer for direction. I know not how to pray; I cannot bend my life to the grand end of doing good; I go on constantly seeking my own pleasure, pursuing the gratification of my own desires. I forget God, and will not God forget me?* And, meantime, I know the greatness of Jehovah; I acknowledge the perfection of His word; I adore the purity of the Christian faith; my theory is right, my practice horribly wrong.'

The Christmas holidays came, and she and Anne returned to the parsonage, and to that happy home circle in which alone their natures expanded; amongst all other people they shrivelled up more or less. Indeed, there were only one or two strangers who could be admitted among the sisters without producing the same result. Emily and Anne were bound up in their lives and interests like twins. The former from reserve, the latter from timidity, avoided all friendships and intimacies beyond their family. Emily was impervious to influence; she never came in contact with public opinion, and her own decision of what was right and fitting was a law for her conduct and appearance, with which she allowed no one to interfere. Her love was poured out on Anne, as Charlotte's was on her. But the affection among all the three was stronger than either death or life.

'E.' was eagerly welcomed by Charlotte, freely admitted by Emily, and kindly received by Anne, whenever she could visit them; and this Christmas she had promised to do so, but her coming had to be delayed on account of a little domestic accident detailed in the following letter:—

'Dec. 29. 1837.*

'I am sure you will have thought me very remiss, in not sending my promised letter long before now; but I have a sufficient and very melancholy excuse in an accident that befell our old faithful Tabby, a few days after my return home. She was gone out into the village on some errand, when, as she was descending the steep street, her foot slipped on the ice, and she fell; it was dark, and no one saw her mischance, till after a time her groans attracted the attention of a passer-by. She was lifted up and carried into the druggist's near; and, after the examination, it was discovered that she had completely shattered and dislocated one leg. Unfortunately, the fracture could not be set till six o'clock the next morning, as no surgeon was to be had before that time, and she now lies at our house in a very doubtful and dangerous state. Of course we are all exceedingly distressed at the circumstance, for she was like one of our own family. Since the event we have been almost without assistance—a person has dropped in now and then to do the drudgery, but we have as yet been able to procure no regular servant; and, consequently, the whole work of the house, as well as the additional duty of nursing Tabby, falls on ourselves. Under these circumstances I dare not press your visit here, at least until she is pronounced out of danger; it would be too selfish of me. Aunt wished me to give you this information before, but papa and all the rest were anxious I should delay until we saw whether matters took a more settled aspect, and I myself kept putting it off from day to day, most bitterly reluctant to give up all the pleasure I had anticipated so long. However, remembering what you told me, namely, that you had commended the matter to a higher decision than ours, and that you were resolved to submit with resignation to that decision, whatever it might be, I hold it my duty to yield also, and to be silent; it may be all for the best. I fear, if you had been here during this severe weather, your visit would have been of no advantage to you, for the moors are blockaded with snow, and you would never have been able to get out. After this disappointment, I never dare reckon with certainty on the enjoyment of a pleasure again; it seems as if some fatality stood between you and me. I am not good enough for you, and you must be kept from the contamination of too intimate society. I would urge your visit yet—I would entreat and press it—but the thought comes across me, should Tabby die while you are in the house, I should never forgive myself. No! it must not be, and in a thousand ways the consciousness of that mortifies and disappoints me most keenly. And I am not the only one who is disappointed. All in the house were looking to your visit with eagerness. Papa says he highly approves of my friendship with you, and he wishes me to continue it through life.'

A good neighbour of the Brontës—a clever, intelligent Yorkshire woman,* who keeps a druggist's shop in Haworth, and from her occupation, her experience, and excellent sense, holds the position of village doctress and nurse, and, as such, has been a friend, in many a time of trial, and sickness, and death, in the households round—told me a characteristic little incident connected with Tabby's fractured leg. Mr Brontë is truly generous and regardful of all deserving claims. Tabby had lived with them for ten or twelve years, and was, as Charlotte expressed it, 'one of the family.' But, on the other hand, she was past the age for any very active service, being nearer seventy than sixty at the time of the accident; she had a sister living in the village; and the savings she had accumulated, during many years' service, formed a competency for one in her rank of life. Or if, in this time of sickness, she fell short of any comforts which her state rendered necessary, the parsonage could supply them. So reasoned Miss Branwell, the prudent, not to say anxious aunt; looking to the limited contents of Mr Brontë's purse, and the unprovided-for future of her nieces; who were, moreover, losing the relaxation of the holidays, in close attendance upon Tabby.

Miss Branwell urged her views upon Mr Brontë as soon as the immediate danger to the old servant's life was over. He refused at first to listen to the careful advice; it was repugnant to his liberal nature. But Miss Branwell persevered; urged economical motives; pressed on his love for his daughters. He gave way. Tabby was to be removed to her sister's, and there nursed and cared for, Mr Brontë coming in with his aid when her own resources fell short. This decision was communicated to the girls. There were symptoms of a quiet, but sturdy rebellion, that winter afternoon, in the small precincts of Haworth Parsonage. They made one unanimous and stiff remonstrance. Tabby had tended them in their childhood; they, and none other, should tend her in her infirmity and age. At tea-time, they were sad and silent, and the meal went away untouched by any of the three. So it was at breakfast; they did not waste many words on the subject, but each word they did utter was weighty. They 'struck' eating till the resolution was rescinded, and Tabby was allowed to remain, a helpless invalid entirely dependent upon them. Herein was the strong feeling of Duty being paramount to Pleasure, which lay at the foundation of Charlotte's character, made most apparent; for we have seen how she yearned for her friend's company; but it was to be obtained only by shrinking from what she esteemed right, and that she never did, whatever might be the sacrifice.

She had another weight on her mind this Christmas. I have said that the air of Dewsbury Moor* did not agree with her, though she herself was hardly aware how much her life there was affecting her health. But Anne had begun to suffer just before the holidays, and Charlotte watched over her younger sisters with the jealous vigilance of some wild creature, that changes her very nature if danger threatens her young. Anne had a slight cough, a pain at her side, a difficulty of breathing. Miss W—— considered it as little more than a common cold; but Charlotte felt every indication of incipient consumption as a stab at her heart, remembering Maria and Elizabeth, whose places once knew them, and should know them no more.

Stung by anxiety for this little sister, she upbraided Miss W—— for her fancied indifference to Anne's state of health. Miss W—— felt these reproaches keenly, and wrote to Mr Brontë about them.* He immediately replied most kindly, expressing his fear that Charlotte's apprehensions and anxieties respecting her sister had led her to give utterance to over-excited expressions of alarm. Through Miss W——'s kind consideration, Anne was a year longer at school than her friends intended. At the close of the half-year Miss W—— sought for the opportunity of an explanation of each other's words, and the issue proved that 'the falling out of faithful friends, renewing is of love.'* And so ended the first, last, and only difference Charlotte ever had with good, kind Miss W——.

Still her heart had received a shock in the perception of Anne's delicacy; and all these holidays she watched over her with the longing, fond anxiety, which is so full of sudden pangs of fear.

Emily had given up* her situation in the Halifax school, at the expiration of six months of arduous trial, on account of her health, which could only be re-established by the bracing moorland air and free life of home. Tabby's illness had preyed on the family resources. I doubt whether Branwell was maintaining himself at this time. For some unexplained reason, he had given up the idea of becoming a student of painting at the Royal Academy, and his prospects in life were uncertain, and had yet to be settled. So Charlotte had quietly to take up her burden of teaching again, and return to her previous monotonous life.

Brave heart, ready to die in harness! She went back to her work, and made no complaint, hoping to subdue the weakness that was gaining ground upon her. About this time, she would turn sick and trembling at any sudden noise, and could hardly repress her screams when startled. This showed a fearful degree of physical weakness in one who was generally so self-controlled; and the medical man, whom at length, through Miss W——'s entreaty, she was led to consult, insisted on her return to the parsonage. She had led too sedentary a life, he said; and the soft summer air, blowing round her home, the sweet company of those she loved, the release, the freedom of life in her own family, were needed, to save either reason or life. So, as One higher than she had over-ruled that for a time she might relax her strain, she returned to Haworth; and after a season of utter quiet, her father sought for her the enlivening society of her two friends, Mary and Martha T. At the conclusion of the following letter, written to the then absent E., there is, I think, as pretty a glimpse of a merry group of young people as need be; and like all descriptions of doing, as distinct from thinking or feeling, in letters, it saddens one in proportion to the vivacity of the picture of what was once, and is now utterly swept away.

'Haworth, June 9. 1838.

'I received your packet of despatches on Wednesday; it was brought me by Mary and Martha, who have been staying at Haworth for a few days; they leave us to-day. You will be surprised at the date of this letter.* I ought to be at Dewsbury Moor, you know; but I stayed as long as I was able, and at length I neither could nor dared stay any longer. My health and spirits had utterly failed me, and the medical man whom I consulted enjoined me, as I valued my life, to go home. So home I went, and the change has at once roused and soothed me; and I am now, I trust, fairly in the way to be myself again.

'A calm and even mind like yours cannot conceive the feelings of the shattered wretch who is now writing to you, when, after weeks of mental and bodily anguish not to be described, something like peace began to dawn again. Mary is far from well. She breathes short, has a pain in her chest, and frequent flushings of fever. I cannot tell you what agony these symptoms give me; they remind me too strongly of my two sisters, whom no power of medicine could save. Martha is now very well; she has kept in a continual flow of good humour during her stay here, and has consequently been very fascinating. . . .

'They are making such a noise about me I cannot write any more. Mary is playing on the piano; Martha is chattering as fast as her little tongue can run; and Branwell is standing before her, laughing at her vivacity.'

Charlotte grew much stronger in this quiet, happy period at home. She paid occasional visits to her two great friends, and they in return came to Haworth. At one of their houses, I suspect, she met with the person to whom the following letter refers—some one having a slight resemblance to the character of 'St John,' in the last volume of 'Jane Eyre,' and, like him, in holy orders.*

'March 12. 1839.

. . . . 'I had a kindly leaning towards him, because he is an amiable and well-disposed man. Yet I had not, and could not have, that intense attachment which would make me willing to die for him; and if ever I marry, it must be in that light of adoration that I will regard my husband. Ten to one I shall never have the chance again; but *n'importe*. Moreover, I was aware that he knew so little of me he could hardly be conscious to whom he was writing. Why! it would startle him to see me in my natural home character; he would think I was a wild, romantic enthusiast indeed. I could not sit all day long making a grave face before my husband. I would laugh, and satirize, and say whatever came into my head first. And if he were a clever man, and loved me, the whole world, weighed in the balance against his smallest wish, should be light as air.'

So that—her first proposal of marriage—was quietly declined and put on one side. Matrimony did not enter into the scheme of her life, but good, sound, earnest labour did; the question, however, was as yet undecided in what direction she should employ her forces. She had been discouraged in literature; her eyes failed her in the minute kind of drawing which she practised when she wanted to express an idea; teaching seemed to her at this time, as it does to most women at all times, the only way of earning an independent livelihood. But neither she nor her sisters were naturally fond of children. The hieroglyphics of childhood were an unknown language to them, for they had never been much with those younger than themselves. I am inclined to think, too, that they had not the happy knack of imparting information, which seems to be a separate gift from the faculty of acquiring it; a kind of sympathetic tact, which instinctively perceives the difficulties that impede comprehension in a child's mind, and that yet are too vague and unformed for it, with its half-developed powers of expression, to explain by words. Consequently teaching very young children was anything but a 'delightful task'* to the three Brontë sisters. With older girls, verging on womanhood, they might have done better, especially if these had any desire for improvement. But the education which the village clergyman's daughters had received, did not as yet qualify them to undertake the charge of advanced pupils. They knew but little French, and were not proficients in music; I doubt whether Charlotte could play at all. But they were all strong again, and, at any rate, Charlotte and Anne must put their shoulders to the wheel. One daughter was needed at home, to stay with Mr Brontë and Miss Branwell; to be the young and active member in a household of four, whereof three—the father, the aunt, and faithful Tabby—were past middle age. And Emily, who suffered and drooped more than her sisters when away from Haworth, was the one appointed to remain. Anne was the first to meet with a situation.*

'April 15th, 1839.*

'I could not write to you in the week you requested, as about that time we were very busy in preparing for Anne's departure. Poor child! she left us last Monday; no one went with her; it was her own wish that she might be allowed to go alone, as she thought she could manage better and summon more courage if thrown entirely upon her own resources. We have had one letter from her since she went. She expresses herself very well satisfied, and says that Mrs —— is extremely kind; the two eldest children alone are under her care, the rest are confined to the nursery, with which and its occupants she has nothing to do. . . . . I hope she'll do. You would be astonished what a sensible, clever letter she writes; it is only the talking part that I fear. But I do seriously apprehend that Mrs —— will sometimes conclude that she has a natural impediment in her speech. For my own part, I am as yet "wanting a situation," like a housemaid out of place. By the way, I have lately discovered I have quite a talent for cleaning, sweeping up hearths, dusting rooms, making beds, &c.; so, if everything else fails, I can turn my hand to that, if anybody will give me good wages for little labour. I won't be a cook; I hate cooking. I won't be a nurserymaid, nor a lady's maid, far less a lady's companion, or a mantua-maker,* or a straw-bonnet maker, or a taker-in of plain work. I won't be anything but a housemaid. . . . . With regard to my visit to G., I have as yet received no invitation; but if I should be asked, though I should feel it a great act of self-denial to refuse, yet I have almost made up my mind to do so, though the society of the T.s is one of the most rousing pleasures I have ever known. Good-bye, my darling E., &c.

'P. S.—Strike out that word "darling;" it is humbug. Where's the use of protestations? We've known each other, and liked each other, a good while; that's enough.'

Not many weeks after this was written, Charlotte also became engaged as a governess.* I intend carefully to abstain from introducing the names of any living people, respecting whom I may have to tell unpleasant truths, or to quote severe remarks from Miss Brontë's letters; but it is necessary that the difficulties she had to encounter in her various phases of life, should be fairly and frankly made known, before the force 'of what was resisted'* can be at all understood. I was once speaking to her about 'Agnes Grey'*—the novel in which her sister Anne pretty literally describes her own experience as a governess—and alluding more particularly to the account of the stoning of the little nestlings in the presence of the parent birds. She said that none but those who had been in the position of a governess could ever realise the dark side of 'respectable' human nature; under no great temptation to crime, but daily giving way to selfishness and ill-temper, till its conduct towards those dependent on it sometimes amounts to a tyranny of which one would rather be the victim than the inflicter. We can only trust in such cases that the employers err rather from a density of perception and an absence of sympathy, than from any natural cruelty of disposition. Among several things of the same kind, which I well remember, she told me what had once occurred to herself. She had been entrusted with the care of a little boy, three or four years old, during the absence of his parents on a day's excursion, and particularly enjoined to keep him out of the stable-yard. His elder brother, a lad of eight or nine, and not a pupil of Miss Brontë's, tempted the little fellow into the forbidden place. She followed, and tried to induce him to come away; but, instigated by his brother, he began throwing stones at her, and one of them hit her so severe a blow on the temple that the lads were alarmed into obedience. The next day, in full family conclave, the mother asked Miss Brontë what occasioned the mark on her forehead. She simply replied, 'An accident, ma'am,' and no further inquiry was made; but the children (both brothers and sisters) had been present, and honoured her for not 'telling tales.' From that time, she began to obtain influence over all, more or less, according to their different characters; and as she insensibly gained their affection, her own interest in them was increasing. But one day, at the children's dinner, the small truant of the stable-yard, in a little demonstrative gush, said, putting his hand in hers, 'I love 'ou, Miss Brontë.' Whereupon, the mother exclaimed, before all the children, 'Love the *governess*, my dear!'

The family into which she first entered was, I believe, that of a wealthy Yorkshire manufacturer. The following extracts from her correspondence at this time will show how painfully the restraint of her new mode of life pressed upon her. The first is from a letter to Emily, beginning with one of the tender expressions in which, in spite of 'humbug,' she indulged herself. 'Mine dear love,' 'Mine bonnie love,' are her terms of address to this beloved sister

'June 8th, 1839.*

'I have striven hard to be pleased with my new situation. The country, the house and the grounds are, as I have said, divine; but, alack-a-day! there is such a thing as seeing all beautiful around you—pleasant woods, winding white paths, green lawns, and blue sunshiny sky—and not having a free moment or a free thought left to enjoy them. The children are constantly with me. As for correcting them, I quickly found that was out of the question; they are to do as they like. A complaint to the mother only brings black looks on myself, and unjust, partial excuses to screen the children. I have tried that plan once, and succeeded in it so notably, I shall try no more. I said in my last letter that Mrs —— did not know me. I now begin to find she does not intend to know me; that she cares nothing about me, except to contrive how the greatest possible quantity of labour may be got out of me; and to that end she overwhelms me with oceans of needlework; yards of cambric to hem, muslin nightcaps to make, and, above all things, dolls to dress. I do not think she likes me at all, because I can't help being shy in such an entirely novel scene, surrounded as I have hitherto been by strange and constantly changing faces. . . . . . I used to think I should like to be in the stir of grand folks' society; but I have had enough of it—it is dreary work to look on and listen. I see more clearly than I have ever done before, that a private governess has no existence, is not considered as a living rational being, except as connected with the wearisome duties she has to fulfil. . . . . . . One of the pleasantest afternoons I have spent here—indeed, the only one at all pleasant—was when Mr —— walked out with his children, and I had orders to follow a little behind. As he strolled on through his fields, with his magnificent Newfoundland dog at his side, he looked very like what a frank, wealthy, Conservative gentleman ought to be. He spoke freely and unaffectedly to the people he met, and, though he indulged his children and allowed them to tease himself far too much, he would not suffer them grossly to insult others.'

(WRITTEN IN PENCIL TO A FRIEND.)

'July, 1839.*

'I cannot procure ink, without going into the drawing-room, where I do not wish to go. . . . . . I should have written to you long since, and told you every detail of the utterly new scene into which I have lately been cast, had I not been daily expecting a letter from yourself, and wondering and lamenting that you did not write; for you will remember it was your turn. I must not bother you too much with my sorrows, of which, I fear, you have heard an exaggerated account. If you were near me, perhaps I might be tempted to tell you all, to grow egotistical, and pour out the long history of a private governess's trials and crosses in her first situation. As it is, I will only ask you to imagine the miseries of a reserved wretch like me, thrown at once into the midst of a large family, at a time when they were particularly gay—when the house was filled with company—all strangers—people whose faces I had never seen before. In this state I had charge given me of a set of pampered, spoilt, turbulent children, whom I was expected constantly to amuse, as well as to instruct. I soon found that the constant demand on my stock of animal spirits reduced them to the lowest state of exhaustion; at times I felt—and, I suppose, seemed—depressed. To my astonishment, I was taken to task on the subject by Mrs —— with a sternness of manner and a harshness of language scarcely credible; like a fool, I cried most bitterly. I could not help it; my spirits quite failed me at first. I thought I had done my best—strained every nerve to please her; and to be treated in that way, merely because I was shy and sometimes melancholy, was too bad. At first I was for giving all up and going home. But, after a little reflection, I determined to summon what energy I had, and to weather the storm. I said to myself, "I have never yet quitted a place without gaining a friend; adversity is a good school; the poor are born to labour, and the dependent to endure." I resolved to be patient, to command my feelings, and to take what came; the ordeal, I reflected, would not last many weeks, and I trusted it would do me good. I recollected the fable of the willow and the oak;* I bent quietly, and now, I trust, the storm is blowing over me. Mrs —— is generally considered an agreeable woman; so she is, I doubt not, in general society. She behaves somewhat more civilly to me now than she did at first, and the children are a little more manageable; but she does not know my character, and she does not wish to know it. I have never had five minutes' conversation with her since I came, except while she was scolding me. I have no wish to be pitied, except by yourself; if I were talking to you I could tell you much more.'

(TO EMILY, ABOUT THIS TIME.)*

'Mine bonnie love, I was as glad of your letter as tongue can express: it is a real, genuine pleasure to hear from home; a thing to be saved till bed-time, when one has a moment's quiet and rest to enjoy it thoroughly. Write whenever you can. I could like to be at home. I could like to work in a mill. I could like to feel some mental liberty. I could like this weight of restraint to be taken off. But the holidays will come. Coraggio.'

Her temporary engagement in this uncongenial family ended in the July of this year; not before the constant strain upon her spirits and strength had again affected her health; but when this delicacy became apparent in palpitations and shortness of breathing, it was treated as affectation—as a phase of imaginary indisposition, which could be dissipated by a good scolding. She had been brought up rather in a school of Spartan endurance than in one of maudlin self-indulgence, and could bear many a pain and relinquish many a hope in silence.

After she had been at home about a week, her friend proposed that she should accompany her in some little excursion, having pleasure alone for its object. She caught at the idea most eagerly at first; but her hope stood still, waned, and had almost disappeared before, after many delays, it was realised. In its fulfilment at last, it was a favourable specimen of many a similar air-bubble dancing before her eyes in her brief career, in which stern realities, rather than pleasures, formed the leading incidents.

'July 26th, 1839.*

'Your proposal has almost driven me "clean daft"—if you don't understand that ladylike expression, you must ask me what it means when I see you. The fact is, an excursion with you anywhere,—whether to Cleathorpe or Canada,—just by ourselves, would be to me most delightful. I should, indeed, like to go; but I can't get leave of absence for longer than a week, and I'm afraid that would not suit you—must I then give it up entirely? I feel as if I *could not;* I never had such a chance of enjoyment before; I do want to see you and talk to you, and be with you. When do you wish to go? Could I meet you at Leeds? To take a gig from Haworth to B., would be to me a very serious increase of expense, and I happen to be very low in cash. Oh! rich people seem to have many pleasures at their command which we are debarred from! However, no repining.

'Say when you go, and I shall be able in my answer to say decidedly whether I can accompany you or not. I must—I will—I'm set upon it—I'll be obstinate and bear down all opposition.

'P. S.—Since writing the above, I find that aunt and papa have determined to go to Liverpool for a fortnight, and take us all with them. It is stipulated, however, that I should give up the Clea-thorpe scheme. I yield reluctantly.'

I fancy that, about this time, Mr Brontë found it necessary, either from failing health or the increased populousness of the parish, to engage the assistance of a curate.* At least, it is in a letter written this summer that I find mention of the first of a succession of curates, who henceforward revolved round Haworth Parsonage, and made an impression on the mind of one of its inmates which she has conveyed pretty distinctly to the world. The Haworth curate brought his clerical friends and neighbours about the place, and for a time the incursions of these, near the parsonage tea-time, formed occurrences by which the quietness of the life there was varied, sometimes pleasantly, sometimes disagreeably. The little adventure recorded at the end of the following letter is uncommon in the lot of most women, and is a testimony in this case to the unusual power of attraction—though so plain in feature—which Charlotte possessed, when she let herself go in the happiness and freedom of home.

'August 4th, 1839.*

'The Liverpool journey is yet a matter of talk, a sort of castle in the air; but, between you and me, I fancy it is very doubtful whether it will ever assume a more solid shape. Aunt—like many other elderly people—likes to talk of such things; but when it comes to putting them into actual execution, she rather falls off. Such being the case, I think you and I had better adhere to our first plan of going somewhere together, independently of other people. I have got leave to accompany you for a week—at the utmost a fortnight—but no more. Where do you wish to go? Burlington,* I should think, from what M. says, would be as eligible a place as any. When do you set off? Arrange all these things according to your convenience; I shall start no objections. The idea of seeing the *sea*—of being near it—watching its changes by sunrise, sunset, moonlight, and noon-day—in calm, perhaps in storm—fills and satisfies my mind. I shall be discontented at nothing. And then I am not to be with a set of people with whom I have nothing in common—who would be nuisances and bores; but with you, whom I like and know, and who know me.

'I have an odd circumstance to relate to you: prepare for a hearty laugh!* The other day, Mr ——, a vicar, came to spend the day with us, bringing with him his own curate. The latter gentleman, by name Mr B., is a young Irish clergyman, fresh from Dublin University. It was the first time we had any of us seen him, but, however, after the manner of his countrymen, he soon made himself at home. His character quickly appeared in his conversation; witty, lively, ardent, clever too; but deficient in the dignity and discretion of an Englishman. At home, you know, I talk with ease, and am never shy—never weighed down and oppressed by that miserable *mauvaise honte** which torments and constrains me elsewhere. So I conversed with this Irishman, and laughed at his jests; and, though I saw faults in his character, excused them because of the amusement his originality afforded. I cooled a little, indeed, and drew in towards the latter part of the evening, because he began to season his conversation with something of Hibernian flattery, which I did not quite relish. However, they went away, and no more was thought about them. A few days after, I got a letter, the direction of which puzzled me, it being in a hand I was not accustomed to see. Evidently, it was neither from you nor Mary, my only correspondents. Having opened and read it, it proved to be a declaration of attachment and proposal of matrimony, expressed in the ardent language of the sapient young Irishman! I hope you are laughing heartily. This is not like one of my adventures, is it? It more nearly resembles Martha's. I am certainly doomed to be an old maid. Never mind. I made up my mind to that fate ever since I was twelve years old.

'Well! thought I, I have heard of love at first sight, but this beats all! I leave you to guess what my answer would be, convinced that you will not do me the injustice of guessing wrong.'

On the 14th of August she still writes from Haworth:—*

'I have in vain packed my box, and prepared everything for our anticipated journey. It so happens that I can get no conveyance this week or the next. The only gig let out to hire in Haworth, is at Harrogate, and likely to remain there, for aught I can hear. Papa decidedly objects to my going by the coach, and walking to B., though I am sure I could manage it. Aunt exclaims against the weather, and the roads, and the four winds of heaven, so I am in a fix, and, what is worse, so are *you*. On reading over, for the second or third time, your last letter (which, by the by, was written in such hieroglyphics that, at the first hasty perusal, I could hardly make out two consecutive words), I find you intimate that if I leave this journey till Thursday I shall be too late. I grieve that I should have so inconvenienced you; but I need not talk of either Friday or Saturday now, for I rather imagine there is small chance of my ever going at all. The elders of the house have never cordially acquiesced in the measure; and now that impediments seem to start up at every step, opposition grows more open. Papa, indeed, would willingly indulge me, but this very kindness of his makes me doubt whether I ought to draw upon it; so, though I could battle out aunt's discontent, I yield to papa's indulgence. He does not say so, but I know he would rather I stayed at home; and aunt meant well too, I dare say, but I am provoked that she reserved the expression of her decided disapproval till all was settled between you and myself. Reckon on me no more; leave me out in your calculations; perhaps I ought, in the beginning, to have had prudence sufficient to shut my eyes against such a prospect of pleasure, so as to deny myself the hope of it. Be as angry as you please with me for disappointing you. I did not intend it, and have only one thing more to say—if you do not go immediately to the sea, will you come to see us at Haworth? This invitation is not mine only, but papa's and aunt's.'

However, a little more patience, a little more delay, and she enjoyed the pleasure she had wished for so much. She and her friend went to Easton* for a fortnight in the latter part of September. It was here she received her first impressions of the sea.

'Oct. 24th.*

'Have you forgotten the sea by this time, E.? Is it grown dim in your mind? Or can you still see it, dark, blue, and green, and foam-white, and hear it roaring roughly when the wind is high, or rushing softly when it is calm?*  . . . I am as well as need be, and very fat. I think of Easton very often, and of worthy Mr H.,* and his kind-hearted help-mate, and of our pleasant walks to H—— Wood, and to Boynton, our merry evenings, our romps with little Hancheon, &c., &c. If we both live, this period of our lives will long be a theme for pleasant recollection. Did you chance, in your letter to Mr H., to mention my spectacles? I am sadly inconvenienced by the want of them. I can neither read, write, nor draw with comfort in their absence. I hope Madame won't refuse to give them up. . . . . Excuse the brevity of this letter, for I have been drawing all day, and my eyes are so tired it is quite a labour to write.'

But, as the vivid remembrance of this pleasure died away, an accident occurred to make the actual duties of life press somewhat heavily for a time.

'December 21st, 1839.

'We are at present, and have been during the last month, rather busy, as, for that space of time, we have been without a servant, except a little girl to run errands. Poor Tabby became so lame that she was at length obliged to leave us. She is residing with her sister, in a little house of her own, which she bought with her savings a year or two since. She is very comfortable, and wants nothing; as she is near, we see her very often. In the meantime, Emily and I are sufficiently busy, as you may suppose: I manage the ironing, and keep the rooms clean; Emily does the baking, and attends to the kitchen. We are such odd animals, that we prefer this mode of contrivance to having a new face amongst us. Besides, we do not despair of Tabby's return, and she shall not be supplanted by a stranger in her absence. I excited aunt's wrath very much by burning the clothes, the first time I attempted to iron; but I do better now. Human feelings are queer things; I am much happier black-leading the stoves, making the beds, and sweeping the floors at home, than I should be living like a fine lady anywhere else. I must indeed drop my subscription to the Jews,* because I have no money to keep it up. I ought to have announced this intention to you before, but I quite forgot I was a subscriber. I intend to force myself to take another situation when I can get one, though I *hate* and *abhor* the very thoughts of governess-ship. But I must do it; and, therefore, I heartily wish I could hear of a family where they need such a commodity as a governess.'

# CHAPTER IX

THE year 1840 found all the Brontës living at home, except Anne. As I have already intimated, for some reason with which I am unacquainted, the plan of sending Branwell to study at the Royal Academy had been relinquished; probably, it was found, on inquiry, that the expenses of such a life were greater than his father's slender finances could afford, even with the help which Charlotte's labours at Miss W——'s gave, by providing for Anne's board and education. I gather from what I have heard, that Branwell must have been severely disappointed when the plan fell through. His talents were certainly very brilliant, and of this he was fully conscious, and fervently desired, by their use, either in writing or drawing, to make himself a name. At the same time, he would probably have found his strong love of pleasure and irregular habits a great impediment in his path to fame; but these blemishes in his character were only additional reasons why he yearned after a London life, in which he imagined he could obtain every stimulant to his already vigorous intellect, while at the same time he would have a license of action to be found only in crowded cities. Thus his whole nature was attracted towards the metropolis; and many an hour must he have spent poring over the map of London, to judge from an anecdote which has been told me.* Some traveller for a London house of business came to Haworth for a night; and, according to the unfortunate habit of the place, the brilliant 'Patrick' was sent for to the inn, to beguile the evening by his intellectual conversation and his flashes of wit. They began to talk of London; of the habits and ways of life there; of the places of amusement; and Branwell informed the Londoner of one or two short cuts from point to point, up narrow lanes or back streets; and it was only towards the end of the evening that the traveller discovered, from his companion's voluntary confession, that he had never set foot in London at all.

At this time, the young man seemed to have his fate in his own hands. He was full of noble impulses, as well as of extraordinary gifts; not accustomed to resist temptation, it is true, from any higher motive than strong family affection, but showing so much power of attachment to all about him that they took pleasure in believing that, after a time, he would 'right himself,' and that they should have pride and delight in the use he would then make of his splendid talents. His aunt especially made him her great favourite. There are always peculiar trials in the life of an only boy in a family of girls. He is expected to act a part in life; to *do*, while they are only to *be*; and the necessity of their giving way to him in some things, is too often exaggerated into their giving way to him in all, and thus rendering him utterly selfish. In the family about whom I am writing, while the rest were almost ascetic in their habits, Branwell was allowed to grow up self-indulgent; but, in early youth, his power of attracting and attaching people was so great, that few came in contact with him who were not so much dazzled by him as to be desirous of gratifying whatever wishes he expressed. Of course, he was careful enough not to reveal anything before his father and sisters of the pleasures he indulged in; but his tone of thought and conversation became gradually coarser, and, for a time, his sisters tried to persuade themselves that such coarseness was a part of manliness, and to blind themselves by love to the fact that Branwell was worse than other young men. At present, though he had, they were aware, fallen into some errors, the exact nature of which they avoided knowing; still he was their hope and their darling; their pride, who should some time bring great glory to the name of Brontë.

He and his sister Charlotte were both slight and small of stature, while the other two were of taller and larger make. I have seen Branwell's profile;* it is what would be generally esteemed very handsome; the forehead is massive, the eye well set, and the expression of it fine and intellectual; the nose too is good; but there are coarse lines about the mouth, and the lips, though of handsome shape, are loose and thick, indicating self-indulgence, while the slightly retreating chin conveys an idea of weakness of will. His hair and complexion were sandy. He had enough of Irish blood in him to make his manners frank and genial, with a kind of natural gallantry about them. In a fragment of one of his manuscripts* which I have read, there is a justness and felicity of expression which is very striking. It is the beginning of a tale, and the actors in it are drawn with much of the grace of characteristic portrait-painting, in perfectly pure and simple language, which distinguishes so many of Addison's papers in the 'Spectator.'* The fragment is too short to afford the means of judging whether he had much dramatic talent, as the persons of the story are not thrown into conversation. But altogether the elegance and composure of style are such as one would not have expected from this vehement and ill-fated young man. He had a stronger desire for literary fame burning in his heart, than even that which occasionally flashed up in his sisters'. He tried various outlets for his talents. He wrote and sent poems to Wordsworth and Coleridge,* who both expressed kind and laudatory opinions, and he frequently contributed verses to the *Leeds Mercury*. In 1840, he was living at home, employing himself in occasional composition of various kinds, and waiting till some occupation, for which he might be fitted without any expensive course of preliminary training, should turn up; waiting, not impatiently; for he saw society of one kind (probably what he called 'life') at the Black Bull; and at home he was as yet the cherished favourite.

Miss Branwell was unaware of the fermentation of unoccupied talent going on around her. She was not her nieces' confidante— perhaps no one so much older could have been; but their father, from whom they derived not a little of their adventurous spirit, was silently cognisant of much of which she took no note. Next to her nephew, the docile, pensive Anne was her favourite. Of her she had taken charge from her infancy; she was always patient and tractable, and would submit quietly to occasional oppression, even when she felt it keenly. Not so her two elder sisters; they made their opinions known, when roused by any injustice. At such times, Emily would express herself as strongly as Charlotte, although perhaps less frequently. But, in general, notwithstanding that Miss Branwell might be occasionally unreasonable, she and her nieces went on smoothly enough; and though they might now and then be annoyed by petty tyranny, she still inspired them with sincere respect, and not a little affection. They were, moreover, grateful to her for many habits she had enforced upon them, and which in time had become second nature: order, method, neatness in everything; a perfect knowledge of all kinds of household work; an exact punctuality, and obedience to the laws of time and place, of which no one but themselves, I have heard Charlotte say, could tell the value in after-life; with their impulsive natures, it was positive repose to have learnt implicit obedience to external laws. People in Haworth have assured me that, according to the hour of day—nay, the very minute—could they have told what the inhabitants of the parsonage were about. At certain times the girls would be sewing in their aunt's bed-room—the chamber which, in former days, before they had outstripped her in their learning, had served them as a school-room; at certain (early) hours they had their meals; from six to eight, Miss Branwell read aloud to Mr Brontë; at punctual eight, the household assembled to evening prayers in his study; and by nine he, the aunt, and Tabby, were all in bed,—the girls free to pace up and down (like restless wild animals) in the parlour, talking over plans and projects, and thoughts of what was to be their future life.

At the time of which I write, the favourite idea was that of keeping a school. They thought that, by a little contrivance, and a very little additional building, a small number of pupils, four or six, might be accommodated in the parsonage. As teaching seemed the only profession open to them, and as it appeared that Emily at least could not live away from home, while the others also suffered much from the same cause, this plan of school-keeping presented itself as most desirable. But it involved some outlay; and to this their aunt was averse. Yet there was no one to whom they could apply for a loan of the requisite means, except Miss Branwell, who had made a small store out of her savings, which she intended for her nephew and nieces eventually, but which she did not like to risk. Still, this plan of school-keeping remained uppermost; and in the evenings of this winter of 1839–40, the alterations that would be necessary in the house, and the best way of convincing their aunt of the wisdom of their project, formed the principal subject of their conversation.

This anxiety weighed upon their minds rather heavily, during the months of dark and dreary weather. Nor were external events, among the circle of their friends, of a cheerful character. In January, 1840, Charlotte heard of the death of a young girl* who had been a pupil of hers, and a school-fellow of Anne's, at the time when the sisters were together at Roe Head; and had attached herself very strongly to the latter, who, in return, bestowed upon her much quiet affection. It was a sad day when the intelligence of this young creature's death arrived. Charlotte wrote thus on January 12th, 1840:—

'Your letter, which I received this morning, was one of painful
interest. Anne C., it seems, is *dead;* when I saw her last, she was
a young, beautiful, and happy girl; and now "life's fitful fever" is
over with her, and she "sleeps well."* I shall never see her again.
It is a sorrowful thought; for she was a warm-hearted, affectionate
being, and I cared for her. Wherever I seek for her now in this
world, she cannot be found, no more than a flower or a leaf which
withered twenty years ago. A bereavement of this kind gives one a
glimpse of the feeling those must have who have seen all drop
round them, friend after friend, and are left to end their pilgrimage
alone. But tears are fruitless, and I try not to repine.'

During this winter, Charlotte employed her leisure hours in
writing a story.* Some fragments of the manuscript yet remain, but
it is in too small a hand to be read without great fatigue to the eyes;
and one cares the less to read it, as she herself condemned it, in
the preface to the 'Professor,' by saying that in this story she had
got over such taste as she might once have had for the 'ornamental
and redundant in composition.' The beginning, too, as she ac-
knowledges, was on a scale commensurate with one of Richardson's
novels, of seven or eight volumes. I gather some of these particulars from a copy of a letter,* apparently in reply to one from
Wordsworth, to whom she had sent the commencement of the
story, sometime in the summer of 1840.

'Authors are generally very tenacious of their productions, but I
am not so much attached to this but that I can give it up without
much distress. No doubt, if I had gone on, I should have made
quite a Richardsonian concern of it. . . . I had materials in my head
for half-a-dozen volumes. . . . . Of course, it is with considerable
regret I relinquish any scheme so charming as the one I have
sketched. It is very edifying and profitable to create a world out of
your own brain, and people it with inhabitants, who are so many
Melchisedecs, and have no father nor mother* but your own
imagination. . . . I am sorry I did not exist fifty or sixty years ago,
when the "Ladies' Magazine" was flourishing like a green bay
tree.* In that case, I make no doubt, my aspirations after literary
fame would have met with due encouragement, and I should have

had the pleasure of introducing Messrs Percy and West into the very best society, and recording all their sayings and doings in double-columned close-printed pages..... I recollect, when I was a child, getting hold of some antiquated volumes, and reading them by stealth with the most exquisite pleasure. You give a correct description of the patient Grisels* of those days. My aunt was one of them; and to this day she thinks the tales of the "Ladies' Magazine" infinitely superior to any trash of modern literature. So do I; for I read them in childhood, and childhood has a very strong faculty of admiration, but a very weak one of criticism..... I am pleased that you cannot quite decide whether I am an attorney's clerk or a novel-reading dressmaker. I will not help you at all in the discovery; and as to my handwriting, or the lady-like touches in my style and imagery, you must not draw any conclusion from that—I may employ an amanuensis. Seriously, sir, I am very much obliged to you for your kind and candid letter. I almost wonder you took the trouble to read and notice the novelette of an anonymous scribe, who had not even the manners to tell you whether he was a man or a woman, or whether his "C. T."* meant Charles Timms or Charlotte Tomkins.'

There are two or three things noticeable in the letter from which these extracts are taken. The first is the initials with which she had evidently signed the former one to which she alludes. About this time, to her more familiar correspondents, she occasionally calls herself 'Charles Thunder,' making a kind of pseudonym for herself out of her Christian name, and the meaning of her Greek surname. In the next place, there is a touch of assumed smartness, very different from the simple, womanly, dignified letter which she had written to Southey, under nearly similar circumstances, three years before. I imagine the cause of this difference to be twofold. Southey, in his reply to her first letter, had appealed to the higher parts of her nature, in calling her to consider whether literature was, or was not, the best course for a woman to pursue. But the person to whom she addressed this one had evidently confined himself to purely literary criticisms; besides which, her sense of humour was tickled by the perplexity which her correspondent felt as to whether he was addressing a man or a woman. She rather wished to encourage the former idea; and, in consequence, possibly, assumed something of the flippancy which very probably existed in her brother's style of conversation, from whom she would derive her notions of young manhood, not likely, as far as refinement was concerned, to be improved by the other specimens she had seen, such as the curates whom she afterwards represented in 'Shirley.'

These curates were full of strong, High-Church feeling. Belligerent by nature, it was well for their professional character that they had, as clergymen, sufficient scope for the exercise of their warlike propensities. Mr Brontë, with all his warm regard for Church and State, had a great respect for mental freedom; and, though he was the last man in the world to conceal his opinions, he lived in perfect amity with all the respectable part of those who differed from him. Not so the curates. Dissent was schism, and schism was condemned in the Bible.* In default of turbaned Saracens, they entered on a crusade against Methodists in broadcloth; and the consequence was that the Methodists and Baptists refused to pay the church-rates. Miss Brontë thus describes the state of things at this time:—*

'Little Haworth has been all in a bustle about church-rates, since you were here. We had a stirring meeting in the schoolroom. Papa took the chair, and Mr C. and Mr W. acted as his supporters, one on each side. There was violent opposition, which set Mr C.'s Irish blood in a ferment, and if papa had not kept him quiet, partly by persuasion and partly by compulsion, he would have given the Dissenters their kale through the reek—a Scotch proverb,* which I will explain to you another time. He and Mr W. both bottled up their wrath for that time, but it was only to explode with redoubled force at a future period. We had two sermons on dissent, and its consequences, preached last Sunday—one in the afternoon by Mr W., and one in the evening by Mr C. All the Dissenters were invited to come and hear, and they actually shut up their chapels, and came in a body; of course the church was crowded. Mr W. delivered a noble, eloquent, High-Church, Apostolical-Succession discourse, in which he banged the Dissenters most fearlessly and unflinchingly. I thought they had got enough for one while, but it was nothing to the dose that was thrust down their throats in the evening. A keener, cleverer, bolder, and more heart-stirring harangue than that which Mr C. delivered from Haworth pulpit, last Sunday evening, I never heard. He did not rant; he did not cant;

he did not whine; he did not sniggle;* he just got up and spoke with the boldness of a man who was impressed with the truth of what he was saying, who has no fear of his enemies, and no dread of consequences. His sermon lasted an hour, yet I was sorry when it was done. I do not say that I agree either with him, or with Mr W., either in all or in half their opinions. I consider them bigoted, intolerant, and wholly unjustifiable on the ground of common sense. My conscience will not let me be either a Puseyite or a Hookist; *mais*, if I were a Dissenter, I would have taken the first opportunity of kicking, or of horse-whipping both the gentlemen for their stern, bitter attack on my religion and its teachers. But in spite of all this, I admired the noble integrity which could dictate so fearless an opposition against so strong an antagonist.

'P. S.—Mr W. has given another lecture at the Keighley Mechanics' Institution,* and papa has also given a lecture; both are spoken of very highly in the newspapers, and it is mentioned as a matter of wonder that such displays of intellect should emanate from the village of Haworth, "situated among the bogs and mountains, and, until very lately, supposed to be in a state of semi-barbarism." Such are the words of the newspaper.'

To fill up the account of this outwardly eventless year, I may add a few more extracts from the letters entrusted to me.

'May 15th, 1840.

'Do not be over-persuaded to marry a man you can never respect*—I do not say *love;* because, I think, if you can respect a person before marriage, moderate love at least will come after; and as to intense *passion*, I am convinced that that is no desirable feeling. In the first place, it seldom or never meets with a requital; and, in the second place, if it did, the feeling would be only temporary: it would last the honeymoon, and then, perhaps, give place to disgust, or indifference worse, perhaps, than disgust. Certainly this would be the case on the man's part; and on the woman's—God help her, if she is left to love passionately and alone.

'I am tolerably* well convinced that I shall never marry at all. Reason tells me so, and I am not so utterly the slave of feeling but that I can *occasionally hear* her voice.'

'June 2nd, 1840.*

'M. is not yet come to Haworth; but she is to come, on the condition that I first go and stay a few days there. If all be well, I shall go next Wednesday. I may stay at G—— until Friday or Saturday, and the early part of the following week I shall pass with you, if you will have me—which last sentence indeed is nonsense, for as I shall be glad to see you, so I know you will be glad to see me. This arrangement will not allow much time, but it is the only practicable one which, considering all the circumstances, I can effect. Do not urge me to stay more than two or three days, because I shall be obliged to refuse you. I intend to walk to Keighley, there to take the coach as far as B——, then to get some one to carry my box, and to walk the rest of the way to G——. If I manage this, I think I shall contrive very well. I shall reach B. by about five o'clock, and then I shall have the cool of the evening for the walk. I have communicated the whole arrangement to M. I desire exceedingly to see both her and you. Good-bye.

C. B.

C. B.

C. B.

C. B.

'If you have any better plan to suggest I am open to conviction, provided your plan is practicable.'

'August 20th, 1840.*

'Have you seen anything of Miss H. lately? I wish they, or somebody else, would get me a situation. I have answered advertisements without number, but my applications have met with no success.

'I have got another bale of French books from G. containing upwards of forty volumes. I have read about half. They are like the rest, clever, wicked, sophistical, and immoral. The best of it is, they give one a thorough idea of France and Paris, and are the best substitute for French conversation that I have met with.

'I positively have nothing more to say to you, for I am in a stupid humour. You must excuse this letter not being quite as long as your own. I have written to you soon that you might not look after the postman in vain. Preserve this writing as a curiosity in caligraphy—I think it is exquisite—all brilliant black blots, and utterly illegible letters.

'CALIBAN.'*

' "The wind bloweth where it listeth.* Thou hearest the sound thereof, but canst not tell whence it cometh, nor whither it goeth." That, I believe, is Scripture,* though in what chapter or book, or whether it be correctly quoted, I can't possibly say. However, it behoves me to write a letter to a young woman of the name of E., with whom I was once acquainted, "in life's morning march, when my spirit was young."* This young woman wished me to write to her some time since, though I have nothing to say—I e'en put it off, day by day, till at last, fearing that she will "curse me by her gods,"* I feel constrained to sit down and tack a few lines together, which she may call a letter or not, as she pleases. Now, if the young woman expects sense in this production, she will find herself miserably disappointed. I shall dress her a dish of salmagundi—I shall cook a hash—compound a stew—toss up an *omelette soufflée à la Française*, and send it her with my respects. The wind, which is very high up in our hills of Judea, though, I suppose, down in the Philistine flats of B. parish it is nothing to speak of, has produced the same effects on the contents of my knowledge-box that a quaigh of usquebaugh does upon those of most other bipeds. I see everything *couleur de rose*, and am strongly inclined to dance a jig, if I knew how. I think I must partake of the nature of a pig or an ass—both which animals are strongly affected by a high wind. From what quarter the wind blows I cannot tell, for I never could in my life; but I should very much like to know how the great brewing-tub of Bridlington Bay works, and what sort of yeasty froth rises just now on the waves.

'A woman of the name of Mrs B., it seems, wants a teacher. I wish she would have me; and I have written to Miss W. to tell her so. Verily, it is a delightful thing to live here at home, at full liberty to do just what one pleases. But I recollect some scrubby old fable about grasshoppers and ants, by a scrubby old knave yclept Æsop; the grasshoppers sang all the summer, and starved all the winter.

'A distant relation of mine, one Patrick Branwell, has set off to seek his fortune in the wild, wandering, adventurous, romantic, knight-errant-like capacity of clerk on the Leeds and Manchester Railroad.* Leeds and Manchester—where are they? Cities in the wilderness—like Tadmor, alias Palmyra*—are they not?

'There is one little trait respecting Mr W. which lately came to my knowledge, which gives a glimpse of the better side of his character. Last Saturday night he had been sitting an hour in the parlour with Papa; and, as he went away, I heard Papa say to him "What is the matter with you? You seem in very low spirits to-night." "Oh, I don't know. I've been to see a poor young girl, who, I'm afraid, is dying." "Indeed, what is her name?" "Susan Bland, the daughter of John Bland, the superintendent." Now Susan Bland is my oldest and best scholar in the Sunday-school; and, when I heard that, I thought I would go as soon as I could to see her. I did go on Monday afternoon, and found her on her way to that "bourn whence no traveller returns."* After sitting with her some time, I happened to ask her mother, if she thought a little port wine would do her good. She replied that the doctor had recommended it, and that when Mr W. was last there, he had brought them a bottle of wine and jar of preserves. She added, that he was always good-natured to poor folks, and seemed to have a deal of feeling and kind-heartedness about him. No doubt, there are defects in his character, but there are also good qualities. . . . . God bless him! I wonder who, with his advantages, would be without his faults. I know many of his faulty actions, many of his weak points; yet, where I am, he shall always find rather a defender than an accuser. To be sure, my opinion will go but a very little way to decide his character; what of that? People should do right as far as their ability extends. You are not to suppose, from all this, that Mr W. and I are on very amiable terms; we are not at all. We are distant, cold, and reserved. We seldom speak; and when we do, it is only to exchange the most trivial and common-place remarks.'

The Mrs B. alluded to in this letter, as in want of a governess, entered into a correspondence with Miss Brontë, and expressed herself much pleased with the letters she received from her; with the 'style and candour of the application,' in which Charlotte had taken care to tell her, that if she wanted a showy, elegant, or fashionable person, her correspondent was not fitted for such a situation. But Mrs B. required her governess to give instructions in music and singing, for which Charlotte was not qualified; and, accordingly, the negotiation fell through. But Miss Brontë was not one to sit down in despair after disappointment. Much as she disliked the life of a private governess, it was her duty to relieve her father of the burden of her support, and this was the only way open to her. So she set to advertising and inquiring with fresh vigour.

In the mean time, a little occurrence took place, described in one of her letters, which I shall give, as it shows her instinctive aversion to a particular class of men, whose vices some have supposed she looked upon with indulgence. The extract tells all that need be known, for the purpose I have in view, of the miserable pair to whom it relates.*

'You remember Mr and Mrs ——?* Mrs —— came here the other day, with a most melancholy tale of her wretched husband's drunken, extravagant, profligate habits. She asked Papa's advice; there was nothing she said but ruin before them. They owed debts which they could never pay. She expected Mr ——'s instant dismissal from his curacy; she knew, from bitter experience, that his vices were utterly hopeless. He treated her and her child savagely; with much more to the same effect. Papa advised her to leave him for ever, and go home, if she had a home to go to. She said, this was what she had long resolved to do; and she would leave him directly, as soon as Mr B. dismissed him. She expressed great disgust and contempt towards him, and did not affect to have the shadow of regard in any way. I do not wonder at this, but I *do* wonder she should ever marry a man towards whom her feelings must always have been pretty much the same as they are now. I am morally certain no decent woman could experience anything but aversion towards such a man as Mr ——. Before I knew, or suspected his character, and when I rather wondered at his versatile talents, I felt it in an uncontrollable degree. I hated to talk with him—hated to look at him; though as I was not certain that there was substantial reason for such a dislike, and thought it absurd to trust to mere instinct, I both concealed and repressed the feeling as much as I could; and, on all occasions, treated him with as much civility as I was mistress of. I was struck with Mary's expression of a similar feeling at first sight; she said, when we left him, "That is a hideous man, Charlotte!" I thought "he is indeed." '

# CHAPTER X

EARLY in March, 1841, Miss Brontë obtained her second and last situation as a governess.* This time she esteemed herself fortunate in becoming a member of a kind-hearted and friendly household. The master of it, she especially regarded as a valuable friend, whose advice helped to guide her in one very important step of her life. But as her definite acquirements were few, she had to eke them out by employing her leisure time in needlework; and altogether her position was that of 'bonne' or nursery governess, liable to repeated and never-ending calls upon her time. This description of uncertain, yet perpetual employment, subject to the exercise of another person's will at all hours of the day, was peculiarly trying to one whose life at home had been full of abundant leisure. *Idle* she never was in any place, but of the multitude of small talks, plans, duties, pleasures, &c., that make up most people's days, her home life was nearly destitute. This made it possible for her to go through long and deep histories of feeling and imagination, for which others, odd as it sounds, have rarely time. This made it inevitable that—later on, in her too short career—the intensity of her feeling should wear out her physical health. The habit of 'making out,' which had grown with her growth, and strengthened with her strength, had become a part of her nature. Yet all exercise of her strongest and most characteristic faculties was now out of the question. She could not (as while she was at Miss W——'s) feel, amidst the occupations of the day, that when evening came, she might employ herself in more congenial ways. No doubt, all who enter upon the career of a governess have to relinquish much; no doubt, it must ever be a life of sacrifice; but to Charlotte Brontë it was a perpetual attempt to force all her faculties into a direction for which the whole of her previous life had unfitted them. Moreover, the little Brontës had been brought up motherless; and from knowing nothing of the gaiety and the sportiveness of childhood—from never having experienced caresses or fond attentions themselves—they were ignorant of the very nature of infancy, or how to call out its engaging qualities. Children were to them the troublesome necessities of humanity;

they had never been drawn into contact with them in any other way. Years afterwards, when Miss Brontë came to stay with us, she watched our little girls perpetually; and I could not persuade her that they were only average specimens of well brought up children. She was surprised and touched by any sign of thoughtfulness for others, of kindness to animals, or of unselfishness on their part; and constantly maintained that she was in the right, and I in the wrong, when we differed on the point of their unusual excellence. All this must be borne in mind while reading the following letters. And it must likewise be borne in mind—by those who, surviving her, look back upon her life from their mount of observation,—how no distaste, no suffering ever made her shrink from any course which she believed it to be her duty to engage in.

'March 3rd, 1841.*

'I told you some time since, that I meant to get a situation, and when I said so my resolution was quite fixed. I felt that however often I was disappointed, I had no intention of relinquishing my efforts. After being severely baffled two or three times,—after a world of trouble, in the way of correspondence and interviews,—I have at length succeeded, and am fairly established in my new place.

\* \* \* \* \*

'The house is not very large, but exceedingly comfortable and well regulated; the grounds are fine and extensive. In taking the place, I have made a large sacrifice in the way of salary, in the hope of securing comfort,—by which word I do not mean to express good eating and drinking, or warm fire, or a soft bed, but the society of cheerful faces, and minds and hearts not dug out of a lead-mine, or cut from a marble quarry. My salary is not really more than 16*l.* per annum,* though it is nominally 20*l.*, but the expense of washing will be deducted therefrom. My pupils are two in number, a girl of eight, and a boy of six. As to my employers, you will not expect me to say much about their characters when I tell you that I only arrived here yesterday. I have not the faculty of telling an individual's disposition at first sight. Before I can venture to pronounce on a character, I must see it first under various lights and from various points of view. All I can say therefore is, both Mr and Mrs —— seem to me good sort of people. I have as yet had no cause to complain of want of considerateness or civility. My pupils are wild and unbroken, but apparently well-disposed. I wish I may be able to say as much next time I write to you. My earnest wish and endeavour will be to please them. If I can but feel that I am giving satisfaction, and if at the same time I can keep my health, I shall, I hope, be moderately happy. But no one but myself can tell how hard a governess's work is to me—for no one but myself is aware how utterly averse my whole mind and nature are for the employment. Do not think that I fail to blame myself for this, or that I leave any means unemployed to conquer this feeling. Some of my greatest difficulties lie in things that would appear to you comparatively trivial. I find it so hard to repel the rude familiarity of children. I find it so difficult to ask either servants or mistress for anything I want, however much I want it. It is less pain for me to endure the greatest inconvenience than to go into the kitchen to request its removal. I am a fool. Heaven knows I cannot help it!

'Now can you tell me whether it is considered improper for governesses to ask their friends to come and see them. I do not mean, of course, to stay, but just for a call of an hour or two? If it is not absolute treason, I do fervently request that you will contrive, in some way or other, to let me have a sight of your face. Yet I feel, at the same time, that I am making a very foolish and almost impracticable demand; yet this is only four miles from B——!'

'March '41.*

'You must excuse a very short answer to your most welcome letter; for my time is entirely occupied. Mrs —— expected a good deal of sewing from me. I cannot sew much during the day, on account of the children, who require the utmost attention. I am obliged, therefore, to devote the evenings to this business. Write to me often; very long letters. It will do both of us good. This place is far better than ——, but God knows, I have enough to do to keep a good heart in the matter. What you said has cheered me a little. I wish I could always act according to your advice. Home-sickness affects me sorely. I like Mr —— extremely. The children are over-indulged, and consequently hard at times to manage. *Do, do*, do come and see me; if it be a breach of etiquette, never mind.

If you can only stop an hour, come. Talk no more about my forsaking you; my darling, I could not afford to do it. I find it is not in my nature to get on in this weary world without sympathy and attachment in some quarter; and seldom indeed do we find it. It is too great a treasure to be ever wantonly thrown away when once secured.'

Miss Brontë had not been many weeks in her new situation before she had a proof of the kind-hearted hospitality of her employers. Mr —— wrote to her father and urgently invited him to come and make acquaintance with his daughter's new home, by spending a week with her in it; and Mrs —— expressed great regret when one of Miss Brontë's friends drove up to the house to leave a letter or parcel, without entering. So she found that all her friends might freely visit her, and that her father would be received with especial gladness. She thankfully acknowledged this kindness in writing to urge her friend afresh to come and see her; which she accordingly did.

'June, 1841.*

'You can hardly fancy it possible, I dare say, that I cannot find a quarter of an hour to scribble a note in; but so it is; and when a note is written, it has to be carried a mile to the post, and that consumes nearly an hour, which is a large portion of the day. Mr and Mrs —— have been gone a week. I heard from them this morning. No time is fixed for their return, but I hope it will not be delayed long, or I shall miss the chance of seeing Anne this vacation.* She came home, I understand, last Wednesday, and is only to be allowed three weeks' vacation, because the family she is with are going to Scarborough. *I should like to see her,* to judge for myself of the state of her health. I dare not trust any other person's report, no one seems minute enough in their observations. I should very much have liked you to have seen her. I have got on very well with the servants and children so far; yet it is dreary, solitary work. You can tell as well as me the lonely feeling of being without a companion.'

Soon after this was written, Mr and Mrs —— returned, in time to allow Charlotte to go and look after Anne's health, which, as she found to her intense anxiety, was far from strong. What could she do, to nurse and cherish up this little sister, the youngest of them all? Apprehension about her brought up once more the idea of keeping a school. If, by this means, they three could live together, and maintain themselves, all might go well. They would have some time of their own, in which to try again and yet again at that literary career, which, in spite of all baffling difficulties, was never quite set aside as an ultimate object; but far the strongest motive with Charlotte was the conviction that Anne's health was so delicate that it required a degree of tending which none but her sister could give. Thus she wrote during those midsummer holidays.

'Haworth, July 19th, 1841.*

'We waited long and anxiously for you, on the Thursday that you promised to come. I quite wearied my eyes with watching from the window, eye-glass in hand, and sometimes spectacles on nose. However, you are not to blame; . . . and as to disappointment, why, all must suffer disappointment at some period or other of their lives. But a hundred things I had to say to you will now be forgotten, and never said. There is a project hatching in this house, which both Emily and I anxiously wished to discuss with you. The project is yet in its infancy, hardly peeping from its shell; and whether it will ever come out a fine full-fledged chicken, or will turn addle and die before it cheeps, is one of those considerations that are but dimly revealed by the oracles of futurity. Now, don't be nonplussed by all this metaphorical mystery. I talk of a plain and every-day occurrence, though, in Delphic style, I wrap up the information in figures of speech concerning eggs, chickens, et-cætera, etcæterorum.* To come to the point: Papa and aunt talk, by fits and starts, of our—id est, Emily, Anne and myself—commencing a school! I have often, you know, said how much I wished such a thing; but I never could conceive where the capital was to come from for making such a speculation. I was well aware, indeed, that aunt had money, but I always considered that she was the last person who would offer a loan for the purpose in question. A loan, however, she *has* offered, or rather intimates that she perhaps *will* offer in case pupils can be secured, an eligible situation obtained, &c. This sounds very fair, but still there are matters to be

considered which throw something of a damp upon the scheme. I do not expect that aunt will sink more than 150*l.* in such a venture; and would it be possible to establish a respectable (not by any means a *showy*) school, and to commence housekeeping with a capital of only that amount? Propound the question to your sister, if you think she can answer it; if not, don't say a word on the subject. As to getting into debt, that is a thing we could none of us reconcile our mind to for a moment. We do not care how modest, how humble our commencement be, so it be made on sure grounds, and have a safe foundation. In thinking of all possible and impossible places where we could establish a school, I have thought of Burlington, or rather of the neighbourhood of Burlington. Do you remember whether there was any other school there besides that of Miss ——? This is, of course, a perfectly crude and random idea. There are a hundred reasons why it should be an impracticable one. We have no connections, no acquaintances there; it is far from home, &c. Still, I fancy the ground in the East Riding is less fully occupied than in the West. Much inquiry and consideration will be necessary, of course, before any place is decided on; and I fear much time will elapse before any plan is executed......
Write as soon as you can. I shall not leave my present situation till my future prospects assume a more fixed and definite aspect.'

A fortnight afterwards, we see that the seed has been sown which was to grow up into a plan materially influencing her future life.

'August 7th, 1841.*

'This is Saturday evening; I have put the children to bed; now I am going to sit down and answer your letter. I am again by myself—housekeeper and governess—for Mr and Mrs —— are staying at ——. To speak truth, though I am solitary while they are away, it is still by far the happiest part of my time. The children are under decent control, the servants are very observant and attentive to me, and the occasional absence of the master and mistress relieves me from the duty of always endeavouring to seem cheerful and conversable. Martha ——, it appears, is in the way of enjoying great advantages;* so is Mary, for you will be surprised to hear that she is returning immediately to the Continent with her brother; not, however, to stay there, but to take a month's tour and recreation. I have had a long letter from Mary, and a packet containing a present of a very handsome black silk scarf, and a pair of beautiful kid gloves, bought at Brussels. Of course, I was in one sense pleased with the gift—pleased that they should think of me so far off, amidst the excitements of one of the most splendid capitals of Europe; and yet it felt irksome to accept it. I should think Mary and Martha have not more than sufficient pocket-money to supply themselves. I wish they had testified their regard by a less expensive token. Mary's letters spoke of some of the pictures and cathedrals she had seen—pictures the most exquisite, cathedrals the most venerable. I hardly know what swelled to my throat as I read her letter: such a vehement impatience of restraint and steady work; such a strong wish for wings—wings such as wealth can furnish; such an urgent thirst to see, to know, to learn; something internal seemed to expand bodily for a minute. I was tantalised by the consciousness of faculties unexercised,—then all collapsed, and I despaired. My dear, I would hardly make that confession to any one but yourself; and to you, rather in a letter than *vivâ voce*. These rebellious and absurd emotions were only momentary; I quelled them in five minutes. I hope they will not revive, for they were acutely painful. No further steps have been taken about the project I mentioned to you, nor probably will be for the present; but Emily, and Anne, and I, keep it in view. It is our polar star, and we look to it in all circumstances of despondency. I begin to suspect I am writing in a strain which will make you think I am unhappy. This is far from being the case; on the contrary, I know my place is a favourable one, for a governess. What dismays and haunts me sometimes, is a conviction that I have no natural knack for my vocation. If teaching only were requisite, it would be smooth and easy; but it is the living in other people's houses—the estrangement from one's real character—the adoption of a cold, rigid, apathetic exterior, that is painful. . . . You will not mention our school project at present. A project not actually commenced is always uncertain. Write to me often, my dear Nell; you *know* your letters are valued. Your "loving child" (as you choose to call me so),

'C. B.

'P. S. I am well in health; don't fancy I am not; but I have one aching feeling at my heart (I must allude to it, though I had resolved not to). It is about Anne; she has so much to endure: far, far more than I ever had. When my thoughts turn to her, they always see her as a patient, persecuted stranger. I know what concealed susceptibility is in her nature, when her feelings are wounded. I wish I could be with her, to administer a little balm. She is more lonely—less gifted with the power of making friends, even than I am. Drop the subject.'

She could bear much for herself; but she could not patiently bear the sorrows of others, especially of her sisters; and again, of the two sisters, the idea of the little, gentle, youngest suffering in lonely patience, was insupportable to her. Something must be done. No matter if the desired end were far away; all time was lost in which she was not making progress, however slow, towards it. To have a school, was to have some portion of daily leisure, uncontrolled but by her own sense of duty; it was for the three sisters, loving each other with so passionate an affection, to be together under one roof, and yet earning their own subsistence; above all, it was to have the power of watching over those two whose life and happiness were ever to Charlotte far more than her own. But no trembling impatience should lead her to take an unwise step in haste. She inquired in every direction she could, as to the chances which a new school might have of success. In all there seemed more establishments like the one which the sisters wished to set up than could be supported. What was to be done? Superior advantages must be offered. But how? They themselves abounded in thought, power, and information; but these are qualifications scarcely fit to be inserted in a prospectus. Of French they knew something; enough to read it fluently, but hardly enough to teach it in competition with natives, or professional masters. Emily and Anne had some knowledge of music; but here again it was doubtful whether, without more instruction, they could engage to give lessons in it.

Just about this time, Miss W—— was thinking of relinquishing her school at Dewsbury Moor; and offered to give it up in favour of her old pupils, the Brontës. A sister of hers* had taken the active management since the time when Charlotte was a teacher; but the number of pupils had diminished; and, if the Brontës undertook it, they would have to try and work it up to its former state of prosperity. This, again, would require advantages on their part which they did not at present possess, but which Charlotte caught a glimpse of. She resolved to follow the clue, and never to rest till she had reached a successful issue. With the forced calm of a suppressed eagerness, that sends a glow of desire through every word of the following letter, she wrote to her aunt thus.

'Sept. 29th, 1841.*

'DEAR AUNT,

'I have heard nothing of Miss W—— yet since I wrote to her, intimating that I would accept her offer. I cannot conjecture the reason of this long silence, unless some unforeseen impediment has occurred in concluding the bargain. Meantime, a plan has been suggested and approved by Mr and Mrs ——' (the father and mother of her pupils) 'and others, which I wish now to impart to you. My friends recommend me, if I desire to secure permanent success, to delay commencing the school for six months longer, and by all means to contrive, by hook or by crook, to spend the intervening time in some school on the continent. They say schools in England are so numerous, competition so great, that without some such step towards attaining superiority, we shall probably have a very hard struggle, and may fail in the end. They say, moreover, that the loan of 100*l*., which you have been so kind as to offer us, will, perhaps, not be all required now, as Miss W—— will lend us the furniture; and that, if the speculation is intended to be a good and successful one, half the sum, at least, ought to be laid out in the manner I have mentioned, thereby insuring a more speedy repayment both of interest and principal.

'I would not go to France or to Paris. I would go to Brussels, in Belgium.* The cost of the journey there, at the dearest rate of travelling, would be 5*l*.; living is there little more than half as dear as it is in England, and the facilities for education are equal or superior to any other place in Europe. In half a year, I could acquire a thorough familiarity with French. I could improve greatly in Italian, and even get a dash of German; *i.e.*, providing my health continued as good as it is now. Mary is now staying at Brussels, at a first-rate establishment there. I should not think of

going to the Château de Kokleberg,* where she is resident, as the
terms are much too high; but if I wrote to her, she, with the assistance
of Mrs Jenkins, the wife of the British Consul,* would be able to
secure me a cheap and decent residence and respectable protection. I
should have the opportunity of seeing her frequently; she would make
me acquainted with the city; and, with the assistance of her cousins,*
I should probably be introduced to connections far more improving,
polished, and cultivated, than any I have yet known.

'These are advantages which would turn to real account, when we
actually commenced a school; and, if Emily could share them with
me, we could take a footing in the world afterwards which we can
never do now. I say Emily instead of Anne; for Anne might take
her turn at some future period, if our school answered. I feel certain,
while I am writing, that you will see the propriety of what I say.
You always like to use your money to the best advantage. You are
not fond of making shabby purchases; when you do confer a favour,
it is often done in style; and, depend upon it, 50*l.*, or 100*l.*, thus
laid out, would be well employed. Of course, I know no other friend
in the world to whom I could apply, in this subject, except yourself.
I feel an absolute conviction that, if this advantage were allowed us,
it would be the making of us for life. Papa will, perhaps, think it a
wild and ambitious scheme; but who ever rose in the world without
ambition? When he left Ireland to go to Cambridge University, he
was as ambitious as I am now. I want us *all* to get on. I know we
have talents, and I want them to be turned to account. I look to you,
aunt, to help us. I think you will not refuse. I know, if you consent,
it shall not be my fault if you ever repent your kindness.'

This letter was written from the house in which she was residing
as governess. It was some little time before an answer came. Much
had to be talked over between the father and aunt in Haworth
Parsonage. At last consent was given. Then, and not till then, she
confided her plan to an intimate friend. She was not one to talk
over-much about any project, while it remained uncertain—to speak
about her labour, in any direction, while its result was doubtful.

'Nov. 2nd, 1841.

'Now let us begin to quarrel. In the first place, I must consider
whether I will commence operations on the defensive, or the

offensive. The defensive, I think. You say, and I see plainly, that your feelings have been hurt by an apparent want of confidence on my part. You heard from others of Miss W——'s overtures before I communicated them to you myself. This is true. I was deliberating on plans important to my future prospects. I never exchanged a letter with you on the subject. True again. This appears strange conduct to a friend, near and dear, long-known, and never found wanting. Most true. I cannot give you my *excuses* for this behaviour; this word *excuse* implies confession of a fault, and I do not feel that I have been in fault. The plain fact is, I *was* not, I am not now, certain of my destiny. On the contrary, I have been most uncertain, perplexed with contradictory schemes and proposals. My time, as I have often told you, is fully occupied; yet I had many letters to write, which it was absolutely necessary should be written. I knew it would avail nothing to write to you then to say I was in doubt and uncertainty—hoping this, fearing that, anxious, eagerly desirous to do what seemed impossible to be done. When I thought of you in that busy interval, it was to resolve, that you should know all when my way was clear, and my grand end attained. If I could, I would always work in silence and obscurity, and let my efforts be known by their results. Miss W—— did most kindly propose that I should come to Dewsbury Moor, and attempt to revive the school her sister had relinquished. She offered me the use of her furniture.* At first, I received the proposal cordially, and prepared to do my utmost to bring about success; but a fire was kindled in my very heart, which I could not quench. I so longed to increase my attainments—to become something better than I am; a glimpse of what I felt, I showed to you in one of my former letters—only a glimpse; Mary cast oil upon the flames—encouraged me, and in her own strong, energetic language, heartened me on. I longed to go to Brussels; but how could I get? I wished for one, at least, of my sisters to share the advantage with me. I fixed on Emily. She deserved the reward, I knew. How could the point be managed? In extreme excitement, I wrote a letter home, which carried the day. I made an appeal to aunt for assistance, which was answered by consent. Things are not settled; yet it is sufficient to say we have a *chance* of going for half a year. Dewsbury Moor is relinquished. Perhaps, fortunately so.* In my secret soul, I believe there is no cause to regret it. My plans for the future are bounded to this intention: if I once get to Brussels, and if my health is spared, I will do my best to make the utmost of every advantage that shall come within my reach. When the half-year is expired, I will do what I can.

\* \* \* \* \*

'Believe me, though I was born in April, the month of cloud and sunshine, I am not changeful. My spirits are unequal, and sometimes I speak vehemently, and sometimes I say nothing at all; but I have a steady regard for you, and if you will let the cloud and shower pass by, be sure the sun is always behind, obscured, but still existing.'

At Christmas she left her situation, after a parting with her employers, which seems to have affected and touched her greatly. 'They only made too much of me,' was her remark, after leaving this family; 'I did not deserve it.'\*

All four children hoped to meet together at their father's house this December. Branwell expected to have a short leave of absence from his employment as a clerk on the Leeds and Manchester Railway, in which he had been engaged for five months.\* Anne arrived before Christmas-day. She had rendered herself so valuable in her difficult situation, that her employers vehemently urged her return, although she had announced her resolution to leave them; partly on account of the harsh treatment she had received, and partly because her stay at home, during her sisters' absence in Belgium, seemed desirable, when the age of the three remaining inhabitants of the parsonage was taken into consideration.

After some correspondence and much talking over plans at home, it seemed better, in consequence of letters which they received from Brussels giving a discouraging account of the schools there, that Charlotte and Emily should go to an institution at Lille, in the north of France, which was highly recommended by Baptist Noel,\* and other clergymen. Indeed, at the end of January, it was arranged that they were to set off for this place in three weeks, under the escort of a French lady, then visiting in London. The terms were 50*l.* each pupil, for board and French alone, but a separate room was to be allowed for this sum; without this indulgence, it was lower. Charlotte writes:—

'I considered it kind in aunt to consent to an extra sum for a separate room. We shall find it a great privilege in many ways. I regret the change from Brussels to Lille on many accounts, chiefly that I shall not see Martha. Mary has been indefatigably kind in providing me with information. She has grudged no labour, and scarcely any expense, to that end. Mary's price is above rubies.* I have, in fact, two friends—you and her—staunch and true, in whose faith and sincerity I have as strong a belief as I have in the Bible. I have bothered you both—you especially; but you always get the tongs and heap coals of fire upon my head. I have had letters to write lately to Brussels, to Lille, and to London. I have lots of chemises, night-gowns, pocket-handkerchiefs, and pockets to make;* besides clothes to repair. I have been, every week since I came home, expecting to see Branwell, and he has never been able to get over yet. We fully expect him, however, next Saturday. Under these circumstances how can I go visiting? You tantalize me to death with talking of conversations by the fireside. Depend upon it, we are not to have any such for many a long month to come. I get an interesting impression of old age upon my face; and when you see me next I shall certainly wear caps and spectacles.'

## CHAPTER XI

I AM not aware of all the circumstances which led to the relinquishment of the Lille plan. Brussels had had from the first a strong attraction for Charlotte; and the idea of going there, in preference to any other place, had only been given up in consequence of the information received of the second-rate character of its schools. In one of her letters reference has been made to Mrs Jenkins, the wife of the chaplain of the British Embassy. At the request of his brother—a clergyman,* living not many miles from Haworth, and an acquaintance of Mr Brontë's—she made much inquiry, and at length, after some discouragement in her search, heard of a school which seemed in every respect desirable. There was an English lady, who had long lived in the Orleans family,* amidst the various fluctuations of their fortunes, and who, when the Princess Louise was married to King Leopold, accompanied her to Brussels, in the capacity of reader. This lady's granddaughter was receiving her education at the pensionnat of Madame Héger;* and so satisfied was the grandmother with the kind of instruction given, that she named the establishment, with high encomiums, to Mrs Jenkins; and, in consequence, it was decided that, if the terms suited, Miss Brontë and Emily should proceed thither. M. Héger informs me* that, on receipt of a letter from Charlotte, making very particular inquiries as to the possible amount of what are usually termed 'extras,' he and his wife were so much struck by the simple earnest tone of the letter, that they said to each other:—'These are the daughters of an English pastor, of moderate means, anxious to learn with an ulterior view of instructing others, and to whom the risk of additional expense is of great consequence. Let us name a specific sum, within which all expenses shall be included.'

This was accordingly done; the agreement was concluded, and the Brontës prepared to leave their native county for the first time, if we except the melancholy and memorable residence at Cowan Bridge. Mr Brontë determined to accompany his daughters. Mary and her brother, who were experienced in foreign travelling, were also of the party. Charlotte first saw London in the day or two they now stopped there; and, from an expression in one of her subsequent letters, they all, I believe, stayed at the Chapter Coffee House, Paternoster Row—a strange, old-fashioned tavern, of which I shall have more to say hereafter.*

Mary's account* of their journey is thus given.

'In passing through London, she seemed to think our business was and ought to be, to see all the pictures and statues we could. She knew the artists, and knew where other productions of theirs were to be found. I don't remember what we saw except St Paul's. Emily was like her in these habits of mind, but certainly never took her opinion, but always had one to offer. . . . I don't know what Charlotte thought of Brussels. We arrived in the dark, and went next morning to our respective schools to see them. We were of course, much preoccupied, and our prospects gloomy. Charlotte used to like the country round Brussels. "At the top of every hill you see something." She took long solitary walks on the occasional holidays.'

Mr Brontë took his daughters to the Rue d'Isabelle, Brussels; remained one night at Mr Jenkins'; and straight returned to his wild Yorkshire village.

What a contrast to that must the Belgian capital have presented to those two young women thus left behind! Suffering acutely from every strange and unaccustomed contact—far away from their beloved home, and the dear moors beyond—their indomitable will was their great support. Charlotte's own words, with regard to Emily, are:—*

'After the age of twenty, having meantime studied alone with diligence and perseverance, she went with me to an establishment on the continent. The same suffering and conflict ensued, heightened by the strong recoil of her upright heretic and English spirit from the gentle Jesuitry of the foreign and Romish system. Once more she seemed sinking, but this time she rallied through the mere force of resolution: with inward remorse and shame she looked back on her former failure, and resolved to conquer, but the victory cost her dear. She was never happy till she carried her hard-won knowledge back to the remote English village, the old parsonage-house, and desolate Yorkshire hills.'

They wanted learning. They came for learning. They would learn. Where they had a distinct purpose to be achieved in intercourse with their fellows, they forgot themselves; at all other times they were miserably shy. Mrs Jenkins told me that she used to ask them to spend Sundays and holidays with her, until she found that they felt more pain than pleasure from such visits. Emily hardly ever uttered more than a monosyllable. Charlotte was sometimes excited sufficiently to speak eloquently and well—on certain subjects; but before her tongue was thus loosened, she had a habit of gradually wheeling round on her chair, so as almost to conceal her face from the person to whom she was speaking.

And yet there was much in Brussels to strike a responsive chord in her powerful imagination. At length she was seeing somewhat of that grand old world of which she had dreamed. As the gay crowds passed by her, so had gay crowds paced those streets for centuries, in all their varying costumes. Every spot told an historic tale,* extending back into the fabulous ages when Jan and Jannika, the aboriginal giant and giantess, looked over the wall, forty feet high, of what is now the Rue Villa Hermosa, and peered down upon the new settlers who were to turn them out of the country in which they had lived since the deluge. The great solemn Cathedral of St Gudule,* the religious paintings, the striking forms and ceremonies of the Romish Church—all made a deep impression on the girls, fresh from the bare walls and simple worship of Haworth Church. And then they were indignant with themselves for having been susceptible of this impression, and their stout Protestant hearts arrayed themselves against the false Duessa* that had thus imposed upon them.

The very building they occupied as pupils, in Madame Héger's pensionnat, had its own ghostly train of splendid associations, marching for ever, in shadowy procession, through and through the ancient rooms, and shaded alleys of the gardens. From the splendour of to-day in the Rue Royale, if you turn aside, near the statue of the General Beliard, you look down four flights of broad stone steps upon the Rue d'Isabelle.* The chimneys of the houses in it are below your feet. Opposite to the lowest flight of steps, there is a large old mansion facing you, with a spacious walled garden behind and to the right of it. In front of this garden, on the same side as the mansion, and with great boughs of trees sweeping over their lowly roofs, is a row of small, picturesque, old-fashioned cottages, not unlike, in degree and uniformity, to the almshouses so often seen in an English country town. The Rue d'Isabelle looks as though it had been untouched by the innovations of the builder for the last three centuries; and yet any one might drop a stone into it from the back windows of the grand modern hotels in the Rue Royale, built and furnished in the newest Parisian fashion.

In the thirteenth century, the Rue d'Isabelle was called the Fossé-aux-Chiens; and the kennels for the ducal hounds occupied the place where Madame Héger's pensionnat now stands. A hospital (in the ancient large meaning of the word) succeeded to the kennel. The houseless and the poor, perhaps the leprous, were received, by the brethren of a religious order, in a building on this sheltered site; and what had been a fosse for defence, was filled up with herb-gardens and orchards for upwards of a hundred years. Then came the aristocratic guild of the cross-bow men—that company the members whereof were required to prove their noble descent untainted for so many generations, before they could be admitted into the guild; and, being admitted, were required to swear a solemn oath, that no other pastime or exercise should take up any part of their leisure, the whole of which was to be devoted to the practice of the noble art of shooting with the cross-bow. Once a year a grand match was held, under the patronage of some saint, to whose church-steeple was affixed the bird, or semblance of a bird, to be hit by the victor.[1] The conqueror in the game was Roi des Arbalétriers for the coming year, and received a jewelled decoration accordingly, which he was entitled to wear for twelve months; after which he restored it to the guild, to be again striven for. The family of him who died during the year that he was king, were bound to present the decoration to the church of the patron saint of the guild, and to furnish a similar prize to be contended

---

[1] Scott describes the sport, 'Shooting at the Popinjay,' 'as an ancient game formerly practised with archery, but at this period (1679) with fire-arms. This was the figure of a bird decked with parti-coloured feathers, so as to resemble a popinjay or parrot. It was suspended to a pole, and served for a mark at which the competitors discharged their fusees and carbines in rotation, at the distance of seventy paces. He whose ball brought down the mark held the proud title of Captain of the Popinjay for the remainder of the day, and was usually escorted in triumph to the most respectable change-house in the neighbourhood, where the evening was closed with conviviality, conducted under his auspices, and, if he was able to maintain it, at his expense.'—*Old Mortality*.*

for afresh. These noble cross-bow men of the middle ages formed a sort of armed guard to the powers in existence, and almost invariably took the aristocratic, in preference to the democratic side, in the numerous civil dissensions of the Flemish towns. Hence they were protected by the authorities, and easily obtained favourable and sheltered sites for their exercise-ground. And thus they came to occupy the old fosse, and took possession of the great orchard of the hospital, lying tranquil and sunny in the hollow below the rampart.

But, in the sixteenth century, it became necessary to construct a street through the exercise-ground of the 'Arbalétriers du Grand Serment,' and, after much delay, the company were induced by the beloved Infanta Isabella to give up the requisite plot of ground. In recompense for this, Isabella—who herself was a member of the guild, and had even shot down the bird, and been queen in 1615—made many presents to the arbalétriers; and, in return, the grateful city, which had long wanted a nearer road to St Gudule, but been baffled by the noble archers, called the street after her name. She, as a sort of indemnification to the arbalétriers, caused a 'great mansion' to be built for their accommodation in the new Rue d'Isabelle. This mansion was placed in front of their exercise-ground, and was of a square shape. On a remote part of the walls, may still be read—

PHILLIPPO IIII. HISPAN. REGE. ISABELLA-CLARA-EUGENIA HISPAN. INFANS. MAGNÆ GULDÆ REGINA GULDÆ FRATRIBUS POSUIT.

In that mansion were held all the splendid feasts of the Grand Serment des Arbalétriers. The master-archer lived there constantly, in order to be ever at hand to render his services to the guild. The great saloon was also used for the court balls and festivals, when the archers were not admitted. The Infanta caused other and smaller houses to be built in her new street, to serve as residences for her 'garde noble;' and for her 'garde bourgeoise,' a small habitation each, some of which still remain, to remind us of English almshouses. The 'great mansion,' with its quadrangular form; the spacious saloon—once used for the archducal balls, where the dark, grave Spaniards mixed with the blond nobility of Brabant and Flanders—now a school-room for Belgian girls; the cross-bow men's archery-ground—all are there—the pensionnat of Madame Héger.

This lady* was assisted in the work of instruction by her husband—a kindly, wise, good, and religious man—whose acquaintance I am glad to have made, and who has furnished me with some interesting details, from his wife's recollections and his own, of the two Miss Brontës during their residence in Brussels. He had the better opportunities of watching them, from his giving lessons in the French language and literature in the school. A short extract from a letter, written to me by a French lady resident in Brussels,* and well qualified to judge, will help to show the estimation in which he is held.

'Je ne connais pas personnellement M. Héger, mais je sais qu'il est peu de caractères aussi nobles, aussi admirables que le sien. Il est un des membres les plus zélés de cette Société de S. Vincent de Paul* dont je t'ai déjà parlé, et ne se contente pas de servir les pauvres et les malades, mais leur consacre encore les soirées. Après des journées absorbées tout entières par les devoirs que sa place lui impose, il réunit les pauvres, les ouvriers, leur donne des cours gratuits, et trouve encore le moyen de les amuser en les instruisant. Ce dévouement te dira assez que M. Héger est profondement et ouvertement religieux. Il a des manières franches et avenantes; il se fait aimer de tous ceux qui l'approchent, et surtout des enfants. Il a la parole facile, et possède à un haut degré l'éloquence du bon sens et du cœur. Il n'est point auteur. Homme de zèle et de conscience, il vient de se démettre des fonctions élevées et lucratives qu'il exerçait à l'Athénée, celles de Préfet des Etudes, parce qu'il ne peut y réaliser le bien qu'il avait espéré, introduire l'enseignement religieux dans le programme des études. J'ai vu une fois Madame Héger, qui a quelque chose de froid et de compassé dans son maintien, et qui prévient peu en sa faveur. Je la crois pourtant aimée et appréciée par ses élèves.'

There were from eighty to a hundred pupils in the pensionnat, when Charlotte and Emily Brontë entered in February 1842.

M. Héger's account is that they knew nothing of French.* I suspect they knew as much (or as little), for all conversational purposes, as any English girls do, who have never been abroad, and have only learnt the idioms and pronunciation from an Englishwoman. The two sisters clung together, and kept apart from the herd of happy, boisterous, well-befriended Belgian girls, who, in their turn, thought the new English pupils wild and scared-looking, with strange, odd, insular ideas about dress; for Emily had taken a fancy to the fashion, ugly and preposterous even during its reign, of gigot sleeves, and persisted in wearing them long after they were 'gone out.' Her petticoats, too, had not a curve or a wave in them, but hung down straight and long, clinging to her lank figure. The sisters spoke to no one but from necessity. They were too full of earnest thought, and of the exile's sick yearning, to be ready for careless conversation or merry game. M. Héger, who had done little but observe, during the few first weeks of their residence in the Rue d'Isabelle, perceived that with their unusual characters, and extraordinary talents, a different mode must be adopted from that in which he generally taught French to English girls. He seems to have rated Emily's genius as something even higher than Charlotte's; and her estimation of their relative powers was the same. Emily had a head for logic, and a capability of argument, unusual in a man, and rare indeed in a woman, according to M. Héger. Impairing the force of this gift, was a stubborn tenacity of will, which rendered her obtuse to all reasoning where her own wishes, or her own sense of right, was concerned. 'She should have been a man—a great navigator,' said M. Héger in speaking of her. 'Her powerful reason would have deduced new spheres of discovery from the knowledge of the old; and her strong imperious will would never have been daunted by opposition or difficulty; never have given way but with life.' And yet, moreover, her faculty of imagination was such that, if she had written a history, her view of scenes and characters would have been so vivid, and so powerfully expressed, and supported by such a show of argument, that it would have dominated over the reader, whatever might have been his previous opinions, or his cooler perceptions of its truth. But she appeared egotistical and exacting compared to Charlotte, who was always unselfish (this is M. Héger's testimony); and in the anxiety of the elder to make her younger sister contented, she allowed her to exercise a kind of unconscious tyranny over her.

After consulting with his wife, M. Héger told them that he meant to dispense with the old method of grounding in grammar, vocabulary, &c., and to proceed on a new plan—something similar to what he had occasionally adopted with the elder among his French and Belgian pupils. He proposed to read to them some of

the master-pieces of the most celebrated French authors* (such as
Casimir de la Vigne's poem on the 'Death of Joan of Arc,' parts of
Bossuet, the admirable translation of the noble letter of St Ignatius
to the Roman Christians in the 'Bibliothèque Choisie des Pères de
l'Église,' &c.), and after having thus impressed the complete effect
of the whole, to analyse the parts with them, pointing out in what
such or such an author excelled, and where were the blemishes. He
believed that he had to do with pupils capable, from their ready
sympathy with the intellectual, the refined, the polished, or the
noble, of catching the echo of a style, and so reproducing their own
thoughts in a somewhat similar manner.

After explaining his plan to them, he awaited their reply. Emily
spoke first; and said that she saw no good to be derived from it;
and that, by adopting it, they should lose all originality of thought
and expression. She would have entered into an argument on the
subject, but for this, M. Héger had no time. Charlotte then spoke;
she also doubted the success of the plan; but she would follow out
M. Héger's advice, because she was bound to obey him while she
was his pupil. Before speaking of the results, it may be desirable
to give an extract from one of her letters, which shows some of her
first impressions of her new life.

'Brussels, 1842 (May?).*

'I was twenty-six years old a week or two since; and at this ripe
time of life I am a school-girl, and, on the whole, very happy in
that capacity. It felt very strange at first to submit to authority
instead of exercising it—to obey orders instead of giving them; but
I like that state of things. I returned to it with the same avidity
that a cow, that has long been kept on dry hay, returns to fresh
grass. Don't laugh at my simile. It is natural to me to submit, and
very unnatural to command.

'This is a large school, in which there are about forty externes,
or day pupils, and twelve pensionnaires, or boarders. Madame
Héger, the head, is a lady of precisely the same cast of mind,
degree of cultivation, and quality of intellect as Miss ——. I think
the severe points are a little softened, because she has not been
disappointed, and consequently soured. In a word, she is a married
instead of a maiden lady. There are three teachers in the school—
Mademoiselle Blanche, Mademoiselle Sophie, and Mademoiselle

Marie. The two first have no particular character. One is an old maid, and the other will be one. Mademoiselle Marie is talented and original, but of repulsive and arbitrary manners, which have made the whole school, except myself and Emily, her bitter enemies. No less than seven masters attend, to teach the different branches of education—French, Drawing, Music, Singing, Writing, Arithmetic, and German. All in the house are Catholics except ourselves, one other girl, and the gouvernante of Madame's children, an Englishwoman,* in rank something between a lady's-maid and a nursery governess. The difference in country and religion makes a broad line of demarcation between us and all the rest. We are completely isolated in the midst of numbers. Yet I think I am never unhappy; my present life is so delightful, so congenial to my own nature, compared to that of a governess. My time, constantly occupied, passes too rapidly. Hitherto both Emily and I have had good health, and therefore we have been able to work well. There is one individual of whom I have not yet spoken—M. Héger, the husband of Madame. He is professor of rhetoric, a man of power as to mind, but very choleric and irritable in temperament. He is very angry with me just at present, because I have written a translation which he chose to stigmatize as *"peu correct."** He did not tell me so, but wrote the word on the margin of my book, and asked, in brief stern phrase, how it happened that my compositions were always better than my translations? adding that the thing seemed to him inexplicable. The fact is, some weeks ago, in a high-flown humour, he forbade me to use either dictionary or grammar in translating the most difficult English compositions into French. This makes the task rather arduous, and compels me every now and then to introduce an English word, which nearly plucks the eyes out of his head when he sees it. Emily and he don't draw well together at all. Emily works like a horse, and she has had great difficulties to contend with—far greater than I have had. Indeed, those who come to a French school for instruction ought previously to have acquired a considerable knowledge of the French language, otherwise they will lose a great deal of time, for the course of instruction is adapted to natives and not to foreigners; and in these large establishments they will not change their ordinary course for one or two strangers. The few private lessons that M. Héger has vouchsafed to give us, are, I suppose, to be considered a great favour; and I can perceive they have already excited much spite and jealousy in the school.

'You will abuse this letter for being short and dreary, and there are a hundred things which I want to tell you, but I have not time. Brussels is a beautiful city. The Belgians hate the English. Their external morality is more rigid than ours. To lace the stays without a handkerchief on the neck is considered a disgusting piece of indelicacy.'

The passage in this letter where M. Héger is represented as prohibiting the use of dictionary or grammar, refers, I imagine, to the time I have mentioned, when he determined to adopt a new method of instruction in the French language, of which they were to catch the spirit and rhythm rather from the ear and the heart, as its noblest accents fell upon them, than by over-careful and anxious study of its grammatical rules. It seems to me a daring experiment on the part of their teacher; but, doubtless, he knew his ground; and that it answered is evident in the composition of some of Charlotte's *devoirs*,\* written about this time. I am tempted, in illustration of this season of mental culture, to recur to a conversation which I had with M. Héger on the manner in which he formed his pupils' style, and to give a proof of his success, by copying a *devoir* of Charlotte's with his remarks upon it.

He told me that one day this summer (when the Brontës had been for about four months receiving instruction from him) he read to them Victor Hugo's celebrated portrait of Mirabeau,\* 'mais, dans ma leçon je me bornais à ce qui concerne *Mirabeau orateur*. C'est après l'analyse de ce morceau, considéré surtout du point de vue du fond, de la disposition, de ce qu'on pourrait appeler *la charpente* qu'ont été faits les deux portraits que je vous donne.' He went on to say that he had pointed out to them the fault in Victor Hugo's style as being exaggeration in conception, and, at the same time, he had made them notice the extreme beauty of his 'nuances' of expression. They were then dismissed to choose the subject of a similar kind of portrait. This selection M. Héger always left to them; for 'it is necessary,' he observed, 'before sitting down to write on a subject, to have thoughts and feelings about it. I cannot tell on what subject your heart and mind have been excited. I must leave that to you.' The marginal comments, I need

hardly say, are M. Héger's; the words in italics are Charlotte's, for
which he substitutes a better form of expression, which is placed
between brackets.

## IMITATION.*

### PORTRAIT DE PIERRE L'HERMITE. CHARLOTTE
### BRONTË

'De temps en temps, il paraît sur la terre des
hommes destinés à être les instruments [prédestinés]
de grands changements moraux ou politiques, ~~dans~~
~~leur siécle.~~ Quelquefois c'est un conquérant, un
Alexandre ou un Attila, qui passe comme un ou-
ragan, et purifie l'atmosphère moral, comme l'orage
purifie l'atmosphère physique; quelquefois, c'est un
révolutionnaire, un Cromwell, ou un Robespierre,
qui fait expier par un roi ˄ les vices de toute une
dynastie; quelquefois c'est un enthousiaste religieux
comme Mahomet, ou Pierre l'Hermite, qui, avec le
seul levier de la pensée, soulève des nations entières,
les déracine et les transplante dans des climats
nouveaux, *peuplant l'Asie avec les habitants de l'Europe.* Pierre l'Hermite était gentilhomme de Picardie,
en France, pourquoi donc n'a-t-il passé sa vie comme
les autres gentilhommes, ses contemporains, ont passé
la leur, à table, à la chasse, dans son lit, sans s'inquiéter
de Saladin, ou de ses Sarrasins? N'est-ce pas, parce
qu'il y a dans certaines natures, *une ardeur* [un foyer
d'activité] indomptable qui ne leur permet pas de
rester inactives, *qui les force à se remuer afin d'exercer
les facultés puissantes, qui même en dormant sont prêtes,
comme Sampson, à briser les nœuds qui les retiennent?*

'Pierre prit la profession des armes; *si son ardeur
avait été de cette espèce* [s'il n'avait eu que cette
ardeur vulgaire] qui provient d'une robuste santé, *il
aurait* [c'eut] été un brave militaire, et rien de plus;
mais son ardeur était celle de l'âme, sa flamme était
pure et elle s'élevait vers le ciel.

Pourquoi cette
suppression?

les fautes et

Ce détail ne con-
vient qu'á Pierre.

Inutile,
quand vous écri-
vez en français.

Vous avez
commencé à
parler de
Pierre: vous
êtes entrée dans
le sujet: mar-
chez au but.

'*Sans doute* [Il est vrai que] la jeunesse de Pierre *était* [fut] troublée par passions orageuses; les natures puissantes sont extrèmes en tout, elles ne connaissent la tiédeur ni dans le bien, ni dans le mal; Pierre donc chercha d'abord avidement la gloire qui se flétrit et les plaisirs qui trompent, mais *il fit bientôt la découverte* [bientôt il s'aperçut] que ce qu'il poursuivait n'était qu'une illusion à laquelle il ne pourrait jamais atteindre; il retourna donc sur ses pas, il recommença le voyage de la vie, mais cette fois il évita le chemin spacieux qui mène à la perdition et il prit le chemin étroit qui mène à la vie; *puisque* [comme] le trajet était long et difficile il jeta la casque et les armes du soldat, et se vêtit de l'habit simple du moine. A la vie militaire succéda la vie monastique, car les extrèmes se touchent, et *chez l'homme sincère* la sincérité du repentir amène [nécessairement à la suite] *avec lui* la rigueur de la pénitence. [Voilà donc Pierre devenu moine!]

Inutile, quand vous avez dit illusion.

'Mais *Pierre* [il] avait en lui un principe qui l'empêchait de rester long-temps inactif, ses idées, sur quel sujet *qu'il soit* [que ce fût] ne pouvaient pas être bornées; il ne lui suffisait pas que lui-même fût religieux, que lui-même fût convaincu de la réalité de Christianismé (sic), il fallait que toute l'Europe, que toute l'Asie, partageât sa conviction et professât la croyance de la Croix. La Piété [fervente] élevée par le Génie, nourrie par la Solitude, *fit naître une espèce d'inspiration* [exalta son âme jusqu'à l'inspiration] *dans son ame*, et lorsqu'il quitta sa cellule et reparut dans le monde, il portait comme Moïse l'empreinte de la Divinité sur son front, et *tout* [tous] reconnurent en lui la véritable apôtre de la Croix.

'Mahomet n'avait jamais remué les molles nations de l'Orient comme alors Pierre remua les peuples austères de l'Occident; il fallait que cette éloquence fût d'une force presque miraculeuse *qui pouvait* [presqu'elle] persuad*er* [ait] aux rois de vendre leurs

royaumes *afin de procurer* [pour avoir] des armes et
des soldats *pour aider* [à offrir] à Pierre dans la guerre
sainte qu'il voulait livrer aux infidèles. La puissance
de Pierre [l'Hermite] n'était nullement une puissance physique, car la nature, ou pour mieux dire,
Dieu est impartial dans la distribution de ses dons;
il accorde à l'un de ses enfants la grâce, la beauté, les
perfections corporelles, à l'autre l'esprit, la grandeur
morale. Pierre donc était un homme petit, d'une
physionomie peu agréable; mais il avait ce courage,
cette constance, cet enthousiasme, cette energie de
sentiment qui écrase toute opposition, et qui fait que
la volonté d'un seul homme devient la loi de toute
une nation. Pour se former une juste idée de l'influence qu'exerça cet homme sur les *caractères*
[choses] et les idées de son temps, il faut se le
représenter au milieu de l'armée des croisées dans
son double rôle de prophète et de guerrier; le pauvre
hermite, vêtu *du pauvre* [de l'humble] habit gris est
là plus puissant qu'un roi; il est entouré *d'une* [de la]
multitude [avide] une multitude qui ne voit que lui,
tandis que lui, il ne voit que le ciel; ses yeux levés
semblent dire, "Je vois Dieu et les anges, et j'ai
perdu de vue la terre!"

'*Dans ce moment le* [mais ce] pauvre *habit* [froc] gris
est pour lui comme le manteau d'Élijah; il l'enveloppe
d'inspiration; *il* [Pierre] lit dans l'avenir; il voit Jérusa-
lem délivrée; [il voit] le saint sépulcre libre; il voit le
Croissant argent est arraché du Temple, et l'Oriflamme
et la Croix rouge sont établi à sa place; non-seulement
Pierre voit ces merveilles, mais il les fait voir à tous
ceux qui l'entourent; il ravive l'espérance et le courage
dans [tous ces corps épuisés de fatigues et de priva-
tions]. La bataille ne sera livrée que demain, mais la
victoire est décidée ce soir. Pierre a promis; et les
Croisés se fient à sa parole, comme les Israëlites se
fiaient à celle de Moïse et de Josué.'

As a companion portrait to this, Emily chose to depict Harold on the eve of the battle of Hastings.* It appears to me that her *devoir* is superior to Charlotte's in power and in imagination, and fully equal to it in language; and that this, in both cases, considering how little practical knowledge of French they had when they arrived at Brussels in February, and that they wrote without the aid of dictionary or grammar, is unusual and remarkable. We shall see the progress Charlotte had made, in ease and grace of style, a year later.

In the choice of subjects left to her selection, she frequently took characters and scenes from the Old Testament, with which all her writings show that she was especially familiar. The picturesqueness and colour (if I may so express it), the grandeur and breadth of its narrations, impressed her deeply. To use M. Héger's expression, 'Elle était nourrie de la Bible.'* After he had read De la Vigne's poem on Joan of Arc, she chose the 'Vision and Death of Moses on Mount Nebo'* to write about; and, in looking over this *devoir*, I was much struck with one or two of M. Héger's remarks. After describing, in a quiet and simple manner, the circumstances under which Moses took leave of the Israelites, her imagination becomes warmed, and she launches out into a noble strain, depicting the glorious futurity of the Chosen People, as, looking down upon the Promised Land, he sees their prosperity in prophetic vision. But, before reaching the middle of this glowing description, she interrupts herself to discuss for a moment the doubts that have been thrown on the miraculous relations of the Old Testament. M. Héger remarks, 'When you are writing, place your argument first in cool, prosaic language; but when you have thrown the reins on the neck of your imagination, do not pull her up to reason.' Again, in the vision of Moses, he sees the maidens leading forth their flocks to the wells at eventide, and they are described as wearing flowery garlands. Here the writer is reminded of the necessity of preserving a certain verisimilitude: Moses might from his elevation see mountains and plains, groups of maidens and herds of cattle, but could hardly perceive the details of dress, or the ornaments of the head.

When they had made further progress, M. Héger took up a more advanced plan, that of synthetical teaching. He would read to them various accounts of the same person or event, and make them notice the points of agreement and disagreement. Where they were different, he would make them seek the origin of that difference by causing them to examine well into the character and position of each separate writer, and how they would be likely to affect his conception of truth. For instance, take Cromwell. He would read Bossuet's description of him in the 'Oraison Funèbre de la Reine d'Angleterre,'* and show how in this he was considered entirely from the religious point of view, as an instrument in the hands of God, pre-ordained to His work. Then he would make them read Guizot, and see how, in his view, Cromwell was endowed with the utmost power of free will, but governed by no higher motive than that of expediency; while Carlyle regarded him as a character regulated by a strong and conscientious desire to do the will of the Lord. Then he would desire them to remember that the Royalist and Commonwealth man had each their different opinions of the great Protector. And from these conflicting characters he would require them to sift and collect the elements of truth, and try to unite them into a perfect whole.

This kind of exercise delighted Charlotte. It called into play her powers of analysis, which were extraordinary, and she very soon excelled in it.

Wherever the Brontës could be national they were so, with the same tenacity of attachment which made them suffer as they did whenever they left Haworth. They were Protestant to the backbone in other things beside their religion, but pre-eminently so in that. Touched as Charlotte was by the letter of St Ignatius before alluded to, she claimed equal self-devotion, and from as high a motive, for some of the missionaries of the English Church sent out to toil and to perish on the poisonous African coast, and wrote as an 'imitation,' 'Lettre d'un Missionnaire, Sierra Léone, Afrique.'*

Something of her feeling, too, appears, in the following letter:—

'Brussels, 1842.*

'I consider it doubtful whether I shall come home in September or not. Madame Héger has made a proposal for both me and Emily to stay another half year, offering to dismiss her English master, and take me as English teacher; also to employ Emily some part of each day in teaching music to a certain number of the pupils. For these services we are to be allowed to continue our studies in French and German, and to have board, &c., without paying for it; no salaries, however, are offered. The proposal is kind, and in a great selfish city like Brussels, and a great selfish school, containing nearly ninety pupils (boarders and day pupils included), implies a degree of interest which demands gratitude in return. I am inclined to accept it. What think you? I don't deny I sometimes wish to be in England, or that I have brief attacks of home-sickness; but, on the whole, I have borne a very valiant heart so far; and I have been happy in Brussels, because I have always been fully occupied with the employments that I like. Emily is making rapid progress in French, German, music, and drawing. Monsieur and Madame Héger begin to recognise the valuable parts of her character, under her singularities. If the national character of the Belgians is to be measured by the character of most of the girls in this school, it is a character singularly cold, selfish, animal, and inferior. They are very mutinous and difficult for the teachers to manage; and their principles are rotten to the core. We avoid them, which it is not difficult to do, as we have the brand of Protestantism and Anglicism upon us. People talk of the danger which Protestants expose themselves to, in going to reside in Catholic countries, and thereby running the chance of changing their faith. My advice to all Protestants who are tempted to do anything so besotted as turn Catholics, is, to walk over the sea on to the Continent; to attend mass sedulously for a time; to note well the mummeries thereof; also the idiotic, mercenary aspect of all the priests; and *then*, if they are still disposed to consider Papistry in any other light than a most feeble, childish piece of humbug, let them turn Papists at once— that's all. I consider Methodism, Quakerism, and the extremes of High and Low Churchism foolish, but Roman Catholicism beats them all. At the same time, allow me to tell you, that there are some Catholics who are as good as any Christians can be to whom the Bible is a sealed book, and much better than many Protestants.'

When the Brontës first went to Brussels, it was with the intention of remaining there for six months, or until the *grandes vacances*\* began in September. The duties of the school were then suspended for six weeks or two months, and it seemed a desirable period for their return. But the proposal mentioned in the foregoing letter altered their plans. Besides, they were happy in the feeling that they were making progress in all the knowledge they had so long been yearning to acquire. They were happy, too, in possessing friends whose society had been for years congenial to them; and in occasional meetings with these, they could have the inexpressible solace to residents in a foreign country—and peculiarly such to the Brontës—of talking over the intelligence received from their respective homes—referring to past, or planning for future days. 'Mary' and her sister, the bright, dancing, laughing Martha, were parlour-boarders in an establishment just beyond the barriers of Brussels.* Again, the cousins of these friends* were resident in the town; and at their house Charlotte and Emily were always welcome, though their overpowering shyness prevented their more valuable qualities from being known, and generally kept them silent. They spent their weekly holiday with this family, for many months; but at the end of the time, Emily was as impenetrable to friendly advances as at the beginning; while Charlotte was too physically weak (as 'Mary' has expressed it) to 'gather up her forces' sufficiently to express any difference or opposition of opinion, and had consequently an assenting and deferential manner, strangely at variance with what they knew of her remarkable talents and decided character. At this house, the T.s and the Brontës could look forward to meeting each other pretty frequently. There was another English family* where Charlotte soon became a welcome guest, and where, I suspect, she felt herself more at her ease than either at Mrs Jenkins', or the friends' whom I have first mentioned.

An English physician, with a large family of daughters, went to reside at Brussels, for the sake of their education. He placed them at Madame Héger's* school in July, 1842, not a month before the beginning of the *grandes vacances* on August 15th. In order to make the most of their time, and become accustomed to the language, these English sisters went daily, through the holidays, to the pensionnat in the Rue d'Isabelle. Six or eight boarders remained, besides the Miss Brontës. They were there during the whole time, never even having the break to their monotonous life, which passing an occasional day with a friend would have afforded them; but devoting themselves with indefatigable diligence to the different studies in which they were engaged. Their position in the school appeared, to these new comers, analogous to what is often called that of a parlour-boarder.* They prepared their French, drawing, German, and literature for their various masters; and to these occupations Emily added that of music, in which she was somewhat of a proficient; so much so as to be qualified to give instruction in it to the three younger sisters of my informant.

The school was divided into three classes. In the first, were from fifteen to twenty pupils; in the second, sixty was about the average number—all foreigners, excepting the two Brontës and one other; in the third, there were from twenty to thirty pupils. The first and second classes occupied a long room, divided by a wooden partition; in each division were four long ranges of desks; and at the end was the *estrade*, or platform for the presiding instructor. On the last row, in the quietest corner, sat Charlotte and Emily, side by side, so deeply absorbed in their studies as to be insensible to any noise or movement around them. The school-hours were from nine to twelve (the luncheon hour), when the boarders and half-boarders—perhaps two-and-thirty girls—went to the refectoire (a room with two long tables, having an oil-lamp suspended over each), to partake of bread and fruit; the *externes*, or morning pupils, who had brought their own refreshment with them, adjourning to eat it in the garden. From one to two, there was fancy-work—a pupil reading aloud some light literature in each room; from two to four, lessons again. At four, the *externes* left; and the remaining girls dined in the refectoire, M. and Madame Héger presiding. From five to six there was recreation; from six to seven preparation for lessons; and, after that succeeded the *lecture pieuse**—Charlotte's nightmare. On rare occasions, M. Héger himself would come in, and substitute a book of a different and more interesting kind. At eight, there was a slight meal of water and *pistolets* (the delicious little Brussels rolls),* which was immediately followed by prayers, and then to bed.

The principal bed-room was over the long classe, or school-room. There were six or eight narrow beds on each side of the apartment, every one enveloped in its white draping curtain; a long drawer, beneath each, served for a wardrobe, and between each was a stand for ewer, basin, and looking-glass. The beds of the two Miss Brontës were at the extreme end of the room, almost as private and retired as if they had been in a separate apartment.

During the hours of recreation, which were always spent in the garden, they invariably walked together, and generally kept a profound silence; Emily, though so much the taller, leaning on her sister. Charlotte would always answer when spoken to, taking the lead in replying to any remark addressed to both; Emily rarely spoke to any one. Charlotte's quiet, gentle manner never changed. She was never seen out of temper for a moment; and occasionally, when she herself had assumed the post of English teacher, and the impertinence or inattention of her pupils was most irritating, a slight increase of colour, a momentary sparkling of the eye, and more decided energy of manner, were the only outward tokens she gave of being conscious of the annoyance to which she was subjected. But this dignified endurance of hers subdued her pupils, in the long run, far more than the voluble tirades of the other mistresses. My informant adds:—'The effect of this manner was singular. I can speak from personal experience. I was at that time high-spirited and impetuous, not respecting the French mistresses; yet, to my own astonishment, at one word from her, I was perfectly tractable; so much so, that at length, M. and Madame Héger invariably preferred all their wishes to me through her; the other pupils did not, perhaps, love her as I did, she was so quiet and silent, but all respected her.'

With the exception of that part which describes Charlotte's manner as English teacher—an office which she did not assume for some months later—all this description of the school life of the two Brontës refers to the commencement of the new scholastic year in October 1842; and the extracts I have given convey the first impression which the life at a foreign school, and the position of the two Miss Brontës therein, made upon an intelligent English girl of sixteen. I will make a quotation* from 'Mary's' letter referring to this time.

'The first part of her time at Brussels was not uninteresting. She spoke of new people and characters, and foreign ways, of the pupils and teachers. She knew the hopes and prospects of the teachers, and mentioned one who was very anxious to marry, "she was getting so old." She used to get her father or brother (I forget which) to be the bearer of letters to different single men, who she thought might be persuaded to do her the favour, saying that her only resource was to become a sister of charity if her present employment failed, and that she hated the idea. Charlotte naturally looked with curiosity to people of her own condition. This woman almost frightened her. "She declares there is nothing she can turn to, and laughs at the idea of delicacy,—and she is only ten years older than I am!" I did not see the connection till she said, "Well, Polly, I should hate being a sister of charity; I suppose that would shock some people, but I should." I thought she would have as much feeling as a nurse as most people, and more than some. She said she did not know how people could bear the constant pressure of misery, and never to change except to a new form of it. It would be impossible to keep one's natural feelings. I promised her a better destiny than to go begging any one to marry her, or to lose her natural feelings as a sister of charity. She said, "My youth is leaving me; I can never do better than I have done, and I have done nothing yet." At such times she seemed to think that most human beings were destined by the pressure of worldly interests to lose one faculty and feeling after another "till they went dead altogether. I hope I shall be put in my grave as soon as I'm dead; I don't want to walk about so." Here we always differed. I thought the degradation of nature she feared was a consequence of poverty, and that she should give her attention to earning money. Sometimes she admitted this, but could find no means of earning money. At others she seemed afraid of letting her thoughts dwell on the subject, saying it brought on the worst palsy of all. Indeed in her position nothing less than entire constant absorption in petty money matters could have scraped together a provision.

'Of course artists and authors stood high with Charlotte, and the best thing after their works would have been their company. She used very inconsistently to rail at money and money-getting, and then wish she was able to visit all the large towns in Europe, see all the sights, and know all the celebrities. This was her notion of literary fame,—a passport to the society of clever people. . . . When she had become acquainted with the people and ways at Brussels her life became monotonous, and she fell into the same hopeless state as at Miss W——'s, though in a less degree. I wrote to her, urging her to go home or elsewhere; she had got what she wanted (French), and there was at least novelty in a new place, if no improvement. That if she sank into deeper gloom she would soon not have energy to go, and she was too far from home for her friends to hear of her condition and order her home as they had done from Miss W——'s. She wrote that I had done her a great service, that she should certainly follow my advice, and was much obliged to me. I have often wondered at this letter. Though she patiently tolerated advice, she could always quietly put it aside, and do as she thought fit. More than once afterwards she mentioned the "service" I had done her. She sent me 10*l.* to New Zealand,* on hearing some exaggerated accounts of my circumstances, and told me she hoped it would come in seasonably; it was a debt she owed me "for the service I had done her." I should think 10*l.* was a quarter of her income. The "service" was mentioned as an apology, but kindness was the real motive.'

The first break in this life of regular duties and employments came heavily and sadly. Martha—pretty, winning, mischievous, tricksome Martha—was taken ill suddenly at the Château de Koekelberg. Her sister tended her with devoted love; but it was all in vain; in a few days she died.* Charlotte's own short account of this event is as follows:—*

'Martha T.'s illness was unknown to me till the day before she died. I hastened to Koekleberg the next morning—unconscious that she was in great danger—and was told that it was finished. She had died in the night. Mary was taken away to Bruxelles. I have seen Mary frequently since. She is in no ways crushed by the event; but while Martha was ill, she was to her more than a mother—more than a sister: watching, nursing, cherishing her so tenderly, so unweariedly. She appears calm and serious now; no bursts of violent emotion; no exaggeration of distress. I have seen Martha's grave—the place where her ashes lie in a foreign country.'

Who that has read 'Shirley' does not remember the few lines—perhaps half a page—of sad recollection?*

'He has no idea that little Jessy will die young, she is so gay, and chattering, and arch—original even now; passionate when provoked, but most affectionate if caressed; by turns gentle and rattling; exacting yet generous; fearless . . . . yet reliant on any who will help her. Jessy, with her little piquant face, engaging prattle, and winning ways, is made to be a pet.

\* \* \*

'Do you know this place? No, you never saw it; but you recognise the nature of these trees, this foliage—the cypress, the willow, the yew. Stone crosses like these are not unfamiliar to you, nor are these dim garlands of everlasting flowers. Here is the place; green sod and a grey marble head-stone—Jessy sleeps below. She lived through an April day; much loved was she, much loving. She often, in her brief life, shed tears—she had frequent sorrows; she smiled between, gladdening whatever saw her. Her death was tranquil and happy in Rose's guardian arms, for Rose had been her stay and defence through many trials; the dying and the watching English girls were at that hour alone in a foreign country, and the soil of that country gave Jessy a grave. \* \* \* \*

'But, Jessy, I will write about you no more. This is an autumn evening, wet and wild. There is only one cloud in the sky; but it curtains it from pole to pole. The wind cannot rest; it hurries sobbing over hills of sullen outline, colourless with twilight and mist. Rain has beat all day on that church tower' (Haworth): 'it rises dark from the stony enclosure of its graveyard: the nettles, the long grass, and the tombs all drip with wet. This evening reminds me too forcibly of another evening some years ago: a howling, rainy autumn evening too—when certain who had that day performed a pilgrimage to a grave new made in a heretic cemetery, sat near a wood fire on the hearth of a foreign dwelling. They were merry and social, but they each knew that a gap, never to be filled, had been made in their circle. They knew they had lost something whose absence could never be quite atoned for, so long as they lived; and they knew that heavy falling rain was soaking into the wet earth which covered their lost darling; and that the sad, sighing gale was mourning above her buried head. The fire warmed them; Life and Friendship yet blessed them: but Jessy lay cold, coffined, solitary—only the sod screening her from the storm.'

This was the first death that had occurred in the small circle of Charlotte's immediate and intimate friends since the loss of her two sisters long ago. She was still in the midst of her deep sympathy with 'Mary,' when word came from home that her aunt, Miss Branwell, was ailing—was very ill.\* Emily and Charlotte immediately resolved to go home straight, and hastily packed up for England, doubtful whether they should ever return to Brussels or not, leaving all their relations with M. and Madame Héger, and the pensionnat, uprooted, and uncertain of any future existence. Even before their departure, on the morning after they received the first intelligence of illness—when they were on the very point of starting—came a second letter, telling them of their aunt's death. It could not hasten their movements, for every arrangement had been made for speed. They sailed from Antwerp; they travelled night and day, and got home on a Tuesday morning. The funeral and all was over, and Mr Brontë and Anne were sitting together, in quiet grief for the loss of one who had done her part well in their household for nearly twenty years, and earned the regard and respect of many who never knew how much they should miss her till she was gone. The small property which she had accumulated, by dint of personal frugality and self-denial, was bequeathed to her nieces. Branwell, her darling, was to have had his share; but his reckless expenditure had distressed the good old lady, and his name was omitted in her will.*

When the first shock was over, the three sisters began to enjoy the full relish of meeting again, after the longest separation they had had in their lives. They had much to tell of the past, and much to settle for the future. Anne had been for some little time in a situation,* to which she was to return at the end of the Christmas holidays. For another year or so they were again to be all three apart; and, after that, the happy vision of being together and opening a school was to be realised. Of course they did not now look forward to settling at Burlington, or any other place which would take them away from their father; but the small sum which they each independently possessed would enable them to effect such alterations in the parsonage-house at Haworth as would adapt it to the reception of pupils. Anne's plans for the interval were fixed. Emily quickly decided to be the daughter to remain at home. About Charlotte there was much deliberation and some discussion.

Even in all the haste of their sudden departure from Brussels, M. Héger had found time to write a letter of sympathy to Mr Brontë on the loss which he had just sustained; a letter containing such a graceful appreciation of the daughters' characters, under the form of a tribute of respect to their father, that I should have been tempted to copy it, even had there not also been a proposal made in it respecting Charlotte, which deserves a place in the record of her life.*

'*Au Révérend Monsieur Brontë, Pasteur Évangélique, &c. &c.*

'Samedi, 5 9^{bre.}

'MONSIEUR,

'Un évènement bien triste décide mesdemoiselles vos filles à retourner brusquement en Angleterre, ce départ qui nous afflige beaucoup a cependant ma complète approbation; il est bien naturel qu'elles cherchent à vous consoler de ce que le ciel vient de vous ôter, en se serrant autour de vous, pour mieux vous faire apprécier ce que le ciel vous a donné et ce qu'il vous laisse encore. J'espère que vous me pardonnerez, Monsieur, de profiter de cette circon-stance pour vous faire parvenir l'expression de mon respect; je n'ai pas l'honneur de vous connaître personnellement, et cependant j'éprouve pour votre personne un sentiment de sincère vénération, car en jugeant un père de famille par ses enfants on ne risque pas de se tromper, et sous ce rapport l'éducation et les sentiments que nous avons trouvés dans mesdemoiselles vos filles n'ont pu que nous donner une très-haute idée de votre mérite et de votre caractère. Vous apprendrez sans doute avec plaisir que vos en-fants ont fait du progrès très-remarquable dans toutes les branches de l'enseignement, et que ces progrès sont entièrement dû à leur amour pour le travail et à leur persévérance; nous n'avons eu que bien peu à faire avec de pareilles élèves; leur avancement est votre œuvre bien plus que la nôtre; nous n'avons pas eu à leur apprendre le prix du temps et de l'instruction, elles avaient appris tout cela dans la maison paternelle, et nous n'avons eu, pour notre part, que le faible mérite de diriger leurs efforts et de fournir un aliment convenable à la louable activité que vos filles ont puisées dans votre exemple et dans vos leçons. Puissent les éloges méritées que nous donnons à vos enfants vous être de quelque consolation dans le malheur que vous afflige; c'est là notre espoir en vous écrivant, et ce sera, pour Mesdemoiselles Charlotte et Emily, une douce et belle récompense de leurs travaux.

'En perdant nos deux chères élèves, nous ne devons pas vous cacher que nous éprouvons à la fois et du chagrin et de l'inquiétude; nous sommes affligés parce que cette brusque séparation vient briser l'affection presque paternelle que nous leur avons vouée, et notre peine s'augmente à la vue de tant de travaux interrompues, de tant de choses bien commencées, et qui ne demandent que quelque temps encore pour être menées à bonne fin. Dans un an, chacune de vos demoiselles eût été entièrement prémunie contre les éventualités de l'avenir; chacune d'elles acquérait à la fois et l'instruction et la science d'enseignement; Mlle Emily allait apprendre le piano; recevoir les leçons du meilleur professeur que nous ayons en Belgique, et déjà elle avait elle-même de petites élèves; elle perdait donc à la fois un reste d'ignorance et un reste plus gênant encore de timidité; Mlle Charlotte commençait à donner des leçons en français, et d'acquérir cette assurance, cet aplomb si nécessaire dans l'enseignement; encore un an tout au plus et l'œuvre était achevée et bien achevée. Alors nous aurions pu, si cela vous eût convenu, offrir à mesdemoiselles vos filles ou du moins à l'une des deux une position qui eût été dans ses goûts, et qui lui eût donné cette douce indépendance si difficile à trouver pour une jeune personne. Ce n'est pas, croyez le bien, Monsieur, ce n'est pas ici pour nous une question d'intérêt personnel, c'est une question d'affection; vous me pardonnerez si nous vous parlons de vos enfants, si nous nous occupons de leur avenir, comme si elles faisaient partie de notre famille; leurs qualités personnelles, leur bon vouloir, leur zèle extrême sont les seules causes qui nous poussent à nous hasarder de la sorte. Nous savons, Monsieur, que vous peserez plus mûrement et plus sagement que nous la conséquence qu'aurait pour l'avenir une interruption complète dans les études de vos deux filles; vous déciderez ce qu'il faut faire, et vous nous pardonnerez notre franchise, si vous daignez considérer que le motif qui nous fait agir est une affection bien désintéressée et qui s'affligerait beaucoup de devoir déjà se résigner à n'être plus utile à vos chers enfants.

'Agréez, je vous prie, Monsieur, l'expression respectueuse de mes sentiments de haute considération.

'C. HÉGER.'

There was so much truth, as well as so much kindness in this letter—it was so obvious that a second year of instruction would be far more valuable than the first, that there was no long hesitation before it was decided that Charlotte should return to Brussels.

Meanwhile, they enjoyed their Christmas all together inexpressibly. Branwell was with them; that was always a pleasure at this time; whatever might be his faults, or even his vices, his sisters yet held him up as their family hope, as they trusted that he would some day be their family pride. They blinded themselves to the magnitude of the failings of which they were now and then told, by persuading themselves that such failings were common to all men of any strength of character; for, till sad experience taught them better, they fell into the usual error of confounding strong passions with strong character.

Charlotte's friend came over to see her, and she returned the visit. Her Brussels life must have seemed like a dream, so completely, in this short space of time, did she fall back into the old household ways; with more of household independence than she could ever have had during her aunt's lifetime. Winter though it was, the sisters took their accustomed walks on the snow-covered moors; or went often down the long road to Keighley, for such books as had been added to the library there during their absence from England.

# CHAPTER XII

TOWARDS the end of January, the time came for Charlotte to return to Brussels. Her journey thither was rather disastrous. She had to make her way alone; and the train from Leeds to London, which should have reached Euston-square early in the afternoon, was so much delayed that it did not get in till ten at night.* She had intended to seek out the Chapter Coffee-house, where she had stayed before, and which would have been near the place where the steam-boats lay; but she appears to have been frightened by the idea of arriving at an hour which, to Yorkshire notions, was so late and unseemly; and taking a cab, therefore, at the station, she drove straight to the London Bridge Wharf, and desired a waterman to row her to the Ostend packet, which was to sail the next morning. She described to me, pretty much as she has since described it in 'Villette,'* her sense of loneliness, and yet her strange pleasure in the excitement of the situation, as in the dead of that winter's night she went swiftly over the dark river to the black hull's side, and was at first refused leave to ascend to the deck. 'No passengers might sleep on board,' they said, with some appearance of disrespect. She looked back to the lights and subdued noises of London—that 'Mighty Heart'* in which she had no place—and, standing up in the rocking boat, she asked to speak to some one in authority on board the packet. He came, and her quiet simple statement of her wish, and her reason for it, quelled the feeling of sneering distrust in those who had first heard her request; and impressed the authority so favourably that he allowed her to come on board, and take possession of a berth. The next morning she sailed; and at seven on Sunday evening she reached the Rue d'Isabelle once more; having only left Haworth on Friday morning at an early hour.

Her salary was 16*l.* a year;* out of which she had to pay for her German lessons, for which she was charged as much (the lessons being probably rated by time) as when Emily learnt with her and divided the expense; viz., ten francs a month. By Miss Brontë's own desire, she gave her English lessons in the *classe*, or school-room, without the supervision of Madame or M. Héger.* They offered to be present, with a view to maintain order among the unruly Belgian girls; but she declined this, saying that she would rather enforce discipline by her own manner and character than be indebted for obedience to the presence of a *gendarme*. She ruled over a new school-room, which had been built on the space in the play-ground adjoining the house. Over that First Class she was *surveillante* at all hours; and henceforward she was called *Madem-oiselle* Charlotte, by M. Héger's orders. She continued her own studies, principally attending to German, and to Literature; and every Sunday she went alone to the German and English chapels.* Her walks too were solitary, and principally taken in the allée défendue,* where she was secure from intrusion. This solitude was a perilous luxury to one of her temperament; so liable as she was to morbid and acute mental suffering.

On March 6th, 1843, she writes thus:—*

'I am settled by this time, of course. I am not too much overloaded with occupation; and besides teaching English, I have time to improve myself in German. I ought to consider myself well off, and to be thankful for my good fortunes. I hope I am thankful; and if I could always keep up my spirits, and never feel lonely, or long for companionship, or friendship, or whatever they call it, I should do very well. As I told you before, M. and Madame Héger are the only two persons in the house for whom I really experience regard and esteem, and, of course, I cannot be always with them, nor even very often. They told me, when I first returned, that I was to consider their sitting-room my sitting-room also, and to go there whenever I was not engaged in the school-room. This, however, I cannot do. In the day-time it is a public room, where music-masters and mistresses are constantly passing in and out; and in the evening, I will not, and ought not to intrude on M. and Madame Héger and their children.* Thus I am a good deal by myself, out of school-hours; but that does not signify. I now regularly give English lessons to M. Héger and his brother-in-law.* They get on with wonderful rapidity; especially the first. He already begins to speak English very decently. If you could see and hear the efforts I make to teach them to pronounce like English-men, and their unavailing attempts to imitate, you would laugh to all eternity.

'The Carnival is just over, and we have entered upon the gloom and abstinence of Lent. The first day of Lent we had coffee without milk for breakfast; vinegar and vegetables, with a very little salt fish, for dinner; and bread for supper. The Carnival was nothing but masking and mummery. M. Héger took me and one of the pupils into the town to see the masks. It was animating to see the immense crowds, and the general gaiety, but the masks were nothing. I have been twice to the D.s' (those cousins of 'Mary's' of whom I have before made mention). 'When she leaves Bruxelles, I shall have nowhere to go to. I have had two letters from Mary. She does not tell me she has been ill, and she does not complain; but her letters are not the letters of a person in the enjoyment of great happiness. She has nobody to be as good to her as M. Héger is to me; to lend her books; to converse with her sometimes, &c.

'Good-bye. When I say so, it seems to me that you will hardly hear me; all the waves of the Channel heaving and roaring between must deaden the sound.'

From the tone of this letter, it may easily be perceived that the Brussels of 1843 was a different place from that of 1842. Then she had Emily for a daily and nightly solace and companion. She had the weekly variety of a visit to the family of the D.s; and she had the frequent happiness of seeing 'Mary' and Martha. Now Emily was far away in Haworth—where she, or any other loved one, might die, before Charlotte, with her utmost speed, could reach them, as experience, in her aunt's case, had taught her. The D.s were leaving Brussels; so, henceforth, her weekly holiday would have to be passed in the Rue d'Isabelle, or so she thought. 'Mary' was gone off on her own independent course; Martha alone remained—still and quiet for ever, in the cemetery beyond the Porte de Louvain. The weather, too, for the first few weeks after Charlotte's return, had been piercingly cold; and her feeble constitution was always painfully sensitive to an inclement season. Mere bodily pain, however acute, she could always put aside; but too often ill-health assailed her in a part far more to be dreaded. Her depression of spirits, when she was not well, was pitiful in its extremity. She was aware that it was constitutional, and could reason about it; but no reasoning prevented her suffering mental agony, while the bodily cause remained in force.

The Hégers have discovered, since the publication of 'Villette,'* that at this beginning of her career as English teacher in their school, the conduct of her pupils was often impertinent and mutinous in the highest degree. But of this they were unaware at the time, as she had declined their presence, and never made any complaint. Still, it must have been a depressing thought to her at this period, that her joyous, healthy, obtuse pupils were so little answerable to the powers she could bring to bear upon them; and though, from their own testimony, her patience, firmness, and resolution, at length obtained their just reward, yet, with one so weak in health and spirits, the reaction after such struggles as she frequently had with her pupils, must have been very sad and painful.

She thus writes to her friend E.:—

'April, 1843.*

'Is there any talk of your coming to Brussels? During the bitter cold weather we had through February, and the principal part of March, I did not regret that you had not accompanied me. If I had seen you shivering as I shivered myself, if I had seen your hands and feet as red and swelled as mine were, my discomfort would just have been doubled. I can do very well under this sort of thing; it does not fret me; it only makes me numb and silent; but if you were to pass a winter in Belgium, you would be ill. However, more genial weather is coming now, and I wish you were here. Yet I never have pressed you, and never would press you too warmly to come. There are privations and humiliations to submit to; there is monotony and uniformity of life; and, above all, there is a constant sense of solitude in the midst of numbers. The Protestant, the foreigner, is a solitary being, whether as teacher or pupil. I do not say this by way of complaining of my own lot; for though I acknowledge that there are certain disadvantages in my present position, what position on earth is without them? And, whenever I turn back to compare what I am with what I was—my place here with my place at Mrs ——'s for instance—I am thankful. There was an observation in your last letter which excited, for a moment, my wrath. At first, I thought it would be folly to reply to it, and I would let it die. Afterwards, I determined to give one answer, once for all. "Three or four people," it seems, "have the idea that the future *époux* of Mademoiselle Brontë is on the Continent." These people are wiser than I am. They could not believe that I crossed the sea merely to return as teacher to Madame Héger's. I must have some more powerful motive than respect for my master and mistress, gratitude for their kindness, &c., to induce me to refuse a salary of 50*l.* in England, and accept one of 16*l.* in Belgium. I must, forsooth, have some remote hope of entrapping a husband somehow, or somewhere. If these charitable people knew the total seclusion of the life I lead,—that I never exchange a word with any other man than Monsieur Héger, and seldom indeed with him,—they would, perhaps, cease to suppose that any such chimerical and groundless notion had influenced my proceedings. Have I said enough to clear myself of so silly an imputation? Not that it is a crime to marry, or a crime to wish to be married; but it is an imbecility, which I reject with contempt, for women, who have neither fortune nor beauty, to make marriage the principal object of their wishes and hopes, and the aim of all their actions; not to be able to convince themselves that they are unattractive, and that they had better be quiet, and think of other things than wedlock.'

The following is an extract, from one of the few letters which have been preserved, of her correspondence with her sister Emily.

'May 29. 1843.*

'I get on here from day to day in a Robinson-Crusoe-like sort of way, very lonely, but that does not signify. In other respects, I have nothing substantial to complain of, nor is this a cause for complaint. I hope you are well. Walk out often on the moors. My love to Tabby. I hope she keeps well.'

And about this time she wrote to her father.

'June 2nd, 1843.

'I was very glad to hear from home. I had begun to get low-spirited at not receiving any news, and to entertain indefinite fears that something was wrong. You do not say anything about your own health, but I hope you are well, and Emily also. I am afraid she will have a good deal of hard work to do now that Hannah'* (a servant-girl who had been assisting Tabby) 'is gone. I am exceedingly glad to hear that you still keep Tabby' (considerably upwards of seventy). 'It is an act of great charity to her, and I do not think it will be unrewarded, for she is very faithful, and will always serve you, when she has occasion, to the best of her abilities; besides, she will be company for Emily, who, without her, would be very lonely.'

I gave a *devoir*, written after she had been four months under M. Héger's tuition. I will now copy out another, written nearly a year later, during which the progress made appears to me very great.

'31 Mai, 1843.*

'SUR LA MORT DE NAPOLÉON

'Napoléon naquit en Corse et mourut à Ste Hélène. Entre ces deux îles rien qu'un vaste et brûlant désert et l'océan immense. Il naquit fils d'un simple gentilhomme, et mourut empereur, mais sans couronne et dans les fers. Entre son berceau et sa tombe qu'y a-t-il? la carrière d'un soldat parvenu, des champs de bataille, une mer de sang, un trône, puis du sang encore, et des fers. Sa vie, c'est l'arc en ciel; les deux points extrêmes touchent la terre, la comble lumineuse mesure les cieux. Sur Napoléon au berceau une mère brillait; dans la maison paternelle il avait des frères et des sœurs; plus tard dans son palais il eut une femme qui l'aimait. Mais sur son lit de mort Napoléon est seul; plus de mère, ni de frère, ni de sœur, ni de femme, ni d'enfant!! D'autres ont dit et rediront ses exploits, moi, je m'arrête à contempler l'abandonnement de sa dernière heure!

'Il est là, exilé et captif, enchaîné sur un écueil. Nouveau Prométhée, il subit le châtiment de son orgueil! Prométhée avait voulu être Dieu et Créateur; il déroba le feu du Ciel pour animer le corps qu'il avait formé. Et lui, Buonaparte, il a voulu créer, non pas un homme, mais un empire, et pour donner une existence, une âme, à son œuvre gigantesque, il n'a pas hésité à arracher la vie à des nations entières. Jupiter indigné de l'impiété de Prométhée, le riva vivant à la cime du Caucase. Ainsi, pour punir l'ambition rapace de Buonaparte, la Providence l'a enchaîné, jusqu'à ce que la mort s'en suivit, sur un roc isolé de l'Atlantique. Peut-être là aussi a-t-il senti lui fouillant le flanc cet insatiable vautour dont parle la fable, peut-être a-t-il souffert aussi cette soif du cœur, cette faim de l'âme, qui torturent l'exilé, loin de sa famille et de sa patrie. Mais parler ainsi n'est-ce pas attribuer gratuitement à Napoléon une humaine faiblesse qu'il n'éprouva jamais? Quand donc s'est-il laissé enchaîner par un lien d'affection? Sans doute d'autres conquérants ont hésité dans leur carrière de gloire, arrêtés par un obstacle d'amour ou d'amitié, retenus par la main d'une femme, rappelés par la voix d'un ami—lui, jamais! Il n'eut pas besoin, comme Ulysse, de se lier au mât du navire, ni de se boucher les oreilles avec de la cire; il ne redoutait pas le chant des Sirènes—il le dédaignait; il se fit marbre et fer pour exécuter ses grands projets. Napoléon ne se regardait pas comme un homme, mais comme l'incarnation d'un peuple. Il n'aimait pas; il ne considérait ses amis et ses proches que comme des instruments auxquels il tint, tant qu'ils furent utiles, et qu'il jeta de côté quand ils cessèrent de l'être. Qu'on ne se permette donc pas d'approcher du sépulcre du Corse avec sentiments de pitié, ou de souiller de larmes la pierre qui couvre ses restes, son âme répudierait tout cela. On a dit, je le sais, qu'elle fut cruelle la main qui le sépara de sa femme et de son enfant. Non, c'était une main qui, comme la sienne, ne tremblait ni de passion ni de crainte, c'était la main d'un homme froid, convaincu, qui avait su deviner Buonaparte; et voici ce que disait cet homme que la défaite n'a pu humilier, ni la victoire enorgueillir. "Marie-Louise n'est pas la femme de Napoléon; c'est la France que Napoléon a épousée; c'est la France qu'il aime, leur union enfante la perte de l'Europe; voilà le divorce que je veux; voilà l'union qu'il faut briser."

'La voix des timides et des traîtres protesta contre cette sentence. "C'est abuser de droit de la victoire! C'est fouler aux pieds le vaincu! Que l'Angleterre se montre clémente, qu'elle ouvre ses bras pour recevoir comme hôte son ennemi désarmé." L'Angleterre aurait peut-être écouté ce conseil, car partout et toujours il y a des âmes faibles et timorées bientôt séduites par la flatterie ou effrayées par le reproche. Mais la Providence permit qu'un homme se trouvât qui n'a jamais su ce que c'est que la crainte; qui aima sa patrie mieux que sa renommée; impénétrable devant les menaces, inaccessible aux louanges, il se présenta devant le conseil de la nation, et levant son front tranquille et haut, il osa dire: "Que la trahison se taise! car c'est trahir que de conseiller de temporiser avec Buonaparte. Moi je sais ce que sont ces guerres dont l'Europe saigne encore, comme une victime sous le couteau du boucher. Il faut en finir avec Napoléon Buonaparte. Vous vous effrayez à tort d'un mot si dur! Je n'ai pas de magnanimité, dit-on? Soit! que m'importe ce qu'on dit de moi? Je n'ai pas ici à me faire une réputation de héros magnanime, mais à guérir, si la cure est possible, l'Europe qui se meurt, épuisée de ressources et de sang, l'Europe dont vous négligez les vrais intérêts, préoccupés que vous êtes d'une vaine renommée de clémence. Vous êtes faibles. Eh bien! je viens vous aider. Envoyez Buonaparte à Ste Hélène! n'hésitez pas, ne cherchez pas un autre endroit; c'est le seul convenable. Je vous le dis, j'ai réfléchi pour vous; c'est là qu'il doit être, et non pas ailleurs. Quant à Napoléon, homme, soldat, je n'ai rien contre lui; c'est un Lion Royal, auprès de qui vous n'êtes que des Chacals. Mais Napoléon Empereur, c'est autre chose, je l'extirperai du sol de l'Europe." Et celui qui parla ainsi toujours sut garder sa promesse, celle-là comme toutes les autres. Je l'ai dit, et je le répète, cet homme est l'égal de Napoléon par le génie; comme trempe de caractère, comme droiture, comme élévation de pensée et de but, il est d'une tout autre espèce. Napoléon Buonaparte était avide de renommée et de gloire; Arthur Wellesley ne se soucie ni de l'une ni de l'autre; l'opinion publique, la popularité, étaient choses de grand valeur aux yeux de Napoléon; pour Wellington l'opinion publique est une rumeur, un rien que le souffle de son inflexible volonté fait disparaître comme une bulle de savon. Napoléon flattait le peuple; Wellington le brusque; l'un cherchait les applaudissements, l'autre ne se soucie que du témoignage de sa conscience; quand elle approuve, c'est assez; toute autre louange l'obsède. Aussi ce peuple, qui adorait Buonaparte, s'irritait, s'insurgeait contre la morgue de Wellington; parfois il lui témoigna sa colère et sa haine par des grognements, par des hurlements de bêtes fauves; et alors, avec une impassibilité de sénateur romain, le moderne Coriolan, toisait du regard l'émeute furieuse; il croisait ses bras nerveux sur sa large poitrine, et seul, debout sur son seuil, il attendait, il bravait cette tempête populaire dont les flots venaient mourir à quelques pas de lui: et quand la foule, honteuse de sa rebellion, venait lécher les pieds du maître, le hautain patricien méprisait l'hommage d'aujourd'hui comme la haine d'hier, et dans les rues de Londres, et devant son palais ducal d'Apsley, il repoussait d'un genre plein de froid dédain l'incommode empressement du peuple enthousiaste. Cette fierté néanmoins n'excluait pas en lui une rare modestie; partout il se soustrait à l'éloge; se dérobe au panégyrique; jamais il ne parle de ses exploits, et jamais il ne souffre qu'un autre que lui en parle en sa présence. Son caractère égale en grandeur et surpasse en vérité celui de tout autre héros ancien ou moderne. La gloire de Napoléon crût en une nuit, comme la vigne de Jonas, et il suffit d'un jour pour la flétrir; la gloire de Wellington est comme les vieux chênes qui ombragent le château de ses pères sur les rives du Shannon; le chêne croît lentement; il lui faut du temps pour pousser vers le ciel ses branches noueuses, et pour enfoncer dans le sol ces racines profondes qui s'enchevêtrent dans les fondements solides de la terre; mais alors, l'arbre séculaire, inébranlable comme le roc où il a sa base, brave et la faux du temps et l'effort des vents et des tempêtes. Il faudra peut-être un siècle à l'Angleterre pour qu'elle connaisse la valeur de son héros. Dans un siècle, l'Europe entière saura combien Wellington a de droits à sa reconnaissance.'

How often in writing this paper 'in a strange land,'* must Miss Brontë have thought of the old childish disputes in the kitchen of Haworth parsonage, touching the respective merits of Wellington and Buonaparte! Although the title given to her *devoir* is, 'On the Death of Napoleon,' she seems yet to have considered it a point of honour rather to sing praises to an English hero than to dwell on the character of a foreigner, placed as she was among those who cared little either for England or for Wellington. She now felt that she had made great progress towards obtaining proficiency in the French language, which had been her main object in coming to Brussels. But to the zealous learner 'Alps on Alps arise.'* No sooner is one difficulty surmounted than some other desirable attainment appears, and must be laboured after. A knowledge of German now became her object; and she resolved to compel herself to remain in Brussels till that was gained. The strong yearning to go home came upon her; the stronger self-denying will forbade. There was a great internal struggle; every fibre of her heart quivered in the strain to master her will; and, when she conquered herself, she remained, not like a victor calm and supreme on the throne, but like a panting, torn, and suffering victim. Her nerves and her spirits gave way. Her health became much shaken.*

'Brussels, August 1st, 1843.*

'If I complain in this letter, have mercy and don't blame me, for, I forewarn you, I am in low spirits, and that earth and heaven are dreary and empty to me at this moment. In a few days our vacation will begin; everybody is joyous and animated at the prospect, because everybody is to go home. I know that I am to stay here during the five weeks that the holidays last, and that I shall be much alone during that time, and consequently get downcast, and find both days and nights of a weary length. It is the first time in my life that I have really dreaded the vacation. Alas! I can hardly write, I have such a dreary weight at my heart; and I do so wish to go home. Is not this childish? Pardon me, for I cannot help it. However, though I am not strong enough to bear up cheerfully, I can still bear up; and I will continue to stay (D. V.) some months longer, till I have acquired German; and then I hope to see all your faces again. Would that the vacation were well over! it will pass so slowly. Do have the Christian charity to write me a long, long letter; fill it with the minutest details; nothing will be uninteresting. Do not think it is because people are unkind to me that I wish to leave Belgium; nothing of the sort. Everybody is abundantly civil, but home-sickness keeps creeping over me. I cannot shake it off. Believe me, very merrily, vivaciously, gaily, yours,

'C. B.'

The *grandes vacances* began soon after the date of this letter, when she was left in the great deserted pensionnat, with only one teacher for companion. This teacher, a Frenchwoman, had always been uncongenial to her;* but, left to each other's sole companionship, Charlotte soon discovered that her associate was more profligate, more steeped in a kind of cold, systematic sensuality, than she had before imagined it possible for a human being to be; and her whole nature revolted from this woman's society. A low nervous fever was gaining upon Miss Brontë. She had never been a good sleeper, but now she could not sleep at all. Whatever had been disagreeable, or obnoxious, to her during the day, was presented when it was over with exaggerated vividness to her disordered fancy. There were causes for distress and anxiety in the news from home, particularly as regarded Branwell. In the dead of the night, lying awake at the end of the long deserted dormitory, in the vast and silent house, every fear respecting those whom she loved, and who were so far off in another country, became a terrible reality, oppressing her and choking up the very life-blood in her heart. Those nights were times of sick, dreary, wakeful misery; precursors of many such in after years.

In the day-time, driven abroad by loathing of her companion and by the weak restlessness of fever, she tried to walk herself into such a state of bodily fatigue as would induce sleep. So she went out, and with weary steps would traverse the Boulevards and the streets, sometimes for hours together; faltering and resting occasionally on some of the many benches placed for the repose of happy groups, or for solitary wanderers like herself. Then up again—anywhere but to the pensionnat—out to the cemetery where Martha lay—out beyond it, to the hills whence there is nothing to be seen but fields as far as the horizon. The shades of evening made her retrace her footsteps—sick for want of food, but not hungry; fatigued with long continued exercise—yet restless still, and doomed to another weary, haunted night of sleeplessness. She would thread the streets in the neighbourhood of the Rue d'Isabelle, and yet avoid it and its occupant, till as late an hour as she dared be out. At last, she was compelled to keep her bed for some days, and this compulsory rest did her good. She was weak, but less depressed in spirits than she had been, when the school re-opened, and her positive practical duties recommenced.

She writes thus:—

'October 13th, 1843.*

'Mary is getting on well, as she deserves to do. I often hear from her. Her letters and yours are one of my few pleasures. She urges me very much to leave Brussels and go to her;* but, at present, however tempted to take such a step, I should not feel justified in doing so. To leave a certainty for a complete uncertainty, would be to the last degree imprudent. Notwithstanding that, Brussels is indeed desolate to me now. Since the D.s left, I have had no friend. I had, indeed, some very kind acquaintances in the family of a

Dr ——, but they too are gone now. They left in the latter part of August, and I am completely alone. I cannot count the Belgians anything. It is a curious position to be so utterly solitary in the midst of numbers. Sometimes the solitude oppresses me to an excess. One day, lately, I felt as if I could bear it no longer, and I went to Madame Héger, and gave her notice. If it had depended on her, I should certainly have soon been at liberty; but M. Héger, having heard of what was in agitation, sent for me the day after, and pronounced with vehemence his decision, that I should not leave. I could not, at that time, have persevered in my intention without exciting him to anger; so I promised to stay a while longer. How long that will be, I do not know. I should not like to return to England to do nothing. I am too old for that now; but if I could hear of a favourable opportunity for commencing a school, I think I should embrace it. We have as yet no fires here, and I suffer much from cold; otherwise, I am well in health. Mr —— will take this letter to England. He is a pretty-looking and pretty behaved young man, apparently constructed without a backbone; by which I don't allude to his corporeal spine, which is all right enough, but to his character.

'I get on here after a fashion;* but now that Mary D. has left Brussels, I have nobody to speak to, for I count the Belgians as nothing. Sometimes I ask myself how long shall I stay here; but as yet I have only asked the question; I have not answered it. However, when I have acquired as much German as I think fit, I think I shall pack up bag and baggage, and depart. Twinges of home-sickness cut me to the heart, every now and then. To-day the weather is glaring, and I am stupified with a bad cold and headache. I have nothing to tell you. One day is like another in this place. I know you, living in the country, can hardly believe it is possible life can be monotonous in the centre of a brilliant capital like Brussels; but so it is. I feel it most on holidays, when all the girls and teachers go out to visit, and it sometimes happens that I am left, during several hours, quite alone, with four great desolate school-rooms at my disposition. I try to read, I try to write; but in vain. I then wander about from room to room, but the silence and loneliness of all the house weighs down one's spirits like lead. You will hardly believe that Madame Héger (good and kind as I have described her) never comes near me on these occasions.* I own, I was astonished the first time I was left alone thus; when everybody else was enjoying the pleasures of a fête day with their friends, and she knew I was quite by myself, and never took the least notice of me. Yet, I understand, she praises me very much to everybody, and says what excellent lessons I give. She is not colder to me than she is to the other teachers; but they are less dependent on her than I am. They have relations and acquaintances in Bruxelles. You remember the letter she wrote me, when I was in England? How kind and affectionate that was? is it not odd? In the meantime, the complaints I make at present are a sort of relief which I permit myself. In all other respects I am well satisfied with my position, and you may say so to people who inquire after me (if any one does). Write to me, dear, whenever you can. You do a good deed when you send me a letter, for you comfort a very desolate heart.'

One of the reasons for the silent estrangement between Madame Héger and Miss Brontë, in the second year of her residence at Brussels, is to be found in the fact, that the English Protestant's dislike of Romanism increased with her knowledge of it, and its effects upon those who professed it; and when occasion called for an expression of opinion from Charlotte Brontë, she was uncompromising truth. Madame Héger, on the opposite side, was not merely a Roman Catholic, she was *dévote*. Not of a warm or impulsive temperament, she was naturally governed by her conscience, rather than by her affections; and her conscience was in the hands of her religious guides. She considered any slight thrown upon her church as blasphemy against the Holy Truth; and, though she was not given to open expression of her thoughts and feelings, yet her increasing coolness of behaviour showed how much her most cherished opinions had been wounded. Thus, although there was never any explanation of Madame Héger's change of manner, this may be given as one great reason why, about this time, Charlotte was made painfully conscious of a silent estrangement between them; an estrangement of which, perhaps, the former was hardly aware. I have before alluded to intelligence from home, calculated to distress Charlotte exceedingly with fears respecting Branwell, which I shall speak of more at large when the realisation of her worst apprehensions came to affect the daily life of herself and her sisters. I allude to the subject again here, in order that the reader may remember the gnawing, private cares, which she had to bury in her own heart; and the pain of which could only be smothered for a time under the diligent fulfilment of present duty. Another dim sorrow was faintly perceived at this time. Her father's eyesight began to fail; it was not unlikely that he might shortly become blind; more of his duty must devolve on a curate, and Mr Brontë, always liberal, would have to pay at a higher rate than he had heretofore done for this assistance.

She wrote thus to Emily:—

'Dec. 1st, 1843.*

'This is Sunday morning. They are at their idolatrous "messe," and I am here, that is in the Refectoire. I should like uncommonly to be in the dining-room at home, or in the kitchen, or in the back kitchen. I should like even to be cutting up the hash, with the clerk and some register people* at the other table, and you standing by, watching that I put enough flour, not too much pepper, and, above all, that I save the best pieces of the leg of mutton for Tiger and Keeper,* the first of which personages would be jumping about the dish and carving-knife, and the latter standing like a devouring flame on the kitchen-floor. To complete the picture, Tabby blowing the fire, in order to boil the potatoes to a sort of vegetable glue! How divine are these recollections to me at this moment! Yet I have no thought of coming home just now. I lack a real pretext for doing so; it is true this place is dismal to me, but I cannot go home without a fixed prospect when I get there; and this prospect must not be a situation; that would be jumping out of the frying pan into the fire. *You* call yourself idle! absurd, absurd! .... Is papa well? Are you well? and Tabby? You ask about Queen Victoria's visit to Brussels.* I saw her for an instant flashing through the Rue Royale in a carriage and six, surrounded by soldiers. She was laughing and talking very gaily. She looked a little stout, vivacious lady, very plainly dressed, not much dignity or pretension about her. The Belgians liked her very well on the whole. They said she enlivened the sombre court of King Leopold, which is usually as gloomy as a conventicle. Write to me again soon. Tell me whether papa really wants me very much to come home, and whether you do likewise. I have an idea that I should be of no use there—a sort of aged person upon the parish. I pray, with heart and soul, that all may continue well at Haworth; above all in our grey half-inhabited house. God bless the walls thereof! Safety, health, happiness, and prosperity to you, papa, and Tabby. Amen.

'C. B.'

Towards the end of this year (1843) various reasons* conspired with the causes of anxiety which have been mentioned, to make her feel that her presence was absolutely and imperatively required at home, while she had acquired all that she proposed to herself in coming to Brussels the second time; and was, moreover, no longer regarded with the former kindliness of feeling by Madame Héger. In consequence of this state of things, working down with sharp edge into a sensitive mind, she suddenly announced to that lady her immediate intention of returning to England. Both M. and Madame Héger agreed that it would be for the best, when they learnt only that part of the case which she could reveal to them—namely, Mr Brontë's increasing blindness. But as the inevitable moment of separation from people and places, among which she had spent so many happy hours, drew near, her spirits gave way; she had the natural presentiment that she saw them all for the last time, and she received but a dead kind of comfort from being reminded by her friends that Brussels and Haworth were not so very far apart; that access from one place to the other was not so difficult or impracticable as her tears would seem to predicate; nay, there was some talk of one of Madame Héger's daughters being sent to her as a pupil if she fulfilled her intention of trying to begin a school. To facilitate her success in this plan, should she ever engage in it, M. Héger gave her a kind of diploma, dated from, and sealed with the seal of the Athénée Royal de Bruxelles, certifying that she was perfectly capable of teaching the French language, having well studied the grammar and composition thereof, and, moreover, having prepared herself for teaching by studying and practising the best methods of instruction. This certificate is dated December 29th, 1843, and on the 2nd of January, 1844, she arrived at Haworth.

On the 23rd of the month she writes as follows:—*

'Every one asks me what I am going to do, now that I am returned home; and every one seems to expect that I should immediately commence a school. In truth it is what I should wish to do. I desire it above all things. I have sufficient money for the undertaking, and I hope now sufficient qualifications to give me a fair chance of success; yet I cannot yet permit myself to enter upon life—to touch the object which seems now within my reach, and which I have been so long straining to attain. You will ask me why? It is on papa's account; he is now, as you know, getting old, and it grieves me to tell you that he is losing his sight. I have felt for some months that I ought not to be away from him; and I feel now that it would be too selfish to leave him (at least, as long as Branwell and Anne are absent), in order to pursue selfish interests of my own. With the help of God, I will try to deny myself in this matter, and to wait.

'I suffered much before I left Brussels. I think, however long I live, I shall not forget what the parting with M. Héger cost me. It grieved me so much to grieve him who has been so true, kind, and disinterested a friend. At parting he gave me a kind of diploma certifying my abilities as a teacher, sealed with the seal of the Athénée Royal, of which he is professor. I was surprised also at the degree of regret expressed by my Belgian pupils, when they knew I was going to leave. I did not think it had been in their phlegmatic nature. . . . . . . I do not know whether you feel as I do, but there are times now when it appears to me as if all my ideas and feelings, except a few friendships and affections, are changed from what they used to be; something in me, which used to be enthusiasm, is tamed down and broken. I have fewer illusions; what I wish for now is active exertion—a stake in life. Haworth seems such a lonely, quiet spot, buried away from the world. I no longer regard myself as young—indeed, I shall soon be twenty-eight; and it seems as if I ought to be working and braving the rough realities of the world, as other people do. It is, however, my duty to restrain this feeling at present, and I will endeavour to do so.'

Of course her absent sister and brother obtained a holiday to welcome her return home, and in a few weeks she was spared to pay a visit to her friend at B. But she was far from well or strong, and the short journey of fourteen miles seems to have fatigued her greatly.

Soon after she came back to Haworth, in a letter to one of the household in which she had been staying,* there occurs this passage:—'Our poor little cat has been ill two days, and is just dead. It is piteous to see even an animal lying lifeless. Emily is sorry.' These few words relate to points in the characters of the two sisters, which I must dwell upon a little. Charlotte was more than commonly tender in her treatment of all dumb creatures, and they, with that fine instinct so often noticed, were invariably attracted towards her. The deep and exaggerated consciousness of her personal defects—the constitutional absence of hope, which made her slow to trust in human affection, and consequently slow to respond to any manifestation of it—made her manner shy and constrained to men and women, and even to children. We have seen something of this trembling distrust of her own capability of inspiring affection, in the grateful surprise she expresses at the regret felt by her Belgian pupils at her departure. But not merely were her actions kind, her words and tones were ever gentle and caressing, towards animals; and she quickly noticed the least want of care or tenderness on the part of others towards any poor brute creature. The readers of 'Shirley'* may remember that it is one of the tests which the heroine applies to her lover.

'Do you know what soothsayers I would consult?' . . . . . . '. . . . . . The little Irish beggar that comes barefoot to my door; the mouse that steals out of the cranny in my wainscot; the bird in frost and snow that pecks at my window for a crumb; the dog that licks my hand and sits beside my knee. . . . . I know somebody to whose knee the black cat loves to climb, against whose shoulder and cheek it likes to purr. The old dog always comes out of his kennel and wags his tail, and whines affectionately when somebody passes.' [For 'somebody' and 'he,' read 'Charlotte Brontë' and 'she.'] 'He quietly strokes the cat, and lets her sit while he conveniently can; and when he must disturb her by rising, he puts her softly down, and never flings her from him roughly: he always whistles to the dog, and gives him a caress.'

The feeling, which in Charlotte partook of something of the nature of an affection, was, with Emily, more of a passion. Some one speaking of her to me,* in a careless kind of strength of expression, said, 'she never showed regard to any human creature; all her love was reserved for animals.' The helplessness of an animal was its passport to Charlotte's heart; the fierce, wild, intractability of its nature was what often recommended it to Emily. Speaking of her dead sister, the former told me that from her many traits in Shirley's character were taken; her way of sitting on the rug reading, with her arm round her rough bull-dog's neck; her calling to a strange dog, running past, with hanging head and lolling tongue, to give it a merciful draught of water, its maddened snap at her, her nobly stern presence of mind, going right into the kitchen, and taking up one of Tabby's red-hot Italian irons to sear the bitten place, and telling no one, till the danger was well-nigh over, for fear of the terrors that might beset their weaker minds. All this, looked upon as a well-invented fiction in 'Shirley,' was written down by Charlotte with streaming eyes; it was the literal true account of what Emily had done.* The same tawny bull-dog (with his 'strangled whistle'), called 'Tartar' in 'Shirley,' was 'Keeper' in Haworth parsonage; a gift to Emily.* With the gift came a warning. Keeper was faithful to the depths of his nature as long as he was with friends; but he who struck him with a stick or whip, roused the relentless nature of the brute, who flew at his throat forthwith, and held him there till one or the other was at the point of death. Now Keeper's household fault was this. He loved to steal up-stairs, and stretch his square, tawny limbs, on the comfortable beds, covered over with delicate white counterpanes. But the cleanliness of the parsonage arrangements was perfect; and this habit of Keeper's was so objectionable, that Emily, in reply to Tabby's remonstrances, declared that, if he was found again transgressing, she herself, in defiance of warning and his well-known ferocity of nature, would beat him so severely that he would never offend again. In the gathering dusk of an autumn evening, Tabby came, half triumphantly, half tremblingly, but in great wrath, to tell Emily that Keeper was lying on the best bed, in drowsy voluptuousness. Charlotte saw Emily's whitening face, and set mouth, but dared not speak to interfere; no one dared when Emily's eyes glowed in that manner out of the paleness of her face, and when her lips were so compressed into stone. She went up-stairs, and Tabby and Charlotte stood in the gloomy passage below, full of the dark shadows of coming night. Down-stairs came Emily, dragging after her the unwilling Keeper, his hind legs set in a heavy attitude of resistance, held by the 'scuft of his neck,' but

growling low and savagely all the time. The watchers would fain
have spoken, but durst not, for fear of taking off Emily's attention,
and causing her to avert her head for a moment from the enraged
brute. She let him go, planted in a dark corner at the bottom of
the stairs; no time was there to fetch stick or rod, for fear of the
strangling clutch at her throat—her bare clenched fist struck
against his red fierce eyes, before he had time to make his spring,
and, in the language of the turf, she 'punished him'* till his eyes
were swelled up, and the half-blind, stupified beast was led to his
accustomed lair, to have his swollen head fomented and cared for
by the very Emily herself. The generous dog owed her no grudge;
he loved her dearly ever after; he walked first among the mourners
to her funeral; he slept moaning for nights at the door of her empty
room, and never, so to speak, rejoiced, dog fashion, after her death.
He, in his turn, was mourned over by the surviving sister. Let us
somehow hope, in half Red Indian creed, that he follows Emily
now; and, when he rests, sleeps on some soft white bed of dreams,
unpunished when he awakens to the life of the land of shadows.

Now we can understand the force of the words, 'Our poor little
cat is dead. Emily is sorry.'

## CHAPTER XIII

THE moors were a great resource this spring; Emily and Charlotte walked out on them perpetually, 'to the great damage of our shoes, but I hope, to the benefit of our health.'* The old plan of school-keeping was often discussed in these rambles; but in-doors they set with vigour to shirt-making for the absent Branwell, and pondered in silence over their past and future life. At last they came to a determination.

'I have seriously entered into the enterprise of keeping a school*—or rather, taking a limited number of pupils at home. That is, I have begun in good earnest to seek for pupils. I wrote to Mrs ——' (the lady with whom she had lived as governess, just before going to Brussels) 'not asking her for her daughter—I cannot do that—but informing her of my intention. I received an answer from Mr —— expressive of, I believe, sincere regret that I had not informed them a month sooner, in which case, he said, they would gladly have sent me their own daughter, and also Colonel S.'s, but that now both were promised to Miss C. I was partly disappointed by this answer, and partly gratified; indeed, I derived quite an impulse of encouragement from the warm assurance that if I had but applied a little sooner they would certainly have sent me their daughter. I own, I had misgivings that nobody would be willing to send a child for education to Haworth. These misgivings are partly done away with. I have written also to Mrs B. and have enclosed the diploma which M. Héger gave me before I left Brussels. I have not yet received her answer, but I wait for it with some anxiety. I do not expect that she will send me any of her children, but if she would, I dare say she could recommend me other pupils. Unfortunately, she knows us only very slightly. As soon as I can get an assurance of only *one* pupil, I will have cards of terms printed, and will commence the repairs necessary in the house. I wish all that to be done before winter. I think of fixing the board and English education at 25*l.* per annum.'*

Again, at a later date, July 24th, in the same year, she writes:—*

'I am driving on with my small matter as well as I can. I have written to all the friends on whom I have the slightest claim, and to some on whom I have no claim; Mrs B. for example. On her, also, I have actually made bold to call. She was exceedingly polite; regretted that her children were already at school at Liverpool; thought the undertaking a most praiseworthy one, but feared I should have some difficulty in making it succeed on account of the *situation*. Such is the answer I receive from almost every one. I tell them the *retired situation* is, in some points of view, an advantage; that were it in the midst of a large town I could not pretend to take pupils on terms so moderate (Mrs B. remarked that she thought the terms very moderate), but that, as it is, not having house-rent to pay, we can offer the same privileges of education that are to be had in expensive seminaries, at little more than half their price; and as our number must be limited, we can devote a large share of time and pains to each pupil. Thank you for the very pretty little purse you have sent me. I make to you a curious return in the shape of half a dozen cards of terms. Make such use of them as your judgment shall dictate. You will see that I have fixed the sum at 35*l.*, which I think is the just medium, considering advantages and disadvantages.'

This was written in July; August, September, and October passed away, and no pupils were to be heard of. Day after day, there was a little hope felt by the sisters until the post came in. But Haworth village was wild and lonely, and the Brontës but little known, owing to their want of connections. Charlotte writes on the subject, in the early winter months, to this effect:—*

'I, Emily, and Anne, are truly obliged to you for the efforts you have made in our behalf; and if you have not been successful, you are only like ourselves. Every one wishes us well; but there are no pupils to be had. We have no present intention, however, of breaking our hearts on the subject, still less of feeling mortified at defeat. The effort must be beneficial, whatever the result may be, because it teaches us experience, and an additional knowledge of this world. I send you two more circulars.'

A month later, she says:—*

'We have made no alterations yet in our house. It would be folly to do so, while there is so little likelihood of our ever getting pupils. I fear you are giving yourself too much trouble on our account. Depend upon it, if you were to persuade a mama to bring her child to Haworth, the aspect of the place would frighten her, and she would probably take the dear girl back with her, instanter. We are glad that we have made the attempt, and we will not be cast down because it has not succeeded.'

There were, probably, growing up in each sister's heart, secret unacknowledged feelings of relief, that their plan had not succeeded. Yes! a dull sense of relief that their cherished project had been tried and had failed. For that house, which was to be regarded as an occasional home for their brother, could hardly be a fitting residence for the children of strangers. They had, in all likelihood, become silently aware that his habits were such as to render his society at times most undesirable. Possibly, too, they had, by this time, heard distressing rumours concerning the cause of that remorse and agony of mind,* which at times made him restless and unnaturally merry, at times rendered him moody and irritable.

In January, 1845, Charlotte says:*—'Branwell has been quieter and less irritable, on the whole, this time than he was in summer. Anne is, as usual, always good, mild, and patient.' The deep-seated pain which he was to occasion to his relations had now taken a decided form, and pressed heavily on Charlotte's health and spirits. Early in this year, she went to H. to bid good-bye to her dear friend 'Mary,' who was leaving England for Australia.*

Branwell, I have mentioned, had obtained the situation of a private tutor. Anne was also engaged as governess in the same family, and was thus a miserable witness to her brother's deterioration of character at this period. Of the causes of this deterioration I cannot speak; but the consequences were these. He went home for his holidays reluctantly, stayed there as short a time as possible, perplexing and distressing them all by his extraordinary conduct— at one time in the highest spirits, at another, in the deepest depression—accusing himself of blackest guilt and treachery, without specifying what they were; and altogether evincing an irritability of disposition bordering on insanity.

Charlotte and Emily suffered acutely from his mysterious behaviour. He expressed himself more than satisfied with his situation; he was remaining in it for a longer time than he had ever done in any kind of employment before; so that for some time* they could not conjecture that anything there made him so wilful, and restless, and full of both levity and misery. But a sense of something wrong connected with him, sickened and oppressed them. They began to lose all hope in his future career. He was no longer the family pride; an indistinct dread, caused partly by his own conduct, partly by expressions of agonising suspicion in Anne's letters home, was creeping over their minds that he might turn out their deep disgrace. But, I believe, they shrank from any attempt to define their fears, and spoke of him to each other as little as possible. They could not help but think, and mourn, and wonder.

'Feb. 20th, 1845.*

'I spent a week at H., not very pleasantly; headache, sickliness, and flatness of spirits, made me a poor companion, a sad drag on the vivacious and loquacious gaiety of all the other inmates of the house. I never was fortunate enough to be able to rally, for as much as a single hour, while I was there. I am sure all, with the exception perhaps of Mary, were very glad when I took my departure. I begin to perceive that I have too little life in me, now-a-days, to be fit company for any except very quiet people. Is it age, or what else, that changes me so?'

Alas! she hardly needed to have asked this question. How could she be otherwise than 'flat-spirited,' 'a poor companion,' and a 'sad drag' on the gaiety of those who were light-hearted and happy! Her honest plan for earning her own livelihood had fallen away, crumbled to ashes; after all her preparations, not a pupil had offered herself; and, instead of being sorry that this wish of many years could not be realised, she had reason to be glad. Her poor father, nearly sightless, depended upon her cares in his blind helplessness; but this was a sacred pious charge, the duties of which she was blessed in fulfilling. The black gloom hung over what had once been the brightest hope of the family—over Branwell, and the mystery in which his wayward conduct was enveloped. Somehow and sometime, he would have to turn to his home as a hiding place for shame; such was the sad foreboding of his sisters. Then how could she be cheerful, when she was losing her dear and noble 'Mary,' for such a length of time and distance of space that her heart might well prophesy that it was 'for ever'? Long before, she had written of Mary T.,* that she 'was full of feelings noble, warm, generous, devoted, and profound. God bless her! I never hope to see in this world a character more truly noble. She would *die* willingly for one she loved. Her intellect and attainments are of the very highest standard.' And this was the friend whom she was to lose! Hear that friend's account of their final interview:—

'When I last saw Charlotte (Jan. 1845), she told me she had quite decided to stay at home. She owned she did not like it. Her health was weak. She said she should like any change at first, as she had liked Brussels at first, and she thought that there must be some possibility for some people of having a life of more variety and more communion with human kind, but she saw none for her. I told her very warmly, that she ought not to stay at home; that to spend the next five years at home, in solitude and weak health, would ruin her; that she would never recover it. Such a dark shadow came over her face when I said, "Think of what you'll be five years hence!" that I stopped, and said "Don't cry, Charlotte!" She did not cry, but went on walking up and down the room, and said in a little while, "But I intend to stay, Polly" '*

A few weeks after she parted from Mary, she gives this account of her days at Haworth.

'March 24th, 1845.

'I can hardly tell you how time gets on at Haworth. There is no event whatever to mark its progress. One day resembles another; and all have heavy, lifeless physiognomies. Sunday, baking-day, and Saturday, are the only ones that have any distinctive mark. Meantime, life wears away. I shall soon be thirty; and I have done nothing yet. Sometimes I get melancholy at the prospect before and behind me. Yet it is wrong and foolish to repine. Undoubtedly, my duty directs me to stay at home for the present. There was a time when Haworth was a very pleasant place to me; it is not so now. I feel as if we were all buried here. I long to travel; to work; to live a life of action. Excuse me, dear, for troubling you with my fruitless wishes. I will put by the rest, and not trouble you with them. You *must* write to me. If you knew how welcome your letters are, you would write very often. Your letters, and the French newspapers, are the only messengers that come to me from the outer world beyond our moors; and very welcome messengers they are.'

One of her daily employments was to read to her father, and it required a little gentle diplomacy on her part to effect this duty; for there were times when the offer of another to do what he had been so long accustomed to do for himself, reminded him only too painfully of the deprivation under which he was suffering. And, in secret, she, too, dreaded a similar loss for herself. Long-continued ill health, a deranged condition of the liver, her close application to minute drawing and writing in her younger days, her now habitual sleeplessness at nights, the many bitter noiseless tears she had shed over Branwell's mysterious and distressing conduct—all these causes were telling on her poor eyes; and about this time she thus writes to M. Héger:—*

'Il n'y a rien que je crains comme le désœuvrement, l'inertie, la léthargie des facultés. Quand le corps est paresseux l'esprit souffre cruellement; je ne connaîtrais pas cette léthargie, si je pouvais écrire. Autrefois je passais des journées, des semaines, des mois entiers à écrire, et pas tout-à-fait sans fruit, puisque Southey et Coleridge, deux de nos meilleurs auteurs, à qui j'ai envoyé certains manuscrits, en ont bien voulu témoigner leur approbation; mais à présent, j'ai la vue trop faible; si j'écrivais beaucoup je deviendrais aveugle. Cette faiblesse de vue est pour moi une terrible privation; sans cela, savez-vous ce que je ferais, Monsieur? J'écrirais un livre et je le dédierais à mon maître de littérature, au seul maître que j'aie jamais eu—à vous, Monsieur! Je vous ai dit souvent en français combien je vous respecte, combien je suis redevable à votre bonté, à vos conseils. Je voudrais le dire une fois en anglais. Cela ne se peut pas; il ne faut pas y penser. La carrière des lettres m'est fermée........ N'oubliez pas de me dire comment vous vous portez, comment Madame et les enfants se portent. Je compte bientôt avoir de vos nouvelles; cette idée me souris, car le souvenir de vos bontés ne s'effacera jamais de ma mémoire, et tant que ce souvenir durera, le respect que vous m'avez inspiré durera aussi. Agréez, Monsieur,' &c.

It is probable, that even her sisters and most intimate friends did not know of this dread of ultimate blindness which beset her at this period. What eyesight she had to spare she reserved for the use of her father. She did but little plain-sewing; not more writing than could be avoided; and employed herself principally in knitting.

'April 2nd, 1845.

'I see plainly it is proved to us that there is scarcely a draught of unmingled happiness to be had in this world. ——'s illness comes with ——'s marriage.* Mary T. finds herself free, and on that path to adventure and exertion to which she has so long been seeking admission. Sickness, hardship, danger are her fellow travellers—her inseparable companions. She may have been out of the reach of these S. W. N. W. gales, before they began to blow, or they may have spent their fury on land, and not ruffled the sea much. If it has been otherwise, she has been sorely tossed, while we have been sleeping in our beds, or lying awake thinking about her. Yet these real, material dangers, when once past, leave in the mind the satisfaction of having struggled with difficulty, and overcome it. Strength, courage, and experience are their invariable results; whereas, I doubt whether suffering purely mental has any good result, unless it be to make us by comparison less sensitive to physical suffering. . . . . . . Ten years ago, I should have laughed at your account of the blunder you made in mistaking the bachelor doctor for a married man. I should have certainly thought you scrupulous over-much, and wondered how you could possibly regret being civil to a decent individual, merely because he happened to be single, instead of double. Now, however, I can perceive that your scruples are founded on common sense. I know that if women wish to escape the stigma of husband-seeking, they must act and look like marble or clay—cold, expressionless, bloodless; for every appearance of feeling, of joy, sorrow, friendliness, antipathy, admiration, disgust, are alike construed by the world into the attempt to hook a husband. Never mind! well-meaning women have their own consciences to comfort them after all. Do not, therefore, be too much afraid of showing yourself as you are, affectionate and good-hearted; do not too harshly repress sentiments and feelings excellent in themselves, because you fear that some puppy may fancy that you are letting them come out to fascinate him; do not condemn yourself to live only by halves, because if you showed too much animation some pragmatical thing in breeches might take it into his pate to imagine that you designed to dedicate your life to his inanity. Still, a composed, decent, equable deportment is a capital treasure to a woman, and that you possess. Write again soon, for I feel rather fierce, and want stroking down.'

'June 13th, 1845.*

'As to the Mrs ——, who, you say, is like me, I somehow feel no leaning to her at all. I never do to people who are said to be like me, because I have always a notion that they are only like me in the disagreeable, outside, first-acquaintance part of my character; in those points which are obvious to the ordinary run of people, and which I know are not pleasing. You say she is "clever"—"a clever person." How I dislike the term! It means rather a shrewd, very ugly, meddling, talking woman. . . . . . . . . I feel reluctant to leave papa for a single day. His sight diminishes weekly; and can it be wondered at that, as he sees the most precious of his faculties leaving him, his spirits sometimes sink? It is so hard to feel that his few and scanty pleasures must all soon go. He has now the greatest difficulty in either reading or writing; and then he dreads the state of dependence to which blindness will inevitably reduce him. He fears that he will be nothing in his parish. I try to cheer him; sometimes I succeed temporarily, but no consolation can restore his sight, or atone for the want of it. Still he is never peevish; never impatient; only anxious and dejected.'

For the reason just given, Charlotte declined an invitation to the only house to which she was now ever asked to come. In answer to her correspondent's reply to this letter, she says:—*

'You thought I refused you coldly, did you? It was a queer sort of coldness, when I would have given my ears to say Yes, and was obliged to say No. Matters, however, are now a little changed.

Anne is come home, and her presence certainly makes me feel more
at liberty. Then, if all be well, I will come and see you. Tell me only
when I must come. Mention the week and the day. Have the kindness
also to answer the following queries, if you can. How far is it from
Leeds to Sheffield?* Can you give me a notion of the cost? Of course,
when I come, you will let me enjoy your own company in peace, and
not drag me out a-visiting. I have no desire at all to see your curate.
I think he must be like all the other curates I have seen; and they seem
to me a self-seeking, vain, empty race. At this blessed moment, we
have no less than three of them in Haworth parish—and there is not
one to mend another. The other day, they all three, accompanied by
Mr S.,* dropped, or rather rushed, in unexpectedly to tea. It was
Monday' (baking-day), 'and I was hot and tired; still, if they had
behaved quietly and decently, I would have served them out their tea
in peace; but they began glorifying themselves, and abusing Dissenters
in such a manner, that my temper lost its balance, and I pronounced
a few sentences sharply and rapidly, which struck them all dumb.
Papa was greatly horrified also, but I don't regret it.'

On her return from this short visit to her friend, she travelled with
a gentleman in the railway carriage,* whose features and bearing
betrayed him, in a moment, to be a Frenchman. She ventured to ask
him if such was not the case; and, on his admitting it, she further
inquired if he had not passed a considerable time in Germany, and
was answered that he had; her quick ear detected something of the
thick guttural pronunciation, which, Frenchmen say, they are able to
discover even in the grandchildren of their countrymen who have
lived any time beyond the Rhine. Charlotte had retained her skill in
the language by the habit of which she thus speaks to M. Héger:—*

'Je crains beaucoup d'oublier le français—j'apprends tous les
jours une demie page de français par cœur, et j'ai grand plaisir à
apprendre cette leçon. Veuillez présenter à Madame l'assurance de
mon estime; je crains que Marie, Louise et Claire ne m'aient déjà
oubliées; mais je vous reverrai un jour; aussitôt que j'aurais gagné
assez d'argent pour aller à Bruxelles, j'y irai.'

And so her journey back to Haworth, after the rare pleasure of
this visit to her friend, was pleasantly beguiled by conversation

with the French gentleman; and she arrived at home refreshed and happy. What to find there?

It was ten o'clock when she reached the parsonage. Branwell was there, unexpectedly, very ill. He had come home a day or two before, apparently for a holiday; in reality, I imagine, because some discovery had been made which rendered his absence imperatively desirable. The day of Charlotte's return, he had received a letter from Mr ——, sternly dismissing him, intimating that his proceedings were discovered, characterising them as bad beyond expression, and charging him, on pain of exposure, to break off immediately, and for ever, all communication with every member of the family.*

Whatever may have been the nature and depth of Branwell's sins,—whatever may have been his temptation, whatever his guilt,—there is no doubt of the suffering which his conduct entailed upon his poor father and his innocent sisters. The hopes and plans they had cherished long, and laboured hard to fulfil, were cruelly frustrated; henceforward their days were embittered and the natural rest of their nights destroyed by his paroxysms of remorse. Let us read of the misery caused to his poor sisters in Charlotte's own affecting words:—*

'We have had sad work with Branwell. He thought of nothing but stunning or drowning his agony of mind. No one in this house could have rest; and, at last, we have been obliged to send him from home for a week, with some one to look after him.* He has written to me this morning, expressing some sense of contrition .... but as long as he remains at home, I scarce dare hope for peace in the house. We must all, I fear, prepare for a season of distress and disquietude. When I left you, I was strongly impressed with the feeling that I was going back to sorrow.'

'August, 1845.

'Things here at home are much as usual; not very bright as it regards Branwell, though his health, and consequently his temper, have been somewhat better this last day or two, because he is now *forced* to abstain.'

'I have delayed writing, because I have no good news to communicate. My hopes ebb low indeed about Branwell. I sometimes fear he will never be fit for much. The late blow to his prospects and feelings has quite made him reckless. It is only absolute want of means that acts as any check to him. One ought, indeed, to hope to the very last; and I try to do so, but occasionally hope in his case seems so fallacious.'

'Nov. 4th, 1845.

'I hoped to be able to ask you to come to Haworth. It almost seemed as if Branwell had a chance of getting employment* and I waited to know the result of his efforts in order to say, dear ——, come and see us. But the place (a secretaryship to a railway committee) is given to another person. Branwell still remains at home; and while *he* is here, *you* shall not come. I am more confirmed in that resolution the more I see of him. I wish I could say one word to you in his favour, but I cannot. I will hold my tongue. We are all obliged to you for your kind suggestion about Leeds; but I think our school schemes are, for the present, at rest.'

'Dec. 31st, 1845.*

'You say well, in speaking of ——,* that no sufferings are so awful as those brought on by dissipation; alas! I see the truth of this observation daily proved. —— and —— must have as weary and burdensome a life of it in waiting upon their unhappy brother. It seems grievous, indeed, that those who have not sinned should suffer so largely.'

In fact,* all their latter days blighted with the presence of cruel, shameful suffering,—the premature deaths of two at least of the sisters,—all the great possibilities of their earthly lives snapped short,—may be dated from Midsummer 1845.

For the last three years of Branwell's life, he took opium habitually, by way of stunning conscience; he drank, moreover, whenever he could get the opportunity. The reader may say that I have mentioned his tendency to intemperance long before. It is true; but it did not become habitual, as far as I can learn, until after he was dismissed from his tutorship.* He took opium, because it made him forget for a time more effectually than drink; and, besides, it was more portable. In procuring it he showed all the cunning of the opium-eater.* He would steal out while the family were at church—to which he had professed himself too ill to go—and manage to cajole the village druggist out of a lump; or, it might be, the carrier had unsuspiciously brought him some in a packet from a distance. For some time before his death he had attacks of delirium tremens of the most frightful character; he slept in his father's room, and he would sometimes declare that either he or his father should be dead before morning. The trembling sisters, sick with fright, would implore their father not to expose himself to this danger; but Mr Brontë is no timid man, and perhaps he felt that he could possibly influence his son to some self-restraint, more by showing trust in him than by showing fear. The sisters often listened for the report of a pistol in the dead of the night, till watchful eye and hearkening ear grew heavy and dull with the perpetual strain upon their nerves. In the mornings young Brontë would saunter out, saying, with a drunkard's incontinence of speech, 'The poor old man and I have had a terrible night of it; he does his best—the poor old man! but it's all over with me.'*

# CHAPTER XIV

In the course of this sad autumn of 1845, a new interest came up; faint, indeed, and often lost sight of in the vivid pain and constant pressure of anxiety respecting their brother. In the biographical notice of her sisters, which Charlotte prefixed to the edition of 'Wuthering Heights' and 'Agnes Grey,' published in 1850*—a piece of writing unique, as far as I know, in its pathos and its power—she says:—

'One day in the autumn of 1845, I accidentally lighted on a MS volume of verse, in my sister Emily's hand-writing. Of course, I was not surprised, knowing that she could and did write verse: I looked it over, and something more than surprise seized me—a deep conviction that these were not common effusions, nor at all like the poetry women generally write. I thought them condensed and terse, vigorous and genuine. To my ear they had also a peculiar music, wild, melancholy, and elevating. My sister Emily was not a person of demonstrative character, nor one on the recesses of whose mind and feelings even those nearest and dearest to her could, with impunity, intrude unlicensed: it took hours to reconcile her to the discovery I had made, and days to persuade her that such poems merited publication. . . . . . . Meantime, my younger sister quietly produced some of her own compositions, intimating that since Emily's had given me pleasure, I might like to look at hers. I could not but be a partial judge, yet I thought that these verses too had a sweet sincere pathos of their own. We had very early cherished the dream of one day being authors. . . . . We agreed to arrange a small selection of our poems, and, if possible, get them printed. Averse to personal publicity, we veiled our own names under those of Currer, Ellis, and Acton Bell;* the ambiguous choice being dictated by a sort of conscientious scruple at assuming Christian names, positively masculine, while we did not like to declare ourselves women, because—without at the time suspecting that our mode of writing and thinking was not what is called "feminine,"—we had a vague impression that authoresses are liable to be looked on with prejudice; we noticed how critics sometimes use for their chastisement the weapon of personality, and for their reward, a flattery, which is not true praise. The bringing out of our little book was hard work. As was to be expected, neither we nor our poems were at all wanted; but for this we had been prepared at the outset; though inexperienced ourselves, we had read the experience of others. The great puzzle lay in the difficulty of getting answers of any kind from the publishers to whom we applied. Being greatly harassed by this obstacle, I ventured to apply to the Messrs Chambers, of Edinburgh,* for a word of advice; *they* may have forgotten the circumstances, but *I* have not, for from them I received a brief and business-like, but civil and sensible reply, on which we acted, and at last made way.'

I inquired from Mr Robert Chambers, and found, as Miss Brontë conjectured, that he had entirely forgotten the application which had been made to him and his brother for advice; nor had they any copy or memorandum of the correspondence.

There is an intelligent man living in Haworth,* who has given me some interesting particulars relating to the sisters about this period. He says:—

'I have known Miss Brontë, as Miss Brontë, a long time; indeed, ever since they came to Haworth in 1819. But I had not much acquaintance with the family till about 1843, when I began to do a little in the stationery line. Nothing of that kind could be had nearer than Keighley before I began. They used to buy a great deal of writing paper, and I used to wonder whatever they did with so much. I sometimes thought they contributed to the Magazines. When I was out of stock, I was always afraid of their coming; they seemed so distressed about it, if I had none. I have walked to Halifax (a distance of 10 miles) many a time, for half a ream of paper, for fear of being without it when they came. I could not buy more at a time for want of capital. I was always short of that. I did so like them to come when I had anything for them; they were so much different to anybody else; so gentle and kind, and so very quiet. They never talked much. Charlotte sometimes would sit and inquire about our circumstances so kindly and feelingly! . . . . Though I am a poor working man (which I have never felt to be any degradation), I could talk with her with the greatest freedom. I always felt quite at home with her. Though I never had any school education, I never felt the want of it in her company.'

The publishers to whom she finally made a successful application for the production of 'Currer, Ellis, and Acton Bell's poems,' were Messrs Aylott and Jones,* Paternoster Row. Mr Aylott has kindly placed the letters which she wrote to them on the subject at my disposal. The first is dated January 28th, 1846, and in it she inquires if they will publish one volume octavo of poems; if not at their own risk, on the author's account. It is signed 'C. Brontë.' They must have replied pretty speedily, for on January 31st she writes again:—

'Gentlemen,

'Since you agree to undertake the publication of the work respecting which I applied to you, I should wish now to know, as soon as possible, the cost of paper and printing. I will then send the necessary remittance, together with the manuscript. I should like it to be printed in one octavo volume, of the same quality of paper and size of type as Moxon's last edition of Wordsworth.* The poems will occupy, I should think, from 200 to 250 pages They are not the production of a clergyman, nor are they exclusively of a religious character; but I presume these circumstances will be immaterial. It will, perhaps, be necessary that you should see the manuscript, in order to calculate accurately the expense of publication; in that case I will send it immediately. I should like, however, previously, to have some idea of the probable cost; and if, from what I have said, you can make a rough calculation on the subject, I should be greatly obliged to you.'

In her next letter, February 6th, she says:—

'You will perceive that the poems are the work of three persons, relatives—their separate pieces are distinguished by their respective signatures.'

She writes again on February 15th; and on the 16th she says:—

'The MS will certainly form a thinner volume than I had anticipated. I cannot name another model which I should like it precisely to resemble, yet, I think, a duodecimo form, and a somewhat reduced, though still *clear* type, would be preferable. I only stipulate for *clear* type, not too small; and good paper.'

On February 21st she selects the 'long primer type' for the poems, and will remit 31*l*. 10*s*. in a few days.

Minute as the details conveyed in these notes are, they are not trivial, because they afford such strong indications of character. If the volume was to be published at their own risk, it was necessary that the sister conducting the negotiation should make herself acquainted with the different kinds of type, and the various sizes of books. Accordingly she bought a small volume,* from which to learn all she could on the subject of preparation for the press. No half-knowledge—no trusting to other people for decisions which she could make for herself; and yet a generous and full confidence, not misplaced, in the thorough probity of Messrs Aylott and Jones. The caution in ascertaining the risk before embarking in the enterprise, and the prompt payment of the money required, even before it could be said to have assumed the shape of a debt, were both parts of a self-reliant and independent character. Self-contained also was she. During the whole time that the volume of poems was in the course of preparation and publication, no word was written telling anyone, out of the household circle, what was in progress.

I have had some of the letters placed in my hands, which she addressed to her old school-mistress, Miss W——.* They begin a little before this time. Acting on the conviction, which I have all along entertained, that where Charlotte Brontë's own words could be used, no others ought to take their place, I shall make extracts from this series, according to their dates.

'Jan. 30th, 1846.*

'My dear Miss W——,

'I have not yet paid my visit to ——; it is, indeed, more than a year since I was there, but I frequently hear from E., and she did not fail to tell me that you were gone into Worcestershire; she was unable, however, to give me your exact address. Had I known it, I should have written to you long since. I thought you would wonder how we were getting on, when you heard of the railway panic; and you may be sure that I am very glad to be able to answer your kind inquiries by an assurance that our small capital is as yet undiminished. The York and Midland* is, as you say, a very good line; yet, I confess to you, I should wish, for my own part, to be wise in time. I cannot think that even the very best lines will continue for many years at their present premiums; and I have been most anxious for us to sell our shares ere it be too late, and to secure the proceeds in some safer, if, for the present, less profitable investment. I cannot, however, persuade my sisters to regard the affair precisely from my point of view; and I feel as if I would rather run the risk of loss than hurt Emily's feelings by acting in direct opposition to her opinion. She managed in a most handsome and able manner for me, when I was in Brussels, and prevented by distance from looking after my own interests; therefore, I will let her manage still, and take the consequences. Disinterested and energetic she certainly is; and if she be not quite so tractable or open to conviction as I could wish, I must remember perfection is not the lot of humanity; and as long as we can regard those we love, and to whom we are closely allied, with profound and never-shaken esteem, it is a small thing that they should vex us occasionally by what appear to us unreasonable and headstrong notions.

'You, my dear Miss W——, know, full as well as I do, the value of sisters' affection to each other; there is nothing like it in this world, I believe, when they are nearly equal in age, and similar in education, tastes, and sentiments. You ask about Branwell; he never thinks of seeking employment, and I begin to fear that he has rendered himself incapable of filling any respectable station in life; besides, if money were at his disposal, he would use it only to his own injury; the faculty of self-government is, I fear, almost destroyed in him. You ask me if I do not think that men are strange beings? I do, indeed. I have often thought so; and I think, too, that the mode of bringing them up is strange: they are not sufficiently guarded from temptation. Girls are protected as if they were something very frail or silly indeed, while boys are turned loose on the world as if they, of all beings in existence, were the wisest and least liable to be led astray. I am glad you like Bromsgrove, though, I dare say, there are few places you would *not* like, with Mrs M. for a companion. I always feel a peculiar satisfaction when I hear of your enjoying yourself, because it proves that there really is such a thing as retributive justice even in this world. You worked hard; you denied yourself all pleasure, almost all relaxation, in your youth, and in the prime of life; now you are free, and that while you have still, I hope, many years of vigour and health in which you can enjoy freedom. Besides, I have another and very egotistical motive for being pleased; it seems that even "a lone woman" can be happy, as well as cherished wives and proud mothers. I am glad of that. I speculate much on the existence of unmarried and never-to-be-married women now-a-days; and I have already got to the point of considering that there is no more respectable character on this earth than an unmarried woman, who makes her own way through life quietly, perseveringly, without support of husband or brother; and who, having attained the age of forty-five or upwards, retains in her possession a well-regulated mind, a disposition to enjoy simple pleasures, and fortitude to support inevitable pains, sympathy with the sufferings of others, and willingness to relieve want as far as her means extend.'

During the time that the negotiation with Messrs Aylott and Co. was going on, Charlotte went to visit her old school-friend, with whom she was in such habits of confidential intimacy; but neither then nor afterwards, did she ever speak to her of the publication of the poems; nevertheless, this young lady suspected that the sisters wrote for Magazines; and in this idea she was confirmed when, on one of her visits to Haworth, she saw Anne with a number of 'Chambers's Journal,'* and a gentle smile of pleasure stealing over her placid face as she read.

'What is the matter?' asked the friend. 'Why do you smile?'

'Only because I see they have inserted one of my poems,' was the quiet reply; and not a word more was said on the subject.

To this friend Charlotte addressed the following letters:—

'March 3rd, 1846.*

'I reached home a little after two o'clock, all safe and right yesterday; I found papa very well; his sight much the same. Emily and Anne were gone to Keighley to meet me; unfortunately, I had returned by the old road, while they were gone by the new, and we missed each other. They did not get home till half-past four, and were caught in the heavy shower of rain which fell in the afternoon. I am sorry to say Anne has taken a little cold in consequence, but I hope she will soon be well. Papa was much cheered by my report of Mr C.'s opinion, and of old Mrs E.'s experience; but I could perceive he caught gladly at the idea of deferring the operation a few months longer. I went into the room where Branwell was, to speak to him, about an hour after I got home; it was very forced work to address him. I might have spared myself the trouble, as he took no notice, and made no reply; he was stupified. My fears were not vain. I hear that he got a sovereign while I have been away, under pretence of paying a pressing debt; he went immediately and changed it at a public-house, and has employed it as was to be expected. —— concluded her account by saying he was a "hopeless being;" it is too true. In his present state it is scarcely possible to stay in the room where he is. What the future has in store I do not know.'

'March 31st, 1846.*

'Our poor old servant Tabby had a sort of fit, a fortnight since, but is nearly recovered now. Martha' (the girl they had to assist poor old Tabby, and who remains still the faithful servant at the parsonage) 'is ill with a swelling in her knee, and obliged to go home. I fear it will be long before she is in working condition again. I received the number of the "Record"* you sent. . . . . I read D'Aubigné's letter. It is clever, and in what he says about Catholicism very good. The Evangelical Alliance part is not very practicable, yet certainly it is more in accordance with the spirit of the Gospel to preach unity among Christians than to inculcate mutual intolerance and hatred. I am very glad I went to —— when I did, for the changed weather has somewhat changed my health and strength since. How do you get on? I long for mild south and west winds. I am thankful papa continues pretty well, though often made very miserable by Branwell's wretched conduct. There— there is no change but for the worse.'

Meanwhile the printing of the volume of poems was quietly proceeding. After some consultation and deliberation the sisters had determined to correct the proofs themselves. Up to March 28th the publishers had addressed their correspondent as

C. Brontë, Esq.; but at this time some 'little mistake occurred,' and she desired Messrs Aylott and Co. in future to direct to her real address, '*Miss* Brontë,' &c. She had, however, evidently left it to be implied that she was not acting on her own behalf, but as agent for the real authors, since in a note dated April 6th, she makes a proposal on behalf of 'C., E., and A. Bell,' which is to the following effect, that they are preparing for the press a work of fiction, consisting of three distinct and unconnected tales, which may be published either together, as a work of three volumes, of the ordinary novel size, or separately, as single volumes, as may be deemed most advisable. She states, in addition, that it is not their intention to publish these tales on their own account; but that the authors direct her to ask Messrs Aylott and Co. whether they would be disposed to undertake the work, after having, of course, by due inspection of the MS, ascertained that its contents are such as to warrant an expectation of success. To this letter of inquiry the publishers replied speedily, and the tenor of their answer may be gathered from Charlotte's, dated April 11th.

'I beg to thank you, in the name of C., E., and A. Bell, for your obliging offer of advice. I will avail myself of it, to request information on two or three points. It is evident that unknown authors have great difficulties to contend with, before they can succeed in bringing their works before the public. Can you give me any hint as to the way in which these difficulties are best met? For instance, in the present case, where a work of fiction is in question, in what form would a publisher be most likely to accept the MS? Whether offered as a work of three vols., or as tales which might be published in numbers, or as contributions to a periodical?

'What publishers would be most likely to receive favourably a proposal of this nature?

'Would it suffice to *write* to a publisher on the subject, or would it be necessary to have recourse to a personal interview?

'Your opinion and advice on these three points, or on any other which your experience may suggest as important, would be esteemed by us as a favour.'

It is evident from the whole tenor of this correspondence, that the truthfulness and probity of the firm of publishers with whom she had to deal in this, her first literary venture, were strongly impressed upon her mind, and was followed by the inevitable consequence of reliance on their suggestions. And the progress of the poems was not unreasonably lengthy or long drawn out. On April 20th she writes to desire that three copies may be sent to her, and that Messrs Aylott will advise her as to the reviewers to whom copies ought to be sent.

I give the next letter as illustrating the ideas of these girls as to what periodical reviews or notices led public opinion.*

'The poems to be neatly done up in cloth. Have the goodness to send copies and advertisements, *as early as possible*, to each of the undermentioned periodicals.

' "Colburn's New Monthly Magazine."
' "Bentley's Magazine."
' "Hood's Magazine."
' "Jerrold's Shilling Magazine."
' "Blackwood's Magazine."
' "The Edinburgh Review."
' "Tait's Edinburgh Magazine."
' "The Dublin University Magazine."

'Also to the "Daily News" and to the "Britannia" newspapers.

'If there are any other periodicals to which you have been in the habit of sending copies of works, let them be supplied also with copies. I think those I have mentioned will suffice for advertising.'

In compliance with this latter request, Messrs Aylott suggest that copies and advertisements of the work should be sent to the 'Athenæum,' 'Literary Gazette,' 'Critic,' and 'Times;' but in her reply Miss Brontë says, that she thinks the periodicals she first mentioned will be sufficient for advertising in at present, as the authors do not wish to lay out a larger sum than two pounds in advertising, esteeming the success of a work dependent more on the notice it receives from periodicals than on the quantity of advertisements. In case of any notice of the poems appearing, whether favourable or otherwise, Messrs Aylott and Co. are requested to send her the name and number of those periodicals in which such notices appear; as otherwise, since she has not the opportunity of seeing periodicals regularly, she may miss reading the critique. 'Should the poems be remarked upon favourably, it is my intention to appropriate a further sum for advertisements. If, on the other hand, they should pass unnoticed or be condemned, I consider it would be quite useless to advertise, as there is nothing either in the title of the work, or the names of the authors, to attract attention from a single individual.'

I suppose the little volume of poems was published some time about the end of May, 1846.\* It stole into life; some weeks passed over, without the mighty murmuring public discovering that three more voices were uttering their speech. And, meanwhile, the course of existence moved drearily along from day to day with the anxious sisters, who must have forgotten their sense of authorship in the vital care gnawing at their hearts. On June 17th, Charlotte writes:—

'Branwell declares that he neither can nor will do anything for himself; good situations have been offered him, for which, by a fortnight's work, he might have qualified himself, but he will do nothing, except drink and make us all wretched.'

In the 'Athenæum' of July 4th, under the head of Poetry for the Million, came a short review of the poems of C., E., and A. Bell. The reviewer assigns to Ellis the highest rank of the three 'brothers,' as he supposes them to be; he calls Ellis 'a fine, quaint spirit;' and speaks of 'an evident power of wing that may reach heights not here attempted.' Again, with some degree of penetration, the reviewer says, that the poems of Ellis 'convey an impression of originality beyond what his contributions to these volumes embody.' Currer Bell is placed midway between Ellis and Acton. But there is little in the review to strain out, at this distance of time, as worth preserving. Still, we can fancy with what interest it was read at Haworth Parsonage, and how the sisters would endeavour to find out reasons for opinions, or hints for the future guidance of their talents.

I call particular attention to the following letter of Charlotte's, dated July 10th, 1846.\* To whom it was written, matters not; but the wholesome sense of duty in it—the sense of the supremacy of that duty which God, in placing us in families, has laid out for us, seems to deserve especial regard in these days.

'I see you are in a dilemma, and one of a peculiar and difficult nature. Two paths lie before you; you conscientiously wish to choose the right one, even though it be the most steep, straight, and rugged; but you do not know which is the right one; you cannot decide whether duty and religion command you to go out into the cold and friendless world, and there to earn your living by governess drudgery, or whether they enjoin your continued stay with your aged mother, neglecting, *for the present*, every prospect of independency for yourself, and putting up with daily inconvenience, sometimes even with privations. I can well imagine, that it is next to impossible for you to decide for yourself in this matter, so I will decide it for you. At least, I will tell you what is my earnest conviction on the subject; I will show you candidly how the question strikes me. The right path is that which necessitates the greatest sacrifice of self-interest—which implies the greatest good to others; and this path, steadily followed, will lead, I believe, in time, to prosperity and to happiness; though it may seem, at the outset, to tend quite in a contrary direction. Your mother is both old and infirm; old and infirm people have but few sources of happiness—fewer almost than the comparatively young and healthy can conceive; to deprive them of one of these is cruel. If your mother is more composed when you are with her, stay with her. If she would be unhappy in case you left her, stay with her. It will not apparently, as far as short-sighted humanity can see, be for your advantage to remain at ——, nor will you be praised and admired for remaining at home to comfort your mother; yet, probably, your own conscience will approve you, and if it does, stay with her. I recommend you to do what I am trying to do myself.'

The remainder of this letter is only interesting to the reader as it conveys a peremptory disclaimer of the report that the writer was engaged to be married to her father's curate*—the very same gentleman to whom, eight years afterwards, she was united; and who, probably, even now, although she was unconscious of the fact, had begun his service to her, in the same tender and faithful spirit as that in which Jacob served for Rachel. Others may have noticed this, though she did not.

A few more notes remain of her correspondence 'on behalf of the Messrs Bell' with Mr Aylott. On July 15th she says, 'I suppose, as you have not written, no other notices have yet appeared, nor has the demand for the work increased. Will you favour me with a line stating whether *any*, or how many copies have yet been sold?'*

But few, I fear; for, three days later, she wrote the following:—

'The Messrs Bell desire me to thank you for your suggestion respecting the advertisements. They agree with you that, since the season is unfavourable, advertising had better be deferred. They are obliged to you for the information respecting the number of copies sold.'

On July 23rd she writes to the Messrs Aylott:—

'The Messrs Bell would be obliged to you to post the enclosed note in London. It is an answer to the letter you forwarded, which contained an application for their autographs from a person who professed to have read and admired their poems.* I think I before intimated, that the Messrs Bell are desirous for the present of remaining unknown, for which reason they prefer having the note posted in London to sending it direct, in order to avoid giving any clue to residence, or identity by post-mark, &c.'

Once more, in September, she writes,* 'As the work has received no farther notice from any periodical, I presume the demand for it has not greatly increased.'

In the biographical notice of her sisters,* she thus speaks of the failure of the modest hopes vested in this publication. 'The book was printed; it is scarcely known, and all of it that merits to be known are the poems of Ellis Bell. The fixed conviction I held, and hold, of the worth of these poems, has not, indeed, received the confirmation of much favourable criticism; but I must retain it notwithstanding.'

END OF THE FIRST VOLUME

# VOLUME II

## CHAPTER I

DURING this summer of 1846, while her literary hopes were waning, an anxiety of another kind was increasing. Her father's eyesight had become seriously impaired by the progress of the cataract which was forming. He was nearly blind. He could grope his way about, and recognise the figures of those he knew well, when they were placed against a strong light; but he could no longer see to read; and thus his eager appetite for knowledge and information of all kinds was severely balked. He continued to preach. I have heard that he was led up into the pulpit, and that his sermons were never so effective as when he stood there, a grey sightless old man, his blind eyes looking out straight before him, while the words that came from his lips had all the vigour and force of his best days. Another fact has been mentioned to me, curious as showing the accurateness of his sensation of time. His sermons had always lasted exactly half an hour. With the clock right before him, and with his ready flow of words, this had been no difficult matter so long as he could see. But it was the same when he was blind; as the minute-hand came to the point, marking the expiration of the thirty minutes, he concluded his sermon.

Under his great sorrow he was always patient. As in times of far greater affliction, he enforced a quiet endurance of his woe upon himself. But so many interests were quenched by this blindness that he was driven inwards, and must have dwelt much on what was painful and distressing in regard to his only son. No wonder that his spirits gave way, and were depressed. For some time before this autumn, his daughters had been collecting all the information they could respecting the probable success of operations for cataract performed on a person of their father's age. About the end of July, Emily and Charlotte had made a journey to

Manchester for the purpose of searching out an operator; and there
they heard of the fame of the late Mr Wilson* as an oculist. They
went to him at once, but he could not tell, from description,
whether the eyes were ready for being operated upon or not. It
therefore became necessary for Mr Brontë to visit him; and
towards the end of August, Charlotte brought her father to him.
He determined at once to undertake the operation, and recommended them to comfortable lodgings kept by an old servant of
his. These were in one of numerous similar streets of small
monotonous-looking houses, in a suburb of the town. From thence
the following letter is dated, on August 21st, 1846:—*

'I just scribble a line to you to let you know where I am, in order
that you may write to me here, for it seems to me that a letter from
you would relieve me from the feeling of strangeness I have in this
big town. Papa and I came here on Wednesday; we saw Mr Wilson,
the oculist, the same day; he pronounced papa's eyes quite ready
for an operation, and has fixed next Monday for the performance
of it. Think of us on that day! We got into our lodgings yesterday.
I think we shall be comfortable; at least, our rooms are very good,
but there is no mistress of the house (she is very ill, and gone out
into the country), and I am somewhat puzzled in managing about
provisions; we board ourselves. I find myself excessively ignorant.
I can't tell what to order in the way of meat. For ourselves I could
contrive, papa's diet is so very simple; but there will be a nurse
coming in a day or two, and I am afraid of not having things good
enough for her. Papa requires nothing, you know, but plain beef
and mutton, tea and bread and butter; but a nurse will probably
expect to live much better; give me some hints, if you can. Mr
Wilson says we shall have to stay here for a month at least. I
wonder how Emily and Anne will get on at home with Branwell.
They, too, will have their troubles. What would I not give to have
you here! One is forced, step by step, to get experience in the
world; but the learning is so disagreeable. One cheerful feature in
the business is that Mr Wilson thinks most favourably of the case.'

'August 26th, 1846.*

'The operation is over; it took place yesterday. Mr Wilson
performed it; two other surgeons assisted. Mr Wilson says, he

considers it quite successful; but papa cannot yet see anything. The affair lasted precisely a quarter of an hour; it was not the simple operation of couching, Mr C. described, but the more complicated one of extracting the cataract. Mr Wilson entirely disapproves of couching.* Papa displayed extraordinary patience and firmness; the surgeons seemed surprised. I was in the room all the time, as it was his wish that I should be there; of course, I neither spoke nor moved till the thing was done, and then I felt that the less I said, either to papa or the surgeons, the better. Papa is now confined to his bed in a dark room, and is not to be stirred for four days; he is to speak and be spoken to as little as possible. I am greatly obliged to you for your letter, and your kind advice, which gave me extreme satisfaction, because I found I had arranged most things in accordance with it, and, as your theory coincides with my practice, I feel assured the latter is right. I hope Mr Wilson will soon allow me to dispense with the nurse; she is well enough, no doubt, but somewhat too obsequious; and not, I should think, to be much trusted; yet I was obliged to trust her in some things . . . .

'Greatly was I amused by your account of ——'s flirtations; and yet something saddened also. I think Nature intended him for something better than to fritter away his time in making a set of poor, unoccupied spinsters unhappy. The girls, unfortunately, are forced to care for him, and such as him, because while their minds are mostly unemployed, their sensations are all unworn, and, consequently, fresh and green; and he, on the contrary, has had his fill of pleasure, and can with impunity make a mere pastime of other people's torments. This is an unfair state of things; the match is not equal. I only wish I had the power to infuse into the souls of the persecuted a little of the quiet strength of pride—of the supporting consciousness of superiority (for they are superior to him because purer)—of the fortifying resolve of firmness to bear the present, and wait the end. Could all the virgin population of —— receive and retain these sentiments, he would eventually have to vail his crest before them. Perhaps, luckily, their feelings are not so acute as one would think, and the gentleman's shafts consequently don't wound so deeply as he might desire. I hope it is so.'

A few days later, she writes thus:* 'Papa is still lying in bed, in a dark room, with his eyes bandaged. No inflammation ensued, but still it appears the greatest care, perfect quiet, and utter privation of light are necessary to ensure a good result from the operation. He is very patient, but, of course, depressed and weary. He was allowed to try his sight for the first time yesterday. He could see dimly. Mr Wilson seemed perfectly satisfied, and said all was right. I have had bad nights from the toothache since I came to Manchester.'

All this time, notwithstanding the domestic anxieties which were harassing them—notwithstanding the ill-success of their poems— the three sisters were trying that other literary venture, to which Charlotte made allusion in one of her letters to the Messrs Aylott. Each of them had written a prose tale, hoping that the three might be published together. 'Wuthering Heights' and 'Agnes Grey' are before the world. The third—Charlotte's contribution—is yet in manuscript, but will be published shortly after the appearance of this memoir.* The plot in itself is of no great interest; but it is a poor kind of interest that depends upon startling incidents rather than upon dramatic development of character; and Charlotte Brontë never excelled one or two sketches of portraits which she has given in 'The Professor,' nor, in grace of womanhood, ever surpassed one of the female characters there described. By the time she wrote this tale, her taste and judgment had revolted against the exaggerated idealisms of her early girlhood, and she went to the extreme of reality, closely depicting characters as they had shown themselves to her in actual life: if there they were strong even to coarseness,—as was the case with some that she had met with in flesh and blood existence,—she 'wrote them down an ass;'* if the scenery of such life as she saw was for the most part wild and grotesque, instead of pleasant or picturesque, she described it line for line. The grace of the one or two scenes and characters, which are drawn rather from her own imagination than from absolute fact, stand out in exquisite relief from the deep shadows and wayward lines of others, which call to mind some of the portraits of Rembrandt.

The three tales had tried their fate in vain together; at length they were sent forth separately, and for many months with still-continued ill-success. I have mentioned this here, because, among the dispiriting circumstances connected with her anxious visit to Manchester, Charlotte told me that her tale came back

upon her hands, curtly rejected by some publisher, on the very day
when her father was to submit to his operation. But she had the
heart of Robert Bruce* within her, and failure upon failure daunted
her no more than him. Not only did 'The Professor' return again
to try his chance among the London publishers, but she began, in
this time of care and depressing inquietude,—in those grey, weary,
uniform streets, where all faces, save that of her kind doctor, were
strange and untouched with sunlight to her,—there and then did
the brave genius begin 'Jane Eyre.'* Read what she herself
says:—'Currer Bell's book found acceptance nowhere, nor any
acknowledgment of merit, so that something like the chill of
despair began to invade his heart.' And, remember, it was not the
heart of a person who, disappointed in one hope, can turn with
redoubled affection to the many certain blessings that remain.
Think of her home, and the black shadow of remorse lying over
one in it, till his very brain was mazed, and his gifts and his life
were lost;—think of her father's sight hanging on a thread;—of her
sisters' delicate health, and dependence on her care;—and then
admire as it deserves to be admired, the steady courage which
could work away at 'Jane Eyre,' all the time 'that the one-volume
tale was plodding its weary round in London.'

Some of her surviving friends consider that an incident which
she heard, when at school at Miss W——'s, was the germ of the
story of 'Jane Eyre.'* But of this nothing can be known, except by
conjecture. Those to whom she spoke upon the subject of her
writings are dead and silent; and the reader may probably have
noticed, that in the correspondence from which I have quoted,
there has been no allusion whatever to the publication of her
poems, nor is there the least hint of the intention of the sisters to
publish any tales. I remember, however, many little particulars
which Miss Brontë gave me, in answer to my inquiries respecting
her mode of composition, &c. She said, that it was not every day
that she could write. Sometimes weeks or even months elapsed
before she felt that she had anything to add to that portion of her
story which was already written. Then, some morning she would
waken up, and the progress of her tale lay clear and bright before
her, in distinct vision. When this was the case, all her care was to
discharge her household and filial duties, so as to obtain leisure to
sit down and write out the incidents and consequent thoughts,

which were, in fact, more present to her mind at such times than her actual life itself. Yet notwithstanding this 'possession' (as it were), those who survive, of her daily and household companions, are clear in their testimony, that never was the claim of any duty, never was the call of another for help, neglected for an instant. It had become necessary to give Tabby—now nearly eighty years of age—the assistance of a girl. Tabby relinquished any of her work with jealous reluctance, and could not bear to be reminded, though ever so delicately, that the acuteness of her senses was dulled by age. The other servant might not interfere with what she chose to consider her exclusive work. Among other things, she reserved to herself the right of peeling the potatoes for dinner; but as she was growing blind, she often left in those black specks, which we in the North call the 'eyes'* of the potato. Miss Brontë was too dainty a housekeeper to put up with this; yet she could not bear to hurt the faithful old servant, by bidding the younger maiden go over the potatoes again, and so reminding Tabby that her work was less effectual than formerly. Accordingly she would steal into the kitchen, and quietly carry off the bowl of vegetables, without Tabby's being aware, and breaking off in the full flow of interest and inspiration in her writing, carefully cut out the specks in the potatoes, and noiselessly carry them back to their place. This little proceeding may show how orderly and fully she accomplished her duties, even at those times when the 'possession' was upon her.

Any one who has studied her writings,—whether in print or in her letters; any one who has enjoyed the rare privilege of listening to her talk, must have noticed her singular felicity in the choice of words. She herself, in writing her books, was solicitous on this point. One set of words was the truthful mirror of her thoughts; no others, however apparently identical in meaning, would do. She had that strong practical regard for the simple holy truth of expression, which Mr Trench has enforced,* as a duty too often neglected. She would wait patiently, searching for the right term, until it presented itself to her. It might be provincial, it might be derived from the Latin; so that it accurately represented her idea, she did not mind whence it came; but this care makes her style present the finish of a piece of mosaic. Each component part, however small, has been dropped into the right place. She never wrote down a sentence until she clearly understood what she wanted to say, had deliberately chosen the words, and arranged them in their right order. Hence it comes that, in the scraps of paper covered with her pencil writing which I have seen, there will occasionally be a sentence scored out, but seldom, if ever, a word or an expression. She wrote on these bits of paper in a minute hand, holding each against a piece of board, such as is used in binding books, for a desk. This plan was necessary for one so short-sighted as she was; and, besides, it enabled her to use pencil and paper, as she sat near the fire in the twilight hours, or if (as was too often the case) she was wakeful for hours in the night. Her finished manuscripts were copied from these pencil scraps, in clear, legible, delicate hand-writing, almost as easy to read as print.*

The sisters retained the old habit, which was begun in their aunt's life-time, of putting away their work at nine o'clock, and beginning their steady pacing up and down the sitting room. At this time, they talked over the stories they were engaged upon, and discussed their plots. Once or twice a week, each read to the others what she had written, and heard what they had to say about it. Charlotte told me, that the remarks made had seldom any effect in inducing her to alter her work, so possessed was she with the feeling that she had described reality; but the readings were of great and stirring interest to all, taking them out of the gnawing pressure of daily-recurring cares, and setting them in a free place. It was on one of these occasions, that Charlotte determined to make her heroine plain, small, and unattractive, in defiance of the accepted canon.

The writer of the beautiful obituary article on 'the death of Currer Bell,'* most likely learnt from herself what is there stated, and which I will take the liberty of quoting, about 'Jane Eyre.'

'She once told her sisters that they were wrong—even morally wrong—in making their heroines beautiful as a matter of course. They replied that it was impossible to make a heroine interesting on any other terms. Her answer was, "I will prove to you that you are wrong; I will show you a heroine as plain and as small as myself, who shall be as interesting as any of yours." Hence "Jane Eyre," said she in telling the anecdote: "but she is not myself, any further than that." As the work went on, the interest deepened to the writer. When she came to "Thornfield" she could not stop.

Being short-sighted to excess, she wrote in little square paper-books, held close to her eyes, and (the first copy) in pencil. On she went, writing incessantly for three weeks; by which time she had carried her heroine away from Thornfield, and was herself in a fever which compelled her to pause.'

This is all, I believe, which can now be told respecting the conception and composition of this wonderful book, which was, however, only at its commencement when Miss Brontë returned with her father to Haworth, after their anxious expedition to Manchester.

They arrived at home about the end of September. Mr Brontë was daily gaining strength, but he was still forbidden to exercise his sight much. Things had gone on more comfortably while she was away than Charlotte had dared to hope, and she expresses herself thankful for the good ensured and the evil spared during her absence.

Soon after this some proposal, of which I have not been able to gain a clear account, was again mooted for Miss Brontë's opening a school* at some place distant from Haworth. It elicited the following fragment of a characteristic reply:—*

'Leave home!—I shall neither be able to find place nor employment, perhaps, too, I shall be quite past the prime of life, my faculties will be rusted, and my few acquirements in a great measure forgotten. These ideas sting me keenly sometimes; but, whenever I consult my conscience, it affirms that I am doing right in staying at home, and bitter are its upbraidings when I yield to an eager desire for release. I could hardly expect success if I were to err against such warnings. I should like to hear from you again soon. Bring —— to the point, and make him give you a clear, not a vague, account of what pupils he really could promise; people often think they can do great things in that way till they have tried; but getting pupils is unlike getting any other sort of goods.'

Whatever might be the nature and extent of this negotiation, the end of it was that Charlotte adhered to the decision of her conscience, which bade her remain at home, as long as her presence could cheer or comfort those who were in distress, or had the slightest influence over him who was the cause of it. The next

extract gives us a glimpse into the cares of that home. It is from a
letter dated December 15th.*

'I hope you are not frozen up: the cold here is dreadful. I do not
remember such a series of North-Pole days. England might really
have taken a slide up into the Arctic Zone; the sky looks like ice;
the earth is frozen; the wind is as keen as a two-edged blade. We
have all had severe colds and coughs in consequence of the
weather. Poor Anne has suffered greatly from asthma, but is now,
I am glad to say, rather better. She had two nights last week when
her cough and difficulty of breathing were painful indeed to hear
and witness, and must have been most distressing to suffer; she
bore it, as she bears all affliction, without one complaint, only
sighing now and then when nearly worn out. She has an
extraordinary heroism of endurance. I admire, but I certainly could
not imitate her.' . . . 'You say I am to "tell you plenty." What
would you have me say? Nothing happens at Haworth; nothing, at
least, of a pleasant kind. One little incident occurred about a week
ago, to sting us to life; but if it gives no more pleasure for you to
hear, than it did for us to witness, you will scarcely thank me for
adverting to it. It was merely the arrival of a sheriff's officer on a
visit to B., inviting him either to pay his debts or take a trip to
York.* Of course his debts had to be paid. It is not agreeable to
lose money, time after time, in this way; but where is the use of
dwelling on such subjects? It will make him no better.'

'December 28th.*

'I feel as if it was almost a farce to sit down and write to you
now, with nothing to say worth listening to; and indeed, if it were
not for two reasons, I should put off the business at least a
fortnight hence. The first reason is, I want another letter from you,
for your letters are interesting, they have something in them; some
results of experience and observation; one receives them with
pleasure, and reads them with relish; and these letters I cannot
expect to get, unless I reply to them. I wish the correspondence
could be managed so as to be all on one side. The second reason
is derived from a remark in your last, that you felt lonely,
something as I was at Brussels, and that consequently you had a
peculiar desire to hear from old acquaintance. I can understand and

sympathise with this. I remember the shortest note was a treat to me, when I was at the above-named place; therefore I write. I have also a third reason: it is a haunting terror lest you should imagine I forget you—that my regard cools with absence. It is not in my nature to forget your nature; though I dare say, I should spit fire and explode sometimes if we lived together continually; and you, too, would get angry, and then we should get reconciled and jog on as before. Do you ever get dissatisfied with your own temper when you are long fixed to one place, in one scene, subject to one monotonous species of annoyance? I do: I am now in that unenviable frame of mind; my humour, I think, is too soon overthrown, too sore, too demonstrative and vehement. I almost long for some of the uniform serenity you describe in Mrs ——'s disposition; or at least, I would fain have her power of self-control and concealment; but I would not take her artificial habits and ideas along with her composure. After all I should prefer being as I am. . . . You do right not to be annoyed at any maxims of conventionality you meet with. Regard all new ways in the light of fresh experience for you: if you see any honey, gather it.' . . . . 'I don't, after all, consider that we ought to despise everything we see in the world, merely because it is not what we are accustomed to. I suspect, on the contrary, that there are not unfrequently substantial reasons underneath for customs that appear to us absurd; and if I were ever again to find myself amongst strangers, I should be solicitous to examine before I condemned. Indiscriminating irony and fault-finding are just *sumphishness** and that is all. Anne is now much better, but papa has been for near a fortnight far from well with the influenza; he has at times a most distressing cough, and his spirits are much depressed.'

So ended the year 1846.

# CHAPTER II

THE next year opened with a spell of cold dreary weather, which told severely on a constitution already tried by anxiety and care. Miss Brontë describes herself as having utterly lost her appetite, and as looking 'grey, old, worn and sunk,'* from her sufferings during the inclement season. The cold brought on severe toothache; toothache was the cause of a succession of restless miserable nights; and long wakefulness told acutely upon her nerves, making them feel with redoubled sensitiveness all the harass of her oppressive life. Yet she would not allow herself to lay her bad health to the charge of an uneasy mind; 'for after all,' said she at this time, 'I have many, many things to be thankful for.' But the real state of things may be gathered from the following extracts from her letters.*

'March 1st.

'Even at the risk of appearing very exacting, I can't help saying that I should like a letter as long as your last, every time you write. Short notes give one the feeling of a very small piece of a very good thing to eat,—they set the appetite on edge, and don't satisfy it,—a letter leaves you more contented; and yet, after all, I am very glad to get notes; so don't think, when you are pinched for time and materials, that it is useless to write a few lines; be assured, a few lines are very acceptable as far as they go; and though I like long letters, I would by no means have you to make a task of writing them . . . . I really should like you to come to Haworth, before I again go to B——. And it is natural and right that I should have this wish. To keep friendship in proper order, the balance of good offices must be preserved, otherwise a disquieting and anxious feeling creeps in, and destroys mutual comfort. In summer and in fine weather, your visit here might be much better managed than in winter. We could go out more, be more independent of the house and of our room. Branwell has been conducting himself very badly lately. I expect, from the extravagance of his behaviour, and from mysterious hints he drops (for he never will speak out plainly), that we shall be hearing news of fresh debts contracted by him soon. My health is better: I lay the blame of its feebleness on the cold weather, more than on an uneasy mind.'

'March 24th, 1847.

'It is at Haworth, if all be well, that we must next see each other again. I owe you a grudge for giving Miss W—— some very exaggerated account about my not being well, and setting her on to urge my leaving home as quite a duty. I'll take care not to tell you next time, when I think I am looking specially old and ugly; as if people could not have that privilege, without being supposed to be at the last gasp! I shall be thirty-one next birthday. My youth is gone like a dream; and very little use have I ever made of it. What have I done these last thirty years? Precious little.'

The quiet, sad year stole on. The sisters were contemplating near at hand, and for a long time, the terrible effects of talents misused and faculties abused in the person of that brother, once their fond darling and dearest pride. They had to cheer the poor old father, into whose heart all trials sank the deeper, because of the silent stoicism of his endurance. They had to watch over his health, of which, whatever was its state, he seldom complained. They had to save, as much as they could, the precious remnants of his sight. They had to order the frugal household with increased care, so as to supply wants and expenditure utterly foreign to their self-denying natures. Though they shrank from over-much contact with their fellow-beings, for all whom they met they had kind words, if few; and when kind actions were needed, they were not spared, if the sisters at the Parsonage could render them. They visited the parish-schools duly; and often were Charlotte's rare and brief holidays of a visit from home shortened by her sense of the necessity of being in her place at the Sunday-school.

In the intervals of such a life as this, 'Jane Eyre' was making progress. 'The Professor' was passing slowly and heavily from publisher to publisher. 'Wuthering Heights' and 'Agnes Grey' had been accepted by another publisher,* 'on terms somewhat im-poverishing to the two authors;' a bargain to be alluded to more fully hereafter. It was lying in his hands, awaiting his pleasure for its passage through the press, during all the months of early summer.

The piece of external brightness to which the sisters looked during these same summer months, was the hope that the friend to whom so many of Charlotte's letters are addressed, and who was her chosen companion, whenever circumstances permitted them to be together, as well as a favourite with Emily and Anne, would be able to pay them a visit at Haworth. Fine weather had come in May, Charlotte writes, and they hoped to make their visitor decently comfortable. Their brother was tolerably well, having got to the end of a considerable sum of money which he became possessed of in the spring,* and therefore under the wholesome restriction of poverty. But Charlotte warns her friend that she must expect to find a change in his appearance, and that he is broken in mind; and ends her note of entreating invitation by saying, 'I pray for fine weather, that we may get out while you stay.'*

At length the day was fixed.

'Friday will suit us very well. I *do* trust nothing will now arise to prevent your coming. I shall be anxious about the weather on that day; if it rains, I shall cry. Don't expect me to meet you; where would be the good of it? I neither like to meet, nor to be met. Unless, indeed, you had a box or a basket for me to carry; then there would be some sense in it. Come in black, blue, pink, white or scarlet, as you like. Come shabby or smart; neither the colour nor the condition signifies; provided only the dress contain E——, all will be right.'

But there came the first of a series of disappointments to be borne. One feels how sharp it must have been to have wrung out the following words.

'May 20th.*

'Your letter of yesterday did indeed give me a cruel chill of disappointment. I cannot blame you, for I know it was not your fault. I do not altogether exempt —— from reproach. . . . . This is bitter, but I feel bitter. As to going to B——, I will not go near the place till you have been to Haworth. My respects to all and sundry, accompanied with a large amount of wormwood and gall, from the effusion of which you and your mother are alone excepted.—C. B.

'You are quite at liberty to tell —— what I think, if you judge proper. Though it is true I may be somewhat unjust, for I am deeply annoyed. I thought I had arranged your visit tolerably comfortable for you this time. I may find it more difficult on another occasion.'

I must give one sentence from a letter written about this time,* as it shows distinctly the clear strong sense of the writer.

'I was amused by what she says respecting her wish that, when she marries, her husband will, at least, have a will of his own, even should he be a tyrant. Tell her, when she forms that aspiration again, she must make it conditional: if her husband has a strong will, he must also have strong sense, a kind heart, and a thoroughly correct notion of justice; because a man with a *weak brain* and a *strong will*, is merely an intractable brute; you can have no hold of him; you can never lead him right. A *tyrant* under any circumstances is a curse.'

Meanwhile, 'The Professor' had met with many refusals from different publishers; some, I have reason to believe, not over-courteously worded in writing to an unknown author, and none alleging any distinct reasons for its rejection. Courtesy is always due; but it is, perhaps, hardly to be expected that, in the press of business in a great publishing house, they should find time to explain why they decline particular works. Yet, though one course of action is not to be wondered at, the opposite may fall upon a grieved and disappointed mind with all the graciousness of dew; and I can well sympathise with the published account which 'Currer Bell' gives,* of the feelings experienced on reading Messrs Smith and Elder's letter containing the rejection of 'The Professor.'

'As a forlorn hope, he tried one publishing house more. Ere long, in a much shorter space than that on which experience had taught him to calculate, there came a letter, which he opened in the dreary anticipation of finding two hard hopeless lines, intimating that "Messrs Smith and Elder were not disposed to publish the MS," and, instead, he took out of the envelope a letter of two pages. He read it trembling. It declined, indeed, to publish that tale for business reasons, but it discussed its merits and demerits, so courteously, so considerately, in a spirit so rational, with a discrimination so enlightened, that this very refusal cheered the author better than a vulgarly-expressed acceptance would have done. It was added, that a work in three volumes would meet with careful attention.'

Mr Smith* has told me a little circumstance connected with the reception of this manuscript, which seems to me indicative of no ordinary character. It came (accompanied by the note given below) in a brown paper parcel, to 65, Cornhill. Besides the address to Messrs Smith and Co., there were on it those of other publishers to whom the tale had been sent, not obliterated, but simply scored through, so that Messrs Smith at once perceived the names of some of the houses in the trade to which the unlucky parcel had gone, without success.

TO MESSRS SMITH AND ELDER.

'July 15th, 1847.

'Gentlemen,—I beg to submit to your consideration the accompanying manuscript. I should be glad to learn whether it be such as you approve, and would undertake to publish at as early a period as possible. Address, Mr Currer Bell, under cover to Miss Brontë, Haworth, Bradford, Yorkshire.'

Some time elapsed before an answer was returned.

A little circumstance may be mentioned here, though it belongs to a somewhat earlier period, as showing Miss Brontë's inexperience of the ways of the world, and willing deference to the opinion of others. She had written to a publisher about one of her manuscripts, which she had sent him, and, not receiving any reply, she consulted her brother as to what could be the reason for the prolonged silence. He at once set it down to her not having enclosed a postage-stamp in her letter. She accordingly wrote again, to repair her former omission, and apologise for it.

TO MESSRS SMITH AND ELDER.

'August 2nd, 1847.

'Gentlemen,—About three weeks since, I sent for your consideration a MS entitled "The Professor, a tale by Currer Bell." I should be glad to know whether it reached your hands safely, and likewise to learn, at your earliest convenience, whether it be such as you can undertake to publish.—I am, Gentlemen, yours respectfully,

'CURRER BELL.

'I enclose a directed cover for your reply.'

This time her note met with a prompt answer; for, four days later, she writes (in reply to the letter which she afterwards characterised in the Preface to the second edition of 'Wuthering Heights,'* as containing a refusal so delicate, reasonable, and courteous, as to be more cheering than some acceptances):

'Your objection to the want of varied interest in the tale is, I am aware, not without grounds;* yet it appears to me that it might be published without serious risk, if its appearance were speedily followed up by another work from the same pen, of a more striking and exciting character. The first work might serve as an introduction, and accustom the public to the author's name; the success of the second might thereby be rendered more probable. I have a second narrative in three volumes, now in progress, and nearly completed, to which I have endeavoured to impart a more vivid interest than belongs to "The Professor." In about a month I hope to finish it, so that if a publisher were found for "The Professor," the second narrative might follow as soon as was deemed advisable; and thus the interest of the public (if any interest was roused) might not be suffered to cool. Will you be kind enough to favour me with your judgment on this plan?'

While the minds of the three sisters were in this state of suspense, their long-expected friend came to pay her promised visit. She was with them at the beginning of the glowing August of that year. They were out on the moors for the greater part of the day, basking in the golden sunshine, which was bringing on an unusual plenteousness of harvest, for which, somewhat later, Charlotte expressed her earnest desire that there should be a thanksgiving service in all the churches.* August was the season of glory for the neighbourhood of Haworth. Even the smoke, lying in the valley between that village and Keighley, took beauty from the radiant colours on the moors above, the rich purple of the heather bloom calling out an harmonious contrast in the tawny golden light that, in the full heat of summer evenings, comes stealing everywhere through the dun atmosphere of the hollows. And up, on the moors, turning away from all habitations of men, the royal ground on which they stood would expand into long swells of amethyst-tinted hills, melting away into aërial tints; and the fresh and fragrant scent of the heather, and the 'murmur of innumerable bees,'* would lend a poignancy to the relish with which they welcomed their friend to their own true home on the wild and open hills.

There, too, they could escape from the Shadow in the house below.

Throughout this time—during all these confidences—not a word was uttered to their friend of the three tales in London; two accepted and in the press—one trembling in the balance of a publisher's judgment; nor did she hear of that other story 'nearly completed,' lying in manuscript in the grey old parsonage down below. She might have her suspicions that they all wrote with an intention of publication some time; but she knew the bounds which they set to themselves in their communications; nor could she, nor can any one else, wonder, at their reticence, when remembering how scheme after scheme had failed, just as it seemed close upon accomplishment.

Mr Brontë, too, had his suspicions of something going on; but, never being spoken to, he did not speak on the subject, and consequently his ideas were vague and uncertain, only just pro-phetic enough to keep him from being actually stunned when, later on, he heard of the success of 'Jane Eyre;' to the progress of which we must now return.

TO MESSRS SMITH AND ELDER.

'August 24th.

'I now send you per rail a MS entitled "Jane Eyre," a novel in three volumes, by Currer Bell. I find I cannot prepay the carriage of the parcel, as money for that purpose is not received at the small station-house where it is left. If, when you acknowledge the receipt of the MS, you would have the goodness to mention the amount charged on delivery, I will immediately transmit it in postage stamps. It is better in future to address Mr Currer Bell, under cover to Miss Brontë, Haworth, Bradford, Yorkshire, as there is a risk of letters otherwise directed not reaching me at present. To save trouble, I enclose an envelope.'

'Jane Eyre' was accepted, and printed and published by October 16th.

While it was in the press, Miss Brontë went to pay a short visit to her friend at B——. The proofs were forwarded to her there, and she occasionally sat at the same table with her friend, correcting them; but they did not exchange a word on the subject.

Immediately on her return to the Parsonage, she wrote:—

'September.*

'I had a very wet, windy walk home from Keighley; but my fatigue quite disappeared when I reached home, and found all well. Thank God for it.

'My boxes came safe this morning. I have distributed the presents. Papa says I am to remember him most kindly to you. The screen* will be very useful, and he thanks you for it. Tabby was charmed with her cap. She said, "She never thought o' naught o' t' sort as Miss —— sending her aught, and, she is sure, she can never thank her enough for it." I was infuriated on finding a jar in my trunk. At first I hoped it was empty, but when I found it heavy and replete, I could have hurled it all the way back to B——. However the inscription A. B. softened me much. It was at once kind and villanous in you to send it. You ought first to be tenderly kissed, and then afterwards as tenderly whipped. Emily is just now on the floor of the bed-room where I am writing, looking at her apples. She smiled when I gave the collar to her as your present, with an expression at once well-pleased and slightly surprised. All send their love.—Yours, in a mixture of anger and love.'

When the manuscript* of 'Jane Eyre' had been received by the future publishers of that remarkable novel, it fell to the share of a gentleman connected with the firm* to read it first. He was so powerfully struck by the character of the tale, that he reported his impression in very strong terms to Mr Smith, who appears to have been much amused by the admiration excited. 'You seem to have been so enchanted, that I do not know how to believe you,' he laughingly said. But when a second reader, in the person of a clear-headed Scotchman, not given to enthusiasm, had taken the MS home in the evening, and became so deeply interested in it, as to sit up half the night to finish it, Mr Smith's curiosity was sufficiently excited to prompt him to read it for himself; and great as were the praises which had been bestowed upon it, he found that they had not exceeded the truth.

On its publication,* copies were presented to a few private literary friends. Their discernment had been rightly reckoned upon. They were of considerable standing in the world of letters; and one and all returned expressions of high praise along with their thanks for the book. Among them was the great writer of fiction for whom Miss Brontë felt so strong an admiration; he immediately appreciated, and, in a characteristic note to the publishers, acknowledged its extraordinary merits.

The Reviews were more tardy,* or more cautious. The 'Athenæum' and the 'Spectator' gave short notices, containing qualified admissions of the power of the author. The 'Literary Gazette' was uncertain as to whether it was safe to praise an unknown author. The 'Daily News' declined accepting the copy which had been sent, on the score of a rule 'never to review novels;' but a little later on, there appeared a notice of the 'Bachelor of the Albany,' in that paper; and Messrs Smith and Elder again forwarded a copy of 'Jane Eyre' to the Editor, with a request for a notice. This time the work was accepted; but I am not aware what was the character of the article upon it.

The 'Examiner'* came forward to the rescue, as far as the opinions of professional critics were concerned. The literary articles in that paper were always remarkable for their genial and generous appreciation of merit; nor was the notice of 'Jane Eyre' an exception; it was full of hearty, yet delicate and discriminating praise. Otherwise, the press in general did little to promote the sale of the novel; the demand for it among librarians had begun before the appearance of the review in the 'Examiner;' the power and fascination of the tale itself made its merits known to the public, without the kindly finger-posts of professional criticism; and, early in December, the rush began for copies.

I will insert two or three of Miss Brontë's letters to her publishers, in order to show how timidly the idea of success was received by one so unaccustomed to adopt a sanguine view of any subject in which she was individually concerned. The occasions on which these notes were written, will explain themselves.

MESSRS SMITH, ELDER, AND CO.

'Oct. 19th, 1847.

'Gentlemen,—The six copies of "Jane Eyre" reached me this morning. You have given the work every advantage which good paper, clear type, and a seemly outside can supply;—if it fails, the fault will lie with the author,—you are exempt.

'I now await the judgment of the press and the public. I am, Gentlemen, yours respectfully,

'C. BELL.'

MESSRS SMITH, ELDER, AND CO.

'Oct. 26th, 1847.

'Gentlemen,—I have received the newspapers. They speak quite as favourably of "Jane Eyre" as I expected them to do. The notice in the "Literary Gazette" seems certainly to have been indited in rather a flat mood, and the "Athenæum" has a style of its own, which I respect, but cannot exactly relish; still when one considers that journals of that standing have a dignity to maintain which would be deranged by a too cordial recognition of the claims of an obscure author, I suppose there is every reason to be satisfied.

'Meantime a brisk sale would be effectual support under the hauteur of lofty critics. I am, Gentlemen, yours respectfully,

'C. BELL.'

MESSRS SMITH, ELDER, AND CO.

'Nov. 13th, 1847.

'Gentlemen,—I have to acknowledge the receipt of yours of the 11th inst., and to thank you for the information it communicates. The notice from the "People's Journal" also duly reached me, and this morning I received the "Spectator." The critique in the "Spectator" gives that view of the book which will naturally be taken by a certain class of minds; I shall expect it to be followed by other notices of a similar nature. The way to detraction has been pointed out, and will probably be pursued. Most future notices will in all likelihood have a reflection of the "Spectator" in them. I fear this turn of opinion will not improve the demand for the book—but time will show. If "Jane Eyre" has any solid worth in it, it ought to weather a gust of unfavourable wind. I am, Gentlemen, yours respectfully,

'C. BELL.'

MESSRS SMITH, ELDER, AND CO.

'Nov. 30, 1847.

'Gentlemen,—I have received the "Economist," but not the "Examiner"; from some cause that paper has missed, as the "Spectator" did on a former occasion; I am glad, however, to learn through your letter, that its notice of "Jane Eyre" was favourable, and also that the prospects of the work appear to improve.

'I am obliged to you for the information respecting "Wuthering Heights."* I am, Gentlemen, yours respectfully,

'C. BELL.'

TO MESSRS SMITH, ELDER, AND CO.

'Dec. 1st, 1847.

'Gentlemen,—The "Examiner" reached me to-day: it had been missent on account of the direction, which was to Currer Bell, care of Miss Brontë. Allow me to intimate that it would be better in future not to put the name of Currer Bell on the outside of communications; if directed simply to Miss Brontë they will be more likely to reach their destination safely. Currer Bell is not known in the district, and I have no wish that he should become known. The notice in the "Examiner" gratified me very much; it appears to be from the pen of an able man who has understood what he undertakes to criticise; of course, approbation from such a quarter is encouraging to an author, and I trust it will prove beneficial to the work.—I am, Gentlemen, yours respectfully,

'C. BELL.

'I received likewise seven other notices from provincial papers enclosed in an envelope. I thank you very sincerely for so punctually sending me all the various criticisms on "Jane Eyre." '

'Dec. 10th, 1847.

'Gentlemen,—I beg to acknowledge the receipt of your letter
enclosing a bank post bill,* for which I thank you. Having already
expressed my sense of your kind and upright conduct, I can now
only say that I trust you will always have reason to be as well
content with me as I am with you. If the result of any future
exertions I may be able to make should prove agreeable and
advantageous to you, I shall be well satisfied; and it would be a
serious source of regret to me if I thought you ever had reason to
repent being my publishers.

'You need not apologise, Gentlemen, for having written to me
so seldom; of course I am always glad to hear from you, but I am
truly glad to hear from Mr Williams likewise; he was my first
favourable critic; he first gave me encouragement to persevere as
an author, consequently I naturally respect him and feel grateful
to him.

'Excuse the informality of my letter, and believe me, Gentlemen,
yours very respectfully,

'CURRER BELL.'

There is little record remaining of the manner in which the first
news of its wonderful success reached and affected the one heart of
the three sisters. I once asked Charlotte—we were talking about the
description of Lowood school, and she was saying that she was not
sure whether she should have written it, if she had been aware how
instantaneously it would have been identified with Cowan Bridge—
whether the popularity to which the novel attained had taken her by
surprise. She hesitated a little, and then said: 'I believed that what had
impressed me so forcibly when I wrote it, must make a strong
impression on any one who read it. I was not surprised at those who
read "Jane Eyre" being deeply interested in it; but I hardly expected
that a book by an unknown author could find readers.'

The sisters had kept the knowledge of their literary ventures
from their father, fearing to increase their own anxieties and
disappointment by witnessing his; for he took an acute interest in
all that befell his children, and his own tendency had been towards
literature in the days when he was young and hopeful. It was true

he did not much manifest his feelings in words; he would have thought that he was prepared for disappointment as the lot of man, and that he could have met it with stoicism; but words are poor and tardy interpreters of feelings to those who love one another, and his daughters knew how he would have borne ill-success worse for them than for himself. So they did not tell him what they were undertaking. He says now that he suspected it all along, but his suspicions could take no exact form, as all he was certain of was, that his children were perpetually writing—and not writing letters. We have seen how the communications from their publishers were received 'under cover to Miss Brontë.' Once, Charlotte told me, they overheard the postman meeting Mr Brontë, as the latter was leaving the house, and inquiring from the parson where one Currer Bell could be living, to which Mr Brontë replied that there was no such person in the parish. This must have been the misadventure to which Miss Brontë alludes in the beginning of her correspondence with Mr Aylott.

Now, however, when the demand for the work had assured success to 'Jane Eyre,' her sisters urged Charlotte to tell their father of its publication. She accordingly went into his study one afternoon after his early dinner, carrying with her a copy of the book, and two or three reviews, taking care to include a notice adverse to it.

She informed me that something like the following conversation took place between her and him. (I wrote down her words the day after I heard them; and I am pretty sure they are quite accurate.)

'Papa, I've been writing a book.'

'Have you, my dear?'

'Yes, and I want you to read it.'

'I am afraid it will try my eyes too much.'

'But it is not in manuscript; it is printed.'

'My dear! you've never thought of the expense it will be! It will be almost sure to be a loss, for how can you get a book sold? No one knows you or your name.'

'But, papa, I don't think it will be a loss; no more will you, if you will just let me read you a review or two, and tell you more about it.'

So she sate down and read some of the reviews to her father; and then, giving him the copy of 'Jane Eyre' that she intended for him, she left him to read it. When he came in to tea, he said, 'Girls, do you know Charlotte has been writing a book, and it is much better than likely?'*

But while the existence of Currer Bell, the author, was like a piece of a dream to the quiet inhabitants of Haworth Parsonage, who went on with their uniform household life, their cares for their brother being its only variety,—the whole reading-world of England was in a ferment to discover the unknown author. Even the publishers of 'Jane Eyre' were ignorant whether Currer Bell was a real or an assumed name,—whether it belonged to a man or a woman. In every town people sought out the list of their friends and acquaintances, and turned away in disappointment. No one they knew had genius enough to be the author. Every little incident mentioned in the book was turned this way and that to answer, if possible, the much-vexed question of sex. All in vain. People were content to relax their exertions to satisfy their curiosity, and simply to sit down and greatly admire.

I am not going to write an analysis of a book with which every one who reads this biography is sure to be acquainted; much less a criticism upon a work, which the great flood of public opinion has lifted up from the obscurity in which it first appeared, and laid high and safe on the everlasting hills of fame.

Before me lies a packet of extracts from newspapers and periodicals, which Mr Brontë has sent me. It is touching to look them over, and see how there is hardly any notice, however short and clumsily worded, in any obscure provincial paper, but what has been cut out and carefully ticketed with its date by the poor, bereaved father,—so proud when he first read them—so desolate now. For one and all are full of praise of this great, unknown genius, which suddenly appeared amongst us. Conjecture as to the authorship ran about like wild-fire. People in London, smooth and polished as the Athenians of old,* and like them 'spending their time in nothing else, but either to tell or to hear some new thing,' were astonished and delighted to find that a fresh sensation, a new pleasure, was in reserve for them in the uprising of an author, capable of depicting with accurate and Titanic power the strong, self-reliant, racy, and individual characters which were not, after all, extinct species, but lingered still in existence in the North. They thought that there was some exaggeration mixed with the peculiar force of delineation. Those nearer to the spot, where the scene of the story was apparently laid, were sure, from the very truth and accuracy of the writing, that the writer was no Southron; for though 'dark, and cold, and rugged is the North,'* the old strength of the Scandinavian races yet abides there, and glowed out in every character depicted in 'Jane Eyre.' Farther than this, curiosity, both honourable and dishonourable, was at fault.

When the second edition appeared, in the January of the following year, with the dedication to Mr Thackeray,* people looked at each other and wondered afresh. But Currer Bell knew no more of William Makepeace Thackeray as an individual man— of his life, age, fortunes, or circumstances—than she did of those of Mr Michael Angelo Titmarsh. The one had placed his name as author upon the title-page of 'Vanity Fair,' the other had not. She was thankful for the opportunity of expressing her high admiration of a writer, whom, as she says, she regarded 'as the social regenerator of his day—as the very master of that working corps who would restore to rectitude the warped state of things. . . . . His wit is bright, his humour attractive, but both bear the same relation to his serious genius, that the mere lambent sheet-lightning, playing under the edge of the summer cloud, does to the electric death-spark hid in its womb.'

Anne Brontë had been more than usually delicate all the summer, and her sensitive spirit had been deeply affected by the great anxiety of her home. But now that 'Jane Eyre' gave such indications of success, Charlotte began to plan schemes of future pleasure,—perhaps relaxation from care, would be the more correct expression,—for their darling younger sister, the 'little one' of the household. But, although Anne was cheered for a time by Charlotte's success, the fact was, that neither her spirits nor her bodily strength were such as to incline her to much active exertion, and she led far too sedentary a life, continually stooping either over her book, or work, or at her desk. 'It is with difficulty,' writes her sister,* 'that we can prevail upon her to take a walk, or induce her to converse. I look forward to next summer with the confident intention that she shall, if possible, make at least a brief sojourn at the sea-side.' In this same letter is a sentence, telling how dearly home, even with its present terrible drawback, lay at the roots of her heart; but it is too much blended with reference to the affairs of others to bear quotation.

Any author of a successful novel is liable to an inroad of letters from unknown readers, containing commendation—sometimes of so fulsome and indiscriminating a character as to remind the recipient of Dr Johnson's famous speech to one who offered presumptuous and injudicious praise*—sometimes saying merely a few words, which have power to stir the heart 'as with the sound of a trumpet,'* and in the high humility they excite, to call forth strong resolutions to make all future efforts worthy of such praise; and occasionally containing that true appreciation of both merits and demerits, together with the sources of each, which forms the very criticism and help for which an inexperienced writer thirsts. Of each of these kinds of communication Currer Bell received her full share; and her warm heart, and true sense and high standard of what she aimed at, affixed to each its proper value. Among other letters of hers, some to Mr G. H. Lewes* have been kindly placed by him at my service; and as I know Miss Brontë highly prized his letters of encouragement and advice, I shall give extracts from her replies, as their dates occur, because they will indicate the kind of criticism she valued, and also because throughout, in anger, as in agreement and harmony, they show her character, unblinded by any self-flattery, full of clear-sighted modesty as to what she really did well, and what she failed in, grateful for friendly interest, and only sore and irritable when the question of sex in authorship was, as she thought, roughly or unfairly treated. As to the rest, the letters speak for themselves, to those who know how to listen, far better than I can interpret their meaning into my poorer and weaker words. Mr Lewes has politely sent me the following explanation of that letter of his, to which the succeeding one of Miss Brontë is a reply.

'When "Jane Eyre" first appeared, the publishers courteously sent me a copy. The enthusiasm with which I read it, made me go down to Mr Parker, and propose to write a review of it for "Frazer's Magazine."* He would not consent to an unknown novel—for the papers had not yet declared themselves—receiving such importance, but thought it might make one on *Recent Novels: English and French*—which appeared in *Frazer, December*, 1847.

Meanwhile I had written to Miss Brontë to tell her the delight with which her book filled me; and seem to have "sermonized" her, to judge from her reply.'

TO G. H. LEWES, ESQ.

'Nov. 6th, 1847.

'Dear Sir,—Your letter reached me yesterday; I beg to assure you, that I appreciate fully the intention with which it was written, and I thank you sincerely both for its cheering commendation and valuable advice.

'You warn me to beware of melodrama, and you exhort me to adhere to the real. When I first began to write, so impressed was I with the truth of the principles you advocate, that I determined to take Nature and Truth as my sole guides, and to follow in their very footprints; I restrained imagination, eschewed romance, repressed excitement; over-bright colouring, too, I avoided, and sought to produce something which should be soft, grave, and true.

'My work (a tale in one volume) being completed, I offered it to a publisher. He said it was original, faithful to nature, but he did not feel warranted in accepting it; such a work would not sell. I tried six publishers in succession; they all told me it was deficient in "startling incident" and "thrilling excitement," that it would never suit the circulating libraries, and as it was on those libraries the success of works of fiction mainly depended, they could not undertake to publish what would be overlooked there.

' "Jane Eyre" was rather objected to at first, on the same grounds, but finally found acceptance.

'I mention this to you, not with a view of pleading exemption from censure, but in order to direct your attention to the root of certain literary evils. If, in your forthcoming article in "Frazer," you would bestow a few words of enlightenment on the public who support the circulating libraries, you might, with your powers, do some good.

'You advise me, too, not to stray far from the ground of experience, as I become weak when I enter the region of fiction; and you say, "real experience is perennially interesting, and to all men."

'I feel that this also is true; but, dear Sir, is not the real experience of each individual very limited? And, if a writer dwells upon that solely or principally, is he not in danger of repeating himself, and also of becoming an egotist? Then, too, imagination is a strong, restless faculty, which claims to be heard and exercised: are we to be quite deaf to her cry, and insensate to her struggles? When she shows us bright pictures, are we never to look at them, and try to reproduce them? And when she is eloquent, and speaks rapidly and urgently in our ear, are we not to write to her dictation?

'I shall anxiously search the next number of "Frazer" for your opinions on these points.——Believe me, dear Sir, yours gratefully,

'C. BELL.'

But while gratified by appreciation as an author, she was cautious as to the person from whom she received it; for much of the value of the praise depended on the sincerity and capability of the person rendering it. Accordingly, she applied to Mr Williams (a gentleman connected with her publishers' firm) for information as to who and what Mr Lewes was. Her reply, after she had learnt something of the character of her future critic, and while awaiting his criticism, must not be omitted. Besides the reference to him, it contains some amusing allusions to the perplexity which began to be excited respecting the 'identity of the brothers Bell,' and some notice of the conduct of another publisher* towards her sisters, which I refrain from characterising, because I understand that truth is considered a libel in speaking of such people.

TO W. S. WILLIAMS, ESQ.

'Nov. 10th, 1847.

'Dear Sir,——I have received the "Britannia," and the "Sun," but not the "Spectator,"* which I rather regret, as censure, though not pleasant, is often wholesome.

'Thank you for your information regarding Mr Lewes. I am glad to hear that he is a clever and sincere man: such being the case, I can await his critical sentence with fortitude; even if it goes against me, I shall not murmur; ability and honesty have a right to condemn, where they think condemnation is deserved. From what you say, however, I trust rather to obtain at least a modified approval.

'Your account of the various surmises respecting the identity of the brothers Bell, amused me much: were the enigma solved, it would probably be found not worth the trouble of solution; but I will let it alone; it suits ourselves to remain quiet, and certainly injures no one else.

'The reviewer who noticed the little book of poems, in the "Dublin Magazine,"* conjectured that the *soi-disant* three personages were in reality but one, who, endowed with an unduly prominent organ of self-esteem, and consequently impressed with a somewhat weighty notion of his own merits, thought them too vast to be concentrated in a single individual, and accordingly divided himself into three, out of consideration, I suppose, for the nerves of the much-to-be-astounded public! This was an ingenious thought in the reviewer,—very original and striking, but not accurate. We are three.

'A prose work, by Ellis and Acton, will soon appear:* it should have been out, indeed, long since; for the first proof-sheets were already in the press at the commencement of last August, before Currer Bell had placed the MS of "Jane Eyre" in your hands. Mr ——, however, does not do business like Messrs Smith and Elder; a different spirit seems to preside at —— Street, to that which guides the helm at 65, Cornhill. . . . . My relatives have suffered from exhausting delay and procrastination, while I have to acknowledge the benefits of a management at once business-like and gentleman-like, energetic and considerate.

'I should like to know if Mr —— often acts as he has done to my relations, or whether this is an exceptional instance of his method. Do you know, and can you tell me anything about him? You must excuse me for going to the point at once, when I want to learn anything: if my questions are impertinent, you are, of course, at liberty to decline answering them.—I am, yours respectfully,

'C. Bell.'

### TO G. H. LEWES, ESQ.

'Nov. 22nd, 1847.

'Dear Sir,—I have now read "Ranthorpe."* I could not get it till a day or two ago; but I have got it and read it at last; and in reading

"Ranthorpe," I have read a new book,—not a reprint—not a reflection of any other book, but a *new book*.

'I did not know such books were written now. It is very different to any of the popular works of fiction: it fills the mind with fresh knowledge. Your experience and your convictions are made the reader's; and to an author, at least, they have a value and an interest quite unusual. I await your criticism on "Jane Eyre" now with other sentiments than I entertained before the perusal of "Ranthorpe."

'You were a stranger to me. I did not particularly respect you. I did not feel that your praise or blame would have any special weight. I knew little of your right to condemn or approve. *Now* I am informed on these points.

'You will be severe; your last letter taught me as much. Well! I shall try to extract good out of your severity: and besides, though I am now sure you are a just, discriminating man, yet, being mortal, you must be fallible; and if any part of your censure galls me too keenly to the quick—gives me deadly pain—I shall for the present disbelieve it, and put it quite aside, till such time as I feel able to receive it without torture.—I am, dear Sir, yours very respectfully,

                                        'C. BELL.'

In December, 1847, 'Wuthering Heights' and 'Agnes Grey' appeared.* The first-named of these stories has revolted many readers by the power with which wicked and exceptional characters are depicted. Others, again, have felt the attraction of remarkable genius, even when displayed on grim and terrible criminals. Miss Brontë herself says, with regard to this tale, 'Where delineation of human character is concerned, the case is different. I am bound to avow that she had scarcely more practical knowledge of the peasantry amongst whom she lived, than a nun has of the country-people that pass her convent gates. My sister's disposition was not naturally gregarious: circumstances favoured and fostered her tendency to seclusion; except to go to church, or to take a walk on the hills, she rarely crossed the threshold of home. Though her feeling for the people round her was benevolent, intercourse with them she never sought, nor, with very few exceptions, ever experienced; and yet she knew them, knew their ways, their language, their family histories; she could hear of them with interest, and talk of them with detail, minute, graphic and accurate; but *with* them she rarely exchanged a word. Hence it ensued, that what her mind had gathered of the real concerning them, was too exclusively confined to those tragic and terrible traits, of which, in listening to the secret annals of every rude vicinage, the memory is sometimes compelled to receive the impress. Her imagination, which was a spirit more sombre than sunny—more powerful than sportive—found in such traits material whence it wrought creations like Heathcliff, like Earnshaw, like Catherine. Having formed these beings, she did not know what she had done. If the auditor of her work, when read in manuscript, shuddered under the grinding influence of natures so relentless and implacable—of spirits so lost and fallen; if it was complained that the mere hearing of certain vivid and fearful scenes banished sleep by night, and disturbed mental peace by day, Ellis Bell would wonder what was meant, and suspect the complainant of affectation. Had she but lived, her mind would of itself have grown like a strong tree—loftier, straighter, wider-spreading—and its matured fruits would have attained a mellower ripeness and sunnier bloom; but on that mind time and experience alone could work; to the influence of other intellects it was not amenable.'

Whether justly or unjustly, the productions of the two younger Miss Brontës were not received with much favour at the time of their publication. 'Critics failed to do them justice. The immature, but very real, powers revealed in "Wuthering Heights," were scarcely recognised; its import and nature were misunderstood; the identity of its author was misrepresented: it was said that this was an earlier and ruder attempt of the same pen which had produced "Jane Eyre." ' . . . . 'Unjust and grievous error! We laughed at it at first, but I deeply lament it now.'

Henceforward Charlotte Brontë's existence becomes divided into two parallel currents—her life as Currer Bell, the author; her life as Charlotte Brontë, the woman. There were separate duties belonging to each character—not opposing each other; not impossible, but difficult to be reconciled. When a man becomes an author, it is probably merely a change of employment to him. He takes a portion of that time which has hitherto been devoted to some other study or pursuit; he gives up something of the legal or medical profession, in which he has hitherto endeavoured to serve others, or relinquishes part of the trade or business by which he has been striving to gain a livelihood; and another merchant, or lawyer, or doctor, steps into his vacant place, and probably does as well as he. But no other can take up the quiet regular duties of the daughter, the wife, or the mother, as well as she whom God has appointed to fill that particular place: a woman's principal work in life is hardly left to her own choice; nor can she drop the domestic charges devolving on her as an individual, for the exercise of the most splendid talents that were ever bestowed. And yet she must not shrink from the extra responsibility implied by the very fact of her possessing such talents. She must not hide her gift in a napkin;* it was meant for the use and service of others. In a humble and faithful spirit must she labour to do what is not impossible, or God would not have set her to do it.

I put into words what Charlotte Brontë put into actions.

The year 1848 opened with sad domestic distress. It is necessary, however painful, to remind the reader constantly of what was always present to the hearts of father and sisters at this time. It is well that the thoughtless critics, who spoke of the sad and gloomy views of life presented by the Brontës in their tales, should know how such words were wrung out of them by the living recollection of the long agony they suffered. It is well, too, that they who have objected to the representation of coarseness and shrank from it with repugnance, as if such conceptions arose out of the writers, should learn, that, not from the imagination—not from internal conception—but from the hard cruel facts, pressed down, by external life, upon their very senses, for long months and years together, did they write out what they saw, obeying the stern dictates of their consciences. They might be mistaken. They might err in writing at all, when their afflictions were so great that they could not write otherwise than they did of life. It is possible that it would have been better to have described only good and pleasant people, doing only good and pleasant things (in which case they could hardly have written at any time): all I say is, that never, I believe, did women, possessed of such wonderful gifts, exercise them with a fuller feeling of responsibility for their use. As to mistakes, they stand now—as authors as well as women—before the judgment-seat of God.

'Jan. 11th, 1848.

'We have not been very comfortable here at home lately. Branwell has, by some means, contrived to get more money from the old quarter,* and has led us a sad life. . . . Papa is harassed day and night; we have little peace; he is always sick; has two or three times fallen down in fits; what will be the ultimate end, God knows. But who is without their drawback, their scourge, their skeleton behind the curtain? It remains only to do one's best, and endure with patience what God sends.'

I suppose that she had read Mr Lewes' review on 'Recent Novels,' when it appeared in the December of the last year, but I find no allusion to it till she writes to him on January 12th, 1848.

'Dear Sir,—I thank you then sincerely for your generous review; and it is with a sense of double content I express my gratitude, because I am now sure the tribute is not superfluous or obtrusive. You were not severe on "Jane Eyre;" you were very lenient. I am glad you told me my faults plainly in private, for in your public notice you touch on them so lightly, I should perhaps have passed them over, thus indicated, with too little reflection.

'I mean to observe your warning about being careful how I undertake new works; my stock of materials is not abundant, but very slender; and, besides, neither my experience, my acquirements, nor my powers, are sufficiently varied to justify my ever becoming a frequent writer. I tell you this, because your article in "Frazer" left in me an uneasy impression that you were disposed to think better of the author of "Jane Eyre" than that individual deserved;* and I would rather you had a correct than a flattering opinion of me, even though I should never see you.

'If I ever *do* write another book, I think I will have nothing of what you call "melodrama;" I *think* so, but I am not sure. I *think*, too, I will endeavour to follow the counsel which shines out of Miss Austen's "mild eyes," "to finish more and be more subdued;" but neither am I sure of that. When authors write best, or, at least, when they write most fluently, an influence seems to waken in them, which becomes their master—which will have its own way—putting out of view all behests but its own, dictating certain words, and insisting on their being used, whether vehement or measured in their nature; new-moulding characters, giving unthought-of turns to incidents, rejecting carefully-elaborated old ideas, and suddenly creating and adopting new ones.

'Is it not so? And should we try to counteract this influence? Can we indeed counteract it?

'I am glad that another work of yours will soon appear;* most curious shall I be to see whether you will write up to your own principles, and work out your own theories. You did not do it altogether in "Ranthorpe"—at least not in the latter part; but the first portion was, I think, nearly without fault; then it had a pith, truth, significance in it, which gave the book sterling value; but to write so, one must have seen and known a great deal, and I have seen and known very little.

'Why do you like Miss Austen so very much? I am puzzled on that point. What induced you to say that you would have rather written "Pride and Prejudice," or "Tom Jones," than any of the Waverley Novels?

'I had not seen "Pride and Prejudice" till I read that sentence of yours, and then I got the book. And what did I find? An accurate daguerreotyped portrait of a commonplace face; a carefully-fenced, highly-cultivated garden, with neat borders and delicate flowers; but no glance of a bright vivid physiognomy, no open country, no fresh air, no blue hill, no bonny beck. I should hardly like to live with her ladies and gentlemen, in their elegant but confined houses. These observations will probably irritate you, but I shall run the risk.

'Now I can understand admiration of George Sand;* for though I never saw any of her works which I admired throughout (even "Consuelo," which is the best, or the best that I have read, appears to me to couple strange extravagance with wondrous excellence), yet she has a grasp of mind, which, if I cannot fully comprehend, I can very deeply respect; she is sagacious and profound;—Miss Austen is only shrewd and observant.

'Am I wrong—or, were you hasty in what you said? If you have time, I should be glad to hear further on this subject; if not, or if you think the question frivolous, do not trouble yourself to reply.—I am, yours respectfully,

'C. BELL.'

'Jan. 18th, 1848.

'Dear Sir,—I must write one more note, though I had not intended to trouble you again so soon. I have to agree with you, and to differ from you.

'You correct my crude remarks on the subject of the "influence"; well, I accept your definition of what the effects of that influence should be; I recognise the wisdom of your rules for its regulation. . . . . . .

'What a strange lecture comes next in your letter! You say I must familiarise my mind with the fact, that "Miss Austen is not a poetess, has no 'sentiment' (you scornfully enclose the word in inverted commas), no eloquence, none of the ravishing enthusiasm of poetry,—and then you add, I *must* "learn to acknowledge her as *one of the greatest artists, of the greatest painters of human character*, and one of the writers with the nicest sense of means to an end that ever lived."

'The last point only will I ever acknowledge.

'Can there be a great artist without poetry?

'What I call—what I will bend to, as a great artist then—cannot be destitute of the divine gift. But by *poetry*, I am sure, you understand something different to what I do, as you do by "sentiment." It is *poetry*, as I comprehend the word, which elevates that masculine George Sand, and makes out of something coarse, something Godlike. It is "sentiment," in my sense of the term—sentiment jealously hidden, but genuine, which extracts the venom from that formidable Thackeray, and converts what might be only corrosive poison into purifying elixir.

'If Thackeray did not cherish in his large heart deep feeling for his kind, he would delight to exterminate; as it is, I believe, he wishes only to reform. Miss Austen being, as you say, without "sentiment," without *poetry*, maybe *is* sensible, real (more *real* than *true*), but she cannot be great.

'I submit to your anger, which I have now excited (for have I not questioned the perfection of your darling?); the storm may pass over me. Nevertheless, I will, when I can (I do not know when that will be, as I have no access to a circulating library), diligently peruse all Miss Austen's works, as you recommend. . . . . You must forgive me for not always being able to think as you do, and still believe me, yours gratefully,

'C. BELL.'

I have hesitated a little, before inserting the following extract from a letter to Mr Williams, but it is strikingly characteristic; and the criticism contained in it is, from that circumstance, so interesting (whether we agree with it or not), that I have determined to do so, though I thereby displace the chronological order of the letters, in order to complete this portion of a correspondence which is very valuable, as showing the purely intellectual side of her character.

TO W. S. WILLIAMS, ESQ.

'April 26th, 1848.

'My dear Sir,—I have now read "Rose, Blanche, and Violet," and I will tell you, as well as I can, what I think of it. Whether it is an improvement on "Ranthorpe" I do not know, for I liked "Ranthorpe" much; but at any rate, it contains more of a good thing. I find in it the same power, but more fully developed.

'The author's character is seen in every page, which makes the book interesting—far more interesting than any story could do; but it is what the writer himself says that attracts, far more than what he puts into the mouths of his characters. G. H. Lewes is, to my perception, decidedly the most original character in the book. . . . . The didactic passages seem to me the best—far the best—in the work; very acute, very profound, are some of the views there given, and very clearly they are offered to the reader. He is a just thinker; he is a sagacious observer; there is wisdom in his theory, and, I doubt not, energy in his practice. But why, then, are you often provoked with him while you read? How does he manage, while teaching, to make his hearer feel as if his business was, not quietly to receive the doctrines propounded, but to combat them? You acknowledge that he offers you gems of pure truth; why do you keep perpetually scrutinising them for flaws?

'Mr Lewes, I divine, with all his talents and honesty, must have some faults of manner; there must be a touch too much of dogmatism; a dash extra of confidence in him, sometimes. This you think while you are reading the book; but when you have closed it and laid it down, and sat a few minutes collecting your thoughts, and settling your impressions, you find the idea or feeling predominant in your mind to be pleasure at the fuller acquaintance you have made with a fine mind and a true heart, with high abilities and manly principles. I hope he will not be long ere he publishes another book. His emotional scenes are somewhat too uniformly vehement: would not a more subdued style of treatment often have produced a more masterly effect? Now and then Mr Lewes takes a French pen into his hand,* wherein he differs from Mr Thackeray, who always uses an English quill. However, the French pen does not far mislead Mr Lewes; he guides it with British muscles. All honour to him for the excellent general tendency of his book!

'He gives no charming picture of London literary society, and especially the female part of it; but all coteries, whether they be literary, scientific, political, or religious, must, it seems to me, have a tendency to change truth into affectation. When people belong to a clique, they must, I suppose, in some measure, write, talk, think, and live for that clique; a harassing and narrowing necessity. I trust, the press and the public show themselves disposed to give the book the reception it merits; and that is a very cordial one, far beyond anything due to a Bulwer or D'Israeli production.'*

Let us return from Currer Bell to Charlotte Brontë. The winter in Haworth had been a sickly season. Influenza had prevailed amongst the villagers, and when there was a real need for the presence of the clergyman's daughters, they were never found wanting, although they were shy of bestowing mere social visits on the parishioners. They had themselves suffered from the epidemic; Anne severely, as in her case it had been attended with cough and fever enough to make her elder sisters very anxious about her.

There is no doubt that the proximity of the crowded churchyard rendered the Parsonage unhealthy, and occasioned much illness to its inmates. Mr Brontë represented the unsanitary state of Haworth pretty forcibly to the Board of Health;* and, after the requisite visits from their officers, obtained a recommendation that all future interments in the churchyard should be forbidden, a new graveyard opened on the hill-side, and means set on foot for obtaining a water-supply to each house, instead of the weary, hard-worked housewives having to carry every bucketful, from a distance of several hundred yards, up a steep street. But he was baffled by the rate-payers; as, in many a similar instance, quantity carried it against quality, numbers against intelligence. And thus we find that illness often assumed a low typhoid form in Haworth, and fevers of various kinds visited the place with sad frequency.

In February, 1848, Louis Philippe was dethroned. The quick succession of events at that time called forth the following expression of Miss Brontë's thoughts on the subject, in a letter addressed to Miss W——, and dated March 31st.*

'I remember well wishing my lot had been cast in the troubled times of the late war, and seeing in its exciting incidents a kind of stimulating charm, which it made my pulse beat fast to think of: I remember even, I think, being a little impatient, that you would not fully sympathise with my feelings on those subjects; that you heard my aspirations and speculations very tranquilly, and by no means seemed to think the flaming swords could be any pleasant addition to Paradise.* I have now outlived youth; and though I dare not say that I have outlived all its illusions—that the romance is quite gone from Life—the veil fallen from Truth, and that I see both in naked reality—yet certainly, many things are not what they were ten years ago: and amongst the rest, "the pomp and circumstance of war"* have quite lost in my eyes their fictitious glitter. I have still no doubt that the shock of moral earthquakes wakens a vivid sense of life, both in nations and individuals; that the fear of dangers on a broad national scale, diverts men's minds momentarily from brooding over small private perils, and for the time gives them something like largeness of views; but as little doubt have I, that convulsive revolutions put back the world in all that is good, check civilisation, bring the dregs of society to its surface; in short, it appears to me, that insurrections and battles are the acute diseases of nations, and that their tendency is to exhaust, by their violence, the vital energies of the countries where they occur. That England may be spared the spasms, cramps, and frenzy-fits now contorting the Continent, and threatening Ireland, I earnestly pray.* With the French and Irish I have no sympathy. With the Germans and Italians I think the case is different; as different as the love of freedom is from the lust for license.'

Her birthday came round. She wrote to the friend whose birthday was within a week of hers; wrote the accustomed letter:* but reading it with our knowledge of what she had done, we perceive the difference between her thoughts and what they were a year or two ago, when she said 'I have done nothing.' There must have been a modest consciousness of having 'done something' present in her mind, as she wrote this year:—

'I am now thirty-two. Youth is gone—gone,—and will never come back: can't help it .... It seems to me, that sorrow must come some time to everybody, and those who scarcely taste it in their youth, often have a more brimming and bitter cup to drain in after life; whereas, those who exhaust the dregs early, who drink the lees before the wine, may reasonably hope for more palatable draughts to succeed.'

The authorship of 'Jane Eyre' was as yet a close secret in the Brontë family; not even this friend, who was all but a sister, knew more about it than the rest of the world. She might conjecture, it is true, both from her knowledge of previous habits, and from the suspicious fact of the proofs having been corrected at B——,* that some literary project was afoot; but she knew nothing, and wisely said nothing, until she heard a report from others, that Charlotte Brontë was an author—had published a novel! Then she wrote to her; and received the two following letters; confirmatory enough, as it seems to me now, in their very vehemence and agitation of intended denial, of the truth of the report.

'April 28th, 1848.

'Write another letter, and explain that last note of yours distinctly. If your allusions are to myself, which I suppose they are, understand this,—I have given no one a right to gossip about me, and am not to be judged by frivolous conjectures, emanating from any quarter whatever. Let me know what you heard, and from whom you heard it.'

'May 3rd, 1848.*

'All I can say to you about a certain matter is this: the report—if report there be—and if the lady, who seems to have been rather mystified, had not dreamt what she fancied had been told to her—must have had its origin in some absurd misunderstanding. I have given *no one* a right either to affirm, or to hint, in the most distant manner, that I was "publishing"—(humbug!) Whoever has said it—if any one has, which I doubt—is no friend of mine. Though twenty books were ascribed to me, I should own none. I scout the idea utterly. Whoever, after I have distinctly rejected the charge, urges it upon me, will do an unkind and an ill-bred thing. The most profound obscurity is infinitely preferable to vulgar notoriety; and that notoriety I neither seek nor will have. If then any B—an, or G—an, should presume to bore you on the subject,—to ask you what "novel" Miss Brontë has been "publishing," you can just say, with the distinct firmness of which you are perfect mistress, when you choose, that you are authorised by Miss Brontë to say, that she repels and disowns every accusation of the kind. You may add, if you please, that if any one has her confidence, you believe you have, and she has made no drivelling confessions to you on the subject. I am at a loss to conjecture from what source this rumour has come; and, I fear, it has far from a friendly origin. I am not certain, however, and I should be very glad if I could gain certainty. Should you hear anything more, please let me know. Your offer of "Simeon's Life"* is a very kind one, and I thank you for it. I dare say Papa would like to see the work very much, as he knew Mr Simeon. Laugh or scold A—— out of the publishing notion; and believe me, through all chances and changes, whether calumniated or let alone,—Yours faithfully,

'C. BRONTË.'

The reason why Miss Brontë was so anxious to preserve her secret, was, I am told, that she had pledged her word to her sisters that it should not be revealed through her.

The dilemmas attendant on the publication of the sisters' novels, under assumed names, were increasing upon them. Many critics insisted on believing, that all the fictions published as by three Bells were the works of one author,* but written at different periods of his development and maturity. No doubt, this suspicion affected the reception of the books. Ever since the completion of Anne Brontë's tale of 'Agnes Grey,' she had been labouring at a second, 'The Tenant of Wildfell Hall.'* It is little known; the subject—the deterioration of a character, whose profligacy and ruin took their rise in habits of intemperance, so slight as to be only considered 'good fellowship'—was painfully discordant to one who would fain have sheltered herself from all but peaceful and religious ideas. 'She had' (says her sister of that gentle 'little one'), 'in the course of her life, been called on to contemplate near at hand, and for a long time, the terrible effects of talents misused and faculties abused; hers was naturally a sensitive, reserved, and dejected nature; what she saw sank very deeply into her mind; it did her harm. She brooded over it till she believed it to be a duty to reproduce every detail (of course, with fictitious characters, incidents, and situations), as a warning to others. She hated her work but would pursue it. When reasoned with on the subject, she regarded such reasonings as a temptation to self-indulgence. She must be honest; she must not varnish, soften, or conceal. This well-meant resolution brought on her misconstruction, and some abuse, which she bore, as it was her custom to bear whatever was unpleasant, with mild, steady patience. She was a very sincere and practical Christian, but the tinge of religious melancholy communicated a sad shade to her brief, blameless life.'

In the June of this year, 'The Tenant of Wildfell Hall' was sufficiently near its completion to be submitted to the person* who had previously published for Ellis and Acton Bell.

In consequence of his mode of doing business, considerable annoyance was occasioned both to Miss Brontë and to them. The circumstances, as detailed in a letter of hers to a friend in New Zealand, were these:—One morning, at the beginning of July, a communication was received at the Parsonage from Messrs Smith and Elder, which disturbed its quiet inmates not a little, as, though the matter brought under their notice was merely referred to as one which affected their literary reputation, they conceived it to have a bearing likewise upon their character. 'Jane Eyre' had had a great run in America, and a publisher there had consequently bid high for early sheets of the next work by 'Currer Bell.' These Messrs Smith and Elder had promised to let him have. He was therefore greatly astonished, and not well pleased, to learn that a similar agreement had been entered into with another American house, and that the new tale was very shortly to appear. It turned out, upon inquiry, that the mistake had originated in Acton and Ellis

Bell's publisher having assured this American house that, to the best of his belief, 'Jane Eyre,' 'Wuthering Heights,' and 'The Tenant of Wildfell Hall' (which he pronounced superior to either of the other two) were all written by the same author.

Though Messrs Smith and Elder distinctly stated in their letter that they did not share in such 'belief,' the sisters were impatient till they had shown its utter groundlessness, and set themselves perfectly straight. With rapid decision, they resolved that Charlotte and Anne should start for London that very day, in order to prove their separate identity to Messrs Smith and Elder, and demand from the credulous publisher his reasons for a 'belief' so directly at variance with an assurance which had several times been given to him. Having arrived at this determination, they made their preparations with resolute promptness. There were many household duties to be performed that day; but they were all got through. The two sisters each packed up a change of dress in a small box, which they sent down to Keighley by an opportune cart; and after early tea, they set off to walk thither—no doubt in some excitement; for, independently of the cause of their going to London, it was Anne's first visit there. A great thunderstorm overtook them on their way that summer evening to the station; but they had no time to seek shelter. They only just caught the train at Keighley, arrived at Leeds, and were whirled up by the night train to London.*

About eight o'clock on the Saturday morning, they arrived at the Chapter Coffee-house, Paternoster Row—a strange place, but they did not well know where else to go. They refreshed themselves by washing, and had some breakfast. Then they sat still for a few minutes, to consider what next should be done.

When they had been discussing their project in the quiet of Haworth Parsonage the day before, and planning the mode of setting about the business on which they were going to London, they had resolved to take a cab, if they should find it desirable, from their inn to Cornhill; but, amidst, the bustle and 'queer state of inward excitement'* in which they found themselves, as they sat and considered their position on the Saturday morning,* they quite forgot even the possibility of hiring a conveyance; and when they set forth, they became so dismayed by the crowded streets, and the impeded crossings, that they stood still repeatedly, in complete despair of making progress, and were nearly an hour in walking the half-mile they had to go. Neither Mr Smith nor Mr Williams knew that they were coming; they were entirely unknown to the publishers of 'Jane Eyre,' who were not, in fact, aware whether the 'Bells' were men or women, but had always written to them as to men.

On reaching Mr Smith's, Charlotte put his own letter into his hands; the same letter which had excited so much disturbance at Haworth Parsonage only twenty-four hours before. 'Where did you get this?' said he,—as if he could not believe that the two young ladies dressed in black, of slight figures and diminutive stature, looking pleased yet agitated, could be the embodied Currer and Acton Bell, for whom curiosity had been hunting so eagerly in vain. An explanation ensued, and Mr Smith at once began to form plans for their amusement and pleasure during their stay in London. He urged them to meet a few literary friends at his house; and this was a strong temptation to Charlotte, as amongst them were one or two of the writers whom she particularly wished to see; but her resolution to remain unknown induced her firmly to put it aside.

The sisters were equally perserving in declining Mr Smith's invitations to stay at his house. They refused to leave their quarters, saying they were not prepared for a long stay.

When they returned back to their inn, poor Charlotte paid for the excitement of the interview, which had wound up the agitation and hurry of the last twenty-four hours, by a racking headache and harassing sickness. Towards evening, as she rather expected some of the ladies of Mr Smith's family to call, she prepared herself for the chance by taking a strong dose of sal-volatile, which roused her a little, but still, as she says, she was 'in grievous bodily case,' when their visitors were announced, in full evening costume. The sisters had not understood that it had been settled that they were to go to the Opera, and therefore were not ready. Moreover, they had no fine elegant dresses either with them, or in the world. But Miss Brontë resolved to raise no objections in the acceptance of kindness. So, in spite of headache and weariness, they made haste to dress themselves in their plain high-made country garments.

Charlotte says, in an account which she gives to her friend of this visit to London, describing the entrance of her party into the Opera-house:—

'Fine ladies and gentlemen glanced at us, as we stood by the box-door, which was not yet opened, with a slight, graceful superciliousness, quite warranted by the circumstances. Still I felt pleasurably excited in spite of headache, sickness, and conscious clownishness; and I saw Anne was calm and gentle, which she always is. The performance was Rossini's "Barber of Seville,"*— very brilliant, though I fancy there are things I should like better. We got home after one o'clock. We had never been in bed the night before; had been in constant excitement for twenty-four hours; you may imagine we were tired. The next day, Sunday, Mr Williams came early to take us to church; and in the afternoon Mr Smith and his mother* fetched us in a carriage, and took us to his house to dine.

'On Monday we went to the Exhibition of the Royal Academy, the National Gallery, dined again at Mr Smith's, and then went home to tea with Mr Williams at his house.

'On Tuesday morning, we left London, laden with books Mr Smith had given us, and got safely home. A more jaded wretch than I looked, it would be difficult to conceive. I was thin when I went, but I was meagre indeed when I returned, my face looking grey and very old, with strange deep lines ploughed in it—my eyes stared unnaturally. I was weak and yet restless. In a while, however, these bad effects of excitement went off, and I regained my normal condition.'*

The impression Miss Brontë made upon those with whom she first became acquainted during this visit to London, was of a person with clear judgment and fine sense; and though reserved, possessing unconsciously the power of drawing out others in conversation. She never expressed an opinion without assigning a reason for it; she never put a question without a definite purpose; and yet people felt at their ease in talking with her. All conversation with her was genuine and stimulating; and when she launched forth in praise or reprobation of books, or deeds, or works of art, her eloquence was indeed burning. She was thorough in all that she said or did; yet so open and fair in dealing with a subject, or contending with an opponent, that instead of rousing resentment, she merely convinced her hearers of her earnest zeal for the truth and right.

Not the least singular part of their proceedings was the place at which the sisters had chosen to stay.

Paternoster Row was for many years sacred to publishers. It is a narrow flagged street, lying under the shadow of St Paul's. The dull warehouses on each side are mostly occupied at present by wholesale booksellers; if they be publishers' shops, they show no attractive front to the dark and narrow street. Half-way up, on the left-hand side, is the Chapter Coffee-house. I visited it last June.* It was then unoccupied. It had the appearance of a dwelling-house, two hundred years old or so, such as one sometimes sees in ancient country towns; the ceilings of the small rooms were low, and had heavy beams running across them; the walls were wainscotted breast high; the staircase was shallow, broad, and dark, taking up much space in the centre of the house. This then was the Chapter Coffee-house, which, a century ago, was the resort of all the booksellers and publishers; and where the literary hacks, the critics, and even the wits, used to go in search of ideas or employment. This was the place about which Chatterton wrote,* in those delusive letters he sent to his mother at Bristol, while he was starving in London. 'I am quite familiar at the Chapter Coffee-house, and know all the geniuses there.' Here he heard of chances of employment; here his letters were to be left.

Years later, it became the tavern frequented by university men and country clergymen, who were up in London for a few days, and, having no private friends or access into society, were glad to learn what was going on in the world of letters, from the conversation which they were sure to hear in the Coffee-room. In Mr Brontë's few and brief visits to town, during his residence at Cambridge, and the period of his curacy in Essex, he had stayed at this house; hither he had brought his daughters, when he was convoying them to Brussels; and here they came now, from very ignorance where else to go. It was a place solely frequented by men; I believe there was but one female servant in the house. Few people slept there; some of the stated meetings of the Trade were held in it, as they had been for more than a century; and, occasionally, country booksellers, with now and then a clergyman, resorted to it; but it was a strange desolate place for the Miss Brontës to have gone to, from its purely business and masculine aspect. The old 'grey-haired elderly man,' who officiated as waiter, seems to have been touched from the very first with the quiet simplicity of the two ladies, and he tried to make them feel comfortable and at home in the long, low, dingy room up stairs, where the meetings of the Trade were held. The high narrow windows looked into the gloomy Row; the sisters, clinging together on the most remote window-seat, (as Mr Smith tells me he found them, when he came, that Saturday evening, to take them to the Opera,) could see nothing of motion, or of change, in the grim, dark houses opposite, so near and close, although the whole breadth of the Row was between. The mighty roar of London was round them, like the sound of an unseen ocean, yet every footfall on the pavement below might be heard distinctly in that unfrequented street. Such as it was, they preferred remaining at the Chapter Coffee-house, to accepting the invitation which Mr Smith and his mother urged upon them; and, in after years, Charlotte says:—

'Since those days, I have seen the West End, the parks, the fine squares; but I love the City far better. The City seems so much more in earnest; its business, its rush, its roar, are such serious things, sights, sounds. The City is getting its living—the West End but enjoying its pleasure. At the West End you may be amused; but in the City you are deeply excited.' (*Villette*, vol. i. p. 89.)*

Their wish had been to hear Dr Croly* on the Sunday morning, and Mr Williams escorted them to St Stephen's, Walbrook; but they were disappointed, as Dr Croly did not preach. Mr Williams also took them (as Miss Brontë has mentioned) to drink tea at his house. On the way thither, they had to pass through Kensington Gardens, and Miss Brontë was much 'struck with the beauty of the scene, the fresh verdure of the turf, and the soft rich masses of foliage.' From remarks on the different character of the landscape in the South to what it was in the North, she was led to speak of the softness and varied intonation of the voices of those with whom she conversed in London, which seem to have made a strong impression on both sisters. All this time those who came in contact with the 'Miss Browns' (another pseudonym, also beginning with B), seem only to have regarded them as shy and reserved little country-women, with not much to say. Mr Williams tells me that on the night when he accompanied the party to the Opera, as Charlotte ascended the flight of stairs leading from the grand entrance up to the lobby of the first tier of boxes, she was so much struck with the architectural effect of the splendid decorations of that vestibule and saloon, that involuntarily she slightly pressed his arm and whispered, 'You know I am not accustomed to this sort of thing.' Indeed, it must have formed a vivid contrast to what they were doing and seeing an hour or two earlier the night before, when they were trudging along, with beating hearts and high-strung courage, on the road between Haworth and Keighley, hardly thinking of the thunderstorm that beat about their heads, for the thoughts which filled them of how they would go straight away to London, and prove that they were really two people, and not one impostor. It was no wonder that they returned to Haworth utterly fagged and worn out, after the fatigue and excitement of this visit.

The next notice I find of Charlotte's life at this time is of a different character to anything telling of enjoyment.

'July 28th.

'Branwell is the same in conduct as ever. His constitution seems much shattered. Papa, and sometimes all of us, have sad nights with him. He sleeps most of the day, and consequently will lie awake at night. But has not every house its trial?'

While her most intimate friends were yet in ignorance of the fact of her authorship of 'Jane Eyre,' she received a letter from one of them, making inquiries about Casterton School. It is but right to give her answer, written on August 28th, 1848.*

'Since you wish to hear from me while you are from home, I will write without further delay. It often happens that when we linger at first in answering a friend's letter, obstacles occur to retard us to an inexcusably late period. In my last, I forgot to answer a question which you asked me, and was sorry afterwards for the omission. I will begin, therefore, by replying to it, though I fear what information I can give will come a little late. You said Mrs —— had some thoughts of sending —— to school, and wished to know whether the Clergy Daughters' School at Casterton was an eligible place. My personal knowledge of that institution is very much out of date, being derived from the experience of twenty years ago. The establishment was at that time in its infancy, and a sad ricketty infancy it was. Typhus fever decimated the school periodically[1]; and consumption and scrofula, in every variety of form, bad air and water, bad and insufficient diet can generate, preyed on the ill-fated pupils. It would not *then* have been a fit place for any of Mrs ——'s children; but I understand it is very much altered for the better since those days. The school is removed from Cowan's Bridge (a situation as unhealthy as it was picturesque—low, damp, beautiful with wood and water) to Casterton. The accommodations, the diet, the discipline, the system of tuition—all are, I believe, entirely altered and greatly improved. I was told that such pupils as behaved well, and remained at the school till their educations were finished, were provided with situations as governesses, if they wished to adopt the vocation, and much care was exercised in the selection; it was added, that they were also furnished with an excellent wardrobe on leaving Casterton. . . . . . The oldest family in Haworth failed lately,* and have quitted the neighbourhood where their fathers resided before them for, it is said, thirteen generations. . . . Papa, I am most thankful to say, continues in very good health, considering his age; his sight, too, rather, I think, improves than deteriorates. My sisters likewise are pretty well.'

But the dark cloud was hanging over that doomed household, and gathering blackness every hour.

On October the 9th, she thus writes:—

'The past three weeks have been a dark interval in our humble home. Branwell's constitution had been failing fast all the summer; but still neither the doctors nor himself thought him so near his end as he was. He was entirely confined to his bed but for one single day, and was in the village two days before his death. He died, after twenty minutes' struggle, on Sunday morning, September 24th. He was perfectly conscious till the last agony came on. His mind had undergone the peculiar change which frequently

---

[1] Mr W. W. Carus Wilson wishes me to mention that this statement is a mistake. He says they have only had typhus fever twice in the school (either at Cowan Bridge or at Casterton) since its institution in 1823.*

precedes death, two days previously; the calm of better feelings filled it; a return of natural affection marked his last moments. He is in God's hands now; and the All-Powerful is likewise the All-Merciful. A deep conviction that he rests at last—rests well after his brief, erring, suffering, feverish life*—fills and quiets my mind now. The final separation, the spectacle of his pale corpse, gave me more acute, bitter pain than I could have imagined. Till the last hour comes, we never know how much we can forgive, pity, regret a near relative. All his vices were and are nothing now. We remember only his woes. Papa was acutely distressed at first, but, on the whole, has borne the event well. Emily and Anne are pretty well, though Anne is always delicate, and Emily has a cold and cough at present. It was my fate to sink at the crisis, when I should have collected my strength. Headache and sickness came on first on the Sunday; I could not regain my appetite. Then internal pain attacked me. I became at once much reduced. It was impossible to touch a morsel. At last, bilious fever declared itself. I was confined to bed a week,—a dreary week. But thank God! health seems now returning. I can sit up all day, and take moderate nourishment. The doctor said at first, I should be very slow in recovering, but I seemed to get on faster than he anticipated. I am truly *much better*.'

I have heard, from one who attended Branwell in his last illness,* that he resolved on standing up to die. He had repeatedly said, that as long as there was life there was strength of will to do what it chose; and when the last agony began, he insisted on assuming the position just mentioned.*

'Oct. 29th, 1848.*

'I think I have now nearly got over the effects of my late illness, and am almost restored to my normal condition of health. I sometimes wish that it was a little higher, but we ought to be content with such blessings as we have, and not pine after those that are out of our reach. I feel much more uneasy about my sister than myself just now. Emily's cold and cough are very obstinate. I fear she has pain in her chest, and I sometimes catch a shortness in her breathing, when she has moved at all quickly. She looks very thin and pale. Her reserved nature occasions me great uneasiness of mind. It is useless to question her; you get no answers. It is still more useless to recommend remedies; they are never adopted. Nor can I shut my eyes to Anne's great delicacy of constitution. The late sad event has, I feel, made me more apprehensive than common. I cannot help feeling much depressed sometimes. I try to leave all in God's hands; to trust in His goodness; but faith and resignation are difficult to practise under some circumstances. The weather has been most unfavourable for invalids of late; sudden changes of temperature, and cold penetrating winds have been frequent here. Should the atmosphere become more settled, perhaps a favourable effect might be produced on the general health, and these harassing colds and coughs be removed. Papa has not quite escaped, but he has so far stood it better than any of us. You must not mention my going to —— this winter. I could not, and would not, leave home on any account. Miss —— has been for some years out of health now. These things make one *feel*, as well as *know*, that this world is not our abiding-place.* We should not knit human ties too close, or clasp human affections too fondly. They must leave us, or we must leave them, one day. God restore health and strength to all who need it!'

I go on now with her own affecting words in the biographical notice of her sisters.*

'But a great change approached. Affliction came in that shape which to anticipate is dread; to look back on, grief. In the very heat and burden of the day, the labourers failed over their work.* My sister Emily first declined.... Never in all her life had she lingered over any task that lay before her, and she did not linger now. She sank rapidly. She made haste to leave us..... Day by day, when I saw with what a front she met suffering, I looked on her with an anguish of wonder and love. I have seen nothing like it; but, indeed, I have never seen her parallel in anything. Stronger than a man, simpler than a child, her nature stood alone. The awful point was, that, while full of ruth for others, on herself she had no pity; the spirit was inexorable to the flesh; from the trembling hand, the unnerved limbs, the fading eyes, the same service was exacted as they had rendered in health. To stand by and witness this, and not dare to remonstrate, was a pain no words can render.'

In fact, Emily never went out of doors after the Sunday succeeding Branwell's death. She made no complaint; she would not endure questioning; she rejected sympathy and help.* Many a

time did Charlotte and Anne drop their sewing, or cease from their
writing, to listen with wrung hearts to the failing step, the laboured
breathing, the frequent pauses, with which their sister climbed the
short staircase; yet they dared not notice what they observed, with
pangs of suffering even deeper than hers. They dared not notice it
in words, far less by the caressing assistance of a helping arm or
hand. They sat, still and silent.

'Nov. 23rd, 1848.

'I told you Emily was ill, in my last letter. She has not rallied
yet. She is *very* ill. I believe, if you were to see her, your
impression would be that there is no hope. A more hollow, wasted,
pallid aspect I have not beheld. The deep tight cough continues;
the breathing after the least exertion is a rapid pant; and these
symptoms are accompanied by pain in the chest and side. Her
pulse, the only time she allowed it to be felt, was found to beat 115
per minute. In this state she resolutely refuses to see a doctor; she
will give no explanation of her feelings, she will scarcely allow her
feelings to be alluded to. Our position is, and has been for some
weeks, exquisitely painful. God only knows how all this is to
terminate. More than once, I have been forced boldly to regard the
terrible event of her loss as possible, and even probable. But nature
shrinks from such thoughts. I think Emily seems the nearest thing
to my heart in the world.'

When a doctor had been sent for, and was in the very house,
Emily refused to see him.* Her sisters could only describe to him
what symptoms they had observed; and the medicines which he
sent she would not take, denying that she was ill.

'Dec. 10th, 1848.*

'I hardly know what to say to you about the subject which now
interests me the most keenly of anything in this world, for, in
truth, I hardly know what to think myself. Hope and fear fluctuate
daily. The pain in her side and chest is better; the cough, the
shortness of breath, the extreme emaciation continue. I have
endured, however, such tortures of uncertainty on this subject that,
at length, I could endure it no longer; and as her repugnance to
seeing a medical man continues immutable,—as she declares "no

poisoning doctor" shall come near her,—I have written, unknown to her, to an eminent physician in London,* giving as minute a statement of her case and symptoms as I could draw up, and requesting an opinion. I expect an answer in a day or two. I am thankful to say, that my own health at present is very tolerable. It is well such is the case; for Anne, with the best will in the world to be useful, is really too delicate to do or bear much. She, too, at present, has frequent pain in the side. Papa is also pretty well, though Emily's state renders him very anxious.

'The ——s (Anne Brontë's former pupils)* were here about a week ago. They are attractive and stylish-looking girls. They seemed overjoyed to see Anne: when I went into the room, they were clinging round her like two children—she, meantime, looking perfectly quiet and passive. . . . . I. and H. took it into their heads to come here. I think it probable offence was taken on that occasion,—from what cause I know not; and as, if such be the case, the grudge must rest upon purely imaginary grounds,—and since, besides, I have other things to think about, my mind rarely dwells upon the subject. If Emily were but well, I feel as if I should not care who neglected, misunderstood, or abused me. I would rather *you* were not of the number either. The crab-cheese* arrived safely. Emily has just reminded me to thank you for it: it looks very nice. I wish she were well enough to eat it.'

But Emily was growing rapidly worse. I remember Miss Brontë's shiver at recalling the pang she felt when, after having searched in the little hollows and sheltered crevices of the moors for a lingering spray of heather—just one spray, however withered—to take in to Emily, she saw that the flower was not recognised by the dim and indifferent eyes. Yet, to the last, Emily adhered tenaciously to her habits of independence. She would suffer no one to assist her. Any effort to do so roused the old stern spirit. One Tuesday morning, in December, she arose and dressed herself as usual, making many a pause, but doing everything for herself, and even endeavouring to take up her employment of sewing: the servants looked on, and knew what the catching, rattling breath, and the glazing of the eye too surely foretold; but she kept at her work; and Charlotte and Anne, though full of unspeakable dread, had still the faintest spark of hope. On that morning Charlotte wrote thus,—probably in the very presence of her dying sister:—

'Tuesday.*

'I should have written to you before, if I had had one word of hope to say; but I have not. She grows daily weaker. The physician's opinion was expressed too obscurely to be of use. He sent some medicine, which she would not take. Moments so dark as these I have never known. I pray for God's support to us all. Hitherto He has granted it.'

The morning drew on to noon. Emily was worse: she could only whisper in gasps. Now, when it was too late, she said to Charlotte, 'If you will send for a doctor, I will see him now.' About two o'clock she died.

'Dec. 21st, 1848.*

'Emily suffers no more from pain or weakness now. She never will suffer more in this world. She is gone, after a hard, short conflict. She died on *Tuesday*, the very day I wrote to you. I thought it very possible she might be with us still for weeks; and a few hours afterwards, she was in eternity. Yes; there is no Emily in time or on earth now. Yesterday we put her poor, wasted, mortal frame quietly under the church pavement. We are very calm at present. Why should we be otherwise? The anguish of seeing her suffer is over; the spectacle of the pains of death is gone by; the funeral day is past. We feel she is at peace. No need now to tremble for the hard frost and the keen wind. Emily does not feel them. She died in a time of promise. We saw her taken from life in its prime. But it is God's will, and the place where she is gone is better than that she has left.

'God has sustained me, in a way that I marvel at, through such agony as I had not conceived. I now look at Anne, and wish she were well and strong; but she is neither; nor is Papa. Could you now come to us for a few days? I would not ask you to stay long. Write and tell me if you could come next week, and by what train. I would try to send a gig for you to Keighley. You will, I trust, find us tranquil. Try to come. I never so much needed the consolation of a friend's presence. Pleasure, of course, there would be none for you in the visit, except what your kind heart would teach you to find in doing good to others.'

As the old, bereaved father and his two surviving children followed the coffin to the grave, they were joined by Keeper, Emily's fierce, faithful bull-dog.* He walked alongside of the mourners, and into the church, and stayed quietly there all the time that the burial service was being read. When he came home, he lay down at Emily's chamber door, and howled pitifully for many days. Anne Brontë drooped and sickened more rapidly from that time; and so ended the year 1848.

# CHAPTER III

AN article on 'Vanity Fair' and 'Jane Eyre' had appeared in the Quarterly Review of December, 1848.* Some weeks after, Miss Brontë wrote to her publishers, asking why it had not been sent to her; and conjecturing that it was unfavourable, she repeated her previous request, that whatever was done with the laudatory, all critiques adverse to the novel might be forwarded to her without fail. The Quarterly Review was accordingly sent. I am not aware that Miss Brontë took any greater notice of the article than to place a few sentences out of it in the mouth of a hard and vulgar woman in 'Shirley,'* where they are so much in character, that few have recognised them as a quotation. The time when the article was read was good for Miss Brontë; she was numbed to all petty annoyances by the grand severity of Death. Otherwise she might have felt more keenly than they deserved the criticisms which, while striving to be severe, failed in logic, owing to the misuse of prepositions; and have smarted under conjectures as to the authorship of 'Jane Eyre,' which, intended to be acute, were merely flippant. But flippancy takes a graver name when directed against an author by an anonymous writer. We call it then cowardly insolence.

Every one has a right to form his own conclusion respecting the merits and demerits of a book. I complain not of the judgment which the reviewer passes on 'Jane Eyre.' Opinions as to its tendency varied then as they do now. While I write, I receive a letter from a clergyman in America* in which he says: 'We have in our sacred of sacreds a special shelf, highly adorned, as a place we delight to honour, of novels which we recognise as having had a good influence on character, *our* character. Foremost is "Jane Eyre." '

Nor do I deny the existence of a diametrically opposite judgment. And so (as I trouble not myself about the reviewer's style of composition) I leave his criticisms regarding the merits of the work on one side. But when—forgetting the chivalrous spirit of the good and noble Southey, who said: 'In reviewing anonymous works myself, when I have known the authors I have never mentioned them, taking it for granted they had sufficient reasons for avoiding the publicity'—the Quarterly reviewer goes on into gossiping conjectures as to who Currer Bell really is, and pretends to decide on what the writer may be from the book, I protest with my whole soul against such want of Christian charity. Not even the desire to write a 'smart article,' which shall be talked about in London, when the faint mask of the anonymous can be dropped at pleasure if the cleverness of the review be admired—not even this temptation can excuse the stabbing cruelty of the judgment. Who is he that should say of an unknown woman: 'She must be one who for some sufficient reason has long forfeited the society of her sex'? Is he one who has led a wild and struggling and isolated life,—seeing few but plain and outspoken Northerns, unskilled in the euphuisms* which assist the polite world to skim over the mention of vice? Has he striven through long weeping years to find excuses for the lapse of an only brother; and through daily contact with a poor lost profligate, been compelled into a certain familiarity with the vices that his soul abhors? Has he, through trials, close following in dread march through his household, sweeping the hearthstone bare of life and love, still striven hard for strength to say, 'It is the Lord! let Him do what seemeth to Him good'—and sometimes striven in vain, until the kindly Light returned? If through all these dark waters the scornful reviewer have passed clear, refined, free from stain,—with a soul that has never in all its agonies, cried 'lama sabachthani,'—still, even then let him pray with the Publican rather than judge with the Pharisee.*

'Jan. 10th, 1849.*

'Anne had a very tolerable day yesterday, and a pretty quiet night last night, though she did not sleep much. Mr Wheelhouse ordered the blister to be put on again. She bore it without sickness. I have just dressed it, and she is risen and come down stairs. She looks somewhat pale and sickly. She has had one dose of the cod-liver oil; it smells and tastes like train oil.* I am trying to hope, but the day is windy, cloudy, and stormy. My spirits fall at intervals very low; then I look where you counsel me to look, beyond earthly tempests and sorrows. I seem to get strength, if not consolation. It will not do to anticipate. I feel that hourly. In the night, I awake and long for morning: then my heart is wrung. Papa continues much the same; he was very faint when he came down to breakfast. . . . Dear E——, your friendship is some comfort to me. I am thankful for it. I see few lights through the darkness of the present time; but amongst them the constancy of a kind heart attached to me is one of the most cheering and serene.'

'Jan. 15th, 1849.

'I can scarcely say that Anne is worse, nor can I say she is better. She varies often in the course of a day, yet each day is passed pretty much the same. The morning is usually the best time; the afternoon and the evening the most feverish. Her cough is the most troublesome at night, but it is rarely violent. The pain in her arm still disturbs her. She takes the cod-liver oil and the carbonate of iron regularly; she finds them both nauseous, but especially the oil. Her appetite is small indeed. Do not fear that I shall relax in my care of her. She is too precious not to be cherished with all the fostering strength I have. Papa, I am thankful to say, has been a good deal better this last day or two.

'As to your queries about myself, I can only say, that if I continue as I am I shall do very well. I have not yet got rid of the pains in my chest and back. They oddly return with every change of weather; and are still sometimes accompanied with a little soreness and hoarseness, but I combat them steadily with pitch plasters and bran tea. I should think it silly and wrong indeed not to be regardful of my own health at present; it would not do to be ill *now*.

'I avoid looking forward or backward, and try to keep looking upward. This day is not the time to regret, dread, or weep. What I have and ought to do is very distinctly laid out for me; what I want, and pray for, is strength to perform it. The days pass in a slow, dark march; the nights are the test; the sudden wakings from restless sleep, the revived knowledge that one lies in her grave, and another not at my side, but in a separate and sick bed. However, God is over all.'

'Jan. 22nd, 1849.*

'Anne really did seem to be a little better during some mild days last week, but to-day she looks very pale and languid again. She perseveres with the cod-liver oil, but still finds it very nauseous.

'She is truly obliged to you for the soles for her shoes, and finds them extremely comfortable. I am to commission you to get her just such a respirator as Mrs —— had. She would not object to give a higher price, if you thought it better. If it is not too much trouble, you may likewise get me a pair of soles; you can send them and the respirator when you send the box. You must put down the price of all, and we will pay you in a Post Office order. "Wuthering Heights" was given to you. I have sent —— neither letter nor parcel. I had nothing but dreary news to write, so preferred that others should tell her. I have not written to —— either. I cannot write, except when I am quite obliged.'

'Feb. 11th, 1849.*

'We received the box and its contents quite safely to-day. The penwipers are very pretty, and we are very much obliged to you for them. I hope the respirator will be useful to Anne, in case she should ever be well enough to go out again. She continues very much in the same state—I trust not greatly worse, though she is becoming very thin. I fear it would be only self-delusion to fancy her better. What effect the advancing season may have on her, I know not; perhaps the return of really warm weather may give nature a happy stimulus. I tremble at the thought of any change to cold wind or frost. Would that March were well over! Her mind seems generally serene, and her sufferings hitherto are nothing like Emily's. The thought of what may be to come grows more familiar to my mind; but it is a sad, dreary guest.'

'March 16th, 1849.

'We have found the past week a somewhat trying one; it has not been cold, but still there have been changes of temperature whose effect Anne has felt unfavourably. She is not, I trust, seriously worse, but her cough is at times very hard and painful, and her strength rather diminished than improved. I wish the month of March was well over. You are right in conjecturing that I am somewhat depressed; at times I certainly am. It was almost easier to bear up when the trial was at its crisis than now. The feeling of Emily's loss does not diminish as time wears on; it often makes itself most acutely recognised. It brings too an inexpressible sorrow with it; and then the future is dark. Yet I am well aware it will not do either to complain or sink, and I strive to do neither. Strength, I hope and trust, will yet be given in proportion to the burden; but the pain of my position is not one likely to lessen with habit. Its solitude and isolation are oppressive circumstances, yet I do not wish for any friend to stay with me; I could not do with any one—not even *you*—to share the sadness of the house; it would rack me intolerably. Meantime, judgment is still blent with mercy. Anne's sufferings still continue mild. It is my nature, when left alone, to struggle on with a certain perseverance, and I believe God will help me.'

Anne had been delicate all her life; a fact which perhaps made her father and sister less aware than they would otherwise have been, of the true nature of those fatal first symptoms. Yet they seem to have lost but little time before they sent for the first advice that could be procured.* She was examined with the stethoscope, and the dreadful fact was announced that her lungs were affected, and that tubercular consumption had already made considerable progress. A system of treatment was prescribed, which was afterwards ratified by the opinion of Dr Forbes.*

For a short time they hoped that the disease was arrested. Charlotte—herself ill with a complaint that severely tried her spirits—was the ever-watchful nurse of this youngest, last sister. One comfort was that Anne was the patientest, gentlest invalid that could be. Still, there were hours, days, weeks of inexpressible anguish to be borne; under the pressure of which Charlotte could only pray: and pray she did, right earnestly. Thus she writes on March 24th:—*

'Anne's decline is gradual and fluctuating; but its nature is not doubtful. . . . . In spirit she is resigned: at heart she is, I believe, a true Christian. . . . . May God support her and all of us through the trial of lingering sickness, and aid her in the last hour, when the struggle which separates soul from body must be gone through! We saw Emily torn from the midst of us when our hearts clung to her with intense attachment. . . . . She was scarce buried when Anne's health failed. . . . . These things would be too much, if Reason, unsupported by Religion, were condemned to bear them alone. I have cause to be most thankful for the strength that has hitherto been vouchsafed both to my father and to myself. God, I think, is specially merciful to old age; and, for my own part, trials, which in perspective would have seemed to me quite intolerable, when they actually came I endured without prostration. Yet I must confess that, in the time which has elapsed since Emily's death, there have been moments of solitary, deep, inert affliction, far harder to bear than those which immediately followed our loss. The crisis of bereavement has an acute pang which goads to exertion; the desolate after-feeling sometimes paralyses. I have learnt that we are not to find solace in our own strength; we must seek it in God's omnipotence. Fortitude is good; but fortitude itself must be shaken under us, to teach us how weak we are!'

All through this illness of Anne's, Charlotte had the comfort of being able to talk to her about her state; a comfort rendered inexpressibly great by the contrast which it presented to the recollection of Emily's rejection of all sympathy. If a proposal for Anne's benefit was made, Charlotte could speak to her about it, and the nursing and the dying sister could consult with each other as to its desirability. I have seen but one of Anne's letters; it is the only time we seem to be brought into direct personal contact with this gentle, patient girl. In order to give the requisite preliminary explanation, I must state that the family of friends, to which E——belonged, proposed that Anne should come to them; in order to try what change of air and diet, and the company of kindly people could do towards restoring her to health. In answer to this proposal, Charlotte writes:—

'March 24th.*

'I read your kind note to Anne, and she wishes me to thank you sincerely for your friendly proposal. She feels, of course, that it would not do to take advantage of it, by quartering an invalid upon the inhabitants of ——; but she intimates there is another way in which you might serve her, perhaps with some benefit to yourself as well as to her. Should it, a month or two hence, be deemed advisable that she should go either to the sea-side, or to some inland watering-place—and should papa be disinclined to move, and I consequently be obliged to remain at home—she asks, could you be her companion? Of course I need not add that in case of such an arrangement being made, you would be put to no expense.

This, dear E., is Anne's proposal; I make it to comply with her wish; but for my own part, I must add that I see serious objections to your accepting it—objections I cannot name to her. She continues to vary; is sometimes worse, and sometimes better, as the weather changes; but, on the whole, I fear she loses strength. Papa says her state is most precarious; she may be spared for some time, or a sudden alteration might remove her before we are aware. Were such an alteration to take place while she was far from home, and alone with you, it would be terrible. The idea of it distresses me inexpressibly, and I tremble whenever she alludes to the project of a journey. In short, I wish we could gain time, and see how she gets on. If she leaves home, it certainly should not be in the capricious month of May, which is proverbially trying to the weak. June would be a safer month. If we could reach June, I should have good hopes of her getting through the summer. Write such an answer to this note as I can show Anne. You can write any additional remarks to me on a separate piece of paper. Do not consider yourself as confined to discussing only our sad affairs. I am interested in all that interests you.'

### FROM ANNE BRONTË .*

'April 5th, 1849.

'My dear Miss ——,—I thank you greatly for your kind letter, and your ready compliance with my proposal, as far as the *will* can go at least. I see, however, that your friends are unwilling that you should undertake the responsibility of accompanying me under present circumstances. But I do not think there would be any great responsibility in the matter. I know, and everybody knows, that you would be as kind and helpful as any one could possibly be, and I hope I should not be very troublesome. It would be as a companion, not as a nurse, that I should wish for your company; otherwise I should not venture to ask it. As for your kind and often-repeated invitation to ——, pray give my sincere thanks to your mother and sisters, but tell them I could not think of inflicting my presence upon them as I now am. It is very kind of them to make so light of the trouble, but still there must be more or less, and certainly no pleasure, from the society of a silent invalid stranger. I hope, however, that Charlotte will by some means make it possible to accompany me after all. She is certainly very delicate, and greatly needs a change of air and scene to renovate her constitution. And then your going with me before the end of May, is apparently out of the question, unless you are disappointed in your visitors; but I should be reluctant to wait till then, if the weather would at all permit an earlier departure. You say May is a trying month, and so say others. The earlier part is often cold enough, I acknowledge, but, according to my experience, we are almost certain of some fine warm days in the latter half, when the laburnums and lilacs are in bloom; whereas June is often cold, and July generally wet. But I have a more serious reason than this for my impatience of delay. The doctors say that change of air or removal to a better climate would hardly ever fail of success in consumptive cases, if the remedy were taken *in time;* but the reason why there are so many disappointments is, that it is generally deferred till it is too late. Now I would not commit this error; and to say the truth, though I suffer much less from pain and fever than I did when you were with us, I am decidedly weaker, and very much thinner. My cough still troubles me a good deal, especially in the night, and what seems worse than all, I am subject to great shortness of breath on going up stairs or any slight exertion. Under these circumstances, I think there is no time to be lost. I have no horror of death: if I thought it inevitable, I think I could quietly resign myself to the prospect, in the hope that you, dear Miss ——, would give as much of your company as you possibly could to Charlotte, and be a sister to her in my stead. But I wish it would please God to spare me, not only for Papa's and Charlotte's sakes, but because I long to do some good in the world before I leave it. I have many schemes in my head for future practice—humble and limited indeed—but still I should not like them all to come to nothing, and myself to have lived to so little purpose. But God's will be done. Remember me respectfully to your mother and sisters, and believe me, dear Miss ——, yours most affectionately,

'ANNE BRONTË.'

It must have been about this time that Anne composed her last verses,* before 'the desk was closed, and the pen laid aside for ever.'

## I.

'I hoped that with the brave and strong
    My portioned task might lie;
To toil amid the busy throng,
    With purpose pure and high.

## II.

'But God has fixed another part,
    And He has fixed it well:
I said so with my bleeding heart,
    When first the anguish fell.

## III.

'Thou God, hast taken our delight,
    Our treasured hope, away;
Thou bid'st us now weep through the night,
    And sorrow through the day.

## IV.

'These weary hours will not be lost,
    These days of misery,—
These nights of darkness, anguish-tost,—
    Can I but turn to Thee.

## V.

'With secret labour to sustain
    In humble patience every blow;
To gather fortitude from pain,
    And hope and holiness from woe.

## VI.

'Thus let me serve Thee from my heart,
    Whate'er may be my written fate;
Whether thus early to depart,
    Or yet a while to wait.

## VII.

'If Thou should'st bring me back to life,
    More humbled I should be;
More wise—more strengthened for the strife,
    More apt to lean on Thee.

## VIII.

'Should death be standing at the gate,
    Thus should I keep my vow;
But, Lord, whatever be my fate,
    Oh let me serve Thee now!'

I take Charlotte's own words as the best record of her thoughts and feelings during all this terrible time.

'April 12th.*

'I read Anne's letter to you; it was touching enough, as you say. If there were no hope beyond this world,—no eternity,—no life to come,—Emily's fate, and that which threatens Anne, would be heart-breaking. I cannot forget Emily's death-day; it becomes a more fixed, a darker, a more frequently recurring idea in my mind than ever. It was very terrible. She was torn, conscious, panting, reluctant, though resolute, out of a happy life. But it *will not do* to dwell on these things.

'I am glad your friends object to your going with Anne: it would never do. To speak truth, even if your mother and sisters had consented, I never could. It is not that there is any laborious attention to pay her; she requires, and will accept, but little nursing; but there would be hazard, and anxiety of mind, beyond what you ought to be subject to. If, a month or six weeks hence, she continues to wish for a change as much as she does now, I shall (D.V.) go with her myself. It will certainly be my paramount duty; other cares must be made subservient to that. I have consulted Mr T——: he does not object, and recommends Scarborough, which was Anne's own choice. I trust affairs may be so ordered, that you may be able to be with us at least part of the time . . . . Whether in lodgings or not, I should wish to be boarded. Providing oneself is, I think, an insupportable nuisance. I don't like keeping provisions in a cupboard, locking up, being pillaged, and all that. It is a petty, wearing annoyance.'

The progress of Anne's illness was slower that that of Emily's had been; and she was too unselfish to refuse trying means, from which, if she herself had little hope of benefit, her friends might hereafter derive a mournful satisfaction.

'I began to flatter myself she was getting strength.* But the change to frost has told upon her; she suffers more of late. Still her illness has none of the fearful rapid symptoms which appalled in Emily's case. Could she only get over the spring, I hope summer may do much for her, and then early removal to a warmer locality for the winter might, at least, prolong her life. Could we only reckon upon another year, I should be thankful; but can we do this for the healthy? A few days ago I wrote to have Dr Forbes' opinion .... He warned us against entertaining sanguine hopes of recovery. The cod-liver oil he considers a peculiarly efficacious medicine. He, too, disapproved of change of residence for the present. There is some feeble consolation in thinking we are doing the very best that can be done. The agony of forced, total neglect, is not now felt, as during Emily's illness. Never may we be doomed to feel such agony again. It was terrible. I have felt much less of the disagreeable pains in my chest lately, and much less also of the soreness and hoarseness. I tried an application of hot vinegar, which seemed to do good.'

'May 1st.

'I was glad to hear that when we go to Scarborough, you will be at liberty to go with us, but the journey and its consequences still continue a source of great anxiety to me; I must try to put it off two or three weeks longer if I can: perhaps by that time the milder season may have given Anne more strength,—perhaps it will be otherwise; I cannot tell. The change to fine weather has not proved beneficial to her so far. She has sometimes been so weak, and suffered so much from pain in the side, during the last few days, that I have not known what to think. . . . . She may rally again, and be much better, but there must be *some* improvement before I can feel justified in taking her away from home. Yet to delay is painful; for, as is *always* the case, I believe, under her circumstances, she seems herself not half conscious of the necessity for such delay. She wonders, I believe, why I don't talk more about the journey: it grieves me to think she may even be hurt by my seeming tardiness. She is very much emaciated,—far more than when you were with us; her arms are no thicker than a little child's. The least exertion brings a shortness of breath. She goes out a little every day, but we creep rather than walk. . . . . Papa continues pretty well;—I hope I shall be enabled to bear up. So far, I have reason for thankfulness to God.'

May had come, and brought the milder weather longed for; but Anne was worse for the very change. A little later on, it became colder, and she rallied, and poor Charlotte began to hope that, if May were once over, she might last for a long time. Miss Brontë wrote to engage the lodgings at Scarborough,*—a place which Anne had formerly visited with the family to whom she was governess. They took a good-sized sitting-room, and an airy double-bedded room (both commanding a sea-view), in one of the best situations of the town. Money was as nothing in comparison with life; besides, Anne had had a small legacy left to her by her godmother, and they felt that she could not better employ this than in obtaining what might prolong life, if not restore health. On May 16th, Charlotte writes:—*

'It is with a heavy heart I prepare: and earnestly do I wish the fatigue of the journey were well over. It may be borne better than I expect; for temporary stimulus often does much; but when I see the daily increasing weakness, I know not what to think. I fear you will be shocked when you see Anne; but be on your guard, dear E——, not to express your feelings; indeed, I can trust both your self-possession and your kindness. I wish my judgment sanctioned the step of going to Scarborough, more fully than it does. You ask how I have arranged about leaving Papa. I could make no special arrangement. He wishes me to go with Anne, and would not hear of Mr N——'s coming, or any thing of that kind; so I do what I believe is for the best, and leave the result to Providence.'

They planned to rest and spend a night at York; and at Anne's desire, arranged to make some purchases there. Charlotte ends the letter to her friend, in which she tells her all this, with—

'May 23rd.

'I wish it seemed less like a dreary mockery in us to talk of buying bonnets, &c. Anne was very ill yesterday. She had difficulty of breathing all day, even when sitting perfectly still. To-day she seems better again. I long for the moment to come when the experiment of the sea-air will be tried. Will it do her good? I cannot tell; I can only wish. Oh! if it would please God to strengthen and revive Anne, how happy we might be together: His will, however, be done!'

The two sisters left Haworth on Thursday, May 24th. They were to have done so the day before, and had made an appointment with their friend to meet them at the Leeds station, in order that they might all proceed together. But on Wednesday morning Anne was so ill, that it was impossible for the sisters to set out; yet they had no means of letting their friend know of this, and she consequently arrived at the Leeds station at the time specified. There she sate waiting for several hours. It struck her as strange at the time—and it almost seems ominous to her fancy now—that twice over, from two separate arrivals on the line by which she was expecting her friends, coffins were carried forth, and placed in hearses which were in waiting for their dead, as she was waiting for one, in four days to become so.

The next day she could bear suspense no longer, and set out for Haworth, reaching there just in time to carry the feeble, fainting invalid into the chaise which was waiting to take them down to Keighley. The servant who stood at the Parsonage gates, saw Death written on her face, and spoke of it. Charlotte saw it and did not speak of it,—it would have been giving the dread too distinct a form; and if this last darling yearned for the change to Scarborough, go she should, however Charlotte's heart might be wrung by impending fear. The lady who accompanied them, Charlotte's beloved friend of more than twenty years, has kindly written out for me the following account of the journey—and of the end.*

'She left her home May 24th, 1849—died May 28th. Her life was calm, quiet, spiritual: *such* was her end. Through the trials and fatigues of the journey, she evinced the pious courage and fortitude of a martyr. Dependence and helplessness were ever with her a far sorer trial than hard, racking pain.

'The first stage of our journey was to York; and here the dear invalid was so revived, so cheerful, and so happy, we drew consolation, and trusted that at least temporary improvement was to be derived from the change which *she* had so longed for, and her friends had so dreaded for her.

'By her request we went to the Minster, and to her it was an overpowering pleasure; not for its own imposing and impressive grandeur only, but because it brought to her susceptible nature a vital and overwhelming sense of omnipotence. She said, while gazing at the structure, "If finite power can do this, what is the . . . ?"

and here emotion stayed her speech, and she was hastened to a less exciting scene.

'Her weakness of body was great, but her gratitude for every mercy was greater. After such an exertion as walking to her bed-room, she would clasp her hands and raise her eyes in silent thanks, and she did this not to the exclusion of wonted prayer, for that too was performed on bended knee, ere she accepted the rest of her couch.

'On the 25th we arrived at Scarborough; our dear invalid having, during the journey, directed our attention to every prospect worthy of notice.

'On the 26th she drove on the sands for an hour; and lest the poor donkey should be urged by its driver to a greater speed than her tender heart thought right, she took the reins, and drove herself. When joined by her friend, she was charging the boy-master of the donkey to treat the poor animal well. She was ever fond of dumb things, and would give up her own comfort for them.

'On Sunday, the 27th, she wished to go to church, and her eye brightened with the thought of once more worshipping her God amongst her fellow-creatures. We thought it prudent to dissuade her from the attempt, though it was evident her heart was longing to join in the public act of devotion and praise.

'She walked a little in the afternoon, and meeting with a sheltered and comfortable seat near the beach, she begged we would leave her, and enjoy the various scenes near at hand, which were new to us but familiar to her. She loved the place, and wished us to share her preference.

'The evening closed in with the most glorious sunset ever witnessed. The castle on the cliff stood in proud glory gilded by the rays of the declining sun. The distant ships glittered like burnished gold; the little boats near the beach heaved on the ebbing tide, inviting occupants. The view was grand beyond description. Anne was drawn in her easy chair to the window, to enjoy the scene with us. Her face became illumined almost as much as the glorious scene she gazed upon. Little was said, for it was plain that her thoughts were driven by the imposing view before her to penetrate forwards to the regions of unfading glory. She again thought of public worship, and wished us to leave her, and join those who were assembled at the House of God. We declined, gently urging the duty and pleasure of staying with her, who was now so dear and so feeble. On returning to her place near the fire, she conversed with her sister upon the propriety of returning to their home. She did not wish it for her own sake, she said; she was fearing others might suffer more if her decease occurred where she was. She probably thought the task of accompanying her lifeless remains on a long journey was more than her sister could bear—more than the bereaved father could bear, were she borne home another, and a third tenant of the family-vault in the short space of nine months.

'The night was passed without any apparent accession of illness. She rose at seven o'clock, and performed most of her toilet herself, by her expressed wish. Her sister always yielded such points, believing it was the truest kindness not to press inability when it was not acknowledged. Nothing occurred to excite alarm till about 11 A.M. She then spoke of feeling a change. "She believed she had not long to live. Could she reach home alive, if we prepared immediately for departure?" A physician was sent for. Her address to him was made with perfect composure. She begged him to say "How long he thought she might live;—not to fear speaking the truth, for she was not afraid to die." The doctor reluctantly admitted that the angel of death was already arrived, and that life was ebbing fast. She thanked him for his truthfulness, and he departed to come again very soon. She still occupied her easy chair, looking so serene, so reliant: there was no opening for grief as yet, though all knew the separation was at hand. She clasped her hands, and reverently invoked a blessing from on high; first upon her sister, then upon her friend, to whom she said, "Be a sister in my stead. Give Charlotte as much of your company as you can." She then thanked each for her kindness and attention.

'Ere long the restlessness of approaching death appeared, and she was borne to the sofa; on being asked if she were easier, she looked gratefully at her questioner, and said, "It is not *you* who can give me ease, but soon all will be well, through the merits of our Redeemer."* Shortly after this, seeing that her sister could hardly restrain her grief, she said, "Take courage, Charlotte; take courage." Her faith never failed, and her eye never dimmed till about two o'clock, when she calmly and without a sigh passed from the temporal to the eternal. So still and so hallowed were her last hours and moments. There was no thought of assistance or of dread. The doctor came and went two or three times. The hostess knew that death was near, yet so little was the house disturbed by the presence of the dying, and the sorrow of those so nearly bereaved, that dinner was announced as ready, through the half-opened door, as the living sister was closing the eyes of the dead one. She could now no more stay the welled-up grief of her sister with her emphatic and dying "Take courage," and it burst forth in brief but agonizing strength. Charlotte's affection, however, had another channel, and there it turned in thought, in care, and in tenderness. There was bereavement, but there was not solitude;—sympathy was at hand, and it was accepted. With calmness came the consideration of the removal of the dear remains to their home resting-place. This melancholy task, however, was never performed; for the afflicted sister decided to lay the flower in the place where it had fallen. She believed that to do so would accord with the wishes of the departed. She had no preference for place. She thought not of the grave, for that is but the body's goal, but of all that is beyond it.

'Her remains rest,

"Where the south sun warms the now dear sod,
"Where the ocean billows lave and strike the steep and turf-
        covered rock." '*

Anne died on the Monday. On the Tuesday Charlotte wrote to her father; but knowing that his presence was required for some annual Church solemnity at Haworth, she informed him that she had made all necessary arrangements for the interment, and that the funeral would take place so soon, that he could hardly arrive in time for it. The surgeon who had visited Anne on the day of her death, offered his attendance, but it was respectfully declined.

A lady* from the same neighbourhood as E—— was staying in Scarborough at this time; she, too, kindly offered sympathy and assistance; and when that solitary pair of mourners (the sister and the friend) arrived at the church, this lady was there, in unobtrusive presence, not the less kind because unobtrusive.

Mr Brontë wrote to urge Charlotte's longer stay at the sea-side. Her health and spirits were sorely shaken; and much as he naturally longed to see his only remaining child, he felt it right to persuade her to take, with her friend, a few more weeks' change of scene,*—though even that could not bring change of thought.

The younger servant,* Martha Brown, who has been occasionally alluded to in these memoirs, who was with Miss Brontë in her last days, and who still remains the faithful servant at Haworth Parsonage, has recently sent me a few letters which she received from her dearly-loved mistress: one of them I will insert here, as it refers to this time.

'June 5th, 1849.

'DEAR MARTHA,

'I was very much pleased with your note, and glad to learn that all at home are getting on pretty well. It will still be a week or ten days before I return, and you must not tire yourself too much with the cleaning.

'My sister Anne's death could not be otherwise than a great trouble to me, though I have known for many weeks that she could not get better. She died very calmly and gently: she was quite sensible to the last. About three minutes before she died she said she was very happy, and believed she was passing out of earth into heaven. It was not her custom to talk much about religion; but she was very good, and I am certain she is now in a far better place than any this world contains.

'I mean to send one of the boxes home this week, as I have more luggage than is convenient to carry about. Give my best love to Tabby.

'I am, dear Martha,
'Your sincere friend,
'C. BRONTË .'

'July, 1849.*

'I intended to have written a line to you to-day, if I had not received yours. We did indeed part suddenly; it made my heart ache that we were severed without the time to exchange a word; and yet perhaps it was better. I got here a little before eight o'clock. All was clean and bright, waiting for me. Papa and the servants were well; and all received me with an affection which should have consoled. The dogs seemed in strange ecstasy. I am certain they regarded me as the harbinger of others. The dumb creatures thought that as I was returned, those who had been so long absent were not far behind.

'I left Papa soon, and went into the dining-room: I shut the door—I tried to be glad that I was come home. I have always been glad before—except once*—even then I was cheered. But this time joy was not to be the sensation. I felt that the house was all silent—the rooms were all empty. I remembered where the three were laid—in what narrow dark dwellings—never more to reappear on earth. So the sense of desolation and bitterness took possession of me. The agony that *was to be undergone*, and *was not* to be avoided, came on. I underwent it, and passed a dreary evening and night, and a mournful morrow; to-day I am better.

'I do not know how life will pass, but I certainly do feel confidence in Him who has upheld me hitherto. Solitude may be cheered, and made endurable beyond what I can believe. The great trial is when evening closes and night approaches. At that hour, we used to assemble in the dining-room—we used to talk. Now I sit by myself—necessarily I am silent. I cannot help thinking of their last days, remembering their sufferings, and what they said and did, and how they looked in mortal affliction. Perhaps all this will become less poignant in time.

'Let me thank you once more, dear E——, for your kindness to me, which I do not mean to forget. How did you think all looking at your home? Papa thought me a little stronger; he said my eyes were not so sunken.'

'July 14th, 1849.

'I do not much like giving you an account of myself. I like better to go out of myself, and talk of something more cheerful. My cold, wherever I got it, whether at Easton or elsewhere, is not vanished yet. It began in my head, then I had a sore throat, and then a sore chest, with a cough, but only a trifling cough, which I still have at times. The pain between my shoulders likewise amazed me much. Say nothing about it, for I confess I am too much disposed to be nervous. This nervousness is a horrid phantom. I dare communicate no ailment to Papa; his anxiety harasses me inexpressibly.

'My life is what I expected it to be. Sometimes when I wake in the morning, and know that Solitude, Remembrance, and Longing are to be almost my soul companions all day through—that at night I shall go to bed with them, that they will long keep me sleepless—that next morning I shall wake to them again,—sometimes, Nell, I have a heavy heart of it. But crushed I am not, yet; nor robbed of elasticity, nor of hope, nor quite of endeavour. I have some strength to fight the battle of life. I am aware, and can acknowledge, I have many comforts, many mercies. Still I can *get on*. But I do hope and pray, that never may you, or any one I love, be placed as I am. To sit in a lonely room—the clock ticking loud through a still house—and have open before the mind's eye the record of the last year, with its shocks, sufferings, losses—is a trial.

'I write to you freely, because I believe you will hear me with moderation—that you will not take alarm or think me in any way worse off than I am.'

# CHAPTER IV

THE tale of 'Shirley' had been begun soon after the publication of 'Jane Eyre.' If the reader will refer to the account I have given of Miss Brontë's school-days at Roe Head, he will there see how every place surrounding that house was connected with the Luddite riots, and will learn how stories and anecdotes of that time were rife among the inhabitants of the neighbouring villages; how Miss W—— herself, and the elder relations of most of her schoolfellows, must have known the actors in those grim disturbances. What Charlotte had heard there as a girl came up in her mind when, as a woman, she sought a subject for her next work; and she sent to Leeds for a file of the 'Mercuries' of 1812, '13 and '14; in order to understand the spirit of those eventful times.* She was anxious to write of things she had known and seen; and among the number was the West Yorkshire character, for which any tale laid among the Luddites would afford full scope. In 'Shirley' she took the idea of most of her characters from life, although the incidents and situations were, of course, fictitious. She thought that if these last were purely imaginary, she might draw from the real without detection, but in this she was mistaken; her studies were too closely accurate. This occasionally led her into difficulties. People recognised themselves, or were recognised by others, in her graphic descriptions of their personal appearance, and modes of actions and turns of thought; though they were placed in new positions, and figured away* in scenes far different to those in which their actual life had been passed. Miss Brontë was struck by the force or peculiarity of the character of some one whom she knew; she studied it, and analysed it with subtle power; and having traced it to its germ, she took that germ as the nucleus of an imaginary character, and worked outwards;—thus reversing the process of analysation, and unconsciously reproducing the same external development. The 'three curates'* were real living men, haunting Haworth and the neighbouring district; and so obtuse in perception that, after the first burst of anger at having their ways and habits chronicled was over, they rather enjoyed the joke of calling each other by the names she had given them. 'Mrs Pryor' was well known to many who loved the original dearly. The whole family of the Yorkes were, I have been assured, almost daguerreo-types.* Indeed, Miss Brontë told me that, before publication, she had sent those parts of the novel in which these remarkable persons are introduced, to one of the sons; and his reply, after reading it, was simply that 'she had not drawn them strong enough.' From those many-sided sons, I suspect, she drew all that there was of truth in the characters of the heroes in her first two works. They, indeed, were almost the only young men she knew intimately, besides her brother. There was much friendship, and still more confidence, between the Brontë family and them—although their intercourse was often broken and irregular. There was never any warmer feeling on either side.

The character of Shirley herself is Charlotte's representation of Emily. I mention this because all that I, a stranger, have been able to learn about her has not tended to give either me, or my readers, a pleasant impression of her. But we must remember how little we are acquainted with her, compared to that sister, who, out of her more intimate knowledge, says that she 'was genuinely good, and truly great,'* and who tried to depict her character in Shirley Keeldar, as what Emily Brontë would have been, had she been placed in health and prosperity.

Miss Brontë took extreme pains with 'Shirley.' She felt that the fame she had acquired imposed upon her a double responsibility. She tried to make her novel like a piece of actual life,—feeling sure that if she but represented the product of personal experience and observation truly, good would come out of it in the long run. She carefully studied the different reviews and criticisms that had appeared on 'Jane Eyre,' in hopes of extracting precepts and advice from which to profit.

Down into the very midst of her writing came the bolts of death. She had nearly finished the second volume of her tale when Branwell died,—after him Emily,—after her Anne;—the pen, laid down when there were three sisters living and loving, was taken up when one alone remained. Well might she call the first chapter that she wrote after this, 'The Valley of the Shadow of Death.'

I knew in part what the unknown author of 'Shirley' must have suffered, when I read those pathetic words which occur at the end of this and the beginning of the succeeding chapter:—*

'Till break of day, she wrestled with God in earnest prayer.

'Not always do those who dare such divine conflict prevail. Night after night the sweat of agony may burst dark on the forehead; the supplicant may cry for mercy with that soundless voice the soul utters when its appeal is to the Invisible. "Spare my beloved," it may implore. "Heal my life's life. Rend not from me what long affection entwines with my whole nature. God of Heaven—bend—hear—be clement!" And after this cry and strife, the sun may rise and see him worsted. That opening morn, which used to salute him with the whisper of zephyrs, the carol of skylarks, may breathe, as its first accents, from the dear lips which colour and heat have quitted,—"Oh! I have had a suffering night. This morning I am worse. I have tried to rise. I cannot. Dreams I am unused to have troubled me."

'Then the watcher approaches the patient's pillow, and sees a new and strange moulding of the familiar features, feels at once that the insufferable moment draws nigh, knows that it is God's will his idol should be broken, and bends his head, and subdues his soul to the sentence he cannot avert, and scarce can bear. . . . .

'No piteous, unconscious moaning sound—which so wastes our strength that, even if we have sworn to be firm, a rush of unconquerable tears sweeps away the oath—preceded her waking. No space of deaf apathy followed. The first words spoken were not those of one becoming estranged from this world, and already permitted to stray at times into realms foreign to the living.'

She went on with her work steadily. But it was dreary to write without any one to listen to the progress of her tale,—to find fault or to sympathise,—while pacing the length of the parlour in the evenings, as in the days that were no more. Three sisters had done this,—then two, the other sister dropping off from the walk,—and now one was left desolate, to listen for echoing steps that never came,—and to hear the wind sobbing at the windows, with an almost articulate sound.

But she wrote on, struggling against her own feelings of illness; 'continually recurring feelings of slight cold; slight soreness in the throat and chest, of which, do what I will,' she writes, 'I cannot get rid.'*

In August there arose a new cause for anxiety, happily but temporary.

'Aug. 23rd, 1849.*

'Papa has not been well at all lately. He has had another attack of bronchitis. I felt very uneasy about him for some days—more wretched indeed than I care to tell you. After what has happened, one trembles at any appearance of sickness; and when anything ails Papa, I feel too keenly that he is the *last*—the only near and dear relative I have in the world. Yesterday and to-day he has seemed much better, for which I am truly thankful. . . . . . .

'From what you say of Mr ——, I think I should like him very much. —— wants shaking to be put out about his appearance. What does it matter whether her husband dines in a dress-coat or a market-coat, provided there be worth, and honesty, and a clean shirt underneath?'

'Sept. 10th, 1849.

'My piece of work is at last finished, and despatched to its destination. You must now tell me when there is a chance of your being able to come here. I fear it will now be difficult to arrange, as it is so near the marriage-day. Note well, it would spoil all my pleasure, if you put yourself or any one else to inconvenience to come to Haworth. But when it is *convenient*, I shall be truly glad to see you. . . . Papa, I am thankful to say, is better, though not strong. He is often troubled with a sensation of nausea. My cold is very much less troublesome, I am sometimes quite free from it. A few days since, I had a severe bilious attack, the consequence of sitting too closely to my writing; but it is gone now. It is the first from which I have suffered since my return from the sea-side. I had them every month before.'

'Sept. 13th, 1849.*

'If duty and the well-being of others require that you should stay at home, I cannot permit myself to complain; still, I am very, *very* sorry that circumstances will not permit us to meet just now. I would without hesitation come to ——, if Papa were stronger; but uncertain as are both his health and spirits, I could not possibly prevail on myself to leave him now. Let us hope that when we do see each other, our meeting will be all the more pleasurable for being delayed. Dear E——, you certainly have a heavy burden laid on your shoulders, but such burdens, if well borne, benefit the character; only we must take the *greatest, closest, most watchful* care not to grow proud of our strength, in case we should be enabled to bear up under the trial. That pride, indeed, would be a sign of radical weakness. The strength, if strength we have, is certainly never in our own selves; it is given us.'

TO W. S. WILLIAMS, ESQ.

'Sept. 21st, 1849.

'My dear Sir,—I am obliged to you for preserving my secret, being at least as anxious as ever (*more* anxious I cannot well be) to keep quiet. You asked me in one of your letters lately, whether I thought I should escape identification in Yorkshire. I am so little known, that I think I shall. Besides, the book is far less founded on the Real, than perhaps appears. It would be difficult to explain to you how little actual experience I have had of life, how few persons I have known, and how very few have known me.

'As an instance how the characters have been managed, take that of Mr Helstone.* If this character had an original, it was in the person of a clergyman who died some years since at the advanced age of eighty. I never saw him except once—at the consecration of a church—when I was a child of ten years old. I was then struck with his appearance, and stern, martial air. At a subsequent period, I heard him talked about in the neighbourhood where he had resided: some mention him with enthusiasm—others with detestation. I listened to various anecdotes, balanced evidence against evidence, and drew an inference. The original of Mr Hall I have seen; he knows me slightly; but he would as soon think I had closely observed him or taken him for a character—he would as soon, indeed, suspect me of writing a book—a novel—as he would his dog, Prince. Margaret Hall called "Jane Eyre" a "wicked book," on the authority of the "Quarterly;" an expression which, coming from her, I will here confess, struck somewhat deep. It opened my eyes to the harm the "Quarterly" had done. Margaret would not have called it "wicked," if she had not been told so.

'No matter,—whether known or unknown—misjudged, or the contrary,—I am resolved not to write otherwise. I shall bend as my powers tend. The two human beings who understood me, and whom I understood, are gone: I have some that love me yet, and whom I love, without expecting, or having a right to expect, that they shall perfectly understand me. I am satisfied; but I must have my own way in the matter of writing. The loss of what we possess nearest and dearest to us in this world, produces an effect upon the character: we search out what we have yet left that can support, and, when found, we cling to it with a hold of new-strung tenacity. The faculty of imagination lifted me when I was sinking, three months ago; its active exercise has kept my head above water since; its results cheer me now, for I feel they have enabled me to give pleasure to others. I am thankful to God, who gave me the faculty; and it is for me a part of my religion to defend this gift, and to profit by its possession.—Yours sincerely,

'CHARLOTTE BRONTË.'

At the time when this letter was written, both Tabby and the young servant whom they had to assist her were ill in bed; and with the exception of occasional aid, Miss Brontë had all the household work to perform, as well as to nurse the two invalids.

The serious illness of the younger servant was at its height, when a cry from Tabby called Miss Brontë into the kitchen, and she found the poor old woman of eighty laid on the floor, with her head under the kitchen-grate; she had fallen from her chair in attempting to rise. When I saw her, two years later, she described to me the tender care which Charlotte had taken of her at this time; and wound up her account of 'how her own mother could not have had more thought for her nor Miss Brontë had,' by saying, 'Eh! she's a good one—she *is!*'

But there was one day when the strung nerves gave way—when, as she says,* 'I fairly broke down for ten minutes; sat and cried like a fool. Tabby could neither stand nor walk. Papa had just been declaring that Martha was in imminent danger. I was myself depressed with headache and sickness. That day I hardly knew what to do, or where to turn. Thank God! Martha is now convalescent: Tabby, I trust, will be better soon. Papa is pretty well. I have the satisfaction of knowing that my publishers are delighted with what I sent them. This supports me. But life is a battle. May we all be enabled to fight it well!'

The kind friend, to whom she thus wrote, saw how the poor over-taxed system needed bracing, and accordingly sent her a shower-bath—a thing for which she had long been wishing. The receipt of it was acknowledged as follows:—

'Sept. 28th, 1849.

'. . . Martha is now almost well, and Tabby much better. A huge monster package, from "Nelson, Leeds,"* came yesterday. You want chastising roundly and soundly. Such are the thanks you get for all your trouble. . . . Whenever you come to Haworth, you shall certainly have a thorough drenching in your own shower-bath. I have not yet unpacked the wretch. Yours, as you deserve,

'C. B.'

There was misfortune of another kind impending over her. There were some railway shares, which, so early as 1846, she had told Miss W—— she wished to sell, but had kept because she could not persuade her sisters to look upon the affair as she did, and so preferred running the risk of loss, to hurting Emily's feelings by acting in opposition to her opinion. The depreciation of these same shares was now verifying Charlotte's soundness of judgment. They were in the York and North-Midland Company,* which was one of Mr Hudson's pet lines, and had the full benefit of his peculiar system of management. She applied to her friend and publisher, Mr Smith, for information on the subject; and the following letter is in answer to his reply:—

'Oct. 4th, 1849.

'My dear Sir,—I must not *thank* you for, but acknowledge the receipt of your letter. The business is certainly very bad; worse than I thought, and much worse than my father has any idea of. In fact, the little railway property I possessed, according to original prices, formed already a small competency for me, with my views and habits. Now, scarcely any portion of it can, with security, be calculated upon. I must open this view of the case to my father by degrees; and, meanwhile, wait patiently till I see how affairs are likely to turn. . . . . However the matter may terminate, I ought perhaps to be rather thankful than dissatisfied. When I look at my own case, and compare it with that of thousands besides, I scarcely

see room for a murmur. Many, very many, are by the late strange
railway system deprived almost of their daily bread. Such then as
have only lost provision laid up for the future, should take care
how they complain. The thought that "Shirley" has given pleasure
at Cornhill, yields me much quiet comfort. No doubt, however,
you are, as I am, prepared for critical severity; but I have good
hopes that the vessel is sufficiently sound of construction to weather
a gale or two, and to make a prosperous voyage for you in the end.'

Towards the close of October in this year, she went to pay a visit
to her friend; but her enjoyment in the holiday, which she had so
long promised herself when her work was completed, was dead-
ened by a continual feeling of ill-health; either the change of air or
the foggy weather produced constant irritation at the chest.
Moreover, she was anxious about the impression which her second
work would produce on the public mind. For obvious reasons, an
author is more susceptible to opinions pronounced on the book
which follows a great success, than he has ever been before.
Whatever be the value of fame, he has it in his possession, and is
not willing to have it dimmed or lost.

'Shirley' was published on October 26th.

When it came out, but before reading it, Mr Lewes wrote to tell
her of his intention of reviewing it in the 'Edinburgh.' Her
correspondence with him had ceased for some time: much had
occurred since.

TO G. H. LEWES, ESQ.

'Nov. 1st, 1849.

'My dear Sir,—It is about a year and a half since you wrote to
me; but it seems a longer period, because since then it has been
my lot to pass some black milestones in the journey of life. Since
then there have been intervals when I have ceased to care about
literature and critics and fame; when I have lost sight of whatever
was prominent in my thoughts at the first publication of "Jane
Eyre;" but now I want these things to come back vividly, if
possible: consequently, it was a pleasure to receive your note. I
wish you did not think me a woman. I wish all reviewers believed
"Currer Bell" to be a man; they would be more just to him. You

will, I know, keep measuring me by some standard of what you deem becoming to my sex; where I am not what you consider graceful, you will condemn me. All mouths will be open against that first chapter; and that first chapter is true as the Bible, nor is it exceptionable. Come what will, I cannot, when I write, think always of myself and of what is elegant and charming in feminity; it is not on those terms, or with such ideas, I ever took pen in hand: and if it is only on such terms my writing will be tolerated, I shall pass away from the public and trouble it no more. Out of obscurity I came, to obscurity I can easily return. Standing afar off, I now watch to see what will become of "Shirley." My expectations are very low, and my anticipations somewhat sad and bitter; still, I earnestly conjure you to say honestly what you think; flattery would be worse than vain; there is no consolation in flattery. As for condemnation I cannot, on reflection, see why I should much fear it; there is no one but myself to suffer therefrom, and both happiness and suffering in this life soon pass away. Wishing you all success in your Scottish expedition,*—I am, dear Sir, yours sincerely,

'C. BELL.'

Miss Brontë, as we have seen, had been as anxious as ever to preserve her incognito in 'Shirley.' She even fancied that there were fewer traces of a female pen in it than in 'Jane Eyre;' and thus, when the earliest reviews were published, and asserted that the mysterious writer must be a woman,* she was much disappointed. She especially disliked the lowering of the standard by which to judge a work of fiction, if it proceeded from a feminine pen; and praise mingled with pseudo-gallant allusions to her sex, mortified her far more than actual blame.

But the secret, so jealously preserved, was oozing out at last. The publication of 'Shirley' seemed to fix the conviction that the writer was an inhabitant of the district where the story was laid. And a clever Haworth man, who had somewhat risen in the world, and gone to settle in Liverpool, read the novel, and was struck with some of the names of places mentioned, and knew the dialect in which parts of it were written. He became convinced that it was the production of some one in Haworth. But he could not imagine who in that village could have written such a work except Miss Brontë. Proud of his conjecture, he divulged the suspicion (which

was almost certainty) in the columns of a Liverpool paper; thus the
heart of the mystery came slowly creeping out; and a visit to London,
which Miss Brontë paid towards the end of the year 1849, made it
distinctly known. She had been all along on most happy terms with
her publishers; and their kindness had beguiled some of those weary,
solitary hours which had so often occurred of late, by sending for her
perusal boxes of books more suited to her tastes than any she could
procure from the circulating library at Keighley. She often writes such
sentences as the following, in her letters to Cornhill:—*

'I was indeed very much interested in the books you sent.
"Eckermann's Conversations with Goëthe," "Guesses at Truth,"
"Friends in Council," and the little work on English social life,
pleased me particularly, and the last not least. We sometimes take
a partiality to books as to characters, not on account of any brilliant
intellect or striking peculiarity they boast, but for the sake of
something good, delicate, and genuine. I thought that small book
the production of a lady, and an amiable, sensible woman, and I
liked it. You must not think of selecting any more works for me
yet; my stock is still far from exhausted.

'I accept your offer respecting the "Athenæum;" it is a paper I
should like much to see, providing that you can send it without
trouble. It shall be punctually returned.'

In a letter to her friend she complains of the feelings of illness
from which she was seldom or never free.

'Nov. 16th, 1849.

'You are not to suppose any of the characters in "Shirley"
intended as literal portraits. It would not suit the rules of art, nor
of my own feelings, to write in that style. We only suffer reality to
*suggest*, never to *dictate*. The heroines are abstractions, and the
heroes also. Qualities I have seen, loved, and admired, are here and
there put in as decorative gems, to be preserved in that setting.
Since you say you could recognise the originals of all except the
heroines, pray whom did you suppose the two Moors to represent?* I send you a couple of reviews;* the one is in the
"Examiner," written by Albany Fonblanque, who is called the

most brilliant political writer of the day, a man whose dictum is much thought of in London. The other, in the "Standard of Freedom," is written by William Howitt, a Quaker! . . . I should be pretty well, if it were not for headaches and indigestion. My chest has been better lately.'

In consequence of this long-protracted state of languor, headache, and sickness, to which the slightest exposure to cold added sensations of hoarseness and soreness at the chest, she determined to take the evil in time, as much for her father's sake as for her own, and to go up to London and consult some physician there. It was not her first intention to visit anywhere; but the friendly urgency of her publishers prevailed, and it was decided that she was to become the guest of Mr Smith. Before she went, she wrote two characteristic letters about 'Shirley,' from which I shall take a few extracts.*

' "Shirley" makes her way. The reviews shower in fast. . . . The best critique which has yet appeared is in the "Revue des Deux Mondes,"* a sort of European Cosmopolitan periodical, whose head-quarters are at Paris. Comparatively few reviewers, even in their praise, evince a just comprehension of the author's meaning. Eugène Forçade, the reviewer in question, follows Currer Bell through every winding, discerns every point, discriminates every shade, proves himself master of the subject, and lord of the aim. With that man I would shake hands, if I saw him. I would say, "You know me, Monsieur; I shall deem it an honour to know you." I could not say so much of the mass of the London critics. Perhaps I could not say so much to five hundred men and women in all the millions of Great Britain. That matters little. My own conscience I satisfy first; and having done that, if I further content and delight a Forçade, a Fonblanque, and a Thackeray, my ambition has had its ration; it is fed; it lies down for the present satisfied; my faculties have wrought a day's task, and earned a day's wages. I am no teacher; to look on me in that light is to mistake me. To teach is not my vocation. What I *am*, it is useless to say. Those whom it concerns feel and find it out. To all others I wish only to be an obscure, steady-going, private character. To you, dear E——, I wish to be a sincere friend. Give me your faithful regard; I willingly dispense with admiration.'

'Nov. 26th.

'It is like you to pronounce the reviews not good enough, and belongs to that part of your character which will not permit you to bestow unqualified approbation on any dress, decoration, &c., belonging to you. Know that the reviews are superb; and were I dissatisfied with them, I should be a conceited ape. Nothing higher is ever said, *from perfectly disinterested motives*, of any living authors. If all be well, I go to London this week; Wednesday, I think. The dressmaker has done my small matters pretty well, but I wish you could have looked them over, and given a dictum. I insisted on the dresses being made quite plainly.'

At the end of November she went up to the 'big Babylon,' and was immediately plunged into what appeared to her a whirl; for changes, and scenes, and stimulus which would have been a trifle to others, were much to her.* As was always the case with strangers, she was a little afraid at first of the family into which she was now received, fancying that the ladies looked on her with a mixture of respect and alarm; but in a few days, if this state of feeling ever existed, her simple, shy, quiet manners, her dainty personal and household ways, had quite done away with it, and she says that she thinks they begin to like her, and that she likes them much, for 'kindness is a potent heart-winner.' She had stipulated that she should not be expected to see many people. The recluse life she had led, was the cause of a nervous shrinking from meeting any fresh face, which lasted all her life long. Still, she longed to have an idea of the personal appearance and manners of some of those whose writings or letters had interested her. Mr Thackeray was accordingly invited to meet her,* but it so happened that she had been out for the greater part of the morning, and, in consequence, missed the luncheon hour at her friend's house. This brought on a severe and depressing head-ache in one accustomed to the early, regular hours of a York-shire Parsonage; besides the excitement of meeting, hearing, and sitting next a man to whom she looked up with such admira-tion as she did to the author of 'Vanity Fair,' was of itself overpowering to her frail nerves. She writes about this dinner as follows:—

'Dec. 10th, 1849.*

'As to being happy, I am under scenes and circumstances of excitement; but I suffer acute pain sometimes,—mental pain, I mean. At the moment Mr Thackeray presented himself, I was thoroughly faint from inanition, having eaten nothing since a very slight breakfast, and it was then seven o'clock in the evening. Excitement and exhaustion made savage work of me that evening. What he thought of me I cannot tell.'

She told me how difficult she found it, this first time of meeting Mr Thackeray, to decide whether he was speaking in jest or in earnest, and that she had (she believed) completely misunderstood an inquiry of his, made on the gentlemen's coming into the drawing-room.* He asked her 'if she had perceived the secret of their cigars;' to which she replied literally, discovering in a minute afterwards, by the smile on several faces, that he was alluding to a passage in 'Jane Eyre.' Her hosts took pleasure in showing her the sights of London. On one of the days which had been set apart for some of these pleasant excursions, a severe review of 'Shirley' was published in the 'Times.'* She had heard that her book would be noticed by it, and guessed that there was some particular reason for the care with which her hosts mislaid it on that particular morning. She told them that she was aware why she might not see the paper. Mrs Smith at once admitted that her conjecture was right, and said that they had wished her to go to the day's engagement before reading it. But she quietly persisted in her request to be allowed to have the paper. Mrs Smith took her work, and tried not to observe the countenance, which the other tried to hide between the large sheets; but she could not help becoming aware of tears stealing down the face and dropping on the lap. The first remark Miss Brontë made was to express her fear lest so severe a notice should check the sale of the book, and injuriously affect her publishers. Wounded as she was, her first thought was for others. Later on (I think that very afternoon) Mr Thackeray called; she suspected (she said) that he came to see how she bore the attack on 'Shirley;' but she had recovered her composure, and conversed very quietly with him: he only learnt from the answer to his direct inquiry that she had read the 'Times' ' article. She acquiesced in the recognition of herself as the authoress of 'Jane Eyre,' because she perceived that there were some advantages to be derived from dropping her pseudonym. One result was an acquaintance with Miss Martineau.* She had sent her the novel just published, with a curious note, in which Currer Bell offered a copy of 'Shirley' to Miss Martineau, as an acknowledgment of the gratification *he* had received from her works. From 'Deerbrook' *he* had derived a new and keen pleasure, and experienced a genuine benefit. In *his* mind 'Deerbrook,' &c.

Miss Martineau, in acknowledging this note and the copy of 'Shirley,' dated her letter from a friend's house in the neighbourhood of Mr Smith's residence; and when, a week or two afterwards, Miss Brontë found how near she was to her correspondent, she wrote, in the name of Currer Bell, to propose a visit to her. Six o'clock, on a certain Sunday afternoon (Dec. 10th), was the time appointed. Miss Martineau's friends had invited the unknown Currer Bell to their early tea; they were ignorant whether the name was that of a man or a woman; and had had various conjectures as to sex, age, and appearance. Miss Martineau had, indeed, expressed her private opinion pretty distinctly by beginning her reply, to the professedly masculine note referred to above, with 'Dear Madam;' but she had addressed it to 'Currer Bell, Esq.' At every ring the eyes of the party turned towards the door. Some stranger (a gentleman, I think) came in; for an instant they fancied he was Currer Bell, and indeed an Esq.; he stayed some time—went away. Another ring; 'Miss Brontë' was announced; and in came a young-looking lady, almost child-like in stature, 'in a deep mourning dress, neat as a Quaker's, with her beautiful hair smooth and brown, her fine eyes blazing with meaning, and her sensible face indicating a habit of self-control.' She came,—hesitated one moment at finding four or five people assembled,—then went straight to Miss Martineau with intuitive recognition, and with the freemasonry of good feeling and gentle breeding, she soon became as one of the family seated round the tea-table; and, before she left, she told them, in a simple, touching manner, of her sorrow and isolation, and a foundation was laid for her intimacy with Miss Martineau.

After some discussion on the subject,* and a stipulation that she should not be specially introduced to any one, some gentlemen were invited by Mr Smith to meet her at dinner the evening before she left town. Her natural place would have been at the bottom of the table by her host; and the places of those who were to be her neighbours were arranged accordingly; but, on entering the dining-room, she quickly passed up so as to sit next to the lady of the house, anxious to shelter herself near some one of her own sex. This slight action arose out of the same womanly seeking after protection on every occasion, when there was no moral duty involved in asserting her independence, that made her about this time write as follows:* 'Mrs —— watches me very narrowly when surrounded by strangers. She never takes her eye from me. I like the surveillance; it seems to keep guard over me.'

Respecting this particular dinner-party she thus wrote to the Brussels schoolfellow of former days,* whose friendship had been renewed during her present visit to London:—

'The evening after I left you passed better than I expected. Thanks to my substantial lunch and cheering cup of coffee, I was able to wait the eight o'clock dinner with complete resignation,* and to endure its length quite courageously, nor was I too much exhausted to converse; and of this I was glad, for otherwise I know my kind host and hostess would have been much disappointed. There were only seven gentlemen at dinner besides Mr Smith, but of these five were critics—men more dreaded in the world of letters than you can conceive. I did not know how much their presence and conversation had excited me till they were gone, and the reaction commenced. When I had retired for the night, I wished to sleep—the effort to do so was vain. I could not close my eyes. Night passed; morning came, and I rose without having known a moment's slumber. So utterly worn out was I when I got to Derby, that I was again obliged to stay there all night.'

'Dec. 17th.*

'Here I am at Haworth once more. I feel as if I had come out of an exciting whirl. Not that the hurry and stimulus would have seemed much to one accustomed to society and change, but to me they were very marked. My strength and spirits too often proved quite insufficient to the demand on their exertions. I used to bear up as long as I possibly could, for, when I flagged, I could see Mr Smith became disturbed; he always thought that something had been said or done to annoy me—which never once happened, for I met with perfect good breeding even from antagonists—men who had done their best or worst to write me down. I explained to him, over and over again, that my occasional silence was only failure of the power to talk, never of the will. . . . .

'Thackeray is a Titan of mind. His presence and powers impress one deeply in an intellectual sense; I do not see him or know him as a man. All the others are subordinate. I have esteem for some, and, I trust, courtesy for all. I do not, of course, know what they thought of me, but I believe most of them expected me to come out in a more marked, eccentric, striking light. I believe they desired more to admire and more to blame. I felt sufficiently at my ease with all but Thackeray; with him I was fearfully stupid.'

She returned to her quiet home, and her noiseless daily duties.* I was anxious to know from her friend 'Mary,' if, in the letters which Charlotte wrote to her, she had ever spoken with much pleasure of the fame which she had earned. To this and some similar inquiries Mary answers,—

'She thought literary fame a better introduction than any other, and this was what she wanted it for. When at last she got it, she lamented that it was of no use. "Her solitary life had disqualified her for society. She had become unready, nervous, excitable, and either incapable of speech, or talked vapidly." She wrote me this concerning her late visits to London. Her fame, when it came, seemed to make no difference to her. She was just as solitary, and her life as deficient in interest as before. "For swarms of people I don't care," she wrote; and then implied that she had had glimpses of a pleasanter life, but she had come back to her work at home. She never criticised her books to me, farther than to express utter weariness of them, and the labour they had given her.'

Her father had quite enough of the spirit of hero-worship in him to make him take a vivid pleasure in the accounts of what she had heard and whom she had seen. It was on the occasion of one of her visits to London that he had desired her to obtain a sight of Prince Albert's armoury,* if possible. I am not aware whether she managed to do this; but she went to one or two of the great national armouries in order that she might describe the stern steel harness and glittering swords to her father, whose imagination was forcibly struck by the idea of such things; and often afterwards, when his spirits flagged and the languor of old age for a time got the better of his indomitable nature, she would again strike on the measure wild,* and speak about the armies of strange weapons she had seen in London, till he resumed his interest in the old subject, and was his own keen, warlike, intelligent self again.

# CHAPTER V

HER life at Haworth was so unvaried that the postman's call was the event of her day. Yet she dreaded the great temptation of centring all her thoughts upon this one time, and losing her interest in the smaller hopes and employments of the remaining hours. Thus she conscientiously denied herself the pleasure of writing letters too frequently, because the answers (when she received them) took the flavour out of the rest of her life; or the disappointment, when the replies did not arrive, lessened her energy for her home duties.

The winter of this year in the north was hard and cold; it affected Miss Brontë's health less than usual, however, probably because the change and medical advice she had taken in London had done her good; probably, also, because her friend had come to pay her a visit, and enforced that attention to bodily symptoms which Miss Brontë was too apt to neglect, from a fear of becoming nervous herself about her own state, and thus infecting her father. But she could scarcely help feeling much depressed in spirits as the anniversary of her sister Emily's death came round; all the recollections connected with it were painful, yet there were no outward events to call off her attention, and prevent them from pressing hard upon her. At this time, as at many others, I find her alluding in her letters* to the solace which she found in the books sent her from Cornhill.

'What, I sometimes ask, could I do without them? I have recourse to them as to friends; they shorten and cheer many an hour that would be too long and too desolate otherwise; even when my tired sight will not permit me to continue reading, it is pleasant to see them on the shelf, or on the table. I am still very rich, for my stock is far from exhausted. Some other friends have sent me books lately. The perusal of Harriet Martineau's "Eastern Life"* has afforded me great pleasure; and I have found a deep and interesting subject of study in Newman's work on the "Soul." Have you read this work? It is daring,—it may be mistaken,—but it is pure and elevated. Froude's "Nemesis of Faith" I did not like;

I thought it morbid; yet in its pages, too, are found sprinklings of truth.'

By this time, 'Airedale, Wharfedale, Calderdale, and Ribblesdale'* all knew the place of residence of Currer Bell. She compared herself to the ostrich hiding its head in the sand; and says that she still buries hers in the heath of Haworth moors; but 'the concealment is but self-delusion.'*

Indeed it was. Far and wide in the West Riding had spread the intelligence that Currer Bell was no other than a daughter of the venerable clergyman of Haworth; the village itself caught up the excitement.

'Mr ——, having finished "Jane Eyre," is now crying out for the "other book;" he is to have it next week. . . . Mr —— has finished "Shirley;" he is delighted with it. John ——'s wife seriously thought him gone wrong in the head, as she heard him giving vent to roars of laughter as he sat alone, clapping and stamping on the floor. He would read all the scenes about the curates aloud to papa.' . . . 'Martha came in yesterday, puffing and blowing, and much excited. "I've heard sich news!" she began. "What about?" "Please ma'am, you've been and written two books—the grandest books that ever was seen. My father has heard it at Halifax, and Mr G—— T—— and Mr G—— and Mr M—— at Bradford; and they are going to have a meeting at the Mechanics' Institute, and to settle about ordering them." "Hold your tongue, Martha, and be off." I fell into a cold sweat. "Jane Eyre" will be read by J—— B——, by Mrs T——, and B——. Heaven help, keep, and deliver me!' . . . 'The Haworth people have been making great fools of themselves about "Shirley;" they have taken it in an enthusiastic light. When they got the volumes at the Mechanics' Institute, all the members wanted them. They cast lots for the whole three, and whoever got a volume was only allowed to keep it two days, and was to be fined a shilling per diem for longer detention. It would be mere nonsense and vanity to tell you what they say.'

The tone of these extracts is thoroughly consonant with the spirit of Yorkshire and Lancashire people, who try as long as they can to conceal their emotions of pleasure under a bantering exterior, almost as if making fun of themselves. Miss Brontë was extremely touched, in the secret places of her warm heart, by the way in which those who had known her from her childhood were proud and glad of her success. All round about the news had spread; strangers came 'from beyond Burnley'* to see her, as she went quietly and unconsciously into church; and the sexton 'gained many a half-crown' for pointing her out.

But there were drawbacks to this hearty and kindly appreciation which was so much more valuable than fame. The January number of the 'Edinburgh Review' had contained the article on 'Shirley,'* of which her correspondent, Mr Lewes, was the writer. I have said that Miss Brontë was especially anxious to be criticised as a writer, without relation to her sex as a woman. Whether right or wrong, her feeling was strong on this point. Now although this review of 'Shirley' is not disrespectful towards women,* yet the headings of the first two pages ran thus: 'Mental Equality of the Sexes?' 'Female Literature,' and through the whole article the fact of the author's sex is never forgotten.

A few days after the review appeared, Mr Lewes received the following note,*—rather in the style of Anne Countess of Pembroke, Dorset, and Montgomery.

TO G. H. LEWES, ESQ.

'I can be on my guard against my enemies, but God deliver me from my friends!

'CURRER BELL.'

In some explanatory notes on her letters to him, with which Mr Lewes has favoured me, he says:—

'Seeing that she was unreasonable because angry, I wrote to remonstrate with her on quarrelling with the severity and frankness of a review, which certainly was dictated by real admiration and real friendship: even under its objections the friend's voice could be heard.'

The following letter is her reply:—

TO G. H. LEWES, ESQ.

'Jan. 19th, 1850.

'My dear Sir,—I will tell you why I was so hurt by that review in the "Edinburgh"; not because its criticism was keen or its blame sometimes severe; not because its praise was stinted (for, indeed, I think you give me quite as much praise as I deserve), but because after I had said earnestly that I wished critics would judge me as an *author*, not as a woman, you so roughly—I even thought so cruelly—handled the question of sex. I dare say you meant no harm, and perhaps you will not now be able to understand why I was so grieved at what you will probably deem such a trifle; but grieved I was, and indignant too.

'There was a passage or two which you did quite wrong to write.

'However, I will not bear malice against you for it; I know what your nature is: it is not a bad or unkind one, though you would often jar terribly on some feelings with whose recoil and quiver you could not possibly sympathise. I imagine you are both enthusiastic and implacable, as you are at once sagacious and careless; you know much and discover much, but you are in such a hurry to tell it all you never give yourself time to think how your reckless eloquence may affect others; and, what is more, if you knew how it did affect them, you would not much care.

'However, I shake hands with you: you have excellent points; you can be generous. I still feel angry, and think I do well to be angry; but it is the anger one experiences for rough play rather than for foul play.—I am yours, with a certain respect, and more chagrin,

'CURRER BELL.'

As Mr Lewes says, 'the tone of this letter is cavalier.' But I thank him for having allowed me to publish what is so characteristic of one phase of Miss Brontë's mind. Her health, too, was suffering at this time. 'I don't know what heaviness of spirit has beset me of late,' (she writes,* in pathetic words, wrung out of the sadness of her heart,) 'made my faculties dull, made rest weariness, and occupation burdensome. Now and then, the silence of the house, the solitude of the room, has pressed on me with a weight I found it difficult to bear, and recollection has not failed to be as alert, poignant, obtrusive, as other feelings were languid. I attribute this state of things partly to the weather. Quicksilver invariably falls

low in storms and high winds, and I have ere this been warned of
approaching disturbance in the atmosphere by a sense of bodily
weakness, and deep, heavy mental sadness, such as some would call
*presentiment*,—presentiment indeed it is, but not at all supernatural.
. . . . I cannot help feeling something of the excitement of expectation till the post hour comes, and when, day after day, it brings
nothing, I get low. This is a stupid, disgraceful, unmeaning state
of things. I feel bitterly vexed at my own dependence and folly;
but it is so bad for the mind to be quite alone, and to have none
with whom to talk over little crosses and disappointments, and to
laugh them away. If I could write, I dare say I should be better,
but I cannot write a line. However (by God's help), I will contend
against this folly.

'I had a letter* the other day from ——. Some things in it
nettled me, especially an unnecessarily earnest assurance that, in
spite of all I had done in the writing line, I still retained a place in
her esteem. My answer took strong and high ground at once. I said
I had been troubled by no doubts on the subject; that I
neither did her nor myself the injustice to suppose there was
anything in what I had written to incur the just forfeiture of
esteem. . . . .

'A few days since, a little incident happened which curiously
touched me. Papa put into my hands a little packet of letters and
papers,*—telling me that they were mamma's, and that I might
read them. I did read them, in a frame of mind I cannot describe.
The papers were yellow with time, all having been written before
I was born: it was strange now to peruse, for the first time, the
records of a mind whence my own sprang; and most strange, and
at once sad and sweet, to find that mind of a truly fine, pure, and
elevated order. They were written to papa before they were
married. There is a rectitude, a refinement, a constancy, a modesty,
a sense, a gentleness about them indescribable. I wished that she
had lived, and that I had known her. . . . All through this month
of February, I have had a crushing time of it. I could not escape
from or rise above certain most mournful recollections,—the last
days, the sufferings, the remembered words—most sorrowful to
me, of those who, Faith assures me, are now happy. At evening
and bed-time, such thoughts would haunt me, bringing a weary
heartache.'

The reader may remember the strange prophetic vision, which dictated a few words, written on the occasion of the death of a pupil of hers in January, 1840:*

'Wherever I seek for her now in this world, she cannot be found; no more than a flower or a leaf which withered twenty years ago. A bereavement of this kind gives one a glimpse of the feeling those must have, who have seen all drop round them—friend after friend, and are left to end their pilgrimage alone.'

Even in persons of naturally robust health, and with no

'Ricordarsi di tempo felice
Nella miseria—'*

to wear, with slow dropping but perpetual pain, upon their spirits, the nerves and appetite will give way in solitude. How much more must it have been so with Miss Brontë, delicate and frail in constitution, tried by much anxiety and sorrow in early life, and now left to face her life alone! Owing to Mr Brontë's great age, and long-formed habits of solitary occupation when in the house, his daughter was left to herself for the greater part of the day. Ever since his serious attacks of illness, he had dined alone; a portion of her dinner, regulated by strict attention to the diet most suitable for him, being taken into his room by herself. After dinner she read to him for an hour or so, as his sight was too weak to allow of his reading long to himself. He was out of doors among his parishioners for a good part of each day; often for a longer time than his strength would permit. Yet he always liked to go alone, and consequently her affectionate care could be no check upon the length of his walks to the more distant hamlets which were in his cure. He would come back occasionally utterly fatigued, and be obliged to go to bed, questioning himself sadly as to where all his former strength of body had gone to. His strength of will was the same as ever. That which he resolved to do he did, at whatever cost of weariness; but his daughter was all the more anxious from seeing him so regardless of himself and his health.

The hours of retiring for the night had always been early in the Parsonage; now family prayers were at eight o'clock; directly after which Mr Brontë and old Tabby went to bed, and Martha was not long in following. But Charlotte could not have slept if she had gone,—could not have rested on her desolate couch. She stopped up,—it was very tempting,—late and later; striving to beguile the lonely night with some employment, till her weak eyes failed to read or to sew, and could only weep in solitude over the dead that were not. No one on earth can even imagine what those hours were to her. All the grim superstitions of the North had been implanted in her during her childhood by the servants who believed in them. They recurred to her now,—with no shrinking from the spirits of the Dead, but with such an intense longing once more to stand face to face with the souls of her sisters, as no one but she could have felt. It seemed as if the very strength of her yearning should have compelled them to appear. On windy nights, cries, and sobs, and wailings seemed to go round the house, as of the dearly-beloved vainly striving to force their way to her. Some one conversing with her once objected, in my presence, to that part of 'Jane Eyre' in which she hears Rochester's voice crying out to her in a great crisis of her life, he being many, many miles distant at the time. I do not know what incident was in Miss Brontë's recollection when she replied, in a low voice, drawing in her breath, 'But it is a true thing; it really happened.'*

The reader, who has even faintly pictured to himself her life at this time,—the solitary days,—the waking, watching nights,—may imagine to what a sensitive pitch her nerves were strung, and how such a state was sure to affect her health.

It was no bad thing for her that about this time various people began to go over to Haworth, curious to see the scenery described in 'Shirley,' if a sympathy with the writer, of a more generous kind than to be called mere curiosity, did not make them wish to know whether they could not in some way serve or cheer one who had suffered so deeply.

Among this number were Sir James and Lady Kay Shuttleworth.* Their house lies over the crest of the moors which rise above Haworth, at about a dozen miles' distance as the crow flies, though much further by the road. But, according to the acceptation of the word in that uninhabited district, they were neighbours, if they so willed it. Accordingly, Sir James and his wife drove over one morning, at the beginning of March, to call upon Miss Brontë and her father. Before taking leave, they pressed her to visit them at Gawthorpe Hall, their residence on the borders of East Lancashire. After some hesitation, and at the urgency of her father, who was extremely anxious to procure for her any change of scene and society that was offered, she consented to go. On the whole, she enjoyed her visit very much, in spite of her shyness, and the difficulty she always experienced in meeting the advances of those strangers whose kindness she did not feel herself in a position to repay.

She took great pleasure in the 'quiet drives to old ruins and old halls, situated among older hills and woods;* the dialogues by the old fireside in the antique oak-paneled drawing-room, while they suited him, did not too much oppress and exhaust me. The house, too, is much to my taste; near three centuries old, grey, stately, and picturesque. On the whole, now that the visit is over, I do not regret having paid it. The worst of it is, that there is now some menace hanging over my head of an invitation to go to them in London during the season. This, which would be a great enjoyment to some people, is a perfect terror to me. I should highly prize the advantages to be gained in an extended range of observation; but I tremble at the thought of the price I must necessarily pay in mental distress and physical wear and tear.'

On the same day on which she wrote the above, she sent the following letter to Mr Smith.

'March 16th, 1850.

'I return Mr H——'s note,* after reading it carefully. I tried very hard to understand all he says about art; but, to speak truth, my efforts were crowned with incomplete success. There is a certain jargon in use amongst critics on this point through which it is physically and morally impossible to me to see daylight. One thing, however, I see plainly enough, and that is, Mr Currer Bell needs improvement, and ought to strive after it; and this (D. V.) he honestly intends to do—taking his time, however, and following as his guides Nature and Truth. If these lead to what the critics call art, it is all very well; but if not, that grand desideratum has no chance of being run after or caught. The puzzle is, that while the people of the South object to my delineation of Northern life and manners, the people of Yorkshire and Lancashire approve.

They say it is precisely the contrast of rough nature with highly artificial cultivation which forms one of their main characteristics. Such, or something very similar, has been the observation made to me lately, whilst I have been from home, by members of some of the ancient East Lancashire families, whose mansions lie on the hilly border-land between the two counties. The question arises, whether do the London critics, or the old Northern squires, understand the matter best?

'Any promise you require respecting the books shall be willingly given, provided only I am allowed the Jesuit's principle of a mental reservation, giving licence to forget and promise whenever oblivion shall appear expedient. The last two or three numbers of "Pendennis" will not, I dare say, be generally thought sufficiently exciting, yet I like them. Though the story lingers, (for me) the interest does not flag. Here and there we feel that the pen has been guided by a tired hand, that the mind of the writer has been somewhat chafed and depressed by his recent illness,* or by some other cause; but Thackeray still proves himself greater when he is weary than other writers are when they are fresh. The public, of course, will have no compassion for his fatigue, and make no allowance for the ebb of inspiration; but some true-hearted readers here and there, while grieving that such a man should be obliged to write when he is not in the mood, will wonder that, under such circumstances, he should write so well. The parcel of books will come, I doubt not, at such time as it shall suit the good pleasure of the railway officials to send it on,—or rather to yield it up to the repeated and humble solicitations of Haworth carriers;—till when I wait in all reasonable patience and resignation, looking with docility to that model of active self-helpfulness "Punch" kindly offers the "Women of England," in his "Unprotected Female." '*

The books lent her by her publishers were, as I have before said, a great solace and pleasure to her. There was much interest in opening the Cornhill parcel. But there was pain too; for, as she untied the cords, and took out the volumes one by one, she could scarcely fail to be reminded of those who once, on similar occasions looked on so eagerly. 'I miss familiar voices, commenting mirthfully and pleasantly; the room seems very still—very empty; but yet there is consolation in remembering that Papa will take pleasure in some of the books. Happiness quite unshared can scarcely be called happiness; it has no taste.'* She goes on to make remarks upon the kind of books sent.

'I wonder how you can choose so well; on no account would I forestall the choice. I am sure any selection I might make for myself would be less satisfactory than the selection others so kindly and judiciously make for me; besides, if I knew all that was coming, it would be comparatively flat. I would much rather not know.

'Amongst the especially welcome works are "Southey's Life,"* the "Women of France," Hazlitt's "Essays," Emerson's "Representative Men;" but it seems invidious to particularise when all are good. . . . . I took up a second small book, Scott's "Suggestions on Female Education;" that, too, I read, and with unalloyed pleasure. It is very good; justly thought, and clearly and felicitously expressed. The girls of this generation have great advantages; it seems to me that they receive much encouragement in the acquisition of knowledge, and the cultivation of their minds; in these days, women may be thoughtful and well read, without being universally stigmatised as "Blues" and "Pedants." Men begin to approve and aid, instead of ridiculing or checking them in their efforts to be wise. I must say that, for my own part, whenever I have been so happy as to share the conversation of a really intellectual man, my feeling has been, not that the little I knew was accounted a superfluity and impertinence, but that I did not know enough to satisfy just expectation. I have always to explain, "In me you must not look for great attainments: what seems to you the result of reading and study is chiefly spontaneous and intuitive." . . . . Against the teaching of some (even clever) men, one instinctively revolts. They may possess attainments, they may boast varied knowledge of life and of the world; but if of the finer perceptions, of the more delicate phases of feeling, they be destitute and incapable, of what avail is the rest? Believe me, while hints well worth consideration may come from unpretending sources, from minds not highly cultured, but naturally fine and delicate, from hearts kindly, feeling, and unenvious, learned dictums delivered with pomp and sound may be perfectly empty, stupid, and contemptible. No man ever yet "by aid of Greek climbed Parnassus,"* or taught others to climb it. . . . .

'I enclose for your perusal a scrap of paper which came into my hands without the knowledge of the writer. He is a poor working man of this village*—a thoughtful, reading, feeling being, whose mind is too keen for his frame, and wears it out. I have not spoken to him above thrice in my life, for he is a Dissenter, and has rarely come in my way. The document is a sort of record of his feelings, after the perusal of "Jane Eyre;" it is artless and earnest; genuine and generous. You must return it to me, for I value it more than testimonies from higher sources. He said, "Miss Brontë, if she knew he had written it, would scorn him;" but, indeed, Miss Brontë does not scorn him; she only grieves that a mind of which this is the emanation, should be kept crushed by the leaden hand of poverty—by the trials of uncertain health, and the claims of a large family.

'As to the "Times," as you say, the acrimony of its critique has proved, in some measure, its own antidote; to have been more effective, it should have been juster. I think it has had little weight up here in the North: it may be that annoying remarks, if made, are not suffered to reach my ear; but certainly, while I have heard little condemnatory of "Shirley," more than once have I been deeply moved by manifestations of even enthusiastic approbation. I deem it unwise to dwell much on these matters; but for once I must permit myself to remark, that the generous pride many of the Yorkshire people have taken in the matter, has been such as to awake and claim my gratitude,—especially since it has afforded a source of reviving pleasure to my father in his old age. The very curates, poor fellows! show no resentment: each characteristically finds solace for his own wounds in crowing over his brethren. Mr Donne was, at first, a little disturbed; for a week or two he was in disquietude, but he is now soothed down; only yesterday I had the pleasure of making him a comfortable cup of tea, and seeing him sip it with revived complacency. It is a curious fact that, since he read "Shirley," he has come to the house oftener than ever, and been remarkably meek and assiduous to please. Some people's natures are veritable enigmas: I quite expected to have had one good scene at least with him; but as yet nothing of the sort has occurred.'

# CHAPTER VI

DURING the earlier months of this spring, Haworth was extremely unhealthy. The weather was damp, low fever was prevalent, and the household at the Parsonage suffered along with its neighbours. Charlotte says,* 'I have felt it (the fever) in frequent thirst and infrequent appetite; Papa too, and even Martha, have complained.' This depression of health produced depression of spirits, and she grew more and more to dread the proposed journey to London with Sir James and Lady Kay Shuttleworth. 'I know what the effect and what the pain will be, how wretched I shall often feel, and how thin and haggard I shall get; but he who shuns suffering will never win victory. If I mean to improve, I must strive and endure... Sir James has been a physician, and looks at me with a physician's eye: he saw at once that I could not stand much fatigue, nor bear the presence of many strangers. I believe he would partly understand how soon my stock of animal spirits was brought to a low ebb; but none—not the most skilful physician—can get at more than the outside of these things: the heart knows its own bitterness, and the frame its own poverty, and the mind its own struggles. Papa is eager and restless for me to go; the idea of a refusal quite hurts him.'

But the sensations of illness in the family increased; the symptoms were probably aggravated, if not caused, by the immediate vicinity of the church-yard, 'paved with rain-blackened tombstones.'* On April 29th she writes:—

'We have had but a poor week of it at Haworth. Papa continues far from well; he is often very sickly in the morning, a symptom which I have remarked before in his aggravated attacks of bronchitis; unless he should get much better, I shall never think of leaving him to go to London. Martha has suffered from tic-douloureux, with sickness and fever, just like you. I have a bad cold, and a stubborn sore throat; in short, everybody but old Tabby is out of sorts. When —— was here,* he complained of a sudden headache, and the night after he was gone I had something similar, very bad,—lasting about three hours.'

A fortnight later she writes:—*

'I did not think Papa well enough to be left, and accordingly begged Sir James and Lady Kay Shuttleworth to return to London without me. It was arranged that we were to stay at several of their friends' and relatives' houses on the way; a week or more would have been taken up on the journey. I cannot say that I regret having missed this ordeal; I would as lief have walked among red-hot plough-shares; but I do regret one great treat, which I shall now miss. Next Wednesday is the anniversary dinner of the Royal Literary Fund Society,* held in Freemasons' Hall. Octavian Blewitt, the secretary, offered me a ticket for the ladies' gallery. I should have seen all the great literati and artists gathered in the hall below, and heard them speak; Thackeray and Dickens are always present among the rest. This cannot now be. I don't think all London can afford another sight to me so interesting.'

It became requisite, however, before long, that she should go to London on business;* and as Sir James Kay Shuttleworth was detained in the country by indisposition, she accepted Mrs Smith's invitation to stay quietly at her house, while she transacted her affairs.

In the interval between the relinquishment of the first plan and the adoption of the second, she wrote the following letter to one who was much valued among her literary friends:—

'May 22nd.*

'I had thought to bring the "Leader" and the "Athenæum" myself this time, and not to have to send them by post, but it turns out otherwise; my journey to London is again postponed, and this time indefinitely. Sir James Kay Shuttleworth's state of health is the cause—a cause, I fear, not likely to be soon removed.....
Once more, then, I settle myself down in the quietude of Haworth Parsonage, with books for my household companions and an occasional letter for a visitor; a mute society, but neither quarrelsome, nor vulgarising, nor unimproving.

'One of the pleasures I had promised myself consisted in asking you several questions about the "Leader," which is really, in its way, an interesting paper. I wanted, amongst other things, to ask you the real names of some of the contributors,* and also what

Lewes writes besides his "Apprenticeship of Life." I always think the article headed "Literature" is his. Some of the communications in the "Open Council" department are odd productions; but it seems to me very fair and right to admit them. Is not the system of the paper altogether a novel one? I do not remember seeing anything precisely like it before.

'I have just received yours of this morning; thank you for the enclosed note. The longings for liberty and leisure which May sunshine wakens in you, stir my sympathy. I am afraid Cornhill is little better than a prison for its inmates on warm spring or summer days. It is a pity to think of you all toiling at your desks in such genial weather as this. For my part, I am free to walk on the moors; but when I go out there alone, everything reminds me of the times when others were with me, and then the moors seem a wilderness, featureless, solitary, saddening. My sister Emily had a particular love for them, and there is not a knoll of heather, not a branch of fern, not a young bilberry-leaf, not a fluttering lark or linnet, but reminds me of her. The distant prospects were Anne's delight, and when I look round, she is in the blue tints, the pale mists, the waves and shadows of the horizon. In the hill-country silence, their poetry comes by lines and stanzas into my mind: once I loved it; now I dare not read it, and am driven often to wish I could taste one draught of oblivion, and forget much that, while mind remains, I never shall forget. Many people seem to recall their departed relatives with a sort of melancholy complacency, but I think these have not watched them through lingering sickness, nor witnessed their last moments: it is these reminiscences that stand by your bedside at night, and rise at your pillow in the morning. At the end of all, however, exists the Great Hope. Eternal Life is theirs now.'

She had to write many letters, about this time, to authors who sent her their books, and strangers who expressed their admiration of her own. The following was in reply to one of the latter class, and was addressed to a young man at Cambridge:—

'May 23rd, 1850.*

'Apologies are indeed unnecessary for a "reality of feeling, for a genuine unaffected impulse of the spirit," such as prompted you to write the letter which I now briefly acknowledge.

'Certainly it is "something to me" that what I write should be acceptable to the feeling heart and refined intellect; undoubtedly it is much to me that my creations (such as they are) should find harbourage, appreciation, indulgence, at any friendly hand, or from any generous mind. You are very welcome to take Jane, Caroline, and Shirley for your sisters, and I trust they will often speak to their adopted brother when he is solitary, and soothe him when he is sad. If they cannot make themselves at home in a thoughtful, sympathetic mind, and diffuse through its twilight a cheering, domestic glow, it is their fault; they are not, in that case, so amiable, so benignant, not so *real* as they ought to be. If they *can*, and can find household altars in human hearts, they will fulfil the best design of their creation, in therein maintaining a genial flame, which shall warm but not scorch, light but not dazzle.

'What does it matter that part of your pleasure in such beings has its source in the poetry of your own youth rather than in any magic of theirs? What, that perhaps, ten years hence, you may smile to remember your present recollections, and view under another light both "Currer Bell" and his writings? To me this consideration does not detract from the value of what you now feel. Youth has its romance, and maturity its wisdom, as morning and spring have their freshness, noon and summer their power, night and winter their repose. Each attribute is good in its own season. Your letter gave me pleasure, and I thank you for it.

'CURRER BELL.'

Miss Brontë went up to town at the beginning of June, and much enjoyed her stay there;* seeing very few persons, according to the agreement she made before she went; and limiting her visit to a fortnight, dreading the feverishness and exhaustion which were the inevitable consequences of the slightest excitement upon her susceptible frame.

'June 12th.

'Since I wrote to you last, I have not had many moments to myself, except such as it was absolutely necessary to give to rest. On the whole, however, I have thus far got on very well, suffering much less from exhaustion than I did last time.

'Of course I cannot give you in a letter a regular chronicle of how my time has been spent. I can only just notify what I deem three of its chief incidents;—a sight of the Duke of Wellington at the Chapel Royal* (he is a real grand old man), a visit to the House of Commons (which I hope to describe to you some day when I see you), and last, not least, an interview with Mr Thackeray.* He made a morning call, and sat above two hours. Mr Smith only was in the room the whole time. He described it afterwards as a "queer scene," and I suppose it was. The giant sate before me; I was moved to speak to him of some of his short-comings (literary of course); one by one the faults came into my head, and one by one I brought them out, and sought some explanation or defence. He did defend himself, like a great Turk and heathen; that is to say, the excuses were often worse than the crime itself. The matter ended in decent amity; if all be well, I am to dine at his house this evening.

'I have seen Lewes too. . . . . I could not feel otherwise to him than half-sadly, half-tenderly,—a queer word that last, but I use it because the aspect of Lewes's face almost moves me to tears; it is so wonderfully like Emily,*—her eyes, her features, the very nose, the somewhat prominent mouth, the forehead,—even, at moments, the expression: whatever Lewes says, I believe I cannot hate him. Another likeness I have seen, too, that touched me sorrowfully. You remember my speaking of a Miss K.,* a young authoress, who supported her mother by writing? Hearing that she had a longing to see me, I called on her yesterday. . . . . She met me half-frankly, half-tremblingly; we sat down together, and when I had talked with her five minutes, her face was no longer strange, but mournfully familiar;—it was Martha¹ in every lineament. I shall try to find a moment to see her again. . . . . I do not intend to stay here, at the furthest, more than a week longer; but at the end of that time I cannot go home, for the house at Haworth is just now unroofed; repairs were become necessary.'

That same day,* June 12th, she wrote Martha the following letter. I give these letters with particular pleasure, as they show her peculiarly womanly character; and the care with which they have been preserved, and the reverence with which they are looked

¹ The friend of her youth, who died at Brussels.

upon, serves to give the lie to Rochefoucauld's celebrated maxim.*
Charlotte Brontë was a heroine to her servant Martha,—and to
those who knew her best.

'London, June 12th, 1850.

'DEAR MARTHA,

'I have not forgotten my promise of writing to you, though a
multitude and variety of engagements have hitherto prevented me
from fulfilling it.

'It appears, from a letter I received from Papa this morning, that
you are now all in the bustle of unroofing; and I look with much
anxiety on a somewhat clouded sky, hoping and trusting that it will
not rain till all is covered in.

'You and Martha Redman are to take care not to break your
backs with attempting to lift and carry heavy weights; also you are
not foolishly to run into draughts, go out without caps or bonnets,
or otherwise take measures to make yourselves ill. I am rather
curious to know how you have managed about a sleeping-place for
yourself and Tabby.

'You must not expect that I should give you any particular
description of London, as that would take up a good deal of time,
and I have only a few minutes to spare. I shall merely say that it is
a Babylon of a place, and just now particularly gay and noisy, as this
is what is called the height of the London season, and all the fine
people are in town. I saw a good many lords and ladies at the Opera
a few nights since,* and, except for their elegant dresses, do not
think them either much better or much worse than other people.

'In answer to this, you may, when you have time, write me a few
lines, in which you may say how Papa is, how you and Tabby are,
how the house is getting on, and how —— prospers.

'With kind regards to Tabby, and Martha Redman,

'I am, dear Martha,

'Your sincere friend,

'C. BRONTË.'

She soon followed her letter to the friend to whom it was
written; but her visit was a very short one, for, in accordance with
a plan made before leaving London, she went on to Edinburgh* to
join the friends with whom she had been staying in town. She

remained only a few days in Scotland, and those were principally spent in Edinburgh, with which she was delighted, calling London a 'dreary place' in comparison.

'My stay in Scotland' (she wrote some weeks later)* 'was short, and what I saw was chiefly comprised in Edinburgh and the neighbourhood, in Abbotsford, and in Melrose,* for I was obliged to relinquish my first intention of going from Glasgow to Oban, and thence through a portion of the Highlands; but though the time was brief, and the view of objects limited, I found such a charm of situation, association, and circumstance, that I think the enjoyment experienced in that little space equalled in degree, and excelled in kind, all which London yielded during a month's sojourn. Edinburgh, compared to London, is like a vivid page of history compared to a large dull treatise on political economy;* and as to Melrose and Abbotsford, the very names possess music and magic.'

And again, in a letter to a different correspondent, she says:—*

'I would not write to you immediately on my arrival at home, because each return to this old house brings with it a phase of feeling which it is better to pass through quietly before beginning to indite letters. The six weeks of change and enjoyment are past, but they are not lost; memory took a sketch of each as it went by, and, especially, a distinct daguerrotype of the two days I spent in Scotland. Those were two very pleasant days. I always liked Scotland as an idea, but now, as a reality, I like it far better; it furnished me with some hours as happy almost as any I ever spent. Do not fear, however, that I am going to bore you with description; you will, before now, have received a pithy and pleasant report of all things, to which any addition of mine would be superfluous. My present endeavours are directed towards recalling my thoughts, cropping their wings, drilling them into correct discipline, and forcing them to settle to some useful work: they are idle, and keep taking the train down to London, or making a foray over the Border—especially are they prone to perpetrate that last excursion; and who, indeed, that has once seen Edinburgh, with its couchant crag-lion, but must see it again in dreams, waking or sleeping? My dear sir, do not think I blaspheme, when I tell you that your great London, as compared to Dun-Edin, "mine own romantic town,"* is as prose compared to poetry, or as a great rumbling, rambling, heavy epic compared to a lyric, brief, bright, clear, and vital as a flash of lightning. You have nothing like Scott's monument, or, if you had that, and all the glories of architecture assembled together, you have nothing like Arthur's Seat, and, above all, you have not the Scotch national character; and it is that grand character after all which gives the land its true charm, its true greatness.'

On her return from Scotland, she again spent a few days with her friends, and then made her way to Haworth.

'July 15th.*

'I got home very well, and full glad was I that no insuperable obstacle had deferred my return one single day longer. Just at the foot of Bridgehouse hill, I met John—staff in hand; he fortunately saw me in the cab, stopped, and informed me he was setting off to B——, by Mr Brontë's orders, to see how I was, for that he had been quite miserable ever since he got Miss ——'s letter. I found, on my arrival, that Papa had worked himself up to a sad pitch of nervous excitement and alarm, in which Martha and Tabby were but too obviously joining him. . . . . The house looks very clean, and, I think, is not damp; there is, however, still a great deal to do in the way of settling and arranging,—enough to keep me disagreeably busy for some time to come. I was truly thankful to find Papa pretty well, but I fear he is just beginning to show symptoms of a cold: my cold continues better. . . . . An article in a newspaper I found awaiting me on my arrival, amused me; it was a paper published while I was in London. I enclose it to give you a laugh: it professes to be written by an Author jealous of Authoresses.* I do not know who he is, but he must be one of those I met. . . . . The "ugly men," giving themselves "Rochester airs," is no bad hit; some of those alluded to will not like it.'

While Miss Brontë was staying in London, she was induced to sit for her portrait to Richmond.* It is a crayon drawing; in my judgment an admirable likeness, though, of course, there is some difference of opinion on the subject; and, as usual, those best acquainted with the original were least satisfied with the resemblance. Mr Brontë thought that it looked older than Charlotte did, and that her features had not been flattered; but he acknowledged that the expression was wonderfully good and life-like. She sent the following amusing account of the arrival of the portrait to the donor:—

'Aug. 1st.

'The little box for me came at the same time as the large one for Papa. When you first told me that you had had the Duke's picture framed,* and had given it to me, I felt half provoked with you for performing such a work of supererogation, but now, when I see it again, I cannot but acknowledge that, in so doing, you were felicitously inspired. It is his very image, and, as Papa said when he saw it, scarcely in the least like the ordinary portraits; not only the expression, but even the form of the head is different, and of a far nobler character. I esteem it a treasure. The lady who left the parcel for me was, it seems, Mrs Gore.* The parcel contained one of her works, "The Hamiltons," and a very civil and friendly note, in which I find myself addressed as "Dear Jane." Papa seems much pleased with the portrait, as do the few other persons who have seen it, with one notable exception; viz., our old servant, who tenaciously maintains that it is not like—that it is too old-looking; but as she, with equal tenacity, asserts that the Duke of Wellington's picture is a portrait of "the Master" (meaning Papa), I am afraid not much weight is to be ascribed to her opinion; doubtless she confuses her recollections of me as I was in childhood with present impressions. Requesting always to be very kindly remembered to your mother and sisters, I am, yours very thanklessly (according to desire),

'C. BRONTË.'

It may easily be conceived that two people living together as Mr Brontë and his daughter did, almost entirely dependent on each other for society, and loving each other deeply (although not demonstratively)—that these two last members of a family would have their moments of keen anxiety respecting each other's health. There is not one letter of hers which I have read, that does not contain some mention of her father's state in this respect. Either she thanks God with simple earnestness that he is well, or some infirmities of age beset him, and she mentions the fact, and then winces away from it, as from a sore that will not bear to be touched. He, in his turn, noted every indisposition of his one remaining child, exaggerated its nature, and sometimes worked himself up into a miserable state of anxiety, as in the case she refers to, when, her friend having named in a letter to him that his daughter was suffering from a bad cold, he could not rest till he despatched a messenger, to go, 'staff in hand,' a distance of fourteen miles, and see with his own eyes what was her real state, and return and report.

She evidently felt that this natural anxiety on the part of her father and friend increased the nervous depression of her own spirits, whenever she was ill; and in the following letter she expresses her strong wish that the subject of her health should be as little alluded to as possible.

'Aug. 7th.

'I am truly sorry that I allowed the words to which you refer to escape my lips, since their effect on you has been unpleasant; but try to chase every shadow of anxiety from your mind, and, unless the restraint be very disagreeable to you, permit me to add an earnest request that you will broach the subject to me no more. It is the undisguised and most harassing anxiety of others that has fixed in my mind thoughts and expectations which must canker wherever they take root; against which every effort of religion or philosophy must at times totally fail; and subjugation to which is a cruel and terrible fate—the fate, indeed, of him whose life was passed under a sword suspended by a horse-hair.* I have had to entreat Papa's consideration on this point. My nervous system is soon wrought on. I should wish to keep it in rational strength and coolness; but to do so I must determinedly resist the kindly-meant, but too irksome expression of an apprehension, for the realization or defeat of which I have no possible power to be responsible. At present, I am pretty well. Thank God! Papa, I trust, is no worse, but he complains of weakness.'

# CHAPTER VII

HER father was always anxious to procure every change that was possible for her, seeing, as he did, the benefit which she derived from it, however reluctant she might have been to leave her home and him beforehand. This August she was invited to go for a week to the neighbourhood of Bowness,* where Sir James Kay Shuttleworth had taken a house; but she says,* 'I consented to go, with reluctance, chiefly to please Papa, whom a refusal on my part would much have annoyed; but I dislike to leave him. I trust he is not worse, but his complaint is still weakness. It is not right to anticipate evil, and to be always looking forward with an apprehensive spirit; but I think grief is a two-edged sword, it cuts both ways; the memory of one loss is the anticipation of another.'

It was during this visit at the Briery—Lady Kay Shuttleworth having kindly invited me to meet her there—that I first made acquaintance with Miss Brontë.* If I copy out part of a letter, which I wrote soon after this to a friend, who was deeply interested in her writings, I shall probably convey my first impressions more truly and freshly than by amplifying what I then said into a longer description.

'Dark when I got to Windermere station; a drive along the level road to Low-wood; then a stoppage at a pretty house, and then a pretty drawing-room, in which were Sir James and Lady Kay Shuttleworth, and a little lady in a black-silk gown, whom I could not see at first for the dazzle in the room; she came up and shook hands with me at once. I went up to unbonnet, &c.; came down to tea; the little lady worked away and hardly spoke, but I had time for a good look at her. She is (as she calls herself) *undeveloped*, thin, and more than half a head shorter than I am; soft brown hair, not very dark; eyes (very good and expressive, looking straight and open at you) of the same colour as her hair; a large mouth; the forehead square, broad, and rather overhanging. She has a very sweet voice; rather hesitates in choosing her expressions, but when chosen they seem without an effort admirable, and just befitting the occasion; there is nothing overstrained, but perfectly simple.

. . . . After breakfast, we four* went out on the lake, and Miss Brontë agreed with me in liking Mr Newman's "Soul," and in liking "Modern Painters,"* and the idea of the "Seven Lamps;" and she told me about Father Newman's lectures at the Oratory in a very quiet, concise, graphic way. . . . . She is more like Miss —— than any one in her ways—if you can fancy Miss —— to have gone through suffering enough to have taken out every spark of merriment, and to be shy and silent from the habit of extreme, intense solitude. Such a life as Miss Brontë's I never heard of before. —— described her home to me as in a village of grey stone houses, perched up on the north side of a bleak moor, looking over sweeps of bleak moors, &c. &c.

'We were only three days together; the greater part of which was spent in driving about, in order to show Miss Brontë the Westmoreland scenery, as she had never been there before. We were both included in an invitation to drink tea quietly at Fox How;* and I then saw how severely her nerves were taxed by the effort of going amongst strangers. We knew beforehand that the number of the party would not exceed twelve; but she suffered the whole day from an acute headache brought on by apprehension of the evening.

'Briery Close was situated high above Low-wood, and of course commanded an extensive view and wide horizon. I was struck by Miss Brontë's careful examination of the shape of the clouds and the signs of the heavens, in which she read, as from a book, what the coming weather would be. I told her that I saw she must have a view equal in extent at her own home. She said that I was right, but that the character of the prospect from Haworth was very different; that I had no idea what a companion the sky became to any one living in solitude,—more than any inanimate object on earth,—more than the moors themselves.'

The following extracts convey some of her own impressions and feelings respecting this visit:—*

'You said I should stay longer than a week in Westmoreland; you ought by this time to know me better. Is it my habit to keep dawdling at a place long after the time I first fixed on for departing? I have got home, and I am thankful to say Papa seems,—to say the least,—no worse than when I left him, yet I wish he were stronger. My visit passed off very well; I am very glad I went. The scenery is, of course, grand; could I have wandered about amongst those hills *alone*, I could have drank in all their beauty; even in a carriage with company, it was very well. Sir James was all the while as kind and friendly as he could be: he is in much better health. . . . . Miss Martineau was from home; she always leaves her house at Ambleside during the Lake season, to avoid the influx of visitors to which she would otherwise be subject.

'If I could only have dropped unseen out of the carriage, and gone away by myself in amongst those grand hills and sweet dales, I should have drank in the full power of this glorious scenery. In company, this can hardly be. Sometimes, while —— was warning me against the faults of the artist-class, all the while vagrant artist instincts were busy in the mind of his listener.

'I forgot to tell you that, about a week before I went to Westmoreland, there came an invitation to Harden Grange;* which, of course, I declined. Two or three days after, a large party made their appearance here, consisting of Mrs F——, and sundry other ladies and two gentlemen; one tall and stately, black-haired and whiskered, who turned out to be Lord John Manners,—the other not so distinguished-looking, shy, and a little queer, who was Mr Smythe, the son of Lord Strangford. I found Mrs F. a true lady in manners and appearance, very gentle and unassuming. Lord John Manners brought in his hand a brace of grouse for Papa, which was a well-timed present: a day or two before Papa had been wishing for some.'

To these extracts I must add one other from a letter referring to this time. It is addressed to Miss W——, the kind friend of both her girlhood and womanhood, who had invited her to spend a fortnight with her at her cottage lodgings.

'Haworth, Sept. 27th, 1850.

'When I tell you that I have already been to the Lakes this season, and that it is scarcely more than a month since I returned, you will understand that it is no longer within my option to accept your kind invitation. I wish I could have gone to you. I have already had my excursion, and there is an end of it. Sir James Kay Shuttleworth is residing near Windermere, at a house called the

"Briery," and it was there I was staying for a little time this August. He very kindly showed me the neighbourhood, *as it can be seen from a carriage*, and I discerned that the Lake country is a glorious region, of which I had only seen the similitude in dreams, waking or sleeping. Decidedly I find it does not agree with me to prosecute the search of the picturesque in a carriage. A waggon, a spring-cart, even a post-chaise might do; but the carriage upsets everything. I longed to slip out unseen, and to run away by myself in amongst the hills and dales. Erratic and vagrant instincts tormented me, and these I was obliged to control, or rather suppress, for fear of growing in any degree enthusiastic, and thus drawing attention to the "lioness"—the authoress.

'You say that you suspect I have formed a large circle of acquaintance by this time. No: I cannot say that I have. I doubt whether I possess either the wish or the power to do so. A few friends I should like to have, and these few I should like to know well; if such knowledge brought proportionate regard, I could not help concentrating my feelings; dissipation, I think, appears synonymous with dilution. However, I have, as yet, scarcely been tried. During the month I spent in London in the spring, I kept very quiet, having the fear of lionising before my eyes. I only went out once to dinner; and once was present at an evening party; and the only visits I have paid have been to Sir James Kay Shuttleworth's and my publisher's. From this system I should not like to depart; as far as I can see, indiscriminate visiting tends only to a waste of time and a vulgarising of character. Besides, it would be wrong to leave Papa often; he is now in his seventy-fifth year, the infirmities of age begin to creep upon him; during the summer he has been much harassed by chronic bronchitis, but I am thankful to say that he is now somewhat better. I think my own health has derived benefit from change and exercise.

'Somebody in D——* professes to have authority for saying that "when Miss Brontë was in London she neglected to attend Divine service on the Sabbath, and in the week spent her time in going about to balls, theatres, and operas." On the other hand, the London quidnuncs make my seclusion a matter of wonder, and devise twenty romantic fictions to account for it. Formerly I used to listen to report with interest, and a certain credulity; but I am now grown deaf and sceptical: experience has taught me how absolutely devoid of foundation her stories may be.'

I must now quote from the first letter I had the privilege of receiving from Miss Brontë. It is dated August the 27th.

'Papa and I have just had tea; he is sitting quietly in his room, and I in mine; "storms of rain" are sweeping over the garden and churchyard: as to the moors, they are hidden in thick fog. Though alone, I am not unhappy; I have a thousand things to be thankful for, and, amongst the rest, that this morning I received a letter from you, and that this evening I have the privilege of answering it.

'I do not know the "Life of Sydney Taylor;"* whenever I have the opportunity I will get it. The little French book you mention shall also take its place on the list of books to be procured as soon as possible. It treats a subject interesting to all women—perhaps, more especially to single women; though, indeed, mothers, like you, study it for the sake of their daughters. The "Westminster Review" is not a periodical I see regularly, but some time since I got hold of a number—for last January, I think—in which there was an article entitled "Woman's Mission"* (the phrase is hackneyed), containing a great deal that seemed to me just and sensible. Men begin to regard the position of woman in another light than they used to do; and a few men, whose sympathies are fine and whose sense of justice is strong, think and speak of it with a candour that commands my admiration. They say, however—and, to an extent, truly—that the amelioration of our condition depends on ourselves. Certainly there are evils which our own efforts will best reach; but as certainly there are other evils—deep-rooted in the foundations of the social system—which no efforts of ours can touch; of which we cannot complain; of which it is advisable not too often to think.

'I have read Tennyson's "In Memoriam,"* or rather part of it; I closed the book when I had got about half way. It is beautiful; it is mournful; it is monotonous. Many of the feelings expressed bear, in their utterance, the stamp of truth; yet, if Arthur Hallam had been somewhat nearer Alfred Tennyson,—his brother instead of his friend,—I should have distrusted this rhymed, and measured, and printed monument of grief. What change the lapse of years may work I do not know; but it seems to me that bitter sorrow, while recent, does not flow out in verse.

'I promised to send you Wordsworth's "Prelude,"* and, accordingly, despatch it by this post; the other little volume shall follow in a day or two. I shall be glad to hear from you whenever you have time to write to me, *but you are never, on any account, to do this except when inclination prompts and leisure permits.* I should never thank you for a letter which you had felt it a task to write.'

A short time after we had met at the Briery, she sent me the volume of Currer, Ellis, and Acton Bell's poems; and thus alludes to them in the note that accompanied the parcel:—*

'The little book of rhymes was sent by way of fulfilling a rashly-made promise; and the promise was made to prevent you from throwing away four shillings in an injudicious purchase. I do not like my own share of the work, nor care that it should be read: Ellis Bell's I think good and vigorous, and Acton's have the merit of truth and simplicity. Mine are chiefly juvenile productions; the restless effervescence of a mind that would not be still. In those days, the sea too often "wrought and was tempestuous,"* and weed, sand, shingle—all turned up in the tumult. This image is much too magniloquent for the subject, but you will pardon it.'

Another letter of some interest was addressed, about this time, to a literary friend, on Sept. 5th:—*

'The reappearance of the "Athenæum" is very acceptable, not merely for its own sake,—though I esteem the opportunity of its perusal a privilege,—but because, as a weekly token of the remembrance of friends, it cheers and gives pleasure. I only fear that its regular transmission may become a task to you; in this case, discontinue it at once.

'I did indeed enjoy my trip to Scotland, and yet I saw little of the face of the country; nothing of its grander or finer scenic features; but Edinburgh, Melrose, Abbotsford—these three in themselves sufficed to stir feelings of such deep interest and admiration, that neither at the time did I regret, nor have I since regretted, the want of wider space over which to diffuse the sense of enjoyment. There was room and variety enough to be very happy, and "enough," the proverb says, "is as good as a feast." The queen, indeed, was right to climb Arthur's Seat with her husband and children.* I shall not soon forget how I felt when, having reached its summit, we all sat down and looked over the city—towards the sea and Leith, and the Pentland Hills. No doubt you are proud of being a native of Scotland,—proud of your country, her capital, her children, and her literature. You cannot be blamed.

'The article in the "Palladium"* is one of those notices over which an author rejoices trembling. He rejoices to find his work finely, fully, fervently appreciated, and trembles under the responsibility such appreciation seems to devolve upon him. I am counselled to wait and watch—D.V., I will do so; yet it is harder to wait with the hands bound, and the observant and reflective faculties at their silent and unseen work, than to labour mechanically.

'I need not say how I felt the remarks on "Wuthering Heights;" they woke the saddest yet most grateful feelings; they are true, they are discriminating, they are full of late justice, but it is very late—alas! in one sense, *too* late. Of this, however, and of the pang of regret for a light prematurely extinguished, it is not wise to speak much. Whoever the author of this article may be, I remain his debtor.

'Yet, you see, even here, "Shirley" is disparaged in comparison with "Jane Eyre;" and yet I took great pains with "Shirley." I did not hurry; I tried to do my best, and my own impression was that it was not inferior to the former work; indeed, I had bestowed on it more time, thought, and anxiety: but great part of it was written under the shadow of impending calamity; and the last volume, I cannot deny, was composed in the eager, restless endeavour to combat mental sufferings that were scarcely tolerable.

'You sent the tragedy of "Galileo Galilei," by Samuel Brown,* in one of the Cornhill parcels; it contained, I remember, passages of very great beauty. Whenever you send any more books (but that must not be till I return what I now have) I should be glad if you would include amongst them the "Life of Dr Arnold." Do you know also the "Life of Sydney Taylor?" I am not familiar even with the name, but it has been recommended to me as a work meriting perusal. Of course, when I name any book, it is always understood that it should be quite convenient to send it.'

# CHAPTER VIII

It was thought desirable about this time, to republish 'Wuthering Heights' and 'Agnes Grey,' the works of the two sisters, and Charlotte undertook the task of editing them.*

She wrote to Mr Williams, September 29th, 1850, 'It is my intention to write a few lines of remark on "Wuthering Heights," which, however, I propose to place apart as a brief preface before the tale. I am likewise compelling myself to read it over, for the first time of opening the book since my sister's death. Its power fills me with renewed admiration; but yet I am oppressed: the reader is scarcely ever permitted a taste of unalloyed pleasure; every beam of sunshine is poured down through black bars of threatening cloud; every page is surcharged with a sort of moral electricity; and the writer was unconscious of all this—nothing could make her conscious of it.

'And this makes me reflect,—perhaps I am too incapable of perceiving the faults and peculiarities of my own style.

'I should wish to revise the proofs, if it be not too great an inconvenience to send them. It seems to me advisable to modify the orthography of the old servant Joseph's speeches; for though, as it stands, it exactly renders the Yorkshire dialect to a Yorkshire ear, yet I am sure Southerns must find it unintelligible; and thus one of the most graphic characters in the book is lost on them.*

'I grieve to say that I possess no portrait of either of my sisters.'*

To her own dear friend, as to one who had known and loved her sisters, she writes still more fully respecting the painfulness of her task.*

'There is nothing wrong, and I am writing you a line as you desire, merely to say that I *am* busy just now. Mr Smith wishes to reprint some of Emily's and Anne's works, with a few little additions from the papers they have left; and I have been closely engaged in revising, transcribing, preparing a preface, notice, &c. As the time for doing this is limited, I am obliged to be industrious. I found the task at first exquisitely painful and depressing; but regarding it in the light of a *sacred duty*, I went on, and now can bear it better. It is work, however, that I cannot do in the evening, for if I did, I should have no sleep at night. Papa, I am thankful to say, is in improved health, and so, I think, am I; I trust you are the same.

'I have just received a kind letter from Miss Martineau. She has got back to Ambleside, and had heard of my visit to the Lakes. She expressed her regret, &c., at not being at home.

'I am both angry and surprised at myself for not being in better spirits; for not growing accustomed, or at least resigned, to the solitude and isolation of my lot. But my late occupation left a result for some days, and indeed still, very painful. The reading over of papers, the renewal of remembrances, brought back the pang of bereavement, and occasioned a depression of spirits well nigh intolerable. For one or two nights, I scarcely knew how to get on till morning; and when morning came, I was still haunted with a sense of sickening distress. I tell you these things, because it is absolutely necessary to me to have some relief. You will forgive me, and not trouble yourself, or imagine that I am one whit worse than I say. It is quite a mental ailment, and I believe and hope is better now. I think so, because I can speak about it, which I never can when grief is at its worst.

'I thought to find occupation and interest in writing, when alone at home, but hitherto my efforts have been vain; the deficiency of every stimulus is so complete. You will recommend me, I dare say, to go from home; but that does no good, even could I again leave Papa with an easy mind (thank God! he is still better). I cannot describe what a time of it I had after my return from London, Scotland, &c. There was a reaction that sunk me to the earth; the deadly silence, solitude, desolation, were awful; the craving for companionship, the hopelessness of relief, were what I should dread to feel again.

'Dear ——, when I think of you, it is with a compassion and tenderness that scarcely cheer me. Mentally, I fear, you also are too lonely and too little occupied. It seems our doom, for the present at least. May God in his mercy help us to bear it!'

During her last visit to London, as mentioned in one of her letters, she had made the acquaintance of her correspondent, Mr Lewes. That gentleman says:—*

'Some months after' (the appearance of the review of 'Shirley' in the 'Edinburgh'), 'Currer Bell came to London, and I was invited to meet her at your house. You may remember, she asked you not to point me out to her, but allow her to discover me if she could. She *did* recognise me almost as soon as I came into the room. You tried me in the same way; I was less sagacious. However, I sat by her side a great part of the evening, and was greatly interested by her conversation. On parting we shook hands, and she said, "We are friends now, are we not?" "Were we not always, then?" I asked. "No! not always," she said significantly; and that was the only allusion she made to the offending article. I lent her some of Balzac's and George Sand's novels* to take with her into the country; and the following letter* was written when they were returned:—

' "I am sure you will have thought me very dilatory in returning the books you so kindly lent me. The fact is, having some other books to send, I retained yours to enclose them in the same parcel.

' "Accept my thanks for some hours of pleasant reading. Balzac was for me quite a new author; and in making his acquaintance, through the medium of 'Modeste Mignon,' and 'Illusions perdues,' you cannot doubt I have felt some interest. At first I thought he was going to be painfully minute, and fearfully tedious; one grew impatient of his long parade of detail, his slow revelation of unimportant circumstances, as he assembled his personages on the stage; but by and by I seemed to enter into the mystery of his craft, and to discover, with delight, where his force lay: is it not in the analysis of motive, and in a subtle perception of the most obscure and secret workings of the mind? Still, admire Balzac as we may, I think we do not like him; we rather feel towards him as towards an ungenial acquaintance who is for ever holding up in strong light our defects, and who rarely draws forth our better qualities.

' "Truly, I like George Sand better.

' "Fantastic, fanatical, unpractical enthusiast as she often is—far from truthful as are many of her views of life—misled, as she is apt to be, by her feelings—George Sand has a better nature than M. de Balzac; her brain is larger, her heart warmer than his. The 'Lettres d'un Voyageur' are full of the writer's self; and I never felt so strongly, as in the perusal of this work, that most of her very faults spring from the excess of her good qualities: it is this excess which has often hurried her into difficulty, which has prepared for her enduring regret.

' "But I believe her mind is of that order which disastrous experience teaches, without weakening or too much disheartening; and, in that case, the longer she lives the better she will grow. A hopeful point in all her writings is the scarcity of false French sentiment; I wish I could say its absence; but the weed flourishes here and there, even in the 'Lettres.' "

'I remember the good expression of disgust which Miss Brontë made use of in speaking to me of some of Balzac's novels: "They leave such a bad taste in my mouth." '

The reader will notice that most of the letters from which I now quote are devoted to critical and literary subjects. These were, indeed, her principal interests at this time; the revision of her sisters' works, and writing a short memoir of them, was the painful employment of every day during the dreary autumn of 1850. Wearied out by the vividness of her sorrowful recollections, she sought relief in long walks on the moors. A friend of hers,* who wrote to me on the appearance of the eloquent article in the 'Daily News' upon the 'Death of Currer Bell,' gives an anecdote which may well come in here.

'They are mistaken in saying she was too weak to roam the hills for the benefit of the air. I do not think any one, certainly not any woman, in this locality, went so much on the moors as she did, when the weather permitted. Indeed, she was so much in the habit of doing so, that people, who live quite away on the edge of the common, knew her perfectly well. I remember on one occasion an old woman saw her at a little distance, and she called out, "How! Miss Brontë! Hey yah (have you) seen ought o' my cofe (calf)?" Miss Brontë told her she could not say, for she did not know it. "Well!" she said, "Yah know, it's getting up like nah (now), between a cah (cow) and a cofe—what we call a stirk, yah know, Miss Brontë; will yah turn it this way if yah happen to see't, as yah're going back, Miss Brontë? nah *do*, Miss Brontë." '

It must have been about this time that a visit was paid to her by some neighbours,* who were introduced to her by a mutual friend.

This visit has been described in a letter from which I am permitted to give extracts, which will show the impression made upon strangers by the character of the country round her home, and other circumstances. "Though the weather was drizzly, we resolved to make our long-planned excursion to Haworth; so we packed ourselves into the buffalo-skin, and that into the gig, and set off about eleven. The rain ceased, and the day was just suited to the scenery,—wild and chill,—with great masses of cloud glooming over the moors, and here and there a ray of sunshine covertly stealing through, and resting with a dim magical light upon some high bleak village; or darting down into some deep glen, lighting up the tall chimney, or glistening on the windows and wet roof of the mill which lies couching in the bottom. The country got wilder and wilder as we approached Haworth; for the last four miles we were ascending a huge moor, at the very top of which lies the dreary black-looking village of Haworth. The village-street itself is one of the steepest hills I have ever seen, and the stones are so horribly jolting that I should have got out and walked with W——, if possible, but, having once begun the ascent, to stop was out of the question. At the top was the inn where we put up, close by the church; and the clergyman's house, we were told, was at the top of the churchyard. So through that we went,—a dreary, dreary place, literally *paved* with rain-blackened tombstones, and all on the slope; for at Haworth there is on the highest height a higher still, and Mr Brontë's house stands considerably above the church. There was the house before us, a small, oblong stone house, with not a tree to screen it from the cutting wind; but how were we to get at it from the churchyard we could not see! There was an old man in the churchyard, brooding like a Ghoul over the graves, with a sort of grim hilarity on his face. I thought he looked hardly human; however, he was human enough to tell us the way; and presently we found ourselves in the little bare parlour. Presently the door opened, and in came a superannuated mastiff,\* followed by an old gentleman very like Miss Brontë, who shook hands with us, and then went to call his daughter. A long interval, during which we coaxed the old dog, and looked at a picture of Miss Brontë, by Richmond, the solitary ornament of the room, looking strangely out of place on the bare walls, and at the books on the little shelves, most of them evidently the gift of the authors since Miss Brontë's celebrity. Presently she came in, and welcomed us very kindly, and took me upstairs to take off my bonnet, and herself brought me water and towels. The uncarpeted stone stairs and floors, the old drawers propped on wood, were all scrupulously clean and neat. When we went into the parlour again, we began talking very comfortably, when the door opened and Mr Brontë looked in; seeing his daughter there, I suppose he thought it was all right, and he retreated to his study on the opposite side of the passage; presently emerging again to bring W—— a country newspaper. This was his last appearance till we went. Miss Brontë spoke with the greatest warmth of Miss Martineau, and of the good she had gained from her. Well! we talked about various things; the character of the people,—about her solitude, &c., till she left the room to help about dinner, I suppose, for she did not return for an age. The old dog had vanished; a fat curly-haired dog honoured us with his company for some time, but finally manifested a wish to get out, so we were left alone. At last she returned, followed by the maid and dinner, which made us all more comfortable; and we had some very pleasant conversation, in the midst of which time passed quicker than we supposed, for at last W—— found that it was half-past three, and we had fourteen or fifteen miles before us. So we hurried off, having obtained from her a promise to pay us a visit in the spring; and the old gentleman having issued once more from his study to say good-bye, we returned to the inn, and made the best of our way homewards.

'Miss Brontë put me so in mind of her own "Jane Eyre." She looked smaller than ever, and moved about so quietly, and noiselessly, just like a little bird, as Rochester called her,* barring that all birds are joyous, and that joy can never have entered that house since it was first built; and yet, perhaps, when that old man married, and took home his bride, and children's voices and feet were heard about the house, even that desolate crowded grave-yard and biting blast could not quench cheerfulness and hope. Now there is something touching in the sight of that little creature entombed in such a place, and moving about herself like a spirit, especially when you think that the slight still frame encloses a force of strong fiery life, which nothing has been able to freeze or extinguish.'

In one of the preceding letters, Miss Brontë referred to an article in the 'Palladium,' which had rendered what she considered the due meed of merit to 'Wuthering Heights,' her sister Emily's tale. Her own works were praised, and praised with discrimination, and she was grateful for this. But her warm heart was filled to the brim with kindly feelings towards him who had done justice to the dead. She anxiously sought out the name of the writer; and having discovered that it was Mr Sydney Dobell, he immediately became one of her

'Peculiar people whom Death had made dear.'*

She looked with interest upon everything he wrote; and before long we shall find that they corresponded.

### TO W. S. WILLIAMS, ESQ.

'Oct. 25th.

'The box of books came last night, and, as usual, I have only gratefully to admire the selection made: "Jeffrey's Essays,"* "Dr Arnold's Life," "The Roman," "Alton Locke," these were all wished for and welcome.

'You say I keep no books; pardon me—I am ashamed of my own rapaciousness: I have kept "Macaulay's History," and Wordsworth's "Prelude," and Taylor's "Philip Van Artevelde." I soothe my conscience by saying that the two last—being poetry—do not count. This is a convenient doctrine for me: I meditate acting upon it with reference to the "Roman," so I trust nobody in Cornhill will dispute its validity or affirm that "poetry" has a value, except for trunk-makers.*

'I have already had "Macaulay's Essays," "Sydney Smith's Lectures on Moral Philosophy," and "Knox on Race." Pickering's work on the same subject I have not seen; nor all the volumes of Leigh Hunt's Autobiography. However, I am now abundantly supplied for a long time to come. I liked Hazlitt's Essays much.

'The autumn, as you say, has been very fine. I and solitude and memory have often profited by its sunshine on the moors.

'I had felt some disappointment at the non-arrival of the proof-sheets of "Wuthering Heights;" a feverish impatience to complete the revision is apt to beset me. The work of looking over papers, &c., could not be gone through with impunity, and with unaltered spirits; associations too tender, regrets too bitter, sprang out of it. Meantime, the Cornhill books now, as heretofore, are my best medicine,—affording a solace which could not be yielded by the very same books procured from a common library.

'Already I have read the greatest part of the "Roman;" passages in it possess a kindling virtue such as true poetry alone can boast; there are images of genuine grandeur; there are lines that at once stamp themselves on the memory. Can it be true that a new planet has risen on the heaven, whence all stars seemed fast fading? I believe it is; for this Sydney or Dobell speaks with a voice of his own, unborrowed, unmimicked. You hear Tennyson, indeed, sometimes, and Byron sometimes, in some passages of the "Roman;" but then again you have a new note,—nowhere clearer than in a certain brief lyric,* sang in a meeting of minstrels, a sort of dirge over a dead brother;—*that* not only charmed the ear and brain, it soothed the heart.'

The following extract will be read with interest as conveying her thoughts after the perusal of Dr Arnold's Life:—

'Nov. 6th.*

'I have just finished reading the "Life of Dr Arnold;" but now when I wish, according to your request, to express what I think of it, I do not find the task very easy; proper terms seem wanting. This is not a character to be dismissed with a few laudatory words; it is not a one-sided character; pure panegyric would be inappropriate. Dr Arnold (it seems to me) was not quite saintly; his greatness was cast in a mortal mould; he was a little severe, almost a little hard; he was vehement and somewhat oppugnant. Himself the most indefatigable of workers, I know not whether he could have understood, or made allowance for, a temperament that required more rest; yet not to one man in twenty thousand is given his giant faculty of labour; by virtue of it he seems to me the greatest of working men. Exacting he might have been, then, on this point; and granting that he were so, and a little hasty, stern, and positive, those were his sole faults (if, indeed, that can be called a fault which in no shape degrades the individual's own character, but is only apt to oppress and overstrain the weaker nature of his neighbours). Afterwards come his good qualities. About these there is nothing dubious. Where can we find justice, firmness, independence, earnestness, sincerity, fuller and purer than in him?

'But this is not all, and I am glad of it. Besides high intellect and stainless rectitude, his letters and his life attest his possession of the most true-hearted affection. *Without* this, however one might admire, we could not love him; but *with* it I think we love him much. A hundred such men—fifty—nay, ten or five such righteous men might save any country; might victoriously champion any cause.

'I was struck, too, by the almost unbroken happiness of his life; a happiness resulting chiefly, no doubt, from the right use to which he put that health and strength which God had given him, but also owing partly to a singular exemption from those deep and bitter griefs which most human beings are called on to endure. His wife was what he wished; his children* were healthy and promising; his own health was excellent; his undertakings were crowned with success; even death was kind,—for, however sharp the pains of his last hour, they were but brief. God's blessing seems to have accompanied him from the cradle to the grave. One feels thankful to know that it has been permitted to any man to live such a life.

'When I was in Westmoreland last August, I spent an evening at Fox How, where Mrs Arnold and her daughters still reside. It was twilight as I drove to the place, and almost dark ere I reached it; still I could perceive that the situation was lovely. The house looked like a nest half buried in flowers and creepers: and, dusk as it was, I could *feel* that the valley and the hills round were beautiful as imagination could dream.'

If I say again what I have said already before, it is only to impress and re-impress upon my readers the dreary monotony of her life at this time. The dark, bleak season of the year brought back the long evenings, which tried her severely: all the more so, because her weak eyesight rendered her incapable of following any occupation but knitting by candle-light. For her father's sake, as well as for her own, she found it necessary to make some exertion to ward off settled depression of spirits. She accordingly accepted an invitation to spend a week or ten days with Miss Martineau at Ambleside. She also proposed to come to Manchester and see me, on her way to Westmoreland. But, unfortunately, I was from home, and not able therefore to receive her. The friends with whom I was staying* in the South of England (hearing me express my regret that I could not accept her friendly proposal, and aware of the sad state of health and spirits which made some change necessary for her) wrote to desire that she would come and spend a week or two with me at their house. She acknowledged this invitation in a letter to me, dated

'Dec. 13th, 1850.

'My dear Mrs Gaskell,—Miss ——'s kindness and yours is such that I am placed in the dilemma of not knowing how adequately to express my sense of it. *This* I know, however, very well—that if I *could* go and be with you for a week or two in such a quiet south-country house, and with such kind people as you describe, I should like it much. I find the proposal marvellously to my taste; it is the pleasantest, gentlest, sweetest, temptation possible; but, delectable as it is, its solicitations are by no means to be yielded to without the sanction of reason, and therefore I desire for the present to be silent, and to stand back till I have been to Miss Martineau's, and returned home, and considered well whether it is a scheme as right as agreeable.

'Meantime, the mere thought does me good.'

On the 10th of December, the second edition of 'Wuthering Heights' was published. She sent a copy of it to Mr Dobell, with the following letter:—

TO MR DOBELL.

'Haworth, near Keighley, Yorkshire,
'Dec. 8th, 1850.

'I offer this little book to my critic in the "Palladium," and he must believe it accompanied by a tribute of the sincerest gratitude; not so much for anything he has said of myself, as for the noble justice he has rendered to one dear to me as myself—perhaps dearer; and perhaps one kind word spoken for her awakens a deeper, tenderer, sentiment of thankfulness than eulogies heaped on my own head. As you will see when you have read the biographical notice, my sister cannot thank you herself; she is gone out of your sphere and mine, and human blame and praise are nothing to her now. But to me, for her sake, they are something still; it revived me for many a day to find that, dead as she was, the work of her genius had at last met with worthy appreciation.

'Tell me, when you have read the introduction, whether any doubts still linger in your mind respecting the authorship of "Wuthering Heights," "Wildfell Hall," &c.* Your mistrust did me some injustice; it proved a general conception of character such as I should be sorry to call mine; but these false ideas will naturally arise when we only judge an author from his works. In fairness, I must also disclaim the flattering side of the portrait. I am no "young Penthesilea *mediis in millibus*,"* but a plain country parson's daughter.

'Once more I thank you, and that with a full heart.

'C. BRONTË.'

# CHAPTER IX

IMMEDIATELY after the republication of her sister's book she went to Miss Martineau's.*

'I can write to you now, dear E——,* for I am away from home, and relieved, temporarily, at least, by change of air and scene, from the heavy burden of depression which, I confess, has for nearly three months been sinking me to the earth. I never shall forget last autumn! Some days and nights have been cruel; but now, having once told you this, I need say no more on the subject. My loathing of solitude grew extreme; my recollection of my sisters intolerably poignant. I am better now. I am at Miss Martineau's for a week. Her house is very pleasant, both within and without; arranged at all points with admirable neatness and comfort. Her visitors enjoy the most perfect liberty; what she claims for herself she allows them. I rise at my own hour, breakfast alone (she is up at five, takes a cold bath, and a walk by starlight, and has finished breakfast and got to her work by seven o'clock). [I must insert a correction of this mistake as to Miss Martineau's hours; the fact being that Miss Martineau rose at six, and went to work at half-past eight, breakfasting separately from her visitor,—as she says in a letter with which she has favoured me, 'it was my practice to come and speak to C.B. when she sat down to breakfast, and *before* I went to work.']* I pass the morning in the drawing-room—she, in her study. At two o'clock we meet—work, talk, and walk together till five, her dinner-hour, spend the evening together, when she converses fluently and abundantly, and with the most complete frankness. I go to my own room soon after ten,—she sits up writing letters till twelve. She appears exhaustless in strength and spirits, and indefatigable in the faculty of labour. She is a great and a good woman; of course not without peculiarities, but I have seen none as yet that annoy me. She is both hard and warm-hearted, abrupt and affectionate, liberal and despotic. I believe she is not at all conscious of her own absolutism. When I tell her of it, she denies the charge warmly; then I laugh at her. I believe she almost rules Ambleside. Some of the gentry dislike her, but the lower orders have a great regard for her. . . . I thought I should like to spend two or three days with you before going home; so, if it is not inconvenient to you, I will (D.V.) come on Monday and stay till Thursday. . . . . . I have truly enjoyed my visit here. I have seen a good many people, and all have been so marvellously kind; not the least so, the family of Dr Arnold. Miss Martineau I relish inexpressibly.'

Miss Brontë paid the visit she here proposes to her friend, but only remained two or three days. She then returned home, and immediately began to suffer from her old enemy, sickly and depressing headache. This was all the more trying to bear, as she was obliged to take an active share in the household work,—one servant being ill in bed, and the other, Tabby, aged upwards of eighty.

This visit to Ambleside did Miss Brontë much good, and gave her a stock of pleasant recollections, and fresh interests, to dwell upon in her solitary life. There are many references in her letters to Miss Martineau's character and kindness.*

'She is certainly a woman of wonderful endowments, both intellectual and physical; and though I share few of her opinions, and regard her as fallible on certain points of judgment, I must still award her my sincerest esteem. The manner in which she combines the highest mental culture with the nicest discharge of feminine duties filled me with admiration; while her affectionate kindness earned my gratitude.' 'I think her good and noble qualities far outweigh her defects. It is my habit to consider the individual apart from his (or her) reputation, practice independent of theory, natural disposition isolated from acquired opinions. Harriet Martineau's person, practice, and character, inspire me with the truest affection and respect.' 'You ask me whether Miss Martineau made me a convert to mesmerism?* Scarcely; yet I heard miracles of its efficacy, and could hardly discredit the whole of what was told me. I even underwent a personal experiment; and though the result was not absolutely clear, it was inferred that in time I should prove an excellent subject. The question of mesmerism will be discussed with little reserve, I believe, in a forthcoming work of Miss Martineau's; and I have some painful anticipations of the manner in which other subjects, offering less legitimate ground for speculation will be handled.'

Miss Martineau sends me the following account* of the 'personal experiment' to which Miss Brontë refers:—'By the way, for the mesmeric experiment on C. B. I was not responsible. She was strangely pertinacious about that, and I *most* reluctant to bring it before her at all, we being alone, and I having no confidence in her nerves. Day after day she urged me to mesmerize her. I always, and quite truly, pleaded that I was too tired for success, for we had no opportunity till the end of the day. At last, on Sunday evening we returned from early tea somewhere; I could not say I was tired, and she insisted. I stopped the moment she called out that she was under the influence, and I would not resume it.'

Miss Martineau has kindly permitted me to make use of one or two anecdotes which she remembers, and which refer to this period.

'One trait may interest you. Her admiration of Wellington brought it to my mind. One morning I brought her the first page of the chapter on the Peninsular War in my Introductory History,* and said, "Tell me if this will do for a beginning, &c." I read the page or two to her, as we stood before the fire, and she looked up at me and stole her hand into mine, and, to my amazement, the tears were running down her cheeks. She said, "Oh! I do thank you! Oh! we are of one mind! Oh! I thank you for this justice to the man." I saw at once there was a touch of idolatry in the case, but it was a charming enthusiasm. . . . . As to the lecture* about which you ask, C.B. sat sideways to me. It was long, for I got interested and forgot the time. She kept her eyes on me the whole time, till her neck must have ached desperately. She stole up to the little platform on which I was standing, while the people dispersed, and as the light shone down into her eyes, repeated (in my very voice) "Is my son dead?" (Edward III's words at the windmill during the battle of Crecy.) We came home in silence (a very little way). In the drawing-room the first thing I did was to light the lamp, and the first flare showed C. B. with large eyes, staring at me, and repeating "Is my son dead?" '

LETTER FROM C. B. TO MISS W.*

'Your last letter evinced such a sincere and discriminating admiration for Dr Arnold, that perhaps you will not be wholly uninterested in hearing that, during my late visit to Miss Martineau, I saw much more of Fox How and its inmates, and daily admired, in the widow and children of one of the greatest and best men of his time, the possession of qualities the most estimable and endearing. Of my kind hostess herself, I cannot speak in terms too high. Without being able to share all her opinions, philosophical, political, or religious,—without adopting her theories,—I yet find a worth and greatness in herself, and a consistency, benevolence, perseverance in her practice, such as wins the sincerest esteem and affection. She is not a person to be judged by her writings alone, but rather by her own deeds and life, than which nothing can be more exemplary or nobler. She seems to me the benefactress of Ambleside, yet takes no sort of credit to herself for her active and indefatigable philanthropy. The government of her household is admirably administered: all she does is well done, from the writing of a history down to the quietest female occupation. No sort of carelessness or neglect is allowed under her rule, and yet she is not over-strict nor too rigidly exacting: her servants and her poor neighbours love as well as respect her.

'I must not, however, fall into the error of talking too much about her merely because my own mind is just now deeply impressed with what I have seen of her intellectual power and moral worth. Faults she has; but to me they appear very trivial weighed in the balance against her excellences.'

'Your account of Mr A——* tallies exactly with Miss M——'s. She, too, said that placidity and mildness (rather than originality and power) were his external characteristics. She described him as a combination of the antique Greek sage with the modern European man of science. Perhaps it was mere perversity in me to get the notion that torpid veins, and a cold, slow-beating heart, lay under his marble outside. But he is a materialist: he serenely denies us our hope of immortality, and quietly blots from man's future Heaven and the Life to come. That is why a savour of bitterness seasoned my feeling towards him.

'All you say of Mr Thackeray is most graphic and characteristic. He stirs in me both sorrow and anger. Why should he lead so harassing a life? Why should his mocking tongue so perversely deny the better feelings of his better moods?'

For some time, whenever she was well enough in health and spirits, she had been employing herself upon 'Villette;'* but she was frequently unable to write, and was both grieved and angry with herself for her inability. In February, she writes as follows to Mr Smith:—*

'Something you say about going to London; but the words are dreamy, and fortunately I am not obliged to hear or answer them. London and summer are many months away: our moors are all white with snow just now, and little redbreasts come every morning to the window for crumbs. One can lay no plans three or four months beforehand. Besides, I don't deserve to go to London: nobody merits a change or a treat less. I secretly think, on the contrary, I ought to be put in prison, and kept on bread and water in solitary confinement—without even a letter from Cornhill—till I had written a book. One of two things would certainly result from such a mode of treatment pursued for twelve months; either I should come out at the end of that time with a three-volume MS in my hand, or else with a condition of intellect that would exempt me ever after from literary efforts and expectations.'

Meanwhile, she was disturbed and distressed by the publication of Miss Martineau's 'Letters,' &c.; they came down with a peculiar force and heaviness upon a heart that looked, with fond and earnest faith, to a future life as to the meeting-place with those who were 'loved and lost awhile.'*

'Feb. 11th, 1851.*

'My dear Sir,—Have you yet read Miss Martineau's and Mr Atkinson's new work, "Letters on the Nature and Development of Man?" If you have not, it would be worth your while to do so.

'Of the impression this book has made on me, I will not now say much. It is the first exposition of avowed atheism and materialism I have ever read; the first unequivocal declaration of disbelief in the existence of a God or a future life I have ever seen. In judging of such exposition and declaration, one would wish entirely to put aside the sort of instinctive horror they awaken, and to consider them in an impartial spirit and collected mood. This I find it difficult to do. The strangest thing is, that we are called on to rejoice over this hopeless blank—to receive this bitter bereavement as great gain—to welcome this unutterable desolation as a state of pleasant freedom. Who *could* do this if he would? Who *would* do it if he could?

'Sincerely, for my own part, do I wish to find and know the Truth; but if this be Truth, well may she guard herself with mysteries, and cover herself with a veil. If this be Truth, man or woman who beholds her can but curse the day he or she was born. I said, however, I would not dwell on what *I* thought; I wish rather to hear what some other person thinks,—some one whose feelings are unapt to bias his judgment. Read the book, then, in an unprejudiced spirit, and candidly say what you think of it. I mean, of course, if you have time—*not otherwise*.'

And yet she could not bear the contemptuous tone in which this work was spoken of by many critics; it made her more indignant than almost any other circumstance during my acquaintance with her. Much as she regretted the publication of the book, she could not see that it had given any one a right to sneer at an action, certainly prompted by no worldly motive.*

'Your remarks on Miss Martineau* and her book pleased me greatly, from their tone and spirit. I have even taken the liberty of transcribing for her benefit one or two phrases, because I know they will cheer her; she likes sympathy and appreciation (as all people do who deserve them); and most fully do I agree with you in the dislike you express of that hard, contemptuous tone in which her work is spoken of by many critics.'

Before I return from the literary opinions of the author to the domestic interests of the woman, I must copy out what she felt and thought about 'The Stones of Venice.'

' "The Stones of Venice"* seem nobly laid and chiselled. How grandly the quarry of vast marbles is disclosed! Mr Ruskin seems to me one of the few genuine writers, as distinguished from book-makers, of this age. His earnestness even amuses me in certain passages; for I cannot help laughing to think how utilitarians will fume and fret over his deep, serious (and as *they* will think), fanatical reverence for Art. That pure and severe mind you ascribed to him speaks in every line. He writes like a consecrated Priest of the Abstract and Ideal.

'I shall bring with me "The Stones of Venice;" all the foundations of marble and of granite, together with the mighty quarry out of which they were hewn; and, into the bargain, a small assortment of crotchets and dicta—the private property of one John Ruskin, Esq.'

As spring drew on, the depression of spirits to which she was subject began to grasp her again, and 'to crush her with a day- and night-mare.'* She became afraid of sinking as low as she had done in the autumn; and to avoid this, she prevailed on her old friend and school-fellow to come and stay with her for a few weeks in March. She found great benefit from this companionship,—both from the congenial society itself, and from the self-restraint of thought imposed by the necessity of entertaining her and looking after her comfort. On this occasion, Miss Brontë said, 'It will not do to get into the habit of running away from home, and thus temporarily evading an oppression instead of facing, wrestling with and conquering it, or being conquered by it.'

I shall now make an extract from one of her letters, which is purposely displaced as to time.* I quote it because it relates to a third offer of marriage which she had, and because I find that some are apt to imagine, from the extraordinary power with which she represented the passion of love in her novels, that she herself was easily susceptible of it.

'Could I ever feel enough for ——, to accept of him as a husband? Friendship—gratitude—esteem—I have; but each moment he came near me, and that I could see his eyes fastened on me, my veins ran ice. Now that he is away, I feel far more gently towards him; it is only close by that I grow rigid, stiffening with a strange mixture of apprehension and anger, which nothing softens but his retreat, and a perfect subduing of his manner. I did not want to be proud, nor intend to be proud, but I was forced to be so. Most true it is, that we are over-ruled by One above us; that in His hands our very will is as clay in the hands of the potter.'*

I have now named all the offers of marriage she ever received, until that was made which she finally accepted. The gentleman referred to in this letter, retained so much regard for her as to be her friend to the end of her life; a circumstance to his credit and to hers.

Before her friend E—— took her departure, Mr Brontë caught cold, and continued for some weeks much out of health, with an attack of bronchitis. His spirits, too, became much depressed; and all his daughter's efforts were directed towards cheering him.

When he grew better, and had regained his previous strength, she resolved to avail herself of an invitation which she had received some time before, to pay a visit in London.* This year, 1851, was, as every one remembers, the time of the great Exhibition; but even with that attraction in prospect, she did not intend to stay there long; and, as usual, she made an agreement with her friends, before finally accepting their offered hospitality, that her sojourn at their house was to be as quiet as ever, since any other way of proceeding disagreed with her both mentally and physically. She never looked excited except for a moment, when something in conversation called her out; but she often felt so, even about comparative trifles, and the exhaustion of reaction was sure to follow. Under such circumstances, she always became extremely thin and haggard; yet she averred that the change invariably did her good afterwards.

Her preparations in the way of dress for this visit, in the gay time of that gay season, were singularly in accordance with her feminine taste; quietly anxious to satisfy her love for modest, dainty, neat attire, and not regardless of the becoming, yet remembering consistency, both with her general appearance and with her means, in every selection she made.

'By the bye,* I meant to ask you when you went to Leeds, to do a small errand for me, but fear your hands will be too full of business. It was merely this: in case you chanced to be in any shop where the lace cloaks, both black and white, of which I spoke, were sold, to ask their price. I suppose they would hardly like to send a few to Haworth to be looked at; indeed, if they cost very much, it would be useless, but if they are reasonable and they would send them, I should like to see them; and also some chemisettes of small size, (the full woman's size don't fit me) both of simple style for every day and good quality for best.' . . . . 'It appears I could not rest satisfied when I was well off. I told you I had taken one of the black lace mantles, but when I came to try it with the black satin dress, with which I should chiefly want to wear it, I found the effect was far from good; the beauty of the lace was lost, and it looked somewhat brown and rusty; I wrote to Mr ——, requesting him to change it for a *white* mantle of the same price; he was extremely courteous, and sent to London for one, which I have got this morning. The price is less, being but 1*l.* 14*s.* 0*d.*; it is pretty, neat, and light, looks well on black; and upon reasoning the matter over, I came to the philosophic conclusion, that it would be no shame for a person of my means to wear a cheaper thing; so I think I shall take it, and if you ever see it and call it "trumpery" so much the worse.'

'Do you know that I was in Leeds on the very same day with you—last Wednesday? I had thought of telling you where I was going, and having your help and company in buying a bonnet, &c., but then I reflected this would merely be making a selfish use of you, so I determined to manage or mismanage the matter alone. I went to Hurst and Hall's for the bonnet, and got one which seemed grave and quiet there amongst all the splendours; but now it looks infinitely too gay with its pink lining. I saw some beautiful silks of pale sweet colours, but had not the spirit or the means to launch out at the rate of five shillings per yard, and went and bought a black silk at three shillings after all. I rather regret this, because papa says he would have lent me a sovereign if he had known. I believe, if you had been there, you would have forced me to get into debt. . . . I really can no more come to B—— before I go to London than I can fly. I have quantities of sewing to do, as well as household matters to arrange, before I leave, as they will clean, &c., in my absence. Besides, I am grievously afflicted with headache, which I trust to change of air for relieving; but meantime, as it proceeds from the stomach, it makes me very thin and grey; neither you nor anybody else would fatten me up or put me into good condition for the visit; it is fated otherwise. No matter. Calm your passion; yet I am glad to see it. Such spirit seems to prove health. Good bye, in haste.

'Your poor mother is like Tabby, Martha, and Papa; all these fancy I am somehow, by some mysterious process, to be married in London, or to engage myself to matrimony. How I smile internally! How groundless and improbable is the idea! Papa seriously told me yesterday, that if I married and left him he should give up housekeeping and go into lodgings!!!'

I copy the following, for the sake of the few words describing the appearance of the heathery moors in late summer.

TO SYDNEY DOBELL, ESQ.

'May 24th, 1851.

'My dear Sir,—I hasten to send Mrs Dobell* the autograph. It was the word "Album" that frightened me: I thought she wished me to write a sonnet on purpose for it, which I could not do.

'Your proposal respecting a journey to Switzerland is deeply kind; it draws me with the force of a mighty Temptation, but the stern Impossible holds me back. No! I cannot go to Switzerland this summer.

'Why did the editor of the "Eclectic" erase that most powerful and pictorial passage?* He could not be insensible to its beauty; perhaps he thought it profane. Poor man!

'I know nothing of such an orchard-country as you describe. I have never seen such a region. Our hills only confess the coming of summer by growing green with young fern and moss, in secret little hollows. Their bloom is reserved for autumn; then they burn with a kind of dark glow, different, doubtless, from the blush of garden blossom. About the close of next month, I expect to go to London, to pay a brief and quiet visit. I fear chance will not be so propitious as to bring you to town while I am there; otherwise, how glad I should be if you would call. With kind regards to Mrs Dobell,—Believe me, sincerely yours,

'C. BRONTË.'

Her next letter is dated from London.

'June 2nd.

'I came here on Wednesday, being summoned a day sooner than I expected, in order to be in time for Thackeray's second lecture,* which was delivered on Thursday afternoon. This, as you may suppose, was a genuine treat to me, and I was glad not to miss it. It was given in Willis' Rooms, where the Almacks balls are held—a great painted and gilded saloon with long sofas for benches. The audience was said to be the cream of London society, and it looked so. I did not at all expect the great lecturer would know me or notice me under these circumstances, with admiring duchesses and countesses seated in rows before him; but he met me as I entered—shook hands—took me to his mother, whom I had not before seen, and introduced me. She is a fine, handsome, young-looking old lady; was very gracious, and called with one of her grand-daughters next day.

'Thackeray called too, separately. I had a long talk with him, and I think he knows me now a little better than he did; but of this I cannot yet be sure; he is a great and strange man. There is quite a furor for his lectures. They are a sort of essays, characterised by his own peculiar originality and power, and delivered with a finished taste and ease, which is felt, but cannot be described. Just before the lecture began, somebody came behind me, leaned over and said, "Permit me, as a Yorkshireman, to introduce myself." I turned round—saw a strange, not handsome, face, which puzzled me for half a minute, and then I said, "You are Lord Carlisle."* He nodded and smiled; he talked a few minutes very pleasantly and courteously.

'Afterwards came another man with the same plea, that he was a Yorkshireman, and this turned out to be Mr Monckton Milnes.* Then came Dr Forbes, whom I was sincerely glad to see. On Friday, I went to the Crystal Palace; it is a marvellous, stirring, bewildering sight—a mixture of a genii palace, and a mighty bazaar, but it is not much in my way; I liked the lecture better. On Saturday I saw the Exhibition at Somerset House;* about half a dozen of the pictures are good and interesting, the rest of little worth. Sunday—yesterday—was a day to be marked with a white stone; through most of the day I was very happy, without being tired or over-excited. In the afternoon, I went to hear D'Aubigné, the great Protestant French preacher;* it was pleasant—half sweet, half sad—and strangely suggestive, to hear the French language once more. For health, I have so far got on very fairly, considering that I came here far from well.'

The lady, who accompanied Miss Brontë to the lecture of Thackeray's alluded to, says that, soon after they had taken their places, she was aware that he was pointing out her companion to several of his friends, but she hoped that Miss Brontë herself would not perceive it. After some time, however, during which many heads had been turned round, and many glasses put up, in order to look at the author of 'Jane Eyre,' Miss Brontë said, 'I am afraid Mr Thackeray has been playing me a trick;' but she soon became too much absorbed in the lecture to notice the attention which was being paid to her, except when it was directly offered, as in the case of Lord Carlisle and Mr Monckton Milnes. When the lecture was ended, Mr Thackeray came down from the platform, and making his way towards her, asked her for her opinion. This she mentioned to me not many days afterwards,* adding remarks almost identical with those which I subsequently read in 'Villette,' where a similar action on the part of M. Paul Emanuel is related.

'As our party left the Hall, he stood at the entrance; he saw and knew me, and lifted his hat; he offered his hand in passing, and uttered the words "Qu'en dites-vous?"—question eminently characteristic, and reminding me, even in this his moment of triumph, of that inquisitive restlessness, that absence of what I considered desirable self-control, which were amongst his faults. He should not have cared just then to ask what I thought, or what anybody thought; but he *did* care, and he was too natural to conceal, too impulsive to repress his wish. Well! if I blamed his over-eagerness, I liked his *naïveté*. I would have praised him; I had plenty of praise in my heart; but alas! no words on my lips. Who *has* words at the right moment? I stammered some lame expressions; but was truly glad when other people, coming up with profuse congratulations, covered my deficiency by their redundancy.'

As they were preparing to leave the room, her companion saw with dismay that many of the audience were forming themselves into two lines, on each side of the aisle down which they had to pass before reaching the door. Aware that any delay would only make the ordeal more trying, her friend took Miss Brontë's arm in hers, and they went along the avenue of eager and admiring faces During this passage through the 'cream of society,' Miss Brontë's hand trembled to such a degree, that her companion feared lest she should turn faint and be unable to proceed; and she dared not express her sympathy or try to give her strength by any touch or word, lest it might bring on the crisis she dreaded.

Surely, such thoughtless manifestation of curiosity is a blot on the scutcheon of true politeness! The rest of the account of this, her longest visit to London, shall be told in her own words.*

'I sit down to write to you this morning in an inexpressibly flat state; having spent the whole of yesterday and the day before in a gradually increasing headache, which grew at last rampant and violent, ended with excessive sickness, and this morning I am quite weak and washy. I hoped to leave my headaches behind me at Haworth; but it seems I brought them carefully packed in my trunk, and very much have they been in my way since I came. . . . . . Since I wrote last, I have seen various things worth describing; Rachel,* the great French actress, amongst the number. But to-day I really have no pith for the task. I can only wish you good-bye with all my heart.'

'I cannot boast that London has agreed with me well this time; the oppression of frequent headache, sickness, and a low tone of spirits, has poisoned many moments which might otherwise have been pleasant. Sometimes I have felt this hard, and been tempted to murmur at Fate, which condemns me to comparative silence and solitude for eleven months in the year, and in the twelfth, while offering social enjoyment, takes away the vigour and cheerfulness which should turn it to account. But circumstances are ordered for us, and we must submit.'

'Your letter would have been answered yesterday, but I was already gone out before post time, and was out all day. People are very kind, and perhaps I shall be glad of what I have seen afterwards, but it is often a little trying at the time. On Thursday, the Marquis of Westminster* asked me to a great party, to which I was to go with Mrs D——, a beautiful, and, I think, a kind woman too; but this I resolutely declined. On Friday I dined at the ——'s, and met Mrs D—— and Mr Monckton Milnes. On Saturday I went to hear and see Rachel; a wonderful sight—terrible as if the earth had cracked deep at your feet, and revealed a glimpse of hell. I shall never forget it. She made me shudder to the marrow of my bones; in her some fiend has certainly taken up an incarnate home. She is not a woman; she is a snake; she is the ——. On Sunday I went to the Spanish Ambassador's Chapel, where Cardinal Wiseman,* in his archiepiscopal robes and mitre, held a confirmation. The whole scene was impiously theatrical.

Yesterday (Monday) I was sent for at ten to breakfast with Mr Rogers, the patriarch-poet. Mrs D—— and Lord Glenelg were there; no one else: this certainly proved a most calm, refined, and intellectual treat. After breakfast, Sir David Brewster* came to take us to the Crystal Palace. I had rather dreaded this, for Sir David is a man of profoundest science, and I feared it would be impossible to understand his explanations of the mechanism, &c.; indeed, I hardly knew how to ask him questions. I was spared all trouble: without being questioned, he gave information in the kindest and simplest manner. After two hours spent at the Exhibition, and where, as you may suppose, I was *very* tired, we had to go to Lord Westminster's and spend two hours more in looking at the collection of pictures in his splendid gallery.'

To another friend she writes:—*

'—— may have told you that I have spent a month in London this summer. When you come, you shall ask what questions you like on that point, and I will answer to the best of my stammering ability. Do not press me much on the subject of the "Crystal Palace." I went there five times, and certainly saw some interesting things, and the *coup d'œil* is striking and bewildering enough; but I never was able to get up any raptures on the subject, and each renewed visit was made under coercion rather than of my own free will. It is an excessively bustling place; and, after all, its wonders appeal too exclusively to the eye, and rarely touch the heart or head. I make an exception to the last assertion, in favour of those who possess a large range of scientific knowledge. Once I went with Sir David Brewster, and perceived that he looked on objects with other eyes than mine.'

Miss Brontë returned from London by Manchester, and paid us a visit of a couple of days at the end of June. The weather was so intensely hot, and she herself so much fatigued with her London sight-seeing, that we did little but sit in-doors, with open windows, and talk. The only thing she made a point of exerting herself to procure was a present for Tabby. It was to be a shawl, or rather a large handkerchief, such as she could pin across her neck and shoulders, in the old-fashioned country manner. Miss Brontë took great pains in seeking out one which she thought would please the old woman.

On her arrival at home, she addressed the following letter to the friend with whom she had been staying in London:—

'Haworth, July 1st, 1851.

'My dear Mrs Smith,—Once more I am at home, where, I am thankful to say, I found my father very well. The journey to Manchester was a little hot and dusty, but otherwise pleasant enough. The two stout gentlemen, who filled a portion of the carriage when I got in, quitted it at Rugby, and two other ladies and myself had it to ourselves the rest of the way. The visit to Mrs Gaskell formed a cheering break in the journey. Haworth Parsonage is rather a contrast, yet even Haworth Parsonage does not look gloomy in this bright summer weather; it is somewhat still, but with the windows open I can hear a bird or two singing on certain thorn-trees in the garden. My father and the servants think me looking better than when I left home, and I certainly feel better myself for the change. You are too much like your son to render it advisable I should say much about your kindness during my visit. However, one cannot help (like Captain Cuttle)* making a note of these matters. Papa says I am to thank you in his name, and offer you his respects, which I do accordingly.—With truest regards to all your circle, believe me very sincerely yours,

'C. BRONTË.'

'July 8th, 1851.*

'My dear Sir,—Thackeray's last lecture* must, I think, have been his best. What he says about Sterne is true. His observations on literary men, and their social obligations and individual duties, seem to me also true and full of mental and moral vigour.* . . . . . The International Copyright Meeting* seems to have had but a barren result, judging from the report in the Literary Gazette. I cannot see that Sir E. Bulwer and the rest *did* anything; nor can I well see what it is in their power to do. The argument brought forward about the damage accruing to American national literature from the present piratical system, is a good and sound argument, but I am afraid the publishers—honest men—are not yet mentally prepared to give such reasoning due weight. I should think, that which refers to the injury inflicted upon themselves, by an oppressive competition in piracy, would influence them more; but

I suppose, all established matters, be they good or evil, are difficult to change. About the "Phrenological Character"* I must not say a word. Of your own accord, you have found the safest point from which to view it: I will not say "look higher!" I think you see the matter as it is desirable we should all see what relates to ourselves. If I had a right to whisper a word of counsel, it should be merely this: whatever your present self may be, resolve with all your strength of resolution, never to degenerate thence. Be jealous of a shadow of falling off. Determine rather to look above that standard, and to strive beyond it. Everybody appreciates certain social properties, and likes his neighbour for possessing them; but perhaps few dwell upon a friend's capacity for the intellectual, or care how this might expand, if there were but facilities allowed for cultivation, and space given for growth. It seems to me that, even should such space and facilities be denied by stringent circumstances and a rigid fate, still it should do you good fully to know, and tenaciously to remember, that you have such a capacity. When other people overwhelm you with acquired knowledge, such as you have not had opportunity, perhaps not application, to gain—derive not pride, but support from the thought. If no new books had ever been written, some of these minds would themselves have remained blank pages: they only take an impression; they were not born with a record of thought on the brain, or an instinct of sensation on the heart. If I had never seen a printed volume, Nature would have offered my perceptions a varying picture of a continuous narrative, which, without any other teacher than herself, would have schooled me to knowledge, unsophisticated, but genuine.

'Before I received your last, I had made up my mind to tell you that I should expect no letter for three months to come (intending afterwards to extend this abstinence to six months, for I am jealous of becoming dependent on this indulgence: you doubtless cannot see why, because you do not live my life). Nor shall I now expect a letter; but since you say that you would like to write now and then, I cannot say "never write," without imposing on my real wishes a falsehood which they reject, and doing to them a violence, to which they entirely refuse to submit. I can only observe that when it pleases you to write, whether seriously or for a little amusement, your notes, if they come to me, will come where they are welcome. Tell —— I will try to cultivate good spirits, as assiduously as she cultivates her geraniums.'

# CHAPTER X

SOON after she returned home, her friend paid her a visit. While she stayed at Haworth, Miss Brontë wrote the letter from which the following extract is taken. The strong sense and right feeling displayed in it on the subject of friendship, sufficiently account for the constancy of affection which Miss Brontë earned from all those who once became her friends.

TO W. S. WILLIAMS, ESQ.

'July 21st, 1851.

'... I could not help wondering whether Cornhill will ever change for me, as Oxford has changed for you. I have some pleasant associations connected with it now—will these alter their character some day?

'Perhaps they may—though I have faith to the contrary, because, I *think*, I do not exaggerate my partialities; I *think* I take faults along with excellences—blemishes together with beauties. And besides, in the matter of friendship, I have observed that disappointment here arises chiefly, *not* from liking our friends too well, or thinking of them too highly, but rather from an over-estimate of *their* liking for and opinion of *us;* and that if we guard ourselves with sufficient scrupulousness of care from error in this direction, and can be content, and even happy to give more affection than we receive—can make just comparison of circumstances, and be severely accurate in drawing inferences thence, and never let self-love blind our eyes—I think we may manage to get through life with consistency and constancy, unembittered by that misanthropy which springs from revulsions of feeling. All this sounds a little metaphysical, but it is good sense if you consider it. The moral of it is, that if we would build on a sure foundation in friendship, we must love our friends for *their* sakes rather than for *our own;* we must look at their truth to *themselves,* full as much as their truth to *us.* In the latter case, every wound to self-love would be a cause of coldness; in the former, only some painful change in the friend's character and disposition—some fearful breach in his allegiance to his better self—could alienate the heart.

'How interesting your old maiden-cousin's gossip about your parents must have been to you; and how gratifying to find that the reminiscence turned on none but pleasant facts and characteristics! Life must, indeed, be slow in that little decaying hamlet amongst the chalk hills. After all, depend upon it, it is better to be worn out with work in a thronged community, than to perish of inaction in a stagnant solitude: take this truth into consideration whenever you get tired of work and bustle.'

I received a letter from her a little later than this; and though there is reference throughout to what I must have said in writing to her, all that it called forth in reply is so peculiarly characteristic, that I cannot prevail upon myself to pass it over without a few extracts:—

'Haworth, Aug. 6th, 1851.

'My dear Mrs Gaskell,—I was too much pleased with your letter, when I got it at last, to feel disposed to murmur now about the delay.

'About a fortnight ago, I received a letter from Miss Martineau; also a long letter, and treating precisely the same subjects on which yours dwelt, viz., the Exhibition and Thackeray's last lecture. It was interesting mentally to place the two documents side by side—to study the two aspects of mind—to view, alternately, the same scene through two mediums. Full striking was the difference; and the more striking because it was not the rough contrast of good and evil, but the more subtle opposition, the more delicate diversity of different kinds of good. The excellence of one nature resembled (I thought) that of some sovereign medicine—harsh, perhaps, to the taste, but potent to invigorate; the good of the other seemed more akin to the nourishing efficacy of our daily bread. It is not bitter; it is not lusciously sweet; it pleases, without flattering the palate; it sustains, without forcing the strength.

'I very much agree with you in all you say. For the sake of variety, I could almost wish that the concord of opinion were less complete.

'To begin with Trafalgar Square.* My taste goes with yours and Meta's completely on this point. I have always thought it a fine site (and *sight* also). The view from the summit of those steps has ever struck me as grand and imposing—Nelson Column included: the fountains I could dispense with. With respect, also, to the Crystal Palace, my thoughts are precisely yours.

'Then I feel sure you speak justly of Thackeray's lecture. You do well to set aside odious comparisons, and to wax impatient of that trite twaddle about "nothing newness"—a jargon which simply proves, in those who habitually use it, a coarse and feeble faculty of appreciation; an inability to discern the relative value of *originality* and *novelty;* a lack of that refined perception which, dispensing with the stimulus of an ever-new subject, can derive sufficiency of pleasure from freshness of treatment. To such critics, the prime of a summer morning would bring no delight; wholly occupied with railing at their cook for not having provided a novel and piquant breakfast-dish, they would remain insensible to such influences as lie in sunrise, dew, and breeze: therein would be "nothing new."

'Is it Mr ——'s family experience which has influenced your feelings about the Catholics?* I own, I cannot be sorry for this commencing change. Good people—*very* good people—I doubt not, there are amongst the Romanists, but the system is not one which should have such sympathy as *yours.* Look at Popery taking off the mask in Naples!

'I have read the "Saint's Tragedy."* As a "work of art" it seems to me far superior to either "Alton Locke" or "Yeast." Faulty it may be, crude and unequal, yet there are portions where some of the deep chords of human nature are swept with a hand which is strong even while it falters. We see throughout (I *think*) that Elizabeth has not, and never had, a mind perfectly sane. From the time that she was what she herself, in the exaggeration of her humility, calls "an idiot girl," to the hour when she lay moaning in visions on her dying bed, a slight craze runs through her whole existence. This is good: this is true. A sound mind, a healthy intellect, would have dashed the priest's power to the wall; would have defended her natural affections from his grasp, as a lioness defends her young; would have been as true to husband and children, as your leal-hearted little Maggie was to her Frank.* Only

a mind weak with some fatal flaw *could* have been influenced as
was this poor saint's. But what anguish—what struggles! Seldom
do I cry over books; but here, my eyes rained as I read. When
Elizabeth turns her face to the wall—I stopped—there needed no
more.

'Deep truths are touched on in this tragedy—touched on, not
fully elicited; truths that stir a peculiar pity—a compassion hot
with wrath, and bitter with pain. This is no poet's dream: we know
that such things *have* been done; that minds *have* been thus
subjugated, and lives thus laid waste.

'Remember me kindly and respectfully to Mr Gaskell, and
though I have not seen Marianne,* I must beg to include her in
the love I send the others. Could you manage to convey a small
kiss to that dear, but dangerous little person, Julia? She surrepti-
tiously possessed herself of a minute fraction of my heart, which
has been missing ever since I saw her.—Believe me, sincerely and
affectionately yours,

'C. BRONTË.'

The reference which she makes at the end of this letter is to my
youngest little girl, between whom and her a strong mutual
attraction existed. The child would steal her little hand into Miss
Brontë's scarcely larger one, and each took pleasure in this
apparently unobserved caress. Yet once when I told Julia to take
and show her the way to some room in the house, Miss Brontë
shrunk back: 'Do not *bid* her do anything for me,' she said; 'it has
been so sweet hitherto to have her rendering her little kindnesses
*spontaneously*.'

As illustrating her feelings with regard to children I may give
what she says in another of her letters to me.*

'Whenever I see Florence and Julia again I shall feel like a fond
but bashful suitor, who views at a distance the fair personage to
whom, in his clownish awe, he dare not risk a near approach. Such
is the clearest idea I can give you of my feeling towards children
I like, but to whom I am a stranger;—and to what children am I
not a stranger? They seem to me little wonders; their talk,
their ways are all matter of half-admiring, half-puzzled speculation.'

The following is part of a long letter which I received from her, dated September 20th, 1851:—

'. . . Beautiful are those sentences out of James Martineau's sermons;* some of them gems most pure and genuine; ideas deeply conceived, finely expressed. I should like much to see his review of his sister's book. Of all the articles respecting which you question me, I have seen none, except that notable one in the "Westminster" on the Emancipation of Women.* But why are you and I to think (perhaps I should rather say to *feel*) so exactly alike on some points that there can be no discussion between us? Your words on this paper express my thoughts. Well-argued it is,— clear, logical,—but vast is the hiatus of omission; harsh the consequent jar on every finer chord of the soul. What is this hiatus? I think I know; and, knowing, I will venture to say. I think the writer forgets there is such a thing as self-sacrificing love and disinterested devotion. When I first read the paper, I thought it was the work of a powerful-minded, clear-headed woman, who had a hard, jealous heart, muscles of iron, and nerves of bend[1] leather; of a woman who longed for power, and had never felt affection. To many women affection is sweet, and power conquered indifferent— though we all like influence won. I believe J. S. Mill would make a hard, dry, dismal world of it; and yet he speaks admirable sense through a great portion of his article—especially when he says, that if there be a natural unfitness in women for men's employment, there is no need to make laws on the subject; leave all careers open; let them try; those who ought to succeed will succeed, or, at least, will have a fair chance—the incapable will fall back into their right place. He likewise disposes of the "maternity" question very neatly. In short, J. S. Mill's head is, I dare say, very good, but I feel disposed to scorn his heart. You are right when you say that there is a large margin in human nature over which the logicians have no dominion; glad am I that it is so.[2]

---

[1] 'Bend,' in Yorkshire, is strong ox leather.

[2] Mr J. S. Mill, in a letter upon this passage, says: 'I am not the author of the article. I may claim to be its Editor; and I should be proud to be identified with every thought, every sentiment, and every expression in it. The writer is a woman, and the most warm-hearted woman, of the largest and most genial sympathies, and the most forgetful of self in her generous zeal to do honour to others, whom I have ever known.'*

'I send by this post Ruskin's "Stones of Venice," and I hope you and Meta will find passages in it that will please you. Some parts would be dry and technical were it not for the character, the marked individuality which pervades every page. I wish Marianne had come to speak to me at the lecture;* it would have given me such pleasure. What you say of that small sprite Julia, amuses me much. I believe you don't know that she has a great deal of her mama's nature (modified) in her; yet I think you will find she has as she grows up.

'Will it not be a great mistake, if Mr Thackeray should deliver his lectures at Manchester under such circumstances and conditions as will exclude people like you and Mr Gaskell from the number of his audience?* I thought his London-plan too narrow. Charles Dickens would not thus limit his sphere of action.

'You charge me to write about myself. What can I say on that precious topic? My health is pretty good. My spirits are not always alike. Nothing happens to me. I hope and expect little in this world, and am thankful that I do not despond and suffer more. Thank you for inquiring after our old servant; she is pretty well; the little shawl, &c., pleased her much. Papa likewise, I am glad to say, is pretty well; with his and my kindest regards to you and Mr Gaskell—Believe me sincerely and affectionately yours,

'C. BRONTË.'

Before the autumn was far advanced, the usual effects of her solitary life, and of the unhealthy situation of Haworth Parsonage, began to appear in the form of sick headaches, and miserable, starting wakeful nights. She does not dwell on this in her letters; but there is an absence of all cheerfulness of tone, and an occasional sentence forced out of her, which imply far more than many words could say. There was illness all through the Parsonage household—taking its accustomed forms of lingering influenza and low fever; she herself was outwardly the strongest of the family, and all domestic exertion fell for a time upon her shoulders.

TO W. S. WILLIAMS, ESQ.

'Sept. 26th.

'As I laid down your letter, after reading with interest the graphic account it gives of a very striking scene, I could not help feeling with renewed force a truth, trite enough, yet ever impressive; viz., that it is good to be attracted out of ourselves—to be forced to take a near view of the sufferings, the privations, the efforts, the difficulties of others. If we ourselves live in fulness of content, it is well to be reminded that thousands of our fellow-creatures undergo a different lot; it is well to have sleepy sympathies excited, and lethargic selfishness shaken up. If, on the other hand, we be contending with the special grief,—the intimate trial,—the peculiar bitterness with which God has seen fit to mingle our own cup of existence,—it is very good to know that our overcast lot is not singular; it stills the repining word and thought,—it rouses the flagging strength, to have it vividly set before us that there are countless afflictions in the world, each perhaps rivalling—some surpassing—the private pain over which we are too prone exclusively to sorrow.

'All those crowded emigrants had their troubles,—their untoward causes of banishment; you, the looker-on, had "your wishes and regrets,"—your anxieties, alloying your home happiness and domestic bliss; and the parallel might be pursued further, and still it would be true,—still the same; a thorn in the flesh* for each; some burden, some conflict for all.

'How far this state of things is susceptible of amelioration from changes in public institutions,—alterations in national habits,—may and ought to be earnestly considered: but this is a problem not easily solved. The evils, as you point them out, are great, real, and most obvious; the remedy is obscure and vague; yet for such difficulties as spring from over-competition, emigration must be good; the new life in a new country must give a new lease of hope; the wider field, less thickly peopled, must open a new path for endeavour. But I always think great physical powers of exertion and endurance ought to accompany such a step. . . . . I am truly glad to hear that an *original* writer has fallen in your way.* Originality is the pearl of great price* in literature,—the rarest, the most precious claim by which an author can be recommended. Are not your publishing prospects for the coming season tolerably rich and satisfactory? You inquire after "Currer Bell." It seems to me that the absence of his name from your list of announcements will leave no blank, and that he may at least spare himself the disquietude of thinking he is wanted when it is certainly not his lot to appear.

'Perhaps Currer Bell has his secret moan about these matters; but if so, he will keep it to himself. It is an affair about which no words need be wasted, for no words can make a change: it is between him and his position, his faculties and his fate.'

My husband and I were anxious that she should pay us a visit before the winter had set completely in; and she thus wrote, declining our invitation:—

'Nov. 6th.

'If anybody would tempt me from home, you would; but, just now, from home I must not, will not go. I feel greatly better at present than I did three weeks ago. For a month or six weeks about the equinox (autumnal or vernal) is a period of the year which, I have noticed, strangely tries me. Sometimes the strain falls on the mental, sometimes on the physical part of me; I am ill with neuralgic headache, or I am ground to the dust with deep dejection of spirits (not, however, such dejection but I can keep it to myself). That weary time has, I think and trust, got over for this year. It was the anniversary of my poor brother's death, and of my sister's failing health: I need say no more.

'As to running away from home every time I have a battle of this sort to fight, it would not do: besides the "weird" would follow. As to shaking it off, that cannot be. I have declined to go to Mrs ——,* to Miss Martineau, and now I decline to go to you. But listen! do not think that I throw your kindness away; or that it fails of doing the good you desire. On the contrary, the feeling expressed in your letter,—proved by your invitation,—goes *right home* where you would have it to go, and heals as you would have it to heal.

'Your description of Frederika Bremer* tallies exactly with one I read somewhere, in I know not what book. I laughed out when I got to the mention of Frederika's special accomplishment, given by you with a distinct simplicity that, to my taste, is what the French would call "impayable." Where do you find the foreigner who is without some little drawback of this description? It is a pity.'

A visit from Miss W—— at this period did Miss Brontë much good for the time. She speaks of her guest's company as being 'very pleasant,' 'like good wine,'* both to her father and to herself.

But Miss W—— could not remain with her long; and then again
the monotony of her life returned upon her in all its force; the only
events of her days and weeks consisting in the small changes which
occasional letters brought. It must be remembered that her health
was often such as to prevent her stirring out of the house in
inclement or wintry weather. She was liable to sore throat, and
depressing pain at the chest, and difficulty of breathing, on the
least exposure to cold.

A letter from her late visitor touched and gratified her much; it
was simply expressive of gratitude for attention and kindness
shown to her, but it wound up by saying that she had not for many
years experienced so much enjoyment as during the ten days past
at Haworth. This little sentence called out a wholesome sensation
of modest pleasure in Miss Brontë's mind; and she says, 'it did me
good.'*

I find, in a letter to a distant friend,* written about this time, a
retrospect of her visit to London. It is too ample to be considered
as a mere repetition of what she had said before; and, besides, it
shows that her first impressions of what she saw and heard were
not crude and transitory, but stood the tests of time and after-
thought.

'I spent a few weeks in town last summer, as you have heard;
and was much interested by many things I heard and saw there.
What now chiefly dwells in my memory are Mr Thackeray's
lectures, Mademoiselle Rachel's acting, D'Aubigné's, Melville's,
and Maurice's preaching,* and the Crystal Palace.

'Mr Thackeray's lectures you will have seen mentioned and
commented on in the papers; they were very interesting. I could
not always coincide with the sentiments expressed, or the opinions
broached; but I admired the gentlemanlike ease, the quiet humour,
the taste, the talent, the simplicity, and the originality of the
lecturer.

'Rachel's acting transfixed me with wonder, enchained me with
interest, and thrilled me with horror. The tremendous force with
which she expresses the very worst passions in their strongest
essence forms an exhibition as exciting as the bull-fights of Spain,
and the gladiatorial combats of old Rome, and (it seemed to me)
not one whit more moral than these poisoned stimulants to popular

ferocity. It is scarcely human nature that she shows you; it is
something wilder and worse; the feelings and fury of a fiend. The
great gift of genius she undoubtedly has; but, I fear, she rather
abuses it than turns it to good account.

'With all the three preachers I was greatly pleased. Melville
seemed to me the most eloquent, Maurice the most in earnest; had
I the choice, it is Maurice whose ministry I should frequent.

'On the Crystal Palace I need not comment. You must already
have heard too much of it. It struck me at the first with only a
vague sort of wonder and admiration; but having one day the
privilege of going over it in company with an eminent countryman
of yours, Sir David Brewster, and hearing, in his kindly Scotch
accent, his lucid explanation of many things that had been to me
before a sealed book, I began a little better to comprehend it, or at
least a small part of it: whether its final results will equal
expectation, I know not.'

Her increasing indisposition subdued her at last, in spite of all
her efforts of reason and will. She tried to forget oppressive
recollections in writing. Her publishers were importunate for a
new book from her pen. 'Villette' was begun, but she lacked power
to continue it.

'It is not at all likely' (she says)* 'that my book will be ready at
the time you mention. If my health is spared, I shall get on with
it as fast as is consistent with its being done, if not *well*, yet as well
as I can do it. *Not one whit faster*. When the mood leaves me (it
has left me now, without vouchsafing so much as a word or a
message when it will return) I put by the MS and wait till it comes
back again. God knows, I sometimes have to wait long—*very* long
it seems to me. Meantime, if I might make a request to you, it
would be this. Please to say nothing about my book till it is written,
and in your hands. You may not like it. I am not myself elated with
it as far as it is gone, and authors, you need not be told, are always
tenderly indulgent, even blindly partial, to their own. Even if it
should turn out reasonably well, still I regard it as ruin to the
prosperity of an ephemeral book like a novel, to be much talked of
beforehand, as if it were something great. People are apt to
conceive, or at least to profess, exaggerated expectation, such as no

performance can realise; then ensue disappointment and the due revenge, detraction, and failure. If when I write, I were to think of the critics who, I know, are waiting for Currer Bell, ready "to break all his bones or ever he comes to the bottom of the den,"* my hand would fall paralysed on my desk. However, I can but do my best, and then muffle my head in the mantle of Patience, and sit down at her feet and wait.'

The 'mood' here spoken of did not go off; it had a physical origin. Indigestion, nausea, headache, sleeplessness,—all combined to produce miserable depression of spirits. A little event which occurred about this time did not tend to cheer her. It was the death of poor old faithful Keeper, Emily's dog. He had come to the Parsonage in the fierce strength of his youth. Sullen and ferocious, he had met with his master in the indomitable Emily. Like most dogs of his kind, he feared, respected, and deeply loved her who subdued him. He had mourned her with the pathetic fidelity of his nature, falling into old age after her death. And now her surviving sister wrote:* 'Poor old Keeper died last Monday morning; after being ill one night, he went gently to sleep; we laid his old faithful head in the garden. Flossy (the "fat curly-haired dog") is dull and misses him. There was something very sad in losing the old dog; yet I am glad he met a natural fate. People kept hinting he ought to be put away, which neither papa nor I liked to think of.'

When Miss Brontë wrote this, on December 8th, she was suffering from a bad cold, and pain in her side. Her illness increased, and on December 17th, she—so patient, silent, and enduring of suffering—so afraid of any unselfish taxing of others— had to call to her friend E. for help.

'I cannot at present go to see you, but I would be grateful if you could come and see me, even were it only for a few days. To speak truth, I have put on but a poor time of it during this month past. I kept hoping to be better, but was at last obliged to have recourse to a medical man. Sometimes I have felt very weak and low, and longed much for society, but could not persuade myself to commit the selfish act of asking you merely for my own relief. The doctor speaks encouragingly, but as yet I get no better. As the illness has

been coming on for a long time, it cannot, I suppose, be expected
to disappear all at once. I am not confined to bed but I am
weak,—have had no appetite for about three weeks,—and my
nights are very bad. I am well aware myself that extreme and
continuous depression of spirits has had much to do with the origin
of the illness; and I know a little cheerful society would do me
more good than gallons of medicine. If you *can* come, come on
Friday. Write to-morrow and say whether this be possible, and
what time you will be at Keighley, that I may send the gig. I do
not ask you to stay long; a few days is all I request.'

Of course, her friend went; and a certain amount of benefit was
derived from her society, always so grateful to Miss Brontë. But the
evil was now too deep-rooted to be more than palliated for a time by
'the little cheerful society' for which she so touchingly besought.

A relapse came on before long. She was very ill, and the remedies
employed took an unusual effect on her peculiar sensitiveness of
constitution. Mr Brontë was miserably anxious about the state of his
only remaining child, for she was reduced to the last degree of
weakness, as she had been unable to swallow food for above a week
before. She rallied, and derived her sole sustenance from half a
teacup of liquid, administered by tea-spoonfuls, in the course of the
day. Yet she kept out of bed, for her father's sake, and struggled in
solitary patience through her worst hours.

When she was recovering, her spirits needed support, and then
she yielded to her friend's entreaty that she would visit her. All the
time that Miss Brontë's illness had lasted, Miss —— had been
desirous of coming to her; but she refused to avail herself of this
kindness, saying, that 'it was enough to burden herself; that it
would be misery to annoy another;'* and, even at her worst time,
she tells her friend, with humorous glee, how coolly she had
managed to capture one of Miss ——'s letters to Mr Brontë, which
she suspected was of a kind to aggravate his alarm about his
daughter's state, 'and at once conjecturing its tenor, made its
contents her own.'

Happily for all parties, Mr Brontë was wonderfully well this
winter; good sleep, good spirits, and an excellent steady appetite,
all seemed to mark vigour; and in such a state of health, Charlotte

could leave him to spend a week with her friend, without any great anxiety.

She benefited greatly by the kind attentions and cheerful society of the family with whom she went to stay. They did not care for her in the least as 'Currer Bell,' but had known and loved her for years as Charlotte Brontë. To them her invalid weakness was only a fresh claim upon their tender regard, from the solitary woman, whom they had first known as a little, motherless school-girl.

Miss Brontë wrote to me about this time, and told me something of what she had suffered.

'Feb. 6th, 1852.

'Certainly, the past winter has been to me a strange time; had I the prospect before me of living it over again, my prayer must necessarily be, "Let this cup pass from me."\* That depression of spirits, which I thought was gone by when I wrote last, came back again with a heavy recoil; internal congestion ensued, and then inflammation. I had severe pain in my right side, frequent burning and aching in my chest; sleep almost forsook me, or would never come, except accompanied by ghastly dreams; appetite vanished, and slow fever was my continual companion. It was some time before I could bring myself to have recourse to medical advice. I thought my lungs were affected, and could feel no confidence in the power of medicine. When, at last, however, a doctor was consulted, he declared my lungs and chest sound, and ascribed all my sufferings to derangement of the liver, on which organ it seems the inflammation had fallen. This information was a great relief to my dear father, as well as to myself; but I had subsequently rather sharp medical discipline to undergo,\* and was much reduced. Though not yet well, it is with deep thankfulness that I can say, I am *greatly better*. My sleep, appetite, and strength seem all returning.'

It was a great interest to her to be allowed an early reading of 'Esmond;'\* and she expressed her thoughts on the subject, in a criticising letter to Mr Smith, who had given her this privilege.

'Feb. 14th, 1852.

'My dear Sir,—It has been a great delight to me to read Mr Thackeray's work; and I so seldom now express my sense of kindness that, for once, you must permit me, without rebuke, to thank you for a pleasure so rare and special. Yet I am not going to praise either Mr Thackeray or his book. I have read, enjoyed, been interested, and, after all, feel full as much ire and sorrow as gratitude and admiration. And still one can never lay down a book of his without the last two feelings having their part, be the subject or treatment what it may. In the first half of the book, what chiefly struck me was the wonderful manner in which the writer throws himself into the spirit and letter of the times whereof he treats; the allusions, the illustrations, the style, all seem to me so masterly in their exact keeping, their harmonious consistency, their nice, natural truth, their pure exemption from exaggeration. No second-rate imitator can write in that way; no coarse scene-painter can charm us with an illusion so delicate and perfect. But what bitter satire, what relentless dissection of diseased subjects! Well, and this, too, is right, or would be right, if the savage surgeon did not seem so fiercely pleased with his work. Thackeray likes to dissect an ulcer or an aneurism; he has pleasure in putting his cruel knife or probe into quivering, living flesh. Thackeray would not like all the world to be good; no great satirist would like society to be perfect.

'As usual, he is unjust to women, quite unjust. There is hardly any punishment he does not deserve for making Lady Castlewood peep through a keyhole, listen at a door, and be jealous of a boy and a milkmaid. Many other things I noticed that, for my part, grieved and exasperated me as I read; but then, again, came passages so true, so deeply thought, so tenderly felt, one could not help forgiving and admiring.*

\* \* \* \* \*

'But I wish he could be told not to care much for dwelling on the political or religious intrigues of the times. Thackeray, in his heart, does not value political or religious intrigues of any age or date. He likes to show us human nature at home, as he himself daily sees it; his wonderful observant faculty likes to be in action. In him this faculty is a sort of captain and leader; and if ever any passage in his writings lacks interest, it is when this master-faculty is for a time thrust into a subordinate position. I think such is the case in the former half of the present volume. Towards the middle, he throws off restraint, becomes himself, and is strong to the close.

Everything now depends on the second and third volumes. If, in pith and interest, they fall short of the first, a true success cannot ensue. If the continuation be an improvement upon the commencement, if the steam gather force as it rolls, Thackeray will triumph. Some people have been in the habit of terming him the second writer of the day;* it just depends on himself whether or not these critics shall be justified in their award. He need not be the second. God made him second to no man. If I were he, I would show myself as I am, not as critics report me; at any rate, I would do my best. Mr Thackeray is easy and indolent, and seldom cares to do his best. Thank you once more; and believe me yours sincerely,

'C. BRONTË.'

Miss Brontë's health continued such, that she could not apply herself to writing as she wished, for many weeks after the serious attack from which she had suffered. There was not very much to cheer her in the few events that touched her interests during this time. She heard in March of the death of a friend's relation in the Colonies; and we see something of what was the corroding dread at her heart.*

'The news of E——'s death came to me last week in a letter from M——; a long letter, which wrung my heart so, in its simple, strong, truthful emotion, I have only ventured to read it once. It ripped up half-scarred wounds with terrible force. The death-bed was just the same,—breath failing, &c. She fears she shall now, in her dreary solitude, become a "stern, harsh, selfish woman." This fear struck home; again and again have I felt it for myself, and what is *my* position to M——'s? May God help her, as God only can help!'

Again and again, her friend urged her to leave home; nor were various invitations wanting to enable her to do this, when these constitutional accesses of low spirits preyed too much upon her in her solitude. But she would not allow herself any such indulgence, unless it became absolutely necessary from the state of her health. She dreaded the perpetual recourse to such stimulants as change of scene and society, because of the reaction that was sure to follow. As far as she could see, her life was ordained to be lonely, and she must subdue her nature to her life, and, if possible, bring the two into harmony. When she could employ herself in fiction, all was comparatively well. The characters were her companions in the quiet hours, which she spent utterly alone, unable often to stir out of doors for many days together. The interests of the persons in her novels supplied the lack of interest in her own life; and Memory and Imagination found their appropriate work, and ceased to prey upon her vitals. But too frequently she could not write, could not see her people, nor hear them speak; a great mist of headache had blotted them out; they were non-existent to her.

This was the case all through the present spring; and anxious as her publishers were for its completion, 'Villette' stood still. Even her letters to her friend are scarce and brief. Here and there I find a sentence in them which can be extracted, and which is worth preserving.*

'M——'s letter is very interesting; it shows a mind one cannot but truly admire. Compare its serene trusting strength, with poor ——'s vacillating dependence. When the latter was in her first burst of happiness, I never remember the feeling finding vent in expressions of gratitude to God. There was always a continued claim upon your sympathy in the mistrust and doubt she felt of her own bliss. M—— believes; her faith is grateful and at peace; yet while happy in herself, how thoughtful she is for others!'

'March 23rd, 1852.

'You say, dear E——, that you often wish I would chat on paper, as you do. How can I? Where are my materials? Is my life fertile in subjects of chat? What callers do I see? What visits do I pay? No, you must chat, and I must listen, and say "Yes," and "No," and "Thank you!" for five minutes' recreation.

\*     \*     \*     \*     \*

'I am amused at the interest you take in politics. Don't expect to rouse me; to me, all ministries and all oppositions seem to be pretty much alike. D'Israeli was factious as leader of the Opposition; Lord John Russell is going to be factious, now that he has stepped into D'Israeli's shoes. Lord Derby's "Christian love and spirit," is worth three half-pence farthing.'*

TO W. S. WILLIAMS, ESQ.

'March 25th, 1852.

'My dear Sir,—Mr Smith intimated a short time since, that he had some thoughts of publishing a reprint of "Shirley."* Having revised the work, I now enclose the errata. I have likewise sent off to-day, per rail, a return-box of Cornhill books.

'I have lately read with great pleasure, "The Two Families."* This work, it seems, should have reached me in January; but owing to a mistake, it was detained at the Dead Letter Office, and lay there nearly two months. I liked the commencement very much; the close seemed to me scarcely equal to "Rose Douglas." I thought the authoress committed a mistake in shifting the main interest from the two personages on whom it first rests—viz., Ben Wilson and Mary—to other characters of quite inferior conception. Had she made Ben and Mary her hero and heroine, and continued the development of their fortunes and characters in the same truthful natural vein in which she commences it, an excellent, even an original, book might have been the result. As for Lilias and Ronald, they are mere romantic figments, with nothing of the genuine Scottish peasant about them; they do not even speak the Caledonian dialect; they palaver like a fine lady and gentleman.

'I ought long since to have acknowledged the gratification with which I read Miss Kavanagh's "Women of Christianity."* Her charity and (on the whole) her impartiality are very beautiful. She touches, indeed, with too gentle a hand the theme of Elizabeth of Hungary; and, in her own mind, she evidently misconstrues the fact of Protestant charities *seeming* to be fewer than Catholic. She forgets, or does not know, that Protestantism is a quieter creed than Romanism; as it does not clothe its priesthood in scarlet, so neither does it set up its good women for saints, canonise their names, and proclaim their good works. In the records of man, their almsgiving will not perhaps be found registered, but Heaven has its account as well as earth.

'With kind regards to yourself and family, who, I trust, have all safely weathered the rough winter lately past, as well as the east winds, which are still nipping our spring in Yorkshire,—I am, my dear Sir, yours sincerely,

'C. BRONTË.'

'My dear Sir,—The box arrived quite safely, and I very much thank you for the contents, which are most kindly selected.

'As you wished me to say what I thought of "The School for Fathers,"* I hastened to read it. The book seems to me clever, interesting, very amusing, and likely to please generally. There is a merit in the choice of ground, which is not yet too hackneyed; the comparative freshness of subject, character, and epoch give the tale a certain attractiveness. There is also, I think, a graphic rendering of situations, and a lively talent for describing whatever is visible and tangible—what the eye meets on the surface of things. The humour appears to me such as would answer well on the stage; most of the scenes seem to demand dramatic accessories to give them their full effect. But I think one cannot with justice bestow higher praise than this. To speak candidly, I felt, in reading the tale, a wondrous hollowness in the moral and sentiment; a strange dilettante shallowness in the purpose and feeling. After all, "Jack" is not much better than a "Tony Lumpkin," and there is no very great breadth of choice between the clown he *is* and the fop his father would have made him. The grossly material life of the old English fox-hunter, and the frivolous existence of the fine gentleman present extremes, each in its way so repugnant, that one feels half inclined to smile when called upon to sentimentalise over the lot of a youth forced to pass from one to the other; torn from the stables, to be ushered perhaps into the ball-room. Jack dies mournfully indeed, and you are sorry for the poor fellow's untimely end; but you cannot forget that if he had not been thrust into the way of Colonel Penruddock's weapon, he might possibly have broken his neck in a fox-hunt. The character of Sir Thomas Warren is excellent; consistent throughout. That of Mr Addison not bad, but sketchy, a mere outline—wanting colour and finish. The man's portrait is there, and his costume, and fragmentary anecdotes of his life; but where is the man's nature—soul and self? I say nothing about the female characters—not one word; only that Lydia seems to me like a pretty little actress, prettily dressed, gracefully appearing and disappearing and reappearing in a genteel comedy, assuming the proper sentiments of her part with all due tact and naïveté, and—that is all.

'Your description of the model man of business is true enough,
I doubt not; but we will not fear that society will ever be brought
quite to this standard; human nature (bad as it is) has, after all,
elements that forbid it. But the very tendency to such a consum-
mation—the marked tendency, I fear, of the day—produces, no
doubt, cruel suffering. Yet, when the evil of competition passes a
certain limit, must it not in time work its own cure? I suppose it
will, but then through some convulsed crisis, shattering all around
it like an earthquake. Meantime, for how many is life made a
struggle; enjoyment and rest curtailed; labour terribly enhanced
beyond almost what nature can bear! I often think that this world
would be the most terrible of enigmas, were it not for the firm
belief that there is a world to come, where conscientious effort and
patient pain will meet their reward.—Believe me, my dear Sir,
sincerely yours,

'C. BRONTË.'

A letter to her old Brussels schoolfellow gives a short retrospect
of the dreary winter she had passed through.

'Haworth, April 12th, 1852.*

'. . . . . . I struggled through the winter, and the early part of the
spring, often with great difficulty. My friend stayed with me a few
days in the early part of January; she could not be spared longer.
I was better during her visit, but had a relapse soon after she left
me, which reduced my strength very much. It cannot be denied
that the solitude of my position fearfully aggravated its other evils.
Some long stormy days and nights there were, when I felt such a
craving for support and companionship as I cannot express.
Sleepless, I lay awake night after night, weak and unable to occupy
myself. I sat in my chair day after day, the saddest memories my
only company. It was a time I shall never forget; but God sent it,
and it must have been for the best.

'I am better now; and very grateful do I feel for the restoration
of tolerable health; but, as if there was always to be some affliction,
Papa, who enjoyed wonderful health during the whole winter, is
ailing with his spring attack of bronchitis. I earnestly trust it may
pass over in the comparatively ameliorated form in which it has
hitherto shown itself.

'Let me not forget to answer your question about the cataract. Tell your papa that *my* father was seventy at the time he underwent an operation; he was most reluctant to try the experiment; could not believe that, at his age, and with his want of robust strength, it would succeed. I was obliged to be very decided in the matter, and to act entirely on my own responsibility. Nearly six years have now elapsed since the cataract was extracted (it was not merely depressed); he has never once during that time regretted the step, and a day seldom passes that he does not express gratitude and pleasure at the restoration of that inestimable privilege of vision whose loss he once knew.'

I had given Miss Brontë, in one of my letters, an outline of the story on which I was then engaged, and in reply she says:—*

'The sketch you give of your work* (respecting which I am, of course, dumb) seems to me very noble; and its purpose may be as useful in practical result as it is high and just in theoretical tendency. Such a book may restore hope and energy to many who thought they had forfeited their right to both; and open a clear course for honourable effort to some who deemed that they and all honour had parted company in this world.

'Yet—hear my protest!

'Why should she die? Why are we to shut up the book weeping?

'My heart fails me already at the thought of the pang it will have to undergo. And yet you must follow the impulse of your own inspiration. If *that* commands the slaying of the victim, no bystander has a right to put out his hand to stay the sacrificial knife: but I hold you a stern priestess in these matters.'

As the milder weather came on, her health improved, and her power of writing increased. She set herself with redoubled vigour to the work before her; and denied herself pleasure for the purpose of steady labour. Hence she writes to her friend:—

'May 11th.*

'Dear E——,—I must adhere to my resolution of neither visiting nor being visited at present. Stay you quietly at B., till you go to S., as I shall stay at Haworth; as sincere a farewell can be taken

with the heart as with the lips, and perhaps less painful. I am glad
the weather is changed; the return of the south-west wind suits me;
but I hope you have no cause to regret the departure of your
favourite east wind.\* .... I read in a French book\* lately, a
sentence to this effect, that "marriage might be defined as the state
of two-fold selfishness." Let the single therefore take comfort.
Thank you for Mary's letter. She *does* seem most happy; and I
cannot tell you how much more real, lasting, and better-warranted
her happiness seems than ever ——'s did. I think so much of it is
in herself, and her own serene, pure, trusting, religious nature.
——'s always gives me the idea of a vacillating, unsteady rapture,
entirely dependent on circumstances with all their fluctuations. If
Mary lives to be a mother, you will then see a greater difference.

'I wish you, dear E., all health and enjoyment in your visit; and,
as far as one can judge at present, there seems a fair prospect of
the wish being realised.

'Yours faithfully,
'C. Brontë.'

# CHAPTER XI

THE reader will remember that Anne Brontë had been interred in the churchyard of the Old Church at Scarborough. Charlotte had left directions for a tombstone to be placed over her; but many a time during the solitude of the past winter, her sad, anxious thoughts had revisited the scene of that last great sorrow, and she had wondered whether all decent services had been rendered to the memory of the dead, until at last she came to a silent resolution to go and see for herself whether the stone and inscription were in a satisfactory state of preservation.

'Cliffe House, Filey, June 6th, 1852.

'Dear E——, —I am at Filey utterly alone. Do not be angry, the step is right. I considered it, and resolved on it with due deliberation. Change of air was necessary; there were reasons why I should *not* go to the south, and why I should come here. On Friday I went to Scarborough, visited the churchyard and stone.* It must be refaced and relettered; there are five errors. I gave the necessary directions. *That* duty, then, is done; long has it lain heavy on my mind; and that was a pilgrimage I felt I could only make alone.

'I am in our old lodgings at Mrs Smith's; not, however, in the same rooms, but in less expensive apartments. They seemed glad to see me, remembered you and me very well, and, seemingly, with great good will. The daughter who used to wait on us is just married. Filey seems to me much altered; more lodging-houses— some of them very handsome—have been built; the sea has all its old grandeur. I walk on the sands a good deal, and try *not* to feel desolate and melancholy. How sorely my heart longs for you, I need not say. I have bathed once; it seemed to do me good. I may, perhaps, stay here a fortnight. There are as yet scarcely any visitors. A Lady Wenlock is staying at the large house of which you used so vigilantly to observe the inmates. One day I set out with intent to trudge to Filey Bridge, but was frightened back by two cows. I mean to try again some morning. I left Papa well. I have been a good deal troubled with headache, and with some pain in the side since I came here, but I feel that this has been owing to the cold wind, for very cold has it been till lately; at present I feel better. Shall I send the papers to you as usual? Write again directly, and tell me this, and anything and everything else that comes into your mind.

'Believe me, yours faithfully,

'C. BRONTË.'

'Filey, June 16th, 1852.

'Dear E——, —Be quite easy about me. I really think I am better for my stay at Filey; that I have derived more benefit from it than I dared to anticipate. I believe, could I stay here two months, and enjoy something like social cheerfulness as well as exercise and good air, my health would be quite renewed. This, however, cannot possibly be; but I am most thankful for the good received. I stay here another week.

'I return ——'s letter.* I am sorry for her: I believe she suffers; but I do not much like her style of expressing herself. . . . . Grief as well as joy manifests itself in most different ways in different people; and I doubt not she is sincere and in earnest when she talks of her "precious, sainted father;" but I could wish she used simpler language.'

Soon after her return from Filey, she was alarmed by a very serious and sharp attack of illness with which Mr Brontë was seized. There was some fear, for a few days, that his sight was permanently lost, and his spirits sank painfully under this dread.

'This prostration of spirits,' writes his daughter,* 'which accompanies anything like a relapse, is almost the most difficult point to manage. Dear E——, you are tenderly kind in offering your society; but rest very tranquil where you are; be fully assured that it is not now, nor under present circumstances, that I feel the lack either of society or occupation; my time is pretty well filled up, and my thoughts appropriated. . . . . I cannot permit myself to comment much on the chief contents of your last; advice is not necessary: as far as I can judge, you seem hitherto enabled to take these trials in a good and wise spirit. I can only pray that such combined strength and resignation may be continued to you.

Submission, courage, exertion, when practicable—these seem to be the weapons with which we must fight life's long battle.'

I suppose that, during the very time when her thoughts were thus fully occupied with anxiety for her father, she received some letter from her publishers, making inquiry as to the progress of the work which they knew she had in hand, as I find the following letter to Mr Williams, bearing reference to some of Messrs Smith and Elder's proposed arrangements.

TO W. S. WILLIAMS, ESQ.

'July 28th, 1852.

'My dear Sir,—Is it in contemplation to publish the new edition of "Shirley" soon? Would it not be better to defer it for a time? In reference to a part of your letter, permit me to express this wish,—and I trust that in doing so, I shall not be regarded as stepping out of my position as an author, and encroaching on the arrangements of business,—viz.: that no announcement of a new work by the author of "Jane Eyre" shall be made till the MS of such work is actually in my publisher's hands. Perhaps we are none of us justified in speaking very decidedly where the future is concerned; but for some too much caution in such calculations can scarcely be observed: amongst this number I must class myself. Nor, in doing so, can I assume an apologetic tone. He does right who does his best.

'Last autumn I got on for a time quickly. I ventured to look forward to spring as the period of publication: my health gave way; I passed such a winter as, having been once experienced, will never be forgotten. The spring proved little better than a protraction of trial. The warm weather and a visit to the sea have done me much good physically; but as yet I have recovered neither elasticity of animal spirits, nor flow of the power of composition. And if it were otherwise, the difference would be of no avail; my time and thoughts are at present taken up with close attendance on my father, whose health is just now in a very critical state, the heat of the weather having produced determination of blood to the head.

'I am, yours sincerely,

'C. BRONTË.'

Before the end of August, Mr Brontë's convalescence became quite established, and he was anxious to resume his duties for some time before his careful daughter would permit him.

On September the 14th, the 'great duke'* died. He had been, as we have seen, her hero from childhood; but I find no further reference to him at this time than what is given in the following extract from a letter to her friend:—*

'I do hope and believe the changes you have been having this summer will do you permanent good, notwithstanding the pain with which they have been too often mingled. Yet I feel glad that you are soon coming home; and I really must not trust myself to say how much I wish the time were come when, without let or hindrance, I could once more welcome you to Haworth. But oh! I don't get on; I feel fretted—incapable—sometimes very low. However, at present, the subject must not be dwelt upon; it presses me too hardly—nearly—and painfully. Less than ever can I taste or know pleasure till this work is wound up. And yet I often sit up in bed at night, thinking of and wishing for you. Thank you for the "Times;" what it said on the mighty and mournful subject was *well* said. All at once the whole nation seems to take a just view of that great character. There was a review too of an American book, which I was glad to see. Read "Uncle Tom's Cabin:" probably, though, you have read it.

'Papa's health continues satisfactory, thank God! As for me, my wretched liver had been disordered again of late, but I hope it is now going to be on better behaviour; it hinders me in working— depresses both power and tone of feeling. I must expect this derangement from time to time.'

Haworth was in an unhealthy state, as usual; and both Miss Brontë and Tabby suffered severely from the prevailing epidemics. The former was long in shaking off the effects of this illness. In vain she resolved against allowing herself any society or change of scene until she had accomplished her labour. She was too ill to write; and with illness came on the old heaviness of heart, recollections of the past, and anticipations of the future. At last Mr Brontë expressed so strong a wish that her friend should be asked to visit her and she felt some little refreshment so absolutely necessary, that on October the 9th she begged her to come to Haworth, just for a single week.

'I thought I would persist in denying myself till I had done my work, but I find it won't do; the matter refuses to progress, and this excessive solitude presses too heavily; so let me see your dear face, E., just for one reviving week.'

But she would only accept of the company of her friend for the exact time specified. She thus writes to Miss W—— on October the 21st:—

'E—— has only been my companion one little week. I would not have her any longer, for I am disgusted with myself and my delays; and consider it was a weak yielding to temptation in me to send for her at all; but in truth, my spirits were getting low—prostrate sometimes—and she has done me inexpressible good. I wonder when I shall see you at Haworth again; both my father and the servants have again and again insinuated a distinct wish that you should be requested to come in the course of the summer and autumn, but I have always turned rather a deaf ear; "not yet," was my thought, "I want first to be free;" work first, then pleasure.'

Miss ——'s visit had done her much good. Pleasant companionship during the day produced, for the time, the unusual blessing of calm repose at night; and, after her friend's departure, she was well enough to 'fall to business,'* and write away, almost incessantly, at her story of 'Villette,' now drawing to a conclusion. The following letter to Mr Smith seems to have accompanied the first part of the MS.

'Oct. 30th, 1852.

'My dear Sir,—You must notify honestly what you think of "Villette" when you have read it. I can hardly tell you how I hunger to hear some opinion besides my own, and how I have sometimes desponded, and almost despaired, because there was no one to whom to read a line, or of whom to ask a counsel. "Jane Eyre" was not written under such circumstances, nor were two-thirds of "Shirley." I got so miserable about it, I could bear no allusion to the book. It is not finished yet; but now I hope. As to the anonymous publication,* I have this to say: If the withholding of the author's name should tend materially to injure the publisher's interest, to interfere with booksellers' orders, &c., I would not press the point; but if no such detriment is contingent, I should be most thankful for the sheltering shadow of an incognito. I seem to dread the advertisements—the large-lettered "Currer Bell's New Novel," or "New Work, by the Author of Jane Eyre." These, however, I feel well enough, are the transcendentalisms of a retired wretch; so you must speak frankly. . . . . I shall be glad to see "Colonel Esmond." My objection to the second volume lay here: I thought it contained decidedly too much History—too little Story.'

In another letter, referring to 'Esmond,' she uses the following words:—*

'The third volume seemed to me to possess the most sparkle, impetus, and interest. Of the first and second my judgment was, that parts of them were admirable; but there was the fault of containing too much History—too little Story. I hold that a work of fiction ought to be a work of creation: that the *real* should be sparingly introduced in pages dedicated to the *ideal*. Plain household bread is a far more wholesome and necessary thing than cake; yet who would like to see the brown loaf placed on the table for dessert? In the second volume, the author gives us an ample supply of excellent brown bread; in his third, only such a portion as gives substance, like the crumbs of bread in a well-made, not too rich, plum-pudding.'

Her letter to Mr Smith, containing the allusion to 'Esmond,' which reminded me of the quotation just given, continues:—

'You will see that "Villette" touches on no matter of public interest. I cannot write books handling the topics of the day; it is of no use trying. Nor can I write a book for its moral. Nor can I take up a philanthropic scheme, though I honour philanthropy; and voluntarily and sincerely veil my face before such a mighty subject as that handled in Mrs Beecher Stowe's work, "Uncle

Tom's Cabin." To manage these great matters rightly, they must be long and practically studied—their bearings known intimately, and their evils felt genuinely; they must not be taken up as a business matter, and a trading speculation. I doubt not, Mrs Stowe had felt the iron of slavery enter into her heart, from childhood upwards, long before she ever thought of writing books. The feeling throughout her work is sincere, and not got up. Remember to be an honest critic of "Villette," and tell Mr Williams to be unsparing: not that I am likely to alter anything, but I want to know his impressions and yours.'

TO G. SMITH, ESQ.

'Nov. 3rd.

'My dear Sir,—I feel very grateful for your letter; it relieved me much, for I was a good deal harassed by doubts as to how "Villette" might appear in other eyes than my own. I feel in some degree authorised to rely on your favourable impressions, because you are quite right where you hint disapprobation. You have exactly hit two points at least where I was conscious of defect;—the discrepancy, the want of perfect harmony, between Graham's boyhood and manhood,—the angular abruptness of his change of sentiment towards Miss Fanshawe. You must remember, though, that in secret he had for some time appreciated that young lady at a somewhat depressed standard—held her a *little* lower than the angels.* But still the reader ought to have been better made to feel this preparation towards a change of mood. As to the publishing arrangements, I leave them to Cornhill. There is, undoubtedly, a certain force in what you say about the inexpediency of affecting a mystery which cannot be sustained; so you must act as you think is for the best. I submit, also, to the advertisements in large letters, but under protest, and with a kind of ostrich-longing for conceal-ment. Most of the third volume is given to the development of the "crabbed Professor's" character. Lucy must not marry Dr John; he is far too youthful, handsome, bright-spirited, and sweet-tem-pered; he is a "curled darling"* of Nature and of Fortune, and must draw a prize in life's lottery. His wife must be young, rich, pretty; he must be made very happy indeed. If Lucy marries anybody, it must be the Professor—a man in whom there is much to forgive, much to "put up with." But I am not leniently disposed towards Miss *Frost:* from the beginning, I never meant to appoint her lines in pleasant places.* The conclusion of this third volume is still a matter of some anxiety: I can but do my best, however. It would speedily be finished, could I ward off certain obnoxious headaches, which, whenever I get into the spirit of my work, are apt to seize and prostrate me......

'Colonel Henry Esmond is just arrived. He looks very antique and distinguished in his Queen Anne's garb;* the periwig, sword, lace, and ruffles are very well represented by the old "Spectator" type.'

In reference to a sentence towards the close of this letter, I may mention what she told me; that Mr Brontë was anxious that her new tale should end well, as he disliked novels which left a melancholy impression upon the mind; and he requested her to make her hero and heroine (like the heroes and heroines in fairy-tales) 'marry, and live very happily ever after.' But the idea of M. Paul Emanuel's death at sea was stamped on her imagination, till it assumed the distinct force of reality; and she could no more alter her fictitious ending than if they had been facts which she was relating. All she could do in compliance with her father's wish was so to veil the fate in oracular words, as to leave it to the character and discernment of her readers to interpret her meaning.

TO W. S. WILLIAMS, ESQ.

'Nov. 6th, 1852.

'My dear Sir,—I must not delay thanking you for your kind letter, with its candid and able commentary on "Villette." With many of your strictures I concur. The third volume may, perhaps, do away with some of the objections; others will remain in force. I do not think the interest culminates anywhere to the degree you would wish. What climax there is does not come on till near the conclusion; and even then, I doubt whether the regular novel- reader will consider the "agony piled sufficiently high" (as the Americans say), or the colours dashed on to the canvass with the proper amount of daring. Still, I fear, they must be satisfied with what is offered: my palette affords no brighter tints; were I to attempt to deepen the reds, or burnish the yellows, I should but botch.

'Unless I am mistaken, the emotion of the book will be found to be kept throughout in tolerable subjection. As to the name of the heroine, I can hardly express what subtility of thought made me decide upon giving her a cold name; but, at first, I called her "Lucy Snowe" (spelt with an "e"); which Snowe I afterwards changed to "Frost." Subsequently, I rather regretted the change, and wished it "Snowe" again. If not too late, I should like the alteration to be made now throughout the MS. A *cold* name she must have; partly, perhaps, on the *"lucus a non lucendo"** principle—partly on that of the "fitness of things," for she has about her an external coldness.

'You say that she may be thought morbid and weak, unless the history of her life be more fully given. I consider that she *is* both morbid and weak at times; her character sets up no pretensions to unmixed strength, and anybody living her life would necessarily become morbid. It was no impetus of healthy feeling which urged her to the confessional,* for instance; it was the semi-delirium of solitary grief and sickness. If, however, the book does not express all this, there must be a great fault somewhere. I might explain away a few other points, but it would be too much like drawing a picture and then writing underneath the name of the object intended to be represented. We know what sort of a pencil* that is which needs an ally in the pen.

'Thanking you again for the clearness and fulness with which you have responded to my request for a statement of impressions, I am, my dear Sir, yours very sincerely,

'C. BRONTË.'

'I trust the work will be seen in MS by no one except Mr Smith and yourself.'

'Nov. 10th, 1852.*

'My dear Sir,—I only wished the publication of "Shirley" to be delayed till "Villette" was nearly ready;* so that there can now be no objection to its being issued whenever you think fit. About putting the MS into type, I can only say that, should I be able to proceed with the third volume at my average rate of composition, and with no more than the average amount of interruptions, I should hope to have it ready in about three weeks. I leave it to you to decide whether it would be better to delay the printing that space of time, or to commence it immediately.* It would certainly be more satisfactory if you were to see the third volume before printing the first and the second; yet, if delay is likely to prove injurious, I do not think it is indispensable. I have read the third volume of "Esmond." I found it both entertaining and exciting to me; it seems to possess an impetus and excitement beyond the other two,—that movement and brilliancy its predecessors sometimes wanted, never fails here. In certain passages, I thought Thackeray used all his powers; their grand, serious force yielded a profound satisfaction. "At last he puts forth his strength," I could not help saying to myself. No character in the book strikes me as more masterly than that of Beatrix; its conception is fresh, and its delineation vivid. It is peculiar; it has impressions of a new kind—new, at least, to me. Beatrix is not, in herself, all bad. So much does she sometimes reveal of what is good and great as to suggest this feeling—you would think she was urged by a fate. You would think that some antique doom presses on her house, and that once in so many generations its brightest ornament was to become its greatest disgrace. At times, what is good in her struggles against this terrible destiny, but the Fate conquers. Beatrix cannot be an honest woman and a good man's wife. She "tries and she *cannot*."* Proud, beautiful, and sullied, she was born what she becomes, a king's mistress. I know not whether you have seen the notice in the "Leader;"* I read it just after concluding the book. Can I be wrong in deeming it a notice tame, cold, and insufficient? With all its professed friendliness, it produced on me a most disheartening impression. Surely, another sort of justice than this will be rendered to "Esmond" from other quarters. One acute remark of the critic is to the effect that Blanche Amory and Beatrix are identical—sketched from the same original! To me they are about as identical as a weazel and a royal tigress of Bengal; both the latter are quadrupeds,—both the former, women. But I must not take up either your time or my own with further remarks. Believe me yours sincerely,

'C. Brontë.,

On a Saturday, a little later in this month, Miss Brontë completed 'Villette,' and sent it off to her publishers.* 'I said my prayers when I had done it. Whether it is well or ill done, I don't know; D.V., I will now try and wait the issue quietly. The book, I think, will not be considered pretentious; nor is it of a character to excite hostility.'

As her labour was ended, she felt at liberty to allow herself a little change. There were several friends anxious to see her and welcome her to their homes: Miss Martineau, Mrs Smith, and her own faithful E——. With the last, in the same letter as that in which she announced the completion of 'Villette,' she offered to spend a week. She began, also, to consider whether it might not be well to avail herself of Mrs Smith's kind invitation, with a view to the convenience of being on the spot to correct the proofs.

The following letter is given, not merely on account of her own criticisms on 'Villette,' but because it shows how she had learned to magnify the meaning of trifles, as all do who live a self-contained and solitary life. Mr Smith had been unable to write by the same post as that which brought the money for 'Villette,' and she consequently received it without a line. The friend with whom she was staying says, that she immediately fancied there was some disappointment about 'Villette,' or that some word or act of hers had given offence; and had not the Sunday intervened,* and so allowed time for Mr Smith's letter to make its appearance, she would certainly have crossed it on her way to London.

'Dec. 6th, 1852.

'My dear Sir,—The receipts have reached me safely. I received the first on Saturday, enclosed in a cover without a line, and had made up my mind to take the train on Monday, and go up to London to see what was the matter, and what had struck my publisher mute. On Sunday morning your letter came, and you have thus been spared the visitation of the unannounced and unsummoned apparition of Currer Bell in Cornhill. Inexplicable delays should be avoided when possible, for they are apt to urge those subjected to their harassment to sudden and impulsive steps.

'I must pronounce you right again, in your complaint of the transfer of interest in the third volume, from one set of characters to another. It is not pleasant, and it will probably be found as unwelcome to the reader, as it was, in a sense, compulsory upon the writer. The spirit of romance would have indicated another

course, far more flowery and inviting; it would have fashioned a
paramount hero, kept faithfully with him, and made him supreme-
ly worshipful; he should have been an idol, and not a mute,
unresponding idol either; but this would have been unlike real
life—inconsistent with truth—at variance with probability. I greatly apprehend, however, that the weakest character in the book is
the one I aimed at making the most beautiful;* and, if this be the
case, the fault lies in its wanting the germ of the *real*—in its being
purely imaginary. I felt that this character lacked substance; I fear
that the reader will feel the same. Union with it resembles too
much the fate of Ixion, who was mated with a cloud.* The
childhood of Paulina is, however, I think, pretty well imagined, but
her. . . .' (the remainder of this interesting sentence is torn off the
letter). 'A brief visit to London becomes thus more practicable, and
if your mother will kindly write, when she has time, and name a
day after Christmas which will suit her, I shall have pleasure,
papa's health permitting, in availing myself of her invitation. I wish
I could come in time to correct some at least of the proofs; it would
save trouble.'

# CHAPTER XII

THE difficulty that presented itself most strongly to me, when I first had the honour of being requested to write this biography, was how I could show what a noble, true, and tender woman Charlotte Brontë really was, without mingling up with her life too much of the personal history of her nearest and most intimate friends. After much consideration of this point, I came to the resolution of writing truly, if I wrote at all; of withholding nothing, though some things, from their very nature, could not be spoken of so fully as others.

One of the deepest interests of her life centres naturally round her marriage, and the preceding circumstances; but more than all other events (because of more recent date, and concerning another as intimately as herself), it requires delicate handling on my part, lest I intrude too roughly on what is most sacred to memory. Yet I have two reasons, which seem to me good and valid ones, for giving some particulars of the course of events which led to her few months of wedded life—that short spell of exceeding happiness. The first is my desire to call attention to the fact that Mr Nicholls* was one who had seen her almost daily for years; seen her as a daughter, a sister, a mistress, and a friend. He was not a man to be attracted by any kind of literary fame. I imagine that this, by itself, would rather repel him when he saw it in the possession of a woman. He was a grave, reserved, conscientious man, with a deep sense of religion, and of his duties as one of its ministers.

In silence he had watched her, and loved her long. The love of such a man—a daily spectator of her manner of life for years—is a great testimony to her character as a woman.

How deep his affection was I scarcely dare to tell, even if I could in words. She did not know—she had hardly begun to suspect—that she was the object of any peculiar regard on his part, when, in this very December, he came one evening to tea.* After tea, she returned from the study to her own sitting-room, as was her custom, leaving her father and his curate together. Presently she heard the study-door open, and expected to hear the succeeding clash of the front door. Instead, came a tap; and, 'like lightning, it flashed upon me what was coming. He entered. He stood before me. What his words were you can imagine; his manner you can hardly realise, nor can I forget it. He made me, for the first time, feel what it costs a man to declare affection when he doubts response. . . . . The spectacle of one, ordinarily so statue-like, thus trembling, stirred, and overcome, gave me a strange shock. I could only entreat him to leave me then, and promise a reply on the morrow. I asked if he had spoken to Papa. He said he dared not. I think I half led, half put him out of the room.'

So deep, so fervent, and so enduring was the affection Miss Brontë had inspired in the heart of this good man! It is an honour to her; and, as such, I have thought it my duty to say thus much, and quote thus fully from her letter about it. And now I pass to my second reason for dwelling on a subject which may possibly be considered by some, at first sight, of too private a nature for publication. When Mr Nicholls had left her, Charlotte went immediately to her father and told him all. He always disapproved of marriages, and constantly talked against them. But he more than disapproved at this time; he could not bear the idea of this attachment of Mr Nicholls to his daughter.* Fearing the consequences of agitation to one so recently an invalid, she made haste to give her father a promise that, on the morrow, Mr Nicholls should have a distinct refusal. Thus quietly and modestly did she, on whom such hard judgments had been passed by ignorant reviewers, receive this vehement, passionate declaration of love,—thus thoughtfully for her father, and unselfishly for herself, put aside all consideration of how she should reply, excepting as he wished!

The immediate result of Mr Nicholls' declaration of attachment was, that he sent in his resignation of the curacy of Haworth; and that Miss Brontë held herself simply passive, as far as words and actions went, while she suffered acute pain from the strong expressions which her father used in speaking of Mr Nicholls, and from the too evident distress and failure of health on the part of the latter. Under these circumstances she, more gladly than ever, availed herself of Mrs Smith's proposal, that she should again visit them in London; and thither she accordingly went in the first week of the year 1853.

From thence I received the following letter. It is with a sad, proud pleasure I copy her words of friendship now.

'Jan. 12th, 1853.

'It is with *you* the ball rests. I have not heard from you since I wrote last; but I thought I knew the reason of your silence, viz. application to work,*—and therefore I accept it, not merely with resignation, but with satisfaction.

'I am now in London, as the date above will show;* staying very quietly at my publisher's, and correcting proofs, &c. Before receiving yours, I had felt, and expressed to Mr Smith, reluctance to come in the way of "Ruth;" not that I think *she* would suffer from contact with "Villette"—we know not but that the damage might be the other way; but I have ever held comparisons to be odious, and would fain that neither I nor my friends should be made subjects for the same. Mr Smith proposes, accordingly, to defer the publication of my book till the 24th inst.; he says that will give "Ruth" the start in the papers daily and weekly, and also will leave free to her all the February magazines. Should this delay appear to you insufficient, speak! and it shall be protracted.

'I dare say, arrange as we may, we shall not be able wholly to prevent comparisons; it is the nature of some critics to be invidious; but we need not care: we can set them at defiance; they *shall* not make us foes, they *shall* not mingle with our mutual feelings one taint of jealousy: there is my hand on that; I know you will give clasp for clasp.

' "Villette" has indeed no right to push itself before "Ruth." There is a goodness, a philanthropic purpose, a social use in the latter, to which the former cannot for an instant pretend; nor can it claim precedence on the ground of surpassing power: I think it much quieter than "Jane Eyre."

\*　　\*　　\*　　\*　　\*　　\*　　\*　　\*

'I wish to see *you*, probably at least as much as you can wish to see *me*, and therefore shall consider your invitation for March as an engagement; about the close of that month, then, I hope to pay you a brief visit. With kindest remembrances to Mr Gaskell and all your precious circle, I am,' &c.

This visit at Mrs Smith's was passed more quietly than any previous one, and was consequently more in accordance with Miss

Brontë's tastes. She saw things rather than persons; and being allowed to have her own choice of sights, she selected the '*real* in preference to the *decorative* side of life.'* She went over two prisons,—one ancient, the other modern,—Newgate and Penton-ville;* over two hospitals, the Foundling and Bethlehem. She was also taken, at her own request, to see several of the great City sights; the Bank, the Exchange, Rothschild's, &c.

The power of vast yet minute organisation always called out her respect and admiration. She appreciated it more fully than most women are able to do. All that she saw during this last visit to London impressed her deeply—so much so as to render her incapable of the immediate expression of her feelings, or of reasoning upon her impressions while they were so vivid. If she had lived, her deep heart would sooner or later have spoken out on these things.

What she saw dwelt in her thoughts, and lay heavy on her spirits. She received the utmost kindness from her hosts, and had the old, warm, and grateful regard for them. But looking back, with the knowledge of what was then the future, which Time has given, one cannot but imagine that there was a toning-down in prepara-tion for the final farewell to these kind friends, whom she saw for the last time on a Wednesday morning in February. She met her friend E—— at Keighley on her return, and the two proceeded to Haworth together.

### TO MARTHA BROWN.*

'Gloucester Terrace, London,
'Jan. 28th, 1853.

'Dear Martha,—If all be well, I hope to come home next Wednesday. I have asked Miss —— to come with me. We shall reach Haworth about half past four o'clock in the afternoon, and I know I can trust you to have things comfortable and in readiness. The table cloths had better be put on the dining-room tables; you will have something prepared that will do for supper,—perhaps a nice piece of cold boiled ham would be as well as anything, as it would come in for breakfast in the morning. The weather has been very changeable here in London. I have often wondered how you and Papa stood it at home; I felt the changes in some degree; but

not half so much as I should have done at Haworth, and have only
had one really bad day of headache and sickness since I came. I
hope you and Tabby have agreed pretty well, and that you have
got help in your work, whenever you have wanted it. Remember
me kindly to Tabby, and believe me, dear Martha,—Your sincere
friend,

'C. BRONTË.'

'Villette'—which, if less interesting as a mere story than 'Jane
Eyre,' displays yet more of the extraordinary genius of the
author—was received with one burst of acclamation. Out of so
small a circle of characters, dwelling in so dull and monotonous an
area as a 'pension,' this wonderful tale was evolved!

See how she receives the good tidings of her success!

'Feb. 15th, 1853.

'I got a budget of no less than seven papers yesterday and to-
day.* The import of all the notices is such as to make my heart
swell with thankfulness to Him who takes note both of suffering,
and work, and motives. Papa is pleased too. As to friends in
general, I believe I can love them still, without expecting them to
take any large share in this sort of gratification. The longer I live,
the more plainly I see that gentle must be the strain on fragile
human nature; it will not bear much.'

I suspect that the touch of slight disappointment, perceptible in
the last few lines, arose from her great susceptibility to an opinion
she valued much,—that of Miss Martineau, who, both in an article
on 'Villette' in the 'Daily News,' and in a private letter to Miss
Brontë, wounded her to the quick by expressions of censure which
she believed to be unjust and unfounded, but which, if correct and
true, went deeper than any merely artistic fault.* An author may
bring himself to believe that he can bear blame with equanimity,
from whatever quarter it comes; but its force is derived altogether
from the character of this. To the public, one reviewer may be the
same impersonal being as another; but an author has frequently a
far deeper significance to attach to opinions. They are the verdicts
of those whom he respects and admires, or the mere words of those
for whose judgment he cares not a jot. It is this knowledge of the

individual worth of the reviewer's opinion, which makes the censures of some sink so deep, and prey so heavily upon an author's heart. And thus, in proportion to her true, firm regard for Miss Martineau, did Miss Brontë suffer under what she considered her misjudgment not merely of writing, but of character.

She had long before asked Miss Martineau to tell her whether she considered that any want of womanly delicacy or propriety was betrayed in 'Jane Eyre.' And on receiving Miss Martineau's assurance that she did not, Miss Brontë entreated her to declare it frankly if she thought there was any failure of this description in any future work of 'Currer Bell's.' The promise then given of faithful truth-speaking, Miss Martineau fulfilled when 'Villette' appeared. Miss Brontë writhed under what she felt to be injustice.[1]

When 'Villette' was on the point of publication she wrote thus to Miss Martineau:—

'Jan. 21st, 1853.

'I know that you will give me your thoughts upon my book, as frankly as if you spoke to some near relative whose good you preferred to her gratification. I wince under the pain of condemnation,—like any other weak structure of flesh and blood; but I love, I honour, I kneel to truth. Let her smite me on the one cheek,—good! the tears may spring to the eyes; but courage! there is the other side, hit again, right sharply.'

'This,' as Miss Martineau observes, 'was the genuine spirit of the woman.'

---

[1] It is but due to Miss Martineau to give some of the particulars of this misunderstanding, as she has written them down for me. It appears that on Miss Brontë's first interview with Miss Martineau in December, 1849, she had expressed pleasure at being able to consult a friend about certain strictures of the reviewers, which she did not understand, and by which she had every desire to profit. 'She said that the reviews sometimes puzzled her, and that some imputed to her what made her think she must be very unlike other people, or cause herself to be misunderstood. She could not make it out at all, and wished that I could explain it. I had not seen that sort of criticism then, I think, but I had heard "Jane Eyre" called "coarse." I told her that love was treated with unusual breadth, and that the kind of intercourse was uncommon, and uncommonly described, but that I did *not* consider the book a coarse one, though I could not answer for it that there were no traits which, on a second leisurely reading, I might not dislike on that ground. She begged me to give it that second reading, and I did on condition that she would regard my criticisms as made through the eyes of her reviewers.'

Miss Martineau, in reply to this adjuration, wrote a letter, part
of which ran as follows:—

'As for the other side of the question which you so desire to
know, I have but one thing to say; but it is not a small one. I do
not like the love, either the kind or the degree of it; and its
prevalence in the book, and effect on the action of it, help to
explain the passages in the reviews which you consulted me about,
and seem to afford *some* foundation for the criticisms they offered.'

Miss Martineau has also allowed me to make use of the passage
referring to the same fault, real or supposed, in her notice of
'Villette' in the 'Daily News.'

'All the female characters, in all their thoughts and lives, are full
of one thing, or are regarded by the reader in the light of that one
thought,—love. It begins with the child of six years old, at the
opening,—a charming picture,—and it closes with it at the last
page; and so dominant is this idea—so incessant is the writer's
tendency to describe the need of being loved,—that the heroine,
who tells her own story, leaves the reader at last under the
uncomfortable impression of her having either entertained a double
love, or allowed one to supersede another without notification of
the transition.* It is not thus in real life. There are substantial,
heartfelt interests for women of all ages, and under ordinary
circumstances, quite apart from love: there is an absence of
introspection, an unconsciousness, a repose in women's lives,—unless under peculiarly unfortunate circumstances,—of which we find
no admission in this book; and to the absence of it may be
attributed some of the criticism which the book will meet with
from readers who are no prudes, but whose reason and taste will
reject the assumption that events and characters are to be regarded
through the medium of one passion only. And here ends all
demur,' &c.

This seems a fitting place to state how utterly unconscious she
was of what was, by some, esteemed coarse in her writings. One
day, during that visit at the Briery when I first met her, the
conversation turned upon the subject of women's writing fiction;
and some one remarked on the fact that, in certain instances,
authoresses had much outstepped the line which men felt to be
proper in works of this kind. Miss Brontë said she wondered how
far this was a natural consequence of allowing the imagination to

work too constantly; Sir James and Lady Kay Shuttleworth and I expressed our belief that such violations of propriety were altogether unconscious on the part of those to whom reference had been made. I remember her grave, earnest way of saying, 'I trust God will take from me whatever power of invention or expression I may have, before He lets me become blind to the sense of what is fitting or unfitting to be said!'

Again she was invariably shocked and distressed when she heard of any disapproval of 'Jane Eyre' on the ground above-mentioned. Some one said to her in London, 'You know, you and I, Miss Brontë, have both written naughty books!'* She dwelt much on this; and, as if it weighed on her mind, took an opportunity to ask Mrs Smith, as she would have asked a mother—if she had not been motherless from earliest childhood—whether, indeed, there was anything so wrong in 'Jane Eyre.'

I do not deny for myself the existence of coarseness here and there in her works, otherwise so entirely noble. I only ask those who read them to consider her life,—which has been openly laid bare before them,—and to say how it could be otherwise. She saw few men; and among these few were one or two with whom she had been acquainted since early girlhood,—who had shown her much friendliness and kindness,—through whose family she had received many pleasures,—for whose intellect she had a great respect,—but who talked before her, if not to her, with as little reticence as Rochester talked to Jane Eyre. Take this in connection with her poor brother's sad life, and the out-spoken people among whom she lived,—remember her strong feeling of the duty of representing life as it really is, not as it ought to be,—and then do her justice for all that she was, and all that she would have been (had God spared her), rather than censure her because circumstances forced her to touch pitch, as it were, and by it her hand was for a moment defiled. It was but skin-deep. Every change in her life was purifying her; it hardly could raise her. Again I cry, 'If she had but lived!'*

The misunderstanding with Miss Martineau on account of 'Villette,' was the cause of bitter regret to Miss Brontë. Her woman's nature had been touched, as she thought, with insulting misconception; and she had dearly loved the person who had thus unconsciously wounded her. It was but in the January just past that she had written as follows,* in reply to a friend, the tenor of whose letter we may guess from this answer:—

'I read attentively all you say about Miss Martineau; the sincerity and constancy of your solicitude touch me very much; I should grieve to neglect or oppose your advice, and yet I do not feel it would be right to give Miss Martineau up entirely. There is in her nature much that is very noble; hundreds have forsaken her[1], more, I fear, in the apprehension that their fair names may suffer, if seen in connection with hers, than from any pure convictions, such as you suggest, of harm consequent on her fatal tenets. With these fair-weather friends I cannot bear to rank; and for her sin, is it not one of those of which God and not man must judge?

'To speak the truth, my dear Miss ——, I believe, if you were in my place, and knew Miss Martineau as I do,—if you had shared with me the proofs of her genuine kindliness, and had seen how she secretly suffers from abandonment,—you would be the last to give her up; you would separate the sinner from the sin, and feel as if the right lay rather in quietly adhering to her in her strait, while that adherence is unfashionable and unpopular, than in turning on her your back when the world sets the example. I believe she is one of those whom opposition and desertion make obstinate in error; while patience and tolerance touch her deeply and keenly, and incline her to ask of her own heart whether the course she has been pursuing may not possibly be a faulty course.'

Kindly and faithful words! which Miss Martineau never knew of; to be repaid in words more grand and tender, when Charlotte lay deaf and cold by her dead sisters.* In spite of their short, sorrowful misunderstanding, they were a pair of noble women and faithful friends.

I turn to a pleasanter subject. While she was in London, Miss Brontë had seen Lawrence's portrait of Mr Thackeray,* and admired it extremely. Her first words, after she had stood before it some time in silence, were, 'And there came up a Lion out of

[1] In reference to this passage, Miss Martineau writes thus:—'There is the unaccountable delusion that I was "deserted" on account of the Atkinson Letters.... Facts are best; so I will only say that I am not aware of having lost any friends whatever by that book, while I have gained a new world of sympathy.'

Judah!' The likeness was by this time engraved, and Mr Smith sent her a copy of it.

TO G. SMITH, ESQ.

'Haworth, Feb. 26th, 1853.

'My dear Sir,—At a late hour yesterday evening, I had the honour of receiving, at Haworth Parsonage, a distinguished guest, none other than W. M. Thackeray, Esq. Mindful of the rites of hospitality, I hung him up in state this morning. He looks superb in his beautiful, tasteful gilded gibbet. For companion he has the Duke of Wellington, (do you remember giving me that picture?) and for contrast and foil Richmond's portrait of an unworthy individual who, in such society, must be nameless. Thackeray looks away from the latter character with a grand scorn, edifying to witness. I wonder if the giver of these gifts will ever see them on the walls where they now hang; it pleases me to fancy that one day he may. My father stood for a quarter of an hour this morning examining the great man's picture. The conclusion of his survey was, that he thought it a puzzling head; if he had known nothing previously of the original's character, he could not have read it in his features. I wonder at this. To me the broad brow seems to express intellect. Certain lines about the nose and cheek betray the satirist and cynic; the mouth indicates a child-like simplicity—perhaps even a degree of irresoluteness, inconsistency—weakness in short, but a weakness not unamiable. The engraving seems to me very good. A certain not quite Christian expression—"not to put too fine a point upon it"—an expression of *spite*, most vividly marked in the original, is here softened, and perhaps a little—a very little—of the power has escaped in this ameliorating process. Did it strike you thus?'

Miss Brontë was in much better health during this winter of 1852–3, than she had been the year before.

'For my part,' (she wrote to me in February)* 'I have thus far borne the cold weather well. I have taken long walks on the crackling snow, and felt the frosty air bracing. This winter has, for me, not been like last winter. December, January, February, '51–2, passed like a long stormy night, conscious of one painful dream, all solitary grief and sickness. The corresponding months in '52–3 have gone over my head quietly and not uncheerfully. Thank God for the change and the repose! How welcome it has been He only knows! My father too has borne the season well; and my book and its reception thus far, have pleased and cheered him.'

In March the quiet Parsonage had the honour of receiving a visit from the then Bishop of Ripon.* He remained one night with Mr Brontë. In the evening, some of the neighbouring clergy were invited to meet him at tea and supper; and during the latter meal, some of the 'curates' began merrily to upbraid Miss Brontë with 'putting them into a book;'* and she, shrinking from thus having her character as authoress thrust upon her at her own table, and in the presence of a stranger, pleasantly appealed to the Bishop as to whether it was quite fair thus to drive her into a corner. His Lordship, I have been told, was agreeably impressed with the gentle unassuming manners of his hostess, and with the perfect propriety and consistency of the arrangements in the modest household. So much for the Bishop's recollection of his visit. Now we will turn to hers.

'March 4th.

'The Bishop has been, and is gone. He is certainly a most charming Bishop; the most benignant gentleman that ever put on lawn sleeves; yet stately too, and quite competent to check encroachments. His visit passed capitally well; and at its close, as he was going away, he expressed himself thoroughly gratified with all he had seen. The Inspector* has been also in the course of the past week; so that I have had a somewhat busy time of it. If you could have been at Haworth to share the pleasures of the company, without having been inconvenienced by the little bustle of the preparation, I should have been *very* glad. But the house was a good deal put out of its way, as you may suppose; all passed, however, orderly, quietly, and well. Martha waited very nicely, and I had a person to help her in the kitchen. Papa kept up, too, fully as well as I expected, though I doubt whether he could have borne another day of it. My penalty came on in a strong headache as soon as the Bishop was gone: how thankful I was that it had patiently waited his departure! I continue stupid to-day: of course, it is the re-action consequent on several days of extra exertion and excitement. It is very well to talk of receiving a Bishop without trouble, but you *must* prepare for him.'

By this time, some of the Reviews had begun to find fault with 'Villette.'* Miss Brontë made her old request.

TO W. S. WILLIAMS, ESQ.*

'My dear Sir,—Were a review to appear, inspired with treble their animus, *pray* do not withhold it from me. I like to see the satisfactory notices,—especially I like to carry them to my father; but I *must* see such as are *un*satisfactory and hostile; these are for my own especial edification;—it is in these I best read public feeling and opinion. To shun examination into the dangerous and disagreeable seems to me cowardly. I long always to know what really *is*, and am only unnerved when kept in the dark. . . . . . . . .

'As to the character of "Lucy Snowe," my intention from the first was that she should not occupy the pedestal to which "Jane Eyre" was raised by some injudicious admirers. She is where I meant her to be, and where no charge of self-laudation can touch her.

'The note you sent this morning from Lady Harriette St Clair, is precisely to the same purport as Miss Mulock's request,*—an application for exact and authentic information respecting the fate of M. Paul Emanuel! You see how much the ladies think of this little man, whom you none of you like. I had a letter the other day, announcing that a lady of some note, who had always determined that whenever she married, her husband should be the counterpart of "Mr Knightley" in Miss Austen's "Emma," had now changed her mind, and vowed that she would either find the duplicate of Professor Emanuel, or remain for ever single! I have sent Lady Harriette an answer so worded as to leave the matter pretty much where it was. Since the little puzzle amuses the ladies, it would be a pity to spoil their sport by giving them the key.'

When Easter, with its duties arising out of sermons to be preached by strange clergymen who had afterwards to be entertained at the Parsonage,—with Mechanics' Institute Meetings, and school tea-drinkings, was over and gone, she came, at the close of April, to visit us in Manchester.* We had a friend, a young lady, staying with us. Miss Brontë had expected to find us alone; and although our friend was gentle and sensible after Miss Brontë's own heart, yet her presence was enough to create a nervous tremor. I was aware that both of our guests were unusually silent; and I saw a little shiver run from time to time over Miss Brontë's frame. I could account for the modest reserve of the young lady; and the next day Miss Brontë told me how the unexpected sight of a strange face had affected her.

It was now two or three years since I had witnessed a similar effect produced on her, in anticipation of a quiet evening at Fox-How; and since then she had seen many and various people in London: but the physical sensations produced by shyness were still the same; and on the following day she laboured under severe headache. I had several opportunities of perceiving how this nervousness was ingrained in her constitution, and how acutely she suffered in striving to overcome it. One evening we had, among other guests, two sisters who sang Scottish ballads exquisitely. Miss Brontë had been sitting quiet and constrained till they began 'The Bonnie House of Airlie,'* but the effect of that and 'Carlisle Yetts,' which followed, was as irresistible as the playing of the Piper of Hamelin. The beautiful clear light came into her eyes; her lips quivered with emotion; she forgot herself, rose, and crossed the room to the piano, where she asked eagerly for song after song. The sisters begged her to come and see them the next morning, when they would sing as long as ever she liked; and she promised gladly and thankfully. But on reaching the house her courage failed. We walked some time up and down the street; she upbraiding herself all the while for folly, and trying to dwell on the sweet echoes in her memory rather than on the thought of a third sister who would have to be faced if we went in. But it was of no use; and dreading lest this struggle with herself might bring on one of her trying headaches, I entered at last and made the best apology I could for her non-appearance. Much of this nervous dread of encountering strangers I ascribed to the idea of her personal ugliness, which had been strongly impressed upon her imagination early in life, and which she exaggerated to herself in a remarkable manner.* 'I notice,' said she, 'that after a stranger has once looked

at my face, he is careful not to let his eyes wander to that part of
the room again!' A more untrue idea never entered into anyone's
head. Two gentlemen who saw her during this visit, without
knowing at the time who she was, were singularly attracted by her
appearance; and this feeling of attraction towards a pleasant
countenance, sweet voice, and gentle timid manners, was so strong
in one as to conquer a dislike he had previously entertained to her
works.

There was another circumstance that came to my knowledge at
this period which told secrets about the finely-strung frame. One
night I was on the point of relating some dismal ghost story,* just
before bed-time. She shrank from hearing it, and confessed that
she was superstitious, and prone at all times to the involuntary
recurrence of any thoughts of ominous gloom which might have
been suggested to her. She said that on first coming to us, she had
found a letter on her dressing-table from a friend in Yorkshire,
containing a story which had impressed her vividly ever since;—
that it mingled with her dreams at night, and made her sleep
restless and unrefreshing.

One day we asked two gentlemen to meet her at dinner,*
expecting that she and they would have a mutual pleasure in
making each other's acquaintance. To our disappointment, she
drew back with timid reserve from all their advances, replying to
their questions and remarks in the briefest manner possible; till at
last they gave up their efforts to draw her into conversation in
despair, and talked to each other and my husband on subjects of
recent local interest. Among these Thackeray's Lectures (which
had lately been delivered in Manchester) were spoken of, and that
on Fielding especially dwelt upon. One gentleman objected to it
strongly, as calculated to do moral harm, and regretted that a man
having so great an influence over the tone of thought of the day,
as Thackeray, should not more carefully weigh his words. The
other took the opposite view. He said that Thackeray described
men from the inside, as it were; through his strong power of
dramatic sympathy, he identified himself with certain characters,
felt their temptations, entered into their pleasures, &c. This
roused Miss Brontë, who threw herself warmly into the discussion; the ice of her reserve was broken, and from that time she
showed her interest in all that was said, and contributed her

share to any conversation that was going on in the course of the evening.

What she said, and which part she took in the dispute about Thackeray's lecture, may be gathered from the following letter, referring to the same subject:—*

'The Lectures arrived safely; I have read them through twice. They must be studied to be appreciated. I thought well of them when I heard them delivered, but now I see their real power, and it is great. The lecture on Swift was new to me;* I thought it almost matchless. Not that by any means I always agree with Mr Thackeray's opinions, but his force, his penetration, his pithy simplicity, his eloquence,—his manly sonorous eloquence—command entire admiration.* . . . Against his errors I protest, were it treason to do so. I was present at the Fielding lecture: the hour spent in listening to it was a painful hour. That Thackeray was wrong in his way of treating Fielding's character and vices, my conscience told me. After reading that lecture, I trebly felt that he was wrong—dangerously wrong. Had Thackeray owned a son, grown, or growing up, and a son, brilliant but reckless—would he have spoken in that light way of courses that lead to disgrace and the grave? He speaks of it all as if he theorised; as if he had never been called on, in the course of his life, to witness the actual consequences of such failings; as if he had never stood by and seen the issue, the final result of it all. I believe, if only once the prospect of a promising life blasted on the outset by wild ways had passed close under his eyes, he never *could* have spoken with such levity of what led to its piteous destruction. Had I a brother yet living, I should tremble to let him read Thackeray's lecture on Fielding. I should hide it away from him. If, in spite of precaution, it should fall into his hands, I should earnestly pray him not to be misled by the voice of the charmer, let him charm never so wisely. Not that for a moment I would have had Thackeray to *abuse* Fielding, or even Pharisaically to condemn his life; but I do most deeply grieve that it never entered into his heart sadly and nearly to feel the peril of such a career, that he might have dedicated some of his great strength to a potent warning against its adoption by any young man. I believe temptation often assails the finest manly natures; as the pecking sparrow or destructive wasp attacks the sweetest and mellowest fruit, eschewing what is sour and crude. The true lover of his race ought to devote his vigour to guard and protect; he should sweep away every lure with a kind of rage at its treachery. You will think this far too serious, I dare say; but the subject is serious, and one cannot help feeling upon it earnestly.'

# CHAPTER XIII

AFTER her visit to Manchester, she had to return to a re-opening of the painful circumstances of the previous winter, as the time drew near for Mr Nicholls' departure from Haworth. A testimonial of respect from the parishioners was presented, at a public meeting, to one who had faithfully served them for eight years:* and he left the place, and she saw no chance of hearing a word about him in the future, unless it was some second-hand scrap of intelligence, dropped out accidentally by one of the neighbouring clergymen.

Early in June* I received the following letter from Miss Brontë:—

'Haworth, June 1st, 1853.

'June is come, and now I want to know if you can come, on Thursday the 9th inst.

'Ever since I was at Manchester, I have been anticipating your visit. Not that I attempt to justify myself in asking you; the place has no attractions, as I told you, here in this house. Papa too takes great interest in the matter. I only pray that the weather may be fine, and that a cold, by which I am now stupified, may be gone before the 9th, so that I may have no let and hindrance in taking you on to the Moors,—the sole, but, with one who loves nature as you do, not despicable resource.

'When you take leave of the domestic circle and turn your back on Plymouth Grove* to come to Haworth, you must do it in the spirit which might sustain you in case you were setting out on a brief trip to the back woods of America. Leaving behind your husband, children and civilisation, you must come out to barbarism, loneliness, and liberty. The change will perhaps do good, if not too prolonged. . . . . Please, when you write, to mention by what train you will come, and at what hour you will arrive at Keighley; for I must take measures to have a conveyance waiting for you at the station, otherwise, as there is no cab stand, you might be inconvenienced and hindered.'

In consequence of this invitation, I promised to pay her a visit on my return from London; but, after the day was fixed, a letter came from Mr Brontë, saying that she was suffering from so severe an attack of influenza, accompanied with such excruciating pain in the head, that he must request me to defer my visit until she was better. While sorry for the cause, I did not regret that my going was delayed till the season when the moors would be all glorious with the purple bloom of the heather; and thus present a scene about which she had often spoken to me. So we agreed that I should not come to her before August or September. Meanwhile, I received a letter from which I am tempted to take an extract, as it shows both her conception of what fictitious writing ought to be, and her always kindly interest in what I was doing.

'July 9th, 1853.

'Thank you for your letter; it was as pleasant as a quiet chat, as welcome as spring showers, as reviving as a friend's visit; in short, it was very like a page of "Cranford."* . . . . . . . . A thought strikes me. Do you, who have so many friends,—so large a circle of acquaintance,—find it easy, when you sit down to write, to isolate yourself from all those ties, and their sweet associations, so as to be your *own woman*, uninfluenced or swayed by the consciousness of how your work may affect other minds; what blame or what sympathy it may call forth? Does no luminous cloud ever come between you and the severe Truth, as you know it in your own secret and clear-seeing soul? In a word, are you never tempted to make your characters more amiable than the Life, by the inclination to assimilate your thoughts to the thoughts of those who always *feel* kindly, but sometimes fail to *see* justly? Don't answer the question; it is not intended to be answered. . . . . . . . .Your account of Mrs Stowe* was stimulatingly interesting. I long to see you, to get you to say it, and many other things, all over again. My father continues better. I am better too; but to-day I have a headache again, which will hardly let me write coherently. Give my dear love to M. and M., dear happy girls as they are. You cannot now transmit my message to F. and J.* I prized the little wild-flower,—not that I think the sender cares for me; she *does* not, and *cannot*, for she does not know me;—but no matter. In my reminiscences she is a person of a certain distinction. I think hers a fine little nature, frank and of genuine promise. I often see her, as she appeared, stepping supreme from the portico towards the carriage, that evening we went to see "Twelfth Night."* I believe in J.'s future; I like what speaks in her movements, and what is written upon her face.'

The following letter was addressed to me soon after my return from a short tour in Normandy:—*

'I was glad to get your little note, glad to hear you were at home again. Not that, practically, it makes much difference to me whether you are in Normandy or Manchester: the shorter distance separates perhaps as effectually as the longer, yet there is a mental comfort in thinking that but thirty miles intervene.

'Come to Haworth as soon as you can: the heath is in bloom now: I have waited and watched for its purple signal as the forerunner of your coming. It will not be quite faded before the 16th, but after that, it will soon grow sere. Be sure to mention the day and hour of your arrival at Keighley.

'My father has passed the summer, not well, yet better than I expected. His chief complaint is of weakness and depressed spirits; the prospect of your visit still affords him pleasure. I am surprised to see how he looks forward to it. My own health has been much better lately.

'I suppose Meta is ere this returned to school again.* This summer's tour will no doubt furnish a lifelong remembrance of pleasure to her and Marianne. Great would be the joy of the little ones at seeing you all home again.

'I saw in the papers the death of Mr S.,* of scarlet fever, at his residence in Wales. Was it not there you left Flossy and Julia? This thought recurred to me, with some chilling fears of what might happen; but I trust that all is safe now. How is poor Mrs S.?

'Remember me very, very kindly to Mr Gaskell and the whole circle. Write when you have time—come at the earliest day, and believe me,

'Yours very truthfully,
'C. BRONTË.'

Towards the latter end of September I went to Haworth. At the risk of repeating something which I have previously said, I will copy out parts of a letter which I wrote at the time.*

'It was a dull, drizzly Indian-inky day, all the way on the railroad to Keighley, which is a rising wool-manufacturing town, lying in a hollow between hills—not a pretty hollow, but more what the Yorkshire people call a "bottom," or "botham." I left Keighley in a car* for Haworth, four miles off—four tough, steep, scrambling miles, the road winding between the wave-like hills that rose and fell on every side of the horizon, with a long illimitable sinuous look, as if they were a part of the line of the Great Serpent, which the Norse legend says girdles the world. The day was lead-coloured; the road had stone factories alongside of it,— grey, dull-coloured rows of stone cottages belonging to these factories, and then we came to poor, hungry-looking fields;—stone fences everywhere, and trees nowhere. Haworth is a long, strag-gling village: one steep narrow street—so steep that the flag-stones with which it is paved are placed end-ways, that the horses' feet may have something to cling to, and not slip down backwards; which if they did, they would soon reach Keighley. But if the horses had cats' feet and claws, they would do all the better. Well, we (the man, horse, car, and I) clambered up this street, and reached the church dedicated to St Autest* (who was he?); then we turned off into a lane on the left, past the curate's lodging at the Sexton's, past the school-house, up to the Parsonage yard-door. I went round the house to the front door, looking to the church;— moors everywhere beyond and above. The crowded grave-yard surrounds the house and small grass enclosure for drying clothes.

'I don't know that I ever saw a spot more exquisitely clean; the most dainty place for that I ever saw. To be sure, the life is like clock-work. No one comes to the house; nothing disturbs the deep repose; hardly a voice is heard; you catch the ticking of the clock in the kitchen, or the buzzing of a fly in the parlour, all over the house. Miss Brontë sits alone in her parlour; breakfasting with her father in his study at nine o'clock. She helps in the housework; for one of their servants, Tabby, is nearly ninety, and the other only a girl. Then I accompanied her in her walks on the sweeping moors: the heather-bloom had been blighted by a thunder-storm a

day or two before, and was all of a livid brown colour, instead of
the blaze of purple glory it ought to have been. Oh! those high, wild,
desolate moors, up above the whole world, and the very realms of
silence! Home to dinner at two. Mr Brontë has his dinner sent* into
him. All the small table arrangements had the same dainty simplicity about them. Then we rested, and talked over the clear, bright
fire; it is a cold country, and the fires were a pretty warm dancing
light all over the house. The parlour has been evidently refurnished
within the last few years, since Miss Brontë's success has enabled
her to have a little more money to spend. Everything fits into, and
is in harmony with, the idea of a country parsonage, possessed by
people of very moderate means. The prevailing colour of the room
is crimson, to make a warm setting for the cold grey landscape
without. There is her likeness by Richmond, and an engraving from
Lawrence's picture of Thackeray; and two recesses, on each side of
the high, narrow, old- fashioned mantel-piece, filled with books,—
books given to her, books she has bought, and which tell of her
individual pursuits and tastes; *not* standard books.

'She cannot see well, and does little beside knitting. The way
she weakened her eyesight was this: when she was sixteen or
seventeen, she wanted much to draw; and she copied nimini-pimini
copper-plate engravings out of annuals, ("stippling," don't the
artists call it?) every little point put in, till at the end of six months
she had produced an exquisitely faithful copy of the engraving. She
wanted to learn to express her ideas by drawing. After she had
tried to *draw* stories, and not succeeded, she took the better mode
of writing; but in so small a hand, that it is almost impossible to
decipher what she wrote at this time.

'But now to return to our quiet hour of rest after dinner. I soon
observed that her habits of order were such that she could not go
on with the conversation, if a chair was out of its place; everything
was arranged with delicate regularity. We talked over the old times
of her childhood; of her elder sister's (Maria's) death,—just like
that of Helen Burns in "Jane Eyre;"* of the desire (almost
amounting to illness) of expressing herself in some way,—writing
or drawing; of her weakened eyesight, which prevented her doing
anything for two years, from the age of seventeen to nineteen; of
her being a governess; of her going to Brussels; whereupon I said
I disliked Lucy Snowe, and we discussed M. Paul Emanuel; and I

told her of ———'s admiration of "Shirley," which pleased her, for the character of Shirley was meant for her sister Emily, about whom she is never tired of talking, nor I of listening. Emily must have been a remnant of the Titans,—great-grand-daughter of the giants who used to inhabit earth. One day, Miss Brontë brought down a rough, common-looking oil-painting, done by her brother, of herself,—a little, rather prim-looking girl of eighteen,—and the two other sisters, girls of sixteen and fourteen, with cropped hair, and sad, dreamy-looking eyes.* . . . . Emily had a great dog,—half mastiff, half bull-dog—so savage, &c. . . . . This dog went to her funeral, walking side by side with her father; and then, to the day of its death, it slept at her room door, snuffing under it, and whining every morning.

'We have generally had another walk before tea, which is at six; at half-past eight, prayers; and by nine, all the household are in bed, except ourselves. We sit up together till ten, or past; and after I go, I hear Miss Brontë come down and walk up and down the room for an hour or so.'

Copying this letter has brought the days of that pleasant visit very clear before me,—very sad in their clearness. We were so happy together; we were so full of interest in each other's subjects. The day seemed only too short for what we had to say and to hear. I understood her life the better for seeing the place where it had been spent—where she had loved and suffered. Mr Brontë was a most courteous host; and when he was with us,—at breakfast in his study, or at tea in Charlotte's parlour,—he had a sort of grand and stately way of describing past times, which tallied well with his striking appearance. He never seemed quite to have lost the feeling that Charlotte was a child to be guided and ruled, when she was present; and she herself submitted to this with a quiet docility that half amused, half astonished me. But when she had to leave the room, then all his pride in her genius and fame came out. He eagerly listened to everything I could tell him of the high admiration I had at any time heard expressed for her works. He would ask for certain speeches over and over again, as if he desired to impress them on his memory.

I remember two or three subjects of the conversations which she and I held in the evenings, besides those alluded to in my letter.

I asked her whether she had ever taken opium, as the description given of its effects in 'Villette' was so exactly like what I had experienced,*—vivid and exaggerated presence of objects, of which the outlines were indistinct, or lost in golden mist, &c. She replied, that she had never, to her knowledge, taken a grain of it in any shape, but that she had followed the process she always adopted when she had to describe anything which had not fallen within her own experience; she had thought intently on it for many and many a night before falling to sleep,—wondering what it was like, or how it would be,—till at length, sometimes after the progress of her story had been arrested at this one point for weeks, she wakened up in the morning with all clear before her, as if she had in reality gone through the experience, and then could describe it, word for word, as it had happened. I cannot account for this psychologically; I only am sure that it was so, because she said it.

She made many inquiries as to Mrs Stowe's personal appearance; and it evidently harmonised well with some theory of hers, to learn that the author of 'Uncle Tom's Cabin' was small and slight. It was another of her theories, that no mixtures of blood produce such fine characters, mentally and morally, as the Scottish and English.

I recollect, too, her saying how acutely she dreaded a charge of plagiarism, when, after she had written 'Jane Eyre,' she read the thrilling effect of the mysterious scream at midnight in Mrs Marsh's story of the 'Deformed.' She also said that, when she read the 'Neighbours,'* she thought every one would fancy that she must have taken her conception of Jane Eyre's character from that of 'Francesca,' the narrator of Miss Bremer's story. For my own part, I cannot see the slightest resemblance between the two characters, and so I told her; but she persisted in saying that Francesca was Jane Eyre married to a good-natured 'Bear' of a Swedish surgeon.

We went, not purposely, but accidentally, to see various poor people in our distant walks. From one we had borrowed an umbrella; in the house of another we had taken shelter from a rough September storm. In all these cottages, her quiet presence was known. At three miles from her home, the chair was dusted for her, with a kindly 'Sit ye down, Miss Brontë;' and she knew what absent or ailing members of the family to inquire after. Her quiet, gentle words, few though they might be, were evidently grateful to those Yorkshire ears. Their welcome to her, though rough and curt, was sincere and hearty.

We talked about the different courses through which life ran. She said, in her own composed manner, as if she had accepted the theory as a fact, that she believed some were appointed beforehand to sorrow and much disappointment; that it did not fall to the lot of all—as Scripture told us—to have their lines fall in pleasant places;* that it was well for those who had rougher paths, to perceive that such was God's will concerning them, and try to moderate their expectations, leaving hope to those of a different doom, and seeking patience and resignation as the virtues they were to cultivate. I took a different view: I thought that human lots were more equal than she imagined; that to some happiness and sorrow came in strong patches of light and shadow (so to speak), while in the lives of others they were pretty equally blended throughout. She smiled, and shook her head, and said she was trying to school herself against ever anticipating any pleasure; that it was better to be brave and submit faithfully; there was some good reason, which we should know in time, why sorrow and disappointment were to be the lot of some on earth. It was better to acknowledge this, and face out the truth in a religious faith.

In connection with this conversation, she named a little abortive plan which I had not heard of till then; how, in the previous July, she had been tempted to join some friends (a married couple and their child)* in an excursion to Scotland. They set out joyfully; she with especial gladness, for Scotland was a land which had its roots deep down in her imaginative affections, and the glimpse of two days at Edinburgh was all she had as yet seen of it. But, at the first stage after Carlisle, the little yearling child was taken with a slight indisposition; the anxious parents fancied that strange diet disagreed with it, and hurried back to their Yorkshire home as eagerly as, two or three days before, they had set their faces northward, in hopes of a month's pleasant ramble.

We parted with many intentions, on both sides, of renewing very frequently the pleasure we had had in being together. We agreed that when she wanted bustle, or when I wanted quiet, we were to let each other know, and exchange visits as occasion required.

I was aware that she had a great anxiety on her mind at this time; and being acquainted with its nature, I could not but deeply admire the patient docility which she displayed in her conduct towards her father.

Soon after I left Haworth, she went on a visit to Miss W——, who was then staying at Hornsea. The time passed quietly and happily with this friend, whose society was endeared to her by every year.

TO MISS W——.*

'Dec. 12th, 1853.

'I wonder how you are spending these long winter evenings. Alone, probably, like me. The thought often crosses me, as I sit by myself, how pleasant it would be if you lived within a walking distance, and I could go to you sometimes, or have you to come and spend a day and night with me. Yes; I did enjoy that week at Hornsea, and I look forward to spring as the period when you will fulfil your promise of coming to visit me. I fear you must be very solitary at Hornsea. How hard to some people of the world it would seem to live your life! how utterly impossible to live it with a serene spirit and an unsoured disposition! It seems wonderful to me, because you are not, like Mrs ——, phlegmatic and impenetrable, but received from nature feelings of the very finest edge. Such feelings, when they are locked up, sometimes damage the mind and temper. They don't with you. It must be partly principle, partly self-discipline, which keep you as you are.'

Of course, as I draw nearer to the years so recently closed, it becomes impossible for me to write with the same fulness of detail as I have hitherto not felt it wrong to use. Miss Brontë passed the winter of 1853-4 in a solitary and anxious manner. But the great conqueror Time was slowly achieving his victory over strong prejudice and human resolve. By degrees Mr Brontë became reconciled to the idea of his daughter's marriage.*

There is one other letter, addressed to Mr Dobell, which developes the intellectual side of her character, before we lose all thought of the authoress in the timid and conscientious woman about to become a wife, and in the too short, almost perfect, happiness of her nine months of wedded life.

> 'Haworth, near Keighley,
> 'Feb. 3rd, 1854.

'My dear Sir,—I can hardly tell you how glad I am to have an opportunity of explaining that taciturnity to which you allude. Your letter came at a period of danger and care, when my father was very ill, and I could not leave his bedside.* I answered no letters at that time, and yours was one of three or four that, when leisure returned to me, and I came to consider their purport, it seemed to me such that the time was past for answering them, and I laid them finally aside. If you remember, you asked me to go to London; it was too late either to go or to decline. I was sure you had left London. One circumstance you mentioned—your wife's illness—which I have thought of many a time, and wondered whether she is better. In your present note you do not refer to her, but I trust her health has long ere now been quite restored.

' "Balder"* arrived safely. I looked at him, before cutting his leaves, with singular pleasure. Remembering well his elder brother, the potent "Roman," it was natural to give a cordial welcome to a fresh scion of the same house and race. I have read him. He impressed me thus: he teems with power; I found in him a wild wealth of life, but I thought his favourite and favoured child would bring his sire trouble—would make his heart ache. It seemed to me, that his strength and beauty were not so much those of Joseph, the pillar of Jacob's age, as of the Prodigal Son, who troubled his father, though he always kept his love.*

'How is it that while the first-born of genius often brings honour, the second almost as often proves a source of depression and care? I could almost prophesy that your third will atone for any anxiety inflicted by this his immediate predecessor.

'There is power in that character of "Balder," and to me a certain horror. Did you mean it to embody, along with force, any of the special defects of the artistic character? It seems to me that those defects were never thrown out in stronger lines. I did not and could not think you meant to offer him as your cherished ideal of the true, great poet; I regarded him as a vividly-coloured picture of inflated self-esteem, almost frantic aspiration; of a nature that has made a Moloch of intellect—offered up, in pagan fires, the natural affections—sacrificed the heart to the brain. Do we not all know that true greatness is simple, self-oblivious, prone to unambitious, unselfish attachments? I am certain you feel this truth in your heart of hearts.

'But if the critics err now (as yet I have seen none of their lucubrations), you shall one day set them right in the second part of "Balder." You shall show them that you too know—better, perhaps, than they—that the truly great man is too sincere in his affections to grudge a sacrifice; too much absorbed in his work to talk loudly about it; too intent on finding the best way to accomplish what he undertakes to think great things of himself— the instrument. And if God places seeming impediments in his way—if his duties sometimes seem to hamper his powers—he feels keenly, perhaps writhes, under the slow torture of hindrance and delay; but if there be a true man's heart in his breast, he can bear, submit, wait patiently.

'Whoever speaks to me of "Balder"—though I live too retired a life to come often in the way of comment—shall be answered according to your suggestion and my own impression. Equity demands that you should be your own interpreter. Goodbye for the present, and believe me,

'Faithfully and gratefully,
'CHARLOTTE BRONTË.'
'Sydney Dobell, Esq.'

A letter to her Brussels school-fellow gives an idea of the external course of things during this winter.

'March 8th.*

'I was very glad to see your handwriting again. It is, I believe, a year since I heard from you. Again and again you have recurred to my thoughts lately, and I was beginning to have some sad presages as to the cause of your silence. Your letter happily does away with all these; it brings, on the whole, glad tidings both of your papa, mama, your sisters, and, last but not least, your dear respected English self.

'My dear father has borne the severe winter very well, a circumstance for which I feel the more thankful as he had many weeks of very precarious health last summer, following an attack from which he suffered in June, and which for a few hours deprived him totally of sight, though neither his mind, speech, nor even his powers of motion, were in the least affected. I can hardly tell you how thankful I was, when, after that dreary and almost despairing interval of utter darkness, some gleam of daylight became visible to him once more. I had feared that paralysis had seized the optic nerve. A sort of mist remained for a long time; and, indeed, his vision is not yet perfectly clear, but he can read, write, and walk about, and he preaches *twice* every Sunday, the curate only reading the prayers. *You* can well understand* how earnestly I wish and pray that sight may be spared him to the end; he so dreads the privation of blindness. His mind is just as strong and active as ever, and politics interest him as they do *your* papa. The Czar, the war, the alliance between France and England*— into all these things he throws himself heart and soul; they seem to carry him back to his comparatively young days, and to renew the excitement of the last great European struggle. Of course my father's sympathies (and mine too) are all with Justice and Europe against Tyranny and Russia.

'Circumstanced as I have been, you will comprehend that I have had neither the leisure nor the inclination to go from home much during the past year. I spent a week with Mrs Gaskell in the spring, and a fortnight with some other friends* more recently, and that includes the whole of my visiting since I saw you last. My life is, indeed, very uniform and retired—more so than is quite healthful either for mind or body; yet I find reason for often-renewed feelings of gratitude, in the sort of support which still comes and cheers me on from time to time. My health, though not unbroken, is, I sometimes fancy, rather stronger on the whole than it was three years ago: headache and dyspepsia are my worst ailments. Whether I shall come up to town this season for a few days I do not yet know; but if I do, I shall hope to call in P. Place.'*

In April she communicated the fact of her engagement to Miss W——.

'Haworth, April 12th.

'My dear Miss W——,—The truly kind interest which you have always taken in my affairs, makes me feel that it is due to you to transmit an early communication on a subject respecting which I have already consulted you more than once. I must tell you then, that since I wrote last, papa's mind has gradually come round to a view very different to that which he once took; and that after some correspondence, and as the result of a visit Mr Nicholls paid here about a week ago, it was agreed that he was to resume the curacy of Haworth, as soon as papa's present assistant* is provided with a situation, and in due course of time he is to be received as an inmate into this house.

'It gives me unspeakable content to see that now my father has once admitted this new view of the case, he dwells on it very complacently. In all arrangements, his convenience and seclusion will be scrupulously respected. Mr Nicholls seems deeply to feel the wish to comfort and sustain his declining years. I think from Mr Nicholls' character I may depend on this not being a mere transitory impulsive feeling, but rather that it will be accepted steadily as a duty, and discharged tenderly as an office of affection. The destiny which Providence in His goodness and wisdom seems to offer me will not, I am aware, be generally regarded as brilliant, but I trust I see in it some germs of real happiness. I trust the demands of both feeling and duty will be in some measure reconciled by the step in contemplation. It is Mr Nicholls' wish that the marriage should take place this summer; he urges the month of July, but that seems very soon.

'When you write to me, tell me how you are . . . I have now decidedly declined the visit to London; the ensuing three months will bring me abundance of occupation; I could not afford to throw away a month . . . Papa has just got a letter from the good and dear Bishop, which has touched and pleased us much; it expresses so cordial an approbation of Mr Nicholls' return to Haworth (respecting which he was consulted), and such kind gratification at the domestic arrangements which are to ensue. It seems his penetration discovered the state of things when he was here in June 1853.'

She expressed herself in other letters, as thankful to One who had guided her through much difficulty and much distress and perplexity of mind; and yet she felt what most thoughtful women do, who marry when the first flush of careless youth is over, that there was a strange, half-sad feeling, in making announcements of an engagement—for cares and fears came mingled inextricably with hopes. One great relief to her mind at this time was derived from the conviction that her father took a positive pleasure in all the thoughts about and preparations for her wedding. He was anxious that things should be expedited, and was much interested in every preliminary arrangement for the reception of Mr Nicholls into the Parsonage as his daughter's husband. This step was rendered necessary by Mr Brontë's great age, and failing sight, which made it a paramount obligation on so dutiful a daughter as Charlotte, to devote as much time and assistance as ever in attending to his wants. Mr Nicholls, too, hoped that he might be able to add some comfort and pleasure by his ready presence, on any occasion when the old clergyman might need his services.

At the beginning of May, Miss Brontë left home to pay three visits before her marriage.* The first was to us. She only remained three days, as she had to go to the neighbourhood of Leeds, there to make such purchases as were required for her marriage.* Her preparations, as she said, could neither be expensive nor extensive; consisting chiefly in a modest replenishing of her wardrobe, some re-papering and re-painting in the Parsonage; and, above all, converting the small flagged passage room, hitherto used only for stores (which was behind her sitting room), into a study for her husband. On this idea, and plans for his comfort, as well as her father's, her mind dwelt a good deal; and we talked them over with the same unwearying happiness which, I suppose, all women feel in such discussions—especially when money considerations call for that kind of contrivance which Charles Lamb speaks of in his 'Essay on Old China,'* as forming so great an addition to the pleasure of obtaining a thing at last.

'Haworth, May 22nd.*

'Since I came home I have been very busy stitching; the little new room is got into order, and the green and white curtains are up; they exactly suit the papering, and look neat and clean enough. I had a letter a day or two since, announcing that Mr Nicholls comes to-morrow. I feel anxious about him; more anxious on one point than I dare quite express to myself. It seems he has again been suffering sharply from his rheumatic affection. I hear this not from himself, but from another quarter. He was ill while I was in Manchester and B——. He uttered no complaint to me; dropped no hint on the subject. Alas! he was hoping he had got the better of it, and I know how this contradiction of his hopes will sadden him. For unselfish reasons he did so earnestly wish this complaint might not become chronic. I fear—I fear; but if he is doomed to suffer, so much the more will he need care and help. Well! come what may, God help and strengthen both him and me! I look forward to to-morrow with a mixture of impatience and anxiety.'

Mr Brontë had a slight illness which alarmed her much. Besides, all the weight of care involved in the household preparations pressed on the bride in this case—not unpleasantly, only to the full occupation of her time. She was too busy to unpack her wedding dresses for several days after they arrived from Halifax; yet not too busy to think of arrangements by which Miss W——'s journey to be present at the marriage could be facilitated.

'I write to Miss W—— to-day.* Would it not be better, dear, if you and she could arrange to come to Haworth on the same day, arrive at Keighley by the same train; then I could order the cab to meet you at the station, and bring you on with your luggage? In this hot weather walking would be quite out of the question, either for you or for her; and I know she would persist in doing it if left to herself, and arrive half killed. I thought it better to mention this arrangement to *you* first, and then, if you liked it, you could settle the time, &c. with Miss W——, and let me know. Be sure and give me timely information, that I may write to the Devonshire Arms* about the cab.

'Mr Nicholls is a kind, considerate fellow. With all his masculine faults, he enters into my wishes about having the thing done quietly, in a way that makes me grateful; and if nobody interferes and spoils his arrangements, he will manage it so that not a soul in Haworth shall be aware of the day. He is so thoughtful, too, about "the ladies,"—that is, you and Miss W——. Anticipating, too, the very arrangements I was going to propose to him about providing for your departure, &c. He and Mr S——* come to —— the evening before; write me a note to let me know they are there; precisely at eight in the morning they will be in the church, and there we are to meet them. Mr and Mrs Grant are asked to the breakfast, not to the ceremony.'

It was fixed that the marriage was to take place on the 29th of June. Her two friends arrived at Haworth Parsonage the day before; and the long summer afternoon and evening were spent by Charlotte in thoughtful arrangements for the morrow, and for her father's comfort during her absence from home. When all was finished—the trunk packed, the morning's breakfast arranged, the wedding-dress laid out,—just at bedtime, Mr Brontë announced his intention of stopping at home while the others went to church.\* What was to be done? Who was to give the bride away? There were only to be the officiating clergyman, the bride and bridegroom, the brides-maid, and Miss W—— present. The Prayer-book was referred to; and there it was seen that the Rubric enjoins that the Minister shall receive 'the woman from her father's or *friend's* hands,' and that nothing is specified as to the sex of the 'friend.' So Miss W——, ever kind in emergency, volunteered to give her old pupil away.

The news of the wedding had slipt abroad before the little party came out of church, and many old and humble friends were there, seeing her look 'like a snow-drop,' as they say. Her dress was white embroidered muslin, with a lace mantle, and white bonnet trimmed with green leaves, which perhaps might suggest the resemblance to the pale wintry flower.

Mr Nicholls and she went to visit his friends and relations in Ireland; and made a tour by Killarney, Glengariff, Tarbert, Tralee, and Cork, seeing scenery, of which she says,\* 'some parts exceeded all I had ever imagined.' . . . . . 'I must say I like my new relations.\* My dear husband, too, appears in a new light in his own country. More than once I have had deep pleasure in hearing his praises on all sides. Some of the old servants and followers of the family tell me I am a most fortunate person; for that I have got one of the best gentlemen in the country. . . . . I trust I feel thankful to God for having enabled me to make what seems a right choice; and I pray to be enabled to repay as I ought the affectionate devotion of a truthful, honourable man.'

Henceforward the sacred doors of home are closed upon her married life. We, her loving friends, standing outside, caught occasional glimpses of brightness, and pleasant peaceful murmurs of sound, telling of the gladness within; and we looked at each other, and gently said, 'After a hard and long struggle—after many cares and many bitter sorrows—she is tasting happiness now!' We thought of the slight astringencies of her character, and how they would turn to full ripe sweetness in that calm sunshine of domestic peace. We remembered her trials, and were glad in the idea that God had seen fit to wipe away the tears from her eyes.* Those who saw her, saw an outward change in her look, telling of inward things.* And we thought, and we hoped, and we prophesied, in our great love and reverence.

But God's ways are not as our ways!

Hear some of the low murmurs of happiness we, who listened, heard:—*

'I really seem to have had scarcely a spare moment since that dim quiet June morning, when you, E——, and myself all walked down to Haworth Church. Not that I have been hurried or oppressed; but the fact is, my time is not my own now; somebody else wants a good portion of it, and says, "We must do so and so." We *do* so and so, accordingly; and it generally seems the right thing. . . . . We have had many callers from a distance, and latterly some little occupation in the way of preparing for a small village entertainment. Both Mr Nicholls and myself wished much to make some response for the hearty welcome and general good-will shown by the parishioners on his return; accordingly, the Sunday and day scholars and teachers, the church-ringers, singers, &c., to the number of five hundred, were asked to tea and supper in the School-room. They seemed to enjoy it much, and it was very pleasant to see their happiness. One of the villagers, in proposing my husband's health, described him as a "*consistent Christian and a kind gentleman.*" I own the words touched me deeply, and I thought (as I know *you* would have thought had you been present) that to merit and win such a character was better than to earn either wealth, or fame, or power. I am disposed to echo that high but simple eulogium. . . . . My dear father was not well when we returned from Ireland. I am, however, most thankful to say that he is better now. May God preserve him to us yet for some years! The wish for his continued life, together with a certain solicitude for his happiness and health, seems, I scarcely know why, even stronger in me now than before I was married. Papa has taken no duty since we returned; and each time I see Mr Nicholls put on gown or surplice, I feel comforted to think that this marriage has secured papa good aid in his old age.'

'September 19th.*

'Yes! I am thankful to say my husband is in improved health and spirits. It makes me content and grateful to hear him from time to time avow his happiness in the brief, plain phrase of sincerity. My own life is more occupied than it used to be: I have not so much time for thinking: I am obliged to be more practical, for my dear Arthur is a very practical, as well as a very punctual and methodical man. Every morning he is in the National School by nine o'clock; he gives the children religious instruction till half-past ten. Almost every afternoon he pays visits amongst the poor parishioners. Of course, he often finds a little work for his wife to do, and I hope she is not sorry to help him. I believe it is not bad for me that his bent should be so wholly towards matters of life and active usefulness— so little inclined to the literary and contemplative. As to his continued affection and kind attentions, it does not become me to say much of them; but they neither change nor diminish.'

Her friend and bridesmaid came to pay them a visit in October. I was to have gone also, but I allowed some little obstacle to intervene, to my lasting regret.

'I say nothing about the war;* but when I read of its horrors, I cannot help thinking that it is one of the greatest curses that ever fell upon mankind. I trust it may not last long, for it really seems to me that no glory to be gained can compensate for the sufferings which must be endured. This may seem a little ignoble and unpatriotic; but I think that as we advance towards middle age, nobleness and patriotism have a different signification to us to that which we accept while young.

'You kindly inquire after Papa. He is better, and seems to gain strength as the weather gets colder; indeed, of late years his health has always been better in winter than in summer. We are all indeed pretty well; and, for my own part, it is long since I have known such comparative immunity from headache, &c., as during the last three months. My life is different from what it used to be. May God make me thankful for it! I have a good, kind, attached husband; and every day my own attachment to him grows stronger.'

Late in the autumn, Sir James Kay Shuttleworth crossed the border-hills that separate Lancashire from Yorkshire, and spent two or three days with them.

About this time, Mr Nicholls was offered a living of much greater value than his curacy at Haworth,* and in many ways the proposal was a very advantageous one; but he felt himself bound to Haworth as long as Mr Brontë lived. Still, this offer gave his wife great and true pleasure, as a proof of the respect in which her husband was held.

'Nov. 29.

'I intended to have written a line yesterday, but just as I was sitting down for the purpose, Arthur called to me to take a walk. We set off, not intending to go far; but, though wild and cloudy, it was fair in the morning; when we had got about half a mile on the moors, Arthur suggested the idea of the waterfall; after the melted snow, he said, it would be fine. I had often wished to see it in its winter power,—so we walked on. It was fine indeed; a perfect torrent racing over the rocks, white and beautiful! It began to rain while we were watching it, and we returned home under a streaming sky. However, I enjoyed the walk inexpressibly, and would not have missed the spectacle on any account.'

She did not achieve this walk of seven or eight miles, in such weather, with impunity. She began to shiver soon after her return home, in spite of every precaution, and had a bad lingering sore-throat and cold, which hung about her, and made her thin and weak.

'Did I tell you* that our poor little Flossy is dead? She drooped for a single day, and died quietly in the night without pain. The loss even of a dog was very saddening; yet, perhaps, no dog ever had a happier life, or an easier death.'

On Christmas-day she and her husband walked to the poor old woman (whose calf she had been set to seek in former and less

happy days), carrying with them a great spice-cake to make glad
her heart. On Christmas-day many a humble meal in Haworth was
made more plentiful by her gifts.

Early in the new year (1855), Mr and Mrs Nicholls went to visit
Sir James Kay Shuttleworth at Gawthorpe. They only remained
two or three days, but it so fell out that she increased her lingering
cold, by a long walk over damp ground in thin shoes.

Soon after her return, she was attacked by new sensations of
perpetual nausea, and ever-recurring faintness. After this state of
things had lasted for some time, she yielded to Mr Nicholls' wish
that a doctor* should be sent for. He came, and assigned a natural
cause for her miserable indisposition; a little patience, and all
would go right. She, who was ever patient in illness, tried hard to
bear up and bear on. But the dreadful sickness increased and
increased, till the very sight of food occasioned nausea. 'A wren
would have starved on what she ate during those last six weeks,'
says one.* Tabby's health had suddenly and utterly given way, and
she died in this time of distress and anxiety respecting the last
daughter of the house she had served so long. Martha tenderly
waited on her mistress, and from time to time tried to cheer her
with the thought of the baby that was coming. 'I dare say I shall
be glad sometime,' she would say;* 'but I am so ill—so weary——'
Then she took to her bed, too weak to sit up. From that last couch
she wrote two notes—in pencil. The first, which has no date, is
addressed to her own 'Dear Nell.'*

'I must write one line out of my weary bed. The news of
M——'s probable recovery came like a ray of joy to me. I am not
going to talk about my sufferings—it would be useless and painful.
I want to give you an assurance, which I know will comfort
you—and that is, that I find in my husband the tenderest nurse,
the kindest support, the best earthly comfort that ever woman had.
His patience never fails, and it is tried by sad days and broken
nights. Write and tell me about Mrs ——'s case; how long was she
ill, and in what way? Papa—thank God!—is better. Our poor old
Tabby is *dead* and *buried*.* Give my kind love to Miss W——. May
God comfort and help you!

'C. B. NICHOLLS.'

The other—also in faint, faint pencil marks—was to her Brussels schoolfellow.

'Feb. 15th.*

'A few lines of acknowledgment your letter *shall* have, whether well or ill. At present I am confined to my bed with illness, and have been so for three weeks. Up to this period, since my marriage, I have had excellent health. My husband and I live at home with my father; of course, I could not leave *him*. He is pretty well, better than last summer. No kinder, better husband than mine, it seems to me, there can be in the world. I do not want now for kind companionship in health and the tenderest nursing in sickness. Deeply I sympathise in all you tell me about Dr W. and your excellent mother's anxiety. I trust he will not risk another operation. I cannot write more now; for I am much reduced and very weak. God bless you all.—Yours affectionately,

'C. B. NICHOLLS.'

I do not think she ever wrote a line again.* Long days and longer nights went by; still the same relentless nausea and faintness, and still borne on in patient trust. About the third week in March there was a change; a low wandering delirium came on; and in it she begged constantly for food and even for stimulants. She swallowed eagerly now; but it was too late. Wakening for an instant from this stupor of intelligence, she saw her husband's woe-worn face, and caught the sound of some murmured words of prayer that God would spare her. 'Oh!' she whispered forth, 'I am not going to die, am I? He will not separate us, we have been so happy.'

Early on Saturday morning, March 31st, the solemn tolling of Haworth church-bell spoke forth the fact of her death to the villagers who had known her from a child, and whose hearts shivered within them as they thought of the two sitting desolate and alone in the old grey house.

# CHAPTER XIV

I HAVE always been much struck with a passage in Mr Forster's Life of Goldsmith.* Speaking of the scene after his death, the writer says:—

'The staircase of Brick Court is said to have been filled with mourners, the reverse of domestic; women without a home, without domesticity of any kind, with no friend but him they had come to weep for; outcasts of that great, solitary, wicked city, to whom he had never forgotten to be kind and charitable.'

This came into my mind when I heard of some of the circumstances attendant on Charlotte's funeral.

Few beyond that sweeping circle of hills knew that she, whom the nations praised far off, lay dead that Easter morning.* Of kith and kin she had more in the grave to which she was soon to be borne, than among the living. The two mourners, stunned with their great grief, desired not the sympathy of strangers. One member out of most of the families in the parish was bidden to the funeral; and it became an act of self-denial in many a poor household to give up to another the privilege of paying their last homage to her; and those who were excluded from the formal train of mourners thronged the churchyard and church, to see carried forth, and laid beside her own people, her whom, not many months ago, they had looked at as a pale white bride, entering on a new life with trembling happy hope.

Among those humble friends who passionately grieved over the dead, was a village girl that had been betrayed* some little time before, but who had found a holy sister in Charlotte. She had sheltered her with her help, her counsel, her strengthening words; had ministered to her needs in her time of trial. Bitter, bitter was the grief of this poor young woman, when she heard that her friend was sick unto death,* and deep is her mourning until this day. A blind girl, living some four miles from Haworth, loved Mrs Nicholls so dearly that, with many cries and entreaties, she implored those about her to lead her along the roads, and over the moor-paths, that she might hear the last solemn words, 'Earth to earth, ashes to ashes, dust to dust; in sure and certain hope of the resurrection to eternal life, through our Lord Jesus Christ.'*

Such were the mourners over Charlotte Brontë's grave.

I have little more to say. If my readers find that I have not said enough, I have said too much. I cannot measure or judge of such a character as hers. I cannot map out vices, and virtues, and debateable land. One who knew her long and well,—the 'Mary' of this Life,—writes thus of her dead friend:—*

'She thought much of her duty, and had loftier and clearer notions of it than most people, and held fast to them with more success. It was done, it seems to me, with much more difficulty than people have of stronger nerves, and better fortunes. All her life was but labour and pain; and she never threw down the burden for the sake of present pleasure. I don't know what use you can make of all I have said. I have written it with the strong desire to obtain appreciation for her. Yet, what does it matter? She herself appealed to the world's judgment for her use of some of the faculties she had,—not the best,—but still the only ones she could turn to strangers' benefit. They heartily, greedily enjoyed the fruits of her labours, and then found out she was much to be blamed for possessing such faculties. Why ask for a judgment on her from such a world?'

But I turn from the critical, unsympathetic public,—inclined to judge harshly because they have only seen superficially and not thought deeply. I appeal to that larger and more solemn public, who know how to look with tender humility at faults and errors; how to admire generously extraordinary genius, and how to reverence with warm, full hearts all noble virtue. To that Public I commit the memory of Charlotte Brontë.

THE END.

# EXPLANATORY NOTES

THE following abbreviations are used throughout these Notes:

Allott    Miriam Allott (ed.), *The Brontës: The Critical Heritage* (1974)

BPM    Brontë Parsonage Museum, Haworth

*BST*    *Brontë Society Transactions* (cited by volume, year, and page)

CB    Charlotte Brontë

Ed. 1, Ed. 2, Ed. 3    the first three editions (all 1857) of *The Life of Charlotte Brontë*

EG    Elizabeth Gaskell

EN    Ellen Nussey

John Rylands    the Rare Books and Manuscript collection, Deansgate Building, John Rylands University Library of Manchester

*Letters*    *The Letters of Mrs Gaskell*, ed. J. A. V. Chapple and Arthur Pollard (1966)

The Life    *The Life of Charlotte Brontë*

MS    the manuscript of *The Life of Charlotte Brontë* in the John Rylands University Library of Manchester; the known additions for the Third Edition (except one page in Manchester Central Public Library) are bound up with this. Other manuscripts are identified by their provenance, e.g. John Rylands MS, BPM MS

WS    *The Brontës: Their Lives, Friendships and Correspondence*, ed. T. J. Wise and J. A. Symington (4 vols., 1932; repr. 1980)

References to the letters of Charlotte Brontë are given as far as possible by date, to allow use with Margaret Smith's Clarendon edition; references are given to Wise and Symington's edition for the other Brontës and for material not readily available elsewhere. The correspondent of a letter is always Ellen Nussey, unless the text or the notes indicates otherwise. Material from the manuscript or from the First Edition is keyed in and out by italicized words from this edition's text. Details of books referred to by author's surname and title are listed in Further Reading. Words are glossed only if not in the *Concise Oxford Dictionary* or if they are used in an obsolete sense.

*Editions*:

Clarendon Brontë:

Charlotte Brontë, *The Professor*, ed. Margaret Smith and Herbert Rosengarten (1987); *Jane Eyre*, ed. Jane Jack and Margaret Smith (1969); *Shirley*, ed. Herbert Rosengarten and Margaret Smith (1979); *Villette*, ed. Herbert Rosengarten and Margaret Smith (1984); Emily Brontë, *Wuthering Heights*, ed. Hilda Marsden and Ian Jack (1976).

World's Classics:

Charlotte Brontë, *The Professor*, ed. Margaret Smith and Herbert Rosengarten (1991); *Jane Eyre*, ed. Margaret Smith (1980); *Shirley*, ed. Herbert Rosengarten and Margaret Smith (1981); *Villette*, ed. Herbert Rosengarten and Margaret Smith (1990); Emily Brontë, *Wuthering Heights*, ed. Ian Jack (1981); Anne Brontë, *Agnes Grey*, ed. Robert Inglesfield and Hilda Marsden (1991); *The Tenant of Wildfell Hall*, ed. Herbert Rosengarten and Margaret Smith (1993).

In references to these editions, where a novel is divided into volumes, each beginning with chapter one, the through chapter number is also given. All page references to the Brontë novels, unless otherwise indicated, are to the World's Classics editions.

*Title-page*: AURORA LEIGH: Elizabeth Barrett Browning (1806–61), *Aurora Leigh* (1857), bk. v, ll. 434, 438–41; in the poem, which has plot similarities to *Jane Eyre*, Aurora is a poet. This epigraph's biblical tone ('God'; 'the nations . . . far off') enforces the woman artist's desolation and is re-echoed by EG in the polarization of CB as woman and artist: EG uses 'the nations praise far off' in her final chapter.

9 *Skipton railway . . . Keighley station*: the railway (properly, the Leeds and Bradford Railway, as given in Ed. 1), opened in 1846, was extended to Keighley and Skipton in 1847. For ease of construction the line followed the river valley where possible. No line was open to Haworth until 1867; closed in 1962, the Keighley and Worth Valley Preservation Society has run a steam service since 1968.

10 *musical world*: John Carrodus (1836–95), violinist, was born at Braithwaite, a few miles west of Keighley.

11 *Haworth Parsonage*: built in 1799; enlarged in the 1860s, it was acquired by the Brontë Society in 1927 and is now the Brontë Parsonage Museum, with the original rooms furnished and decorated as they would have been in the early to mid-1850s; there is also an

extensive display of the Brontë collections. EG's sketch of the Parsonage and the church, with the school building (1832), was engraved as the vol. II frontispiece: it emphasizes the bleakness, before the graveyard was enclosed and trees planted; for a photograph, possibly of the mid-1850s, see Fraser, *CB*, plate 3b.

12 *of upright tombstones*: the church of St Michael and All Angels is almost entirely post-Brontë, having been rebuilt in 1880, except for the West Tower; the church the Brontës knew dated from the late Middle Ages, though its interior had been altered extensively. EG drew her information about the history of the church and parish from a variety of sources (as well as observation); here and on later historical and topographical details, EG's sources have not always been traced: any information would be welcome. The detail below of the 1317 chapel is from John James, *The History and Topography of Bradford* (1841), p. 361.

*'Hic fecit . . . A.D. sexcentissimo'*: the inscription reads: 'Here was built a monastery, founded by Austet in AD 600.' If true, this would have been only three years after St Augustine of Canterbury came to England, predating the conversion of Northumbria in 625. The explanation of a plain error is from Thomas Dunham Whitaker's history of Leeds, *Loidis and Elmete* (1816), pp. 355–6.

14 *on the tablet*: footnote added in Ed. 3. Anne Brontë was born 17 Jan. 1820. Patrick Brontë's statement is from his letter of 20 June 1855 to EG (John Rylands MS). The mural tablets, transcribed for EG by John Greenwood of Haworth and checked by him for Ed. 3 (*Letters*, pp. 368, 457), were taken down shortly before 1860 and the broken pieces buried by order of Arthur Bell Nicholls, CB's widower, to frustrate souvenir hunters: a single tablet was substituted.

16 *enemy draws near*: used in *Shirley*, vol. I, ch. vii (p. 123).

*desire for riches*: MS identifies the man as from Haworth.

*days of Edward III*: the woollen cloth industry was long established before Edward III in the fourteenth century gave it new impetus by encouraging skilled weavers to come to England from the Low Countries. The cloth being sent to Holland to be dyed, James I in 1603 granted Alderman William Cockayne (below) and others the exclusive right of dyeing: the Dutch retaliated by prohibiting imports of English cloth. Under Charles I's so-called arbitrary rule without Parliament (1629–40), Archbishop Laud tried to impose conformity to the doctrines and organization of the Church of England; the cloth-workers of Yorkshire, amongst others, were attracted to Calvinistic doctrines and discipline (the 'Puritans'). Yorkshire was a key area, because of its wealth, in the early stages of the Civil War, and was lost decisively to the King at Marston Moor (1644). Cromwell defeated the Scots at Dunbar (1650).

18 *Lamartine, Kossuth, and Dembinsky*: all three were identified with democratic and nationalist movements: Alphonse Lamartine (1790–1869) in France; Lajos Kossuth (1802–94) in Hungary; Henrik Dembinsky (1791–1864) in Poland. EG found the point about Old Testament names, originally made by T. D. Whitaker (*Loidis and Elmete*, pp. 370–1), in Joseph Hunter, *The Rise of the Old Dissent, Exemplified in the Life of Oliver Heywood* (1842), p. 75.

*days of Charles II*: by the Act of Uniformity (1662) all ministers holding Church of England livings were required to give their consent to 'all and everything contained and prescribed' in the Book of Common Prayer. Some thousand ministers who in conscience could not do so were ejected on St Bartholomew's Day (24 Aug.) 1662.

'*Life of Oliver Heywood*': Joseph Hunter, *The Rise of the Old Dissent, Exemplified in the Life of Oliver Heywood*; the quotation from Rither is on p. 75; the reference above to the abundance of coal and its consequences is from Hunter, pp. 73–4.

19 *husband and myself . . . Addingham*: EG left half a page in MS after 'from Haworth' and William Gaskell wrote in the account (down to 'sympathy or sorrow'). The lines below are from 'Flodden Field' by Richard Jackson.

20 *the seventeenth century*: the 'savage custom of the forest' and the beheadings, the last being in 1650, are from Joseph Hunter, *The Rise of the Old Dissent*, p. 73.

21 *woollen manufacturer*: unidentified; it is not clear whether this is from a printed or an oral source.

*over Blackstone Edge*: on the pack-horse and coach route between Rochdale and Halifax (approximately the modern A58); the Edge marks the division between Lancashire and Yorkshire.

22 '*busy town or crowded mart*': John Keble, 'St Matthew' (*The Christian Year*, 1827).

*recently given me*: EG's informant unidentified; possibly Sir James Kay-Shuttleworth (see p. 337 note).

*threap yo' down th' loan*: 'whip you down the road'.

23 *the Rev. William Grimshaw*: William Grimshaw (1708–63) became perpetual curate of Haworth in 1742; he experienced a personal conversion in 1744 and while remaining in the Church of England,

shared as an evangelical the beliefs and enthusiasm of Wesley and Methodism.

*one Mr Nicholls*: the details about Nicholls are from Joseph Hunter, *The Rise of the Old Dissent*, p. 80.

*Newton, Cowper's friend*: John Newton (1725–1807), after a wild life at sea, underwent a religious conversion in 1748, and came under the influence of Wesley and Whitfield. He became curate at Olney, Buckinghamshire, where he met the poet William Cowper (1731–1800) and they collaborated in the *Olney Hymns*. As EG indicates, she draws on Newton's *Memoirs of the Life of the Late Rev. William Grimshaw* (1799), including his conversion, 2 Sept. 1744 (pp. 24, 36–7); his preaching and the presence of Wesley and Whitfield (pp. 59–60, 69–70); his rebuke to Whitfield (pp. 142–3); his enforcement of church attendance (p. 110); his carrying his own food (p. 119); and the Haworth races (pp. 121–2). The details of Psalm 119 and the horsewhip are either local tradition or EG's own colouring.

24 *Wesley . . . Whitfield*: John Wesley (1703–91), evangelist and leader of Methodism (a development originally within the Church of England, of which Wesley always regarded himself a member); contrasted with the less humane George Whitfield (or Whitefield) (1714–70), who, while part of the Methodist movement, held to strict Calvinist doctrines.

25 *Wesleyan Methodists . . . Baptists . . . worship*: the Methodist chapel was erected in the 1750s and later enlarged; the West Lane Baptist Chapel in 1752 (and enlarged 1775). The quotation from Whitaker (*Loidis and Elmete*, p. 371) is taken from Joseph Hunter, *The Rise of the Old Dissent*, p. 75.

26 *the Black Bull*: at the top of Haworth main street, just below the church.

*Heywood . . . two quotations*: Joseph Hunter, *The Rise of the Old Dissent*, p. 405 n., the first from the antiquarian Ralph Thoresby.

*funeral of Mr Charnock*: James Charnock (d. 1819) succeeded John Richardson (d. 1791) as perpetual curate. The source of EG's information unidentified; 'pawsing' is 'kicking'.

27 *the Saxon law*: a legal code of King Edgar (944–75) laid down the classes of churches and made provision for support of their priests.

*Mr Brontë says*: in a letter to EG, 27 Aug. 1855 (John Rylands MS), prompted by hearing that EG had 'mentioned to a clergyman' that Patrick Brontë had been opposed on his entrance to the living and his salary withheld.

27 *A Yorkshire gentleman*: the Revd J. Hodgson Ramsbotham, a son-in-law of the Revd Samuel Redhead (1778–1845), the minister proposed for Haworth; he wrote to EG, denying her account of the 'Haworth commotions' and giving another, 'in which I don't see any great difference' (*Letters*, p. 453). This passage ('A Yorkshire gentleman . . . won their hearts') added in Ed. 3; manuscript in Manchester Central Public Library.

28 *Dr Scoresby*: William Scoresby (1789–1857); followed his father into the whale fishery; ordained in the 1820s; Vicar of Bradford, 1839–47. EG met him in Sept. 1855, when he gave her information about Patrick Brontë and 'the extraordinary character of the people round Haworth' (*Letters*, p. 872).

*Redhead as perpetual curate*: Redhead was minister at Horton when offered the perpetual curacy of Haworth.

29 *landlord of the inn at the time*: Abraham Wilkinson.

30 *came to preach*: on 21 July 1844.

*have already quoted*: the following passage ('The foregoing account . . . be anything but level') added in Ed. 3; in MS additions (from 'of men, a man to myself' to 'and not infrequently inebriate'). The section about musical talent after 'ecksqueaize' ('There are some things . . . Compulsion they defy') is an insertion within the addition, copied out twice and bound in vol. I of MS at p. 33, with a note to add it 'if not too late'.

31 *of his order*: the sweep in his workaday soot-covered clothes mirrored the professional black coat of the clergyman: hence, given the situation, the joke.

32 *Marcello*: Benedetto Marcello (1686–1739), Venetian composer, noted for his psalm settings. The phrase 'familiar as household words', virtually proverbial, adapts *Henry V*, IV. iii. 52. The Haworth tenor (below) was Thomas Parker (1787–1866); Branwell's portrait of him is in BPM.

*Mr Heap*: the Revd Henry Heap (b. 1790) became Vicar of Bradford on the death of John Crosse (1739–1816), who had been blind for a number of years.

33 *suaviter in modo . . . fortiter in re*: show less of 'gentleness' than 'firmness', less of the 'velvet glove' than the 'iron fist'.

*o' th' Yate*: 'of the Street'; the medieval word commonly survives as 'gate' in street names (e.g. Deansgate, Jubber Gate).

*had then to begin*: the first European Temperance Society was established in Ulster in 1829.

34 *Down in Ireland*: Patrick Brontë (1777–1861) supplied EG with details
of his parentage and early life in a letter (20 June 1855; John Rylands
MS), the first of a series giving details about the family, once EG had
agreed to write the biography. His parents were Hugh Brunty and
Eleanor McClory, Patrick being the eldest child. An early influence
was the biennial preaching visits of John Wesley, important in his
evangelical background, itself emphasized by Patrick's education at St
John's College, Cambridge, where Charles Simeon (see next note) was
Fellow of King's College. After schoolteaching, he entered the family
of the Revd Thomas Tighe (1798) before proceeding to Cambridge
(1802): it was on entry here (1 Oct.) that he first wrote his family
name (written also as Prunty and Pruty) as Brontë, an adaptation of
Nelson's title, Duke of Bronte (in Sicily; conferred 1799 by the King
of Naples). Patrick graduated BA in Apr. 1806; was ordained deacon,
Aug. 1806, and appointed curate at Wethersfield, Essex (through links
with Simeon and the evangelical wing of the Church of England);
ordained priest, Dec. 1807. It is important for Patrick's ministry and
connections (religious and personal) to remember that Methodism
only finally separated itself from the Church of England in the early
nineteenth century and remained an important evangelical presence
in the established church: see Gerald R. Cragg, 'Methodism and the
Evangelical Revival', in *The Church and the Age of Reason* 1648–1789
(1960; rev. 1970), and Alec R. Vidler, 'Christianity in England', in *The
Church in an Age of Revolution* (1961; rev. 1974).

*Cambridge*: at Cambridge, Charles Simeon (1759–1836), Fellow of
King's College and perpetual curate of Holy Trinity, was an important religious influence. Through preaching and example, he promoted
evangelicalism in the Church of England, emphasizing individual
conversion, the rejection of mediation between the individual and
God, and the need to be active witnesses in the world. Simeon
was concerned to get right-minded men into parishes; later, he was a
subscriber to the Clergy Daughters' School (see p. 50 and note).

35 *remaining in his speech*: John Lock and W. T. Dixon claim Patrick's
Ulster accent puzzled his Essex congregation, though it was considerably blunted by the time he went to Yorkshire (*A Man of Sorrow*,
pp. 27, 88); Mary Taylor (see p. 80) noted that CB had 'a strong Irish
accent' as a schoolgirl at Roe Head. EG referred in 1853 to Patrick's
'strong Scotch accent (he comes from the North of Ireland)' (*Letters*,
p. 245). The traditional Irish features (often caricatured) were round
face and nose, with protruding jaw (for Patrick at about 30 years, see
*A Man of Sorrow*, frontispiece).

35 *volunteers . . . Lord Palmerston*: Napoleon had gathered at Boulogne an army to invade England. Henry John Temple, Viscount Palmerston (1784–1865), was at St John's College (MA, 1806); later notable as Secretary at War, Foreign Secretary, and Prime Minister.

*at Hartshead*: between Wethersfield (which he left in Jan. 1809) and Hartshead (where he became perpetual curate in Mar. 1811), Patrick Brontë was curate at Wellington, Shropshire (Jan.–Dec. 1809) and Dewsbury (Dec. 1809–Mar. 1811). Patrick visited his family after ordination as deacon in 1806, but never went to Ireland again.

*Maria Branwell*: Maria Branwell (1783–1821); for details of the Branwell family, see C. W. Hatfield, 'The Relations of Maria Branwell: The Mother of the Brontë Sisters', *BST* 9 (1939), 245–52. Maria was in Yorkshire at the invitation of her aunt, Jane Fennell (see p. 37 note, the Revd John Fennell), to assist at the Wesleyan Academy, Apperley Bridge, near Bradford.

*life of his brother*: John Davy, *Memoirs of the Life of Sir Humphry Davy, Bart.* (2 vols., 1836); the three extracts from the scientist's biography are all in ch. 1 (pp. 9–11).

37 *aunt, Miss Branwell*: Elizabeth Branwell (1776–1842). She had visited her sister in Thornton in 1815 and 1816 and came to Haworth during her sister's last illness (1821), affording 'great comfort' to Patrick Brontë and 'behaving as an affectionate mother to my children' (Patrick Brontë to John Buckworth, 27 Nov. 1821). Patrick Brontë made at least two proposals of marriage, to Mary Burder and Elizabeth Firth, before accepting widowerhood and the permanent residence of Elizabeth. The servants remembered her as fault-finding and 'close', 'a bit of a tyke' (Helen H. Arnold, 'The Reminiscences of Emma Huidekoper Cortazzo: A Friend of Ellen Nussey', *BST*, 13 (1958), 227). She clearly did not care for Haworth: EN remembered her as 'a very small, antiquated little lady' in the 1830s, with 'a horror of the climate . . . and of the stone floors' (WS, i. 111, quoting *Scribner's Monthly*, May 1871). Elizabeth Branwell had a strong sense of responsibility, was crucial to the children's upbringing, and was regarded by them (despite reservations) with affection.

*were Methodists*: the Methodists, like John Wesley himself, long regarded their affiliation as with the Church of England: only at the end of the eighteenth century and the beginning of the nineteenth were separate branches of Methodism established, while other followers of Wesley formed an important evangelical presence within the Anglican Church.

*engagement in 1812*: WS, i. 8–23 prints the nine letters, dated 26 Aug.–5 Dec.; on 3 Nov. 1856 Patrick Brontë wrote to EG that they would demonstrate his wife's 'sound sense, her affectionate disposition, and delicate tact and taste' (John Rylands MS). CB read these letters in 1850: 'The papers were yellow with time, all having been written before I was born. It was strange now to peruse . . . the records of a mind whence my own sprang' (16 Feb.). The Nov. letter (below) is dated the 18th.

*Reverend John Fennel*: John Fennell (1762–1842); as a Methodist, appointed headmaster (1812) of the newly founded Wesleyan Academy, Woodhouse Grove, Apperley Bridge; was shortly after, on taking orders in the Church of England, required to resign. Ordained and curate at Bradford, 1815. Married (1790) Jane Branwell (1753–1829), aunt of Maria and Elizabeth Branwell, whose invitation of Maria to Yorkshire led to the meeting with Patrick Brontë.

38 *'But trust me . . . to be strange'*: *Romeo and Juliet*, II. i. 142–3.

*Kirkstall Abbey*: the finely preserved ruin of a twelfth-century Cistercian abbey, just west of Leeds.

*Cousin Jane . . . clergyman*: Jane Branwell Fennell (1791–1827) was engaged to the Revd William Morgan, friend of Patrick Brontë from their curate days in Wellington, Shropshire.

39 *202l. per annum*: MS has deleted note: '(Clergy list for 1854)', in which the information is given.

*prettily describes*: the letter is dated 18 Nov. 1812; the storm was probably that of 19 Oct., which did great damage.

*Mr Brontë's composing*: Patrick Brontë's writings include two collections of poems, *Cottage Poems* (1811) and *The Rural Minstrel* (1818). Maria possibly refers to 'The Cottager's Hymn' in the former volume.

*'Advice to a Lady'*: 1731, by George, Baron Lyttelton (1709–73).

*elegant and neat*: after 'neat' MS has, deleted: 'and the spelling perfectly correct'.

40 *'The Advantages . . . in Religious Concerns'*: WS, i. 24–7; manuscript in Brotherton Library, Leeds.

*December, 1812*: from Woodhouse Grove, Apperley Bridge. The marriage was at Guiseley; Patrick Brontë and Maria were married by William Morgan; William Morgan and Jane Fennell were then married by Patrick Brontë. Charlotte Branwell on the same day married her cousin Joseph Branwell. There seems no evidence of how EG contacted the Branwell relatives or which they were.

40 *Maria and Elizabeth*: Maria was born 1813 and christened by William Morgan, 23 Apr. 1814; Elizabeth, born 8 Feb. 1815, was christened 26 Aug. by John Fennell.

*in Bradford parish*: in 1815 Patrick Brontë exchanged the living of Hartshead with the Revd Thomas Atkinson of Thornton (his wife was related to Elizabeth Firth, to whom Patrick proposed after his wife's death); the family arrived in Thornton on or before 19 May. A 'chapel of ease' (below), when a parish was large and the distance to the parish church far, provided services within reasonable travelling distance, the curate-in-charge being responsible to the parish priest (here, the Vicar of Bradford). EG stresses it was *episcopal* (i.e. Church of England), since the Nonconformist monuments might suggest it was a dissenting chapel. Ruins of the seventeenth-century old church (Bell Chapel) survive in the graveyard of St James's church (1870); the font (1679) was removed to St James's.

*Lister . . . Hall*: Accepted Lister (d. 1709) and his father Joseph (1627–1709), Nonconformists of the seventeenth-century Puritan tradition. Dr John Hall (1633–1710), of a Puritan family, became Bishop of Bristol and remained within the Church of England, though attacked as a Puritan.

*chapel . . . denomination*: the Nonconformist Kipping Chapel, named after the estate on which it was originally built, was moved to the east end of Thornton in 1769.

*Charlotte . . . Emily Jane, and Anne*: the children were born at the Parsonage, Market Street (plaque), off High Street. Charlotte was christened 29 June by William Morgan; her godparents were Frances Walker and the Revd Thomas Atkinson, and possibly Elizabeth Firth. She was named after her aunt Charlotte Branwell. Branwell was born 26 June 1817 and christened 23 July; Emily Jane born 30 July 1818 and christened 20 Aug., her second name coming from Jane Morgan, one of her godparents; Anne born 17 Jan. 1820 and christened 25 Mar., named after her Branwell grandmother and aunt.

41 *February 25th, 1820*: Patrick Brontë was licensed to Haworth 25 Feb., though the family only moved in April. Haworth was a perpetual curacy (i.e. permanent to the holder for life or as long as he wished), the salary of about £200 p.a. coming from freehold rents; the house was rent free. Patrick supplied EG with the date of 25 Feb. in a document annotated by EG 'Papers & facts relating to parents of C.B.' (John Rylands MS).

*house and garden*: corrected in Ed. 3 from 'goes round house and garden, on all sides but one' (in MS additions); corrected again on p. 99 from '*in a churchyard*—for the parsonage is surrounded by it on three sides—*and with all*'.

*to the children*: this room has been significantly affected by later alterations.

*warm-hearted sisters*: revised in Ed. 3 from 'two rough affectionate warm-hearted, wasteful sisters'. The sisters, Nancy and Sarah Garrs, were from Thornton, where they were first engaged as servants in the Brontë household, afterwards moving with the family to Haworth. EG refers (see p. 47) to them both living in Bradford, though Sarah had emigrated some time before to America. It was Nancy, in later life, who characterized Aunt Branwell (see p. 37 note). These references to waste, intended 'to show that it was from no *stingy* motive that Mr Brontë refused his children . . . meat' (*Letters*, p. 467), provided one of EG's many problems over fact and individual sensitivity: the servants 'make a doleful complaint, & have even been over to see Mr Brontë'. The words complained of were taken out late in the printing of Ed. 3 (*Letters*, p. 463). Patrick Brontë gave the sisters a testimonial, exonerating them from waste and lack of care (WS, iv. 226; BPM MS). Nancy was a mourner at both CB's funeral and at Patrick's in 1861.

42 '*Who mells . . . shoe his goose*': the abbey at Whalley in Lancashire, about 18 miles from Haworth, was begun in the thirteenth century; at the Reformation, some seats from the sedilia or choir were moved to the parish church, including the one EG refers to (choir, south side). The wording (modernized) is: 'Whoso melles [meddles, concerns] him of that all men does, let him come here and shoe the goose' (the carving shows a man at the task).

43 *good old woman*: this 'good old woman' (from Burnley, EG had learnt back in 1850: *Letters*, p. 124) proved particularly troublesome to EG; she is sometimes treated as though solely responsible for the account of the Brontë children and of Patrick Brontë that follows and which EG later substantially altered (see notes, below, for material omitted in Ed. 3). A tradition has grown up that this nurse had a grudge (allegedly because abruptly dismissed by Patrick Brontë) and she was particularly attacked by William Dearden (*Bradford Observer*, 13 and 20 Aug. 1857), ostensibly defending Patrick Brontë but put up to it (so EG believed: *Letters*, p. 468) by Nancy Garrs. As EG insisted, some of the details came directly from CB and others from Haworth people (*Letters*, pp. 455, 467): indeed, during her first meeting with CB in Aug. 1850, EG had heard versions of the sawn chairs and the hearthrug, told her by Lady Kay-Shuttleworth (*Letters*, pp. 124–5). It

seems likely that the nurse, during Mrs Brontë's illness, did observe
certain things (no one has disputed the account of Maria reading to
the other children in the house of sickness) and picked up others,
distorted as gossip, which she told EG and which fitted with EG's
other information and with her sense of Patrick Brontë's eccentricity
(admitted, not without pleasure, by himself: 'I do not deny that I am,
somewhat eccentric'—to EG, 30 July 1857; John Rylands MS). The
details are in two groups: the first concerns waste, a vegetarian diet,
and the boots (seemingly those supplied by the nurse); the second
focuses on Patrick's behaviour (supplied by CB, Lady Kay-Shuttleworth, and Haworth people: perhaps by the nurse also): the pistols,
solitary meals, the gown, the hearthrug, and sawing the chairs. Patrick
Brontë, while generally approving *The Life*, raised the first objections:
specifically he denied the children lived on vegetable food, or that he
fired the pistols or sawed the chairs to express suppressed feelings (to
William Gaskell, 7 Apr. 1857; John Rylands MS). Later he again
denied these things to EG (30 July 1857; John Rylands MS), though
allowing against EG's evident protest that CB was her informant that
CB 'must have been misinform'd'. William Dearden, the unwelcome
champion of Patrick Brontë, was one of Branwell Brontë's friends
from Halifax days (1841); his testimony cannot simply be accepted, in
general because he was one of those who later claimed that Branwell
wrote much of *Wuthering Heights* and in particular because he claims
to be quoting Patrick directly, something Patrick Brontë denied.
However, his version of the silk gown (WS, i. 49–50), claimed to be
from Nancy Garrs, reads like a truer version, though still not grasping
Patrick's fear of a *cotton* dress as more inflammable. Again, indicating
the underlying foundations of these stories, EN recalled (clearly
the true version) that having loaded the pistol at night, Patrick would
discharge it each morning (WS, i. 114; and see also EN on
Patrick's horror of fire: WS, i. 113, 114). Since Patrick himself
repudiated most of the details, EG withdrew them, concerned to
'save Mr Brontë from worry as much as ever I can' (*Letters*, p. 467),
whatever she might believe, with some reason, to the contrary.

43 *I had ever seen*: Ed. 3 omits: '*seen*. In part, I set it down to a fancy Mr
Brontë had of not letting them have flesh-meat to eat. It was from no
wish for saving, for there was plenty and even waste in the
house, with young servants and no mistress to see after them; but he
thought that children should be brought up simply and hardily:
so they had nothing but potatoes for their dinner; but they never
seemed to wish for anything else; *they were good*'. See *Letters*, pp.
466–7.

*Rousseau . . . Day on education*: Jean-Jacques Rousseau (1712–78) set out his ideas on human development in *Émile, or On Education* (1762): the child's distinctive nature and desires being recognized, Émile is nurtured through the freedom of nature rather than the constraints of society. Thomas Day (1748–89), an early enthusiast for Rousseau's educational ideas, educated two girls on these principles: though he may have thought of marrying one of them, the story of Sabrina (below) is apocryphal. Day set out his modified thoughts on education in the vastly popular *History of Sandford and Merton* (3 vols., 1783–9), showing that the principal evil to be guarded against is effeminacy— hence the 'discipline' to which EG's aunt (not identifiable) was subjected.

44 *regarded his daughters*: Ed. 3 omits: '*daughters*; but he went at his object with unsparing earnestness of purpose. Mrs Brontë's nurse told me that one day when the children had been out on the moors, and rain had come on, she thought their feet would be wet, and accordingly she rummaged out some coloured boots which had been given to them by a friend—the Mr Morgan, who married "Cousin Jane," she believes. These little pairs she ranged round the kitchen fire to warm; but, when the children came back, the boots were nowhere to be found; only a very strong odour of burnt leather was perceived. Mr Brontë had come in and seen them; they were too gay and luxurious for his children, and would foster a love of dress; so he had put them into the fire. He spared nothing that offended his antique simplicity. Long before this, some one had given Mrs Brontë a silk gown; either the make, the colour, or the material, was not according to his notions of consistent propriety, and Mrs Brontë in consequence never wore it. But, for all that, she kept it treasured up in her drawers, which were generally locked. One day, however, while in the kitchen, she remembered that she had left the key in her drawer, and, hearing Mr Brontë up-stairs, she augured some ill to her dress, and, running up in haste, she found it cut into shreds.'

*or displeased*: Ed. 3 omits: '*displeased*, but worked off his volcanic wrath by firing pistols out of the back-door in rapid succession. Mrs Brontë, lying in bed up-stairs, would hear the quick explosions, and know that something had gone wrong; but *her sweet nature*'.

*an angry word*: Ed. 3 omits: '*word?*" Now and then his anger took a different form, but still was speechless. Once he got the hearth-rug, and stuffing it up the grate, deliberately set it on fire, and remained in the room in spite of the stench, until it had smouldered and shrivelled away into uselessness. Another time he took some chairs, and sawed away at the backs till they were reduced to the condition of stools.' Mrs Brontë's life was not easy, but that it was generally a happy marriage is suggested by Nancy Garrs's anecdote (from William Dearden: see p. 43 note; but probably to be trusted), when her intended marriage was known (WS, i. 51).

45 *days of the Luddites*: the commercial depression of the late years of the Napoleonic wars and the threat to jobs perceived in new machinery led in 1811–13 to machine-breaking by workers who claimed the mythical Ned Ludd as their leader: see pp. 86–9 and notes. This outbreak is part of the background to *Shirley*.

*was a strike*: unidentified.

46 *September, 1821*: on 15 Sept.; she had been ill since 29 Jan. She was buried 22 Sept., William Morgan officiating.

*age, sex, and station*: Ed. 3 omits: '*and station*. There was one family residing near Haworth who had been remarkably attentive and kind to Mrs Brontë in her illness, and who had paid the children the attention of asking them occasionally to tea; and as the story connected with this family, and which, I suspect, dissolved their intercourse with their neighbours, made a deep impression on Charlotte's mind in her early girlhood, I may as well relate it here. It will serve as a specimen of the wild stories afloat in an isolated village, for as to its truth in minor particulars, I will not vouch; no more did she, the principal event having occurred when she was too young to understand its full import, and the tale having been heard, with the addition, probably, of the whispered exaggerations of the uneducated. The family were Dissenters, professing some rather rigid form of religion. The father was a woollen manufacturer and moderately wealthy; at any rate, their style of living appeared "grand" to the simple children who bounded their ideas by the frugal habits of the parsonage. These people had a green-house, the only one in the neighbourhood; a cumbrous building, with more wood and wall than glass, situated in a garden which was divided from the house by the high road to Haworth. They had a large family; and one of the elder daughters was married to a wealthy manufacturer "beyond Keighley;" she was near her confinement, when she begged that a favourite young sister might go and pay her a visit, and remain with her till her baby was born. The request was complied with; the young girl—fifteen or sixteen years of age—went. She came home, after some weeks spent in her brother-in-law's house, ill and dispirited. Inquiries were made of her by her parents, and it was discovered that she had been seduced by her sister's wealthy husband; and that the consequences of this wickedness would soon become apparent. Her angry and indignant father shut her up in her room, until he could decide how to act; her elder sisters flouted at and scorned her. Only her mother, and she was reported to be a stern woman, had some pity on her. The tale went, that passers along the high-road at night time saw the mother and young daughter walking in the garden, weeping, long after the household were gone to bed. Nay, more; it was whispered that they walked and wept there still, when Miss Brontë told me the tale— though both had long mouldered in their graves. The wild whisperers of this story added, that the cruel father, maddened perhaps by the disgrace which had fallen upon a "religious" family, offered a sum of money to any one who would marry his poor fallen daughter; that a husband was found, who bore her away from Haworth, and broke her heart, so that she died while even yet a child. / Such deep passionate resentment would have seemed not unnatural in a man who took stern pride in his character for religious morality; but the degrading part, after all, was this. The remaining members of the family, elder sisters even, went on paying visits at their wealthy brother-in-law's house, as if his sin was not a hundred-fold more scarlet than the poor young girl's, whose evil-doing had been so hardly resented, and so coarsely hidden. The strong feeling of the country-side still holds the descendants of this family as accursed. They fail in business, or they fail in health. / At this house, I believe, the little Brontës paid their only visits; and these visits ceased before long. / *But the children'*. This story's truth might seem vouched for by *William Dearden* (letter to *Bradford Observer*, note to p. 43) who refers to the pain caused by it amongst the manufacturer's descendants: though he confuses which family's descendants EG refers to. In both Dearden and in EG's account, the reference to descendants and EG's ghostly tradition seem to place the incident back a century, rather than within CB's lifetime. Sarah Fermi convincingly identifies the Haworth family as that of James Greenwood of Bridge House and his son-in-law as William Sugden of Eastwood House, Keighley ('A "Religious" Family Disgraced: New Information on a Passage Deleted from Mrs Gaskell's *Life of Charlotte Brontë*', *BST*, 20 (1992), 289–95).

*Lamb expresses it*: Charles Lamb, 'Mackery End', *Essays of Elia* (1823).

47 *with each other*: Patrick Brontë to EG, 24 July 1855 (John Rylands MS); in the further extract below, the first part ('When mere children . . . of their age') is from the same letter; the second ('A circumstance . . . what I have stated') from Patrick Brontë to EG, 30 July 1855 (John Rylands MS).

47 *a little anecdote*: added in Ed. 3 ('I may add . . . by the resemblance'). The frontispiece portrait to vol. I was an engraving from George Richmond's drawing (see p. 349 and note); it was photographed, on Sir James Kay-Shuttleworth's insistence, by Stewart of Manchester. The 'gentleman' who showed it to Nancy was presumably Sir James.

48 *"Age and experience"*: without denying the interest and strangeness of Patrick Brontë's educational experiment, the children's answers would all be stock ones at the time.

49 *after his children*: for Elizabeth Branwell, see p. 37 note; she was certainly at Haworth during her sister's final illness. Patrick Brontë had simply informed EG that Aunt Branwell came soon after his wife's death (to EG, 20 June 1855; John Rylands MS): she may have returned briefly to Penzance. Some details here, as of the pattens worn indoors, come also in EN's reminiscences (WS, i. 110–16): she presumably supplied them to EG.

*made of stone*: there is a minor contradiction between the account here and that on p. 41, where EG stresses the amount of woodwork in the house; the stairs were of stone. Until CB was left as the only child, there were few carpets and no curtains in the house; EN remembered the hall floor and stairs as sandstoned; when EG visited they were presumably carpeted. Pattens, which Aunt Branwell wore indoors, were undershoes, reinforced with metal, for outdoors wear in bad weather.

50 *was Cowan Bridge*: given as 'Cowan's' throughout Eds. 1 and 2; in Eds. 1 and 2 the first right-hand running headline identified the real with the fictional school of *Jane Eyre*: 'COWAN'S BRIDGE (LOWOOD) SCHOOL'. Cowan Bridge School, near Kirby Lonsdale, then in Westmorland (now Cumbria), was founded by the Revd William Carus Wilson. Good in intention and later successful, especially after moving to a new site at nearby Casterton where it is still established, it was not healthy or well-run in its early days. EG was convinced that CB suffered irreversible physical and emotional damage there. CB spoke of it with bitterness, presenting the school as Lowood in *Jane Eyre*, with Wilson as Mr Brocklehurst: see Clarendon *Jane Eyre*, appendix II. On publication of *The Life*, Mr Wilson's supporters attacked the account of school and of founder, though their arguments often referred to the school after the Brontës' time and its removal to Casterton. EG had, as she states below, received an account from CB on their first meeting (Aug. 1850; *Letters*, pp. 125, 128) and she borrowed reports on the school (*Letters*, pp. 456, 462) as well as visiting both sites: at Cowan Bridge (where now only the former

dormitory survives; plaque to the four sisters), the wing built by Wilson was already destroyed by fire. That Wilson was not popular, despite his philanthropy, is indicated by a spoof prospectus, where promised accomplishments include ventriloquy and the singing teacher doubles as scourge-mistress (*BST*, 11 (1946), 16–28; copy in BPM); Myra Curtis has shown its satirical nature in a comparison with the actual prospectus ('Cowan Bridge School: An Old P-rospectus Re-examined', *BST*, 12 (1953), 187–92). WS (iv, appendix I, pp. 297–344) usefully prints the controversy begun by Wilson's son. EG, as the notes below show, rewrote the episode considerably, correcting, qualifying, but also offering new evidence in support of some statements. She felt hampered in asserting the truth, because many 'who are now offering me testimony in proof of my correctness are poor people ... who say I *may* make use of their names, if absolutely necessary—but that it may seriously injure them if I do'; *Letters*, p. 451, and see also pp. 462–3).

*Report for 1842*: originally borrowed with others by EG from the Revd Henry Shepheard (1809–78), son-in-law of Wilson and chaplain to the school; they included the Report of 1850, in which Wilson withdrew from the Secretaryship (quoted below). Shepheard published *A Vindication of the Clergy Daughters' School and the Rev. W. Carus Wilson* (1857). EG refers (below) to 'schools', because there was also a Servants' School, which trained girls for service. In the Prospectus the 'use of the globes' was of the terrestial globe for geography and the celestial for astronomy. EG agreed (*Letters*, pp. 462–3) that the sums of £3 and £1 successively given as entrance money for clothes was a contradiction; she was unable to check, but £3 is the correct figure.

51 *with Cowan Bridge*: CB took pleasure in reporting (4 Jan. 1848) that a clergyman, recognizing both school and Wilson, said Wilson 'deserved the chastisement he had got'. The immediate identification of Lowood as Cowan Bridge was a point made by those attacking *The Life* (WS, iv. 297).

*some of the notices*: added in Ed. 3 ('In some of the notices ... the subject from her'). EG's first acquaintance with CB (below) was in Aug. 1850.

52 *'Common-place Book'*: in Robert Southey's *The Doctor* (1834–47), two sisters, sent from Cumbria to Dent in the West Riding to learn knitting, dislike the unfamiliar ways of preparing food (Interchapter xxiv, p. 558b (1848 one-vol. edn.)).

*William Carus Wilson*: the Revd William Carus Wilson (1791–1859), son of a wealthy landowner who had been influenced by Simeon at

Cambridge. Wilson himself was ordained in 1816 and given the living of Tunstall, near Kirby Lonsdale, where he founded a charity school. He established the Clergy Daughters' School at Cowan Bridge near Tunstall in 1824; it moved to nearby Casterton in 1833. Patrick Brontë was in part attracted to the school by the founder's evangelicalism. Wilson was a Calvinist, convinced of humanity's sinfulness and of predestination. A distributor of tracts from the age of 8, he wrote and published polemical magazines and tracts (see Gérin, *CB*, pp. 12–14, and *Jane Eyre*, ch. IV). Ill health led him to withdraw from directing the school in 1849 and he settled in the Isle of Wight (memorial in St John's, Newport). The page headline in Ed. 1 (i. 65) was 'THE REV. CARUS WILSON' and he was identified as a 'wealthy' clergyman. Shepheard objected both to the headline and the word 'wealthy' (*Vindication*, pp. 3–4, 8).

53 *perpetual interference*: Ed. 3 omits '*perpetual* and injudicious *interference*'; and in the next paragraph softens '*errors*, which he certainly *committed*' to 'which he was believed to have'.

54 *This original house*: 'This original house . . . now destroyed' added and revised in Ed. 3. Ed. 1 reads: '*school garden*. Running from this building, at right angles with what now remains of the school-house, there was formerly a bobbin-mill connected with the stream, where wooden reels were made out of the alders which grow profusely in such ground as that surrounding Cowan's Bridge. Mr Wilson adapted this mill to his purpose; there were school-rooms on the lower floor, and dormitories on the upper. *The present*'.

55 *been only sixteen*: revised from Ed. 1: '*hand, and*, as far as I can make out, from seventy to eighty pupils.' Shepheard (*Vindication*, p. 8) pointed out the error; Maria and Elizabeth were enrolled respectively as pupils number 17 and 18, CB and Emily as 30 and 44.

*an unnecessary extent*: Ed. 3 substitutes '*inspection*; carried . . . occasionally to a' for Ed. 1: '*inspection*; and his love of authority seems to have led to a great deal of unnecessary and irritating *meddling*'; later in the sentence ('which had sometimes . . . of feeling') added in Ed. 3

56 *admitted as pupils*: Maria and Elizabeth had been admitted, 21 July. CB was admitted on 10 Aug., Emily on 25 Nov.: for the school register entries on their accomplishments, see Gérin, *CB*, p. 1, and *Emily Brontë*, pp. 7–8.

*subject before him*: Ed. 3 omits: '*him*; and when he heard of them, his reply was to the effect that the children were to be trained up to regard higher things than dainty pampering of the appetite, and (apparently unconscious of the fact, that daily loathing and rejection of food is sure to undermine the health) he lectured them on the sin of caring over-much for carnal things'; in the next paragraph, Ed. 3 adds the extenuating particularities of '*children* like the delicate little Brontës' and '*their* feeble appetites . . . inducing a *half starved condition*'; Shepheard had seized on the Brontës' 'thin blood' (*Vindication*, p. 21) to deny that Cowan Bridge undermined their health.

*to Tunstall Church*: St John the Baptist's, mainly early 15th century; the porch is two-storeyed and the girls would have entered its upper room from the gallery (now destroyed) where they sat for services (photograph in Flintoff, *In the Steps of the Brontës*, p. 32).

57 *lingered about her*: Maria, like Elizabeth, died from tuberculosis (consumption); while Cowan Bridge promoted the illness, the sisters had developed it at Haworth. As commonly in the nineteenth century, tuberculosis was passed between family members; Branwell, Emily, and Anne all later died of it.

'*Miss Scatcherd' in 'Jane Eyre'*: a Miss Andrews, who was an underteacher. She had married and emigrated to America; in 1855 she wrote in defence of Carus Wilson and of the school (effectively also a defence of herself): see Shepheard, *Vindication*, pp. 13–14 (where the initials of her first and married name are 'A. H.') and WS, iv. 297–8.

*of Miss Temple*: Miss Ann Evans, superintendent of the school.

58 *applied to her side*: raising blisters, usually by plasters of various substances, including Spanish fly, was done in the belief that the blister's fluid drew blood away from inflammation. With Maria, presumably meant to treat her continued cough.

*in 'Jane Eyre'*: vol. I, ch. ix (CB herself calls it typhus, p. 77). The symptoms of typhus match those described: quick weak pulse; impaired senses; marked bodily weakness. Typhus was particularly dangerous in crowded conditions and to those already weakened by, for example, poor food.

59 *symptoms of this*: Ed. 3 omits: '*of this*; his self-confidence was shaken; he did not understand what kind of illness it could be, that made the girls too dull and heavy to understand remonstrances, or be roused by texts and spiritual exhortation; but caused them to sink away into dull stupor, and half-unconscious listlessness. *He went*'.

*most liberal manner*: the following passage revised from Ed. 1: '*manner*; he even sent for additional advice, in the person of his own brother-in-law, a very clever medical man in Kirby, with whom he had not been on good terms for some time previously; and it was this doctor who tasted and condemned the daily food of the girls *by the expressive'*. Ed. 3 adds the next sentence ('He himself . . . or dangerous'). EG stresses in Ed. 3, by naming Dr Batty and emphasizing the two witnesses, the truth of her account, challenged by Carus Wilson's supporters (see WS, iv. 301, 308; and the eyewitness report that the doctor declared the food 'unfit for pigs': WS, iv. 305).

59 *complain of it*: this housekeeper, who served at the school for twenty years, was still alive in 1857: Shepheard uses her as evidence of the excellence of the food provided, while simultaneously showing that she in fact replaced the bad cook (*Vindication*, p. 15). It is possible that EG met her while gathering materials.

60 *and in estimating*: William Shaen, a lawyer and husband of EG's friend Eliza Fox, advised EG on Ed. 3's revision and at proof-stage sent her alterations which she accepted (*Letters*, pp. 462–3), so this passage ('and in estimating . . . painful impressions') was substituted in Ed. 3 for Ed. 1: *'establishment*. But Mr Wilson seems to have had the unlucky gift of irritating even those to whom he meant kindly, and for whom he was making perpetual sacrifices of time and money, by never showing any respect for their independence of opinion and action. He had, too, so little knowledge of human nature as to imagine that, by constantly reminding the girls of their dependent position, and the fact that they were receiving their education from the charity of others, he could make them lowly and humble. Some of the more sensitive felt this treatment bitterly, and instead of being as grateful as they should have been for the real benefits they were obtaining, their mortified pride rose up from its fall a hundred-fold more strong. Painful impressions sink deep into the hearts of delicate and sickly children. *What the healthy'*. The rest of the paragraph was revised by Shaen in some unspecified way (*Letters*, p. 463). The estimate of Wilson's character was rewritten from Ed. 1: *'quarter of a century afterwards*. She saw only one side, and that the unfavourable side of Mr Wilson; but many of those who knew him, assure me of the wonderful fidelity with which his disagreeable qualities, his spiritual pride, his love of power, his ignorance of human nature and consequent want of tenderness are represented; while, at the same time, they regret that the delineation of these should have obliterated, as it were, nearly all that was noble and conscientious'; the rest of the paragraph added in Ed. 3.

*husband of 'Miss Temple'*: the Revd James Connor, who married Ann Evans, the superintendent of Cowan Bridge School (the model for Miss Temple in *Jane Eyre*) in July 1826; Patrick Brontë often heard

CB speak highly of Miss Evans (to EG, 30 July 1855; John Rylands MS). The extract EG gives is similar to one quoted by Sarah Baldwin, a former pupil of Cowan Bridge, in a letter defending Carus Wilson to the *Halifax Guardian*, 11 July 1857 (WS, iv. 307): the difference between the two versions shows that either Connor wrote independently to EG or else that Sarah Baldwin sent EG his original letter to her. This section being an Ed. 3 addition accounts for the slightly odd effect of reference to the death of 'Miss Temple' last year and then (below) to receiving a letter from her. EG was attempting in July 1855 to contact Mrs Connor, in the hope she might give particulars of Cowan Bridge '& possibly some explanations whh may modify that account . . . in Jane Eyre, which took such strong hold on the public mind' (*Letters*, p. 360). EG's success in tracing Mrs Connor is shown by 'Miss Temple' 's letter, reproduced below.

61 *'Mellany Hane'*: Patrick Brontë spells it 'Melina Hane' (to EG, 30 July 1855; John Rylands MS). Ed. 3 omits the detail (not supplied by Patrick) that she was 'a West Indian', possibly because untrue or possibly because it might suggest identification with Bertha Mason in *Jane Eyre*.

62 *in this fatal year*: Maria died on 6 May, Elizabeth on 15 June. Neither CB nor Emily returned to Cowan Bridge; EG was misled by Patrick Brontë, who informed her they stayed a further year (30 July 1855; John Rylands MS).

*and superficial grounds*: footnote added in Ed. 3.

63 *servant at the parsonage*: Tabitha Aykroyd (Tabby) was in her mid-fifties in 1825. She replaced the Garrs sisters and was servant and member of the family for the rest of her life. This account's detail of the factories driving out the fairies ('But that was . . . she said') is added on the back of MS p. 76 from a later deleted account of Tabby, largely repetition (see p. 99 note). Ed. 2 uniquely adds a footnote after 'in dialect': 'On one occasion, for instance, when some guests were in the parlour, and she thought it necessary to speak rather finely, her exclamation (to express that the chimney was smoking very much) was, "it reeks wi' a' its meet!" ' There is no evidence on who added this or why EG omitted it from Ed. 3.

64 *packet confided to me*: in July 1856 EG got from Nicholls at Haworth, through the determination of Sir James Kay-Shuttleworth, a number of items, including 'a packet about the size of a lady's travelling writing case, full of paper books of different sizes . . . all in . . . indescribably fine writing'; William Gaskell calculated they would make more than fifty volumes if printed (*Letters*, p. 398). These were the Brontës' 'little writings', the childhood productions of CB, Emily,

Anne, and Branwell. EG recognized their importance, both in the children's imaginative play and in CB's creative development; her earliest impression was that they 'give one the idea of creative power carried to the verge of insanity', linking them to the work of Blake as artefacts (*Letters*, p. 398). The writings were returned to Nicholls after being in EG's possession for about a fortnight. The notable thing, given the writings' quantity and the reading difficulty, is how much EG made of her opportunity (see *Letters*, p. 410). She rewrote substantially on the basis of this material: the present chapter, after Tabby is introduced, is virtually free-standing. Subsequently, the writings passed from Nicholls in the 1890s to Clement Shorter and then to T. J. Wise, the bibliographer and forger, who broke them into small lots for sale, with often inaccurate attributions. For CB's 'little writings', see Alexander, *Bibliography*, *Early Writings*, and her edition of *Early Writings*.

64 *fac-simile of a page*: the page is the opening of CB's *The Secret and Lily Hart: Two Tales by Lord Charles Wellesley*, a manuscript booklet of 19,000 words in 16 pages, approximately 4½ by 3½ inches, now in the University of Missouri; transcribed and edited by William Holtz, 1978. EG sent the booklet to George Smith, July 1856, who had the page lithographed (copied on to a printing block direct) rather than reproduced photographically (*Letters*, pp. 398, 400).

66 *of her works*: there survive 25 manuscript booklets by CB, dated between Mar. 1829 and Jan. 1836 (see Alexander, *Bibliography*, section I). CB's catalogue below is now in the Pierpont Morgan Library.

67 '*Little Magazines*': from the first of the 4 volumes of the *Tales of the Islanders*, dated 30 June 1829 (31 June is CB's slip). The volume is now in the New York Public Library.

68 *men in our islands*: as EG notes, most of the men are Tories, with the notable exception of Branwell's Leigh Hunt (1784–1859), liberal journalist and poet. The lists show a certain shrewdness, in the choice of three medical men (Cooper, Halford, and John Abernethy), and indicate the sisters' narrowly conservative views. The chief men can mostly be found in *DNB*: note, though, that Johnny Lockhart figured as John Gibson Lockhart's son in *Blackwood's Magazine*; that Bentinck would be Lord William Bentinck (1774–1839), governor-general, Bengal, 1827; that Christopher North is the literary persona of John Wilson (1785–1854) in *Blackwood's Magazine*, introduced in convivial conversation with both imaginary and real people ('and Co.'; see CB's account in 'The History of the Year 1829', below), including James Hogg (1770–1835), the Ettrick Shepherd.

69 THE YEAR 1829: BPM MS.

"*Blackwood's Magazine*": established by the Edinburgh publisher William Blackwood as a conservative counterblast to the *Edinburgh Review*, *Blackwood's Edinburgh Magazine* (1817–1980) was deeply influential politically and imaginatively upon the Brontës: see Gérin, *CB*, ch. 2. Christopher North, the supposed editor, was a persona of the real one, John Wilson, in his mid-forties in 1829.

70 '*list of painters . . . wish to see*': the list (BPM MS), representative of eighteenth- and early nineteenth-century taste, favours Renaissance and Baroque painters: Guido Reni (1575–1642); Giulio Romano (1492–1546); Titian (*c.*1487–1576); Raphael (1483–1520); Michelangelo (1475–1564); Correggio (1494–1534); Annibale Carracci (1560–1609); Leonardo da Vinci (1452–1519); Fra Bartolommeo (1472/5–1517); Carlo Cignani (1628–1719); Anthony Vandyke (1599–1641); Rubens (1577–1640); Bartolomeo Ramenghi (1484–1542)—Gaskell's 'Ramerghi' is incorrect.

'*Friendship's Offering for 1829*': one of the immensely popular Annuals, published for the Christmas season, that offered verse, prose, and engravings of famous beauties and picturesque scenes; the volume is only 5½ by 3½ inches and the engravings are very finely detailed. CB's manuscript, entitled 'Campbell Castle', is in the Houghton Library, Harvard University; see Alexander, *Bibliography*, no. 46.

'*Tales of the Islanders*': dated 2 Dec. 1829; now in the New York Public Library.

71 *Catholic question*: the King's Speech in Feb. 1829 announced the Government's intention to grant full religious and civil liberties to Catholics. Robert Peel introduced the bill in the House of Commons and in March it went to the Lords: in April (the royal Dukes of Cumberland and Sussex taking part in the final debate) it passed with a majority of 104 (213 : 109). CB's account of the debate is highly coloured.

*the 'Little Magazines'*: BPM MS; it is a separate piece, not from one of the magazines themselves. The Brontës delighted in the exotic and magical of oriental tales, whether directly from the *Thousand and One Nights* or from such imitations as James Ridley's *Tales of the Genii* (1766).

72 *Deus ex Machinâ*: i.e. the Duke of Wellington appears in the nick of time to prevent disaster or to resolve the plot (like Jupiter the Thunderer, intervening as king of the gods, or like a god descending by stage machinery to end a play happily).

72 *the various magazines*: four of the items come from the *Young Men's Magazine* (the first and second from no. 1; the third from no. 6; the fifth from no. 5); *The Green Dwarf* is a separate tale. The first three items are now in BPM; the fourth in the Humanities Research Center, Texas; the location of the fifth is unknown.

73 *Chaldean shepherds*: EG draws on Wordsworth's extended meditation on the imagination's sympathetic power in *The Excursion*, bk. IV: the Chaldean shepherds are at ll. 694 ff., the lonely herdsman at ll. 851–2.

*following relation*: one of the 'diary papers'; now in the Houghton Collection, Harvard University.

74 *bridegroom is coming*: Matthew 6: 10; the following reference to cords, bowl, and pitcher is Ecclesiastes 12: 6.

*following poem*: in 'The Wounded Stag and Other Poems', a manuscript volume dated 19 Jan. 1836.

77 *a country clergyman*: Ed. 3 omits: '*clergyman* (as evinced in his destruction of the coloured boots and the silk gown), *her aunt*'.

*to school again*: Roe Head, near Mirfield, still standing; for CB's drawing of it, see Fraser, *CB*, plate 7a; for a photograph, Barker, *The Brontës*, plate 8. Kirklees (below), originally a priory of Cistercian nuns, passed to the Armitage family in the sixteenth century; in legend, Robin Hood, betrayed by the abbess, shot a last arrow to mark where he should be buried: the 'grave' is extant.

*to the Miss W——*: 'Woolers'. Margaret Wooler (1792–1885) was assisted in her schools at Roe Head and Dewsbury Moor by three of her younger sisters. After retirement she lived at Heckmondwike and Gomersal; her grave is in St Peter's churchyard, Birstall. Notable for good sense, she became an important friend to CB, and they maintained a correspondence throughout CB's life, though nothing like so extensive as that with EN. In 1851 CB declared her to be 'like good wine . . . time improves her, and . . . whatever she may be in person, in mind she is younger than when at Roe Head' (3 Oct.). EG contacted her early when gathering materials and met her in Oct. 1855. CB's letters to her can be livelier than those to EN: EG said she liked them better than any other letters of CB's (12 Nov. 1855; *Letters*, p. 372). The name Wooler was given in full throughout Eds. 1 and 2; Miss Wooler presumably asked EG to veil her identity. EG included the direction to do so to the printers for Ed. 3 (MS additions); one example only escaped EG's revision for Ed. 3 (p. 113). Though Miss Wooler was not one of the noisier objectors to Ed. 1's representation of herself, detailed revision about her needed much attention; the changes, some quite minor, show EG's care throughout the revision process. Small details are revised in the rest of this paragraph from Ed. 1 (e.g. three tiers of windows, for two).

78 *Howley Hall*: between Batley and Morley: built 1590; partly demolished 1730. It was 'Within a walk from' Miss Wooler's house, not 6 miles, in Ed. 1; and, below, the Palm Sunday visit to the well becomes 'formerly' instead of Ed. 1's 'yet'.

*Oakwell Hall*: dated 1583, but considerably altered, and still standing, the Field Head of *Shirley*; EG visited it in Oct. 1855 (photograph in Flintoff, *In the Steps of the Brontës*, p. 47). Norrison Scatcherd, *The History of Morley* (1830) gives details of Henry Batt and his son William (Captain Batt), but is not the source of EG's legend of the bloody footprint. Ed. 3 omits 'rough-looking' before 'pasture-field' in the next sentence and again, three sentences later, before 'field'.

79 *three or four miles*: the distance added in Ed. 3.

80 *year and a half*: Ed. 3 corrects from Ed. 1's 'two years' (as also on pp. 85 and 93).

*'E.'s'*: the first reference to Ellen Nussey (1817–97), whose friendship and correspondence with CB made EG's biography possible in its present form and consequently shaped it. As EG correctly guessed (*Letters*, p. 875) and notes below, EN was the model for Caroline Helstone in *Shirley* (though Caroline also draws on Anne Brontë, CB herself, and CB's juvenilia: *Shirley*, pp. xix–xx). MS gives the name 'Ellen' and her home as 'Birstall' (near Dewsbury; she is buried in St Peter's churchyard, Birstall). EN from the first wanted her name omitted: in July 1856 EG suggested she call her 'simply' Ellen, since initials 'give so little personality—they are so like a mathematical proposition' (*Letters*, p. 396). But 'E.' it was (a couple of Ellens slipped in and survive through Ed. 3); sometimes even the initial is omitted. See further on EN, Whitehead, *CB and Her 'Dearest Nell'*.

*other dear friends*: Mary ('Polly') Taylor (1817–93) and her sister Martha (1819–42). Mary and EN were CB's closest friends. Mary later travelled in Europe and with her sister studied in Brussels while CB and Emily were there; Mary emigrated to New Zealand in 1845, returning in 1860 and living the rest of her life at the family home, the Red House, Gomersal; she is buried in the graveyard of Gomersal parish church. The most outspoken and advanced of the three friends, Mary was sure that CB was the victim of a society where no one thought it 'a strange or wrong state of things that a woman of first rate talents, industry, and integrity should live all her life in a walking nightmare of "poverty and self-suppression" ' (Stevens, *Mary Taylor*, p. 133; which see further on Mary Taylor).

80 *from 'Mary'*: EG contacted Mary Taylor early while gathering material. Mary had kept only one CB letter (the wonderful account of the 1848 London visit with Anne), but she gave her impressions of CB in a letter of 18 Jan. 1856, largely incorporated into *The Life*. A further letter, responding to *The Life*, was used by EG in Ed. 3 (see Stevens, *Mary Taylor*, appendix B, and Easson, *Elizabeth Gaskell*, pp. 141–2).

*Irish accent*: see p. 35 note.

81 *'sick for home . . . tears'*: John Keats (1795–1821), 'Ode to a Nightingale', ll. 66–7 (alluding to the biblical story of Ruth).

*printing characters*: the phrase added at proof-stage in Ed. 1; presumably EG's gloss, in the light of seeing CB's 'little writings'.

82 *being in 1832* : during 1831–2 the struggle for parliamentary reform brought serious civil unrest and the threat of civil war. Charles, Earl Grey (1764–1845), became Prime Minister in 1830; two Reform Bills were defeated in 1831. There was a sense of crisis with the introduction of the third Reform Bill in Dec. 1831; passed twice in the Lords, it was stopped by a procedural amendment in May 1832. CB's reference, below, to its being thrown out is, strictly, inaccurate, but many believed the bill had been killed, and Grey resigned (9 May). He speedily returned to office, King William IV agreed if necessary to create sufficient peers to pass the bill through the Lords, and the Reform Bill passed in the Lords on 4 June 1832. Robert Peel (1788–1850) recognized the reality of political and national situations, earlier in accepting the need for Catholic Emancipation and, in 1832, for parliamentary reform.

83 *'Frazer's Magazine'*: properly *Fraser's Magazine*; spelt 'Frazer's' by CB; EG in MS altered 's' to 'z' to reproduce CB's original accurately. *Fraser's* (1830–82), a monthly, began as a high-spirited miscellany, including original work (Carlyle, Thackeray) and reviews. For *Blackwood's* (below), see p. 69 note.

84 *one at school*: this paragraph and the next added in Ed. 3; its layout in the MS additions clearly suggests it is a further extract from Mary Taylor's first letter to EG, though it may be from the second, itself incorporated in Ed. 3.

85 *'Lectures on Belles Lettres'*: Hugh Blair (1718–1800), *Lectures on Rhetoric and Belles Lettres* (1783).

*so long a task*: reworked from Ed. 1's *'she had* over-tasked so willing a pupil'. This incident, taking account of Miss Wooler's sensibilities, was subjected to a variety of revision. MS has a deleted first version of the 'strike' below, between 'variety of ways' and 'until Miss W——': '*of ways*. They said Miss Wooler might teach whom she liked, for they would not learn from her, while the bad mark remained against Charlotte Brontë's name. They defied the school-rolls, raced round the forbidden fruit-garden, were deaf to the summoning bells, and chose their own time for going to bed *until Miss W——*'. The end of the paragraph's final sentence is revised in Ed. 3 from Ed. 1: '*choosing to consider* Miss Wooler's injustice, in giving Charlotte Brontë a longer task than she could possibly prepare, as a reason for no longer obeying any *of the school regulations*.'

86 '*conter*' . . . *the tales*: the tales, in which Miss Wooler displayed her art of telling (as does EG, who reconstructs them from local history and tradition and from *Shirley*), hark back, as EG notes, to Patrick Brontë's own earlier experiences (see p. 45 and note). They prepare through CB's childhood knowledge for their re-creation in *Shirley* (in writing which CB also pursued the contemporary evidence of the *Leeds Mercury*). In early 1811, with trade seriously affected by the Napoleonic Wars and with Wellington pinned down, before his increasingly triumphant campaign through Spain (hence the 'Peninsular war') and into France (1811–14), employers were attempting to use machinery (the 'shears' referred to) to increase efficiency and were opposed by the workmen. Machine-breaking, by men organized in semi-military fashion and claiming the fictitious Ned Ludd as their leader (hence Luddite), was widespread. William Cartwright's mill was attacked, but not burnt; EG's source for the anecdote of hiding the children in the chimney is untraced. William Horsfall (the manufacturer 'shot down', below) was murdered 27 Apr. 1812. CB drew on Cartwright for Robert Moore in *Shirley*; the attack on the mill is in vol. II, ch. viii (ch. 19), on Moore in vol. III, ch. viii (ch. 31). See also on Ludditism, E. P. Thompson, *The Making of the English Working Class* (Penguin, 1968) and pp. 611–18 in particular for these events.

88 *Yorkshire houses*: MS has deleted passage for 'This was a terrible threat . . . Yorkshire houses'; the deletion is not readable, but probably stylistic revision only is involved.

*Roberson of Heald's Hall*: the Revd Hammond Roberson (1757–1841), who transferred his school to the eighteenth-century Hall at Liversedge in 1795. Christ Church, Liversedge, was consecrated in 1816; both buildings survive. CB used him, as well as elements from her father, for Mr Helstone in *Shirley* (to W. S. Williams, 21 Sept. 1849).

Mary Taylor classed him with 'the black-coated and Tory savages [i.e. clergymen] that kept the people down, and provoked excesses in those days' (to EG, 30 July 1857). On the demonization of Roberson, see E. P. Thompson, *The Making of the English Working Class*, pp. 613–15.

90 *rubric-meeting*: apparently a 'special day or occasion', from the directions given in red (rubrics) for church feasts and special services (cf. 'red-letter day').

91 *principally Independents*: or Congregationalists; with the Presbyterians and Baptists, descendants of the seventeenth-century 'Puritans'; each Independent congregation chose its own minister and doctrinally tended to retain Calvinism; their activities were stimulated by the evangelical and industrial movements of the eighteenth and early nineteenth centuries.

*A friend*: unidentified. MS has one or two words after 'A friend', heavily deleted, which might be a name; on p. 92, before the next extract, several words are heavily deleted in MS that might have included a name.

93 *called "The Lecture"*: established in 1761 by the Revd James Scott, who originally provided his friends with a plain dinner and a notable preacher; held in the week after the second Sunday in June.

*Spite Hall*: not otherwise traced.

94 *correspondence with her*: rest of paragraph added in Ed. 3. Despite EG's claim, EN had not always effaced names and places.

95 *'her times in His hands'*: adapting Psalms 31: 15.

*of this memoir*: as is clear, this paragraph and the two following added in Ed. 3, from Mary Taylor's letter received by EG in May 1857 (*Letters*, p. 449).

*of Cobbett's*: William Cobbett (1763–1835), Tory radical and prolific journalist: now best known for the *Rural Rides* (collected 1830); edited *Cobbett's Political Register* (1802–35).

*meaning conscientiousness*: a reference to the pseudo-science of phrenology, which interpreted character and ability from the shape and development of the head. Conscientiousness was located on the highest part of the head, on either side of firmness (see George Combe, *Elements of Phrenology* (1824), frontispiece and pp. 73–6).

96 *teacher in drawing*: the children were certainly all regularly drawing in 1829; in 1894 it was claimed that Thomas Plummer of Keighley had been their drawing master (Gérin, *Branwell Brontë*, p. 75). Branwell later had lessons from William Robinson (1799–1839) of Leeds.

*a waterfall*: now known as the Brontës' Waterfall, at the meeting of two streams above Haworth: the flow, which depends on rainfall, is now lessened by the reservoir.

*fortnight's absence*: letter dated 18 Oct. 1832. EN gave an account of this visit (in her *Scribner's Monthly* reminiscences, 1871; WS, i. 106–7). The letter reads: 'I arrived at Haworth in perfect safety without the least accident or misfortune. My little sisters ran out of the house to meet me as soon as the carriage came in sight, and they kissed me with as much enthusiasm and pleasure as if I had been away a year. My father, my aunt, and the gentleman of whom my brother had spoken, were all gathered in the living room and I was soon there too. It is often the decree of Heaven that when we lose one happiness, there is another close at hand to take its place. Thus I had to leave beloved friends, yet a short while ago I returned to a family as beloved and precious. Even while you lost me (dare I believe my departure was painful to you?), you awaited the arrival of your brother and your sister. I have given my sisters the apples you so kindly sent them; they say that they are sure that Miss E. is kind and good; they are both extremely impatient to see you; I hope that within a month they will have that pleasure.'

97 *to criticise books*: the following paragraph was expanded in MS from a deleted passage: '*criticise books*. I believe they had but few in the house as a standing library, and those were probably kept in the sanctuary of Mr Brontë's room. I have always imagined that the list of books given in Shirley as those belonging to ____ Rectory was pretty much taken from the catalogue in Haworth Parsonage' (followed by an extract from *Shirley*, close to but not identical with that reproduced).

*of a solid kind*: this would include history and biography of the kind listed by CB (p. 103) and classics, Greek, Latin, and English. Patrick Brontë had both religious and scientific works. The circulating library in Keighley (probably Hudson's, High Street) would provide novels, poetry, and general literature. Although Patrick Brontë joined the Keighley Mechanics' Institute in 1833 this would not, as has been claimed, have given the young Brontës direct access to its rather dull and limited library: see Ian Dewhirst, 'The Rev. Patrick Brontë and the Keighley Mechanics' Institute', *BST*, 14 (1965), 35–7.

*access in 'Shirley'*: the account (vol. II, ch. xi; (ch. 22; p. 389 ) ), refers to Latin and Greek classics. *The Lady's Magazine* founded 1770; Elizabeth Rowe (1674–1737), *Friendship in Death: Twenty Letters from the Dead to the Living* (1728).

98 *upon 'Kenilworth'*: by Sir Walter Scott (1771–1832); published 1821.

   *follows about it*: 1 Jan. 1833.

   *of 1833, she wrote*: 20 June 1833.

99 *obnoxious colour*: i.e. red; until the mid-century change of taste
   promoted by the Pre-Raphaelite painters, red hair was distinctly
   unfashionable.

   *to 'E.'*: 11 Sept. 1833.

   *scribble no longer*: MS has, deleted, a passage about Tabby, essentially
   the account at the opening of Ch. v: one detail from the MS account
   here was added on the back of the earlier MS page (see p. 63 note):
   'There are two facts alluded to in this letter worthy of notice. Mr
   Brontë kept one servant, the "Tabby" herein named. She was
   upwards of forty when she came to live with them, considerably
   before this date. She was a Haworth woman, and distinctly averred
   that in her youth, when there were no mills in the vallies and when
   all the wool spinning was done by hand in the farmhouses round there
   were fairies to be seen every moonlight night in the hollows. "It was
   the mills as had driven them away." She was full of old stories about
   old ways of living, and former inhabitants, decayed gentry who had
   melted away, and their places knew them no more; family tragedies,
   and dark superstitious doom. Tabby was faithfully attached to the
   Brontë family, and their conduct to her was delicate and generous in
   the extreme. I shall hereafter have to relate an instance of Charlotte's
   consideration for her. Meanwhile I must just say that to a visitor in
   that house it *was a great thing*'.

   *deaths in the village*: EG takes the information on weather and deaths
   from CB to EN, 11 Feb. 1834.

   *of her friends says*: only the first sentence appeared in Ed. 1; the rest
   ('Charlotte was certainly . . . more, some less') added in Ed. 3. The
   friend not identified, though possibly Mary Taylor, in which case it
   is part of Mary's letter to EG, 18 Jan. 1856.

100 *to 'Jane Eyre'*: vol. II, ch. x (ch. 25; p. 284).

   *"British Essayists"*: the *British Essayists*, ed. Alexander Chalmers (45
   vols., 1803), collected the eighteenth-century periodical literature,
   including *The Rambler* (1750–2), by Samuel Johnson, and *The Mirror*
   (1779–80) and *The Lounger* (1785–7), both edited by Henry Macken-
   zie (1745–1831).

101 *Stanley . . . O'Connell*: Edward Stanley (1799–1869), politician; as
   Irish Secretary (1830–3) came into political and personal conflict with

O'Connell. Later Earl of Derby and three times Prime Minister. Daniel O'Connell (1775–1847), known as 'The Liberator'; Irish Nationalist. The request below for information about the king's military band came from Branwell, who was interested in music and soldiers.

*June 19th*: 1834.

103  *instruct you*: cf. Luke 16: 31.

*married, is he*: Richard Nussey (1803–72), EN's brother, a millowner; married Elizabeth Charnock.

*to leave ——*: Rydings, the property of EN's uncle Richard Nussey, where EN and her family had lived since 1826, after her father's death. The move to Brookroyd, a quarter-mile away, took place in Sept. 1836 (see Whitehead, *CB and Her 'Dearest Nell'*, for illustrations, pp. 44, 71; both houses survive).

*Wordsworth, and Southey*: the list and the comments are fairly conventional, though CB's recommendation of Shakespeare suggests just how much more conventional EN was than general taste. Milton and Shakespeare are obvious; Pope was less in fashion, over-shadowed by the Romantics, though Byron was suspect for his moral looseness: *Don Juan* (1819–24) passes no strictures on its amorous hero, while *Cain* (1821) sympathetically represents its hero questioning God's providence. James Thomson (1700–48) was author of *The Seasons* (1726–30); Oliver Goldsmith (1730–74), now best known as novelist and dramatist, also wrote 'The Traveller' and 'The Deserted Village'; Thomas Campbell (1777–1844) produced 'Gertrude of Wyoming' and short pieces such as 'The Battle of the Baltic' and 'Lord Ullin's Daughter'. Walter Scott (1771–1832) was still as famous as poet as novelist; Wordsworth (1770–1850) was increasingly seen as the greatest living poet, confirmed by his appointment as Poet Laureate on the death of Robert Southey (1774–1843). The historians are David Hume (1711–76), now best known as a philosopher, whose *History of Great Britain* (1754–61) remained a standard work; the French historian Charles Rollin's *Ancient History* (1730–8) and the French *Universal History, from the Earliest Account of Time* (23 vols., 1736–65), were both early translated into English and became standard works. The biographies are Samuel Johnson, *Lives of the English Poets* (1779–81); James Boswell, *The Life of Samuel Johnson* (1791); Robert Southey, *Life of Nelson* (1813); John Gibson Lockhart, *Life of Robert Burns* (1828); Thomas Moore, *Life of Sheridan* (1825) and *Life of Byron* (1830); Charles Wolfe (1791–1823; author of 'The Burial of Sir

John Moore'), *Remains* (2 vols., 1825): vol. i is a biographical account by John Russell, interspersed with Wolfe's writings. The natural historians are Thomas Bewick (1753–1828), illustrator rather than author of *A General History of Quadrupeds* (1790) and *History of British Birds* (1797, 1804): his woodcuts are recalled by Jane Eyre (vol. i, ch. i; pp. 8–9); John James Audubon (1780–1851), ornithologist and bird illustrator, published *Birds of America* (1827–30) and *Ornithological Biography* (1831–9); Oliver Goldsmith, *Animated Nature* (1774); Gilbert White (1720–93), *The Natural History of Selborne* (1789). Ellen's brothers Joshua (1798–1871) and Henry (1812–67) were both clergymen, being ordained respectively in 1824 and 1835; the former is presumably meant, of whom Mary Taylor wrote tartly to Ellen: 'he no doubt has read as much as you and I put together, and a little bit of Charlotte included' (*c.* Oct. 1842).

103 *her own reading*: MS has, deleted because of the revised account (p. 97) of books: '*own reading*. I do not, as I have said, believe that Mr Brontë himself possessed many volumes, but he, as well as his daughter, was a great reader, and from some public library in Leeds, if from no nearer place, all these books might be obtained.'

104 *Charlotte replies*: 10 Nov. 1834. 'Mr ——' (below) is the Revd Thomas Allbutt (vicar of Dewsbury 1835), who married Marianne, sister of Margaret Wooler; EN's sister might be either Ann (1795–1878) or Mercy Mary (1801–86), the latter more likely, since she had been a sister in the Moravian Community, Fairfield, Manchester.

*and B——*: Birstall. The details about a Bradford meeting and the Haworth gig taken from CB to EN, 12 Jan. 1835.

*March, 1835, she writes*: 13 Mar. 1835.

105 *care greatly about it*: in Dec. 1834 Robert Peel became Prime Minister (with Wellington as Foreign Secretary), after the resignation of Melbourne. In opposition, as in office, the Whigs represented a range of opinions, from radical to conservative (hence Red-hots and Lukewarms). Peel, who had no overall majority and was defeated six times in six weeks, resigned; in Apr. 1835 Melbourne returned as Prime Minister. 'B.' is Henry, Lord Brougham (1778–1868), Lord Chancellor under Melbourne, who was leading the attack on Peel in the Lords; MS gives the name as Baines (Edward Baines, 1774–1848; proprietor, *Leeds Mercury* and Whig MP for Leeds), possibly an attempt to transcribe what EN had deleted.

*landlord of the Black Bull*: Thomas Sugden.

106 *weaker son wanted*: the account of Branwell's social habits and the extentuation of Mr Brontë's paternal negligence ('for Branwell's talents . . . weaker son wanted') are on the back of the sheet (MS, p. 133). In the parentheses above, the phrase 'though in his own family he was always "Branwell" ' was added in Ed. 3 and the information's repetition omitted from p. 145, between 'brilliant "Patrick" ' and 'was sent for'.

*minuteness . . . pre-Raphaelite accuracy*: the artists who formed the Pre-Raphaelite Brotherhood in 1848 aimed for precision of line, brilliancy of colour, and accuracy to nature. EG admired their work and their aesthetic. See Tim Hilton, *The Pre-Raphaelites* (1970); for CB's copying, see Gérin, *CB*, ch. 4, and Christine Alexander and Jane Sellars, *The Art of the Brontës* (1995) (and cf. CB's judgement on this kind of work in *Villette*, ch. 35, p. 500).

*painting of his*: now in the National Portrait Gallery (see Richard Ormond, *Early Victorian Portraits* (2 vols., 1973), i. 57 ff. and ii, no. 98: this work reproduces the then known portraits of the Brontës). The pillar in the painting conceals an unfinished male figure. See also Susan R. Foister, 'The Brontë Portraits', *BST*, 18 (1985), 345–52. The picture is dated by EG *c.*1835, both here and in her original account of CB showing it (*Letters*, p. 249; and below, p. 440), assuming in the latter account that CB was 18; Gérin, *Branwell Brontë*, pp. 80–3, argues for *c.*1838.

107 *the Royal Academy*: Gérin, *Branwell Brontë*, ch. 9 ('London') gives a useful account of the Academy training. Branwell drafted a letter enquiring about entry requirements, with a view to enrolling in autumn 1835. There is no evidence that he even approached the Royal Academy nor indeed any contemporary surviving record that he went to London; EG's language here, at p. 131, and at the opening of Ch. IX, shows she never heard of Branwell going to London. The accounts of the London expedition derive later from Branwell and his biographer, Leyland.

*had lived there*: the anecdote of Branwell's marvellous knowledge of London (below, p. 145) was originally here: it is deleted and written out again later; the deleted version reads: '*lived there* and, once, about this time, a stranger, from London, who staid for a night at the little Haworth Inn, and at the landlord's suggestion, sent for "Patrick" to bear him company, was startled to find that his companion had never been to London although he had just been proving his superior information [just over a line illegible]'.

107 *July 6th, 1835:* 2 July 1835. EG seems to have taken the date from the postmark; the letter is clearly dated. In copying, the date below for leaving home was incorrectly transcribed '27' for '29' (given correctly at the beginning of Ch. VIII). 'Miss W—' (below) is Miss Wooler; 'Polly' is Mary Taylor.

108 *in pleasant places*: Psalms 16: 6; 'lines' = 'appointed lot in life' (the verse continues: 'yea, I have a goodly heritage').

109 *again ventured on*: from CB's Prefatory Note to 'Selections from Poems by Ellis Bell', in the 1850 edition of *Wuthering Heights* (p. 370).

110 *than King Alfred*: the apocryphal story would be best known through Oliver Goldsmith's *History of England* (1771 edn.), i. 75; for its development, see *Alfred the Great*, trans. and ed. Simon Keynes and Michael Lapidge (1983), appendix I.

*to 'make talk'*: Ed. 3 omits: ' "*make talk*." / It was about this time that an event happened in the neighbourhood of Leeds, which excited a good deal of interest. A young lady, who held the situation of governess in a very respectable family, had been wooed and married by a gentleman, holding some subordinate position in the commercial firm to which the young lady's employer belonged. A year after her marriage, during which time she had given birth to a child, it was discovered that he whom she called husband had another wife. Report now says, that this first wife was deranged, and that he had made this an excuse to himself for his subsequent marriage. But, at any rate, the condition of the wife who was no wife—of the innocent mother of the illegitimate child—excited the deepest commiseration; and the case was spoken of far and wide, and at Roe Head among other places. / *Miss W—*'. Compare this with the other omitted tale of seduction (p. 46 and note); here, the omission may be because, apart from possible impropriety or identification of those involved, the obvious similarities with *Jane Eyre* could cast doubt on CB's originality.

111 *that one night*: this paragraph ('She told me . . . a feebler mind') added in Ed. 3; incomplete in MS additions.

*Vol. I, page 20*: vol. I, ch. ii (pp. 16–17), with minor variations and one unacknowledged omission.

112 *of Cowper's letters*: the poet William Cowper's depression acted with his belief in the Calvinistic doctrine of predestination, especially under the influence of the Revd John Newton (p. 23 note), to convince him that he was damned; in 'The Castaway', 1798 (below), Cowper parallels himself to a sailor overboard, who is 'predestined' to

destruction. Cowper's letters, including some that illustrate his religious depression, were published in 1824. For Anne Brontë's religious crisis at Roe Head and the help she received, see Gérin, *Anne Brontë*, pp. 98–101; for Patrick Brontë's humane version of evangelical Calvinism, see WS, i. 169. The following section (' "Mary" says . . . with such subjects') added in Ed. 3; incomplete in MS additions.

*Socinianism, Calvinism*: the sixteenth-century doctrines respectively of Lelio and Faustus Socinus, founders of Unitarianism, who denied the divinity of Jesus; and of John Calvin (1509–64). Calvin taught the absolute corruption of humanity, no one being able by deed or conduct to effect their own salvation; that salvation therefore was by the grace of God, granted through the agency of the Son alone; that the salvation or damnation of everyone was already determined (predestined); and that only those chosen (elected) by God would be saved.

113 *were Tantalus*: Tantalus, in classical mythology, was punished by thirst, the water in which he stood receding whenever he tried to drink (hence, 'tantalized'); the Well of Life, above, echoes Proverbs 10: 11.

*the Repetitions*: i.e. examinations; a reminder of how much of the teaching was rote learning.

*Miss Wooler*: the only survival of Miss Wooler's name in full in Ed. 3

*My dear dear E.*: this and the following extracts come from four letters: the first extract is probably of early 1837; the second (beginning 'Weary with a day's . . .') is probably Oct. 1836; the third (beginning 'You have been very kind . . .') is 26 Sept. 1836; the fourth (beginning 'My life since I saw . . .') is probably of early June 1837.

114 *I saw ——*: EN's brother, George Nussey (1814–85); assisted his brothers in their woollen manufacturing activities (see WS, i. 146, for his physical attractions).

*Huddersfield market-day*: Tuesdays.

*from the window*: after 'window' Ed. 3 omits: 'forbidden to pupils'.

116 *"Life of Oberlin" . . . "Domestic Portraiture"*: Thomas Sims, *Brief Memorials of J. F. Oberlin* (1830); Legh Richmond, *Domestic Portraiture: or, The Successful Application of Religious Principle in the Education of a Family* (1833). Richmond included a memoir (below) of his son, Wilberforce.

*Dewsbury Moor*: the building, known originally as Heald's House, survives (see Gérin, *Anne Brontë*, pp. 108–9); photograph in White-

head, *CB and Her 'Dearest Nell'*, p. 74. The account of the school's
situation and of CB's response modified in Ed. 3 from: '*miles distant.*
Her new residence was a much lower site, and the air much less pure
and exhilarating to one bred at the wild hill-village of Haworth.
Charlotte felt the change extremely, and regretted it not merely on
her own account, but for the sake of her sister Anne. Moreover, *Emily
had*'.

116 *school at Halifax*: Law Hill, Southowram Bank, Halifax, kept
by Elizabeth Patchett (photograph in Gérin, *Emily Brontë*, opposite
p. 72). Emily most likely went there in Sept. 1838: CB misdates her
letter (below and next note) 1836 for 1838 (see Edward Chitham and
Tom Winnifrith, *Brontë Facts and Brontë Problems* (1983), pp. 21–8,
and Jennifer A. Cox, 'Emily at Law Hill, 1838', *BST*, 18 (1984),
267–70). Emily stayed 6 months.

*October 2nd, 1836*: 2 Oct. 1838; misdated 1836 by CB.

117 '*days . . . no more*': Alfred Tennyson (1809–92), 'Tears, idle tears',
from *The Princess* (1847).

*write to Southey*: Robert Southey (1774–1843), Poet Laureate since
1813. Though a prolific poet, he earned his living (supporting his own
family and that of his brother-in-law Coleridge) by reviewing and
prose writing. Coleridge had died in 1834; the Brontë correspondence
(see also pp. 147, 149, and nn.) was with his son, Hartley.

118 *to Wordsworth*: the letter (Dove Cottage Library, Grasmere) was
supplied to EG by Jemima Quillinan, Wordsworth's granddaughter;
it had been passed to her father, Edward Quillinan, by Wordsworth's
wife Mary. Branwell's poem, 'The Struggles of Flesh with Spirit
Scene 1—Infancy' is considerably longer than the 18 stanzas EG
reports it to be (see Stephen Gill, 'A Manuscript of Branwell Brontë,
with Letters of Mrs. Gaskell', *BST*, 15 (1970), 408–11). The letter is
called 'remarkable' in MS and Ed. 1; the word was omitted or
dropped out in Ed. 2. The account of Branwell's letter is an insertion
in MS; hence Southey's reply to CB is made to seem even more
delayed than it was.

119 *not the worst*: for the poem, of about 300 lines, dated 13 Aug. 1836,
see *Poems of CB and Patrick Branwell Brontë*, ed. T. J. Wise and J. A.
Symington (1934), 291–300.

120 *Feb. 20th*: 1837. EN was to make an extended stay in London from
June with her brother John.

121 "*Thy will be done!*": Acts 21: 14.

*French nobleman*: perhaps François de la Motte Fénelon (1651–1715), Archbishop of Cambrai; English interest is shown by Andrew Ramsey's biography of 1723.

*'Mary's' father*: Joshua Taylor (1766–1840), on whom Hunsden Yorke Hunsden in *The Professor* and Hiram Yorke in *Shirley* were based. His brother James (1773–1848) settled in France.

122 *of his Father*: Charles Cuthbert Southey, *Life and Correspondence of Robert Southey* (6 vols., 1849–50). The volume reference was incorrectly printed as 'iv' in Ed. 3.

123 *"faculty of verse"*: adapted from *The Excursion*, I. 78–80; the compliment might be double-edged, since Wordsworth speaks of natural poets who, having the 'vision and the faculty divine', yet lack through education 'the accomplishment of verse'.

*flat and unprofitable*: *Hamlet*, I. ii. 133.

124 *Cuthbert Southey's note*: in Aug. 1850, when EG first met CB: see pp. 352 ff.

126 *Southey's reply*: from the *Life and Correspondence of Robert Southey*, vi. 330; CB annotated it: 'Southey's advice to be kept for ever.'

*Southey was dead*: Southey, who lived at Keswick, died 1843; EG and CB met in the Lakes in Aug. 1850.

127 *comparatively less breezy*: altered in Ed. 3 from '*the* flat and comparatively stagnant *air*'.

*August 27. 1837*: properly, 1838; CB stayed on at Dewsbury Moor until the end of 1838.

*error she says*: 5 and 6 Dec. 1836.

*following letter*: in fact from the same letter as the previous extract (5 and 6 Dec. 1836).

128 *doctrines are true*: CB particularly means the doctrines of predestination and of the impossibility of salvation through one's own actions or by obedience to any moral law (see p. 112 notes).

*God forget me*: biblical in tone, but not a quotation.

*Dec. 29. 1837*: EN annotated it 1837, but Edward Chitham argues for 1836 (*Brontë Facts and Brontë Problems*, pp. 29–30).

130 *Yorkshire woman*: Elizabeth Hardaker (d. 1888).

131 *that . . . Dewsbury Moor*: altered in Ed. 3 from: '*said that Dewsbury Moor* was low and damp, and that the air *did not*'.

131 *Brontë about them*: revised in Ed. 3 from: '*about them*. He immediately sent for his children, who left Dewsbury Moor the next day. Meanwhile, Charlotte had resolved that Anne should never return as a pupil, nor she herself as a governess. But, just before she left, *Miss W—— sought*'; in MS additions. Anne was at Roe Head and Dewsbury Moor from Oct. 1835 to Dec. 1837.

'*the falling out . . . of love*': Richard Edwardes (?1523–66), *Amantium Irae*.

*Emily had given up*: Ed. 1 begins the paragraph: 'Miss Wooler had entreated her to return after the holidays, and she had consented. But, independently of this, *Emily had given*'. Direction for the change given in MS additions. EG, misled by CB's misdating of 1836 for 1838 (see p. 116 note), places Emily's time at Law Hill too early, while correctly giving 6 months as the length of her stay.

132 *date of this letter*: i.e. nineteenth-century idiom for the place where it is dated or written from.

133 *in holy orders*: Henry Nussey, EN's brother, whose identity EG conceals here and by omission from CB's letter that follows. Ordained in 1835, Henry was seeking a wife. In his diary he recorded the refusal of Mary Lutwidge, daughter of his former vicar, and wrote the same day to CB; on 8 Mar. 1839 Henry noted: 'Received an unfavourable reply from "C.B." The will of the Lord be done' (WS, i. 171 note). Like Patrick Brontë, Henry was influenced by Simeon while at Cambridge (see p. 34 note), but he had little real religious enthusiasm and no missionary zeal; despite claims, he is not generally seen as a model for St John Rivers in *Jane Eyre*.

134 '*delightful task*': James Thomson, *The Seasons* ('Spring', ll. 1152–3); the task is teaching, 'to rear the tender thought, | To teach the young idea how to shoot'.

*with a situation*: with the Inghams at Blake Hall, Mirfield (demolished 1955); Anne drew on her experiences for the Bloomfields in *Agnes Grey* (pp. 199–201 include useful information on governesses, including status and salary). The Inghams then had five children.

*April 15th, 1839*: 'Mrs ——' (below twice) is Ingham; 'G.' is Gomersal; 'the T.s', the Taylors.

135 *mantua-maker*: a dress-maker (a mantua was a style of loose gown).

*as a governess*: with the Sidgwicks at Stonegappe, Glusburn, near Lothersdale, 5 miles from Haworth, from May to July 1839. The Sidgwicks then had four children; CB was responsible for Mathilda

(b. 1832) and John (b. 1835): the eldest brother (below) was William (b. 1829). The house is still there.

*'of what was resisted'*: Robert Burns, 'Address to the Unco Guid', l. 64.

*about 'Agnes Grey'*: Anne Brontë's first novel, published 1847; the episode referred to (not quite accurately) is in ch. v (pp. 43–5).

136 *June 8th, 1839*: 'Mrs ——' and 'Mr ——' (below) are Sidgwick.

137 *July, 1839*: 30 June or 1 July. Ed. 3 makes two omissions from this letter: CB describes being thrown into *'a large family*—proud as peacocks and wealthy as Jews—*at a time'*, and in the summary of her employer's character near the end writes: *'in general society*. Her health is sound, her animal spirits good, consequently she is cheerful in company; but, oh! does this compensate for the absence of every fine feeling—of every gentle and delicate sentiment? *She behaves somewhat'*. 'Mrs —— ' (below twice) is Sidgwick.

138 *and the oak*: the oak boasts of his greater strength, but in resisting the storm is blown down while the willow bends and survives.

ABOUT THIS TIME : probably *c.* July 1839.

139 *July 26th, 1839*: 'B.' (below) is Birstall.

140 *of a curate*: Patrick Brontë was 62 in 1839; the population of Haworth itself grew from 4,668 to 6,301 between 1821 and 1841. Patrick had had a curate since 1835, supported financially by the evangelical Pastoral Aid Society. The curate referred to in 1839 was William ('Willy') Weightman (1814–42), dubbed by CB for his complexion and curls 'Celia Amelia'; EG scarcely mentions him, though he not only brought cheerfulness into Haworth, but, as a tolerated flirt, was linked to both EN and Anne Brontë (see Gérin, *Anne Brontë*, ch. 12). His death of cholera was a great shock to all the Brontës. Patrick Brontë's curates were: William Hodgson (1835–37), described by CB as the 'former Curate' in her letter of 4 Aug. 1839; William Weightman (1839–42); James William Smith (1842–4); Joseph Brett Grant (1844–5); Arthur Bell Nicholls (1845–53, 1854–61); James Stuart Cranmer (1847, while Nicholls was in Ireland); George de Renzy (1853–4).

*August 4th, 1839*: 'M.' (below) is Mary Taylor.

*Burlington*: an earlier form of Bridlington, on the Yorkshire coast.

141 *a hearty laugh*: the vicar was William Hodgson, Patrick Brontë's former curate, minister at Christ Church, Colne; his curate was David Bryce, who died Jan. 1840.

141  *mauvaise honte*: 'false shame'.

   *from Haworth*: 'B.' (below) is Birstall.

142  *to Easton*: MS has, deleted, 'and took lodgings there'; they stayed with
   the Hudsons at Easton House Farm, near Bridlington (illustrated in
   Gérin, *CB*, opposite p. 156).

   *Oct. 24th*: 1839.

143  *it is calm*: Patrick Brontë, from inland Haworth, had startled EG by
   describing CB's pleasure in 'the glittering ripple of the sea waves' and
   her rapture in 'the swelling billows' (24 July 1855; John Rylands MS);
   this was CB's first sight of the sea, though delayed by the Hudsons'
   kindness (see also WS, i. 189–90, and the sea imagery of *Villette*, pp.
   42 and 617).

   *worthy Mr H.*: John Hudson; he and his wife Sophia were friends of
   Henry Nussey. Hancheon was Fanny Whipp, niece and later adopted
   daughter of the couple. The wood (below) is Harlequin Wood and
   'Madame' is Madame Booth (presumably the keeper of the Bridlington lodging-house where they stayed after the Hudsons).

   *to the Jews*: to the London Society for Promoting Christianity
   Amongst the Jews, established 1809 (Caroline Helstone in *Shirley*
   shares responsibility for a Jews-basket: see vol. I, ch. vii; pp. 112–13).

145  *anecdote . . . told me*: transferred from earlier: see p. 107 and note.

146  *Branwell's profile*: the bas-relief portrait by Joseph Bentley Leyland
   (1811–51), now displayed in the dining-room, BPM (reproduced
   Gérin, *Branwell Brontë*, frontispiece). In height, Branwell was 'about
   5 ft 3 inches', slight but well proportioned (Gérin, *Branwell Brontë*,
   p. 142).

   *one of his manuscripts*: unidentified.

147  *in the 'Spectator'*: *The Spectator* (1711–12), a daily periodical, founded
   and partly written by Joseph Addison (1672–1719).

   *Wordsworth and Coleridge*: Branwell wrote to Wordsworth at the same
   time as CB wrote to Southey (see p. 118 and note; EG went back and
   inserted Branwell's letter at the correct point chronologically, while
   retaining the reference here). Wordsworth apparently never replied;
   Southey wrote that Wordsworth was 'disgusted' with Branwell's
   letter, 'for it contained gross flattery and plenty of abuse of other
   poets' (WS, i. 156). Coleridge here means Hartley Coleridge (1796–
   1849), the poet's elder son.

148  *a young girl*: Ann Cook (1825–40).

149  *'life's fitful fever . . . sleeps well'*: *Macbeth*, III. ii. 25.

*writing a story*: for the story, see C. W. Hatfield, 'CB and Hartley Coleridge 1840', *BST*, 10 (1940), 15–24. CB's remarks, as quoted, are in the Preface to *The Professor* (p. 1). Samuel Richardson's *Clarissa* (1747–8) and *Sir Charles Grandison* (1753–4), to which CB had alluded in the letter below, are among the longest of novels.

*of a letter*: a draft, to Hartley Coleridge, written on the cover of Hartley Coleridge's reply to Charlotte; the fair copy, presumably written up almost immediately, is dated 10 Dec. 1840. EG's comments are based on her supposition that CB addressed Wordsworth; the humorous tone is appropriate to Hartley Coleridge.

*father nor mother*: Melchizedek, king of Salem and priest (Genesis 14: 18), is seen by St Paul (Hebrews 7: 1–3) as a type of Christ, who as God has neither father nor mother, beginning nor end.

*"Ladies' Magazine"*... *bay tree*: for the *Lady's Magazine*, see p. 97 note; the bay tree, from Psalms 37: 35, proverbial for vigorous growth. Percy and West (below) are characters in a number of CB's 'Angrian' tales.

150 *patient Grisels*: or Griseldas; proverbial name for submissive women: see e.g. Chaucer's 'Clerk's Tale' in *The Canterbury Tales*.

*his "C. T."*: the earliest example in *The Life* of CB referring to possible pseudonyms. In 1840 CB seems to have taken pleasure in comic pseudonyms for letters to EN: 'CHARIVARI' and 'ÇA IRA' are two others. She also used 'Charles Townsend' about this time. 'Charles Thunder' (below) derives from the likeness of 'Brontë' to the Greek word for 'thunder' when transliterated ($\beta\rho\text{o}\upsilon\nu\eta$ = thunder). The playful element here (as elsewhere) is important.

151 *in the Bible*: 1 Corinthians 12: 25. The episode that follows reflects religious tensions of the 1830s and 1840s, as the Church of England's claim to be the state church and hence entitled at the parish level to levy rates for church maintenance, was increasingly challenged by Dissenters. One Anglican response was to accuse Dissenters of schism—the breaking away into factions. The recent Anglo-Catholic movement in the Anglican Church (typified by CB below in Edward Pusey (1800–82) of Oxford and Walter Hook (1798–1875) of Leeds) asserted the authority of the Church of England through an unbroken succession from Christ's Apostles, together with a revival of ceremonies and doctrines in defiance of the Thirty-nine Articles. EG was no doubt amused by the episode, since she could perceive the absurdity of the curates' claims to be based in the true Church, rather than being themselves schismatics from the Catholic Church. See on the

background, W. O. Chadwick, *The Victorian Church* (2 vols., 1966–70), and Alec R. Vidler, *The Church in an Age of Revolution*, ch. 4.

151 *at this time*: 7 or 8 Apr. 1840. 'Mr C.' (below) is John Collins, curate at Keighley, and 'Mr W.' is William Weightman.

*Scotch proverb*: he would have 'let them have it', 'stormed and railed at them'; literally, let them have their broth through the smoke or only eat during a domestic tirade.

152 *did not sniggle*: the original letter has 'snivel' and (below) 'nay' for '*mais*'. It is not certain, given the similarity of their handwritings, but Marianne Gaskell may have transcribed this letter, rather than EG.

*Mechanics' Institution*: founded 1825; Patrick Brontë became a member in 1833. Weightman lectured on 'The Advantage of Classical Studies' and Patrick on 'The Influence of Circumstances'. The newspaper quotation given by CB below is untraced.

*can never respect*: the Revd Osman Parke Vincent (d. 1875); EN wrote of him to CB in April.

*I am tolerably*: MS has, deleted, 5½ lines of the letter at the beginning of this paragraph: 'Your letters are assuming an odd tone. We write of little else but love and marriage and, verily, I have a sort of presentiment that you will be married before you are many years older. I do not want you to reciprocate the compliment because *I am tolerably*'. An example of EG respecting EN's privacy while working on the MS.

153 *June 2nd, 1840*: 'M.' (below) is Mary Taylor; 'G——' (twice) is Gomersal; 'B——' (twice) is Bradford. At the end, EG marked in MS the diminishing size of CB's initials.

*August 20th, 1840*: 'Miss H.' (below) should be 'W.' (more properly, 'W——s', since CB wrote 'Miss Woolers'; hence the plural pronoun that follows). 'G.' is Gomersal.

154 *CALIBAN*: as with the other pseudonyms CB used about this time, the playful element is as important as any identity with Prospero's brutish servant.

*where it listeth*: ?29 Sept. 1840. 'B.' (below) is Batley; 'Mrs B.' is Mrs Thomas Brooke of Huddersfield; 'Mr W.' (thrice) is William Weightman.

*is Scripture*: John 3: 8.

*spirit was young*: Thomas Campbell, 'The Soldier's Dream'.

*"curse . . . by her gods"*: echoing I Samuel 17: 43.

155 *and Manchester Railroad*: Branwell had been tutor with a family near Ulverston for the first 6 months of 1840. The Manchester and Leeds Railway (incorporated 1836) opened the section from Normanton to Hebden Bridge in 1840; Branwell's appointment as Assistant Clerk at Sowerby Bridge at £75 p.a. was confirmed 31 Aug. 1840. The present railway station, built 1876, is half a mile east of the original.

*Tadmor, alias Palmyra*: Palmyra, supposedly founded by Solomon as Tadmor (2 Chronicles 8: 4); a city-state east of Syria, famous for its wealth and power, destroyed by the Romans in the third century AD.

*"bourn . . . no traveller returns"*: *Hamlet*, III. i. 81–2.

156 *whom it relates*: 12 Nov. 1840; the same letter is summarized and quoted from above about negotiations with Mrs Brooke.

*Mr and Mrs ——*: Collins; he was curate to William Busfeild, Rector of Keighley, and one of the supporters of Patrick Brontë at the church-rates meeting earlier in the year. For CB's account of Mrs Collins's reappearance, see her letter to EN, 4 Apr. 1847.

158 *as a governess*: with Mr and Mrs John White of Upperwood House, Rawdon (demolished), 11 miles from Haworth, between Horsforth and Yeadon. The Whites had at least three children; CB was only responsible for two, Sarah Louisa, aged 8, and a boy aged 6, though she was also expected to act as nurse to the baby on occasions. CB was with the Whites from 2 Mar. to 24 Dec. 1841.

159 *March 3rd, 1841*: 'Mr and Mrs ——' (below) are Mr and Mrs White; 'B.' is Brookroyd.

*16l. per annum*: CB, as EG notes, was not well qualified and £20 was not unreasonable, however 'close' the Whites showed themselves in laundry charges; see on salaries the details in *Agnes Grey*, p. 200.

160 *March, '41*: Eds. 1–3 print date as 'March 21st', but MS clearly reads (correctly) 'March, '41'; probably 12 or 22 Mar. 1841. 'better than ——' (below) is Stonegappe; 'Mr ——' is White.

161 *June, 1841*: 10 June. 'Mr and Mrs ——' (below, as in preceding and succeeding paragraphs) are White.

*Anne this vacation*: CB returned to Haworth on 30 June, by when Anne (despite EG's statement below) had already gone back to her post with the Robinsons of Thorp Green where she had been since Mar. 1841.

162 *July 19th, 1841*: MS and Ed. 1 correctly give 19 July; Ed. 2's change to 18 has no authority. 'Miss ——' (below) is Jackson.

162 *Delphic style . . . etcæterorum*: i.e. in the often riddling or obscure manner of the prophecies of the oracle at Delphi; 'etcætera, etcæterorum' = 'and so on and so forth'.

163 *August 7th, 1841*: 'Mr and Mrs ——' (below) are White; 'at ——' is Brook Hall near Tadcaster; 'Martha ——' is Taylor.

   *great advantages*: Martha Taylor had been at school in Brussels since spring 1841; Mary Taylor had been travelling in Europe and was to join Martha at school; the advantages, in education and travel, stimulated CB's desire to acquire French so that languages would be a positive attraction at the Brontës' school.

165 *sister of hers*: Eliza Wooler, who took over the school in 1838.

166 *Sept. 29th, 1841*: 'Mr and Mrs ——' (below) are White.

   *Paris . . . Brussels, in Belgium*: Parisian French would be the best accent to acquire; but Paris was comparatively expensive and (especially in persuading Aunt Branwell to favour the Brussels proposal) its moral reputation was low. The disadvantage of Brussels, despite the prospective companionship of the Taylors, was the poor esteem amongst native French speakers of the accent.

167 *Château de Kokleberg*: the Château de Koekelberg, a school run by Catherine Goussaert (née Phelps); it was not a château, though on the site of one. For its history and situation, see Stevens, *Mary Taylor*, appendix D.

   *Mrs Jenkins . . . British Consul*: wife of the Revd Evan Jenkins, the chaplain (as CB soon learnt), not consul; CB's mistake was 'corrected' in *The Life*, which here reverts to CB's original and EG's MS. It was Mrs Jenkins's unfavourable account of Brussels schools that temporarily switched the destination to Lille. Her son later showed EG round in Brussels (*Letters*, p. 391).

   *of her cousins*: the Dixons, children of Mary Taylor's aunt Laetitia and Abraham Dixon; Mary Dixon (d. 1897) particularly was to befriend CB in the second Brussels period. Mary Taylor called them 'the most united affectionate family' (Stevens, *Mary Taylor*, pp. 39–40).

168 *of her furniture*: Ed. 3 omits: '*her furniture*, for the consideration of her board'.

   *fortunately so*: Ed. 3 omits: '*so*, for it is an obscure, dreary place, not adapted for a school'.

169 *'I did not deserve it'*: 10 Jan. 1842.

   *for five months*: Branwell had now been working for nearly 15 months, since Oct. 1840; he had been transferred in Apr. 1841 from Sowerby

Bridge to Luddenden Foot as 'Clerk in Charge' at a starting salary of £130 p.a. The station has been demolished. At the year end, the accounts showed a shortage; Branwell was dismissed 31 Mar. 1842, the loss being deducted from his salary.

*Baptist Noel*: Baptist Noel (1798–1873), another member of the evangelical network; he was interested in Protestant activities in Europe, including the Evangelical Society of France.

170 *price is above rubies*: Proverbs 31: 10 (echoing 3: 15); below, the 'coals of fire' is from Romans 12: 20 (itself echoing Proverbs 25: 22).

*pockets to make*: cf. *Jane Eyre*: 'little pockets . . . (shaped something like a Highlander's purse) tied in front of their frocks and destined to serve the purpose of a work-bag' (vol. I, ch. v; p. 47).

171 *his brother—a clergyman*: the Revd David Jenkins, Vicar of Pudsey, brother of Evan Jenkins.

*English lady . . . Orleans family*: the English lady as yet unidentified. The Orleans family was a branch of the French royal family. At the Revolution, the then Duke, Louis-Philippe-Joseph (1747–93), supported its principles and, as Philippe Égalité, voted for the King's execution: he was himself executed soon after. Égalité's son, Louis-Philippe (1773–1850) became King of France in 1830; his eldest son died in 1842 and the King himself was exiled in 1848. Louis-Philippe's daughter, Louise-Marie (1812–50), married in 1832 Leopold I, King of the Belgians (uncle of Queen Victoria), who had accepted the throne in 1831, following Belgium's successful 1830 revolution, which separated it from the Dutch Crown.

*pensionnat of Madame Héger*: the school, for boarders and day pupils, at 32 Rue d'Isabelle, kept by Claire Zoë Heger (1804–90); EG's accent on the name is incorrect. Mme Heger, née Parent (she hyphenated the names after marriage), was the second wife of Constantin Heger (see below), whom she married in 1836. The school was established in 1830; in her circular (WS, i. 252) the fee, without extras, was 650 francs ( = £26); CB gives the number of pupils as 52 (p. 178) and nearly 90 (p. 186); EG, taking the latter figure as more fully informed, as from 80 to 100 (p. 176). Mme Heger was the prototype of Mlle Reuter in *The Professor* and of Mme Beck in *Villette*. She was a highly efficient and effective educationalist and manager, who naturally became alienated from CB when, during the second Brussels period, CB's passion for her husband became evident. For a photograph of the school, see Victor Tahon, 'La Rue Isabelle et le Jardin des Arbalétriers', *BST*, 6 (1923), 135 (reproduced in Fraser, *CB*, opposite

p. 181, who also has two photographs of the pensionnat's garden, opposite p. 340); the whole area was redeveloped *c.*1910. See further Gérin, *CB*, ch. 13, and Duthie, *The Foreign Vision of CB*.

171 *M. Héger informs me*: Constantin Georges Heger (1809–96); became a teacher at a boys' academy in 1829, the Athénée Royal in the Rue d'Isabelle, and also at his future wife's school in 1834; the establishments were next door to each other. His first wife and child had died in 1833; he married Mlle Parent in 1836. He was a notable teacher, though he could be highly and disconcertingly emotional. EG met him in Brussels in May 1856 and 'very much indeed I both like and respect him'; his wife, 'understanding I was a friend of Miss Brontë's, refused to see me' (*Letters*, p. 394). The meeting of 1856 confirmed what EG would already assume from *Villette* (given CB's use of autobiographical material in *Jane Eyre* and *Shirley*): that Heger was M. Paul Emanuel and that CB had been in love with him. Clearly, Heger insisted that the love had not been reciprocated; urged EG to read his letters to CB as evidence of his propriety; and as well as giving EG his reminiscences, later sent examples of CB's French exercises and extracts from CB's letters to him. EG was concerned to protect CB's reputation and, given Heger's confidence in her and his married state, not to write anything that would seem like a betrayal of him (see also Gérin, *CB*, appendix A ('EG and M. Heger'). For portraits of Heger, his wife and family, see Gérin, *CB*, opposite p. 204 (also in Fraser, *CB*, opposite p. 181); Heger was bearded when CB knew him. It is useful to remember that Heger was only seven years older than CB; that his wife was twelve years older; and that they had only been married six years when the Brontës came to Brussels.

172 *more to say hereafter*: the Brontës, with Mary and Joseph Taylor, travelled in the first week of Feb. 1842; for the Chapter Coffee House, see pp. 285–6. Martha Taylor was already at the Château de Koekelberg and Mary was to join her.

*Mary's account*: 'Mary's account . . . occasional holidays' added in Ed. 3; cf. CB's knowledge of artists and their works with Branwell's theoretical command of London streets (p. 145) and CB's own list of artists to see (p. 70).

*to Emily, are*: from CB's Prefatory Note to 'Selections from Poems by Ellis Bell' (*Wuthering Heights*, p. 370, with slight variations); the extract is copied out on the back of MS p. 223, EG not interrupting her flow when it could be picked up later.

173 *an historic tale*: EG's source for the legendary giants is not traced; they seem to be unknown in Belgium.

*Cathedral of St Gudule*: the collegiate church (not a cathedral) of St Michael and St Gudule, dating from the thirteenth to the sixteenth centuries; the exterior was restored in 1843.

*the false Duessa*: in Edmund Spenser's *The Faerie Queene* (1589–96), bk. I, Duessa represents the deceitful splendour of the Roman Catholic Church as against the true Protestant purity of Una.

*Beliard . . . Rue d'Isabelle*: Augustin-Daniel Belliard (1769–1832), French Ambassador to Belgium, 1831–2, helped ensure Belgium's independence after the 1830 revolution. The street was named after Isabella of Spain, Archduchess of Austria (1566–1633), the successful and popular governor of the Netherlands after her husband's death.

174 *Old Mortality*: the footnote is written on a small slip of paper (bound up in MS at this point), copied out separately from the main work on the text. The extract is from Scott's novel (1816), ch. 2.

176 *This lady*: this paragraph and the next, clearly written later, are on two pages (both numbered p. 228*) inserted in MS between pp. 228 and 229.

*French lady . . . Brussels*: not identified; her letter reads: 'I don't know M. Heger personally, but I know that there are few natures so noble or so admirable as his. He is one of the most enthusiastic members of that Society of St Vincent de Paul which I mentioned to you before, and not satisfied with helping the poor and the sick, he also sacrifices his evenings to them. After days entirely taken up by the duties his work imposes on him, he gets together the poor, the labourers, and gives them free classes, and finds ways to entertain them even while he teaches them. This commitment shows you clearly that M. Heger is deeply and openly religious. His manner is frank and pleasant; he makes everyone he comes in contact with, and above all children, love him. He is a fluent speaker, and possesses in high degree the eloquence of good sense and heart. He is not an author. A man of enthusiasm and principles, he decided to resign the prestigious and well-paid duties that he undertook at the Athénée, those of Director of Studies, because he could not bring about the good there that he had hoped for, the introduction of religious education in the pro-gramme of study. I have once seen Mme Heger, who has something cold and formal in her make-up, and who scarcely predisposes you in her favour. Even so, I understand her to be loved and valued by her pupils.' The sentence translated above as 'He is not an author' is problematic: MS clearly gives the French as printed and the sentence can, in the context but with difficulty, be rendered as here: but colleagues who teach French can find no parallel usage.

176 *S. Vincent de Paul*: the Frenchman, Vincent de Paul (*c.*1580–1660), dedicated his life to service of the poor; besides the orders of priests and nuns established in his lifetime, the Society of St Vincent de Paul was founded in Paris by Frédéric Ozanam (1833) for laymen committed to charitable work.

*nothing of French*: as is clear from CB's resolution to correspond with EN in French (p. 96), EG is right about their basic if limited grounding: see further Duthie, *The Foreign Vision of CB*, pp. 5–7. It says much for Heger's character and ability that he set about getting these peculiar sisters to achieve their venture's purpose.

178 *French authors*: Casimir Delavigne (1793–1843), 'The Life of Joan of Arc', *Les Messéniennes* (1818–22); Jacques Bénigne Bossuet (1627–1704), preacher and Catholic controversialist; St Ignatius (d. *c.*107), Bishop of Antioch, who wrote seven letters, one to the Romans, on his journey to martyrdom (see *Early Christian Writings*, trans. Maxwell Staniforth (1968), pp. 101–8). For CB's response to French authors at this time and her surviving transcriptions from them (including two from Bossuet), see Duthie, *The Foreign Vision of CB*, ch. 2 and pp. 231–2; BPM has an exercise book containing various extracts. See also Shirley's learning of French with Louis Moore (*Shirley*, vol. III, ch. iv; ch. 27).

*Brussels, 1842 (May?)*: late April or early May from the reference to Charlotte's birthday (21 Apr.). 'Miss ——' (below) is Catherine Wooler; CB's opinion of her was not high, a letter of hers, characterized as 'very like her', being dismissed as 'palaver' (1 Sept. 1851). CB also compared Mme Heger in this letter to another Wooler sister, unfavourably to both (Stevens, *Mary Taylor*, p. 51 note).

179 *one other girl . . . an Englishwoman*: the 'other girl' was Maria Miller, later Mrs Robertson, on whom Ginevra Fanshawe in *Villette* was based. In *Villette*, Lucy Snowe is first employed as gouvernante; Mme Beck 'would have the women of no other country about her own children' (ch. VIII; p. 89).

*"peu correct"*: 'not very correct'. In the description of Heger, EG discreetly omits CB's elaboration: 'a little black ugly being, with a face that varies in expression. Sometimes he borrows the lineaments of an insane tom-cat, sometimes those of a delirious hyena; occasionally, but very seldom, he discards these perilous attractions, and assumes an air not above 100 degrees removed from mild and gentlemanlike.'

180 *Charlotte's devoirs*: more than 25 of CB's *devoirs* or school exercises have survived (see Alexander, *Bibliography*, section IV); they are dated from 18 Apr. 1842 to 6 Oct. 1843. For discussion of Heger's methods, which began from an absolute commitment and 'a tireless and sympathetic study' of each pupil, and of CB's development, see Duthie, *The Foreign Vision of CB*, ch. 2. EG's account is based partly on her conversation with Heger, partly on his letter to her of 22 May 1856, with which he sent 3 exercises plus extracts from CB's letters to him (John Rylands MSS). The exercises were 'Peter the Hermit' (CB's original) and 'The Death of Napoleon' (copy by Heger) and Emily Bronte's 'Harold the Night before Hastings' (copy by Heger).

*of Mirabeau*: the Comte de Mirabeau (1749–91) was a leading figure, particularly through his powerful oratory, in the early stages of the French Revolution; Victor Hugo (1802–85) collected his 'Étude sur Mirabeau' in *Littérature et Philosophie Mêlées* (1834). Heger identifies this source and how he specifically directed them to section VI of the Mirabeau study in his letter of 22 May 1856, from which EG takes his account of the lesson, which reads: 'but, in my lesson I limited myself to what concerned *Mirabeau the orator*. It was after the analysis of this extract, considered variously from the points of view of content, of organization, of what can be called *the framework* that they produced the two portraits that I send you.' CB copied out part of Hugo's 'Mirabeau' (Duthie, *The Foreign Vision of CB*, p. 231). Heger's comments given in English (below) are not from his letter and presumably were noted by EG during their meeting.

181 *IMITATION*: CB's original (John Rylands MS) shows that neither she nor Heger was much concerned at this stage with the formalities of accents: much of the accentuation of this and the other French passages in *The Life* was added successively in the three printed editions; for Ed. 3, EG asked that someone at her publishers 'would look over the French dévoirs' (*Letters*, p. 464). Peter the Hermit (?1050–1115) was a popularist preacher of the First Crusade (1096–9) that ended with the capture of Jerusalem: CB probably drew on Joseph-François Michaud, *Histoire des Croisades* (1819); for a modern account, see Steven Runciman, *A History of the Crusades*, vol. I (1951). In this translation, Heger's marginal comments are given in the text in pointed brackets <>: 'From time to time, there appear on earth men destined to be the [predestined] instruments of great changes, moral or political, ~~in their age~~ <Why this deletion?> Sometimes it is a conqueror, an Alexander or an Attila, who passes like a whirlwind, and purifies the moral atmosphere, as a storm purifies the physical

atmosphere; sometimes, it is a revolutionary, a Cromwell, or a Robespierre, who expiates by a king <the crimes and> the vices of a dynasty; sometimes it is a religious enthusiast like Mahomet, or Peter the Hermit, who, with only the lever of the mind, raises whole nations, uproots them and transplants them to new parts of the world, *peopling Asia with the inhabitants of Europe.* <This detail only applies to Peter.> Peter the Hermit was a gentleman of Picardy, in France <Needless when you are writing in French.>, so why did he not pass his life as other gentlemen, his contemporaries, spent theirs, at table, hunting, in his bed, without worrying himself about Saladin, or his Saracens? Isn't it because there is in some natures, an untamable ardour [a centre of activity] that will not allow them to remain inactive, *that forces them at last to stir themselves up to exercise powerful faculties, which even while sleeping are ready, like Sampson, to burst the knots that restrain them?* <You have begun to speak of Peter: you are into the subject: go to the point.> / Peter became a soldier; *if his ardour had been of that kind* [if he had only had that common enthusiasm] that stems from bodily strength, *he would have* [he had] been for ever a brave soldier, and nothing more; but his ardour was of the soul, his flame was pure and it raised itself towards heaven. / *Without doubt* [It is true that] the youth of Peter *was* [was] disturbed by stormy passions; powerful natures are extreme in everything, they do not recognize lukewarmness, either in good, or in evil; Peter then from the very beginning sought avidly for the glory that fades and the pleasures that deceive, *but he soon discovered* [he soon perceived] that what he was pursuing was only an illusion which he would never attain <Useless when you have said illusion.>; he then retraced his steps, he began life's journey again, but this time he avoided the broad road that leads to destruction and took the narrow road that leads to life; *since* [as] the route was long and difficult he cast away the helmet and weapons of the soldier, and clad himself in the simple habit of a monk. To the military life succeeded the monastic life, for extremes meet, and *in the sincere man* the sincerity of repentance brings along [necessarily in its train] *with it* the stringency of penitence. [And so Peter became a monk!] / But *Peter* [he] had in him a force that prevented him from being inactive long, his thoughts, on whatever subject *it might be* [it was] could not be limited; it was not enough for him that he was himself religious, that he himself was convinced of the truth of Christianity, it was necessary that all Europe, that all Asia, partook of his certainty and professed belief in the Cross. [Fervent] Piety raised by Genius, fed by Solitude, *gave birth to a kind of inspiration* [inspired his soul] *in his soul*, and when he left his cell and reappeared in the world, he bore like Moses the imprint of God in his face, and *all* [all] recognized in him the true apostle of the Cross. / Mahomet had never stirred the indolent nations of the East as Peter then stirred the hardy people of the West; that eloquence must needs be of a near miraculous power *that could* [that almost persuaded] kings to sell their kingdoms *in order to procure* [to get] weapons and troops *to help* [to supply] to Peter in the holy war that he wished to wage against the infidels. The power of Peter [the Hermit] was not in the least a physical power, for nature, or to speak more truly, God is impartial in the distribution of his gifts; he grants to one <u>of his children</u> grace, beauty, bodily perfection, to another intellect, moral greatness. Peter indeed was a small man, of not very agreeable appearance; but he had that courage, that constancy, that enthusiasm, that emotional energy which crushes all opposition, and makes the will of a single man become the law of a whole nation. To form a true idea of the influence that this man exerted over the *characteristics* [things] and ideas of his age, it is necessary to imagine him in the midst of the crusading army in his double role of prophet and warrior; the poor hermit, dressed in his *poor* [lowly] grey habit is there <u>more powerful than a king; he is</u> surrounded <u>by an</u> [by an] [eager] multitude <u>a multitude that looks only to him, while he, he</u> <u>looks only to heaven; his raised eyes</u> seem to say, "I see God and the angels, and I have lost sight of earth!" / *In that moment the* [but that] poor grey *habit* [habit] on him is like the mantle of Elijah; it enfolds him with inspiration; *he* [Peter] reads the future; he sees Jerusalem delivered; [he sees] the holy sepulchre freed; <u>he sees</u> the silver Crescent torn from the Temple, and the Oriflamme and the red Cross established in its place; not only Peter sees these wonders, but he makes all those that surround him see them; he rekindles hope and courage in [all those bodies exhausted by hardship and privations]. The battle will not take place until the morrow, but the victory is decided that evening. Peter promised; and the Crusaders trusted his word, as the Israelites trusted that of Moses and Joshua.'

184 *the battle of Hastings*: original in BMP, dated June 1842. Text in Gérin, *Emily Brontë*, pp. 267–8; translation by Dorothy H. Cornish in 'The Brontës' Study of French', *BST*, 11 (1947), 98. Cf. Frances Henri's exercise, 'King Alfred and the Cakes', in *The Professor*, ch. XVI; pp. 122–3.

'*Elle était nourrie de la Bible*': 'She was nourished on the Bible'. Presumably Heger used the phrase to EG when they met; it is not in his letter of 22 May 1856.

'*Vision . . . on Mount Nebo*': based on Deuteronomy 34. Original in possession of the Heger family, dated 27 July 1843 (EG believed it to

be much earlier). Text and translation by Phyllis Bentley in 'More
Brontë Devoirs', *BST*, 12 (1955), 366–75.

185 '*Oraison . . . la Reine d'Angleterre*': the Funeral Oration on Henrietta
Maria, widow of Charles I, delivered 16 Nov. 1669. Carlyle's account
of Cromwell is in *On Heroes and Hero Worship* (1840); François
Guizot's in his *History of the English Revolution* (pt. 1, *The History of
Charles I* (1826–7) ).

'*Lettre . . . Sierra Léone, Afrique*': this *devoir* seems not to have survived.
MS has, deleted: '*Afrique*. / Her strong feeling against the Roman
Catholic religion was considered as hatred against the Roman Catholics,
and yet I imagine that part of its vehemence arose from the fact that
she was aware of her own susceptibility to some of the influences
employed by its professors, but did not consider that they were such
as ought to prevail against the exercise of free will and reason as the
highest points that can concern a human being. *Something of*'. CB's
response to Catholicism, despite what Heger offered her through the
example of his life and Catholicism's literary traditions, was both
emotionally immature and lacking in intellectual curiosity; she was
drawn to it, yet failed to 'exercise free will and reason' in examining it.

*Brussels, 1842: c.* July, suggested by reference to the close of the first
half-year.

186 *the grandes vacances*: the school year was divided into two halves or
semesters, with only brief breaks at Christmas and Easter; the summer
vacation actually began in mid-August.

187 *barriers of Brussels*: the barriers were customs posts, at what had been
the gates of the city, where tolls were collected on certain goods.

*cousins of these friends*: the Dixons; Mary Taylor referred to a pleasant
evening with them, with CB and Emily (Stevens, *Mary Taylor*, p. 40).

*another English family*: of Dr Thomas and Elizabeth Wheelwright;
they lived at the Hôtel Clusyenaar, Rue Royale, 1842–3. The eldest
of the five daughters, Laetitia (1828–1911), became a friend and
correspondent of CB's; the sisters liked CB, but did not care for
Emily. EG met Laetitia in spring 1856, on her way to Brussels.

*at Madame Héger's*: a MS deletion here shows how EG reworked
material in the process of writing: '*Héger's* in the year immediately
succeeding this annual September holiday. The young ladies well
remember the two English sisters who were found by them just
assuming their new duties of English and Music teacher. They were
immediately attracted by Charlotte's kind and tender manner to the
young newcomers *school*'.

188 *parlour-boarder*: a pupil who took meals and lived with the family rather than with the other boarders.

*lecture pieuse*: 'the pious reading'; a reading from some improving work (cf. *Villette*, ch. XIII; pp. 143–4).

*little Brussels rolls*: the comment is typical of EG's delight (often in marked contrast to CB's) in things continental, not least food; in *The Professor*, Crimsworth stirs his coffee with a pistolet (ch. XIII; p. 102; and see *Villette*, ch. VIII; p. 92).

189 *I will make a quotation*: this long extract ('I will make . . . the real motive') added in Ed. 3.

191 *to New Zealand*: possibly in 1848, when Mary Taylor wrote to CB about 'your cow' (see Stevens, *Mary Taylor*, p. 78, and WS, ii. 248).

*she died*: on 12 Oct. 1842, of cholera, aged 23.

*is as follows*: 10 Nov. 1842.

*sad recollection*: *Shirley*, vol. I, ch. ix (first two extracts); vol. II, ch. xii; ch. 23 (pp. 149, 407–8); Jessy Yorke was modelled on Martha Taylor. Mary Taylor walked out with CB and Emily to the Protestant cemetery on the Chaussée de Louvain on 30 Oct.; the cemetery, described in *The Professor* (ch. XIX; pp. 152–4), has been redeveloped.

192 *was very ill*: EG omits the death of William Weightman from cholera (6 Sept. 1842); Patrick Brontë, in the funeral sermon, spoke of himself and Weightman as 'fellow labourers in the same glorious cause' (*Brontëana*, ed. J. Horsfall Turner (1898), p. 258). Aunt Branwell became ill in mid-October with what CB called an 'internal obstruction' (10 Nov. 1842) and died 29 Oct. 1842. CB and Emily received the first news of her illness on 2 Nov.; they sailed on Sunday, 6 Nov.

193 *in her will*: Aunt Branwell's will (WS, i. 277–8), drawn up on 30 Apr. 1833 before Branwell's behaviour could have been any influence, left personal items to each of the Brontë children (including Branwell) and her money to be divided between the sisters and another niece.

*in a situation*: with the Robinsons of Thorp Green, since Mar. 1841.

194 *record of her life*: given the confusion into which the sisters' hasty departure had thrown Mme Heger's arrangements, the letter is remarkably generous and its suggestion that CB return makes clear that at this stage neither of the Hegers was worried about CB. The letter, in the formal style of the period, reads: '*To the Reverend Mr Brontë, Protestant Minister, &c. &c.* / Saturday, 5 November [1842] / Sir, / A very sad event made your daughters decide to return suddenly to England. This departure, which has saddened us greatly,

nevertheless has my complete approval. It is perfectly natural that they want to console you for what heaven has taken from you, and in gathering around you, for you to appreciate the better what heaven has given you and what it leaves you still. I hope you will forgive me, sir, for taking advantage of this occasion to send my respects to you; I do not have the honour of knowing you personally, and yet I have a feeling of real veneration for you, for in judging the father of a family by his children there is no risk of deceiving oneself, and given this affinity, the education and the feelings that we have found in your daughters, can only give us a very high opinion of your worth and your character. You will no doubt learn with pleasure that your children have made remarkable progress in all branches of their study, and that this progress is entirely due to their love of work and to their perseverance; we have had to do little with such pupils; their progress is your work rather than ours; we have not had to teach them the value of time or of instruction; they had learnt all that in their own home, and we for our part have only the slight credit of directing their efforts and supplying a diet appropriate to the commendable industry that your daughters owe to your example and your teaching. May the well-deserved praises that we give your children be some consolation to you in the unhappiness that afflicts you, and may it be, for Charlotte and Emily, a pleasing and fair reward for their labours. / In losing our two dear students, we ought not to hide from you that we feel at the same time both sorrow and anxiety; we are sorry because this sudden separation comes to destroy the almost fatherly affection that we have given them, and our pain is increased at the sight of so much work disrupted, of so many things well begun, and which only required time to bring them to a successful conclusion. Within a year, each of your daughters would have been entirely provided against all future eventualities; each of them was acquiring at once both knowledge and the art of teaching. Miss Emily was learning the piano; having lessons from the best teacher that we have in Belgium; and already she herself had junior pupils; she was losing simultaneously her remaining ignorance and, what was still more awkward, her shyness. Miss Charlotte was beginning to give lessons in French, and to acquire that assurance, that confidence, so necessary in teaching; only another year, at the most, and the business would have been finished and finished well. Then we would have been able, if you had agreed, to offer your daughters or at least one of them, a post that would be agreeable to them and that would give them that pleasing independence so difficult for a young person to find. This is not, believe me, sir, this is not now a matter of personal interest for us, but a matter of affection; you will pardon me if we talk of your children, if we concern ourselves with their future, as if they were part of our family; their personal qualities, their willingness, their extreme eagerness, are the only reasons that urge us to hazard ourselves in this way. We know, sir, that you will weigh more thoughtfully and more wisely than us the result for their future of a complete interruption in the studies of your two daughters; you will decide what ought to be done, and you will pardon our frankness, if you will only consider that the reason that prompts us is a truly disinterested affection, and one which would be deeply grieved if it were now forced to resign itself to no longer being useful to your dear children. / Accept, I beg you, sir, the respectful expression of my feelings of high regard. / C. HEGER.'

197 *ten at night*: it had been possible to travel from Leeds to London in a single day since 1840, though only in 1846 was it possible without changing; the route was via Derby and Rugby. In her letter to EN, 30 Jan. 1843, CB indicates that the train had been due in at 8 p.m.

*in 'Villette'*: *Villette*, ch. VI (pp. 59–62); see further ch. VII. *The Professor*, ch. VII, also describes the journey.

*that 'Mighty Heart'*: Wordsworth, 'Composed upon Westminster Bridge' (1802).

*16l. a year*: this paragraph was written afterwards on the back of MS p. 255; what is now the immediately following passage ('On March . . . that I was to consider') was crossed out and then recopied (apparently by William Gaskell) to give the necessary continuity. The salary was not unreasonable in itself, since Belgium was cheap and CB was gaining experience; but the German lessons would cost nearly £5 a year and laundry another £2. CB had on occasions to seek money from home. Her German teacher was Mme Mühl, Fräulein Anna Braun in *Villette* (ch. XXVI; pp. 377–8).

*of Madame or M. Héger*: for CB's versions of her early teaching experience, see *The Professor*, chs. VII and X (Crimsworth, as a man, is chaperoned at Mlle Reuter's), and *Villette*, ch. VIII.

198 *German and English chapels*: German and English services were held at the Chapelle Royale (Leopold had remained a Protestant), and English services in the chapel on the Boulevard de l'Observatoire.

*allée défendue*: the garden-walk, forbidden to the pupils, that ran parallel with the wall dividing Mme Heger's from the boys' Athénée Royal; it appears in both *The Professor* and *Villette*.

*she writes thus*: 'the D.s' (below) are the Dixons.

198  *and their children*: at this date the Hegers had three daughters (Marie
Pauline, Louise Florence, Claire Zoë Marie) and a son, Prospère (b.
March 1842); they later had another daughter (Victorie, b. November
1843) and another son (Paul, b. 1846).

  *his brother-in-law*: M. Chapelle; Heger's first wife had been sister of
Chapelle's present wife. He was a music teacher and gave Emily
Brontë piano lessons.

200  *publication of 'Villette'*: CB's publisher secured £100 in 1853 for a
French translation of *Villette* (*Letters*, p. 231). The 1855 version the
Hegers knew (Gérin, *CB*, p. 597) removed CB's pseudonymous place-
name: *La Mâitresse d'Anglais—ou le Pensionnat de Bruxelles* ('The
English Teacher—or The Brussels School').

  *April, 1843*: 'at Mrs ——'s' (below) is 'Mrs Sidgwick's or Mrs
White's'.

201  *May 29. 1843*: apparently a free version by EG, to judge by other
printed versions of it.

  *Hannah*: not otherwise identified; Emily had to take charge of her
younger sister (WS, i. 299).

202  *31 Mai, 1843*: this *devoir*, incorrectly entitled in Eds. 1 and 2 'Sur la
Nom de Napoléon' ('On the Name of Napoleon'), is from a copy
Heger sent EG (CB's original is now in BPM). Complete text and
translation by Margaret Lane in *BST*, 12 (1954), 273–85; the original
has an introduction and minor variants. Napoleon died on St Helena,
1821; his remains had been brought to Paris as recently as Dec. 1840,
for interment in the Hôtel des Invalides. CB refers to his second wife,
Marie Louise of Austria, and his son (d. 1832); the portrait of
Wellington (his 'speech' is CB's invention) includes reference to his
unpopularity during the 1832 Reform Bill crisis. In the myth of
Prometheus, the titan, having stolen heavenly fire to give life to
mankind, was punished by being chained to a rock where an eagle
(rather than CB's vulture) each day devoured his liver; Ulysses, in
Homer, safely heard the luring songs of the Sirens by having himself
tied to his ship's mast while his men rowed, their ears blocked with
wax. For Jonah's gourd, see Jonah 4: 6–7. The *devoir* reads: '31 May
1843. / On the Death of Napoleon. / Napoleon was born in Corsica
and died on St Helena. Between those two islands nothing except a
vast and burning desert and an immense ocean. He was born the son
of a simple gentleman, and died an emperor, though without a crown
and in chains. Between his cradle and his grave, what was there? the
career of an upstart soldier, battlefields, a sea of blood, a throne, then

more blood, and chains. His life was a rainbow; the two ends touch
the earth, the shining height measures the heavens. On Napoleon in
his cradle a mother smiled; in his family home he had brothers and
sisters; later in his palace he had a wife who loved him. But on his
death-bed Napoleon was alone; no mother, neither brother nor sister,
neither wife nor child!! Others have told and retold his deeds; for
myself, I pause to consider the desolation of his last hour! / There he
is, in exile and a prisoner, chained to a rock. Another Prometheus, he
submits to the punishment of his pride! Prometheus had wanted to
be God and Creator; he stole heavenly fire to give life to the body that
he had formed. And Buonaparte, for his part, wished to create, not a
man, but an empire, and to give life, a soul, to his gigantic work, he
did not hesitate to root out the life of whole nations. Jupiter, angry at
the impiety of Prometheus, nailed him living to the summit of the
Caucasus. Likewise, to punish the insatiable ambition of Buonaparte,
Providence fettered him, until death came for him, on an isolated rock
in the Atlantic. Perhaps there he also felt gouging his side that
insatiable vulture of which the myth tells, perhaps he also suffered
that thirst of the heart, that hunger of the soul, which torture the
exile, far from his family and his country. But to talk thus is surely
to attribute gratuitously to Napoleon a human weakness that he never
showed? When did he let himself be restrained by a bond of affection?
Undoubtedly other conquerors have hesitated in their progress of
glory, halted by an obstacle of love or friendship, restrained by a
woman's hand, recalled by the voice of a friend—he, never! He had
no need, like Ulysses, of being bound to the mast of the ship, or to
shut his ears with wax; he did not fear the song of the Sirens—he
scorned it; he made himself marble and iron to carry out his great
plans. Napoleon did not think of himself as a man, but as the
embodiment of a nation. He did not love; he thought of his friends
and those near to him only as instruments which he played on, so long
as they were useful, and which he threw aside when they ceased to be
so. One should not then approach the Corsican's grave with feelings
of pity, nor stain with tears the stone that covers his remains, for his
spirit repudiates all that. It has been said, I know, that the hand was
cruel that separated him from his wife and his child. But no, it was a
hand that, like his own, trembled neither with passion nor with fear,
it was the hand of a cold man, convinced, who had the knowledge to
understand Buonaparte; and this is what that man said, whom neither
defeat could humiliate nor victory swell with pride. "Marie-Louise is
not the wife of Napoleon; it is France that Napoleon has married; it
is France that he loves, their union bringing forth the ruin of Europe;

there's the divorce I want; that's the union that must be broken." /
The voice of the fearful and the treacherous protested against this
sentence. "It is an abuse of the right of victory! It is treading the
vanquished underfoot! England ought to show mercy, she ought to
open her arms to receive with hospitality her disarmed enemy."
England might perhaps have listened to this advice, since everywhere
and always there are feeble and timorous souls easily seduced by
flattery or frightened by blame. But Heaven allowed a man to be
found who had never known what it was to be afraid; who loved his
country better than fame; unmoved in the face of threats, impervious
to praises, he came before the council of the nation, and lifting up his
calm and lofty brow, he dared to say: "Let treason be silent! because
it is treason that advises compromise with Buonaparte. I know what
the wars are from which Europe still bleeds, like a victim under the
butcher's knife. It is necessary to have done with Napoleon Buonaparte. You are frightened of a wrong in such a firm statement! I have
no magnanimity, it is said? So be it! what does it matter what is said
of me? I am not here to make myself a reputation as a magnanimous
hero, but to heal, if a cure is possible, a Europe which is dying,
drained of resources and blood, a Europe of which you neglect the
true interests, preoccupied as you are by the hollow reputation of
mercy. You are weak. Well! I come to help you. Send Buonaparte to
St Helena! do not hesitate, do not look for some other place; it is the
only suitable one. I tell you this; I have thought it out for you; it is
there that he ought to be, and nowhere else. As for Napoleon, the
man, the soldier, I have nothing against him; he is a royal lion, before
whom you are no more than jackals. But Napoleon the Emperor is
quite another thing; I will remove him from the soil of Europe." He
who spoke thus was always known to keep his promise, this one like
all the rest. I have said, and I repeat it, this man is equal to Napoleon
in genius; as for calibre of character, for uprightness, for loftiness of
thought and of purpose, he is quite another species. Napoleon
Buonaparte was eager for fame and glory; Arthur Wellesley cared
nothing for one or the other; public opinion, popularity, were things
of great value in the eyes of Napoleon; for Wellington, public opinion
was mere noise, a nothing that the breath of his inflexible will made
vanish like a soap bubble. Napoleon flattered the people; Wellington
was curt; the one sought applause, the other cared only for the witness
of his conscience; when it approved, that was enough; all other praise
annoyed him. Thus the people, who adored Buonaparte, angered, rose
against the haughtiness of Wellington; for a time, they displayed their
anger against him and their hate by growls, by roaring like wild beasts;

and then, with the impassivity of a Roman senator, the modern Coriolanus scornfully eyed these violent disturbances; he crossed his strong arms over his mighty chest, and alone, before his threshold, he awaited, he outfaced this popular storm of which the waves died out only a step or two from him: and when the crowd, ashamed of its rebellion, came to lick the feet of its master, the haughty patrician scorned the homage of today like the hatred of yesterday, and in the streets of London, and before his ducal palace of Apsley, he repelled with a manner full of cold disdain the unwanted attentions of the enthusiastic crowd. This pride none the less did not prevent in him a rare modesty; above all he shrank from praise; shied away from tributes; never talked of his exploits and never allowed anyone to talk of them in his presence. His character equalled in grandeur and surpassed in sincerity that of all other heroes ancient or modern. The glory of Napoleon sprang up in a night, like the gourd of Jonah, and it needed only a day for it to wither; the glory of Wellington is like the ancient oaks that shade the mansion of his forebears on the banks of the Shannon; the oak grows slowly; it needs time to thrust its knotty branches towards the sky, and to strike into the earth the deep roots that become tangled together in the solid depths of the earth; but then, the age-old tree, unshakeable like the rock on which it has its base, stands against both the scythe of time and the exertion of winds and storms. Perhaps a century will be needed by England for her to recognize the value of her hero. In a hundred years, all Europe will know how much Wellington is entitled to its gratitude.'

205 *'in a strange land'*: the phrase occurs in Exodus 2: 22, 18: 3; Psalms 137: 4; Acts 7: 6.

*'Alps on Alps arise'*: Alexander Pope, *An Essay on Criticism* (1711), l. 232.

206 *became much shaken*: CB was increasingly isolated during her second Brussels year: apart from Emily's absence, Mary Taylor, the Dixons, and the Wheelwrights successively departed; Heger was taken up by his duties and family. The summer vacation took away even the routine of teaching; it was during this time (1 Sept. 1843) that CB went to confession at St Gudule's: however lightly she treats the episode to Emily (2 Sept. 1843; cf. the version in *Villette*, ch. xv; pp. 198–202), she clearly needed to talk in confidence to someone, though not therefore necessarily about Heger. CB gave in her notice in early October, though at Heger's insistence this was withdrawn. Despite all this other strain, EG knew of CB's growing feelings for Heger: she highlights Branwell as a cause of CB's distress (a thematic preparation for Branwell's fate), although Branwell was not dismissed until July

1845 and CB's letters suggest no concern about him in 1843. Again, while EG omits the confession episode (though she probably saw CB's letter to Emily and knew the *Villette* version), she later uses religious difference to explain the increasing estrangement between CB and Mme Heger, though the latter almost certainly knew or suspected CB's feelings.

206 *August 1st, 1843*: properly, 6 Aug. 1843.

*uncongenial to her*: Mlle Blanche, whom CB called 'heartless, insincere, and vindictive' (29 May 1843) and represented in *Villette* as Mlle Zelie St Pierre: 'a Parisian, externally refined—at heart, corrupt' (ch. XIV; pp. 155–6; cf. Mlle Zephyrine in *The Professor*, ch. XII). I am baffled as to the exact nature of her 'profligacy and sensuality', though *Villette* provides hints.

207 *October 13th, 1843*: The 'D.s' (below) are the Dixons (only Mary Dixon in CB's original); 'Dr ——' is Wheelwright; 'Mr ——' is George Dixon.

*go to her*: Mary Taylor was in Germany, teaching English, and learning music, algebra, and German.

208 *after a fashion*: extract from another letter; internal references (e.g. to learning German) indicate late June.

*on these occasions*: MS has, deleted: '*occasions*. She is a reasonable and calm woman. *I own*'.

210 *Dec. 1st, 1843*: misdated by EG: correct date, 1 Oct. 1843.

*register people*: obscure; possibly people informing the clerk of baptisms, marriages, and deaths.

*Tiger and Keeper*: a cat the Brontës had for some time between 1841 and its death in Mar. 1844, and the bulldog identified particularly as Emily's (see p. 214 and note).

*visit to Brussels*: Victoria arrived in the afternoon of 18 Sept.; *The Times* reported that the carriage, which she shared with Prince Albert, King Leopold, and Queen Louise, was drawn by four horses. In CB's description of Victoria about three words are heavily scored through in MS between 'stout' and 'vivacious'.

211 *various reasons*: MS has, deleted and largely illegible, a passage setting out the reasons: they include Mr Brontë's failing sight, already touched on above.

*writes as follows*: the earlier details about the diploma and the Hegers' daughter are from the same letter. The diploma is not known to survive.

212 *had been staying*: 25 Mar. 1844; the cat was Tiger.

213 *readers of 'Shirley'*: Shirley, vol. II, ch. i (ch. 12; p. 218); the quotation copied into MS by William Gaskell in a space left for it.

*of her to me*: informant not identified.

214 *Emily had done*: Shirley, vol. III, ch. v (ch. 28; pp. 496 ff., and particularly pp. 508–10).

*gift to Emily*: there seems no evidence that Keeper was a gift to Emily, though the two developed a particularly close relationship. She drew him 24 Apr. 1838 (see Gérin, *Emily Brontë*, opposite p. 44). Martha Brown (Oct. 1858) had no memory of the incident that follows, but had seen Emily 'separate Keeper from other dogs when fighting'; John Greenwood remembered one of these occasions (T. P. Foley, 'John Elliot Cairnes' Visit to Haworth Parsonage', *BST*, 18 (1984), 293; Gérin, *Emily Brontë*, pp. 146–7); Keeper's collar is in BPM.

215 *'punished him'*: 'gave him a severe beating'; a term from boxing (therefore, the language of 'the ring', not 'the turf'). EG refers below to the Happy Hunting Ground, where Indian and dog are reunited.

216 *of our health*: 7 Apr. 1844.

*keeping a school*: letter of ?10 Aug. 1844 (in July EN, to whom it is written, was still at Haworth). 'Mrs ——' and 'Mr ——' (below) are White; 'Colonel S.' is Stott; 'Miss C.' is Cockhills; 'Mrs B.' is Mrs Busfeild of Keighley.

*25l. per annum*: the sum, soon £35 (below), can be compared with the subsidized £14 of the Clergy Daughters' School and £26 for Mme Heger's pensionnat (Belgium being cheaper); the circular is reproduced in WS, ii. 1, and Gérin, *CB*, p. 273; copies in BPM.

*year, she writes*: by internal reference this should be *c.*22 Aug. 1844. 'Mrs B.' (below twice) is Busfeild.

217 *to this effect*: 2 Oct. 1844.

*she says*: 14 Nov. 1844.

218 *agony of mind*: Branwell Brontë had become tutor to Edmund, son of the Robinsons of Thorp Green (12 miles from York) in Jan. 1843; Anne had been governess there since Mar. 1841. The Revd Edmund Robinson (1800–46), a wealthy evangelical, though ordained in the Church of England did not exercise his ministry; his wife was Lydia, *née* Gisborne (1800–59). Some disquiet about Branwell is clear in CB's letters from the beginning of 1845 (e.g. 13 Jan., below); when he was suddenly dismissed in July 1845, Branwell claimed it was because Mr Robinson had discovered that he and Mrs Robinson were romantically involved. The evidence on this and on subsequent events is tentative

and often conjectural. On her husband's death in May 1846, Mrs Robinson sent someone, apparently her coachman (a strange choice if the mission was delicate or confidential), to Branwell at Haworth. It was soon clear that Mrs Robinson had no intention of marrying Branwell, as Branwell seems to have hoped or expected, though she had money occasionally transmitted to him, that might be regarded either as compensation or as buying off a nuisance. Much of the relationship clearly springs from Branwell's fantasy and his self-pity, though Mrs Robinson cannot be cleared of all blame and may well have originally amused herself with him in some way. In Nov. 1848 Mrs Robinson married, as his second wife, Sir Edward Scott (then aged 55: see 'A Portrait of Lydia Robinson', *BST*, 18 (1981), 29); he died in 1851, she in 1859. The Brontë family, while not extenuating the culpability of Branwell, were convinced that Mrs Robinson had taken the initiative ('his diabolical seducer', Patrick Brontë called her to EG, 2 Apr. 1857; John Rylands MS). EG clearly believed the Brontë version ('that bad woman who corrupted Branwell'; *Letters*, p. 418) and had had independent corroboration of Mrs Robinson's character (*Letters*, p. 432); the threat of a legal action by Mrs Robinson (now Lady Scott) after publication of Ed. 1 led EG's lawyer (without consulting EG, then in Italy) to place a retraction in *The Times* (30 May 1857), and the whole account was extensively revised in Ed. 3 (no changes were made in Ed. 2). For an assessment of the evidence and an account of Branwell's relationship with Mrs Robinson, see Gérin, *Branwell Brontë*, ch. 16; Fraser, *CB*, ch. 12, who corrects Gérin's account; and Barker, *The Brontës*, chs. 16 and 17.

218 *Charlotte says*: 13 Jan. 1845.

*for Australia*: CB visited Mary Taylor at Hunsworth in Feb. 1845 before her departure for New Zealand. Ed. 3 omits: '*for Australia*. But a weight hung over her—the gloom preceding the full knowledge of sin in which her brother was an accomplice; which was dragging him down to confirmed habits of intemperance; yet by which he was so bewitched, that no remonstrance, however stern, on the part of others—no temporary remorse, however keen—could make him shake off the infatuation that bound him. / The story must be told. If I could, I would have avoided it; but not merely is it so well-known to many living as to be, in a manner, public property, but it is possible that, by revealing the misery, the gnawing, life-long misery, the degrading habits, the early death of her partner in guilt—the acute and long-enduring agony of his family—to the wretched woman, who not only survives, but passes about in the gay circles of London society, as a vivacious, well-dressed, flourishing widow, there may be awakened in her some feelings of repentance.' In the next paragraph, the second sentence ('Anne was . . . consequences were these') substituted in Ed. 3 for: '*private tutor*. Full of available talent, a brilliant talker, a good writer, apt at drawing, ready of appreciation, and with a not unhandsome person, he took the fancy of a married woman, nearly twenty years older than himself. It is no excuse for him to say that she began the first advances, and "made love" to him. She was so bold and hardened, that she did it in the very presence of her children, fast approaching to maturity; and they would threaten her that, if she did not grant them such and such indulgences, they would tell their bed-ridden father "how she went on with Mr. Brontë." He was so beguiled by this mature and wicked woman, that he *went home*'. In MS is, deleted, a detail from this latter passage: '*a married woman*, (the wife of a clergyman) *nearly twenty*'. The Robinson children were almost certainly unaware of any impropriety; see CB's comment in 1847 (1 Mar. 1847—and see 10 Dec. 1848, for their visit to Haworth). The evidence of Dr Ryott on the situation at Thorp Green (Gérin, *Branwell Brontë*, pp. 241–2) is worthless.

219 *for some time*: the qualification ('that for some time') added in Ed. 3; below, Ed. 3 adds: 'caused partly by . . . Anne's letters home'.

   *Feb. 20th, 1845*: 'H.' (below) is Hunsworth, where Mary Taylor's grandfather had built a mill and house (1788), which was occupied by Mary's brothers John and Joseph Taylor after their father's death (1840): Mary Taylor was living there after her return to England, Apr. 1844.

220 *written of Mary T.*: of Mary Taylor, to EN, 20 Nov. 1840.

   *"But I intend to stay, Polly"*: MS has, undeleted, Mary Taylor's comment ('She thought much of her duty . . . sake of present pleasure'), transferred with further material from Mary's letter to the final chapter (p. 457).

221 *to M. Héger*: the originals of CB's four letters to Heger are in the British Library, presented by the Heger family in 1913; French text of all four in Gérin, *CB*, appendix D, with translations on pp. 268–70, 274–5, 278, and 291–2. Heger's letters to CB are not known to survive. EG may have seen all four letters when in Brussels; Heger transcribed for her three extracts (in John Rylands), two from that of 24 July 1844 (one of these consists of three separate passages run together and misdated by Heger 24 June) and one from that of 24 Oct. 1844. In these first two extracts, the omission marks ( . . . . . . . ) indicate but do not declare EG's move from the letter of 24 July 1844 to that of 24 Oct. 1844. The extracts read: 'There is nothing I fear as

much as unemployment, inertia, lethargy of the faculties. When the body is idle, the spirit suffers cruelly; I would not experience this lethargy, if I could write. Once I spent days, weeks, whole months in writing, and not altogether without results, since Southey and [Hartley] Coleridge, two of our best writers, to whom I sent some manuscripts, were pleased to express their approval of them; but at present, my eyesight is too weak; if I were to write much, I would go blind. This weakness of the eyes is a terrible privation for me; otherwise, do you know what I would do, monsieur? I would write a book and dedicate it to my literature master, the only master I have ever had—to you, monsieur! I have often said to you in French how much I respect you, how much I am indebted to your kindness, to your advice. I want to say it to you once in English. That is not possible; it must not be thought of. Writing as a career is closed to me. . . . . . Do not forget to tell me how you are getting on, how madame and the children are. I trust to have your news soon; that thought cheers me, for the memory of your kindness will never be blotted from my mind, and as long as that memory lasts, the respect that you have inspired in me will last as well. Accept, monsieur, &c.'

222 ——'s *illness* . . . ——'s *marriage*: George and Henry Nussey. George's illness proved to be a mental disorder that confined him permanently to nursing homes; Henry, now Vicar of Hathersage, married Emily Prescott, 22 May.

223 *June 13th, 1845*: 'Mrs ——' (below) is Mrs William Prescott, a relative of George Nussey's bride; EN had been a bridesmaid.

*letter, she says*: 18 June 1845. EG, glossing Monday's significance, identified her addition as editorial.

224 *Leeds to Sheffield*: a visit to Hathersage as guest of Henry Nussey was proposed; Sheffield was then the nearest railway station.

*all three . . . Mr S.*: the curates were Arthur Bell Nicholls, J. C. Bradley of Oakworth, and J. B. Grant of Oxenhope; 'Mr S.' is J. W. Smith, a former curate of Patrick Brontë's.

*the railway carriage*: Gérin, *CB*, p. 290, finds it necessary to make the man a Belgian, though it is not clear why CB would conceal the fact either from EN or from Heger, to whom she later mentioned the incident (p. 293).

*to M. Héger*: an extract from CB's letter of 24 July 1844 (properly, three passages but written out continuously by Heger); misdated 24 June by Heger. Marie, Louise, and Claire were the eldest of the Hegers' five children (p. 198 note). The extract reads: 'I am terrified

of forgetting my French—I memorize half a page of French by heart
every day, and take much pleasure in learning this lesson. Please give
madame my best respects; I fear that Marie, Louise, and Claire will
have already forgotten me; but I shall meet you again one day; as
soon as I have earned enough money to travel to Brussels, I shall go
there.'

225 *of the family*: the next paragraph ('Whatever may have . . . affecting
words') substituted in Ed. 3 for: 'All the disgraceful details came out.
Branwell was in no state to conceal his agony of remorse, or, strange
to say, his agony of guilty love, from any dread of shame. He gave
passionate way to his feelings; he shocked and distressed those loving
sisters inexpressibly; the blind father sat stunned, sorely tempted to
curse the profligate woman, who had tempted his boy—his only
son—into the deep disgrace of deadly crime. / All the variations of
spirit and of temper—the reckless gaiety, the moping gloom of many
months, were now explained. There was a reason deeper than any
mere indulgence of appetite, to account for his intemperance; he
began his career as an habitual drunkard to drown remorse. / The
pitiable part, as far as he was concerned, was the yearning love he still
bore to the woman who had got so strong a hold upon him. It is true,
that she professed equal love; we shall see how her professions held
good. There was a strange lingering of conscience, when meeting her
clandestinely by appointment at Harrogate some months after, he
refused to consent to the elopement which she proposed; there was
some good left in this corrupted, weak young man, even to the very
last of his miserable days. The case presents the reverse of the usual
features; the man became the victim; the man's life was blighted, and
crushed out of him by suffering, and guilt entailed by guilt; the man's
family were stung by keenest shame. The woman—to think of her
father's pious name—the blood of honourable families mixed in her
veins—her early home, underneath whose roof-tree sat those whose
names are held saintlike for their good deeds,—she goes flaunting
about to this day in respectable society; a showy woman for her age;
kept afloat by her reputed wealth. I see her name in county papers,
as one of those who patronize the Christmas balls; and I hear of her
in London drawing-rooms. Now let us read, not merely of the
suffering of her guilty accomplice, but of the misery she caused to
innocent victims, whose premature deaths may, in part, be laid at her
door.' For Branwell's account of the development of his relationship
with Mrs Robinson, see WS, ii. 64–5; EG's source for Branwell and
Mrs Robinson meeting at Harrogate is not known.

225 *own affecting words*: 31 July 1845: the same letter that describes the
conversation on the train with the Frenchman.

*to look after him*: John Brown the sexton was the 'some one'. Branwell
was, Anne Brontë noted laconically in her diary paper of 31 July 1845,
'very ill on Thursday' (24 July, the day he received Mr Robinson's
dismissal notice); he went to Liverpool and North Wales on 29 July
for a week.

226 *of getting employment*: for Branwell's application to the Manchester and
Hebden Bridge Railway Company, see Gérin, *Branwell Brontë*, pp.
246–7.

*Dec. 31st, 1845*: postmark is 30 Dec., so that or 29 Dec. should be the
date.

*speaking of ——*: Branwell; the blanks below are for Ann and Mercy
Mary, EN's sisters, who had to cope with their brother Joseph
(1797–1846), an alcoholic.

*In fact*: this paragraph (in MS additions) substituted in Ed. 3 for:
'Thus ended the year 1845. / I may as well complete here the
narrative of the outward events of Branwell Brontë's life. A few
months later (I have the exact date, but, for obvious reasons, withhold
it) the invalid husband of the woman with whom he had intrigued,
died. Branwell had been looking forward to this event with guilty
hope. After her husband's death, his paramour would be free; strange
as it seems, the young man still loved her passionately, and now he
imagined the time was come when they might look forwards to being
married, and might live together without reproach or blame. She had
offered to elope with him; she had written to him perpetually; she had
sent him money—twenty pounds at a time; he remembered the
criminal advances she had made; she had braved shame, and her
children's menaced disclosures, for his sake; he thought she must love
him; he little knew how bad a depraved woman can be. Her husband
had made a will, in which what property he left to her was bequeathed
solely on the condition that she should never see Branwell Brontë
again. At the very time when the will was read, she did not know but
that he might be on his way to her, having heard of her husband's
death. She despatched a servant in hot haste to Haworth. He stopped
at the Black Bull, and a messenger was sent up to the parsonage for
Branwell. He came down to the little inn, and was shut up with the
man for some time. Then the groom came out, paid his bill, mounted
his horse, and was off. Branwell remained in the room alone. More
than an hour elapsed before sign or sound was heard; then, those

outside heard a noise like the bleating of a calf, and, on opening the door, he was found in a kind of fit, succeeding to the stupor of grief which he had fallen into on hearing that he was forbidden by his paramour ever to see her again, as, if he did, she would forfeit her fortune. Let her live and flourish! He died, his pockets filled with her letters, which he had carried perpetually about his person, in order that he might read them as often as he wished. He lies dead; and his doom is only known to God's mercy. When I think of him, I change my cry to heaven. Let her live and repent! That same mercy is infinite.' Mr Robinson's will, drawn up in Jan. 1846, made no mention of Branwell; while Mrs Robinson would lose her trusteeship and her income from the estate if she remarried, during her widowhood she was to have full powers and rights, scarcely the provisions of a man convinced of his wife's adultery (see Fraser, *CB*, pp. 238, 254–6, and Barker, *The Brontës*, pp. 492–5); for Branwell's account of Mrs Robinson's messenger (certainly sent to Haworth, as confirmed to EG by local people, whatever Mrs Robinson's motive or the nature of the transaction), see WS, ii. 95–6.

*his tutorship*: 'until after he was dismissed from his tutorship' substituted in Ed. 3 for: '*until after* the commencement of his guilty intimacy with the woman of whom I have been speaking. If I am mistaken on this point, her taste must have been as depraved as her principles.' The directions for this change are in MS additions.

227 *of the opium-eater*: opium, in solid form or suspended in alcohol (laudanum), was freely available as a painkiller and many nineteenth-century addicts first used it medicinally, notably Coleridge and Thomas De Quincey (see Alethea Hayter, *Opium and the Romantic Imagination*, 1968).

*all over with me*: Ed. 3 omits (as directed in MS additions): '*with me*; (whimpering) "it's *her* fault, *her* fault." All that is to be said more about Branwell Brontë, shall be said by Charlotte Brontë herself, not by me.'

228 *published in 1850*: 'Biographical Notice of Ellis and Acton Bell', 1850 (*Wuthering Heights*, pp. 359–60, for the passage below, with minor variations).

*Currer, Ellis, and Acton Bell*: the practice of anonymous or pseudonymous publication was widespread in the nineteenth century; most journalism was anonymous, while pseudonyms were used to project a persona (e.g. John Wilson's 'Christopher North' in *Blackwood's* or Thackeray's 'Michael Angelo Titmarsh') or to separate the author from other professional activities or to avoid (as the Brontës hoped) the 'weapon of personality'. The Brontës had established a long and playful series of pseudonyms (see pp. 150, 154 and notes); their choice also allowed the three authors to be distinguished without being identified, each poem being initialled. It is possible they borrowed 'Bell' from the latest Haworth curate, Arthur Bell Nicholls; 'Currer' was a local name, possibly from Miss Currer of Eshton Hall, though it is also a place-name. Their first surviving use of the names is in CB's letter to Aylott, 6 Apr. 1846, below.

229 *Chambers, of Edinburgh*: William (1800–83) and Robert (1802–71) Chambers, publishers and authors. For EG's contact with Robert Chambers in 1856, see *Letters*, p. 413.

*living in Haworth*: John Greenwood, d. 1863, aged 56. He first informed EG of CB's death; CB spoke of him in 1854 as 'the one *friend* she had in Haworth' (*Letters*, p. 337).

230 *Aylott and Jones*: booksellers and stationers, 8 Paternoster Row (a centre of the booktrade), established in 1828. They had evangelical connections, including the Church Missionary Society and the Church of England Book Hawking Union. While preferring to publish 'classical and theological books' (WS, ii. 80), they undertook work where the author bore the cost, including *The Germ*, the Pre-Raphaelites' journal. EG contacted Aylott in 1856.

*edition of Wordsworth*: Edward Moxon (1801–58) was noted as a publisher of poetry; Wordsworth's last ( = latest) volume was the 1845 Collected Works in one volume.

231 *a small volume*: MS adds: '*volume*, published by Saunders & Otley, entitled "Hints to Authors" '; this was *The Author's Printing and Publishing Assistant* (1839), which connects (p. 35) long primer type with poetry.

*Miss W——*: the letters to Miss Wooler were originally to have come at the end of the previous chapter (Ch. XIII); this introductory paragraph was crossed through in MS and transferred to here.

*Jan. 30th, 1846*: 'to ——' (below) is Brookroyd; 'E.' is EN; 'Mrs M.' is Moore, who later herself set up a school.

232 *York and Midland*: opened 1839 between York and Leeds. The years 1845–7 saw an immense investment in and construction of railways (the Railway Mania), though not without failures of some companies.

233 *'Chambers's Journal'*: no poem by the Brontës has been traced in *Chambers's Journal*; Anne Brontë's 'The Three Guides' appeared in *Fraser's Magazine*, Aug. 1848.

*March 3rd, 1846*: 'Mr C.' (below) is Carr; 'Mrs E.' is Elam; CB had sought information about operations for cataracts. It was Emily who gave the account of Branwell's behaviour.

234 *March 31st, 1846*: 'to ——' (below) is Brookroyd.

the *"Record"*: The Record, 1828–1948; incorporated with the *Church of England Newspaper* in 1949. Jean Henri Merle D'Aubigné (1794–1872) was a Swiss preacher and author of a *History of the Reformation*; his letter was in the issue for 12 Mar. 1846.

236 *led public opinion*: 7 May 1846; CB's next reply (below) is 11 May; and the quotation ('Should the poems be . . .') from a letter of 25 May.

237 *end of May, 1846*: the volume of 165 pages was priced 4s. Aylott's advice about additional copies and advertisements made good sense, since the *Athenaeum*, *Literary Gazette*, and *Critic* were the chief reviewing journals, and despite CB's demur, seems to have been taken, since as well as the *Athenaeum* (below), the *Critic* reviewed *Poems* (4 July 1846); the only other review was in the *Dublin University Magazine* (Oct. 1846): see Allott, nos. 1–3.

*July 10th, 1846*: with financial pressure on the family, including the expenses of George Nussey's medical care, EN was considering whether to go out as a governess; 'at ——' (below) is Brookroyd.

238 *her father's curate*: Arthur Bell Nicholls (1817–1906) was born in Co. Antrim and graduated from Trinity College, Dublin in 1844, when he took deacon's orders; he became a curate at Haworth in 1845 (CB noted him as 'a respectable young man, reads well, and I hope he will give satisfaction'; 26 May 1845) and was ordained priest 20 Sept. 1846. With an interval in 1853–4, because of Patrick Brontë's opposition to his marrying CB, he continued as curate until Patrick's death in 1861. Nicholls then returned to Ireland, took up farming, and married a cousin as his second wife. For Jacob and Rachel, below, see Genesis 28.

239 *yet been sold*: the last words of vol. I of MS as bound up; vol. II of MS begins with the last two paragraphs of Ch. XIV ('Once more in . . . not withstanding').

*admired their poems*: the autograph, for Frederick Enoch of Warwick, is in BPM; reproduced WS, ii. 104.

*September, she writes*: the letter is untraced.

*notice of her sisters*: 'Biographical Notice of Ellis and Acton Bell', 1850 (*Wuthering Heights*, p. 360).

242 *an operator . . . Mr Wilson*: William James Wilson (d. 1855), surgeon; helped found the Manchester Institute for Curing Diseases of the Eye.

   *August 21st, 1846*: from 83 Mount Pleasant, Boundary Street, Oxford Road, Manchester. The lodgings (later Boundary Street West) were kept by Mr and Mrs Ball; demolished in 1945 and the area redeveloped: plaque on Briarfields, Boundary Lane. Photograph in Brian Kay and James Knowles, 'Where "Jane Eyre" and "Mary Barton" Were Born', *BST*, 15 (1967), facing p. 146.

   *August 26th, 1846*: 'Mr C.' (below) is Carr; '——', who flirted, is Joseph Taylor, brother of Mary; the 'virgin population of ——' were in Birstall and Gomersal.

243 *the cataract . . . of couching*: couching, the most popular method, involved depressing the cataract (the opaque horny growth) below the pupil. Patrick Brontë's sensation, conscious through an operation of 15 minutes, was 'of a burning nature—but not intolerable' (Lock and Dixon, *A Man of Sorrow*, p. 389).

   *she writes thus*: 31 Aug. 1846.

244 *of this memoir*: *The Professor* was published by Smith, Elder in June 1857 (*The Life* appeared in March); see the World's Classics 'Note on the Text'. EG's fears that it related especially to Heger were allayed, once she read it; she then favoured publication, not because of its excellence, but as 'a very curious link in her literary history' (*Letters*, p. 403). The portraits (below) would probably include the pensionnat girls (ch. XII); the unsurpassed female character is Frances Henri.

   *'wrote them down an ass'*: echoing *Much Ado about Nothing*, IV. ii. 73–4.

245 *heart of Robert Bruce*: Robert de Bruce (1274–1329), King of Scotland; despite defeats he never lost heart, in legend being inspired by the spider which persisted until it successfully secured its web.

   *begin 'Jane Eyre'*: CB's account that follows, including the quotation about the 'one-volume tale', is from the 'Biographical Notice of Ellis and Acton Bell', 1850 (*Wuthering Heights*, p. 361).

   *story of 'Jane Eyre'*: the paragraph begins in Ed. 1: 'I believe I have already mentioned, that *some*', referring to the deleted anecdote, p. 110 note, the supposed 'germ'. For discussion of CB's use of her own earlier writings and other literary works, see Margaret Smith's Introduction (*Jane Eyre*, pp. vii–xviii). CB drew upon and transformed her feelings for Heger in the Jane–Rochester relationship.

246 *North call the 'eyes'*: 'eyes' is not a dialect word, though 'in the North' was added in MS by William Gaskell.

*Trench has enforced*: Richard Chenevix Trench (1807–86), churchman and philologist; author of *On the Study of Words* (1851) and *English Past and Present* (1855): EG may particularly have in mind the concluding paragraphs of Lecture V in the former.

247 *to read as print*: CB's fair copies of *Jane Eyre*, *Shirley*, and *Villette* are in the British Library; that of *The Professor* in the Pierpont Morgan Library, New York: see their descriptions in the World's Classics' respective 'Note on the Text'. For pencil-written notes towards stories, see Alexander, *Bibliography*, items 487–90.

*writer . . . 'the death of Currer Bell'*: Harriet Martineau (see p. 327 note), in the *Daily News*, 6 Apr. 1855; reprinted *Biographical Sketches*, 1869, and Allott, no. 88. For CB's meetings with Martineau, see later.

248 *opening a school*: EN had proposed to start a school in her own home and asked CB to take joint share. EG discreetly omits EN's part in the venture, to which the rest of the letter refers.

*a characteristic reply*: 14 Oct. 1846. 'Bring ——' (below) is Richard Nussey.

249 *December 15th*: misdated by EG; correct date, 13 Dec. 1846; EN was in Northamptonshire.

*visit to B . . . to York*: Branwell's mounting debts threatened imprisonment in York: see Gérin, *Branwell Brontë*, pp. 269–72.

*December 28th*: the extract below ('I don't, after all . . .') is from the same letter. 'Mrs ——' (below) is Mrs Joshua Nussey.

250 *sumphishness*: 'stupidity' (Northern and Scottish dialect).

251 *'grey, old, worn and sunk'*: 14 Feb. 1847. The following extract ('for after all . . .') is from CB to EN, 1 Mar. 1847, at the end of the letter (below) of that date.

*from her letters*: in the first extract, 'B——' is Brookroyd.

252 *by another publisher*: Thomas Cautley Newby of 72 Mortimer Street, Cavendish Square; his name, though written here and elsewhere in MS, was omitted from *The Life*, as George Smith feared EG's remarks were actionable. Newby's bad practices made EG wish to name and to gibbet him (*Letters*, p. 418; see also pp. 428, 432). The terms (EG quotes from CB's 'Biographical Notice of Ellis and Acton Bell', 1850 (*Wuthering Heights*, p. 361 )) were that Emily and Anne (Newby had rejected *The Professor*) should advance £50 against production costs. Newby delayed production and took advantage of *Jane Eyre*'s success to imply that *Wuthering Heights* and *Agnes Grey* were by the same author (see Gérin, *Emily Brontë*, pp. 209–10, 232).

253 *in the spring*: apparently transmitted through Dr John Crosby, the Robinson family's physician (see Gérin, *Branwell Brontë*, p. 272).

*while you stay*: 12 May 1847. The following letter ('Friday will suit us very well') is of 17 May.

*May 20th*: '———' (below, twice) is Ann, EN's sister, whose acceptance of an invitation from the Swaines of Brier Hall meant EN had to stay and look after their mother; 'B———' is Brookroyd.

254 *written about this time*: 29 June 1847. The subject was Amelia Ringrose, engaged to George Nussey before his illness and later the wife of Mary Taylor's brother, Joseph.

*'Currer Bell' gives*: from the 'Biographical Notice of Ellis and Acton Bell', 1850 (*Wuthering Heights*, p. 361).

255 *Mr Smith*: George Smith (1824–1901) joined Smith, Elder at 65 Cornhill, London, in 1838. The firm, founded by Smith's father in 1816 with Alexander Elder, were publishers and East India agents, dealing in books and magazines, in commercial services, and in banking. In 1846, on his father's death, Smith became head of the firm and despite financial difficulties in 1848, from 1851 there was rapid growth. In 1859 Smith founded the *Cornhill Magazine*, with Thackeray as editor; in 1865, the *Pall Mall Gazette*; and in 1882, the *Dictionary of National Biography*. EG naturally published *The Life* with him, as CB's publisher, and all her subsequent volume publication. He provided material for *The Life* and shaped it significantly. He married Elizabeth, née Blakeway, in 1853; before that his mother, Mrs Alexander Smith (née Elizabeth Murray), kept house for him and acted as hostess at 4 Westbourne Place and then at 76 Gloucester Terrace, Hyde Park Terrace. See further *DNB* and Glynn, *Prince of Publishers*; photograph in Fraser, *CB*, plate 11c; self-caricature on a Valentine to EG in J. G. Sharps, *EG's Observation and Invention* (1970), opposite p. 544. EG recognized in Smith and his mother the prototypes of the Brettons in *Villette*. Part of the account that follows ('had been sent . . . the prolonged silence') in a hand other than EG's in MS.

256 *of 'Wuthering Heights'*: 'Biographical Notice of Ellis and Acton Bell', 1850 (*Wuthering Heights*, p. 361).

*not without grounds*: to Smith and Elder, 6 Aug. 1847.

*in all the churches*: 29 Aug. 1847.

257 *'murmur of innumerable bees'*: Tennyson, 'Come down, O maid, from yonder mountain height', from *The Princess*.

258 *September*: 25 Sept. 1847. 'B———' (below) is Birstall.

*The screen*: a protection for the face when sitting by the fire; though possibly also as a shield for Patrick Brontë's eyes. Emily's apples (below) are a reminder of winter storage of fruit and its need to be regularly checked.

*When the manuscript*: this account of *Jane Eyre* (pp. 258–65: 'When the manuscript . . . hid in its womb') was written separately; it consists of 13 pages, so numbered (pp. 1–13), inserted between pp. 347 and 348 of MS; EG noted (now deleted) on MS p. 347 that material was 'to come in here about Jane Eyre as soon as I have heard from Mr Smith'. See *Letters*, pp. 424, 426. For George Smith's own later account of his reading *Jane Eyre*, see Glynn, *Prince of Publishers*, pp. 50–1.

*connected with the firm*: William Smith Williams (1800–75) was George Smith's literary assistant and general manager of the publishing department. CB found him a congenial correspondent, though she sometimes needed to console him or cheer him up; photograph in Fraser, *CB*, plate 11b. The second reader (below) was James Taylor (d. 1874, aged 57), who went to India in 1851 to take charge of the firm's interests. He was attracted to CB and twice visited Haworth, but CB did not reciprocate his feelings.

259 *On its publication*: this paragraph introduces Thackeray ('the great writer of fiction'), highlighting his generous response, though EG had to omit the details of Thackeray's account (see below and *Letters*, p. 419). William Makepeace Thackeray (1811–63) was making a hit with the serialization of *Vanity Fair* (1847–8), after many years of journalistic drudgery. It was only in 1850 that George Smith became Thackeray's publisher. The paragraph was considerably reworked between MS and printed version: apart from other changes, the sentence 'They were of considerable . . . thanks for the book' occupied a later point in the paragraph. After 'rightly reckoned upon', MS has 'Among the first named [the private literary friends] was the great writer of fiction for whom Miss Brontë felt so strong an admiration. He immediately appreciated its extraordinary merits, and expressed his sense of them in a characteristic note, ending with the words / "It made me cry—to the astonishment of John, who came in with the coals." / The publishers of "Jane Eyre" had reckoned correctly on the discernment of those few private friends to whom they sent copies. They were of considerable literary standing . . . thanks for the book. / But the *Reviews were more tardy*'.

*Reviews were more tardy*: for reviews in weekly papers and journals, see Tom Winnifrith, *The Brontës and Their Background* (1973), appendix C, and Anne Passel, *Charlotte and Emily Brontë: An Annotated Biblio-graphy* (1979): neither is complete. Allott (nos. 7, 9, 10, 12) gives extracts from the *Athenaeum*, the *Examiner*, the *People's Journal*, and the *Spectator*. 'Opinions of the Press', appended to the 3rd edition of *Jane Eyre* (Clarendon, appendix V), includes some of the 'seven provincial newspapers' mentioned in CB to Smith, Elder, 1 Dec. 1847. W. S. Williams helped EG find the reviews (*Letters*, pp. 418–19). *The Bachelor of the Albany* was a comic novel by Marmion Savage (1803–72).

259 *The 'Examiner'*: the *Examiner*, an influential weekly newspaper, pub-lished its review, possibly by Albany Fonblanque, 27 Nov. 1847.

261 *respecting "Wuthering Heights"*: the 'information' not identified. CB had asked W. S. Williams about Newby's business practices.

262 *bank post bill*: bank post bills, issued by the Bank of England, were post-dated, so they could be stopped if stolen in the post. MS has '*bill* for £100'. CB received £500 in all for *Jane Eyre*; she also accepted £500 each for the English copyrights of *Shirley* and *Villette*.

264 *better than likely*: EG's earliest surviving version of this anecdote is in a letter of 25 Aug. 1850, the week in which EG and CB first met. The two versions agree, though the wording of Patrick's judgement shows EG heightening the dialogue; the letter has: 'Children, Charlotte has been writing a book—and I think it is a better one than I expected' (*Letters*, p. 126). Cf. a similar change between the two versions of Tabby on the fairies (p. 99 note; p. 63).

*the Athenians of old*: Acts 17: 21.

265 *'dark . . . rugged is the North'*: a version of Tennyson's 'And dark and true and tender is the North' in 'O swallow, swallow' from *The Princess*. The term 'at fault' below is from hunting, when the hounds lose the scent.

*dedication to Mr Thackeray*: the 2nd edition (22 Jan. 1848) carried the dedication and a Preface (pp. 3–5), from which EG quotes below. Thackeray had married Isabella Shaw in 1836; she became insane and was permanently confined. CB knew nothing about Thackeray's personal circumstances, any more than about Michael Angelo Tit-marsh's (one of Thackeray's pseudonyms). CB's admiration was for *Vanity Fair*, published by Thackeray under his own name. Unfortu-nately, as EG allusively suggests, some people who knew of Thacker-ay's circumstances had supposed *Jane Eyre* to be written by a Thackeray family governess: Thackeray told CB this when thanking her for the dedication and the gossip was repeated in the *Quarterly*

*Review*'s attack (see p. 295 and note). Despite this, the dedication stood in the 3rd and 4th editions.

*writes her sister*: 7 Oct. 1847.

266 *and injudicious praise*: 'I know nobody who blasts by praise as you do' (James Boswell, *Life of Samuel Johnson*, 1 Apr. 1781).

'*as with ... trumpet*': apparently an echo of Sir Philip Sidney, *An Apologie for Poetrie* (1595), whose heart was 'moved more than with a trumpet' at the ballad of Percy and Douglas.

*Mr G. H. Lewes*: George Henry Lewes (1817–78), editor and critic, and scientific popularizer. After the breakdown of his marriage, he and Marian Evans (George Eliot) formed a relationship that lasted from 1854 until his death: through his encouragement, George Eliot began to write fiction. EG knew him slightly, but not liking 'a certain familiarity' in his manner, used George Smith to contact him (*Letters*, pp. 414, 418). See further Rosemary Ashton, *G. H. Lewes: A Life* (1991).

*Mr Parker ... "Frazer's Magazine"*: John William Parker (1792–1870), publisher and printer; for the *Fraser's* review, see Allott, no. 14. Lewes also gave the 2nd edition a favourable notice in the *Westminster Review* (Jan. 1848; Allot, no. 15)

268 *of another publisher*: MS has: 'of Mr Newby's conduct' for 'the conduct of another publisher'.

*"Britannia" ... "Sun" ... "Spectator"*: the reviews were in the issues for 6 Nov. 1847.

269 *in the "Dublin Magazine"*: William Arthur Butler, in his anonymous review (Oct. 1846), was undecided whether the Bells were three or 'but one master spirit' (Allott, p. 63).

*will soon appear*: i.e. the publication of *Wuthering Heights* and *Agnes Grey* as a set of three volumes, *Wuthering Heights* occupying the first two. For the printed letter's 'Mr ——', in this paragraph and the next, MS has 'Newby' deleted, leaving 'N'; MS gave Newby's full address and has, in the gap indicated by dots: 'Mr N[ewby] shuffles, gives his word and breaks it; Messrs Smith and Elder's performance is always better than their promise'.

*now read "Ranthorpe"*: Ranthorpe (1847) draws on Lewes's experience of theatrical and literary life; he later disowned it.

270 '*Agnes Grey' appeared*: EG's account, to p. 271 ('In December ... deeply lament it now'), is on three separate pages in MS, marked to the printer for insertion. CB's account of *Wuthering Heights* (below)

is from the 'Editor's Preface to the New Edition of Wuthering Heights', 1850 (pp. 366–7). CB's following comment ('Critics failed . . . lament it now') is from the 'Biographical Notice of Ellis and Acton Bell', 1850 (*Wuthering Heights*, pp. 361–2).

272 *in a napkin*: from the parable of the talents in Luke (19: 12–27 and in particular 20).

273 *the old quarter*: presumably from Dr Crosby (p. 253 note), with or without the knowledge of Mrs Robinson.

*individual deserved*: in 'Recent Novels: French and English', *Fraser's Magazine*, 36 (Dec. 1847), 686–95, Lewes was enthusiastic, though with reservations about 'melodrama'. The references below to Jane Austen and 'to finish more', not in the review, presumably are picked up from Lewes's letter.

274 *yours will soon appear*: Lewes's novel, *Rose, Blanche, and Violet*, published by Smith, Elder in Apr. 1848.

*George Sand*: pseudonym of Amandine-Aurore-Lucie Dupin (1804–76), prolific novelist. Though often regarded with suspicion for her ideas (particularly on marriage and on love), she was hugely popular in England as well as France (see Patricia Thomson, *George Sand and the Victorians*, 1977). In *Consuelo* (1842–3) the spirit summons of Consuelo by Count Albert (ch. 97) may have influenced Rochester's summoning cry.

277 *pen into his hand*: an English view of French literary characteristics would include amorality, the unrestrainedly emotional, the sexual, and the scientifically analytical. *Rose, Blanche, and Violet* included adultery, prostitution, and suicide (see Ashton, *G. H. Lewes*, pp. 73–5).

*Bulwer or D'Israeli production*: Edward Lytton Bulwer (later Bulwer Lytton) (1803–73) and Benjamin Disraeli (1804–81), both successful as novelists of fashionable society. The form 'D'Israeli', though abandoned by Benjamin, was still commonly used.

*the Board of Health*: for the petitions and Patrick Brontë's letters to the Board of Health in London (1849–51), see Lock and Dixon, *A Man of Sorrow*, pp. 432–8; a proper water supply was only obtained in 1856.

278 *dated March 31st*: to Miss Wooler.

*addition to Paradise*: alluding to the sword set about the garden of Eden to prevent the return of Adam and Eve (Genesis 3: 24).

*"the pomp and circumstance of war"*: *Othello*, III. iii. 359.

*I earnestly pray*: in 1848, the 'Year of Revolutions', the political order established after the defeat of Napoleon began violently to break up. France became a republic and there were widespread demands in Germany, the Austro-Hungarian Empire, and Italy for liberal constitutions or national self-determination. In England, the Chartists, seeking working-class participation in political power, organized a demonstration in May 1848, though the revolution some feared did not come. In Ireland, which was shaken by the Great Famine and the Great Emigration of the 1840s, the 'Young Ireland' movement seemed to threaten armed uprising.

279 *the accustomed letter*: 22 Apr. 1848. EN was born 20 Apr. 1817; CB 21 Apr. 1816.

*corrected at B——*: Brookroyd (EN's house) or Birstall (where the house was).

*May 3rd, 1848*: 'B—an' and 'G—an' (below) are Birstallian and Gomersallian; 'A——' is Ann Nussey.

280 *"Simeon's Life"*: *Memoirs of the Life of Charles Simeon*, ed. William Carus (1847). Simeon had been an important evangelical influence on Patrick Brontë at Cambridge (see p. 34 note).

*works of one author*: the idea was actively promoted by Newby in advertising *Wuthering Heights* and, later in 1848, Anne's *The Tenant of Wildfell Hall* (Allott, p. 11). The success of *Jane Eyre* and the oddity of the Bells' names naturally led reviewers of Emily and Anne's volumes to speculate on identity (see e.g. Allott, pp. 217–18, 227, 230).

*'The Tenant of Wildfell Hall'*: the novel was published at the end of June 1848 and a 2nd printing issued in early Aug. 1848; it was republished in 1854. The central character, Arthur Huntingdon, is based on Branwell Brontë, whose degradation had also been alluded to by CB (*The Professor*, p. 174). Anne Brontë insisted on her desire to tell the truth, however unpalatable (*Tenant*, pp. 3–5), quoting in the 2nd edition's Preface the *Spectator*'s condemnation of 'a marked love of the coarse, if not of the brutal' (8 July 1848; Allott, no. 70). CB's account of Anne's determination is from the 'Biographical Notice of Ellis and Acton Bell', 1850 (*Wuthering Heights*, p. 363).

281 *the person*: MS has 'Mr Newby'. The account of the London visit was significantly reorganized and rewritten between MS and Ed. 1. EG first had one of her daughters copy out in the manuscript CB's letter of 4 Sept. 1848 to Mary Taylor, which describes the visit (John Rylands MS; Stevens, *Mary Taylor*, pp. 176–81); this she meant to

revise before George Smith saw it, taking out what 'was undesirable to have published when I read it over with Mr Gaskell'
(*Letters*, p. 429). She then paraphrased the letter, fully and accurately
(as now in MS), but Smith clearly intervened as elsewhere to reduce
his own role, with respect at least to personal details; EG took the
opportunity, as this only extensive example of rewriting shows, to
make the account more shapely and punchy. No manuscript of the
revised version as printed is known. For the account that begins in
the next paragraph, MS has: 'One Friday morning, in the beginning
of July, a letter from Messrs Smith & Elder was received at Haworth
Parsonage, which disturbed the quiet little inhabitants extremely, as
it implied a suspicion of unfair dealing on the part of Currer and
Acton Bell. The facts of the case were these (according to a letter of
Miss Brontë's, written to her friend in New Zealand.) "Acton Bell"
was on the point of publishing another work "The Tenant of Wildfell
Hall." Now a short time before this Charlotte Brontë had received a
letter from Messrs Smith & Elder, saying that "Jane Eyre" had had a
great run in America, and that a publisher there had consequently bid
high for the next book by "Currer Bell," which they had promised to
let him have. / The letter which arrived this morning at Haworth,
was also from Messrs Smith & Elder to "Currer Bell," but this time
they wrote in suspicion and alarm to their unknown correspondent.
They had heard again from the house in America with whom they
had so lately concluded an agreement, complaining that the first
sheets of a new work by "Currer Bell" had been already received, and
not by their house, but by a rival publisher, and asking the meaning
of such false play. They enclosed an extract from a letter from Mr
Newby, (Acton and Ellis Bell's publisher,) affirming that to the "best
of his knowledge" "Jane Eyre," "Wuthering Heights" and the "Tenant of Wildfell Hall" (the new book) were all the production of one
writer. Mr Newby had been told repeatedly by "Acton & Ellis Bell"
that the works named above were the productions of three different
writers; but I suppose he chose not to believe assertions which would
have deprived him of the power of saying that he had got hold of
"Currer Bell", and thus to obtain the large sum which the American
publishers were ready to offer for the future works of the Author of
"Jane Eyre." / The sisters were annoyed and impatient under the
suspicion of their integrity which Messrs Smith & Elder very
naturally conceived from the circumstances above stated; and with
rapid decision they resolved that Charlotte and Anne should set off
for London *that very day . . . and demand* a reason from Mr Newby
for his statement to the American publisher, which was in such direct

contradiction to what he had been repeatedly told. *Having arrived at this'*. MS then proceeds as in the printed text (with a few minor verbal changes) until the sisters' arrival at Smith, Elder's office: '*written to them as men.* / They found "65 Corn Hill" to be a large booksellers shop in a bustling and noisy street. They went in and walked up to the counter; there were a great many young men and lads here and there. Charlotte said to the first she could accost "May I see Mr Smith?" he hesitated, and enquired if an interview with a subordinate would not answer her purpose; but when she persisted in her request he went to fetch Mr Smith. The two sisters sate down, and waited awhile; beguiling the time by looking at some books on the counter; publications well known to them, as they had received copies of many of them as presents. At last Mr Smith came up, and said dubiously "Did you want to see me, Ma'am?" / "Are you Mr Smith?" replied Miss Brontë looking up at him with her spectacled eyes; a little creature by a tall man. / As soon as she was assured of his identity she put his own letter into his hands: that very letter to "Currer Bell," *which had excited . . . only twenty-four hours before*. Mr Smith's first exclamation, on receiving this letter from her hands, was "Where did you get this?" *as if he could not . . . so eagerly in vain*. Miss Brontë could not help smiling at his queer perplexity; a recognition took place and she gave him her real name, Miss Brontë. Then they were both hurried from the shop into a little bare room ceiled with a great sky-light, and only large enough to hold three chairs and a desk, and explanations were rapidly gone into, and Miss Brontë was introduced to Mr Williams, with whom she had previously corresponded. Mr Smith was full of plans for their amusement and gratification during their stay in London. That very night he said they must go to the Italian Opera; Jenny Lind was to sing. The Academy Exhibition was open, that was well worth seeing. He began to form plans for a meeting between Miss Brontë and Mr Thackeray and Mr Lewes. But she put a stop to this last project (the most tempting of all that were submitted to her,) by a grave explanation that although she should very much like to see Mr Lewes, and still more Mr Thackeray, yet that she and her sisters were as resolved as ever to maintain their incognito; that they had only acknowledged themselves to their publishers, in order to do away with the inconveniences which had arisen from the mystery in which they had shrouded themselves; but that to all the rest of the world they must be "gentlemen" as heretofore. / They were then urged to meet a literary party incognito; they might be introduced as country cousins. The desire to see some of the personages whose names were mentioned was strongly excited;

but as Charlotte found on further examination that such men as Thackeray could hardly be asked on so short a notice, without receiving a hint as to whom they were to meet, she declined even this, as she feared it would end in their being made a show of, "a thing I have ever resolved to avoid. / *The sisters were equally persevering*'.

282 *night train to London*: the 12.20 a.m., by Derby and Rugby. The sisters' expenses are preserved in a notebook (BPM); the cost, including fares, three nights in London and one in Leeds, was £14, when a governess's salary might be £20 (Barker, *The Brontës*, p. 562).

*'queer state of inward excitement'*: this and the quotation below, 'in grievous bodily case', are from CB's letter to Mary Taylor.

*the Saturday morning*: an ordinary business day, in the nineteenth century.

284 *"Barber of Seville"*: at the Royal Italian Opera, Covent Garden, with the soprano Fanny Persiani as Rosina and Antonio Tamburini as Figaro; the programme, which began at 8 p.m., also included an operatic excerpt and a ballet.

*his mother*: throughout the visit, George Smith maintained the sisters' incognito: neither his mother nor other members of his family knew why Smith was entertaining them: yet their politeness and good temper never failed.

*my normal condition*: MS adds: '*condition*. We saw Newby, but of him more another time.' No full account exists of the interview, though later Anne Brontë stressed in the Preface to the 2nd edition of *The Tenant of Wildfell Hall* (dated 22 July) that Acton was not Ellis or Currer, while CB told W. S. Williams (14 Aug. 1848) that Anne intended to offer any future novel to George Smith.

285 *Coffee-house . . . last June*: EG visited the Coffee House on 17 June 1856 with George Smith; later, Smith found a waiter who remembered the Brontës and while eating an 'indifferent dinner', obtained his account of them (*Letters*, pp. 390, 401, 416): see below, where EG presumably quotes Smith's description of the man. The Coffee House was demolished in 1858. Ed. 3 omits: '*Paul's*; at each end there are posts placed, so as to prevent the passage of carriages, and thus preserve a solemn silence for the deliberations of the "Fathers of the Row." '

*which Chatterton wrote*: Thomas Chatterton (1752–70), poet. EG quotes from his letter of 6 May 1770, from which she takes the other details.

286 *Villette, vol. i. p. 89*: ch. VI (pp. 59–60). MS, in the sentence preceding the invitation, describes the invitation as 'kind'; the omission may be

another response to George Smith's susceptibilities or simply a printing error.

*Dr Croly*: George Croly (1780–1860), Irish clergyman and journalist; Rector of St Stephen's, Walbrook.

287 *August 28th, 1848*: to Miss Wooler. 'Mrs ——' (below, twice) is Mrs Susan Carter, sister of Miss Wooler; '——' is Ellen Carter.

288 *its institution in 1823*: in 1838, when two pupils died, and presumably in 1825, when the Brontës were there. The footnote added in Ed. 3; in MS additions.

*Haworth failed lately*: the Greenwoods (see p. 46 note).

289 *rests well . . . feverish life*: echoes *Macbeth*, III. ii. 24–5.

*in his last illness*: EG's informant unidentified. Possibly Martha Brown (who showed EG the graves in the church on her 1853 visit to Haworth: *Letters*, p. 246); her father John Brown, the sexton, who apparently attended Branwell on the Sunday morning, called the family when he realized the end was near. Branwell certainly did not die standing up, though he might earlier have declared some such intention.

*position just mentioned*: Ed. 3 omits: '*mentioned*. I have previously stated, that when his fatal attack came on, his pockets were found filled with old letters from the woman to whom he was attached. He died! she lives still,—in May Fair. The Eumenides, I suppose, went out of existence at the time when the wail was heard, "Great Pan is dead." I think we could better have spared him than those awful Sisters who sting dead conscience into life. / I turn from her for ever. Let us look once more into the Parsonage at Haworth. / "*Oct*'. A direction is given in MS additions to omit from 'I have previously stated' to bottom of the page. The letters in Branwell's pockets (see also p. 226 note) are not mentioned by CB and are unlikely anyway to have been Mrs Robinson's. The Eumenides or Furies in Greek mythology pursued criminals; for the death of the god Pan, see Plutarch, 'The Decline of the Oracles', §17 (*Moral Essays*).

*Oct. 29th, 1848*: 'to ——' (below) is Brookroyd; 'Miss ——' is Heald.

290 *not our abiding-place*: biblical in tone, though not a direct quotation: cf. 1 Chronicles 29: 15 and Hebrews 13: 14.

*notice of her sisters*: 'Biographical Notice of Ellis and Acton Bell', 1850 (*Wuthering Heights*, p. 363).

*heat and burden . . . their work*: echoes Matthew 20: 12, in the parable of the labourers in the vineyard.

290 *sympathy and help*: MS has, deleted: '*and help*. Her conduct was the very essence of stern selfishness. *Many a time*'.

291 *refused to see him*: Dr John Wheelhouse; he had certified Branwell's death (as 'chronic bronchitis' and 'marasmus' i.e. wasting or consumption) and was to do so for Emily.

*Dec. 10th. 1848*: 'The ——' (below) are Robinsons; 'I. and H.' are Joseph and Henry Taylor.

292 *physician in London*: John Epps (1805–69), homoeopathic physician. W. S. Williams had urged the merits of homoeopathy and CB sent Epps an account of Emily's symptoms through Williams (WS, ii. 286, 291–2 and note).

*former pupils*: Elizabeth and Mary Robinson, who had been corresponding with Anne since early 1847.

*crab-cheese*: a thick jam or jelly made from crab-apples.

293 *Tuesday*: 19 Dec. 1848, by reference to Emily's death.

*Dec. 21st, 1848*: properly, 23 Dec. 1848, since Emily's funeral was on 22 Dec.

294 *faithful bull-dog*: EG first had this detail from Martha Brown, in 1853 (*Letters*, p. 246).

295 *December, 1848*: a review primarily of *Vanity Fair* and *Jane Eyre* (84 (Dec. 1848), 153–85), by Elizabeth Rigby (1809–93); she married Sir Charles Eastlake in 1849. W. S. Williams identified the author for CB; EG writes as though author and hence her sex were unknown to her: this may be disingenuous or a strategy to enforce her distinction between critical opinion and biographical speculation: Lady Eastlake was one of those EG intended to 'libel' (*Letters*, p. 418). Rigby, characterizing *Jane Eyre* as 'pre-eminently an anti-Christian composition', touched on the author possibly having been the Thackeray governess, on being a man, or if a woman then one who had 'long forfeited the society of her own sex' (Allott, no. 22). EG's point about the failure of logic through misuse of prepositions is not obvious. The passage below from Southey on anonymous works is from the *Quarterly Review* (98 (Mar. 1856), 486), noted by EG on a sheet now with MS.

*woman in 'Shirley'*: of both Mrs Hardman and her daughter, to Mrs Pryor: vol. II, ch. x (ch. 21; pp. 375–7); the relevant passages are in appendix B of the Clarendon edition, which has as appendix C, CB's 'A Word to the Quarterly' (BPM), originally intended as a preface to *Shirley*.

*a clergyman in America*: not otherwise identified.

296 *euphuisms*: properly, an ornate elaborated style of writing, but EG's habitual form of 'euphemism'.

*judge with the Pharisee*: in MS this sentence has 'a soul' written in by William Gaskell above 'faith', deleted; he also wrote 'in all its agonies, cried "lama sabachthani" ', above something heavily scored through. 'It is the Lord!' is I Samuel 3: 18; 'lama sabachthani' is Christ's cry on the cross ('Why hast thou forsaken me'), Mark 15: 34—EG seems undisturbed by the hyperbole of comparison; see Luke 18: 10–14 for the Publican and the Pharisee.

*Jan. 10th, 1849*: this series of letters, to the end of 16 Mar. 1849, copied out by a hand clearly other than EG's.

*train oil*: i.e. it tasted like whale-oil (used for lamps); the medicines mentioned below include precipitate of iron dissolved in carbonic acid (carbonate of iron) and pitch combined with lard or wax as plasters.

297 *Jan. 22nd, 1849*: 'Mrs ——' (below) is Heald; the two following blanks are respectively Mary Taylor and Ellen Taylor.

298 *Feb. 11th, 1849*: correct date, 16 Feb. 1849.

299 *that could be procured*: Thomas Teale of the Leeds General Infirmary, in Jan. 1849 ('first' = 'best').

*Dr Forbes*: John Forbes (1787–1861), physician, established in London; George Smith had at first proposed Forbes might visit Anne. EG took this whole paragraph with only minor changes from CB to Laetitia Wheelwright, 15 Mar. 1849.

*on March 24th*: to Miss Wooler.

300 *March 24th*: misdated by EG; correct date, 29 Mar. 1849. '——' (below) is Brookroyd.

301 *ANNE BRONTË:* '——' (below) is Brookroyd.

302 *her last verses*: dated 7 and 28 Jan. 1849; the quotation below ('the desk was closed . . .') is CB's note to the verses, amongst the poems appended to the 2nd edition of *Wuthering Heights* (1850).

304 *April 12th*: 'Mr T——' (below) is Teale (see p. 299 note).

*was getting strength*: date uncertain, but late Jan. or more probably early Feb. 1849 (by 1 Feb. CB had heard from Forbes but was still hopeful Anne was benefiting from Dr Teale's regimen).

306 *the lodgings at Scarborough*: 2 The Cliff (Wood's Lodgings on St Nicholas Cliff): see Gérin, *Anne Brontë*, plates 8 and 9; now covered by the Grand Hotel. Anne used the town in *Agnes Grey* under the

disguise of 'A——'; see particularly ch. 24. Anne's godmother (below), Fanny Outhwaite, who died in Feb. 1849, had left her £200.

306  *Charlotte writes*: 'Mr N——' (below) is Arthur Bell Nicholls.

307  *and of the end*: MS has heading, deleted: 'A short account of the last days of dear Anne Brontë'. EG deleted or altered in proof EN's three uses of the 'dear invalid' (to 'her' or 'she'); while near the end 'The dear departed one' was deleted and 'she' substituted in the sentence now beginning: 'She thought not of the grave . . .' EN based the account on her notes (MS Walpole Collection, The King's School, Canterbury).

309  *merits of our Redeemer*: it strikes as slightly odd that while the doctor (not otherwise identified: he did not certify or register the death) came several times, no clergyman was sent for.

310  *"Where the south sun . . . turf-covered rock"*: verses unidentified. The funeral was on 30 May at Christ Church, Vernon Road, and Anne was buried in St Mary's churchyard: the stone (photograph in Flintoff, *In the Steps of the Brontës*, p. 149) still gives her age incorrectly as 28 (for 29).

*A lady*: this paragraph ('A lady . . . because unobtrusive') inserted in Ed. 3; in MS additions.

311  *more weeks' change of scene*: CB and EN stayed in Scarborough until 7 June; they then went to Filey and Bridlington for a week at each.

*The younger servant*: this paragraph and the following letter (in MS additions) inserted in Ed. 3, which omits from end of previous paragraph the introduction to the letter of July 1849: 'Late in June the friends returned homewards,—parting rather suddenly (it would seem) from each other, when their paths diverged.'

*July, 1849*: correct date, 23 June 1849; CB is writing two days after she reached home on 21 June.

312  *glad before—except once*: presumably on her return to find Branwell had been dismissed: p. 225.

314  *of those eventful times*: while it is surprising that CB was allowed to borrow the files, that she did see them is clear from her use of their reports: see the Clarendon *Shirley*, appendix A, and Herbert Rosengarten, 'CB's *Shirley* and the *Leeds Mercury*', *Studies in English Literature*, 16 (1976), 591–600. W. S. Williams had suggested in Dec. 1847 that CB write a novel for serial publication: while refusing, she indicated that she was trying to recast *The Professor* as a three-volume novel: *Shirley* seems to have come out of that attempt (see Clarendon, pp.xiii–xv). The first volume was sent to W. S. Williams on 4 Feb.

1849; the other two were completed before the end of May and by 29 Aug.

*figured away*: 'acted out their parts' (a metaphor from moving in a dance sequence or 'figure').

*The 'three curates'*: Donne was modelled on Joseph Brett Grant; Malone on James William Smith; Sweeting on James Chesterton Bradley. Mrs Pryor has her origins in Margaret Wooler; the Yorkes are portraits of Mary Taylor and her family.

315 *daguerreotypes*: photographs by the process of Jacques Daguerre (1787–1851), first produced in 1838.

'*was . . . truly great*': from CB's 'Biographical Notice of Ellis and Acton Bell', 1850 (*Wuthering Heights*, p. 364); CB included Anne in the phrase as well as Emily.

*the succeeding chapter*: *Shirley*, vol. III, chs. i–ii (chs. 24–5; pp. 441–3).

316 '*I cannot get rid*': 23 Aug. 1849 (part of the following letter).

317 *Aug. 23rd, 1849*: 'Mr ——' (below) is Robert Clapham; '——' is Ann Nussey, who married Clapham, 26 Sept.

*Sept. 13th, 1849*: '——' (below) is Brookroyd.

318 *Mr Helstone*: Helstone is largely based on the Revd Hammond Roberson (see p. 88 and note), who died in 1841; Mr Hall (below) is based on the Revd W. M. Heald (d. 1875), Vicar of Birstall.

319 *as she says*: 24 Sept. 1849.

320 "*Nelson, Leeds*": James Nelson & Sons, stove-grate manufacturers and general ironmongers, Briggate.

*York and North-Midland Company*: incorporated 1836; the first line with which George Hudson (1800–71), the 'Railway King', was associated. Hudson's practices, including paying dividends out of capital, were coming to light in 1849; in 1854 he resigned his chairmanships and retired to the Continent. The Company survived.

322 *your Scottish expedition*: Lewes, as well as lecturing and acting in Edinburgh, was seeking subscribers there for a new periodical, the *Leader* (1850–60).

*must be a woman*: this was conjectured or taken for granted by at least seven of the earliest reviews (31 Oct. to 15 Nov.): see Allott, nos. 24–7, 29, 30, 32).

323 *her letters to Cornhill*: to James Taylor, 6 Nov. 1849. The books mentioned below are Johann Eckermann, *Conversations with Goethe*

(trans. 1849); Augustus and Julius Hare, *Guesses at Truth* (1827; rev. 1837); Arthur Helps, *Friends in Council* (4 series 1847–59); Mrs Whateley, *English Life, Social and Domestic, in the Nineteenth Century* (1847). The *Athenaeum* (1828–1921), published weekly, covered literature, the arts, and science.

323 *Moors to represent*: Robert Moore was based on William Cartwright: see pp. 86 note and 86–8; Louis Moore partly on William Crimsworth in *The Professor*, partly on M. Heger; Hortense Moore on Mlle Haussée, a teacher at the Pensionnat Heger.

*a couple of reviews*: the *Examiner*, 3 Nov. 1849; the *Standard of Freedom*, 10 Nov. 1849. Albany Fonblanque (1793–1872) had edited the *Examiner* until 1847 and still wrote for it; William Howitt (1792–1879) was an author and critic, even though as a Quaker he might be expected to reject all fictions.

324 *a few extracts*: the first is dated 22 Nov. 1849.

*"Revue des Deux Mondes"*: an influential Parisian fortnightly review, founded in 1828 (current as *Revue des Mondes*); 4 (15 Nov. 1849), 714–35 (Allott, no. 33). Eugène Forçade (1820–69), journalist and editor, joined the *Revue* in the 1840s.

325 *much to her*. EG draws in this paragraph on CB to EN, 4 Dec. 1849: the letter includes the phrase 'big Babylon' (above), one CB uses elsewhere to describe London (it was a common semi-humorous cliché); the letter is also the source of the phrase 'kindness is a potent heart-winner'. The phrases 'As was always the case with strangers' and 'of the family into which she was now received' were inserted into Ed. 1 at proof-stage; George Smith, despite EG's wish (*Letters*, pp. 429–30), clearly vetoed details of his domestic arrangements at 4 Westbourne Place, Bayswater. MS has, undeleted: '*much to her*. She was most kindly received at Mr Smith's, and names with grateful obligation, and as circumstances of comfort to which she was not accustomed, the having a fire & candles in her bedroom. *She was at first*'.

*invited to meet her*: on 3 Dec. 1849; for the later accounts by Thackeray (1860) and George Smith (1900), see *The Private Letters and Papers of W. M. Thackeray*, ed. Gordon N. Ray, ii (1945), 611 n. (see also WS, iii. 46–52). Thackeray recalled 'the trembling little frame . . . the great honest eyes'.

326 *Dec. 10th, 1849*: since the postscript is dated Sunday, it ought to be 8 Dec. 1849.

*into the drawing-room*: the custom was for the ladies to go to the drawing-room after dinner, while the men remained to smoke in the dining-room. Thackeray's reference below is to *Jane Eyre*, vol. II, ch. viii (ch. 23; p. 250).

*published in the 'Times'*: 7 Dec. 1849; Allott, no. 35. Occupying almost three columns, the review was sardonic about both plot and characters, concluding that the novel was 'at once the most high flown and the stalest of fictions'.

327 *Miss Martineau*: Harriet Martineau (1802–76) came from a Unitarian family, though herself a free-thinker, and supported herself by writing. Her early works on economics, in fictional form, were immensely successful; the novel, *Deerbrook*, was published 1839. She was severely deaf and scorned the report (below) of CB's 'intuitive recognition' of her, noting in her copy of *The Life*: 'Seeing the [speaking] trumpet'. Her *Autobiography*, published posthumously, gives CB's letter accompanying *Shirley* and an account of their meeting (see Vera Wheatley, *The Life and Work of Harriet Martineau* (1957), pp. 281–3). They met on Sunday, 9 Dec. (not 10) at Richard Martineau's house, Hyde Park Square. EG gave a detailed account shortly after the meeting (*Letters*, pp. 96–7; 20 Dec. 1849); Martineau's description of CB, quoted below, is from her *Daily News* obituary (6 Apr. 1855; Allott, p. 304). Martineau had been canvassed as an author of *Jane Eyre*; CB acknowledged the likeness of their childhood experiences after reading *Household Education* (1849) (Wheatley, *Harriet Martineau*, p. 282).

*on the subject*: MS has: '*subject*, her hosts resolved to ask some gentlemen to *dinner the evening before she left town*. She understood that these visitors were not to be informed of the name of the little country lady staying at Mr Smith's; but somehow they were all pretty well aware that out of the three ladies present one was no other than "Currer Bell." *Her natural*'.

328 *write as follows*: from the letter dated 17 Dec. below: EG changed the tenses from past to present, the letter being written after the visit. 'Mrs ——' (below) is Mrs Alexander Smith, George Smith's mother (see also *Letters*, pp. 429–30).

*schoolfellow of former days*: to Laetitia Wheelwright, 17 Dec. 1849.

*with complete resignation*: the dinner was on Thursday, 13 Dec.; George Smith kept fashionable London hours, of late dinner, whereas CB was used to the main meal about 2 p.m. MS details the newspapers the critics (below) represented: '*were critics*—a formidable band, including the literary Rhadamanthi of the "Times", the "Athenæum", the "Examiner," the "Spectator", and the "Atlas"; *men more*'. Rhadamanthus, in classical mythology, was an uncorruptible judge of the dead.

328 *Dec. 17th*: date uncertain: the postmark is 19 Dec.; the same letter, already quoted above, on Mrs Smith's surveillance.

329 *daily duties*: Ed. 3 adds the rest of the paragraph and the extract from Mary Taylor's letter; in MS additions.

*Prince Albert's armoury*: at Windsor Castle; when her father was out of spirits, CB told him 'over and over again of the different weapons' there (*Letters*, p. 246).

330 *the measure wild*: deliberately romantic in the context, but cf. Walter Scott, *The Lay of the Last Minstrel* ('Introduction', l. 87) and *Marmion* ('Introduction', canto III, l. 152).

331 *in her letters*: extracts from five follow: to James Taylor, 1 Oct. 1849; to EN, 19 Jan. 1850 ('Mr —— having finished "Jane Eyre" . . .'); to EN, 28 Jan. 1850 ('Mr —— has finished "Shirley;" he . . .'); to EN, 4 Feb. 1850 ('Martha came in yesterday . . .'); to EN, 16 Feb. 1850 ('The Haworth people have . . .'). 'Mr ——' (below, twice) is Nicholls; 'John ——' is John Brown; 'Mr G—— T——' is George Taylor; 'Mr G——' is Greenwood; 'Mr M——' is Merrall; 'J—— B——', 'Mrs T——', and 'B——' are John Brown, Mrs Taylor, and Betty.

*"Eastern Life"*: Harriet Martineau, *Eastern Life Present and Past* (3 vols., 1848); Francis William Newman (1805–97), *The Soul* (1849); James Anthony Froude (1818–94), *The Nemesis of Faith* (1849).

332 *'Airedale . . . Ribblesdale'*: i.e. the whole of the area around Haworth.

*'the concealment . . . self-delusion'*: source of reference and quotation, presumably a letter, untraced.

333 *'from beyond Burnley'*: EG possibly refers to Sir James and Lady Kay-Shuttleworth (p. 337 and note), who came from Gawthorpe, near Burnley; the quotations possibly from an untraced letter or from Martha Brown. Misprinted as 'Bromley', Eds. 1 and 2.

*article on 'Shirley'*: the *Edinburgh Review*, 91 (Jan. 1850), 153–73 (Allott, no. 39); Lewes began by considering woman's role and women as artists.

*towards women*: Ed. 3 revised from: *'Now* in this review of "Shirley," the headings'.

*the following note*: Jan. 1850: date not certain, though after the *Edinburgh Review* notice and before 19 Jan. (CB's next letter to Lewes). Anne Clifford (1590–1676), being required by Charles II's secretary to accept his nominee as candidate for Parliament, replied:

'I have been bullied by a usurper; I have been neglected by a court;
but I will not be dictated to by a subject—your man shan't stand.'

334 *she writes*: 16 Feb. 1850.

335 *had a letter*: toned down in Ed. 3 from: 'I had rather a foolish letter';
the writer was Miss Wooler, whose identity is concealed even in MS,
but she may have recognized the letter's contents.

*of letters and papers*: see p. 37 and note.

336 *in January, 1840*: see p. 149.

'*Ricordarsi . . . miseria*: Dante, *Divine Comedy* ('Inferno', canto 5, ll.
122–3): 'recall in misery a time of happiness'; EG has not matched
her sentence's grammar strictly to Dante's.

337 *it really happened*: for a similar incident in CB's juvenilia and for
parallels, see *Jane Eyre*, p. 472 note; for the summons in George
Sand's *Consuelo*, see p. 274 note.

*Sir James and Lady Kay Shuttleworth*: Sir James Kay-Shuttleworth
(né Kay; 1804–77), after practising medicine in Manchester, became
a social reformer in health, education, and the poor law. He married
Janet Shuttleworth (1817–72) in 1842, adding her name to his. The
early seventeenth-century Gawthorpe Hall, near Burnley, was restored by Charles Barry 1850–2: now National Trust. It was through
the Kay-Shuttleworths that EG, who had heard of CB's visit to them
(*Letters*, p. 116), was invited to meet CB. Neither CB nor EG entirely
liked Sir James, though he was important in obtaining materials for
*The Life* which Mr Nicholls was reluctant to part with.

338 *hills and woods*: to W. S. Williams, 16 Mar. 1850. For the London
proposal, see p. 343 below.

*Mr H——'s note*: Thornton Leigh Hunt (1810–73), son of the poet
Leigh Hunt; a journalist, he and G. H. Lewes were recruiting contribu-
tors for their new periodical, the *Leader*; CB refused him on 16 Mar.
Hunt's name, undeleted, is in MS.

339 *of "Pendennis" . . . illness*: *Pendennis* appeared monthly from Nov. 1848 to
Dec. 1850; Thackeray was seriously ill in autumn 1849, George Smith's
dinner to meet CB being one of his first engagements on recovery.

"*Unprotected Female*": CB's reference to 'self-helpfulness' is ironic:
the Unprotected Female (going about independent of any protector)
was a butt of *Punch*: from late 1849 to early 1850 (vols. XVII and XVIII)
a series of scenes depicts her discomfiture when travelling, in London,
at an auction, and so on.

340 *has no taste*: to W. S. Williams, 19 Mar. 1850; the following extract, to end of the chapter, from the same letter.

"*Southey's Life*": this and the following books are: C. C. Southey, *Life and Correspondence of Robert Southey* (6 vols., 1849–50); Julia Kavanagh, *Woman in France during the Eighteenth Century* (2 vols., 1850); William Hazlitt, probably *Winterslow: Essays and Characters Written There* (1850); Ralph Waldo Emerson, *Representative Men* (1850); Alexander John Scott, *Suggestions on Female Education* (1849).

"*by aid . . . climbed Parnassus*": Robert Burns, 'First Epistle to John Lapraik', l. 71.

341 *man of this village*: presumably John Greenwood.

342 *Charlotte says*: 12 Apr. 1850; the following extract ('I know what . . .') is from the same letter.

'*paved with . . . tomb-stones*': from a letter, part of which EG quotes later (see p. 363): Barker, *The Brontës*, pp. 658–9 and note, convincingly argues for its writer being Jane Forster, wife of William Forster of Bradford; she was a sister of Matthew Arnold and CB visited her mother when in the Lakes in Aug. 1850 (see pp. 353, 367).

—— *was here*: Joseph Taylor.

*she writes*: 11 May 1850.

343 *Literary Fund Society*: the Royal Literary Fund (founded 1790) helped distressed authors; Octavian Blewitt (1810–84) had been Secretary since 1839. The dinner was on 17 May (deferred from the Wednesday); Dickens (below) had not attended a dinner since the early 1840s.

*London on business*: about the dividends on her payments from Smith, Elder, invested in Government funds.

*May 22nd*: to James Taylor.

*the contributors*: on the *Leader*, its contributors, and the system of 'Open Council', see Ashton, *G. H. Lewes*, ch. 6.

344 *May 23rd, 1850*: the 'young man' not further identified.

345 *enjoyed her stay there*: George Smith had now moved to 76 Gloucester Terrace (later renumbered 112; photograph in Fraser, *CB*, plate 13d). This paragraph ('Miss Brontë went up to town . . . her susceptible frame') originally in MS on p. 159 (between 'her affairs' and 'In the interval'); deleted and transferred.

346 *the Chapel Royal*: at St James's Palace; services were at 8 a.m. and noon.

*with Mr Thackeray*: that same evening, CB went to dinner at Thackeray's: see his daughter's account of the evening, which was not a success, in *The Private Letters and Papers of W. M. Thackeray*, ed. Ray, ii. 673 n., and in Gérin, *CB*, pp. 433–4.

*wonderfully like Emily*: the likeness is readily apparent (despite Harriet Martineau's marginal comment on Lewes: 'Baboon, most hideous') by a comparison of Emily in Branwell's group portrait (Fraser, *CB*, plate 4a) with Lewes (Ashton, *G. H. Lewes*, plates 18 and 19).

*Miss K.*: Julia Kavanagh (1824–77), novelist and biographical writer.

*That same day*: this paragraph and the letter to Martha Brown added in Ed. 3. The letter itself is incorrectly dated 15 June in Ed. 3 (12 June in MS additions). With this addition some confusion arises: first, the Martha here is not the same as the Martha of the preceding letter to EN; second, the statement (p. 347) that CB 'followed her letter', written before the insertion, refers to EN, not Martha Brown. The addition is not quite complete in MS: it ends with the instruction (not by EG): 'Up to Page 180, Vol II, may be printed off' (i.e. of Ed. 3). '——' (below) is John Greenwood.

347 *Rochefoucauld's celebrated maxim*: François, duc de La Rochefoucauld (1613–80), *Maxims* (1665). The maxim EG has in mind, though, 'That no man is a hero to his servant', is not La Rochefoucauld's but Mme Cornuel's (1605–94).

*Opera a few nights since*: most likely on Saturday, 1 June 1850, either to *The Barber of Seville* at Her Majesty's Theatre or Meyerbeer's *The Huguenots* at Covent Garden.

*to Edinburgh*: EG takes the details and the quotation here from CB to EN, 5 July 1850.

348 *some weeks later*: to Laetitia Wheelwright, 30 July 1850.

*Abbotsford, and in Melrose*: Abbotsford, some 30 miles south of Edinburgh, was the home of Sir Walter Scott; Scott had helped make the nearby ruins of Melrose Abbey a tourist attraction.

*political economy*: i.e. modern economics; in the nineteenth century particularly associated with facts as opposed to human values.

*she says*: to W. S. Williams, 20 July 1850.

*"mine own romantic town"*: unidentified.

349 *July 15th*: 'John ——' (below) is Greenwood; 'B ——' is Brookroyd; 'Miss ——' is EN.

*jealous of Authoresses*: untraced.

*portrait to Richmond*: George Richmond (1809–96), portraitist. The picture, now in the National Portrait Gallery and engraved as the frontispiece to vol. 1 of *The Life*, was a gift to Patrick Brontë from George Smith.

350 *Duke's picture framed*: an engraving by H. T. Ryall (1845) of Antoine Claudet's daguerreotype portrait of 1844; now in BPM.

*Mrs Gore*: Catherine Grace Frances Gore (1799–1861), prolific novelist; *The Hamiltons, or Official Life in* 1830 (1831). MS has 'in Gloucester Terrace', the Smiths' address, after 'me'.

351 *by a horse-hair*: Damocles declared monarchs were the happiest of men; Dionysius of Syracuse invited him to experience that happiness and revealed, after entertaining him to a kingly banquet, a naked sword hanging over his head by a thread.

352 *Bowness*: on Windermere; Briery Close at Low Wood (which survives), on the road to Ambleside, is 3 miles from Windermere station.

*she says*: 16 Aug. 1850.

*with Miss Brontë*: EG's letter that follows is from two sources: the first is given complete in *Letters*, pp. 123–6; the second (the last two paragraphs) is only known from *The Life*. She arrived at Briery Close on 19 Aug. 'Miss ——' (below) is Eliza Fox; '——', who described CB's home, is Lady Kay-Shuttleworth.

353 *we four*: i.e. EG, CB, Sir James, and a Mr Moseley; Lady Kay-Shuttleworth was ill throughout the visit.

*"Modern Painters"*: John Ruskin (1819–1900), *Modern Painters* (5 vols., 1843–60; only vols. i and ii published at this date); *The Seven Lamps of Architecture* (1849). John Henry Newman (1801–90) was prominent in the Anglican Oxford Movement and became a Roman Catholic (1845); established the oratories at Birmingham (1847) and London (1850); 'at the Oratory' is a gloss by EG to her original letter.

*Fox How*: built for Dr Thomas Arnold of Rugby (d. 1842) and home of his family (it survives).

*this visit*: three extracts: to EN, 26 Aug. 1850; from an untraced letter, possibly to W. S. Williams ('If I could only have dropped . . .')—cf. the similar response in the letter to Miss Wooler, 27 Sept., below; to EN, 26 Aug. 1850 ('I forgot to tell you that . . .'). '——' (below), who warned of the artist class, is Sir James Kay-Shuttleworth.

354 *Harden Grange*: 4 miles from Haworth, home of Busfeild Ferrand; the other visitors named below were Lord John Manners (1818–1906) and George Smythe (1818–57), both associated with Disraeli in the 'Young England' party.

355 *in D——*: Dewsbury.

356 *"Life of Sydney Taylor"*: *Selections from the Writings of John Sydney Taylor . . . with a Brief Sketch of his Life* (1843).

*"Woman's Mission"*: *Westminster Review*, 52 (Jan. 1850), 352–78.

*Tennyson's "In Memoriam"*: published 1 June 1850; it appeared anonymously, its subject, Arthur Henry Hallam (1811–33), being identified only by his initials: authorship and subject rapidly became well known and George Smith could have told CB.

357 *Wordsworth's "Prelude"*: Wordsworth had died 13 Apr. 1850 (Tennyson became Poet Laureate in succession, 1850, largely due to the success of *In Memoriam*). *The Prelude*, designed by Wordsworth for posthumous publication, appeared July 1850; EG reported that in the Lakes everyone 'was full of "The Prelude" ' (*Letters*, 27 Aug. 1850, p. 130). The 'other little volume' promised was the Brontës' *Poems*: see below.

*the parcel*: 26 Sept. 1850.

*"wrought . . . tempestuous"*: Jonah 1: 11, 13.

*Sept. 5th*: to James Taylor.

358 *husband and children*: on 30 Aug. 1850, with the four eldest children.

*"Palladium"*: Sept. 1850, pp. 161–75 (Allott, no. 80); an unsigned review by Sydney Dobell (1824–74), poet and critic. Dobell takes Currer Bell to be the single author of all the Brontë novels. In *Shirley*, he found the same qualities as in *Wuthering Heights* and *Jane Eyre*, but the author laboured 'in an exhausted soil'. Dobell gives the two words of advice, 'Wait' and 'Watch', on p. 174.

*Samuel Brown*: *The Tragedy of Galileo Galilei* (1850).

359 *task of editing them*: Smith, Elder brought out the 2nd edition in 1850, with CB contributing a 'Biographical Notice of Ellis and Acton Bell', the 'Editor's Preface' to *Wuthering Heights*, and a 'Prefatory Note' to selections from Emily's poetry (see *Wuthering Heights*, pp. 359–70). For CB's treatment of the text, see the World's Classics and Clarendon editions.

*lost on them*: MS has, deleted: 'on them . . . . . . What the probable quantity of new matter will be, I cannot say exactly, but I think it will not exceed thirty or at the most forty pages. Since it is so inconsiderable, would it not be better to place the title thus— / "Wuthering Heights and Agnes Grey by E. and A. Bell. With a notice of the Authors by Currer Bell, and a selection from their literary remains"? / I grieve'. The new material was 50 pages in all; for the layout of the title-page, see Clarendon, pp. xxxiv–xxxv.

359 *of my sisters*: CB was not correct, since there were certainly the group portrait EG saw (p. 106 and note) and another group portrait seen by a visitor in 1857 (Susan R. Foister, 'The Brontë Portraits', *BST*, 18 (1985), 345–52), plus CB's own portrait of Anne. Presumably CB means none suitable for reproduction.

*of her task*: extracts from two letters to EN: late Sept. 1850; 23 Oct. 1850 ('I am both angry and . . .').

360 *That gentleman says*: again, as is clear from the phrase 'to meet her at your house', Lewes is addressing George Smith (see p. 266 note).

361 *Balzac's and George Sand's novels*: Honoré de Balzac (1799–1850); the two novels identified below are *Modeste Mignon* (1844) and *Lost Illusions* (3 pts., 1837–43). For George Sand, see p. 274 note; *A Traveller's Letters* (serialized 1834–6; vol. pub. 1837) is both autobiography and travel journal. Lewes had written enthusiastically on Sand in English journals since 1842 (see Ashton, *G. H. Lewes*, pp. 52 ff.).

*following letter*: 17 Oct. 1850.

362 *A friend of hers*: possibly John Greenwood of Haworth; EG offered to send him the obituary notice if he had not seen it (*Letters*, p. 337).

*by some neighbours*: Jane Forster (1821–99; née Arnold); see p. 342 note; her letter is dated 3 Oct. 1850.

363 *superannuated mastiff*: Keeper, who was at least 14; the curly-haired dog below is Flossy.

364 *Rochester called her*: as, for example, *Jane Eyre*, vol. II, ch. viii (ch. 23; p. 256); vol. III, ch. i (ch. 27; pp. 314, 317).

365 *'Peculiar . . . made dear'*: unidentified.

*"Jeffrey's Essays"*: this and the following works are: Francis Jeffrey, *Contributions to the Edinburgh Review* (1844); Arthur Stanley, *Life and Correspondence of Thomas Arnold* (1844); Sydney Dobell, *The Roman* (1849); Charles Kingsley, *Alton Locke* (1850); Thomas Macaulay, *History of England from the Accession of James II* (2 vols. 1849—3 vols. came later); Henry Taylor, *Philip Van Artevelde: A Dramatic Romance* (1834); Macaulay, *Critical and Miscellaneous Essays* (1843); Sydney Smith, *Elementary Sketches of Moral Philosophy* (1850); Robert Knox, *The Races of Men* (1850); Charles Pickering, *The Races of Man* (1848); Leigh Hunt, *Autobiography* (1850).

*except for trunk-makers*: waste-paper was used to line trunks; a handy source was unsellable books (cf. Laurence Sterne, *A Sentimental*

*Journey through France and Italy* (1768), 'The Fragment: Paris' (World's Classics, pp. 101–2) ).

366 *brief lyric*: 'Brother, there is a vacant spot', in scene viii (*Collected Poems of Sydney Dobell*, ed. John Nichol (2 vols., 1875), i. 127–9).

*Nov. 6th*: to James Taylor.

367 *His wife . . . his children*: Thomas Arnold married Mary Penrose; they had four daughters and five sons, among them Matthew Arnold. Dr Arnold died (below) from an angina attack.

368 *whom I was staying*: the Shaens, at Crix in Essex, where EG was to spend January (*Letters*, p. 138). 'Miss ——' in CB's reply (below) is one of the Shaen daughters.

369 *"Wildfell Hall," &c.*: in his *Palladium* review (see p. 358 and note), Dobell had insisted that the Bells' novels were the work of one person, despite CB's Preface to *Jane Eyre*'s 3rd edition, stating that this was Currer Bell's only novel.

*mediis in millibus*: 'young Penthesilea in the midst of her army'; Dobell in his review had adapted Virgil, *Aeneid*, i. 491, which CB quotes back to him, denying she is exceptional like the Amazon warrior.

370 *to Miss Martineau's*: at the Knoll, which Martineau had had built for herself, 1845–6: still standing (picture in Wheatley, *The Life and Work of Harriet Martineau*, plate 8).

*you now, dear E——*: 18 Dec. 1850.

*I must insert . . . went to work*: this addition inserted in Ed. 3; in MS additions. Martineau, in her copy of *The Life*, annotated CB's letter, correcting the hours; against the words below 'When I tell her of it', she wrote 'Never did. Imaginary altogether' and against 'then I laugh at her' wrote 'Stuff!' (Wheatley, *The Life and Work of Harriet Martineau*, p. 330; see Wheatley also for Martineau's way of life at Ambleside).

371 *character and kindness*: three extracts follow: to Laetitia Wheelwright, 12 Jan. 1851; to an unidentified correspondent, presumably about Jan. 1851 ('I think her good and noble . . .'); to James Taylor, 15 Jan. 1851 ('You ask me whether . . .'). In MS and Eds. 1–2, before the additional material supplied by Harriet Martineau was inserted ('Miss Martineau sends me . . . my son dead?' "'), the next two extracts (see p. 392 note) followed without a break, making a sequence of five.

*convert to mesmerism*: Martineau was seriously ill from 1839 to 1844 and attributed her recovery to 4 months of hypnotic treatment. She published an account in *Letters on Mesmerism* (1845). For the forthcoming work on mesmerism, see p. 373 note.

372 *the following account*: added (down to paragraph ending 'Is my son dead?') in Ed. 3; in MS additions, except for final sentence.

*Introductory History*: Martineau had completed Charles Knight's *History of the Thirty Years' Peace* (1849) (i.e. 1815–46), and then wrote an *Introduction to the History of the Peace* (1851), covering 1800 to 1815. The Peninsular War chapter is bk. II, ch. vi.

*the lecture*: Martineau regularly lectured to the working people of Ambleside; Edward III had required his son, the Black Prince, to prove himself in battle ('win his spurs') without reinforcements from his father.

*TO MISS W.*: in fact, to James Taylor, 1 Jan. 1851 (MS and Eds. 1–2 have no heading, this being originally one of a sequence of five extracts; see p. 371 note). The passage beginning 'Your account of Mr A——' is from CB to EG, 22 Jan. 1851.

373 *Mr A——*: Henry Atkinson (b. 1815); his interest in mesmerism led to friendship with Martineau; through him she developed her rationalism, and they set out their ideas in *Letters on the Laws of Man's Nature and Development* (1851).

'*Villette*': CB had again offered *The Professor* for publication, but withdrew it, sensing George Smith's acceptance to be from kindness rather than conviction. In the same letter, partly quoted below, she spoke of no novel being in sight, rather than of an interruption of writing. CB, though, clearly felt *The Professor*'s potential (see p. 314 note), and as *Shirley* came out of an attempt to rewrite it, so too *Villette* emerged from the nine-times rejected *Professor*. The Clarendon *Villette* prints (appendix I) four pencil fragments, the first dated Jan. 1850, connected with *Villette*.

*to Mr Smith*: 5 Feb. 1851.

374 '*loved and lost awhile*': J. H. Newman, 'Lead kindly light' (1833; written when an Anglican); EG quotes from memory.

*Feb. 11th, 1851*: to James Taylor.

375 *no worldly motive*: Ed. 3 omits: '*motive*, and which was but one error—the gravity of which she admitted—in the conduct of a person who had, all her life long, been striving, by deep thought and noble words, to serve her kind.'

*on Miss Martineau*: to EG, 28 Mar. 1851.

"*The Stones of Venice*": John Ruskin, *The Stones of Venice* (1851–3); vol. i (to which CB refers) was entitled 'The Foundations' and its first chapter 'The Quarry': hence CB's allusions in what follows. The 'letter' consists of two extracts: to George Smith, 7 Jan. 1851 (where

CB also refers to Newby's continued failure to render any statement of account for her sisters' books: *Letters*, p. 437); to EG, 28 Mar. 1851 ('I shall bring with me . . .').

376 *day- and night-mare*: this and the extract below ('It will not do . . .') apparently from untraced letters.

*displaced as to time*: 9 Apr. 1851. James Taylor (see p. 258 note) is this letter's subject, though strictly he never proposed; CB sensed that during his Haworth visit he would have done so, if encouraged.

*hands of the potter*: Jeremiah 18: 6.

377 *a visit to London*: George Smith's mother invited her in mid-April. The Exhibition of the Industry of All Nations opened 1 May at the Crystal Palace in Hyde Park.

*By the bye*: four extracts, all to EN: 12 Apr. 1851; 23 Apr. 1851 ('It appears I could . . .'); 10 May 1851 ('Do you know that I was . . .'); 21 May 1851 ('I really can no more come . . .'). 'Mr ——' (below) is James Stocks, shawl and lace warehouse, 96 Briggate, Leeds; 'Hurst and Hall' (properly Hunt and Hall), milliners, 42 Commercial Street; 'B——' is Brookroyd.

379 *Mrs Dobell*: Emily Fordham, whom Dobell married in 1844.

*pictorial passage*: a rhapsody comparing Nature to Christ, quoted by Dobell in the letter (21 May) proposing the Swiss holiday.

*Thackeray's second lecture*: Thackeray was lecturing on *The English Humourists of the Eighteenth Century* (pub. 1853); on 29 May the subjects were Congreve and Addison. Willis's Rooms or Almack's were in King Street, St James's; the Almack's balls were managed by a ladies' committee. Thackeray's mother, Anne (née Becher; 1792–1864), had married Henry Carmichael-Smyth after her first husband's death; her grandchildren were Anne and Minny. For George Smith's account of Thackeray ignoring CB's desire to remain incognito, see *The Private Letters and Papers of W. M. Thackeray*, ed. Ray, ii. 784 n.; CB was accompanied by George Smith's mother.

380 *Lord Carlisle*: George Howard, 7th Earl of Carlisle; CB recognized him from an election meeting at Haworth: he had been MP for the West Riding 1832–41 and 1846–8.

*Monckton Milnes*: Richard Monckton Milnes (1809–85), later Lord Houghton, was an important political figure and patron. He was noted for his friendships, with Thackeray, Tennyson, and EG, amongst others; he wrote the first life of Keats. MP for Pontefract.

*Somerset House*: the summer exhibition of the Royal Academy; amongst the paintings were Maclise's *Caxton's Printing Office*, Ward's

*The French Royal Family Confined in the Temple*, and Millais' *The Return of the Dove to the Ark* and *Mariana*.

380 *Protestant French preacher*: Jean D'Aubigné: see p. 234 note.

381 *many days afterwards*: CB went from London to stay with EG in Manchester, travelling on 27 June and returning to Haworth on 30 June. The passage is from *Villette*, ch. XXVII (p. 388).

*her own words*: from three letters, all to EN: 11 June 1851; 19 June 1851 ('I cannot boast that London . . .'); 24 June 1851 ('Your letter would have been . . .').

382 *Rachel*: the stage name of Elisa Felix (1820–58). She was appearing for a season at the St James's Theatre: CB saw her twice, in Eugène Scribe and Ernest Legouvé's *Adrienne Lecouvreur* (7 June) and in Corneille's *Horace* (21 June), a vehicle for Rachel as Camille (the final act, after Camille's death, was omitted). It was as Camille that Rachel stirred CB (CB to Dobell, 28 June 1851): *The Times* praised Rachel's ability to convey an elaborate tale of internal grief without speaking, and declared her Camille to be a martyr to love, who trampled on 'patriotism, fame, honour, and even filial piety, as so many empty baubles' (14 June). She is the model for Vashti in *Villette* (ch. XXIII).

*Marquis of Westminster*: Richard Grosvenor (1795–1869), 2nd marquis. 'Mrs D——' (below) is Davenport, a relation of the Kay-Shuttleworths. The dinner on Friday was at the Kay-Shuttleworths'.

*Cardinal Wiseman*: Nicholas Wiseman (1802–65), Cardinal-Archbishop of Westminster from 1850; CB saw him twice and sent her father a virulent portrait. The Spanish Chapel was in Spanish Place, Manchester Square.

383 *Rogers . . . Glenelg . . . Brewster*: Samuel Rogers (1763–1855), wealthy poet and patron, whose breakfasts were an institution; Charles Grant, Baron Glenelg (1778–1866), politician; Sir David Brewster (1781–1868), scientist.

*she writes*: to Miss Wooler, 14 July 1851. The blank (below) is of course EN.

384 *Captain Cuttle*: in Dickens's *Dombey and Son* (1847–8), Captain Cuttle's catchphrase is 'When found, make a note of'.

*July 8th, 1851*: to George Smith. 'Tell ——' (below) is 'your mother' (in MS; clearly omitted deliberately).

*Thackeray's last lecture*: CB had attended three further lectures (on Steele; on Prior, Gay, and Pope; on Hogarth, Smollett, and Fielding). Thackeray's final lecture was on Sterne and Goldsmith.

*and moral vigour*: MS has, undeleted, a long passage critical of Thackeray's 'trite vein of abuse' against publishers.

*Copyright Meeting*: on 1 July, prompted by a legal ruling that foreigners had copyright protection in Britain, although such rights were not reciprocated. Sir Edward Bulwer repeated the well-known argument that the lack of copyright agreement meant that United States publishers pirated British works rather than encouraging American authors.

385 *"Phrenological Character"*: CB and George Smith (under the names of Mr and Miss Fraser) had had their heads 'read' by Dr J. P. Browne of the Strand: for CB's Character, dated 29 June, see Gérin, *CB*, appendix B.

388 *Trafalgar Square*: laid out 1829–50. Nelson's Column was erected 1840–3, though as yet without Landseer's lions. The steps are of the National Gallery (1832–8).

*about the Catholics*: EG was generally as tolerant of Catholics as of most other varieties of Christianity; 'Mr ——' is Bryan Procter (1787–1874), poet under the name of Barry Cornwall; his daughter, Adelaide Ann (1825–64), also a poet, became a Catholic.

*"Saint's Tragedy"*: by Charles Kingsley (1848), about St Elizabeth of Hungary. *Yeast* (serialized 1848; vol. pub. 1850), like *Alton Locke*, was one of Kingsley's social novels.

*Maggie . . . Frank*: in EG's *The Moorland Cottage* (1850).

389 *Mr Gaskell . . . Marianne*: William Gaskell (1805–84), Unitarian minister at Cross Street Chapel, Manchester and EG's husband; Marianne (1834–1920), their eldest daughter. Julia and Florence (below) are Julia Bradford (1846–1908) and Florence Elizabeth (1842–81), their fourth and third daughters.

*letters to me*: 22 May 1852.

390 *James Martineau's sermons*: James Martineau (1805–1900), Unitarian minister and brother of Harriet Martineau. EG had most likely quoted from his *Endeavours after the Christian Life* (2 vols., 1843–7). He reviewed the *Letters on the Laws of Man's Nature* with considerable asperity in the *Prospective Review*: see Wheatley, *The Life and Work of Harriet Martineau*, pp. 309–10.

*Emancipation of Women*: 'The Enfranchisement of Women', *Westminster Review*, 55 (July 1851), 289–311, ostensibly by John Stuart Mill (1806–73, the philosopher), but actually by Harriet Taylor (1807–58; née Hardy), Mill's companion and collaborator since 1830; they married in 1851.

390 *have ever known*: footnote added in Ed. 3.

391 *to me at the lecture*: Marianne, at school in London, clearly attended one of Thackeray's lectures.

*number of his audience*: details of the arrangements not traced. In London, Thackeray had lectured on weekday mornings; this arrangement, if proposed for Manchester, would prevent business and professional people from attending.

392 *a thorn in the flesh*: 2 Corinthians 12: 7.

*in your way*: probably Miss Bigger, whose *The Fair Carew; or, Husbands and Wives* (1851) CB read soon after.

*pearl of great price*: Matthew 13: 46.

393 *Mrs ——*: Mrs W. E. Forster (née Jane Arnold); CB met her mother and sisters at Fox How while in the Lakes in 1850.

*Frederika Bremer*: correctly Fredrika Bremer (1801–65), Swedish novelist and travel writer; in October, EG reported her 'a quaint droll little lady': her 'special accomplishment' (below) was her habit of '*spitting* right and left . . . and not entirely sparing private houses' (*Letters*, p. 167).

'*like good wine*': from a letter to EN, 3 Oct. 1851.

394 '*it did me good*': presumably a paraphrase from CB to Miss Wooler, 21 Oct. 1851.

*to a distant friend*: to James Taylor (who was in India), 15 Nov. 1851.

*Melville's, and Maurice's preaching*: Henry Melvill (1798–1871), educationalist; preacher at St Margaret's, Lothbury 1850–6. John Frederick Maurice (1805–72), Anglican clergyman and Christian Socialist.

395 *she says*: to George Smith, 28 Nov. 1851.

396 "*to break . . . the den*": adapting Daniel 6: 24.

*surviving sister wrote*: 8 Dec. 1851 (as EG gives below). The description of Flossy in parentheses (below) is EG's gloss.

397 *to annoy another*: 16 Jan. 1851. The anecdote of intercepting the letter (below) is from the same letter, with the pronoun changed from 'mine' to 'her'.

398 "*Let this cup pass from me*": Matthew 26: 39.

*discipline to undergo*: CB was given mercury, a common prescription for liver complaints, in calomel or blue pills: too strong a dose produced feverishness, ulceration of the mouth, and worse.

*an early reading of 'Esmond'*: The History of Henry Esmond; CB had been sent, with Thackeray's approval, the manuscript of the first volume (chs. 1–14). EG's printed text discreetly conceals CB's privilege. MS has: '*allowed* to read part of the manuscript *of*'; in the following letter, EG changed 'Mr Thackeray's manuscript' to 'Mr Thackeray's work'.

399 *and admiring*: MS adds: '*admiring*. I wish there was any one whose word he cared for, to bid him good speed—to tell him to go on courageously with the book; he may yet make it the best thing he has written. *But I*'. Since *Esmond* was issued not serially but complete in 3 vols., this would have revealed CB was referring to Thackeray's manuscript. Again, below, EG substituted 'former half of the present volume' for 'former half of the present work', to make less ambiguous the form in which CB supposedly saw it.

400 *second writer of the day*: Dickens was generally reckoned the first.

*dread at her heart*: Ellen Taylor died in New Zealand on 27 Dec. 1851, so leaving her sister Mary alone there. CB clearly dates her letter to EN 4 Mar. 1852; Joan Stevens suggests convincingly that Mary Taylor's letter arrived in London between 24 Apr. and 8 May 1852 and that CB misdated her letter Mar. for May, a conjecture supported by CB to EN, 18 May 1852, sending on Mary Taylor's letter and two by Ellen Taylor (Stevens, *Mary Taylor*, pp. 106–7).

401 *is worth preserving*: ?10 Mar. 1852. '——' is Mary Gorham, who married the Revd T. S. Hewitt in 1852.

*half-pence farthing*: Lord John Russell had resigned as Prime Minister in Feb. 1852. The Earl of Derby became Prime Minister, with Disraeli (who had led the Opposition in the House of Commons) as Chancellor of the Exchequer. Derby in his statement to the Lords (27 Feb.) stressed the importance of the Church and the diffusion of the Scriptures and of evangelical truth.

402 *a reprint of "Shirley"*: published Nov. 1852, though dated 1853 (for the corrections, see Clarendon, pp. xxxii–xxxv).

*"The Two Families"*: by Mrs S. R. Whitehead, who also wrote *Rose Douglas* (below).

*Kavanagh's "Women of Christianity"*: *Women of Christianity, Exemplary of Acts of Piety and Charity* (1852).

403 *"The School for Fathers"*: by Josepha Gulston, under the pseudonym of Talbot Gwynne. Tony Lumpkin (below) is in Goldsmith's *She Stoops to Conquer*.

404 *April 12th, 1852*: to Laetitia Wheelwright. MS has, deleted, the letter's opening.

405 *she says*: 26 Apr. 1852.

405 *of your work*: EG's *Ruth*, published Jan. 1853.

*May 11th*: 'B.' (below) is Brookroyd; 'S.' is Sussex, where EN was staying with the Gorhams, with whom she had become friendly in the mid-1840s.

406 *east wind*: Ed. 3 omits: '*east wind*. What you say about —— does not surprise me; I have had many little notes (whereof I answer about one in three) breathing the same spirit,—self and child the sole all-absorbing topics, on which the changes are rung even to weariness. But I suppose one must not heed it, or think the case singular. Nor, I am afraid, must one expect her to improve. *I read*'. The reference, to Amelia Taylor and her daughter Emily Martha (1851–8), was deleted because EG had clearly transgressed her ordinance about not mentioning the living adversely. 'Mary' (below) is Mary Gorham.

*a French book*: untraced.

407 *churchyard and stone*: see p. 310 note.

408 ——'s *letter*: Emma Sherwood, whose father's illness and death faced her with the prospect of becoming a governess. MS has, deleted, after 'expressing herself': 'it absolutely reminded me of ——': the blank is for Amelia Walker, school-fellow of CB and EN at Roe Head and prototype of Ginevra Fanshawe in *Villette*; CB found her hideously affected in 1836 and not changed for the better in 1851.

*writes his daughter*: 12 Aug. 1852.

410 '*great duke*': Tennyson, 'Ode on the Death of the Duke of Wellington'. *The Times* gave his obituary over two days (15 and 16 Sept. 1852). The review (below) of Harriet Beecher Stowe's *Uncle Tom's Cabin* was in *The Times* for 3 Sept.

*letter to her friend*: 24 Sept. 1852.

411 '*fall to business*': from a letter to EN, 26 Oct. 1852.

412 *the anonymous publication*: *Villette* was advertised and published as by Currer Bell, author of *Jane Eyre* and *Shirley*.

*the following words*: to George Smith, 10 Nov. 1852. In MS in the first sentence, 'third volume' is written over one word, deleted; in the second sentence, 'first and second' is written over one word, deleted; later in transcribing the letter, EG remembered to conceal CB's privileged sight of Thackeray's manuscript and wrote out directly 'second volume' and 'third'. The whole section ('In another letter . . . given, continues') is on the back of a page in MS, with directions to 'See other side' after 'too little Story'.

413 *a little lower than the angels*: Psalms 8: 5.

"*curled darling*": *Othello*, I. ii. 69.

414 *her lines in pleasant places*: Psalms 16: 6.

*his Queen Anne's garb*: *The History of Henry Esmond* (3 vols., 1852) was printed in a typeface and with the long 's' in imitation of eighteenth-century books to match its period setting.

415 "*lucus a non lucendo*": 'by paradoxical derivation' (Lucy's passionate nature contradicts her chill surname).

*to the confessional*: *Villette*, ch. xv (pp. 198–202); see p. 206 note.

*pencil*: i.e. paintbrush; CB alludes to the classical painter so bad that he needed to write under his picture 'This is a Cock'.

*Nov. 10th, 1852*: to George Smith.

*nearly ready*: since the reissue of *Shirley* would carry advertisements for the new novel.

416 *commence it immediately*: this slightly hazardous process, which speeded publication, was also followed in printing *The Life*.

"*tries and she cannot*": epitomizing what Beatrix says in her interview with Esmond (vol. III, ch. vii); she becomes the mistress of the Old Pretender (James III).

*the "Leader"*: 6 Nov. 1852, p. 1071. Blanche Amory (below) is in Thackeray's *Pendennis* (1848–50).

*to her publishers*: *Villette* was completed on 20 Nov.; the extract that follows is from a letter to EN, 22 Nov. 1852.

417 *the Sunday intervened*: CB would not travel on a Sunday, but there was a postal delivery that day.

418 *the most beautiful*: Paulina de Bassompierre; the child Paulina may have been modelled on Julia Gaskell, hence CB's claim for success there.

*mated with a cloud*: Ixion, in classical mythology, tried to rape Hera, but Zeus substituted a cloud in her shape; he was punished on a burning wheel.

419 *Mr Nicholls*: Arthur Bell Nicholls: see p. 238 note.

*one evening to tea*: on Monday, 13 Dec.; the account is from a letter to EN, 15 Dec. 1852.

420 *to his daughter*: Patrick Brontë's reaction to CB and by letter to Nicholls was violent and bitter. At this stage, CB's objections to Nicholls were grounded on 'uncongeniality in feelings, tastes, principles' (to EN, 18

Dec. 1852). All three took refuge in and used illness tactically. For a time CB and Patrick did not speak to each other; Patrick tried to break the barrier of silence by writing to CB under the guise of Flossy the spaniel: EG saw this letter (BPM) and annotated it.

421 *application to work*: EG had been working on *Ruth*; she feared that if published at the same time as *Villette*, it would suffer in comparative reviews. *Ruth* appeared on 10 Jan. 1853 and *Villette* on 28 Jan.

*the date above will show*: i.e. the place from which the letter is dated.

422 *side of life*: 19 Jan. 1853. The places visited detailed below (except for Rothschilds') came from the same letter.

*Newgate and Pentonville*: the public institutions visited are: Newgate by the Old Bailey (rebuilt 1783); the Model Prison at Pentonville (completed 1842), where those condemned to transportation were taught a trade before being sent out; the Foundling Hospital, Guildford Street (founded 1739), for poor illegitimate children; Bethlehem (popularly Bedlam) Hospital, St George's Fields (founded 1246; rebuilt 1812, enlarged 1832), for the insane, run on humane principles. The commercial institutions are: the Bank of England, Threadneedle Street (founded 1694); the Royal Exchange, facing down Cheapside (founded 1566; building of 1844), home of Lloyd's: the Rothschilds' bank was also in the Exchange.

*MARTHA BROWN*: letter added in Ed. 3; in MS additions, bound up in vol. 1 between pp. 278 and 279, because headed 278, indicating where it was to be inserted in Eds. 1–2's pagination (II. 278).

423 *seven papers . . . and to-day*: CB had already seen five reviews (*Daily News; Examiner; Literary Gazette; Morning Advertiser; Nonconformist*). The seven papers would mainly be weekly journals, published 12 Feb., and including the *Athenaeum; Atlas; Bell's Weekly; Globe* (7 Feb.); *Leader; Spectator;* and *Weekly Chronicle*: see Allott, nos. 41–7. Despite largely favourable notices, *Villette* was not reprinted in CB's lifetime: sales may have been adversely affected by *Shirley*.

*merely artistic fault*: the *Daily News* review appeared on 3 Feb. 1853; for Martineau's letter and the offending passage, see below (for a longer extract from the *Daily News*, see Allott, pp. 172–4). Martineau noted in her copy of *The Life* against EG's phrase, 'expressions of censure': 'One only' and 'In a private letter' (Wheatley, *The Life and Work of Harriet Martineau*, p. 331); she wrote at length to EG (*Letters*, p. 453) about the episode, as a result of which EG inserted the footnote below and the passage 'When "Villette" was on the point . . . end all demur,' &c.' In her *Autobiography*, Martineau, in addition to the quoted comment below after CB's letter to her, noted that CB 'might be weak for once; but her permanent temper was one of humility, candour, integrity and conscientiousness' (quoted Wheatley, p. 326). Martineau's reply to CB (below) obviously should be dated between CB's letter of 21 Jan. 1853 and the *Daily News* review.

425 *of the transition*: i.e. the transference of Lucy's love from John Bretton to M. Paul.

426 *'You know . . . naughty books*: probably Geraldine Jewsbury (1812–80), whom CB met in 1850; Jewsbury's first novel, *Zoë* (1845), was considered 'warm'.

*'If she had but lived!'*: this paragraph is one of the few instances of EG copying a passage out fair (at least that has survived): it clearly was important to get it right; the fair copy is bound at its proper place in MS and the original draft at the end, among the additions and other material. There are a few minor changes of words and phrases, but nothing significant.

427 *written as follows*: to Miss Wooler, 27 Jan. 1853.

*by her dead sisters*: in Martineau's obituary notice, *Daily News*, 6 Apr. 1855.

*portrait of Mr Thackeray*: George Smith commissioned the portrait in 1852 from Samuel Laurence (1812–84); now privately owned. It was engraved (1853) by Frank Holl. The Kings of Israel came from the tribe of Judah (Genesis 49: 8–10); CB also echoes Revelations 5: 5.

*In reference . . . world of sympathy*: footnote added in Ed. 3. Martineau annotated her copy of *The Life* against this letter 'Hallucination!' . . . 'Fie!' By the passage about standing by her, Martineau wrote 'Libel on the world' and 'H.M. did not lose a single friend' (Wheatley, *The Life and Work of Harriet Martineau*, p. 331). Against EG's conclusion that the two women were 'faithful friends', Martineau commented: 'That word was never attained'.

428 *in February*: 24 Feb. 1853.

429 *Bishop of Ripon*: Charles Thomas Longley (1794–1868), Bishop of Ripon 1836–56; later Archbishop of York and then of Canterbury.

*'curates . . . into a book'*: possibly from an untraced letter or by report.

*Inspector*: of the National School.

430 *fault with 'Villette'*: Williams had sent the *Eclectic Review* (March) and the *Guardian* (23 Feb.), to which CB refers in her reply below. Both admitted the novel's power, while finding it unpleasing and neglecting the higher demands of truth: see Allott, nos. 49 and 50.

430 *WILLIAMS, ESQ.*: extracts from three letters, to Williams, 9 Mar. 1853; to EN, 22 Mar. 1853 ('As to the character . . .'); to Williams, 23 Mar. 1853 ('The note you sent . . .').

*St Clair . . . Miss Mulock's request*: Harriet St Clair-Erskine (d. 1867), daughter of the Earl of Rosslyn. Dinah Mulock (1826–87), afterwards Mrs Craik, novelist.

431 *us in Manchester*: CB arrived on 22 Apr.; she went to EN in Birstall on 28 Apr. EG's other guest (below) is unidentified; the sisters who sang are unidentified.

*'The Bonnie House of Airlie'*: a traditional Scottish ballad (see *The English and Scottish Popular Ballads*, ed. F. J. Child, iv (1890), 54–60). 'Carlisle Yetts' (below) is by Allan Cunningham (1784–1842). The Pied Piper is best known from Robert Browning's version (1842).

*a remarkable manner*: the following remark was presumably made in EG's hearing.

432 *dismal ghost story*: EG was famous for her ghost stories; the letter was from EN. EG may echo Wordsworth below in 'mingled with her dreams': cf. *The Prelude*, bk. I, ll. 274 and 400.

*meet her at dinner*: unidentified, though amongst those CB met on this visit was the manufacturer Salis Schwabe (see p. 437).

433 *the same subject*: to George Smith, 26 Mar. 1853.

*Swift was new to me*: Thackeray's first lecture had been on Swift; CB had arrived in London in time to attend the second.

*entire admiration*: MS adds: '*admiration*. I deny, and must deny that Mr Thackeray is very good or amiable, but the man is great, great, but mistaken, full of errors; against *his errors*'.

435 *for eight years*: Nicholls left Haworth on 27 May; he went to a curacy at Kirk Smeaton. He was presented with an inscribed gold watch on 25 May, still in Nicholls's possession in 1900.

*Early in June*: introductory sentence, letter, and 'In consequence of this invitation' added in Ed. 3.

*Plymouth Grove*: 84 Plymouth Grove, to which the Gaskells moved in 1850; now owned by Manchester University.

436 *"Cranford"*: serialized *Household Words*, 1851–3; vol. pub. 1853. CB received the book on 9 June, the day EG should have come, and read it twice, once to herself and once to her father.

*account of Mrs Stowe*: EG met Harriet Beecher Stowe, who was touring Europe, twice while in London: she 'is short and American in her manner, but very true & simple & thoroughly unspoiled & unspoilable' (*Letters*, p. 237).

*M . . . M . . . F . . . J*: EG's daughters, Marianne, Meta, Florence, and Julia. The first two, with EG, were going on a tour of Normandy, while Florence and Julia stayed with Mrs Grace Schwabe in Wales.

437 *"Twelfth Night"*: an amateur performance at the Theatre Royal, Peter Street, Manchester, 25 Apr. 1853, in aid of the Manchester Free Library (*BST*, 15 (1968), 241–3).

*tour in Normandy*: early Sept. 1853 (since the heather blooms on through August, reference to '16th' makes September the month of writing; before 16 Sept., when CB wrote to make arrangements for EG's travel to Haworth). Introductory sentence and letter added in Ed 3.

*to school again*: in Hampstead, North London, where Marianne had been before her.

*death of Mr S.*: Salis Schwabe, a manufacturer and friend of EG, had died at Glyn Garth, Anglesea, on 23 July. CB's concern was not only because scarlet fever was often fatal; EG's only son had died of it in 1845, so she would have particular reason to be anxious for her daughters, staying at Glyn Garth.

438 *wrote at the time*: EG arrived at Haworth on 19 Sept. and stayed four days. The recipient of this letter is unidentified.

*a car*: a wheeled vehicle (CB told EG that the cab would be waiting at Keighley for her).

*St Autest*: see p. 12 and note.

439 *I don't know . . . his dinner sent*: this section cut away in MS and bound up at the end with additions to Ed. 3.

*in "Jane Eyre"*: Ed. 3 omits: '*Eyre;*' of those strange, starved days at school; *of the desire*'.

440 *dreamy-looking eyes*: see p. 106 and note.

441 *what I had experienced*: opium was freely available as a painkiller. Despite CB's denial, the Roe Head Journal (BPM) suggests she had had experience of opium: 'the toil of the day succeeded by this moment of divine leisure had acted on me like opium and was coiling about me a disturbed but fascinating spell such as I never felt before' (Gérin, *CB*, p. 105).

*'Deformed' . . . 'Neighbours'*: Anne Marsh (1791–1874), 'The Deformed', in *Two Old Men's Tales* (1834); Fredrika Bremer, *Neighbours* (*Grannarna*, 1837; trans. 1842): see also p. 274 note on *Consuelo*, and *Jane Eyre*, p. 424 note.

442 *fall in pleasant places*: Psalms 16: 6.

*friends . . . their child*: Joseph Taylor, his wife Amelia, and Emily (b. 1851).

443 *MISS W——*: this series of letters (12 Dec., 3 Feb., 8 Mar.) copied out by another hand (apparently William Gaskell's), the link after the first ('Of course, as I draw . . . months of wedded life') being inserted by EG. After the third letter, William Gaskell wrote out the link sentence ('In April she . . . to Miss W——') and all the section on pp. 447-8 ('She expressed herself . . . obtaining a thing at last'). This copying originally ran continuously, but EG, having obtained or decided to use the letter to Miss Wooler of 12 Apr., deleted from the copying a section 'She expressed herself . . . youth is over, that there' (transferred in due course to present p. 447); then she copied out the letter of 12 Apr., wrote out again the deleted section, and so back into William Gaskell's copying. EG's own hand in MS begins again with the letter of 22 May. The section exemplifies the pains EG was at to incorporate material and to go back over what seemed finished, as well as the help she had from her family.

*his daughter's marriage*: CB and Nicholls, on his initiative, had been in correspondence during autumn 1853; in Jan. 1854 CB, having told her father of the correspondence, met Nicholls. Patrick Brontë accepted what CB was making inevitable and in April CB became engaged. EG herself had been trying secretly, through Richard Monckton Milnes, to get Nicholls a living or a pension so that Patrick's objections to his poverty would be countered (Barker, *The Brontës*, pp. 741-2, 745-6).

444 *not leave his bedside*: Patrick Brontë had had a seizure in June and temporarily lost his sight again.

*"Balder"*: published Dec. 1853; the first of an intended trilogy on the Progress of a Human Being from Doubt to Faith in the modern world.

*kept his love*: for Joseph and Jacob, see Genesis, chs. 37 ff., and particularly chs. 46 ff.; for the Prodigal Son, Luke 15: 11-32.

445 *March 8th*: to Laetitia Wheelwright.

446 *You can well understand*: Laetitia Wheelwright's father had suffered from cataracts: see p. 405.

*The Czar . . . France and England*: the Crimean War began Mar. 1854; England (which declared war 28 Mar.) and France were allied with Turkey against Russia: the crisis had been developing for some time.

*some other friends*: the Joseph Taylors in July 1853: after the aborted Scottish trip, CB stayed with them in Ilkley.

*P. Place*: 29 Phillimore Place, Kensington.

447 *papa's present assistant*: George de Renzy.

448 *visits before her marriage*: for the visit to EG, see Catherine Winkworth's letter, WS, iv. 121–5. CB also visited the Joseph Taylors and EN.

*required for her marriage*: BPM has CB's going-away dress, as well as her wedding bonnet and part of her wedding dress (photographs in Fraser, *CB*, plates 15b and c). BPM also has a fragment of wallpaper with CB's note on the reverse, expressing her preference for it. The marriage settlement, dated 24 May 1854, put all CB's money (£1,678) in trust, the reversion, if she died childless before Nicholls, being not to her husband but to Patrick Brontë; in her will (17 Feb. 1855) CB exercised her right to break this reversionary clause and left Nicholls her property 'absolutely and entirely' (Barker, *The Brontës*, pp. 755–6, 770; Barker prints the trust document in *BST*, 19 (1986), 36–9).

'*Essay on Old China*': in *Last Essays of Elia* (1833).

*May 22nd*: 'B——' (below) is Brookroyd.

449 *to Miss W—— today*: 16 June 1854.

*Devonshire Arms*: Devonshire Arms Inn and Posting House, Church Street, Keighley.

*Mr S——*: the Revd Sutcliffe Sowden; he was to stay at James Grant's in Oxenhope, under 2 miles south of Haworth.

450 *the others went to church*: CB, a fortnight earlier, had told Miss Wooler that only she (Wooler), EN, and Sowden would be present at the ceremony: this could mean that Patrick Brontë's absence had already been agreed, or simply that CB only listed to Miss Wooler those outside the immediate family.

*of which she says*: 28 July 1854.

*my new relations*: to Miss Wooler, 10 July 1854.

451 *the tears from her eyes*: Revelations 7: 17; 21: 4.

*telling of inward things*: CB was pregnant and died partly through complications of the pregnancy: for an assessment, see Barker, *The Brontës*, pp. 769–72 and note 96 in particular.

*we, who listened, heard*: to Miss Wooler, 22 Aug. 1854.

452 *September 19th*: to Miss Wooler.

*nothing about the war*: extracts from two letters, both to Miss Wooler: 6 Dec. 1854; 15 Nov. 1854 ('You kindly inquire after . . .').

453 *curacy at Haworth*: at Padiham, by Sir James Kay-Shuttleworth.

*Did I tell you*: 7 Dec. 1854.

454 *a doctor*: Dr MacTurk of Bradford.

*says one*: unidentified; possibly Martha Brown.

*she would say*: possibly from an untraced letter or from Martha Brown.

*her own 'Dear Nell'*: the reference to Tabby's funeral makes it on or shortly after 21 Feb. 1855. 'M——' (below) is Mercy Mary, EN's sister (she survived to 1886); 'Mrs ——' is Mrs Hewitt (née Mary Gorham): at EN's request she wrote to CB about her illness, much like CB's own, for which CB sent thanks through EN (Feb. 1855).

*is dead and buried*: Tabitha Aykroyd died on 17 Feb., aged 84, and was buried on 21 Feb., near the wall that separates the Parsonage from the churchyard. At the Parsonage since 1825, she had long been a member of the family.

455 *Feb. 15th*: to Laetitia Wheelwright. 'Dr W.' (below) is Laetitia's father, whose sight was again threatened.

*a line again*: while EG knew only the 'two notes' she gives, at least three more survive, written in CB's last illness, one to EN (after that of ?21 Feb., since it thanks Mrs Hewitt for her letter) and two to Amelia Taylor.

456 *Life of Goldsmith*: John Forster (1812–76), *The Life of Oliver Goldsmith* (1848); bk. IV, ch. xxi, p. 330 (7th edn, 1878).

*that Easter morning*: EG heightens the contrast between private and public in CB in this evocation of the day of her death, by use of E. B. Browning's *Aurora Leigh* (see title-page epigraph and note) and by writing of Saturday, 31 March as 'that Easter morning', the public focus of death and resurrection. In 1855, though, Easter Day was Sunday, 8 Apr. and CB was buried on 4 Apr., the Wednesday in Holy Week.

*that had been betrayed*: substituted in Ed. 3 for 'who had been seduced'. Patrick Brontë gave EG both this example and the next, of the blind girl (27 Aug. 1855; John Rylands MS); he used the words 'who had been deceived and deserted'. Friends of the girl had objected to the term 'seduced', possibly through Martha Brown (see *Letters*, p. 470).

*sick unto death*: echoing 2 Kings 20: 1; 2 Chronicles 32: 24; Isaiah, 38: 1

457 *Lord Jesus Christ*: from the service for the Burial of the Dead (Book of Common Prayer), to be said while earth is cast upon the body.

*of her dead friend*: this last extract from Mary Taylor's letter allows EG to emphasize the heroic and tragic nature of CB (stressed in the biblical phrasing and rhythms), even while she herself concludes by challenging a new judgement from a world she deems more ready to understand, because of what they have read, than that characterized by Mary Taylor.

# TEXTUAL VARIANTS

THIS edition is based on the text of the Third Edition. The following list of textual variants gives on the left the reading of the present edition, with its authority; on the right is its form in the Third Edition and from where derived. Where there are more than two forms of a variant, these are given in succession. The following abbreviations are used: MS = the manuscript of *The Life of Charlotte Brontë*, in the John Rylands University Library of Manchester; MS 3 = additions and corrections for the Third Edition, bound with the manuscript of *The Life* (in Manchester Central Library for p. 30); Ed. 1, Ed. 2, Ed. 3 = the three successive 1857 editions of *The Life*; CB's ms = reading from text of a Charlotte Brontë letter; editorial = reading by present editor. See also the Note on the Text.

15 : 20  doubt their power] MS; doubt the power] Eds. 1–3
17 : 28  dictations] MS, Ed. 1; dictation] Eds. 2, 3
28 :  1  but that as] MS 3; but as] Ed. 3
28 :  4  approbation] MS 3; approval] Ed. 3
28 : 12  and their acceptance] MS 3; and the acceptance] Ed. 3
33 : 16  Yate] MS 3; Gate] Ed. 3
41 :  2  her there] MS; her then] Eds. 1–3
47 : 27  her brother and] MS; her brothers and] Eds. 1–3
66 : 21  Queens] MS, Ed. 1; Queen] Eds. 2, 3
70 :  9  one up] MS, Ed. 1; up one] Eds. 2, 3
72 : 10  Geni] MS, Ed. 1; Genii] Eds. 2, 3
83 : 35  Well! but] MS; but] Eds. 1–3
89 : 28  field] MS, Ed. 1; fields] Eds. 2, 3
92 : 33  villages] MS, Ed. 1; villagers] Eds. 2, 3
107 : 36–7  us are unacquainted] MS, Eds. 1, 2; us is unacquainted] Ed. 3
116 :  5  Legh] Ed. 1; Leigh] MS, Eds. 2, 3
118 : 14  following remarkable letter] MS, Ed. 1; following letter] Eds. 2, 3
122 : 28  vol. VI] MS, Eds. 1, 2; vol. iv] Ed. 3
130 : 39  remain, a] editorial; remain a] MS, Eds. 1–3
136 : 37  woods, winding white] MS; woods, white] Eds. 1–3
137 :  5  succeeded in it so] MS; succeeded so] Eds. 1–3
146 : 39  language, which] MS, Ed. 1; language which] Eds. 2, 3
149 : 31  brain] MS; brains] Eds. 1–3
160 : 26  March '41] MS; March 21.] Ed. 1; March 21st.] Eds. 2, 3
162 : 13  19th] MS, Ed. 1; 18th] Eds. 2, 3
165 :  9  Drop the subject.] MS; Drop the subject.'] Ed. 1; 'Drop the subject.'] Eds. 2, 3

165 : 20 those two] MS, Ed. 1; these two] Eds. 2, 3
167 :  3 British Consul] MS; British Chaplain] Eds. 1–3
167 :  4 cheap and decent] MS; cheap decent] Eds. 1–3
167 : 19 apply, in this] MS; apply, on this] Eds. 1–3
168 : 31 get? I] MS, Ed. 1; get there? I] Eds. 2, 3
173 : 38 behind and] MS; behind—and] Eds. 1–3
181 : 10–11 politiques, ~~dans leur siécle~~ Quelquefois] MS; politiques.
              Quelquefois] Eds. 1–3
185 :  4 affect] MS, Ed. 1; effect] Eds. 2, 3
187 : 26 friends'] MS; friends] Eds. 1–3
191 : 20 Koekleberg] MS, Eds. 1, 2; Koekelberg] Ed. 3
206 : 29 for companion] MS; for a companion] Eds. 1–3
208 : 11 a while] MS; a little while] Eds. 1–3
208 : 19 corporeal] MS; corporal] Eds. 1–3
221 : 11 reminded him only] MS, Ed. 1; only reminded him] Eds. 2, 3
224 : 13 Monday' (baking day), 'and] MS; Monday (baking-day), and]
              Eds. 1–3
224 : 32 Marie, Louise et Claire] MS; Marie Louise et Claire] Ed. 1;
              Maria-Louise et Claire] Eds. 2, 3
233 : 35 were gone] MS, Ed. 1; were going] Eds. 2, 3
236 :  1 this, her] MS; this her] Eds. 1–3
237 : 19 Poetry] MS; poetry] Eds. 1–3
237 : 20 Million] MS; million] Eds. 1–3
237 : 27 Currer Bell is] MS, Ed. 1; Currer is] Eds. 2, 3
238 : 27 approve you, and] MS; approve, and] Eds. 1–3
239 : 23 no farther notice] MS; no further notice] Eds. 1–3
243 : 33 eventually] MS; continually] Eds. 1–3
247 : 12 delicate hand-writing] MS; delicate traced writing] Eds. 1–3
247 : 16 beginning] MS, Ed. 1; commencing] Eds. 2, 3
247 : 16 their steady pacing] MS; their study, pacing] Eds. 1–3
247 : 18 discussed their] MS; described their] Eds. 1–3
249 :  9 I am glad] MS; we are glad] Eds. 1–3
249 : 19 it did for] MS, Ed. 1; it does for] Eds. 2, 3
251 : 10 the charge of] MS; the change of] Eds. 1–3
253 : 37 to tell —— what] MS; to tell what] Eds. 1–3
254 : 26 he tried] MS; we tried] Eds. 1–3
256 : 22 roused] MS; aroused] Eds. 1–3
258 : 20 as Miss —— sending] MS; as Miss sending] Eds. 1–3
262 : 19 yours very respectfully] MS; yours respectfully] Eds. 1–3
268 : 22 sisters] MS; sister] Eds. 1–3
269 : 22 relatives] MS; relations] Eds. 1–3
273 : 14 with a sense] MS; with the sense] Eds. 1–3

275 : 27–8 be only corrosive] MS; be corrosive] Eds. 1–3
277 : 11 he guides it] MS; he wields it] Eds. 1–3
277 : 24 and when] MS; and where] Eds. 1–3
278 : 19 from Life] MS; from life] Eds. 1–3
278 : 19 from Truth] MS; from truth] Eds. 1–3
278 : 23 earthquakes wakens a] MS, Ed. 1; earthquakes waken a] Eds. 2, 3
281 : 9 sank] MS; sunk] Eds. 1–3
283 : 34–5 they made haste] MS, Ed.1; they make haste] Eds. 2, 3
288 : 14 educations were] MS; education was] Eds. 1–3
290 : 22 back on, grief] MS; back on grief] Eds. 1–3
291 : 14 pain in the] MS; pains in the] Eds. 1–3
292 : 8 pain in the] MS; pains in the] Eds. 1–3
297 : 11 and the carbonate] MS; and carbonate] Eds. 1–3
297 : 26 This day is] MS; This is] Eds. 1–3
299 : 4 any friend to] MS; any friends to] Eds. 1–3
299 : 35 Reason] MS; reason] Eds. 1–3
299 : 35 Religion] MS; religion] Eds. 1–3
300 : 17 and the dying] MS; and dying] Eds. 1–3
300 : 35 consequently be obliged] MS; consequently obliged] Eds. 1–3
300 : 36 in case of] MS; in the event of] Eds. 1–3
306 : 6 had had a] MS; had a] Eds. 1–3
306 : 16 and your kindness] MS, Ed. 1; and kindness] Eds. 2, 3
307 : 11 one, in] MS; one in] Eds. 1–3
312 : 28 giving you an] MS; giving an] Eds. 1–3
316 : 10 whisper] MS; whispers] Eds. 1–3
322 : 4 is true as] MS, Ed. 1; is as true as] Eds. 2, 3
331 : 7–8 the disappointment] MS, Ed. 1; her disappointment] Eds. 2, 3
332 : 19 news!"] MS, Ed. 1; news!] Eds. 2, 3
337 : 15–6 dearly-beloved vainly] MS; dearly-beloved] Eds. 1–3
339 : 14 lingers, (for] MS, Eds. 1, 2; lingers (for] Ed. 3
339 : 29 kindly offers] MS; friendly offers] Eds. 1–3
341 : 1 'I enclose] editorial; *no paragraph* MS, Eds. 1, 2; I enclose] Ed. 3
346 : 26 we sat down] MS; we sate down] Eds. 1–3
346 : 33 June 12th] MS 3; June 15th] Ed. 3
348 : 22 daguerrotype] CB's ms; daguerreotype] MS, Eds. 1, 2;
        daguerréo-type] Ed. 3
351 : 4 remaining child] editorial; remaining child's] MS, Eds. 1–3
351 : 26 cruel and terrible] MS; cruel terrible] Eds. 1–3
354 : 11 drank] MS, Eds. 1, 2; drunk] Ed. 3
360 : 26 is still better] MS; is better] Eds. 1–3
362 : 32 it's getting] MS; its getting] Eds. 1–3
373 : 17 over-strict nor too] MS, Ed. 1; over-strict or too] Eds. 2, 3

373 : 27–8 modern European man] MS; European modern man] Eds. 1–3
375 : 8–9 I wish rather to hear what] CB's ms; I wish rather to hear rather
        what] MS; I wish to hear, rather, what] Eds. 1–3
378 : 21 spirit or the] MS; spirit nor the] Eds. 1–3
379 : 2 lodgings!!!] MS; lodgings!] Eds. 1–3
379 : 22 garden blossom] MS; garden blossoms] Eds. 1–3
380 : 34–5 lecture of Thackeray's] MS; lecture at Thackeray's] Eds. 1–3
382 : 19 which condemns me] MS; which compels me] Eds. 1–3
383 : 21 than of my] MS; than my] Eds. 1–3
387 : 28 excellence] CB's ms; excellencies] MS; excellences] Eds. 1–3
388 : 26 Saint's] MS; Saints'] Eds. 1–3
388 : 36 the priest's power] MS; the priest-power] Eds. 1–3
389 : 10 subjugated] MS, Ed. 1; subjected] Eds. 2, 3
392 : 36 after "Currer] MS, Ed. 1; after, "Currer] Eds. 2, 3
395 : 12 kindly] MS; friendly] Eds. 1–3
395 : 13 that had been] MS, Ed. 1; that have been] Eds. 2, 3
395 : 32 it is gone] MS, Ed. 1; it has gone] Eds. 2, 3
396 : 18 morning; after] MS; morning, after] Eds. 1–3
396 : 19 night, he] MS; night; he] Eds. 1–3
399 : 6–7 subject or treatment] MS, Ed. 1; subject of treatment] Eds. 2, 3
399 : 9 and letter of] CB's ms; and letters of] MS, Eds. 1–3
399 : 14 illusion] MS; allusion] Eds. 1–3
401 : 6 her own life] MS, Ed. 1; her life] Eds. 2, 3
403 : 36 and disappearing and] MS; and disappearing, and] Eds. 1–3
404 : 10 struggle;] MS, Eds. 1, 2; struggle] Ed. 3
406 : 17 faithfully] MS; sincerely] Eds. 1–3
409 : 15 trust that in] MS; trust in] Eds. 1–3
414 : 28 others will remain] MS; others still remain] Eds. 1–3
415 : 3 subtility] MS; subtlety] Eds. 1–3
430 : 22 Mulock's] MS; Muloch's] Eds. 1–3
430 : 28 Knightley] MS; Knightly] Eds. 1–3
441 : 19 learn] MS; hear] Eds. 1–3
443 : 27 keep] MS; keeps] Eds. 1–3
449 : 24 to *you* first] MS; to you first] Eds. 1–3
451 : 17 been hurried or] MS; been wearied or] Eds. 1–3
452 : 17–8 usefulness—so] MS; usefulness; so] Eds. 1–3
453 : 27–8 sore-throat] MS; sorethroat] Eds. 1–3
454 : 26 my weary bed] MS; my dreary bed] Eds. 1–3
454 : 28 talk about my] MS; talk of my] Eds. 1–3
456 : 11 that sweeping circle] MS; that circle] Eds. 1–3

# INDEX

Many people and places appear in the text only by first name, initial, or a blank. The Index treats them as named on that page; the Explanatory Notes will identify them. Names are indexed as in the text: if misspelt the correct version is given in brackets. The Explanatory Notes are selectively indexed, though all significant material from *The Life*'s manuscript and first edition is covered. Inverted commas indicate fictional characters (their identity with originals should be treated with due caution).

*The Oxford World's Classics Website*

**www.worldsclassics.co.uk**

- Browse the full range of Oxford World's Classics online

- Sign up for our monthly e-alert to receive information on new titles

- Read extracts from the Introductions

- Listen to our editors and translators talk about the world's greatest literature with our Oxford World's Classics audio guides

- Join the conversation, follow us on Twitter at OWC_Oxford

- Teachers and lecturers can order inspection copies quickly and simply via our website

**www.worldsclassics.co.uk**